For Hazel, a book
42 years in the making, but
not as long as our half-century
of a marvelous friendship

David

ps   Pat's was only 48

The Social Conscience of the Early Victorians

F. David Roberts

Stanford University Press
Stanford, California
2002

Stanford University Press

Stanford, California

© 2002 by the Board of Trustees of the

Leland Stanford Junior University

Printed in the United States of America

Library of Congress Cataloging-in-Publication Data

Roberts, F. David.

The social conscience of the early Victorians / F. David Roberts.

p.   cm.

Includes bibliographical references (p.) and index.

ISBN 0-8047-4532-3 (cloth : alk. paper)

1. Great Britain—Social policy—History—19th century.   2. Paternalism—
Great Britain—History—19th century.   3. Charities—Great Britain—
History—19th century.   I. Title.

HN385 .R594   2001

361.6'1'0941—dc21   2002004730

This book is printed on acid-free, archival-quality paper

Original printing 2002

Last figure below indicates year of this printing:

11   10   09   08   07   06   05   04   03   02

Designed and typeset at Stanford University Press in 10/13 Minion

Dedicated to
PATRICIA MACDONALD
fellow historian
and friend of 48 years

Acknowledgments

Acknowledgement is long overdue to the Social Science Research Council and the John Guggenheim Foundation for awarding me year-long grants to study the social conscience of the early Victorians in 1962 and 1966, which helped lay the basis for this book. Both foundations deserve many thanks. Also deserving thanks is Dartmouth College, whose year-long faculty fellowship and many sabbaticals allowed not a few research visits to London, and whose substantial subvention to the Stanford University Press supported this study's publication.

I must also acknowledge the indispensable help of the British Library. From 1951, when I took my first notes in the great round reading room of the British Museum, to 2001, when I checked the last notes to this book in the Library's splendid new building, the staff served me with an almost unbelievably gracious and attentive spirit.

Also helpful were the libraries of Oxford, Cambridge, and London universities in England, and in the United States, the libraries at the University of Washington, Yale, and especially Harvard, whose remarkable holdings on Victorian England were available to me as the spouse of a Harvard librarian. Dartmouth College's Baker Library has been home to me for forty-five years. To all of these libraries, and for the diligence and politeness of their librarians, many, many thanks.

My debt to fellow scholars is great. They both widened my knowledge of Victorian England and made valuable criticisms of my work. Conversations with H. L. Beales of the London School of Economics greatly enhanced my understanding of Congregationalism, while his colleague Theo Barker wisely cautioned me to see the industrial revolution as not so revolutionary. Cambridge's George Kitson Clark, in my visit to his Victorian seminar, broadened my view of Anglicanism. R. A. Lewis of the University of Wales at Bangor proved most constructive in his criticism of earlier drafts of the book, as were John Harrison of the University of Sussex of the final one and E. P.

Thompson of my sketch of paternalism's roots in Tudor, Stuart, and eighteenth-century England. Thompson's summer teaching at Dartmouth College's history department led to some profitable conversations.

In the United States, I gained much from John Clive in the many meetings of the Harvard Victorians—meetings that included the trenchant criticisms of my papers by Harry Hanham. I also learned from many meetings with Iowa's William Aydelotte of the value of a careful counting and analysis of the important votes in Parliament. David Spring of Johns Hopkins read the chapters on paternalism and shrewdly advised me not to be too accepting of the paternalists' claims.

James Winter of the University of British Columbia read earlier versions of the text and made eminently sensible suggestions, as did Perry Curtis of Brown University. Trygve Tholfsen of Teachers College, Columbia University, read all of my drafts, early and late, and proved to be my most diligent and perceptive critic.

And, finally, I owe many thanks to Patricia Macdonald, who helped me in my research in many different ways; to my brother Clayton Roberts, of Ohio State University, who has been straightening out my awkward sentences and catching my historical errors since we were undergraduates; and to my wife, Helene Roberts, editor of *Visual Resources*, who is both an impeccable proofreader and a sharp critic of style. All of the above scholars deserve the most generous of acknowledgments.

Contents

Introduction 1

The Social Conscience of the Early Victorians

Introduction

In 1830, the dominant theme defining the social conscience of the early Victorians was a paternalism that looked largely to property, the Church, and local authorities to govern society. By 1860, the dominant theme of the early Victorian social conscience had become a vision of a laissez-faire society that looked largely to economic laws, self-reliant and benevolent individuals, and voluntary associations to govern society. It was a vision that remained in the ascendance until it was forced to share its dominance with the collectivism of the twentieth century.

Alhough the emergence of a laissez-faire vision was a decisive and significant event, it was not revolutionary: paternalism continued a strong part of the social outlook after 1830, just as a vision of a laissez-faire society had long been a growing force before that date. Also still vigorous was the philanthropic outlook that emerged after the Reformation and that humanitarianism that arose in the eighteenth century. The social conscience of Britain, like its geological structure, consists of various and lasting layers and deposits. Two of the oldest of these deposits, for example, were a belief in a harmonious order ruled by a Divine Providence and the conviction that property was sacred, beliefs dating from medieval times, which eventually formed part of the laissez-faire ideal, although not without first being a crucial part of that early Victorian paternalism with which this study of the social conscience of the early Victorians begins.

The paternalism that the early Victorians inherited was unlike that which existed on the Continent. It was a paternalism based not on monarchy but on land. The English looked to no czar or Kaiser as "father of the people." Queen Victoria was seldom called the "mother of the people"; nor were her predecessors, the sailor king William IV and the profligate George IV, often thought of as "father of the country." Promises of a paternal monarchy suffered grievous harm in 1649 with the beheading of Charles I and died in 1688 with the flight of his son. In the seventeenth century, the landed classes dismantled that centralized rule of royal councils and royal officials so dear to the Stuarts and so integral to the paternal monarchies of the Continent.

But though without a strong monarchical paternalism, England was far from wanting the social and political paternalism of a landed class. The aristocracy of England was the envy of a European nobility that was far poorer in acres and political power. The English lord possessed huge estates based on the law of primogeniture, which ensured that the estate went intact to the eldest son. English peers also sat in the House of Lords, part of a Parliament that was sovereign. As lords lieutenants and magistrates, they ruled the countryside. By weight of local influence, they controlled the M.P.'s who controlled the House of Commons, and they and their brothers, sons, cousins, and friends dominated the law courts, the military, and the wealthiest church in Europe, the Church of England.

The paternalism of the aristocracy had deep roots not only in the social, political, and economic structure but in England's intellectual heritage. The proposition that property had its duties as well as rights was woven into both the feudal form of landholding and the legal thought underlying it. And that the Church had the duty of consoling the poor, teaching the young, admonishing the sinner, and guiding all in both morals and the way to salvation was a medieval inheritance scarcely weakened by the Reformation. Indeed, the idea of the mission of the Church and the paternal duties of landowners were enhanced in the sixteenth century by the writings of Tudor humanists, from Thomas More to Thomas Starkey, furthered in the seventeenth century by Puritan divines and Cambridge Platonists, and kept alive by eighteenth-century philosophers. They formed the basis of the spirited revival of paternalist thought begun by Edmund Burke and Sir Walter Scott and culminating in scores of early Victorian pleas for Church and landowners to do their duties.

So firmly implanted was paternalism by 1830 in the structure and mentality of England that the question of why paternalism persisted is perhaps less puzzling than why it yielded its dominant role after 1830 to a vision of a laissez-faire society.

Five basic ideas defined the vision of a laissez-faire society and are analyzed in Part II. They are (1) the sacredness of property, (2) the rightness of the providential order, (3) the economists' invisible hand that benefits all, (4) a morality of self-reliance, and (5) a voluntarism that both looked to the benevolence of the wealthy and released the energies of the people.

That property as sacred and Providence as harmonious were integral to paternalism did not prevent it from also being integral to the vision of a laissez-faire society. Even political economy, so central to laissez-faire, was not that revolutionary an innovation. By the late eighteenth century, many land-lords had become practicing capitalists and admiringly read Edmund Burke, both the age's leading paternalist and one of its most ardent believers in po-litical economy. And by the 1830s, the early Victorians read Thomas Chalm-ers's *The Christian and Civic Economy*, a synthesis of paternalism and political economy. Not all paternalists, however, accepted the new science; those wed-ded to protectionism could not tolerate its attack on the Corn Law and the Navigation Act. But their attacks availed little as political economy con-quered the press, the universities, the Whigs, and made inroads with Tories and Radicals. For those conquered, it spoke with the authority of Moses and became the center of their vision of a laissez-faire society. But although dra-matic in its triumphs, it was less widespread, less effective, less the center of the new outlook than the morality of self-reliance.

Self-reliance was far more disruptive of paternalism than political econ-omy. Paternalists, to be sure, esteemed highly that self-reliance—patient, en-during, deferential, and stoical—that won awards for those laborers who never asked for poor relief. But the growth of wealth, towns, literacy and up-ward mobility created a new self-reliance—bold, energetic, assertive, and not always deferential—that flourished in towns and spread to the countryside. While leading to no barricades or great agitations, it was still a revolutionary force in all the interstices of society. One of the great conflicts of the age, said John Stuart Mill, was between self-dependence and dependence or protec-tion. In self-improvement and self-reliance, the early Victorians found a rem-edy suitable to an age that was seriously moral and strongly individualistic.

Just as esteemed as self-improvement and self-reliance was the fifth basic idea, voluntarism. Though voluntarism was everywhere popular, few wor-shipped it with more fervor than did the Nonconformists nourished on a ha-tred of a state Church that was long hostile to their religion. They viewed the established Church as established wickedness and the worldly state as every-where corrupting. Only voluntary churches would bring spiritual purity, and only a people acting voluntarily a just society.

The working class had also suffered persecution, also saw the state as op-pressive, and also embraced voluntarism. They feared government. The so-cialists among them, Owenites and Fourierists, looked to communities vol-untarily formed, while the reformers turned to trade unions, friendly, benefit, and building societies, and to consumer cooperatives, all voluntary, all free of government.

The middle classes were also enthusiastic for the voluntary principle. There was scarcely an activity that could not be done by a voluntary society—hospitals, dispensaries, schools, asylums for the homeless, visiting societies for the poor, universities, athenaeums, and the list goes on and on, a veritable sea of voluntary societies, all integral to a laissez-faire society and worth careful analysis.

Part III deals with three pervasive attitudes that, although not a necessary part of a vision of a laissez-faire society, did constitute an important part of the early Victorian social conscience. They are the philanthropic impulse, humanitarianism, and those always ubiquitous qualities of human nature: self-, vested, and class interests. Some readers might wonder why philanthropy is not a part of the voluntarism discussed in Part II, while others might be puzzled as to why philanthropy requires a separate chapter from humanitarianism.

Victorian philanthropy, with its abundance of societies, was in fact a part of voluntarism. But it was much more. In the great philanthropists William Wilberforce and Lord Ashley—and in many more—it transcended voluntarism by calling in no uncertain tones for the intervention of government. Only government, said Wilberforce, could end slavery and the slave trade, and only government could make sure that the theater and press did not corrupt morals. And only government, added Lord Ashley a generation later, could end the evils of child labor, women in mines, harsh lunatic asylums, and disease-ridden towns. Such philanthropic legislation, neither voluntary nor a part of the laissez-faire ideal, was nevertheless a part of the early Victorian social conscience.

Neither was philanthropy exactly synonymous with humanitarianism. The two were, of course, similar. Philanthropic zeal often coincided with humanitarian compassion. But not always. There was a gulf dividing them, a gulf that found unforgettable expression in *Bleak House,* where the age's greatest humanitarian, Charles Dickens, mercilessly caricatured the philanthropic efforts of Mrs. Jellyby, a pretentious evangelical who neglected the suffering around her in her zeal to save the souls of the Booriboula Gha of Africa.

Dickens was only one of the journalists, novelists, poets, dramatists, and painters of London representative of a humanitarianism far removed from the Victorian philanthropy that David Owen, in his magisterial *English Philanthropy, 1660–1960* (1964) said was nearly synonymous with evangelicalism. At the center of humanitarianism was a simple, direct, nearly spontaneous compassion for all who suffered unmerited pain; at the center of philanthropy lay a desire to reform morals, to improve people, and to save souls. Humanitarianism was widespread and diffuse, bursting forth in editorials, pamphlets, poems, novels, and parliamentary speeches on behalf of overworked children, criminals hanged for small offenses, cruelly treated lunatics, and famine-stricken Irish. The philanthropist's efforts were more organized, a matter of societies and subscription lists and with the intent of moral improvement. Despite all their similarities, the differences are great enough to demand separate chapters.

Humanitarianism certainly deserves such. Few principles were invoked more often in press and Parliament in opposition to oppressive landlords, selfish mill owners, and cruel poor law officials than the "dictates of humanity" and "humane feelings." Appeals to humanity were also invoked to counter the steely arguments of economists, the severe moralizing of evangelicals, and the corrupting influence of every kind of vested interest. Humanitarianism, although diffuse, vague, and weak when confronted with powerful interests, nonetheless grew ever more extensive and pervasive. It is an historical force too often neglected and is worth a separate and full analysis.

Even more powerful than both philanthropy and humanitarianism in defining the early Victorian social conscience was the force of self-interest. Whether it took the form of self-, vested, or class interest, it constituted a force unrivalled in Victorian England, a force that after 1834 reduced by millions of pounds the relief given to an ever-increasing number of paupers, and one that in 1854 abolished the General Board of Health, which had succeeded in taking the first steps to lowering England's fearful mortality rate. For a great many Englishmen, it was not the rate of mortality that was fearful but the rates to be paid for sewers and waterworks. And allying with the selfishness of ratepayers were vested interests. Few forces indeed could rival vested interests. Special interests of every kind—landlords, mill owners, railway directors, shippers, lawyers, churchmen—dominated government at every level. Less clearly visible in its self-interest, but underlying the very structure of these interests, were the deep class loyalties of the dominant aristocracy and rising middle classes. No discussion of the social conscience of the early Victorians could omit an analysis of these powerful forces.

So overwhelming, indeed, were self-, vested, and class interests that the early Victorians turned to an equally pervasive and powerful force, that of government. They usually did so unwillingly. Most early Victorians disliked government. Quite astonishing were the numbers in all classes, lower, middle, and upper, who found government a vast evil. But equally astonishing, after 1832, was the rapid growth of government, both central and local. Parliament created more than twenty new central departments full of inspectors and assistant commissioners and passed laws expanding both the central and local government. Greatly increased was a centralization that was widely denounced. The most puzzling of the paradoxes of the early Victorians' social conscience was the advent of a large but ostensibly unwanted government. It is a paradox that has led some historians to see in the impersonal forces of population growth, urbanization, and industrialism, and not in men's ideas and volitions, the defining forces of Victorian Britain.

Part IV examines not only the degree to which government was both distrusted and expanded but the impersonal forces behind its growth. It also examines two ideas that played a role, the idea of a paternal government and the idea of a utilitarian state.

By 1860, the social conscience of the early Victorians had departed considerably from its paternalist ideal to embrace a vision of a laissez-faire society. It was a vision that stayed strong even though it was accompanied by a nearly revolutionary growth of government, a government needed to reduce the many social evils that did not fade before the economists' invisible hand, the rise of a better-educated and more self-reliant working class, and the greater efforts of a Christian philanthropy. The early Victorians inherited from their Georgian ancestors an admirable and often effective paternalist ideal, although not without serious deficiencies and illusions. After 1860, they bequeathed to the late Victorians a vision of a laissez-faire society that was also an admirable and often effective ideal, although also not without serious deficiencies and illusions. It is the aim of the following study to describe and explain these many changes.

PART I

The Tradition of Paternalism

CHAPTER 1

The Idea of Paternalism

When Queen Victoria ascended the throne in 1837, no social outlook was more widespread and deeply rooted in Britain than paternalism. It pervaded the age's novels, poetry, and learned tomes, as well as the speeches and editorials of its politicians and journalists. It was also instinctive to the wealthy and powerful who governed Britain and owned and ran its economy. Given how widespread its appeal was, it varied in form and content. There was no one paternalism. Indeed, the word "paternalism" was never used; "paternal government" and "patriarchal principle," yes, but not "paternalism." Yet there was enough of a common agreement on its basic assumptions to allow later historians to use that term, and even to draw up a model of paternalist ideas.

A MODEL OF PATERNALISM

Almost all Victorian paternalists held four basic assumptions about society: it should be authoritarian, hierarchic, organic, and pluralistic. That it should be authoritarian followed from the very word "paternal." Fathers command and expect to be obeyed, and so do kings, bishops, landlords, justices of the peace, and even constables. In their sphere, they all are sovereign, as fathers are, and if their rule is not authoritarian, confusion follows. Paternal authority must be firm, even severe. The typical paternalist believed in capital punishment, whipping, summary justice for delinquents, and imprisonment for seditious writers.

Confusion would also follow if there was no fixed hierarchy defining the respective place of those many authorities and the subjects they ruled. Paternalists never doubted that God had created a hierarchical society. They decried all leveling measures, all talk of equality, because without inequality there would be no structure by which the wealthy could govern wisely and the poor work and obey. At the heart of the paternalist's hierarchical outlook is a strong belief in dependency, a dependency only possible where there is deference to one's betters.

Less obvious is the paternalist's third assumption, that society should be organic. Although the word "organic" was uncommon, phrases such as "old social bonds," "social ties," and "community" were far from rare; and those ties and bonds were increasingly imperiled by huge, impersonal factories and cities. In rural England, there were personal ties, a sense of mutuality, of being one family, bound all together, each in his or her appointed place. Unlike on the Continent, the many paternalist spheres were relatively autonomous in England, part of a pluralistic rather than centralized paternalism. On the Continent, kings were the fathers and governors of their subjects. In England, property was the single most important source of authority, and since property was widely held, paternalism was exercised in many different spheres, in a mostly pluralistic way, a way Englishmen, proud of their "English Liberties," never doubted was necessary for paternalism. "Property has its duties as well as rights" became a hallmark of the early Victorian paternalists. Since property owners seldom questioned their rights, the emphasis of this maxim was on duties, and three in particular were understood, those of ruling, guiding, and helping. It was certainly the landlord's duty to rule his estate and parish firmly and resolutely—to fine tipplers, jail poachers, transport arsonists, and evict slovenly tenants. As protector of his parish, he also had to suppress crime, riots, and disorder, put the idle to work, and see that vagrants were expelled and the king's peace kept.

It was also the property owner's duty to guide, but this was quite as much the duty of the clergy as, if not more than, of the landlord. The parson preached morality to the poor on Sunday and visited them during the week to urge them to mend their ways. If they did not, many landlords and clergymen would, as magistrate, guide them by severer disciplines. Peers, squires, and parsons were convinced, as fathers are, that they knew what was best for their dependents.

The model paternalist had not only to rule and guide but also to help those in distress: soup kitchens had to be provided in periods of severe want, coal sold cheaply in January, clean cottages made available, with modest rents, and the poor law justly and sternly administered. For social critics (and later historians) anxious to find in paternalism the answer to multiplying social ills, the duty of helping was all important. But to most paternalists, it formed a set of duties less crucial than the duty to rule firmly and guide wisely. One could, after all, only mitigate, not remove, social ills, which were an inevitable part of a providential order.

The inevitability of poverty was one of many attitudes that clustered around the four assumptions and three duties that lay at the core of paternalism. The Bible itself declares that the poor shall never cease out of the land, a dictum constantly cited. Paternalists were not reformers. They had no hope of remaking the world. Evils were as ineradicable as the sinfulness of man. It was a belief that led to a second attitude, a deep conservatism. Most paternalists were nostalgic for a golden age when the lower orders had been deferential, the wealthy benevolent, and society harmonious. Innovation was suspect, particularly innovation coming from the new towns and manufactories, two dangerous dissolvents of a society and a government based on land.

A worship of land and a dislike of monied interests constituted a third attitude common to most, though not all, paternalists. Landowners had deep roots in their localities and firm personal bonds with their dependents, while money was rootless, impersonal, mobile, and free of obligations and duties. The landowner knew his tenants and laborers, could tell the worthy from the unworthy, and claimed to act in terms of a moral, not a cash nexus.

Paternalists thought in ethical terms. Belief in a moral nexus—in fair rents and just prices, in the deserving and undeserving poor, in social betterment through moral improvement—formed a fourth attitude. A sense of a just and moral economy fitted in with a mercantilism that preached protectionism for the landlord and a Church of England whose parish clergy saw in the spiritual and moral regeneration of the individual the solution to England's social evils.

A fifth attitude, deeply ingrained, was hostility to government. It was an ambiguous hostility, one aimed largely at the central government, not the local, at laws intruding on the rights of property, not those repressing seditious literature. Landlords hated centralization but never doubted their right to govern under Parliament's laws as justices of the peace. Many, although not all, also denounced the economists' laissez-faire but loved the adage "Live and let live." Although paternalism was not without its inconsistencies, it nevertheless formed a coherent social outlook, based on common assumptions which were all the stronger for being so inextricably bound up with the dominant institutions of the day, institutions all the more dominant because their roots ran deep into the past.

The roots of two of those institutions—a property that ruled and a Church that guided—had their beginnings in medieval England. It was a medieval past celebrated in the drawings and writings of Augustus Welby Pugin, the romances of Sir Walter Scott, the revival of the Gothic style, and the unstinted praise of the medieval Church by the Cobbetts and Carlyles, a past of barons and bishops faithful in the discharge of their duties, an idealized and not entirely accurate past, but one loved by many Victorians.

Paternalism had been greatly strengthened in Tudor England by a powerful gentry, a nationalized Church, and a stronger monarchy, three pillars supporting a firmly hierarchical and authoritarian society. It was also strengthened by the legislation and the writings of Tudor statesmen and humanists, the statesmen expanding the paternalism of the Crown in Parliament and the humanists making the Christian responsibilities of the stewards of the nation's privileges and wealth far more explicit. The statute books grew fat with acts increasing the paternal role of government. Acts of Parliament decreed what one wore, what one believed, and how the poor were to be treated. On the surface, the monarchy grew ever more paternal, but in reality the peers and gentry in Parliament designed their statutes so that the justices of the peace became the actual paternal rulers of England.

It was the task of the humanists—Thomas Starkey, Robert Crowley, Thomas Elyot, and most especially Sir Thomas More—to see that that paternal rule was virtuous and just. They condemned avariciousness in all its forms—enclosures, rack-renting, evictions, and engrossing—and urged, in the words of Thomas Starkey, "living together in good order, one ever ready to do good to others." And thus do Christian virtues "perfect common weal as every part . . . doth his office in perfect love and unity."[1] The humanists, following Aristotle, found the origins of "the patriarchal state" in the "extensions of the family," a patriarchal state in which, said Elyot, "all property is . . . a trust of God" and in which "the public weal . . . [is] a body, a living compact of the sundry estates and degrees of men."[2]

James I and Charles I desired to complete Tudor paternalism by making the king truly the father—the firm and unquestioned sovereign father—of the commonweal. Proclamations and ordinances, Star Chamber and Councils of the North, and Laudian bishops would bring England a monarchical paternalism on the Continental model. But it was not to be. The two political revolutions of 1647 and 1688 made Parliament sovereign over the nation and the J.P.'s the rulers of the countryside. England's paternalism would be pluralistic, not monolithic, often despotic locally, but less so from the throne.

Two other revolutions, the scientific and the capitalist, appeared to undermine paternalist assumptions. After Newton, Harvey, and Boyle, with assists from Bacon, Hobbes, and Locke, the great chain of being suffered, and the world of humors, essences, and angels yielded to a mechanistic world of forces and atoms. At the same time, the moral economy of just prices and fair rents, of tariffs and monopolies, which accompanied capitalism in the mercantilist seventeenth century, yielded in the eighteenth to the individualism and self-interest of Bernard de Mandeville's *Fable of the Bees* and Adam Smith's *Wealth of Nations*, two affirmations of self-interest that would have been anathema to Tudor humanists. But the pluralistic paternalism of landed estates, Church and parish, J.P.'s and municipal courts, and an array of other local authorities had struck roots.

The Reformation, like the political, scientific, and capitalist revolution modified but did not end the old paternalist values. Henry VIII placed the Church under the king; two centuries later, it was partly under the ministers of the king, who were answerable to Parliament, partly under its bishops and clergy, and partly under those peers and gentry who had the right to appoint to benefices. It was a wealthy Church, yet one whose political position was most ambiguous, at once highly respected by the landed class, whose younger sons manned it, but still as persuaded as ever of its divine mission to guide and instruct and to visit the ill, feed the hungry, and clothe the naked. At the end of the eighteenth century, the Church, the landed estates, and local government constituted the three most powerful and wealthy of England's many institutions, which, in their respective spheres, promised a forceful, just, and benevolent paternal rule.

The promises of a paternal rule, as the nineteenth century began, were expressed in many ways, in sermons, pamphlets, novels, and speeches, as well as in the charges of bishops, the decisions of judges, and the pronouncements of editors. Like the institutions they reflected, traditional paternalist attitudes were everywhere, but they were diffuse and unformed, often no more than a set of maxims and adages. There was no theory of paternalism, none at least that was very explicit, until the French Revolution and sudden industrial, urban, and population growth raised the alarming question of the state of the nation, which forced those most attached to England's dominant institution to transform the paternalist's maxims and customs into a search for a more viable and effective theory.

THEORIES OF PATERNALISM

Between 1823 and 1847, twenty or more authors published thirty or more works espousing paternalist ideas, ranging from the absentee Irish landowner Kenelm Digby's *The Broad Stone of Honour, or, Rules for the Gentlemen of England* to *Friends in Council* by Sir Arthur Helps, secretary to the Privy Council. The same two decades saw an outpouring of novels, pamphlets, and articles championing the same principles. Never before, in so short a time, did so many search for a theory of paternalism with a firm philosophical base.

Easily the most prominent of the twenty were the romantic poets Samuel Taylor Coleridge, Robert Southey, and William Wordsworth. In 1829, Southey published *Sir Thomas More, or, Colloquies on the Progress of Society,* and in 1832, *Essays, Moral and Political*. In 1830, Coleridge's *On the Constitution of the Church and State* placed paternalist theory on the metaphysical foundation of German idealism. In 1835, his *Table Talk* was published, followed in 1839 by the republication of his 1816 *The Statesman's Manual*. Wordsworth meanwhile published as a "Postscript" to his *Collected Poems* of 1835, an incisive essay on the obligations of the higher classes to the lower.

The search for a paternalist theory was not limited to romantic poets. In 1826, in his *The Christian and Civic Economy of Large Towns*, the stern Calvinist divine Thomas Chalmers provided an elaborate blueprint of a paternalism that rested on Church and property and not the state.

Far different in tone were the prodigious writer Kenelm Digby's eleven-volume *Mores Catholicus, or, Age of Faith* (1832–42), which glorified medieval chivalry, and Michael Sadler's works praising contemporary mercantilism. Digby's romantic view of a caring medieval Church and a noble medieval baronage greatly inspired the paternalist fervor of the Young England movement. In *Ireland: Its Evils and Their Remedies* (1839) and *Law of Population* (1830), the Leeds merchant and Tory M.P. Michael Sadler sought an alternative political economy that his biographer Robert Benton Seeley calls a patriarchal system that would "foster, protect, cherish and encourage." No one agreed more with these aims than Richard Oastler, Sadler's ally in the fight for the ten-hour day, who from 1827 to 1841 published forty-one pamphlets that saw in local gentry and parsons the remedies for the problems of factories, pauperism, and slums.[3]

Oastler looked to locality, not to the state, as the basis of paternalism. Far different was Thomas Arnold's embracing of a strong paternal state in his 1833 *Principles of Church Reform* and 1832 *Letters on Social Conditions*, both republished in 1845 in *Miscellaneous Works*. Arnold called for a reformed Church to fuse with a more active state, one that would encourage landlords and manufacturers to ameliorate the sufferings of the poor. It was a view that Thomas Carlyle also expressed in *Chartism* (1839) and *Past and Present* (1843), one in which authority at every level did much more governing, protecting, guiding, and commanding. For William Gladstone, governing and guiding belonged largely to the Church, the more powerful Church that he described in *The State and Its Relations with the Church* (1839) and *Church Principles* (1840). The High Church sentiment alarmed many, although not his future rival Benjamin Disraeli, whose romantic and idealized churchmen, landlords, and manufacturers of *Coningsby* (1844) and *Sybil* (1845) dressed up paternalism in a most stunning garb. Less stunning and far more practical was R. B. Seeley's *The Perils of the Nation* (1843) and *Remedies Suggested for Some of the Evils Which Constitute the Perils of a Nation* (1844), two large manuals as full of explicit directions on how to perform one's paternal duties as was John Sandford's 450-page *Parochialia* (1845) or Arthur Helps's *The Claims of Labour* (1844). Thoroughly paternalist and eminently useful as were these manuals, they lacked a philosophical base. Just such a base was provided by Oxford's William Sewell in his *Christian Politics*, the fullest and most coherent statement of paternalism, one nearest to the model sketched above.

Not nearly so full and comprehensive were F. D. Maurice's *The Kingdom of Christ* (1843) and W. G. Ward's *The Ideal of a Christian Church* (1838), two works that joined those of Coleridge and Gladstone in looking to a revived and expanded Church as the great paternal authority. Also persuaded of the Church's great role were the architect Augustus Welby Pugin's *Contrasts* (1836) and the philanthropist John Minter Morgan's *Christian Commonwealth* (1845). Pugin insisted the Church be Roman Catholic, as it was in his idealized world of medieval ecclesiastical paternalism. Morgan, on the other hand, fuses Owenite and communitarian ideas with the ideals of a powerful paternal Church and the Christian stewardship of the wealthy.

The flowering of paternal ideas from 1827 to 1847 did not spring anew from sterile soil. That soil was prepared by William Paley's *Moral and Political Philosophy* (1785) and Edmund Burke's *Reflections on the Revolution in France* (1790). In 1814, Paley's work was in its twenty-eighth edition and was required reading at Cambridge. The matchless expositor of the age's conventional morality, Paley instructed the various classes of a hierarchical society in the duties of property in a rational, assured, moderate, and almost complacent manner, which, by combining the greatest happiness principle with deism, made God the great utilitarian. It was a paternalism that fitted an age of rural stability, Enlightenment ideas and latitudinarian religion, but one Burke would have found shallow and tepid.

It was Burke's more passionate and profound *Reflections* that started the wave of paternalist writings that flourished between 1827 and 1847. Burke, like Paley, assumed a hierarchical society based on authoritarian landlords, a caring clergy, and obedient laborers, but he did so in a much different manner. Instead of Paley's urbane, self-assured world and mechanistic rationalism, he made a passionate and stirring appeal to feelings of honor and chivalry. Alarmed by the radical talk of French revolutionaries and English radicals of the rights of man and social contracts, Burke responded eloquently with a plea for a more organic and authoritarian society, one in which rich and poor and all in between formed part of what he called "the unalterable relations which Providence had ordained." For Burke "the rich were trustees of those who laboured for them," the guarantors of "those connections . . . that regulate and hold together the community of subordination."[4] Although there was little that was new in Burke's hierarchical and organic view of society, he did place it on a firmer philosophical base. England's paternal institutions, he argued, were eminently useful, because they reflected not only the pragmatic adjustments of the past but an enlarged morality that was part of natural and divine law.

Burke's paternalist ideas had an enormous impact in an age frightened into conservatism by revolution abroad and radicals at home, and by cities full of factories, crime and disorder. In 1816, Coleridge, who venerated Burke and committed much of his writing to memory, stoutly defended a society in which "all classes are interdependent . . . more or less a moral unity, an organic whole." Robert Southey, another admirer of Burke, similarly celebrated "that appointed chain / whose cohesion unites / order to order, rank to rank."[5]

Burke's powerful plea for paternal authority was largely political. There was little in the *Reflections* of the social and economic, and although he does deal with such matters in his *Thoughts and Details on Scarcity* (1795), he does so as a disciple of Adam Smith, not of the Tudor humanists. But after the repeal of the Test Acts, Catholic Emancipation, and the Reform Act of 1832, social issues became more prominent than purely political ones. The early Victorians could now turn to the long-festering evils of rural pauperism, exploited factory children, half-naked women in mines, starving handloom weavers, disease-ridden slums, rising crime, overcrowded prisons, cruel lunatic asylums, drunkenness, and prostitution. The problems were endless and formidable, and they demanded an expanded paternalism. Paley's perfunctory paternalism and Burke's political focus would no longer suffice. A broader, more penetrating theory of paternalism was needed, one that spelled out how property could solve rural and urban distress, how the Church could end ignorance and immorality, and how a paternal government could protect its citizens from the vicissitudes of an industrial society. Above all, property had to solve England's multitudinous evils, for property was everywhere the dominant institution. Property, not government or the Church, was truly sovereign, and to it fell the greatest role of a revived paternalism.

THE SOVEREIGN SPHERE OF PROPERTY

Few institutions were more esteemed than property. The sons of the governing class read of its legality in Blackstone and of its utility in Locke. Its usefulness and profitability were evident to all. It stimulated industry, imposed order on the economy, provided the ruling classes and the Church with their incomes, supported charities of every kind, and defined one's station in life and so, according to Burke, one's duties. Burke added that property must "submit to the dominion of prudence and virtue," otherwise "none will submit to the dominion of the great . . . to the feudal tenure."[6]

Coleridge also made property the centerpiece of his social philosophy. Property not the state must alleviate the suffering of their dependents. "The land is not ours," he declared but is held "in trust for the nation"—a trust since "the law of God [has] connected indissolubly the cultivation of every rood of earth with the watchful labours of men." Land made its owner a "free agent," and only a "free agent" could effect reform. "All reforms or innovation" he insists, "not won from a free agent . . . it were folly to propose or wrong to attempt." That free agents based on property should constitute society's main guide and protector rested in great part on what Coleridge called, in capitals, HOMEBORN FEELINGS, feelings enjoyed only by those who ruled society's many small, personal spheres, in which every man should "measure his efforts by his sphere of action," spheres that Burke insisted were the primary area of moral relations and that Southey celebrated when he urged all Christians "to promote the welfare and happiness of those who are in any way dependent."[7]

It would be difficult to exaggerate the paternalists' attachment to the small sphere where property was sovereign. Both Seeley's patriarchal system and Sewell's *Christian Politics* made property the source of the social control and benevolence most likely to prevail between those who knew one another, as was preeminently the case on the landed estate. Ancient, wealthy, and venerated, the landed estate was so central to paternalist thought and reality that it left little room for the trader and manufacturer.

Coleridge and Southey had little use for either. "The greedy, grasping spirit of commercial and manufacturing ambition and avarice," wrote Southey, "is the root of all our evil"—an astonishing claim, yet one that Coleridge appears to have shared when he wrote, in 1816, "The cause of our distress is the overbalance of the commercial spirit." Landowners were fixed and permanent and gave good governance; commerce sought only "the quickest profit and the least cost."[8] Seeley insisted in his *Perils* that not one in fifty manufacturers was benevolent, and Sewell declared in his *Christian Politics* that, since they belonged to an "inferior class," their growth should be stopped.[9]

Far more realistic were Thomas Carlyle, Thomas Arnold, and Arthur Helps. They knew that, as Carlyle put it, "a changed times" demanded "a changed aristocracy" particularly since England had become the workshop of the world; "if there be no nobleness in manufactures there will never be an aristocracy more." Carlyle saw in the nation's captains of industry an "aristocracy of fact," which Arnold embraced when he pronounced that the "chimneys of Sheffield are of not less value than the domain of the land-lord."[10] No one aware of the massive growth of industrial and urban England could deny that if the paternalism of property were to remain a viable rem-edy, traders and manufacturers must be included. Arthur Helps certainly did, and he thus addressed his *Claims of Labour* largely to them. "Eschew the grandeur and glitter of life," he implored them, "and care for your depend-ents"; don't reduce "your intercourse to mere cash payments" and above all adopt " the rule of the father which is the type of all good government."[11]

The paternalist's view of philanthropy was also mixed and ambivalent. Not a few of them had deep suspicions about its diffuseness and presumptuous-ness, which seemed to encroach on the paternalism of property. Coleridge never found a "trader in philanthropy" who was not "wrong in heart"; Tho-mas Chalmers denounced the "vague and vagrant philanthropy which loses much of its energy in diffuseness"; Sewell called it "promiscuous benevo-lence"; and Carlyle expostulated, "Most sick I am of this sugary jargon of philanthropy."[12] None of the three meant to condemn all philanthropy, and no doubt they were aware that that term was occasionally used to describe the benevolent work of property itself. But they remained suspicious because philanthropy had become identified with two very different outlooks, either the grand visionary scheme of utopian philosophers, like Godwin and Shelley, or the bold and far-reaching efforts of the evangelicals to convert everyone in the world, irrespective of whether they were tepid Anglicans or Africans igno-rant of Jesus. Such grand, visionary schemes could in no way develop the HOMEBORN FEELINGS that the smaller spheres could alone engender. Far-reaching philanthropy not only rivaled the smaller spheres of property but the village and town, and, most alarmingly, the Church's parishes, dioceses, cathedrals, and ecclesiastical courts.

THE PATERNAL MISSION OF THE CHURCH

Devout churchmen had no difficulty with the paternalist outlook. God was after all the greatest of fathers. To preach, instruct, exhort, correct, guide, and love one's neighbors were paternal duties that Jesus demanded of his followers. None of the twenty paternalist writers alluded to doubted the sa-credness of these injunctions. Neither did they doubt the sacredness of the Church of England, which was proud of its divine origins and glorious past, a past that writers as diverse as Cobbett, Oastler, Disraeli, Carlyle, and Pugin found even more glorious in medieval times than in the present. Before the Reformation, before the destruction of monasteries and the subordination of Church to state, churchmen had tended the sick and destitute, cathedral schools had educated the sons of grocers and gentlemen alike; chantries had given spiritual solace, almshouses had succored the poor, and hospitals had tended the sick. The organic community of medieval times had yielded, however, to secular, mammon-worshipping, capitalist England, a contrast that Pugin made vivid in his two drawings in *Contrasts*, one of a medieval town of cathedral spires and handsome churches and abbeys, all ministering to the poor, the other of a modern town full of ugly factories, secular halls, and workhouses whose wardens beat the poor.[13] Southey, in his *Book of the Church*, also presented a nostalgic view of a happy united ecclesiastical society with abbeys dispensing alms and clergy visiting the poor, as did Kenelm Digby more fully and rhapsodically in *Broad Stone* and *Mores Catholicus*. What a wonderful world it was, he wrote, "No lawyers, no manufacturers . . . no speculators," only pious clergymen and devout churchmen praying for and succoring the meek, dependent, obedient, and not overeducated poor.[14] Many early Victorians lost themselves in these lovely evocations of a caring Church, just as they delighted in the picture that Cobbett drew in his *Protestant Reformation* of monasteries that "helped all that were in need," "promoted rectitude in morals," and provided hospitals, fifty to a county, "open to the poor, the aged, the orphan, the widow and the stranger."[15] These were the powerful visions that led many to look to the Church of England to refashion society according to the spiritual ideals of the past.

The Church certainly had the wealth and manpower to do so. With an income of £9 million, some 12,000 benefices, nearly 17,000 clergy, two universities, many schools, many chantries, and chapels, and 61 archdeacons and 26 bishops supervising a multitude of cathedral offices, there seemed little the Church of England could not do. William Wordsworth was persuaded that "ministers . . . of irreproachable manners and morals, thoroughly acquainted with the structure of society" could meet the challenges of the new manufacturing towns.[16] This was not entirely a pipe dream. The clergy, numbering 17,000, were equivalent to nearly two-thirds of England's central bureaucracy, and if one added Nonconformist ministers, they perhaps even outnumbered it. In his *Church and State* (in contrast to his *Table Talk*), with its "Idea of Nationality" and a national Church with its own considerable property, Coleridge envisaged the clerisy as including, not only the Nonconformist clergy, but the learned of every kind, whether in law, medicine, psychology, music, military or civil architecture, or the sciences.[17] It was an idea that Thomas Chalmers and Thomas Arnold promoted, although in a less Platonic and more practical manner and one consonant with political economy. Chalmers's clerisy would include not only ministers, but lay elders, deacons, and schoolteachers, the elders spreading the reforming gospel, the deacons visiting the poor, and the teachers inculcating self-reliance. The indigent were urged to seek jobs or help from kin, because there would be no state relief, and only the blind, halt, diseased, and aged would receive the voluntary charity of the Church.[18]

Thomas Arnold's vision was far different. His clerisy would be part of a Church that would fuse with a more active and Christian state. He would divide large dioceses and multiply the number of bishops, one for every large town. The wealthy parts of the Church would share with the poorer, and there would be no absentee clergy. The reformed "diaconates" would teach the lower orders habits of industry and their superiors their Christian responsibilities.[19] It was a clerisy far too radical for the High Church William Sewell.

Sewell also envisaged multiplying bishops and enlarging the clergy, but in his scheme of things, there would be no redistribution of income and no fusing with the state. The ordained priests of a divinely created and visible Apostolic Church, assisted by strictly supervised sisters of charity and young monks, would bring about a spiritually rejuvenated England. Somewhat similar, yet basically different, was the invisible Church of all believers, clerical and lay, of the evangelicals, who were active in a multitude of lay societies repellent to High Churchmen. They, too, envisaged a Church that, as guardian of the poor, would solve England's social ills by reforming its moral life.

Both High Churchmen and, to a lesser degree, evangelicals were sanguine about what their clerisies could accomplish. Sewell even asked Parliament to transfer administration of the Poor Law to the churches.[20] Whether High or Low Church, whether believing in salvation and grace through the sacraments or by a rebirth through faith, it was the man of God, not the man of property or public office who would thoroughly reform society—and would do so not by act of Parliament, but by the spiritual regeneration of men, a task that belonged to those with the miraculous powers of remaking men.

Increasingly championed as the best way to remake men was education. Confronted both by the rise of radicalism, crime, and urban squalor and by societies demanding a secular and universal education, even paternalists, once fearful that education would unsettle the lower orders, were converted to its necessity. If public education was inevitable, however, the Church had to control it.

Belief in the redeeming powers of the Church colored even the outlook of Christian Socialists such as F. D. Maurice, John Minter Morgan, and J. M. Ludlow (who were, in fact, far more Christian than socialist). Maurice envisaged the Church as the architect of a new society of Christian cooperation, rather than capitalist competition. The key institution for Christian cooperation, Morgan and Ludlow concurred, would be the parish, with its squire and parson, not the state. Ludlow hoped the wealthy and clergy would turn the vestry into a temple of labor for the employment of the jobless, while Morgan wanted such elite-dominated vestries to act as village institutes, each with its labor exchange, reading room, friendly and temperance society, and soup kitchen. The unworthy poor, drunkards, and gamblers would be excluded.[21]

In an age as intensely religious as was early Victorian England, all persuasions saw their churches as a crucial means of forming a better society. As great and earnest as was this vision of a resurgent Church of England, its advocates faced two formidable forces, the Dissenters and the state. Of those attending service on Census Sunday in 1851, only half were Anglican, and far more did not attend at all. Most diverse and multiplying were the Nonconformist sects, Catholics, and those of little belief. For liberal Broad Churchmen like Arnold and Maurice, and for the Coleridge of *Church and State*, the answer was a more comprehensive Church; for High Churchmen, it was an exclusive, proselytizing Church; and for Anglican evangelicals, it was the conversion of the many to form one large Church of the believing. The evangelicals, however, were divided on whether all Nonconformists were among the believing. To fulfill their respective visions, all agreed that the Church should control education. Sewell insisted on it, because he could cooperate neither with a "desecrated, creedless Church-less state" nor with those in "a state of heathenism, heresy and schism." The evangelical Seeley was nearly as exclusive, refusing to cooperate with Dissenters, because he was sure of victory over them.[22] In *Church and State*, Coleridge proposed to include all Protestants in his enlarged clerisy, as did Arnold, except for "Quakers, Unitarians and Catholics." But in his *Table Talk*, Coleridge denounced all sectaries and heresies and called for the exclusion of Dissenters from Oxford and Cambridge and of Catholics from Parliament.[23] Neither Coleridge nor the other Anglicans could square the circle of their visions of one enlarged, paternalist clerisy with the realities of secularism and sectarianism. It was a dilemma resolved only if all agreed on theological truths or on their unimportance. F. D. Maurice, professor of English literature at King's College, London, sought theological agreement. Convinced that man's inner conscience and intuition would reveal Christianity's essential truths, he envisioned a universal Church and a Christian socialism that would replace egotism and competitiveness. It was a forlorn hope. Far from agreeing on essentials, King's College dismissed him for denying eternal damnation. Arnold, like Maurice a tolerant Broad Churchman who sought to bring all together on the basis of essential truths, was also denounced as too radical.[24] Few were the Anglicans, especially the influential ones, who believed in working with Dissenters, much less the Catholics. The idea of a large, comprehensive active clerisy was a will-o'-the-wisp.

Not a will-o'-the-wisp, but infinitely perplexing, was the problem of Church and state. With the 1828 repeal of the Test Acts, the 1829 Catholic Emancipation Act, and the 1832 Reform Act, Dissenters and Catholics became part of a state that was no longer purely Anglican. For Congregationalists and Baptists, as well as for Thomas Chalmers after he broke away from the Church of Scotland in 1847, these were but the first steps to the separation of Church and state. For Chalmers, once a defender of the ecclesiastical estab-lishment, the state would now be little more than a policeman, leaving truly voluntary churches to educate, relieve and ameliorate.[25] Another Scotsman, Thomas Carlyle, had an entirely different view. His "New Downing Street" would organize the clergy into "sacred corporations," because the universal need was for an "Aristocracy and Priesthood, a Governing Class and a Teaching Class"—a vision he had developed in *Past and Present,* with its ide-alized fifteenth-century Abbot Sampson running his monastery like a captain of industry.[26] But Carlyle's secularist tendencies and worship of heroes offered no solution to the Church and state problem.

Coleridge's solution was more complex. Although part of the larger idea of the state, the Church was also separate. The large, active clerisy of the learned constituted a "nationality," with its own property, and it, not government, would manage local affairs. This "democracy," as Coleridge called it, would treat men as individuals, not, as did the state, as classes. In the paternalists' world of local spheres, free of the central state, although not of the Church's rejuvenating spirit, the clerisy would manage parishes and corporations that nourished HOMEBORN FEELINGS.[27] The state, of course, would see to it that the Church of England remained the nation's established Church, although in no way to be controlled by it.

William Sewell agreed that there should be no state control, certainly not by a Parliament gone secular and a state "powerful only for evil," and he and many High Churchmen talked boldly of "the voluntary principle," although without yielding the right of an established Church to Church rates, burial fees, and laws against heresy.[28] Profound ambivalence vis-à-vis the state col-ored most Anglicans' views of the paternal mission of the Church, an am-bivalence Thomas Arnold proposed to end by a bold attempt to fuse Church and state. They were really identical, he declared, the ends of both being a truly Christian commonwealth. Since a "religious society is only a civil soci-ety enlightened," he concluded that "the State in its highest perfection is the Church."[29] Possibly more practical than Arnold's radical solution was J. M. Ludlow's novel proposal that Parliament grant money to all faiths, allowing each to compete in the creation of a paternal society, a formula that the Whigs adopted in 1847 in their grants to Anglican and Nonconformist schools.[30] But grants to all faiths meant grants to false creeds and one more invasion by the state into territory belonging to the Church, an invasion that drove the incisive thinker John Henry Newman to abandon serious thought on social questions. In 1877, he lamented that for fifty years, secular measures such as civil marriages, school boards, and poor laws had substituted "political or social motives for social and personal duties, thereby withdrawing matters of conduct from the jurisdiction of religion."[31] Newman sensed the hopelessness of applying Coleridge's grand idea of a clerisy to a society of both religious diversity and social evils exceeding the Church's capacity to remedy. The only answer seemed to be in a paternal state.

THE SEVERAL SPHERES OF GOVERNMENT

The English had many differing conceptions of government. For most, it was a vague, remote, notion of Crown, Parliament, and the courts, and, more immediately, J.P.'s, mayors, aldermen, vestrymen, and overseers, all part of a gigantic network that ran from Crown to constable, a part of what Burke called a "moral partnership of all those who were united by "connections, natural and civil" into a "chain of subordination." It was a network Sewell spelled out in his *Christian Politics*. The functions and offices of state, he wrote, "should be ramified and extended through all to the very lowest," to the jurymen acting as judges and the school where "the masters act as a sovereign."[32] It was, as Sewell repeatedly claimed, a "pluralistic world."

Neither Burke nor Sewell made a clear distinction between public and private authorities. Schoolmasters were sovereign, as were fathers, landlords, and J.P.'s. A poacher appearing before a petty session held in a country house hardly knew whether the squire who fined him was acting as landlord or J.P. Paternalism saw no sharp lines dividing the public and private authorities, especially in the local sphere, neither in Seeley's "old English parish . . . with its own parson, known and knowing every family, and its publicly chosen overseer" nor in the "corporations and vestries" where Coleridge found his "democracy."[33] In the local sphere, schoolmasters, landlords, and parsons joined publicly appointed J.P.'s, councillors, overseers, sheriffs, and constables to form a network of authorities—each, said Coleridge, reflecting the "Idea of the State." For Oastler, the "excellence" in the English Constitution was that it allowed "every locality to manage its affairs."[34] Oastler did not, of course, object to Parliament passing a Ten Hour Act; nor was Southey at all reticent in urging statute after statute empowering localities to rule paternally, all being part of what Helps called "the happy admixture of central and local authority." But they wanted no centralized bureaucracy. Oastler wanted a

Ten Hour Act but no factory inspectors, Helps wanted regulations on the dwellings of the poor but regulations carried out by property and local officials, and Southey was explicit that landowners and parsons, not government inspectors, would carry out poor laws and educational measures.[35] Thomas Arnold, the advocate of a strong state, wanted local authorities to manage his schemes for public employment of the jobless. There would be no Benthamite commissioners. Day-to-day government for paternalism meant local government, and a local government by private as well as public authorities, authorities more often than not based on property. Property qualified one to be a J.P., an M.P., or alderman; property supported the parson, and great property made the great landlord the local sovereign. Ecclesiastical, legal, family, and titled privileges fused with property in parish, county, and town to form those local centers of that undifferentiated, coalescing power so central to a paternalist's role. Their commitment to locality, when joined to their devotion to property, led paternalist writers to an almost laissez-faire view of government, a view made all the stronger by three strongly held assumptions, that a harmonious natural law regulated society and its economy, that a self-reliant morality should be basic to that society, and that its incidental ills could best be assuaged by the voluntary principle.

That paternalists believed in self-regulating economic laws may seem surprising; but it would not to the many readers of Burke. He never hid his belief in political economy: labor is a "commodity"; "monopoly capital" and "large farms" are a great benefit; "profits, salutary"; and the greater a farmer's avarice, the better. A wise Deity "counsels self interest to the general good," and the laws of commerce were "the laws of Nature and of God." And although government could prevent evil, it could do little "positive good"; statesmen should thus never descend "from province to a parish and . . . a private house."[36] It is little wonder that Adam Smith called Burke his disciple.

Coleridge may have winced at Burke's praise of avarice, but he was just as opposed to government descending to parish and house. He told the gentry that their estates "were secured from all human interference by every principle of law." Although the state might regulate manufactures, land and commerce should enjoy "the unqualified right to do what I like with my own."[37] William Sewell and Robert Southey had too great a disdain of political economy to go with Coleridge's "maxims of trade" and Burke's laissez-faire economics. But they held property to be no less sacrosanct and a divinely ordered society no less harmonious, the harmony arising not from the economists' self-interest but from the identity of interests inherent in doing one's paternal duties.[38] Their writings show that one can develop a paternalist laissez-faire in no way indebted to a hateful political economy.

For Thomas Chalmers, who was known both for his economic writings and his Christian sermons, political economy was anything but hateful, and he had no difficulty incorporating the economists' laissez-faire into the paternalist outlook. Both fitted well his Calvinistic and Scottish individualism, his belief in self-reliance. It was a belief held, in varying degrees, by all paternalists, although by none as resolutely as Chalmers. He believed that schoolmasters, preachers, and elders could so train up the poor to industry and providence that neither state nor church need give them relief.[39] Coleridge and Southey could not go so far, but Coleridge did, in 1816, oppose the payment of relief to the able-bodied because it encouraged imprudence, and Southey proposed giving "the worthless poor no more relief than would prevent them from famine."[40] It was a formula for a minimalist, not a welfare, state. Welfare should be by private charity, not public dole, in keeping with the paternalist's devotion to the voluntary principle. Let there be coal and blanket clubs, soup kitchens and dispensaries, hospitals and orphanages, and schools, all run by the voluntary principle. "In the province of charity," wrote Burke, "the magistrate has nothing at all to do."[41] Few were the paternalists who did not agree with Burke that a charity's rights, especially if a Church charity, were inviolable. That many charities were corrupt, wasteful, and ineffectual did not lead them to demand the interference of government, since their reform would come from the spiritual regeneration of the individual. "I have no faith in Act of Parliament reform," exclaimed Coleridge, "let us become better people." Both Coleridge and Wordsworth believed that better people, acting voluntarily, would end slavery, for Coleridge, by boycotting its products, for Wordsworth, by trusting the slaves' owners to free them.[42] It was better people, not central bureaucrats, to whom Richard Oastler looked for England's salvation. Social problems cried out for spiritual not organizational solutions, for Christians who had had a change of heart, not Poor Law commissioners from London, a view shared by Southey, Sadler, Helps, and Sewell, as well as Carlyle, and also expressed by Burke, for whom "the only sure reform [is] the ceasing to do ill."[43] Christians ceasing to do ill also did not threaten, as Acts of Parliament and government inspectors did, the status quo that Burke taught embodied the wisdom of the past. Paternalists disliked change. In 1816, Coleridge claimed that the aims of government had been realized to an unexampled degree and that government should do little beyond "the withholding of all extrinsic aid . . . to an injurious system."[44] Bacon's apothegm "All innovation is with injury" was a favorite of paternalists; it was quoted by Burke, repeated by Sadler, and almost as popular among them as the injunction "Live and let live."[45]

Yet the paternalists' laissez-faire had its limits. Except for Arnold and possibly Chalmers, they were exceedingly authoritarian on all matters of social disorder, Church privileges, political sedition, and crime. Burke certainly taught the danger of disorder and sedition. He was a firm supporter of Pitt's 1795 repressive measures against radicals. Coleridge insisted that the state could in theory repress heresy and in practice repress lotteries, close theaters on Sunday, and exclude Dissenters from the universities.[46] Southey, ever fearful of sedition and riot, rejoiced in a feudalism with its "superintendence everywhere," and urged that libelers be transported, public houses restricted, vagabonds punished, and the seditious press suppressed. William Sewell who would applaud Southey's every severity, called for "one external authority to harmonize all acts."[47] Though in actuality that external authority would be a Parliament passing laws that the courts, especially local ones, would enforce, in rhetoric many believed it to be the monarchy. Coleridge rejoiced that Europe was turning to "a pure monarchy"; Disraeli saw in a resurgent monarch "the protector of the people"; and Carlyle called for a "King made in the image of God who could a little achieve for the people."[48] But if the rhetoric of monarchy indulged in by almost all the paternalists was no more than a fantasy, their authoritarianism was real. Capital punishment, coercion acts for Ireland, laws against seditious writings, imprisonment for blasphemy, fines for nonattendance at Church, and the locking up of tipplers were all part of a paternalist government firmly rooted in the many statutes that landed M.P.'s enacted and landed J.P.'s enforced.

None of the paternalist writers had a consistent definition of government. They could denounce centralization and bureaucracy but use a centralized Parliament, law courts, and Church to help them rule England. As protectionists, they also embraced the Corn and Navigation laws to help them rule England and in a benevolent spirit supported factory and poor laws. In 1816, Coleridge urged an act to exclude children from factories, and Oastler, although an enemy of centralization, called for a strong Ten Hours Bill, which Michael Sadler proposed in Parliament in line with his belief in a protectionist and mercantilist state. Southey also wished a protectionist state. No paternalist writer was more fertile in government schemes that would constitute a "paternal government," a government Wordsworth would have stand *in loco parentis* to the poor.[49] There was an interventionist strand in paternalist thought, but one largely empowering local property, local government, and local charities to grapple with England's bewildering array of social problems.

It was not until *Latter Day Pamphlets* (1850) that Carlyle looked to a centralized state that would organize labor into industrial regiments, force captains of industry to cooperate, and conscript the clergy into "social corporations."[50] An impetuous and discontented Scotsman steeped in French and

German learning, who had first come to London at the age of thirty-nine, Carlyle lacked the deep roots in the English institutions and vested interests that defined the early Victorian paternalists' concept of a pluralistic society and paternal government rooted in powerful vested interests.

Important as were the more than nearly thirty works published between 1823 and 1847 to the development of paternalism as an idea, they neither reached England's governing classes nor dealt fully and concretely with its social problems. Paternalism as an idea would have had a far less impact but for the press.

CHAPTER 2

Paternalism Made Popular

In the 1830s and 1840s, the quarterlies and monthlies, more than the learned works of Coleridge and Southey, graced the reading tables of England's governing classes; and in Tory households, they would likely be the *Quarterly Review, Blackwood's Magazine,* or *Fraser's Magazine,* three paternalist journals whose writers were not only deep admirers of Coleridge and Southey but willing to deal with workhouses, sewers, lunatic asylums, and factory labor—to bridge the gap between intellectual development and concrete social problems. Also Tory were the *English Review,* the *Oxford and Cambridge Review,* the *British Critic,* the *Christian Remembrancer,* and the *Dublin Magazine.* They published over 300 articles on social questions, articles that provide a large and detailed picture of the idea of Tory paternalism, a picture that thanks to the *Wellesley Index to Victorian Periodicals* now includes the names of sixty-nine of their authors. It is a picture that allows an analysis of the impact on them of three powerful forces, dominant ideas, pressing social problems, and the influence of the social milieu.

The dominant ideas for most of the sixty-nine reviewers were those of Burke, Scott, Coleridge, Southey, and Wordsworth. Of these five none was quoted more often than Burke, especially by *Blackwood's* George Croly (a biographer of Burke) and the *Quarterly Review's* political editor, John Croker. For Croly, Burke was "the noblest philosopher" of the age; for Croker, he was "the greatest authority who ever wrote on political ethics."[1]

For Croly and Croker, who were both sixty in 1840, Burke was the giant of their youth; but for the sixty-seven others, whose average age was thirty-five, Coleridge, Wordsworth, and Walter Scott were the outstanding writers of the age. Scott was especially the hero of contributors to the *Quarterly Review* and *Blackwood's;* the lawyer William Aytoun wrote of reading Scott on the hearth rug, Professor J. D. Blackie recalled "leisure hours pouring over Walter Scott's matchless stories," and for the novelist Samuel Warren, Scott was "the colossus."[2] Scott himself wrote for the *Quarterly Review* in the 1820s, and his son-in-law John Lockhart edited it in the 1840s.

While Scott's tales entranced, it was Coleridge who brought intellectual excitement. Blackie, who remembered Scott's "matchless tales," found Coleridge in 1831 "the greatest figure in the intellectual world of London." A year later, Blackie had a fit "of Wordsworthian fervour," as did *Blackwood's* W. H. Smith, whose Wordsworthian "moral conversion" saved him from Byron. Thomas de Quincy, an important contributor, also esteemed Wordsworth and Coleridge, calling their *Lyrical Ballads* "the greatest event in the unfolding of my mind."[3] *Lyrical Ballads* also led the *Quarterly Review*'s John Croker, as it did De Quincy, to a lifelong friendship with Wordsworth. The great poet was also toasted at many a banquet at *Blackwood's*. J. F. Murray called him "the great ornament of our age."[4]

Blackwood's contributors also admired Robert Southey. Archibald Alison, who wrote fifteen articles on social problems, met Southey, talked with him until midnight, and left with an impression, "never . . . effaced." *Blackwood's* authors' fervent admiration of the Lake Poets was returned by Coleridge's "perfect identity of sentiments, principles, and faith" with *Blackwood's*.[5]

Writers in the *Quarterly Review* also fervently admired the Lake Poets. Its editor, John Gibson Lockhart, said his biographer, "bowed low at the shrine of Wordsworth" and called Southey "a wonderful political writer." Southey, in many articles in the 1820s and 1830s, set the paternalist tone of the *Quarterly Review*, a tone deepened in the 1840s by three articles from a Lord Ashley who was close to, and much influenced by, Southey. Also friends of and influenced by Southey were the *Quarterly Review*'s Henry Milman and Henry Taylor. In an 1842 issue, Taylor told *Quarterly Review* readers that Wordsworth, Coleridge, Southey, and Scott were the "four greatest geniuses in their generation."[6] Dean Lake of Balliol, also a *Quarterly Review* author, certainly felt so, busy as he was in "endeavoring to imbue [W. G. Ward] with Coleridge and Wordsworth," an effort that did indeed influence Ward's very Coleridgean *Ideal of the Christian Church*. Ward contributed articles to the *British Critic*, whose first two editors were John Henry Newman and Thomas Mozley. When the *British Critic* became the *Christian Remembrancer* in 1843, Oxford's R. W. Church wrote "of our own Coleridge."[7] Ward, Church, and Mozley were part of the Tractarian Movement, which was, according to Newman, "Coleridgean." Few were more dominant in the 1830s than Coleridge. John Kemble and Henry Reeve of the *British and Foreign Review* judged Coleridge a greater sage than Locke and "a great luminary."[8] The *British and Foreign Review*, although not Tory, was decidedly Coleridgean, as was *Fraser's Magazine* and the very Tory Young England's *Oxford and Cambridge Review*. J. A. Heraud, *Fraser's* assistant editor in the 1830s, was called "a conscientious follower of Coleridge," and its editor until 1842, William Maginn, confessed that his friend Coleridge had "acted strongly on the mind of the day." Maginn's *Fraser's* denounced the utilitarians for wishing to replace Scott, Coleridge, Wordsworth, and Southey with Bentham, McCulloch, Mill, and Ricardo.[9]

The great impact of Scott and the Lake Poets was as much aesthetic as political. As Blackie shrewdly observed of their impact on *Blackwood's* authors, "they were . . . Tories perhaps less on political than on romantic grounds."[10] Wordsworth in particular wrote little on social questions, yet he taught, said *Blackwood's* W. H. Smith, "the spirit of obedience and reverence . . . the impulse to accept the order of the universe . . . to faithfully discharge the near and known duty."[11] Wordsworth's deep sense of the rightness of nature and God's ways, of the value of simple personal truths and acts of goodness assured countless readers that not all was Benthamite calculus, political economy, and Whig complacency. For that complete paternalist William Sewell, Wordsworth was greater than Coleridge for he took the first "step to the restoration of philosophy . . . in a safe direction."[12]

The problem of intellectual influence is one of great complexity and uncertainty. There is no accurate way of measuring the influence of Coleridge or Southey, even when *Blackwood's* editor, John Wilson, calls Southey a "genius rich and rare."[13] Such comments only suggest a strong affinity between the intellectual and social outlook of Scott, Burke, and the romantic poets and the intellectual and social outlook of the Tory reviewers. It was an affinity that included a reverence for a hierarchical and paternalist society based on land, Church, and locality. Few Tory reviewers doubted that society should be hierarchic and authoritarian, vital aspects of what *Blackwood's* W. H. Smith called "the unalterable nature of our social pyramid." Smith feared equality. So did the *Quarterly Review's* Henry Taylor, who found nothing so "ungenial and unfruitful."[14] High then was his praise of a Wordsworth who "nowhere advocated equality of station." Inequality and subordination were "indispensable," declared *Fraser's*, "where the social structure consists of grades." Also indispensable to these journals was obedience, submission, and dutifulness. "Mankind," asserted Archibald Alison of *Blackwood's*, was "in need of the direction of others as children in school."[15]

Society was also to be as organic as that feudalism which the *Oxford and Cambridge Review* judged the most "perfect form of society since Jewish theocracy." *Fraser's* found in the duke of Richmond's paternalism a shining example of "modern feudal relations," while *Blackwood's* Longueville Jones called it "the highest form of civilization," one that delighted his colleague Alison because it "conferred power . . . on those only who are interested in the welfare of the people," that is, people in small, organic, personal communities immune from the evils of capitalism, centralization, heartless economists, and crass utilitarians who saw society as a mere "collection of atoms."[16] "Society is not a heap of sand," wrote the *Quarterly Review's* William Sewell, "but a plurality in unity," one with hierarchy and authority since without submission "no complete organism can exist."[17] William Sewell defined these organic bodies in the *Quarterly Review* as consisting of landlords "exercising . . . the duties of little monarchs" who were aided in every village by "an ecclesiastical establishment." Together they would constitute a "feudal system" in relation to which "the master of the soil should stand . . . in a fatherly way."[18]

The basis of this feudal system was land. It alone, Croker announced in the *Quarterly Review*, provided the foundation of government. "An absolute necessity," said W. H. Smith in *Blackwood's*, the journal in which De Quincy proclaimed primogeniture and the Church "the basis of our civil constitution."[19] Squire and parson were to rule these organic communities. Their partnership did in fact become a reality in innumerable rural parishes like Wiltshire's Cholderton, the parish of the Reverend Thomas Mozley, editor of the *British Critic*, in which in 1840 he told readers that "property had its duties," duties that land above all could perform, since factories were "houses of bondage" and the steam engine an "enormous calamity," destructive of the "moral units of society." The *Quarterly Review's* William Sewell's solution to Mozley's fears was to "raze . . . to the ground half of an overgrown metropolis."[20]

Few Tory reviewers would have wanted to raze half of London, but most were haunted by the thought of fearsome cities and satanic factories. They looked, as did Wordsworth, to the Church of England as the saving remedy. The reviewers had only enthusiasm for its holy mission, especially the Anglican clergymen who edited and wrote the *English Review*, the *British Critic*, and the *Christian Remembrancer*, all of whom urged the creation of more bishops, priests, and cathedral institutions as well as hospitals, houses of mercy, female penitentiaries, almshouses, and sisters of charity. They also urged that diocesan boards of education should closely supervise their training colleges and the multiplying schools.[21] It was an ambitious scheme, one that *Blackwood's* urged the Church to carry out fearlessly, a scheme that would even meet the evil of pauperism. "The offertory," declared the *English Review*, was the safest remedy of that evil, especially when bishops "lift up the cross and pastoral staff in . . . our crowded towns" and when monasteries trained "Christian warriors" as Wilfred and Ethelred had long ago. The nineteenth century, it said, must return to "the seventh, or sixth, nay even to the first century." Young England's *Oxford and Cambridge Review* also dreamed of medieval monasteries and sisters of charity, while the *Quarterly Review* championed penitentiaries for fallen women.[22]

At the center of the new mission envisioned by High Churchmen was the offertory, the answer, said many, to pauperism. But an offertory that excluded Nonconformists and Catholics as well as secularists and the indifferent could hardly grapple with pauperism. Poverty, however, disturbed them less than secularism and heresy. "Latitudinarianism," said the *Oxford and Cambridge Review*, "is the one most dangerous adversary . . . to national amelioration."[23]

Parliament had once been the great ally of the Church and had voted generous grants for the building of churches. But by 1847 this had changed. A Parliament open to Dissenters and latitudinarians gave grants only to supplement the efforts of church schools, but church schools with a small *c*, since the grants also went to Nonconformist and Catholic schools. The grants also carried restrictions that many High Churchmen found so intolerable that they embraced the voluntary principle and denounced a secular state growing ever more centralized. Even *Fraser's*, which in 1843 called a patriarchal government the best, was constant in denouncing centralization. In an article on a government for New Zealand, it revealed how it squared a patriarchal government with hatred of a centralized state: most power would go to great landlords, considerable power to the established Church, and only some to a legislative council, with no mention at all of an executive and a bureaucracy.[24] Hatred of a centralized state fitted in with the *Oxford and Cambridge Review*'s definition of a patriarchal government as "supervision, care, and kindness . . . in all the relations of society," the *English Review*'s "every man should cultivate the region Providence has assigned him," and the *Quarterly Review*'s "Let each man care for his own part and the whole will take care of itself."[25] It was the medieval dream that for *Blackwood's* and the *Quarterly Review* included noblemen leading regiments of armed men.

The Tory reviewers focus on personal rule within a locality—Burke's "moral partnership" and Coleridge's "HOME BORN FEELINGS"—lay at the heart of the Tories' paternalism, making them suspicious even of the large, diffuse philanthropy that encroached on paternalism's local spheres. The reviewers wrote of "platform philanthropy," "clap-trap philanthropy," and "the pernicious cant of universal philanthropy." They also condemned the "cant of humanity" and, pointing to the evangelicals, "the unctuous silkiness of Exeter Hall." "Philanthropy," said *Blackwood's* S. R. Phillips, "does not work, she talks."[26] In *John Bull*, Phillips also attacked Charles Dickens for his part in "the exertions of modern philanthropy." Dickens's egalitarian humanitarianism also irritated other Tory journals, the *English Review* because of his hostility to "our aristocratic institutions"; the *Oxford and Cambridge Review* for "feelings of brotherhood" and "forgetting religion"; the *British and Foreign Review* for "too much kindness of heart"; and *Blackwood's* for "flashy philanthropy," a philanthropy whose diffuseness, according to most Tory reviewers, undermined the duties of men of rank and station in their localities.[27]

Also threatening to the world of personal duties and localities was the political economists' hard and impersonal cash nexus, although it bothered the Tories' romantic and aesthetic sensibilities more than their actual economic views. How unromantic, how unspiritual, was talk of the iron law of wages, geometrical and arithmetical progressions, and a calculus of pain and pleasure. The axioms of the economists were nevertheless not without some truth. *Blackwood's* Alison had studied political economy with "ardour" while one of its leading reviewers, De

Quincy, author of the *Logic of Political Economy*, wrote in praise of David Ricardo.[28] At the *Quarterly Review*, Croker shared Burke's enthusiasm for Adam Smith and wrote of the "prurience of legislation" and "false and dangerous estimates of government." J. S. Mill's *Political Economy* even won the accolades of the *Christian Remembrancer* and that journal's conclusion that "as direct remedies all legislative enactments must be powerless."[29] Aesthetically and spiritually averse to the economists' selfish principle, as property owners and ardent localists, they nevertheless liked political economy's laissez-faire doctrines.

The paternalist vision of the Tory reviewers, one based on Scott's romanticism, Burke's wisdom of history, Coleridge's metaphysics, and Wordsworth's sensitive poetry wore an attractive and appealing garb. But was it a viable vision? Could it meet the problems of pauperism, child labor, slums, ignorance, crime, and Irish famines?

With one in ten on relief, pauperism posed a most formidable problem, one made all the greater by the Whigs' New Poor Law of 1834 with its harsh *diktat* to the able, no relief except in the workhouse. Though it was a *diktat* that Tory candidates and the press attacked in the parliamentary elections of 1841, the workhouse test it demanded was not all that incompatible with the Tory reviewers' view of the poor. For *Blackwood's* De Quincy, pauperism was "radicated in the nature of man, which is wicked."

Fraser's believed that pauperism arose from individual failings and not the vicissitudes of trade.[30] For Thomas Mozley, writing in the *British Critic*, poverty itself was healthy, since "nothing but the deepest and bitterest poverty will subdue the uneducated classes." "More comfort," he added, would only make "worse the bondage of sin." Mozley ended his article by excusing the legislature and every "rank or order" from "heartless wrong" and concluding that "no one is to blame."[31] *Fraser's* seemed to agree that no one was to blame when it insisted that agriculture requires no "over-anxious interference." *Blackwood's* Croly went even further, pronouncing "the very idea of a poor law a direct contradiction of the principle that man should be a provident animal," a sentiment with which the evangelical Tory Chalmers was in entire agreement.[32]

But not all Tory reviewers agreed with Croly and Chalmers. Despite Croker's warning of "the prurience of legislation," the *Quarterly Review* had an assistant poor law commissioner defend it. *Blackwood's* also had a poor law official write about the new law, but more critically, voicing the Tory squire's hatred of its centralization and its refusal to let local authorities discriminate between the worthy and unworthy poor.[33] The Tory *Fraser's* also objected to its centralization, and to its being "new-fangled." But newfangled it was not in the 1840s but a law that had, by 1838, saved property £12,300,000 in lower poor rates. Quickly made part of the status quo, it soon enjoyed the *"viz inertia"* that *Blackwood's* Charles Neaves called the "principle of conservatism." It is a principle that explains why Tory reviewers opposed a poor law for Scotland.[34]

Viz inertia also influenced the Tory reviewers on child labor. They, as all England, supported Lord Ashley's bill that excluded women and children from coal mines, but beyond that they did not go. The *British Critic* called child labor in agriculture a necessity; *Fraser's* wanted no government interference with seamstresses; the *English Review* urged a trust in private employers, not "precipitous legislation"; and the *Quarterly Review* called critics of the overworking of seamstresses "enthusiasts" and denied that seamstresses were underpaid.[35]

An exception to these tepid views was Lord Ashley's compassion for the exploited in England's factories and workshops. In an 1841 article in the *Quarterly Review*, he described in graphic detail the plight of infants still working 14 and 15 hours a day in many of England's workshops and urged Parliament to "protect the weak," but he did so in a vaguer and less vigorous manner than in his plea that good Christians should "open your treasury, erect churches, send forth missionaries of religion, reverse the conduct of mankind."[36] For Ashley, as for Coleridge, the solution lay in becoming better people. It was also the early hope of Tory paternalists that better people, especially better churchmen—not the government— would lessen widespread ignorance. In 1839, not one of the Tory reviewers, and only a handful of Anglicans and Nonconformists, supported the Whigs' scheme for government grants to and inspection of Anglican and Nonconformist schools. The scheme passed and money (some 80 percent of it) poured into the Anglican schools, money that persuaded many a churchman and Tory to support the government's scheme. But the scheme was inadequate, so much so that even a leading Anglican, Dr. Hook of Leeds, urged, as did others less wedded to the Church, rate-supported schools with excused time for a religious instruction given by a faith of their choice. Only the *Quarterly Review*'s Henry Milman, in 1846, supported Hook. *Fraser's* judged rate-supported schools "impractical," and the *Oxford and Cambridge Review* thought the idea "preposterous." The *English Review* judged it likely to be productive of infidels.[37] All such schemes, warned *Blackwood's* in 1849, encouraged "the hydra-head of dissent," a warning that led the *Quarterly Review* in 1848 to abandon Milman's views for those of the contemporary French statesman and historian François Guizot. All education, declared Guizot, belongs to the "private and voluntary."[38]

A zeal for the private and voluntary also informed the paternalists' view of Ireland. "No direct legislation," announced *Blackwood's* "can affect the social condition of Ireland," a sentiment the *Quarterly Review*'s Croker shared when, after condemning public works, the government use of wastelands for the poor, and any increase in poor relief, he urged, during the famine, a trust in the "active benevolence at work."[39] *Fraser's* was no less sanguine in trusting the "paternal authority" of a clergy and gentry "universally kind, forbearing and considerate," an authority that would teach "obedience," an obedience the *Quarterly Review* embraced since the Irish needed "someone to look up to, to love," and the *Oxford and Cambridge Review* because Ireland's salvation lay "each in his own sphere . . . doing deeds of individual justice and mercy."[40]

Great as was the Tory paternalists' esteem for the private and voluntary, they did leave some room for government, for what Croker called "the protective system," a system that made room for corn laws, agricultural loans to landlords, and subsidies to railways. It was an indirect system, one that protected property that protected the poor.[41] Acts of Parliament, for example, could give the owners of railways great powers, but the owners, not acts of Parliament, should protect the traveler. *Fraser's, Blackwood's*, and the *Quarterly Review* all opposed Gladstone's 1844 Railway Act, which guaranteed that the third class trains be covered, that they run at more than a snail's pace, and that railways' charge reasonable rates. *Fraser's* denounced its "pseudo-humanity" and "Whiggish-radical centralization"; the *Quarterly Review* pronounced it "unjust, uncalled for" and unsettling "to the habits of the poor"; and *Blackwood's* regretted its control from London.[42] No Tory journal demanded an increase in government regulation, although all, given *viz inertia*, supported existing ones.

Only on matters of crime did they depart from *viz inertia*. They wanted less leniency. *Blackwood's*, which insisted that "Justice leans too much to the side of mercy," scoffed at those who said education reduced crime and argued that crime rose wherever capital punishment was abolished. Capital punishment was a favorite with Tory reviewers; the *Oxford and Cambridge Review* because it embodied the principle of retribution, a principle also embodied in harsh prisons. In prison, said *Blackwood's* W. H. Smith, "every inmate should feel an irresistible domination." *Fraser's* would lessen the "no punishment mania" by punishing women for adultery, by whipping beggars, by flogging sailors, and by preserving fagging in the public schools—fagging being part of a "paternal system."[43] Crime, like poverty, arose from man's wickedness and sin.

Cholera did not. It arose from impure water and bad drainage. The first response of Tory reviewers was to do nothing—*viz inertia* again. For the *Quarterly Review's* Dr. Ferguson, the laws were already "sufficiently comprehensive" and the supervision of the squires and clergy adequate.[44] Then came Edwin Chadwick's 1842 report on England's sanitary horrors. The *Quarterly Review* called for legislation, as did *Blackwood's*, only reluctantly, since the answer it prized the most was Lord Francis Egerton's paternal care for the housing and cleanliness of his workers. "Legislation may do something," declared *Blackwood's*, but more could be done by "private exertion." The same reluctance to legislate was a hallmark of the paternalists' social conscience. Even Lord Ashley was reluctant. After giving a most graphic description of the evils of London's housing and no mention of the need for legislation, he merely asked property and "all ranks and professions . . . to consider these evils."[45]

Dr. Guy of *Fraser's*, was less sanguine about all the ranks and professions and less reluctant about government. But then Dr. Guy was a Londoner and *Fraser's* was a very London magazine.[46] Each journal had its unique personality. The *Quarterly Review* was proud, aristocratic, and pontifical, and its articles were tough-minded and conservative; *Blackwood's* was more literary and romantic, satirical and polemical, pouring epithets on Whigs and utilitarians; *Fraser's*, in Bohemian London, was bumptious, spirited, and more sensitive to urban sufferings, although vague as to remedies. The *Oxford and Cambridge Review* was romantic, nostalgic, and medieval. The *English Review*, the *British Critic*, and the *Christian Remembrancer* were obsessed with the age's great religious debates and viewed all social problems from the point of view of embattled churchmen.

All but two of the sixty-nine reviewers came from the upper classes. Three came from the landed gentry, seventeen from the world of business, and nine from the Church. The fathers of five of them were physicians, five were barristers' sons, and three were the sons of army officers. Forty-nine attended university, three went to military colleges, and one earned a medical degree. Almost all experienced authoritarian and patriarchal ways in family and school and intimately knew the rural world of squires and parsons. Alison remembered visits to the poor with his clerical father, a memory "never afterwards effaced."[47] The *Quarterly Review*'s Reverend John Armstrong remembered "ancient rows of alms-houses built before the hurrying tide of commerce."[48] After university, many of them read for the bar. The study of law was no small ingredient in the paternalist's social conscience, and neither was the Church.

Favored with prosperous parents and privileged education, twenty-three became Anglican clergymen, eighteen lawyers, seven landed gentry, seven civil servants, four physicians, two journalists, one a headmaster, and one an artist. All were successful, all involved with vested interests and unselfconsciously so: William Aytoun, a railway solicitor, wrote on railways, and C. D. Brady, an Irish landowner, on Ireland, as did many clergymen on the Church.[49] It is unlikely Aytoun, Brady, and the clergymen expected larger fees, rents, or stipends because of their defense of railways, land, and the Church, but being an intimate part of the same social milieu, they shared its assumptions. How could the clerical editors of the *Christian Remembrancer*, the *English Review*, and the *British Critic*, or the clergymen who defended the Church in the *Quarterly Review, Blackwood's*, and *Fraser's* not be proud of the paternal mission of the Church?

Nor were men of property shy of defending that institution. John Croker, of considerable property, was unabashed in demanding "a scrupulous respect for existing interests" whether that respect took the form of corn laws for the landed or subsidies for railways. "Vested interests," said Southey, "are the key stone of the social edifice."[50]

The Tory reviewers also enjoyed society, a society that had no little influence on their outlook. Lockhart, the editor of the *Quarterly Review*, who dined constantly with peers and politicians, insisted that articles be "by men of the world," men aware of the "thoughts and feelings in the highest and best society." *Blackwood's* Alison also loved society, dined out often, and never more ecstatically than with the archbishop of Canterbury or the duke of Richmond.[51] Their life in society informed them of their readership. "We must look," wrote Lockhart at the *Quarterly Review*, "for an audience to the clergy and country gentry." His colleague Croker was quick to oblige. "As to the Irish Church," he wrote Lockhart, "I have already embarked the *Quarterly* in an unhesitating support."[52] John Blackwood, London's editor of *Blackwood's*, was no less candid in refusing an article on the Corn Law as it would "offend the Duke of Buckingham and that party." The duke was not the only protectionist who called on *Blackwood's* London office; they came in such numbers that Lockhart predicted it would become "a chapel of ease" for the Tory Carlton Club.[53]

Powerful allies to the above journals in making paternalism popular were the London daily newspapers, the *Morning Post, Morning Herald, Evening Standard,* and *St. James Chronicle*, the last three under the control of Stanley Lees Giffard, an Irishman, Tory, proud Anglican, and unstinting in his praise of Burke and Southey. He was ably assisted by Alaric Watts, friend and admirer of Wordsworth, Southey, and Coleridge.[54] The columns of these dailies never wavered in their Tory paternalism, and neither did the *Post* and *Mirror*. Exceeding them all in circulation, at some 22,000, was the mighty *Times*, whose paternalism, if less pure and aristocratic, was quite decided during the 1830s, when, under its owner John Walter II, it listed toward the Tories. It continued to do so in the 1840s under his son, John Walter III, and the editorship of John Delane. Delane, fresh from Oxford and Newman's influence, brought with him young Tories and High Churchmen who made England's *vox populi* the voice of paternalism.[55]

The popular weekly *John Bull* was edited in the 1840s by William Mudford, an admirer of Burke and an intimate of "that extra-ordinary man" Coleridge, and was outdone by few in his Tory paternalism.[56] London's weeklies and dailies also greatly influenced England's burgeoning provincial press, which both had roots in rural England's paternal institutions and borrowed editorials from London. The press and the learned journals were thus without rival in making the deeply rooted tradition of paternalism popular. It was a popularity made even greater by the flood of popular novels and stories that delighted England's millions.

P A T E R N A L I S M   I N   T H E   N O V E L

With books increasingly cheaper and the people more literate, and with no cinema or television, the novel reigned supreme as a source of excitement, adventure, and even enlightenment. It carried readers away from grim row houses to dreams of elegant country homes where dashing baronets won the hands of rich heiresses. It also plunged them into satanic mills and littered alleys, ranging over the entire gamut of society and reflecting the social concepts of a diverse people.

Four kinds of novels reflected the diverse ways paternalism colored English life: romances of the fashionable world, stories of the lower classes, tales of religious and moral edification, and dramas of London life. Romances of the fashionable world won a particularly great popularity, tied in, as they were, with England's old and venerable institutions. Two of their most seasoned practitioners were Catherine Gore and G. P. R. James. In the 1840s, Gore published twenty-four romances and James twenty-eight. Sometimes known as silver fork novels, sometimes as novels of the upper ten thousand, their settings were country houses and vicarages, their heroes from the gentry and nobility, and their plots full of passionate love and fierce quarrels. Like the Hollywood movies of the 1930s, they were a way to escape reality in no way disturbing to one's social conscience. They nevertheless tell much of the setting, institutions, and mores of paternalism.

There were proud earls and wicked squires, stern magistrates and selfless curates, and the worthy and unworthy poor—a world in which everyone knew his or her place. In James's *Charles Tyrrel,* Evard, although he has grown intimate with the noble and wealthy Tyrell, refuses to "seek associating above myself—to take my chance of rising . . . to a society of a high grade," but instead follow his father's advice "to content myself with the middle class."[57]

Such was not the fate of Jervis, the hero of Gore's *Peers and Parvenus.* The son of a laborer, he rises by attending on an earl. A friend then advises him, "Be a village curate rather than a courtly chaplain." He refuses the advice, becomes a courtly chaplain, and proposes marriage to the earl's daughter. He is refused, and his career ends in ruins. He had reached too high.[58] Deference and a sense of one's place, wife to husband or tenant to squire, form a dominant theme in these novels. In his *The Gentleman of the Old School,* James spoke of "the imperceptible shades and grades of life and station . . . from the cottage to the palace." The gentleman of the old school is a landlord and the guardian of the village poor.[59] The silver fork novels used stock characters—the benevolent squire, the kindly parson, and the lady bountiful—to make explicit one's patriarchal duties: in Gore's *Men of Capital,* there are a good and a bad squire; the good one improves cottages, grants allotments, build schools, and abolishes game preserves, while the bad one does nothing.[60]

The clergy always loom large in the novels of the upper ten thousand. It is a compassionate parson in J. F. Murray's *Viceroy* who sees that the poor are well housed and does so because an improved "temporal condition must precede all spiritual regeneration." An Irish journalist, a contributor to *Blackwood's* and not a noted novelist, Murray was one of many authors whose portraits of model landlords and descriptions of a patriarchal society helped condition many to accept as natural that paternalist status quo that, however imperfectly, governed rural England.[61]

In the 1840s, a new species came to rival the silver fork, the novel of the lower classes. Mrs. Trollope's *Michael Armstrong, Factory Boy* (1840) and *Jesse Phillips* (1844) first exposed the cruelties of factory and workhouse. Disraeli's *Coningsby* (1844) and *Sybil* (1845) followed, each a mix of silver fork and lower-class novel, a mix also found in William Sewell's *Hawkstone,* but not in Mrs. Gaskell's *Mary Barton* (1848) and only a little in Charles Kingsley's *Yeast* (1848) and *Alton Locke* (1850). All of these novels presented a dramatic picture of those painful social abuses revealed by endless parliamentary investigations. With varying degrees of verisimilitude, compassion, and melodrama, the novelists transformed these reports of oppression and exploitation into tales that evoked pity.

They also saw the solution to those evils in a more active paternalism. Few did so more ardently than Sewell and Disraeli. Both preached a classic paternalism in their novels. The heroes of both, lamenting that society is so atomistic, look back to the golden age when barons and bishops protected the poor and a monarch ruled over a truly organic and hierarchic society, one in which rank and property did their duties.

There were, however, differences: Sewell's *Hawkstone* (1845) is as narrow and intolerant as Disraeli is broad and comprehensive. The High Church Sewell denounces evangelicals, Dissenters, Chartists, Roman Catholics, teetotalers, "athenaeums," economists, women philanthropists, and manufacturers. His hero Ernest Villiers wishes "it were the old times again when landlords and tenants and labourers all hung together, and we had none of these ugly factories." To achieve this, Villiers rids the town of those evangelicals, Dissenters, Chartists, teetotalers, women philanthropists, and factory workers who had infested it. In their place come bishops, priests, monks, and teachers who teach children "not to rise above a higher sphere than . . . nature has placed them"[62]

Disraeli is more generous. He too has churches, monasteries, and almsgiving landlords, but he also includes Carlyle's captains of industry; and nowhere is he intolerant of Dissent. Disraeli dresses his paternalism in a motley garb, a colorful mix of medievalism and modernism, of conventionalities and idiosyncrasies, all compassionately presented. However unrealistic, few novels rivaled *Sybil* and *Coningsby* in championing a revived paternalism.

But the two novels were not unrivaled as graphic depictions of working-class life. Mrs. Trollope's *Jesse Phillips* gives a fuller and a more balanced picture of the rural poor. Her deep and probing look at the harsh New Poor Law focuses especially on the cruelty of the bastardy clause that excused the father and burdened the mother with upkeep of their bastard child. Her depiction of the workhouse is the best in fiction, less dramatic than that in *Oliver Twist*, but less a caricature, although equally affecting. Mrs. Gaskell's *Mary Barton* is as realistic on urban evils as Mrs. Trollope is on rural ones. Both also rely, as a remedy, on paternalism, although the Manchester-raised and Unitarian Mrs. Gaskell does so more reluctantly. In *Jesse Phillips*, Mrs Trollope writes nostalgically of a time "when resident gentry have familiar personal acquaintance with every poor family." *Jesse Phillips* is the story of the breakdown of such relations, a story of a landlord's son making Jesse Phillips's daughter pregnant and then abandoning her to the workhouse. Ill and confused, she wanders from the workhouse and has the child, which the landlord's son then kills, but for whose murder the magistrates indict the daughter. A benevolent squire and kind clergyman prove her innocent, and all ends happily and paternalistically. *Michael Armstrong, Factory Boy* also has a happy paternalist ending, with a lady bountiful declaring, "let each in his own circle raise his voice . . . AND THESE HORRORS WILL BE REMEDIED."[63]

Mrs. Gaskell in *Mary Barton* can find no other remedy. Neither trade unions, Chartism, nor socialism—not even laissez-faire (under which a painful unemployment occurred)—will do, only a hope that a penitent and wealthy mill owner, Mr. Carson, will create "a perfect understanding . . . between master and men" and recognize that "the interests of one were the interests of all." Later, in Mrs. Gaskell's *North and South* another mill owner, Mr. Thornton, falls in love with a strong willed woman from the south of England, who teaches him the wisdom of paternalism.[64] Model landlords, mill owners, and parsons became the novelist's universal remedy. They certainly appear in Charles Kingsley's *Alton Locke* in his portrait of the almsgiving Lord and Lady Ellerton. They lower rents, improve cottages, grant allotments, and plead with the workers to abandon Chartism. But Kingsley has some doubts, even of Lord Vieuxbois, a kind and patronizing landlord, whose generous poor relief corrupts, making the people "slaves and humbugs." No more pleasing to Kingsley is Lord Minchampstead, whose niggardly relief drives the poor into the workhouse. Doubts about paternalism begin to cloud Kingsley's mind, not helped by his savage satire of both Tractarian and evangelical parsons. With his cutting satire of landlords and clergy, Kingsley knocks down two of his paternalist props, property and the Church. He also will have none of the third prop, the state. He condemns "the bureaucracy of despotic commissioners" and pleads for "a state founded on better things than Acts of Parliament," a sentiment echoed by Sewell and Disraeli. Sewell's hero is scornful of "Acts of Parliament," while in *Coningsby* the wise Sidonia urges England to "think more of community and less of government." Once again a paternalist distrusts government and recommends, in the words of Lord Egremont in *Sybil*, "far greater exertion in our own sphere." But such exertions, as Kingsley realizes in *Yeast*, were often either absent or hard-hearted. All thus becomes "a chaos of noble materials . . . polarized, jarring, chaotic." Kingsley can only, in Carlylean fashion, look to "one inspiring spirit to organize and unite," a plea less convincing to the reader than Tregevara's confession in *Alton Locke*, "I don't see my way out."[65]

Less hesitant of the way out were the third kind of novels, those of religious and moral edification. The characters are all true believers in paternalism. Certainly, Elizabeth Sewell (William's sister) is in *Amy Herbert*, a story of Amy and her mother's visit to a peer's country house. While there, Amy learns that it is the will of God that some are wealthy, that "vulgarity is the wish to be of higher rank," and that contentment comes from visiting the sick. The world of *Amy Herbert* is as elegant and resplendent as in any silver fork novel, but instead of intrigue and worldliness, there are pious homilies on deference and obedience, lessons that also abound in Charlotte Elizabeth's *Helen Fleetwood*. The background of *Helen Fleetwood* is not a peer's country house, but a mill, a mill in which the daughter is overworked and beaten. Helen, a widow, stops her son from rebelling in defense of the daughter. "We are all sinners," Helen says, adding, "enterprize and perseverance won the millowner his wealth," and it is "our duty to submit" to all laws. The son submits, and is rescued by a landowner who is a paragon of paternal virtues.[66]

Some High Church clergymen had a flair for writing novels of edification, as seen in the Reverend Robert Armitage's *Ernest Singleton*, the Reverend Francis Paget's *The Pageant*, and the Reverend William Gresley's *Clement Walton*. These novels have weak plots and endless colloquies and dialogues on the duties of landlords and clergy. A paternalistic orthodoxy centered on Oxford informs them—a High Church paternalism that owes more to Exeter's William Sewell than to Oriel's Newman. What Armitage calls a "shepherd clergy" typifies their paternalism—priests who visit the poor and dying, discipline the erring, and educate the ignorant, a clergy working under a bishop not too proud to visit "the low abodes of misery," a realization of the clerisy envisioned by Coleridge, whom Armitage declared "our favourite." Landlords as "stewards of God" are also important, enjoined, of course, to "see cottages neat and clean," but above all to see to it that true religion is preached. Preaching religion is the social panacea. "The dangers of popular outbreaks will be annihilated," Armitage announces, "in the same ratio that ungodliness is removed." It is doubtful, however, whether the novels of Armitage, Paget, and Gresley did much to combat ungodliness, since probably only one-hundredth of the public read them compared to those breathlessly awaiting the next installment of *Nicholas Nickleby*.[67] Although, like *Sybil* or *Mary Barton*, Dickens's novels, could be considered novels of the working class, they were also much more; nor did they end with paternalist solutions. Paternal benevolence, of course, there was, as in Nicholas's patrons, the Cheeryble brothers, city merchants "who can not allow those who serve well any privation or discomfort," or the converted Scrooge, who becomes "a second father" to Tiny Tim, or the always kind Mr. Pickwick and Oliver Twist's savior Mr. Brownlow. Dickens even ends *Hard Times* with a plea to mill owners "to draw nigh to folks wi' kindness and patience and cheery ways."[68] Dickens, the many-sided reflector of life, could hardly not reflect paternalism, but he did so in a different manner and with strong doubts. His Cheerybles and Pickwicks are not strictly paternalists. Their benevolence is diffuse and individual, not linked to the spheres of the lord's estate and the vicar's parish. It is humanitarian, not authoritarian, part of London's democratic life. The Cheerybles and Pickwicks have no estate, no parish, and no superior rank, but are humble, like Pickwick—"former occupation unknown"—or the Cheerybles whom "thousands would not invite to dinner." They are also broad in their benevolence, like the new Scrooge, to whom "mankind was my business," or the Pickwick who does not distinguish between worthy and unworthy poor but helps all in the debtors' prison.[69]

Dickens also had strong doubts, indeed a strong dislike, of paternalism's authoritarianism. It could be cruel, pompous and patronizing. *Nicholas Nickleby* offers not only the paternalist Cheerybles, but rebelliousness. Nicholas rebels against the schoolmaster Squeers, rebels against his Uncle, and again against Lord Verisopht and Sir Mulberry Hawk, the latter receiving a beating. Dickens suspected all authority, whether that of Bumble the workhouse master in *Oliver Twist*, Mr. Bounderby and Mr. Gradgrind, husband and father to Louisa in *Hard Times*, or the baronet in *The Chimes*, Sir Joseph Bowley. Nowhere is Dickens more hostile to paternalism than in his spirited satire of the pompous Bowley. "I am your perpetual parent," Bowley announces, and "will treat you paternally," especially by "inculcating . . . the one great lesson . . . entire dependence." He expresses his love for his tenants by playing skittles with them, assured that when "a baronet . . . plays skittles the country was coming around."[70] Dickens, a Londoner through and through, found paternalism a pale and tepid answer to the vast suffering of the sprawling metropolis.

Dickens's friend and fellow Londoner Douglas Jerrold was no more buoyant about paternalism. In *St. Giles and St. James,* he mocks arrogant gentry, imperious magistrates, and self-righteous parsons. One magistrate, who calls the poor obdurate and hopeless, declares the novel's hero guilty of a murder he had not committed. Meanwhile, an unctuous parson tells his parishioners of "the social necessity of the many trusting the few" and exhorts them "to be obedient to [those] appointed to guide and protect them."[71]

Although the rhetoric of paternalism won little praise from the skeptical, urbane, and mocking Dickens and Jerrold, it did, surprisingly, win some from the serious, earnest and individualistic Charlotte Brontë, Elizabeth Gaskell, and Harriet Martineau, of Yorkshire, Lancashire, and Norfolk respectively. There is, of course, also some rebellion in Brontë's *Shirley*, and Martineau's *Deerbrook*: Shirley, the heroine, rebels against her uncle and his choice of a gentleman of considerable estate as her husband. Defiant, she instead marries a lowly tutor. Martineau, in *Deerbrook,* has Doctor Hope oppose the ruling lord of the manor with that staunch provincial independence and self-reliance that Gaskell prized in her novels. But none of the three discards paternalism. Dr. Hope is paternalism itself in his plea for "the honest genuine acquaintance with the poor" when the novel ends at his manor house with festivities given with paternal graciousness. *Shirley* also ends with a model paternalist, who speaks of "all the cares and duties of property," visits schools for the poor, and has the clergy organize clothing clubs. At the end a hungry pauper says, "Them that governs mun find a way to help us; they mun mak' fresh oderations."[72]

In marked contrast to Brontë's and Martineau's clothes-dispensing clergy, conscientious doctors, and paupers begging for "fresh oderations" is Theodore Hook's caricature of the Reverend Slobberton Mawks, who "fancied he could domineer over the poor," of Justice Minton who sent "idle dogs" to the treadmill, and of Mrs. Minton who "trumpets piety and charity."[73] All occur in Hook's hilarious *Peregrine Bunce*, a most surprising satire of paternalism, since it comes from the editor, until 1841, of the Tory and High Church *John Bull*. Why is a High Church Tory more irreverent of paternalism than the Unitarian and middle-class Gaskell and Martineau? Two facts help answer the paradox: first, that paternalism was not the preserve of any class or party, and, second, that it did not go down well in London. Hook, like Dickens and Jerrold, was thoroughly a Londoner, and so part of a world of actors and journalists, of cockney comedy, and a busy and a rootless multitude who only read of squires and parson and paternal lords. Paternalism rested on locality, the limited sphere, the known authority; it did not suit a giant metropolis. Gaskell's Manchester, Martineau's Norwich, and Brontë's Keighley were still local spheres. Not so London. Dickens's Harriet Crocker, in *Dombey and Son*, reflects on those "swallowed up in one phase or another of its immensity . . . food for the hospitals, churchyards, the prisons, the river, fever, madness, vice and death."[74] The monster that was London defied paternalist solutions. In the very 1840s that saw the high point of paternalist theory and its greatest dissemination in the press and novels, doubts arose about its viability. Did paternalism actually work? Did it provide an effective solution to proliferating social evils? The answer to those disturbing questions would not come from the learned tomes, editorials, and novels in which paternalism as an idea triumphed, but from estates, churches, and factories—from the villages and towns where paternalism was actually practiced.

CHAPTER 3

The Practice of Paternalism

Social attitudes derive only partly from the writings of intellectuals. They also reflect economic and social interests. How property, classes, and institutions are organized are as important as seminal thinkers. Although intellectual developments are not without a dialectic and power of their own, they are also not free from social forces. The interests and prejudices of landowners were as significant as romantic poets and philosophical idealists in forming the early Victorian social conscience. Indeed, the landowners had much more wealth, power, and social status. The speeches and policies of landlords carried more weight than the rhapsodic dreams of Young England. And it was on their land, in their parishes and counties, that they, as landlords and magistrates, would prove whether paternalism was an effective social outlook, whether land in fact did its duties.

LAND AND ITS DUTIES

It was the opinion of rural England that land did do its duties. Few were the speeches given to agricultural societies, sermons delivered by the clergy and leaders written by rural editors that did not boast of the paternalists' benevolent activities, of beef and ale at Christmas, of coal deliveries and clothing clubs and soup kitchens when distress became acute. And firm and wise too were guidance and control from the landowning magistrates with their stern lectures and stiff sentences to poachers, tipplers, and vagrants. Addressing the Liverpool agricultural association, Lord Stanley promised "bringing together all the classes of the community," while the Reverend C. A. Hulbert told the earl of Dartmouth's tenantry that "property has its duties as well as its privileges." In Devon, the dean of Exeter joined the earl of Devon and Sir Thomas Acland, M.P., in praise of allotments for members of the St. Thomas Labourer's Society, while at Shrewsbury, the duke of Sotheran, the bishop of Lichfield, and Robert Slaney, M.P., presided over the Church Extension Society.[1] At Goodwood, the West Sussex Agricultural Association met, the duke of Richmond presiding, flanked by the earl of Chichester, the bishop of Chichester, the leading gentry, and, at the far end of the hall, for the first time, the laborers, some to receive prizes. The duke told them that "their interests were closely and intimately connected," praised his "honest, industrious tenants," and told them to give the laborers allotments and so "a stake in the hedge." Archdeacon Manning then told them of the social pyramid that God ordained, one in which "the multitude were poor and the few rich."[2]

The meeting was reported in the *Sussex Agricultural Express*, a paper also abounding in reports of a benevolent paternalism. From 1840 to 1846, it reported more than 300 occasions when the wealthy helped the poor. They "regaled the poor with old English fare, roast beef and plum pudding," set aside a field for cricket, rewarded schoolchildren with "hats, bonnets and frocks," and, at Brighton, "an orange, a white ribbon and a small book." In winter, they gave food, fuel, and clothing, either directly, as with the earl of Arundel's 600 loaves of bread and 200 gallons of beer on New Year's Day, or indirectly by charging a penny or two to belong to a clothing and coal club.[3] Although the contemporary rural press provides ample evidence of benevolent paternalism, it also reveals authoritarianism, which was sometimes ruthless. Throughout rural England, the landed classes believed that preventing social unrest required a vigorous discipline by the landlord, the firm admonitions of the clergy, the severity of the magistrate, the moral inculcations of the schoolmaster, and the firm control of poor law guardians. It was an old system, although moving in the 1840s from the conventional, limited, lax paternalism of the eighteenth century to that of the nineteenth, marked by a greater awareness of pressing social evils and an expanded sense of duties to be done. Comparing the paternalist manuals of the 1840s with John Mordaunt's *The Complete Stewart* of 1761 or Thomas Gisborne's *Inquiry into the Duties of Men of the Higher and Middle Classes* of 1794, for example, makes this clear. In Mordaunt, the gentry reside on their estates, mix "affably" with and promote "the comfortable subsistence of [their] tenants," keep vagrants out of the parish, prevent the rich from seizing the poor's land, see justice done, and ensure that poor relief goes only to those unable to work or with large families. Gisborne goes further, favoring fair rents, improved drainage, and long leases for tenants. He also expresses the usual concern to employ the idle—the source "of vice and disorder"—and to be not "unmindful of the infirm and the children of the poor."[4]

By 1838 and Sidney Godolphin Osborne's *Hints to the Charitable*, the duties of the gentry had greatly increased. The landlord now had to do more than simply treat his tenants fairly, do his poor law duties, and see to an improved agriculture. He also had to establish clothing funds, benefit clubs, savings banks, loan funds, and a wives' friendly society. He should also maintain good cottages and good schools. John Sandford expands on and adds to all these duties in his 390-page *Parochialia*.[5]

Although not all landlords measured up to these duties, a great many espoused them in their agricultural meetings, electioneering, and pamphlets, and did so more vigorously than ever after the agricultural riots of the early 1830s and the attacks on the Corn Law of the 1840s put them on the defensive. Corn Law battles had increased landlords' activity, said the *Northampton Mercury*, and a Select Committee concluded in 1843 that the rage for allotments had begun after the riots of 1830 and 1831.[6]

The rage for allotments was more than mere rhetoric. It was one of the more effective ways to place paternalism on an institutional basis, an attempt that looms large in paternalist pamphlets and the *Labourer's Friend Magazine*, as well as in the *Farmer's Magazine* and the rural press. A quarter of an acre, at a nominal rent, for potatoes or turnips or a pig, would do wonders in promoting self-reliance, a self-reliance also furthered by a farthing a week to clothing and coal clubs, savings banks, and clubs for women to save for the birth of a child. Despite widespread pleas to landlords to give laborers allotments, however, the response was limited. They liked the idea in Kent, where 3,000 laborers raised pigs and dug their gardens in their spare time, but not in Norfolk, where commercial farms used gangs of laborers from nearby towns, and in Yorkshire, where landlords disliked allotments. The effort to revive, expand, and institutionalize paternalism, to expand allotments and self-help clubs and schools, was a generous and noble effort—but was it in fact realized?

It is not easy to say. F. M. L. Thompson, the leading authority on the nineteenth-century landed estate calls paternalism a "patchy affair," saying that those in open parishes with no squire experienced little benevolence, and those under the gentry received "less succor and protection" than if "under a magnate."[7]

The dukes of Bedford, Northumberland, Rutland, Grafton, Devonshire, and Argyll all won praise: Bedford for building model cottages, Northumberland and Grafton for renting good cottages with allotments at low rents, Newcastle for granting 2,000 allotments, Devonshire and Argyll for enlightened help to their Irish and Scots tenants during the famine, and Rutland for unaffected friendliness and for his "pride and happiness . . . to reside in the country . . . in daily intercourse with the middle and humbler classes."[8] On acceding to the title in 1847, the young duke of Argyll "lost no time in establishing a personal intercourse with his numerous tenantry." He poured capital into improved farming, replaced thatched hovels with slate-roofed houses, borrowed £10,000 to help them during the famine, and seldom evicted anyone.[9]

Earls too performed their paternal duties: Fitzwilliam by championing better medical relief, Leicester by renting good cottages at a loss, Dartmouth by distributing prizes for spade husbandry, Carlisle by building a reformatory, Devon a county lunatic asylum, and Roseberry cottages with two comfortable apartments.[10] The young Lord Ashley, the embodiment of paternalism, felt only pain at his father's neglect, of the "shocking state of cottages—no school of any kind," and only joy when, as earl of Shaftesbury, he could write, "I determined under God to build one." The vast estates, grand titles, and privileged upbringing of dukes and earls demanded of them a patriarchal largesse. A thousand tenants celebrated the earl of Aberdeen's coming of age, and 700 attended a dinner for the duke of Richmond's son.[11] To receive such adulation, to then become a lord lieutenant, chairman of quarter sessions, and inherit control of several livings, demanded a paternalist outlook, however perfunctory in practice.

A paternalist need not always be benevolent. Authority and command were far more central to the aristocratic role. When the duke of Sutherland offered his male tenants a bounty of £6 to join the army and fight the Russians in 1851, no one volunteered, and an elderly man declared that "we would not expect worse treatment" if the czar and not the Sutherlands had ruled the county over the past fifty years, which had seen 10,000 evictions, many houses destroyed and families broken up, and their places taken by sheep. To work, marry, or worship required the duke's approval.[12]

The marquis of Londonderry was no less imperious. He told his striking coal miners that they were "stupid," "beaten," and "indifferent to my really paternal advice." He evicted them from their cottages in order to make room for strikebreakers from his Irish estates, called on the "civil and military" to defend the "rights of property," and promised to do "my duty to my family and station." Yet the high Tory Lord Londonderry could be solicitous too. Unlike most, including the radical earl of Durham, he refused to work women in his mines. Durham ruled his estates with little benevolence, writes the historian David Spring, and that was also true of the duke of Buckingham. Conversely, the intelligent and generous duke of Bedford was highly benevolent. Paternalism was "a patchy affair," one that even varied within one individual. Sharmon Crawford, M.P., called Londonderry Ireland's best landlord, and the mining inspector Seymour Tremeheere thought him "liberal and effectual for education," whereas Durham was "deficient" in that respect. Even the duke of Sutherland found "no occupation more . . . agreeable than going about among [the poor] . . . rebuking . . . or commending," and doing the duties that his position demanded—but duties that, he confessed, he could not fully perform, since his estates were so vast.[13]

The vast estates and exalted titles of dukes and earls often brought a loftiness and remoteness that did not burden the gentry. The squire's estate proved more personal and intimate, one where tenants and laborers could look up to the squire as the father of the parish. Three such fathers were Norfolk's Sir John Boileau, Suffolk's Henry Bunbury, and Essex's J. J. Strutt. All were agricultural improvers, aware that only greater crops could feed the multiplying parishioners. Boileau, a member of the Royal Society, experimented with crop rotation and improved drainage; Bunbury examined his tenants' various soils, regrouped the farms, advised on crops, and knew every tenant and laborer personally; Strutt gave his tenants a "harangue on capital, labour, and manure"; and all three believed fair rents and wages and winter employment to be economically profitable.[14] All three also promoted allotments, schools, and good cottages, rural paternalism's three indispensable institutions. Bunbury built twenty-eight new cottages and enlarged the old ones, some for the retired; Boileau did the same, as well as teaching tenants to keep them "neat and clean"; and Strutt improved all of his houses. Strutt and Boileau also built new schools. All three saw allotments as the great desideratum. Bunbury wrote an article in their praise in the *Journal of the Royal Society*, urging that they never be over one-half acre, at nominal rents, near the cottage, and free of the poor rate. His ninety-eight allotments netted £4 to £5 a year, and in twenty-eight years, only one cottager failed to pay the rent, evidence of the great moral improvement effected. Strutt, a magistrate, insisted that allotments reduced crime, as did Boileau and Bunbury, both high sheriffs. Boileau called himself "the father of the parish" and "father of the fatherless . . . a peace maker, and teacher of the poor." He held daily prayers with the servants, demanded Church attendance, and would have no Dissenters as tenants. Servants were censured, boys who stole whipped, and striking laborers confronted with the military, lectures on political economy, and, two days later, higher wages. Bunbury was also a believer in political economy and ran his parish with firmness, as did Strutt, although on evangelical lines anathema to Boileau and Bunbury. Strutt denounced balls, parties, and hunting. Aware that he had "all the parish on my hand," he urged all to "do our utmost to improve the religious, moral and temporal state of the poor." He made them attend Church, punished "theft, drunkenness and idleness" and gave fair wages.[15]

Model squires such as Boileau, Bunbury, and Strutt added a warm intimacy to their moral sovereignty. Boileau sat with the sick and every January feasted the poor on beef, plum pudding, and ale, while Strutt saw to it that the aged had tea and sugar and salt butter, and that his wife organized a ladies' lying-in fund. Bunbury expressed his warmth by defending the laborers in the *Bury Post*, declaring that incendiarism arose from "inadequate wages . . . [and] frequent dismissals." The "simple minded, well meaning" laborers, he added were "grateful and full of good feeling." He ended with a purely paternalist exhortation to "let land and cottages . . . at reasonable rates," pay "fair wages," never discharge because of "rain or frost . . . talk with them . . . advise them, and encourage them, [and then] you will have no more fires"[16]

There were more than 3,000 landed gentry in early Victorian England, most of whom did not do as Bunbury exhorted. Suffolk's historian John Glyde sadly recorded in 1852 that Bunbury's letter had not persuaded Suffolk's 423 landowners to give allotments "a fair trial." Most paid only seven or eight shillings in weekly wages, although Lancashire farmers paid thirteen or fourteen. Most cottages were overcrowded and dismal, a source of immorality. In slack seasons, laborers were also "cast upon the parish."[17] In Suffolk, Bunburys were as exceptional as Shaftesburys in Dorset. The diary of Lord Ashley, who became the seventh earl of Shaftesbury in 1851, records his strong resolve to build good cottages. But the same diary also describes "petty proprietors [who] exact five fold rent for a [cottage] five fold inferior in condition," which was not merely done sometimes but "always." Ashley's cryptic "always" and Glyde's "no fair trial" tell a story amply supported by the government's 1843 Report on Women and Children in Agriculture and 1847 Report on Settlement and Removal. Both underline the curse of wretched housing. Witness upon witness, clergymen, doctors, and poor law guardians, describe overcrowded, run-down, leaky cottages, damp and close, whose bedroom for six or seven spawned promiscuity. "In nine villages out of ten," said one witness, "the cottage is still nothing but a slightly improved hovel," a judgment repeated by witnesses from Devon to Northumberland.[18]

Some landlords tore down and some refused to build cottages. In a "close" parish, one owned by one or two landlords, cottagers, if unemployed, ill, or old would, by going on relief, increase the landlord's rates. Not a few landlords therefore either destroyed or refused to build cottages, thus lowering their rates. Nineteen witnesses told the 1847 Select Committee on Settlement that this was widely done, which not a single witness denied. "It has been done very much," was one comment, "in a great many parishes." There was "a great tendency" to do so, and "in many smaller parishes [there were] often no cottages." In Dorset, this was the case "to a very great extent"; in the eastern counties, cottages were "fast diminishing"; and in Suffolk, where there was one proprietor, "they get rid of the poor people." It was not Chartists or agitators against the Corn Law who gave such testimony but poor law guardians, magistrates, and clergymen. And they added "in open parishes . . . cottages are shocking"; throughout England, there was "a great destitution . . . of cottages." It was not only to lower rates that cottages were destroyed or not built. "Many landowners," said one witness, consider them "a nuisance." More and more the evicted cottagers were forced to live three or four or five miles away in towns with no paternal bonds. That there is a "tie between farmers and labourers" said a magistrate, "is a delusion." The two government reports of 1843 and 1847 make it clear that model squires and cottage-building earls were rare and harsh landlords common. Even paternalist journals admitted the fact. "Nor are landlords and farmers," said the *Times*, "apt to care much for cottages"; "the great majority of the owners of landed property," concluded the *Oxford and Cambridge Review*, "have regarded cottages as nuisances . . . [and] diminish their number."[19] Landlords also regarded low rents as a nuisance, as farmers did high wages. Farmers, said the ninety-year-old James Sparshott, "have got hard hearted." He told a select committee in 1837 that a golden age of high wages and each with his "barrel of beer" had given way to low wages and water. Wages ranged from seven to nine shillings a week in the southwest, and from nine to eleven shillings in Sussex and Kent. Low wages were a necessity, declared the farmers, despite the fact that farmers in Northumberland paid twelve to fourteen shillings.[20] It was a mystery, more than one witness said, how the poor survived. It was a mystery solved in part by sending their boys to the fields and their daughters into service, the boys as early as the age of seven, and generally when aged nine or ten. Except for the winter, the hours were from 6 A.M. to 6 P.M. Wages began at 1s. 6d. a week, rising to 3s. 6d.

Wages were low, declared the farmers, because rents were so high and leases so short. Farmers complained loudly to the 1847 and 1848 Select Committee on the Game Law and Agricultural Customs that landowners had the upper hand. Farmers with skill and capital who wanted to rent farms were too numerous, ten to twenty bidding for each farm. The result was high rents and yearly leases, which allowed landlords to raise rents quickly if prices rose. And compensation was seldom given for improvements to a farm when the lease ended, as was standard for urban properties. Asked why there was this disparity, a barrister replied, "The tenants in towns have more power . . . [since] the tenants in the country were a good deal more under the power of the landlord."

The landlords also used their power to preserve game, which was often at the farmer's expense, because the hares and game birds preserved for hunting and the hunting itself often did damage to the farmers' fields, ranging from £2 to £6 per acre. In one district, game destroyed one-fourth of the crop.[21] The landowners, too, had grown hard-hearted. They even sought profits in the quintessential paternalist act, the granting of allotments. "My fear is," declared Sir George Strickland, a Yorkshire M.P., "that this allotment system is an excuse for getting rack rents, very high rents." Quarter-acre allotments were rarely given free. To do so, landowners insisted, would undermine the laborer's self-reliance. For the same reason, paternalist landlords imposed penny and farthing charges for clothing and coal clubs, and even for soup kitchens. How much self-reliance it taught is unknown, but it did show that a cash nexus ruled agriculture, a cash nexus about which two paternalist squires and M.P.'s, Oxfordshire's Joseph Henley and Warwickshire's Charles Newdegate, were unashamed. Both insisted that private contract, not law, should determine whether compensation should be given for a tenant's improvements. Hard bargaining, profits, and market forces, not benevolence, ruled English landowners; their most cherished motto being "live and let live." "Landowners talk much of identity-of-interests and harmony," said W. H. Little in 1845 to the Abergavenny Farm Club, "but however beautiful this may sound . . . it is not . . . true in fact."[22]

Many a landlord would, however, protest that there was another side to the story, that their returns from rents fell short of returns from capital invested in railways, textiles, or government consols ("consolidated annuities"). Except for improved agriculture on good soil, agriculture was not a buoyant source of profit. Furthermore, despite much haggling over leases and complaints about hares and game birds, trust and friendship did, in most cases, bind landlord and tenant, and even informed the laborer's deference. It is for economic historians to determine how profitable land was, how fair the rewards to landlord, tenant, and laborer were, and how exploitative or necessary high rents and low wages. It is, however, most probable that, in most cases, the landlord's rent and the farmer's profits were ample enough for a more generous performance of his paternal duties than was common.

The record of that performance is not distinguished. Many landlords were niggardly, especially when it came to support of schools. Such was certainly the view of the education inspectors who recorded "very poor agricultural schools," "small and ill paid village schools," "one teacher per 111 pupils," "only one in three teachers duly prepared," and "the indifference of the many"; in 1852, in the southwest, "three-fourths of the pupils [were] under ten," the older children being out in the fields.[23]

Not a few in the fields turned to poaching. Ill-educated, mired in poverty, and adventuresome, the young were tempted to steal pheasant eggs, a first step in a poacher's career. After hearing in the beer shop of hares and game birds and hunters destroying crops, poaching seemed no crime. But it was, and the most common of crimes. Nearly one in four of those sent to prison were poachers, most of them sentenced by a summary hearing of one or two landlord J.P.'s, not too knowledgeable in the law. The Home Office reported in 1845 that of 1,849 committals, not only were a great many "illegal," but "there was a great deal of . . . injustice." No other law protecting property, said witnesses to the Select Committee on the Game Laws, was administered so harshly, and so greatly encouraged disrespect for the law.[24] They hardly cemented those bonds that the duke of Richmond celebrated as part of "the old fashioned way."

Once in prison, the poacher became a ward of the state. The landlord as J.P. thus acted for him, as for the insane, in loco parentis. It was a paternal duty resting on a legal basis, whether voting money in quarter sessions for county prisons and lunatic asylums or, as visiting justices, supervising those institutions. It was a duty not always well performed. Although the Lunacy Act of 1845 required all thirty-nine counties to build asylums, only sixteen had done so by 1852; nor did magistrates comply with orders to send the over 9,000 insane who suffered in the grim backrooms of workhouses to licensed institutions. An ingrained aversion to higher rates led to their failure to act genuinely in loco parentis toward the insane and the criminal.[25] "A scene of abject misery," said one prison inspector of a miserable jail; "a dismal, filthy, black hole," reported another; "discreditable" concluded a third, who also found that magistrates refused any schooling as too expensive. Nineteen years after the establishment of the prison inspectors, one of them found the prisons in the southwest and Wales, mired in "inertia and failure." Many J.P.'s took to their duties in loco parentis quite robustly, carrying out the Home Office's policy of separate confinement and the treadmill with a paternal authority and paternal severity. Prison inspectors found flogging and long hours on the treadmills far too common. The J.P.'s at Wells readily built a new prison for separate confinement, but to save expense, built cells only 9 feet by 4 feet 6 inches. J.P.'s in loco parentis could be grim.[26]

The above picture of land doing its paternal duties is partial, focusing on the failings. The same parliamentary reports that tell of rack-renting, squalid cottages, and dismal prisons also tell of the multiplication of medical clubs, improved housing, benefit societies, and good schools. Benevolence, sympathy, and conscientiousness were interwoven with callousness, selfishness, and negligence to form the "patchy" pattern of paternalism at the grass roots. Yet notwithstanding the promotion of clothing clubs, so admirable in intent, many women who worked a field in the rain retired early to bed to allow their one dress to dry, and many, many men never attended church for want of proper clothing.[27] They lived in the counties where a scattering of clothing clubs did little to clothe men earning seven to nine shillings a week.

There was, of course, the New Poor Law of 1834, designed to institutionalize a paternalism that disciplined instead of corrupted, which won the support of most landlords. In 1858, no fewer than fifty-one peers and twenty baronets were chairmen of boards of guardians. Assistant poor law commissioners praised their cooperation, saying: "Lord Dartmouth has given great and valuable support"; "Lord Spencer introduced me to many gentlemen"; "Lord Howe declares himself a convert"; Lord Ebrington "helped me form medical clubs"; the duke of Rutland is "zealous for our cause."[28]

The gentry also pitched in. "All my chairmen but one," boasted an assistant commissioner, "are members of the House." Numerous too were the clergy who chaired boards of guardians, some ninety-one in 1838. The elite of the countryside saw in the New Poor Law a way to do its duties. Peers, M.P.'s, and clergymen presided over nearly one-third of the 528 boards of guardians.[29] They saw in the Poor Law a means to consolidate their power. The historian Anthony Brundage has shown how the law "incorporated the many hierarchically structured deference communities" and so "enhanced the aggregate influence of . . . [the] local magnates."[30] Many of them, along with the gentry and clergy, cooperated in order to be sure that the boundaries and forms of the new unions would leave unscathed their patriarchal position.

The elite performed their duties in harness with farmers and shopkeepers in ways that varied from the refusal of all outdoor relief for the able-bodied to its abundant use, from austere to ample diets, and from well- to ill-ordered workhouses. They could enforce harsh discipline and yet grant generous medical relief. It is again a mixed picture, made more ambiguous because it is not one of a purely local paternalism at work. Much of the improved medical care, improved treatment of the insane, and greater cleanliness and healthiness and order in the workhouse came from a central bureaucracy detested by many a paternalist. It was also government grants and the persuasion of education inspectors that led to more and better parish schools, just as the harangues of lunacy commissioners led to civilized asylums. If left solely to its local base, paternalism would not have been as dynamic or effective.

The landed class was ambivalent toward the central government. Its attitude varied from the deepest hostility to a grudging approval. Individual landlords could even hold differing views, now favoring a central poor law, now opposing a central board of health. They disliked new measures, but as law-abiding Englishmen, they carried them out, if sometimes reluctantly, once they were old ones. Acting on their own, they promoted allotments—a prime symbol of a landed paternalism—so tepidly that an 1843 select committee declared that what was needed was legislation. Indeed, the Labourer's Friend Society, which did the most to promote allotments, was centered in London and northern towns, more a reflection of diffuse philanthropy than of "HOMEBORN" paternalism. The lament of the Labourer's Friend Society was that so few landlords granted allotments.[31] In the end, paternalists in Parliament defeated the compulsory measure. When it came to allotments, they wanted no central government interfering in their local paternalism, not even a partnership as in the cases of the poor law, lunacy, and education. A local paternalism, acting on its own, was capable of individual instances of a wise and benevolent rule, but those instances were too few for paternalism as practiced to solve England's acute, vast, and multiplying social evils. They were evils that also challenged the Church of England and its clergy, who claimed to be the shepherds of their flocks.

THE SHEPHERDS AND THEIR FLOCKS

Some 17,000 to 18,000 ordained priests of the Church of England—over 13,000 of them with benefices and parish churches—considered themselves shepherds enjoined by God to care for the eternal and temporal welfare of the poor. In 1844, the archbishop of Canterbury pronounced that Jesus' injunctions "to preach the gospel . . . and feed His flock" were the twofold aim of the Church. Other bishops added the duty to clothe the naked and visit the sick, citing Matthew's "I am hungered and ye gave me meat . . . naked and ye clothed me." These oft-repeated injunctions led enthusiastic Tractarians, like the Reverend Edward Pusey, to urge the clergy "to penetrate our mines . . . to grapple with our manufacturing system," and the bishop of London to urge the clergy to inspect the homes of the poor, teach them cleanliness, and improve the most miserable of their dwellings. Nothing seemed too heroic for these shepherds. The bishop of Chester asked his clergy to visit 3,000 families a year in addition to the sick and aged. The bishop of Oxford called his clergy "instructors and guides of thought and opinion," who should "promote the general welfare and . . . morals of the people." They should protect women from panderers, limit the sale of liquor, improve prisons, and end brutal sports, and the abuse of charitable trusts.[32] Extensive as were their activities, they did not expect poverty, disease, and crime to end. They indulged in no such hubris. They hoped to console, admonish, and relieve, not to remake society. Poverty was inevitable, man hopelessly sinful. "The poor," said the bishop of Chester citing Deuteronomy 11:15 "shall never cease out of the land." But its inevitability in no way lessened the command to visit the destitute and sick and assuage that suffering that churchmen believed was providential. They considered both the Irish famine and the cholera of 1848 as ordained of God. "Famine, a Rod of God" was a sermon preached by Liverpool's most popular evangelical, the Reverend Hugh M'Neil, a rod whose "merciful object" was to "call . . . the suffering to repentance."

Like the bishops and most clergymen's sermons, M'Neil nowhere called for improved sanitation, only that Christians be penitent and devout. The clergy also accepted as providential the enormous and growing gap between rich and poor. Only a few, like the Reverend W. F. Hook of Leeds, worried about such gross inequalities. He told Archdeacon Samuel Wilberforce that bishops should give up their huge incomes and "become as poor as Ambrose or Augustine." Wilberforce disagreed, replying that not only would there always be poverty but "God has ordained differences of rank."[33]

Three assumptions informed the clergy's view of wealth, that its inequalities were ordained, that it carried with it a Christian stewardship, and that the superior ranks were needed to control and improve the sinful. The first of these assumptions led the Reverend William Gresley to declare that "independence and perfect equality are not good for man . . . [and that] there should be rich and poor . . . in order to call forth . . . self denial, charity, humility." The Reverend Samuel Green agreed, calling poverty God's affliction and "wealth . . . his gift [and] the gradations of society . . . his appointment." The Reverend Arthur Martineau, in a sermon full of Coleridge and Wordsworth, insisted that "each has his appointed station . . . in a framework of society that runs from parent and child, husband and wife, to ruler and ruled.[34]

A Christian stewardship based on wealth should also lead to a generous charity. The rich, announced the bishop of Salisbury, faced "great danger" if they forsook "God's Stewardship," a fact that led the bishop of Llandaff constantly to "inculcate the maxim that property has its duties," which the clergy never tired of preaching. Property had to do its duty, since, however frequent the parish clergy's visitations, and they were none too frequent, they could barely touch England's myriad social ills. The wealthy must also visit the poor, act kindly to servants, be fair to employees, and urge the rich to help the poor. The wealthy were obliged, proclaimed St. Pancras's the Reverend Thomas Dale, "to feed the hungry, to clothe the naked, to provide a refuge for the fatherless, to be the eyes to the blind and feet to the lame."[35] The exemplary lives of the rich should also inspire those beneath them. Clerical and lay would, by the conscientious use of the talents God had given them, mitigate the afflictions that were Adam's curse.

The poor also had duties. They must be sober and industrious, obedient and subordinate. "The book of Providence," said Cheltenham's Reverend Francis Close, "is one grand scheme of subordination." The humble and meek who would inherit the Kingdom of Heaven were even more favored of God than the rich, according to the Reverend Alexander Watson, because the rich had only one advantage in winning salvation, that they had the means of being charitable.

Most clergymen had as sanguine a view of a harmonious society as did the political economists. Providence had decreed, declared the bishop of Chester, that all evils have "a corresponding remedy." Excessive riches did not hurt the poor, said the Reverend Gresley, because "no man however rich can appropriate to himself much more than his proportion of the necessaries of life." The poor were also an absolute boon to the rich, said the Reverend Henry Melville, a very popular London evangelical, since by providing "objects which continually appeal to our compassion," they allowed the rich "to make progress in genuine piety." The High Church Reverend Francis Paget agreed. "If we provide for the sick and needy," he said, "we shall ourselves be delivered in the day of our trouble."[36]

Society was not all harmony, because there were sinners, and they demanded authority. "Submit yourself to every ordinance of man for the Lord's sake" was an unquestioned part of their social outlook. The magistrate "beareth not the sword in vain," announced the Reverend T. R. Bentley, with the Reverend Francis Close seconding him, saying, "Obedience must be obtained, whether by reason . . . or moral suasion or the rod."[37]

The clergy were not shy of the rod. They defended flogging for the erring and workhouses for the indolent. The Reverend Henry Milman wanted the workhouse to be "a place of hardship, of coarse fare and degradation." The shepherds of the flock were more than visitors to the poor. In their manifold duties, often as J.P.'s or poor law guardians, they viewed the Church as central to paternalism, for some as "the lynch pin holding society together," for others as "a great social machine," a "natural link between . . . rich and poor," and "a catholic society divinely instituted for social ends."[38] They managed charities and hospitals and supervised prisons and asylums, all part of what Archdeacon Wilberforce called "your several spheres."

The clergy did not always agree on how to care for their flocks. The chairman of the Andover poor law guardians, the Reverend Christopher Dodson, defended that law before a select committee that in 1846 exposed its cruel workings and meager diets, while the Reverend Thomas Sockett joined other clergymen to denounce it before the 1837 Select Committee on the Poor Law.[39] No, one, however, denounced it more vigorously than West Riding's Parson Bull, ally of the High Tory Richard Oastler in the movement for a ten-hour day and an inveterate foe of centralization. He was a model paternalist, building schools, encouraging sick clubs, and lecturing on temperance when not proclaiming that the poor had a right to God's generous bounty of fertile land. Not many of the clergy shared Bull's hatred of the law; the majority accepted it even though many also agreed with the Reverend C. Waterson, in his *Address on Pauperism*, that the true remedy lay in the principles of the gospel. Even some of the most benevolent, like the Reverend Sidney Godolphin Osborne, supported the New Poor Law, although not without condemning its worst severities.[40]

On boards of guardians throughout England, as guardians, chaplains, and visitors, the Anglican clergy saw that the members of their flock were not ill used. Many were also active founding and running schools. "Train up a child in the way he should go: and when he is old, he will not depart from it," they believed with Proverbs (22:6). The child's soul also required education in Christian truth. To John Keble, inspirer of the Oxford Movement, no duty was so vital and sacred as catechizing young pupils, and the Reverend Robert Armitage of Hereford pronounced the schoolmaster second only to the clergyman in usefulness. Bishop Blomfield of London also saw Church and school as allies in usefulness. "Where a church is built," he announced, "schools . . . are sure to follow, "bringing a combined provision for the spiritual and moral wants of the people . . . [and] cure of its most dangerous disease." More schools, he insisted, would mean fewer prisons, an optimism not shared by Kent's Reverend T. J. Hussey, who feared that overeducation "prematurely develops the intellect until . . . it totters on the verge of insanity." Most clergy, sharing neither Hussey's fears nor Blomfield's optimism, worked to promote education, although only if solidly Anglican—catechism, prayer book, and all—and also only if the secular instruction was limited to reading, writing, morality, and the proper social deference. The bishop of Salisbury saw no need of schooling beyond the age of ten, since "the pressure of poverty demanded their employment."[41] Believing that sinful man's indolence, drinking, and improvidence greatly contributed to his distress, the clergy insisted that the great remedy for that distress would be the stern lessons of industry, sobriety, and frugality, all taught by admonishing clergymen, disciplining employers, and truly Christian schoolmasters.

The above account of the clergymen's views of themselves as shepherds of their flock is drawn from many episcopal charges, sermons, and memoirs. Whether High, Broad, or Low Church, though differing on theology, they believed that, as good shepherds they must visit, aid, console, admonish, educate, and discipline their flock. It was an ideal suitable for rural England, in which the clergyman (supposedly) knew all his parishioners—parishes such as Chilbottom in Hampshire, where the Reverend Richard Durnford gave the poor allotments from his glebe lands, established a school at his own expense, collected fuel for the poor, and chastised farmers who ill treated their laborers. His wife also made daily visits to the poor, whom she regarded as family. She gave the destitute soup, and the sick and weak, wine and medicine. At Oxford's parish of Whitney, the Reverend Charles Jerram was also active, placing all dwellings under his appointed visitors, who aided the residents and supervised them. He built two schoolrooms and an infant school, examined the pupils himself, visited the old and ill, and saw that there was no pugilism in the parish. More active than Durnford or Jerram was Dorset's Sidney Godolphin Osborne, with his coal fund, wives' friendly society, penny clothing fund, benefit clubs, savings bank, and allotments. In parishes like these, and in others in rural England, the clergy showed how much they were a part of paternalism, and how it could alleviate, if not remove, poverty and destitution.[42]

The Church of England had its cathedral towns as well as rural parishes, and its cathedral ideal, an ideal dear to the heart of Edward Denison, bishop of Salisbury. For Denison, "the service of ordination expressly entrusts its ministers with both the guardianship of the poor" and the teaching of the children. To educate the children, he helped establish a diocesan board of education and two teacher training colleges. Convinced that diocesan institutions could mold and control society, he urged that ecclesiastical courts be more active. His canon and secretary of the diocesan board of education, Walter Hamilton, was convinced that cathedrals "ought to be centers of religious education," a vision he carried out after 1854 as bishop of Salisbury. Known as the "bishop of the poor," he gave the 100 neediest a yearly dinner of roast beef and plum pudding. Pleased by the work of both bishops was Sydney Herbert, M.P., of nearby Wilton House. In 1849, Herbert published *Proposals for the Better Application of Cathedral Institutions*. To existing diocesan colleges for training teachers, he proposed adding a pastoral college to educate men for the clergy and a college to educate laymen. There would be a diocesan building society, diocesan inspectors of charities, and "an army of missionaries to combat ignorance and infidelity." It was a noble vision, but one far exceeding both the resources of the diocese and the energy and resolve of its canons and prebends.[43] The early Victorian bishops had great ambitions, and they grew more powerful than ever. In 1838 and 1839, in response to talk of government schools, they took bold action. They established twenty-four diocesan and sub-diocesan boards of education and many colleges for training hundreds of schoolmasters and schoolmistresses to fulfill the Church's resolve to be the educator of the people.

But although bishops had grown in power and assumed bold ambitions, the revenues and zeal were lacking. In 1845, the bishop of Salisbury confessed that the diocesan board of education had run out of money. It was a reality that James Kay-Shuttleworth, secretary to the government's Committee on Education bluntly recognized when he told Lord John Russell, "Neither the clergy nor the laity were equal to the design. They did not care sufficiently for the people . . . and have not made the necessary sacrifices."[44]

The cathedral ideal, like the parochial ideal, had its limits. Since both were at their best mitigating rural evils, how could they meet a flood of urban ones? The Reverend W. F. Hook thought they could, even in Leeds, with 152,000 people, 88,741 of whom lived in Hook's parish, which was nearly seven miles in diameter. The parish had ten churches, seating only 13,000—of which only 5,500 seats were not taken by the renters of pews. Eight churches had no residences for their ministers. There was only one clergyman for 6,000 souls. But Hook was undaunted. He not only built ten new churches but seventeen parsonages for seventeen ministers in seventeen parishes created by an act of Parliament that he had engineered. He also established schoolrooms for 7,500.[45]

Bishop Blomfield faced quite as awesome a challenge in vast London: in Bethnal Green, there was one church for every 35,000 people and one national school for every 70,000. The vast evils did not discourage the energetic and ambitious Blomfield. He supervised the addition of 11 clergymen, 15 schoolmasters, 100 Sunday school teachers, and 101 district visitors to Bethnal Green, all bringing the parish "our holy religion [and] administering to their temporal wants."[46]

Not all towns faced Leeds's and London's vast problems. Cheltenham had 36,000 inhabitants and only two churches in 1825, and few children there attended any school at all. The Reverend Francis Close, a zealous evangelical, then arrived, and by 1841, Cheltenham had six Anglican churches, 17,000 children attending school, and many Church-supported institutions, ranging from orphanages to Magdalen houses.

In his effort to bring Christianity to East London, Blomfield was helped by dedicated clergymen such as Whitechapel's Reverend William Champneys, who built three churches and founded schools for boys and girls and a special one for the ragged. He also formed a shoe-black brigade to employ vagrant boys, an association to promote workers' health, and opened an office to replace pubs as a place for hiring coal whippers (laborers who moved coal using a pulley called a "whip").[47] The work of Hook, Close, and Champneys and their lay helpers appeared to be the first step—however limited—toward the creation of a clerisy that could lessen social evils, but it was a step that drew criticism from Coleridge because of its use of laymen in visiting societies, reducing it, he said, to "a Scotch eldership in disguise."

Coleridge, the deprecator of "traders in philanthropy," might have liked

Close's vast array of societies even less. So might Hook, who, like so many High Churchmen, wished ordained churchmen, not reborn laymen, however devout, to be the ministering shepherds of the flock. He thus concentrated on creating more parishes and more clergy, clergy who, as part of an apostolic Church, could catechize the young, celebrate the sacraments, and ordain sisters of charity. These sisters and young men in religious communities would visit the poor and the sick and teach the young. Hook contributed £400 out of his income of £1,200 to this end and inspired his young clergy to be equally sacrificial. "We lived together to save money," one of them wrote, "rose at six, [to pray] . . . at nine religious instruction . . . to the older scholars . . . [then] visits . . . a service, . . . baptism and burials: and at ten at night we wearily reached home."[48]

Close worked just as tirelessly, only in an evangelical way, as an inveterate organizer of societies. No other town, bragged the *Cheltenham Chronicle*, "possess[ed] a greater number of benevolent institutions." There were societies for orphans, hospitals, dispensaries, missionaries, aid to pastors, fallen women, propagating Christian knowledge, and schools of every kind, societies invariably chaired by the man many called the "Pope of Cheltenham." Idolized by the fashionable and feared by the lowly, the imperious Close would tolerate no error or sin. He had the young radical George Jacob Holyoake imprisoned for blasphemy. Close's social outlook was a fusion of a traditional paternalism with evangelical philanthropy. He was more than a shepherd of his flock, he was their complete patriarch.[49]

Not a few High Churchmen shuddered at Close and his many societies. For the Reverend William Gresley, Close's mortal enemy in theological disputes, there would be "no need of those numerous associations" if all Christians were like the early ones. His friend the Reverend John Sandford, author of *Parochialia*, called voluntary associations a "painful anomaly," since they did work so obviously "the province of the Church." There was no need of such societies, argued the Reverend Francis Paget, whose colleague the Reverend T. J. Hussey said that "the Church ought to be one great club, or benefit society," one that would not form "a selfish vainglorious philanthropy," but care for the poor directly. Only by giving through "the offertory as part of the divine service," added Paget, could one escape "hypocrisy and ostentation" and fulfill "the responsibilities which wealth involves."[50] But to comprehend the poor in the Church as a benefit society, the pew rents that excluded them must end. The High Church bishop of Exeter, who did little to alleviate the poor's suffering, was tireless in denouncing pew rents. His paternalism, like that of most High Churchmen, was Church-centered. It was a paternalism never more evident at the consecration of the Church of St. Barnabas in Pimlico, a consecration attended by Keble, Pusey, Manning, Sewell, Gresley, and Paget. St. Barnabas was for the poor. No pew rents disgraced it. It had schools for boys and girls and a college for resident clergy. Its pastor, the Reverend William Bennet, who called the existence of great wealth and abject poverty a "grievous disease," saw its cure in religion—in more churches and schools, and more colleges of clergymen and sisters of charity. "How better to manifest our love of the poor by . . . living with them . . . as an ecclesiastical body," an act that would "end the spiritual and material destitution in the metropolis."[51] It was a noble vision, and no doubt did some good in Pimlico, but hardly in the metropolis. In the year that St. Barnabas was consecrated, London's diocesan board of education raised only £360 for its 353 schools. Admirable though their aims and worthy their acts, their paternalism, like that of most churchmen, had severe limitations, among which four were increasingly obvious: (1) inadequate revenue, (2) too few caring shepherds, (3) too narrow a focus on saving souls, and (4) too great a fear of disturbing the status quo and the Church's privileges.

The revenues of the Church of England were inadequate in large part because they were poorly distributed. One contemporary estimated its revenue from tithes, lands, fees of all sorts, offerings, lectureships, chaplaincies, and chapels to be £9,450,565. Many voluntary societies, such as the Church Pastoral and Church Building Society and the National Society, raised thousands. Queen Anne's Bounty also helped poorer livings, and by 1849, government grants to Church schools came to £529,000. There was no need to build new churches either, because the existing ones were not full. In London and in northern towns, only one in ten workers attended church. Money was, of course, needed, especially for the parish livings that Hook brought to Leeds and Bennet to Pimlico. Such an invaluable expansion might have occurred had there been a fairer division of the Church's wealth. The bishop of Durham's £19,000 could have supported many a curate. The richer livings, some with incomes of over £1,000, could have helped the 860 curates receiving less than £50 a year. An ecclesiastical commission thought of shifting those ample cathedral incomes, much of which went to idle prebends and canons, to parishes with active pastors, but ended up shifting only £30,000 a year. Meanwhile, seven bishops in the 1840s spent huge sums to rebuild, build anew, or lease new palaces: £4,800 helped the bishop of Oxford build a new residence, and £15,000 went for a new one for the bishop of Ripon.[52] Such expenditures hardly set a good example for those who desired the Church to become the teacher of a rapidly growing population, a task demanding millions of pounds. Such was not forthcoming. Although they received nearly 80 percent of the government's grants for education, every diocesan board of education reported want of funds. The education inspectors praised "the zeal of the clergy" and their "expert assistance" and called them "sacrificial" and "great promoters of elementary education," but then noted "a great deficiency of money" and "a want of adequate . . . funds." The want of funds, said one inspector in 1852, "is constantly growing worse and worse," another in 1853 adding that they are "wholly insufficient." A want of the funds necessary to qualify for a government grant doomed many a poor district to no church school at all, Anglican or Dissenting. The National Society might have helped the Anglican schools, but in 1854, its funds were "in a depressed state."[53]

The shepherds of the flock also lacked the means to fulfill Christ's admonition "feed the hungry and clothe the naked." Except for Christmas benevolence, occasional alms, and the encouragement of clothing, coal, and blanket clubs, and, in crises, soup kitchens, these aspiring shepherds could do little but accept the fact that the government's Poor Law, not the Church's largesse, would care for the poor.

More than money was lacking. The Church lacked the Hooks and Champneys to fulfill its paternal mission. Too many of the clergy were like the Bartons, Gilfils, and "old Mr. Crewes" in George Eliot's *Scenes of Clerical Life* or the Hardinges and Grantleys of Anthony Trollope's *The Warden*. Barton was "plebeian, dim and ineffectual," Gilfils "smoked long pipes and preached short sermons" and dined and hunted with local squires, while Crewe "delivered inaudible sermons" and "made a fortune out of his school and curacy." Trollope's Hardinge was a warden of a charity most of whose income the warden received, and his Grantley an archdeacon as ambitious as the sleekest bishop and adamantly opposed to all reform. George Eliot lovingly portrays Barton, Gilfil, and Crewe as playing a warm and admirable part in village life. But such clergymen were not effective reformers of social ills, and neither did they, or Trollope's clerics, ever entertain such an idea.[54]

Although the clerics in Eliot and Trollope never measured up to the Hooks and Champneys, they were no doubt more representative of the English clergy. Clergymen varied greatly, ranging from foxhunting sybarites and ambitious careerists to earnest evangelicals and devout High Churchmen. Hertforshire's pious Edward Bickersteth, author of sixteen volumes of theology and innumerable pamphlets, was an earnest evangelical who, at four in the afternoon, visited the school or the poor, warning them against novels, dancing, and vain songs; and the equally pious High Churchman Robert Wilberforce worked zealously for a system in which deacons and churchwardens took a more active role in parish life.[55]

George Eliot's portrait of the Reverend Tryan, ever solicitous of the poor, shows how evangelical Anglicans, challenged in part by Dissent and in part by infidelity, reinvigorated the paternalism of the Church, a reinvigoration that in turn helped evoke an equally serious Tractarian movement. But despite these revivals, so few were the model shepherds, and so great the want of funds, that the solving of England's social problems by a Church paternalism was a chimera, something clergymen resolute on saving souls seldom admitted.

Theology and the saving of souls, not the solving of social problems, obsessed the Church's clerics. Among the 50 charges and 350 sermons used for this analysis, only one in four charges and one in twenty sermons dealt with social problems, and then peripherally. Moral themes there were, but they concerned personal behaviour and were overshadowed by theological themes, by Tractarian disquisitions on the need of apostolic authority and ritual and on the saving grace of the sacraments, or by evangelical sermons on the conversion and spiritual edification of individual souls.

Society's status quo, ordained by God, was also not to be disturbed. A Christian need not become obsessed by destitution, child labor, long hours of labor, and exploitation. In 1842, a year of deep depression, the Reverend Close, the pope of Cheltenham, preached only one sermon on the poor. Five of Cheltenham's churches raised only £595 to relieve the many jobless, although in January 1842, the town's handsome assembly rooms hosted twenty balls and many entertainments. The £595 nevertheless led Close to say that the poor could no longer "rail against the Church." Indefatigable in his philanthropic societies, Close never thought of elevating Cheltenham's poorest to a higher status.[56] Neither did most clergymen, according to Hampshire's Reverend Richard Dawes, a model shepherd, renowned for his excellent schools. They were, Dawes declared, really suspicious of a good secular education and would settle for mere "charity schools that would keep the labouring classes . . . entirely apart."[57] The clergy disliked radical change. A few, mostly in northern factory towns, supported the Ten Hour Bill, but the overwhelming majority did not, sensitive as always to property's rights and hostile to the interference of a secular, centralizing government. "The bishops," complained Lord Ashley, "are timid, timeserving, and great worshippers of wealth and power." He could scarcely remember any clergyman who would "maintain the cause of the labourers in the face of the pew holders."[58]

Never was the clergy's hostility to reform greater than when it endangered the Church's privileges—and most particularly against any measure lessening their right to educate the people. When, in 1846, one of their own, W. F. Hook, proposed a plan for rate-supported schools with excused time for religious instruction by either Nonconformist or Anglican pastors, Tractarians and evangelicals alike denounced it with unprecedented anger. The Reverend

Close declared that it would, like the Poor Law, exhaust the rates, the bishop of London that it invaded the Church's sacred domain.[59] But Close and the bishop had no such objection to Treasury grants to their National Society schools, particularly since they received some 80 percent of them. Their attitude to the state was ambivalent and expedient; for it when it helped the Church, against it if it hurt the Church or helped Dissent. In 1843, they supported rate-supported factory schools that they would dominate, and in 1846, they opposed Hook's rate-supported schools, which they could not dominate. In the long run, their jealous regard for their dominance in education seriously delayed the advent of an effective, national tax-supported system of public education.

The Closes and Blomfields were more willing to accept Treasury grants for their schools than were many High Churchmen, who from 1848 to 1853, led by Archdeacon George Denison, attacked the Committee on Education for insisting that laymen share with the clergy the management of small rural schools. For Denison, this squabble over laymen acting as trustees involved "the conflict between the Church and the world," a conflict, said the Reverend Francis Paget, that also involved the Church's relief of the poor through almsgiving. "Acts of Parliament," he exclaimed, "cannot mend it." Some High Churchmen would not even recognize civil or Nonconformist marriages. St. Barnabas's Bennet refused to recognize any marriage "not solemnized by the parish priest."[60]

The paternalism of High Churchmen grew ever more hostile to the paternalism of the state as they pursued their will-o'-the-wisp of a monopoly of England's religious life. They all, including the Hooks and Blomfields, defended the Church's right to burial fees and control of parish cemeteries, since it involved clergymen's powers and incomes. Whether it was over burials or workhouse chaplains being exclusively Anglican, whether education or marriage, the Church's vested interest conflicted with the growth of a paternal government sufficiently comprehensive to be viable.

Paternalism was not of one piece. Its strongest pillar was the paternalism of property; its second strongest, the Church. By 1850, for all the clergy's self-sacrifice, generosity, and compassion and for all their admirably Christian work, they came nowhere near to stemming the flood of abuses and distress brought on by industrialization, urbanization, and an expanding population.

For these very urban problems it would be perhaps wiser to look to Carlyle's captains of industry.

CAPTAINS OF INDUSTRY

Paternalism found expression not only in great dukes and fatherly squires governing rural estates, but in captains of industry presiding over mills run by the side of roaring streams—Samuel Greg's Quarry Bank on the Bollin, Thomas Ashton's Hyde on a tributary of the Mersey, and Henry and Edmund Ashworth's New Eagley on the Irwell.

The Ashworths' commodious mill of Lancashire limestone was flanked by spacious four- and six-room houses of the same glistening stone for its workers, with Henry Ashworth's mansion across the ravine, proudly overlooking the chimneys, chapel spires, and evergreen-clad hills of his New Eagley.

Greg's less elevated mansion at Quarry Bank was still "near at hand to the cottages," allowing "his daughters to give friendly greetings and flowers to the apprentices on their way to church." Ashton at Hyde, also built his workers houses of stone, two-storied, and with a small backyard. Pride in good housing also distinguished the Whitehead brothers' mills, "none destitute of a clock and a small collection of books." The Ashworths rented their houses for £5 a year, more than was charged by the duke of Richmond for his, but then their working-class families' incomes averaged £1 13s. 4d. a week, an amount unheard of in rural Sussex.[61]

The captains of industry were also proud of their schools, churches, chapels, libraries, playgrounds, reading and lecture rooms, and baths and washhouses. The children of Henry Ashworth's workers began their education in infant schools, and after they went to work at the age of nine, they continued to attend school for two hours a day. After the age of thirteen, it was Sunday and night school. Of Ashworth's workers, 98 percent could read and 45 percent could write. His schools taught so much that they caused the visiting Lord John Manners to be "alarmed by all this hotbed of intellect," and Lord Ashley to be thankful that the school's "superior intellects" were rare, since it "would be difficult keeping them in their station."[62]

Lords of the soil, fearful of superior intellects, expressed their paternalism largely in seasonal benevolence, prizes for long service, clothing and coal clubs, and visits of the lady bountiful and the parson; the captains of industry expressed theirs in libraries, Sunday schools, reading and lecture rooms, and temperance societies. A religious education was fundamental to both, an Anglican one for rural children, Anglican and Nonconformist for the urban ones. The Ashworths were Quakers, the Gregs and Ashtons Unitarians, the Whiteheads Methodist. Ashworth, no less autocratic than the duke of Richmond, required not only attendance at church but sobriety, industry, respectability and cleanliness; rule boards on factory walls promoted "the virtues of thrift, order, promptitude and perseverance." Shoddy work, swearing, and loitering earned a heavy fine, and industry and morality ample rewards. He personally inspected their houses and evicted the slovenly. As did Robert Owen at New Lanark, he had special constables to suppress immorality. "We exercise a control . . . over them," he told the Factory Commission, "for their moral and social improvement."[63]

The paternal autocracy of the captains of industry flourished in small towns, where a Samuel Oldknow could, as his biographer wrote, "control and direct the life of the community" and a Josiah Wedgewood could end the "notion" that the workers could "do what they please." Both were strict disciplinarians, firm in governing, not just on moral grounds, but because discipline was necessary for factory work. Sidney Pollard argues that the village mill paternalism was functional. The need for water power forced the mills into remote areas, the remote areas forced them to supply houses, churches, and other services for their new recruits to the industrial army, an army that also needed training and discipline, and hence Sunday and day schools that indoctrinated the young in hard work, thrift, and respectability. "It required a man of Napoleonic nerve and ambition to subdue the refractory temper of work people," Andrew Ure wrote in his *The Philosophy of Manufactures* (1835).[64] Autocratic rule was not alone functional, so were benevolence and friendly intercourse. Ashworth estimated that "the order and content" of each worker was worth £50. Particularly profitable was the friendly intercourse in chapels, Sunday schools, and lecture halls, where Ashworth in 1844 discoursed on the evils of the Corn Law. Samuel Greg of Quarry Bank overflowed with geniality when he met his workers at the Sunday school, as did his son at games—quoits, trap, and cricket—and when he taught them geography and natural history, "those excelling winning the silver cross."[65]

Scotland also had its village mill paternalists, the "young and athletic, affable and generous" Archibald Buchanan, who joined the young in sports; James Finlay whose workforce included 200 teetotalers and not one drunkard; and most famous and paternal of all, New Lanark's Robert Owen and David Dale.

Paternalism even emerged, though less vigorously, in the cities. In Liverpool, the Northshore Mill had excellent schools, good housing, a medical program, and a yearly boating excursion for 600 children "of good conduct." Every week, one of the three owners (Anglican, Methodist and Unitarian) read the church service to their employees. In Manchester, Mr. Morris sought to lessen the distance between master and men in his mill with a library, class and coffee rooms, lectures, and industrial training—including household duties for the girls. Some 300 joined his temperance society, and all showed "docility and growing desire for instruction."[66]

The captains of industry, at ease with the functional aims of paternal benevolence and discipline, were less so with much of its rhetoric. Often Nonconformist and mostly self-made, they were strongly individualistic and would have their workers the same. W. R. Greg, mill owner turned author and reviewer for the *Edinburgh* and *Westminster* reviews denounced deference and servility as feudal, while Henry Ashworth insisted that calculated self-interest, not *noblesse oblige,* should rule.[67] There was in this a harmony of interests, since educated, well-treated workers increased profits. It was a thesis repeated and amplified by their two great publicists, Andrew Ure, Glasgow's professor of chemistry, and the journalist W. C. Taylor. Ure in *The Philosophy of Manufactures* and Taylor in *Notes of a Tour in the Manufacturing Districts* told all England of the Ashworths and Gregs and many others. Although free of the platitudes about property's duties and workers' deference, Ure did urge "a paternal concern for children" and the setting of good examples, holding that "like master like man" was true of mills as of families. He joined Ashworth in emphasizing an identity of interests. "Godliness is great gain" proclaimed the exuberant Ure who called the factory system the laborers' "grand palladium." Its mill owners, he added, were less proud and self-important and more egalitarian than landlords, a point with which W. C. Taylor entirely concurred when he contrasted the independence of Lancashire men, who gave "not one inch . . . in homage to wealth," with a deferential peasantry. Taylor never speaks of subordination, condescension, rank, and station, but of those qualities—equality, liberty, and identity of interests—that were stronger in manufacturing than in agriculture, a position the reverse of that held by E. S. Cayley, an agricultural publicist from Yorkshire. Cayley argued that landlords had stronger "inducements . . . to live in intimacy and Christian kindness." Not so, said Taylor, claiming that manufacturers had invested so greatly in floating capital, in machinery, that they had to keep their men happy and efficient. The landlord, however, enjoy a huge fixed capital and so could evict and let the land lie fallow.[68] Economic circumstances themselves forced the manufacturers to embrace paternalism, a position even *Fraser's* held in 1844 when it announced "there is no such thing as arcadian happiness," since harsh farmers separate laborers from the landlord. The *Eclectic Review* also believed that manufacturers, not landlords, had "a direct interest in educating and elevating the poor"[69]

For Taylor and the *Eclectic* and for the Quaker Ashworth and the Unitarians Greg and Ashton, the poor not only had to become good and profitable

workers but good, Christian men and women. These Bible-reading manufacturers also desired to create godly men, men worthy of the new Jerusalem,
self-reliant, law-abiding citizens of the new, purer, more equal Christian
commonwealth. The paternalism of the captains of industry was also an expression of a puritan vision of a godly society, one ranging from the mille-
narianism of the former Methodist Robert Owen to the vision of a laissez-
faire society whose citizens followed the teachings of Jesus.

Many of the English of the 1840s found a model for such a society in Lowell, Massachusetts. Charles Dickens, James Silk Buckingham, and the *Westminster*, *Eclectic*, and *Athenaeum* were among the many authors, M.P.'s, and
periodicals that extolled Lowell's virtues.[70] None of the writings of Coleridge
or Southey or any other authors rivaled these accounts of Lowell in popular-
izing paternalism. From the least feudal of countries came a model of paternalism far more vivid that any of England's landed estates—the only descriptions rivaling it were accounts of the Ashworths and Gregs, not of Boileau or
Bunbury.[71] Not paternalist rhetoric but model houses, schools, baths, and
lecture halls expressed the paternalism of the captains of industry.

It was an ideal Coleridge and Southey had not foreseen, but one welcomed
by Carlyle and Disraeli, Disraeli seeing in it old feudal ways and Carlyle England's salvation. After visiting the mills of Ashworth and Leeds's John Marshall, Disraeli created Mr. Millbank of *Coningsby* and Mr. Trafford of *Sybil*,
two exemplary and benevolent industrialists. At Marshall's flax mill, Disraeli
found a colossal factory in the Egyptian style, with 34-foot columns, a flat
roof upon which grass grew and sheep grazed, and schools and lecture halls,
where Marshall lectured on "the duties that attach to . . . property," duties
that in the hands of "the aristocracy of the land and the aristocracy of the
loom" would create a "union among the people of every station." To achieve
this, Marshall gave the jobless allotments, promoted education and friendly
societies, and was generous to the public infirmary.[72] His efforts were of little
avail. Few other mill owners joined in, the workers had little time for allotments, and the destitution was too vast.

The paternalism of village factories was ill suited for burgeoning Leeds and
Manchester or for gigantic London. In W. H. Eliot's *The Story of the
"Cheeryble" Grants of Manchester* and in Lord John Manner's account of
Manchester's mills, there are no reports of their sponsoring housing, schools,
or churches. They did contribute to mechanics institutes, churches, charities,
and "ameliorative public movements," and William Grant gave alms to the
poor every morning. But large cities demanded a more general benevolence.
"In the country district" wrote James Stuart, a factory inspector and convinced paternalist, "the owners . . . pay scrupulous attention to the wants of

the population . . . [but] the factory owner in a town knows little . . . of the people." Elizabeth Stone, in her novel *William Langshawe, Cotton Lord* (1842), also saw the advantages of the village factory. But she noted, as Stuart did not, that "in secluded districts" they became "the only magistrate . . . and the lord paramount . . . with none to restrain them," the result being a "tyrannical despot."[73]

Wealth as well as a countryside setting promoted a manufacturing paternalism. Model factories were a function of both capital and environment. "Great capitalists," insisted W. C. Taylor "are more equitable and merciful . . . than persons of limited fortunes." Landlords with poor soil and manufacturers with slim margins could not afford benevolence. The perfect formula, then, for a viable industrial paternalist was capital, a rural village, and religious earnestness, a formula that Titus Salt filled to perfection. A Congregationalist Sunday school teacher of great wealth, he moved his firm from crowded Bradford to "Saltaire," a town and mill that he created on the river Aire. Its 3,000 operatives worked in a huge, well-ventilated commodious mill, lived in 850 three-bedroom stone houses with gardens—the cost, £106,552—worshipped in a church costing £16,000, and were educated in schools that cost £7,000 and were "unrivalled for beauty, size and equipment." There were steam-driven machines for washing and drying clothes and forty-five almshouses, rent free, with income, for the aged or infirm of "good moral character." Salt also provided festivals and games on his estate for the operatives and feasted them royally.[74]

There were not many Saltaires in Britain, or many Ashworths and Gregs. There were, however, over 4,800 factories, thousands of collieries, and even more thousands of workshops, a fact that the factory inspector Leonard Horner knew well, and a fact that he wished the economist Nassau Senior to know well. The Factory Act, he told Senior, was not passed for the Gregs and Ashtons but for "the very many millowners whose standard of morality is low . . . whose governing principle is to make money and who do not give a straw for the children." Horner himself preached paternalism to the mill owners, urging them to supply good schooling. They did not. Disheartened, he lamented that in an eight-by-four-mile area around Oldham, with 105,000 people (90,000 wage earners), there was "not one day school for the humbler ranks [nor] . . . one medical charity." He found nine out of ten of the factory schools that did exist "a mockery of education," and eleven years after the 1833 Factory Act, illegal overworking of children was extensive.[75] He praised factory owners who "in many instances" treated their workers more generously than did landowners, a judgment that the Tory *Fraser's Magazine* supported, claiming that manufacturers had learned that their success depended on the "improvement of their work people." The *Examiner* also said that mill owners were kinder than landowners while the *Westminster* contrasted "the suffering hidden in the rustic cabin" with the "solid comfort and modest plenty" of the "square brick cottage of the artisan." Furthermore, the evils the workers suffered came not from "the warm, well ventilated, well lit, well paying factory but from overcrowded and disease ridden towns." The author of the *Westminster* article was W. R. Greg, himself a former mill owner, and hence not without a strong bias. Not all factory owners fitted Horner's claim that such owners were more benevolent than landlords. Not a few were less so, and especially those in workshops not covered by the Factory Act. "A want of consideration for the employed is widely spread," Horner concluded.[76]

That owners of workshops did little or nothing for their workers is fully corroborated by the six volumes of the Royal Commission on Women and Children in Mines and Manufactures. They presented a picture of exploitation, callous indifference, and cruel neglect that equals government reports of landlords' harshness.

The most scandalous exposures came from the mines, five- and six-year-olds opening and shutting trapdoors, and eight- and nine-year-olds dragging baskets in narrow seams, both for twelve hours and more; and, most shocking, half-naked women and totally naked men, fornication, accidents, and abusive parents and butties who beat the children—all occurring in mines largely owned by great landlords, landlords with paternalist outlooks. Some, like Lord Balcarres said he would have excluded women except that it would have created a disturbance. Lord Buccleuch, however, did exclude women, and no disturbance followed, only "increased morale." Buccleuch was an exception, as were the one mine owner in ten who supplied adequate schools.[77] In the three volumes on mines, not one in fifty mine owners evidenced a care for the housing and schooling of their workers, nor was the ratio any better for workshop masters: again poignant scenes of the exploitation of children, of seven- and eight-year-olds as "teers" in print works, who worked all night and collapsed, or young dressmakers and milliners stitching the night through to meet rush orders, of ten-year-olds in lace shops working fourteen- and fifteen-hour days, and of pottery boys vomiting from poisonous dyes.[78]

The commission's selection of these cases of exploitation may have overshadowed the more salutary features of workshop employment—the solid earnings of a family at work, constant jobs, dry and warm places of work, and perhaps a chance for advancement—but the general picture is of workshops with few amenities, and almost nothing done for schooling, health, and housing. Carlyle's belief that captains of industry could solve the condition of

England question was a noble one, and insofar as it assumed a benevolent at-tititude on the part of the masters, an admirable one. But there were still only about 50 or 60 model factory owners among some 4,800, and only a few score of good mine owners and workshop masters among several thousands. The government reports of the 1830s and 1840s should have disabused careful readers of a sanguine trust in property doing its duty.

PART II

The Vision of a Laissez-Faire Society

CHAPTER 4

The Triumph of Political Economy

The question of the day, proclaimed Benjamin Disraeli in 1847, was "whether society was to be governed by the pedantic application of . . . political economy or . . . by practical men." "In every question," he added, "these two principles come into perpetual collision."[1]

Disraeli was not alone in recognizing that two distinct outlooks divided early Victorian England. "There is . . . a great contest begun," announced the *Economist*, between "interference and non-interference." The *Oxford and Cambridge Review* saw it as "a conflict between the principle of patriarchal government" and the "harsh indifferentism of . . . political economy." For John Stuart Mill, it was a contest between "two modes of social existence," the "free" and the "protective," and for Thomas Babington Macaulay, a contest between a "patriarchal, meddling" and a "let-things alone" government.[2]

That political economy—only six decades old when Victoria became queen—should have challenged a paternalistic outlook that was centuries old and universally pervasive was nothing short of remarkable.

THE BIRTH OF POLITICAL ECONOMY

Political economy in England was born in 1776 with Adam Smith's *Wealth of Nations* and achieved, after many important works, near universal acceptance with John Stuart Mill's *Principles of Political Economy* of 1848. It was an intellectual event rivaled only by evangelicalism in defining the social conscience of the early Victorians. That political economy was born with the *Wealth of Nations*, many would question, since there were studies in the seventeenth and early eighteenth centuries of particular economic questions. In those years, men like Thomas Mun, Sir William Petty, John Locke, and David Hume did pioneering work on particular economic questions, on the quantity theory of money, the balance of trade, and the correct poor laws. They sought the true theory of rent, discussed the division of labor, and examined how the cost of labor influenced prices.[3] Adam Smith could, as Newton said of himself, see further because he stood on the shoulders of his predecessors. He also saw much more broadly, viewing the economy in its entirety, seeing its many interconnections and its defining principles, all richly illustrated with historical examples. It was a survey that, although too diffuse to constitute a cogent theory, nevertheless was united by two themes that were to inspire innumerable readers, a trenchant and persisting criticism of mercantilist restrictions and a protectionist government, and an optimistic belief in that "simple system of natural liberty" in which an individual's free, spontaneous, and selfish action, guided by an invisible hand, would best promote a nation's wealth and the people's well-being.

After Adam Smith, the floodgates opened. Jeremy Bentham published his *Defense of Usury* (1787), Thomas Malthus his *Essay on Population* (1793), and David Ricardo his *Principles of Political Economy* (1817), and scores more works, too numerous to cite, also appeared. Bentham's work won him notoriety as a political economist, and Malthus's had enormous impact, but it was Ricardo's *Principles* that took the most gigantic steps forward. The French, whose physiocrats first developed theoretical political economy, were critical of Adam Smith for his lack of theory. "No more," said France's J. B. Say of the *Wealth of Nations*, "than a confused assembly of the sanest principles of political economy."[4]

Ricardo's *Principles* was no "confused assembly" but a rigidly logical theory, one with laws defining the distribution of wealth, rent, prices, wages, and profits, laws that, like Smith's invisible hand, underlay the "natural identity of interests" that would, if only the government adopted a policy of laissez-faire, yield the greatest wealth and well-being. It was a theory seemingly so logical, and so persuasive, that it won a multitude of followers, ranging from the leading economists to lecturers at mechanics institutes.

James Mill in his *Elements of Political Economy* (1821) and John Ramsey McCulloch in his *Principles of Political Economy* (1825) were Ricardians and were widely read, although not as widely as Mrs. Marcet's *Conversations on Political Economy* and Harriet Martineau's *Illustrations of Political Economy*.[5] The youth of England were to be trained in axioms of political economy, axioms not solely Ricardian. Political economy was hardly taught except by Dugald Stewart at Edinburgh University. There were no professorships of political economy until they were established at Cambridge in 1817, Oxford in 1825, and shortly thereafter at London University's King's College, the civil service's Hailebury College, and Trinity College, Dublin. One was even established at Queen's College in Galway.[6]

Political economy quickly penetrated the learned journals, promulgated by the Ricardians McCulloch and Senior, with 81 and 29 articles respectively in the Whig *Edinburgh Review*, by Peronnet Thompson with 108 and J. S. Mill with 53 in the Utilitarian *Westminster Review*, and even by the Ricardian Thomas De Quincy in the Tory *Blackwood's* and the economist George Poulett Scrope in the *Quarterly Review*. Scrope contributed 21 articles and De Quincy 73, including three on "Ricardo Made Easy."[7] It also soon penetrated the popular press—London's *Globe, Morning Chronicle, Examiner*, and *Spectator*, and, in the provinces, great papers like the *Manchester Guardian* and the *Leeds Mercury*. J. S. Mill contributed over 400 items to the press. McCulloch lectured on it in London in 1824 to prominent Whigs and Tories. Political economy was the rage of London, observed McCulloch; it was in "high fashion with the blue stocking ladies," declared Maria Edgeworth; and the Whig diarist George Greville declared that "all men had become political economists."[8] Henry Brougham's Society for the Diffusion of Useful Knowledge made it the centerpiece of their inexpensive publications and spread its truth wide and far in their mechanics institutes, as did the widely read *Chamber's Edinburgh Journal*. And most crucially it invaded Parliament.

From 1821 to 1868, 52 of the 109 members of the Political Economy Club were in Parliament, where they joined perhaps an equal number—men like George Poulett Scrope, Richard Cobden, and Joseph Hume—who, although not members, were deeply versed in political economy. The economists in Parliament were an active group—some of them holding government office, such as C. E. Poulett Thomson and John Bowring at the Board of Trade. Others chaired select committees, proposing bills and speaking often. Ricardo, a member from 1819 to 1823, taught many M.P.'s the truths of the new science and, according to Henry Brougham "carried great weight." In Lord Melbourne's Whig cabinet of 1835, four were members of the Political Economy Club.[9]

The ideas of the political economists had indeed made many triumphs and spread widely. But as their publications grew vast, so their outlooks grew more varied. There was no one political economy. How could political economy be influential if it had no agreed-upon vision? The problem was twofold: first the challenge of the protectionist and the popular schools to orthodoxy and secondly the divisions between the orthodox themselves. If these challenges were powerful and the divisions among economists deep, how could political economy create a social conscience solidly based on the vision of a laissez-faire society?

The challenge was not, however, that powerful nor the divisions that deep. The protectionists had some trenchant things to say, particularly Michael Sadler's criticisms of Malthus's theory of population and Sadler's defense of the ten-hour day. E. S. Cayley also made telling criticism of laissez-faire in his writings on the cause of agricultural distress and the need for protection. So, too, did George Frederick Muntz and Mathias and Thomas Attwood in their demand for a more inflationary money supply. Anna Gambles reveals the vigor, imagination, variety, and extensiveness of protectionists' arguments on a vast array of issues, but as trenchant as were their criticisms, their writings and speeches fell far short of presenting a theory that was sufficiently developed and coherent to pose a serious challenge to political economy's central assumptions.[10]

Neither did the popular school of political economy that, taking its lead from Ricardo's claim that labor gives all products their value, argued that a much greater share of those products should therefore go to labor. The two most popular advocates of this argument, Thomas Hodgskin and William Thompson, were better economists than any of the protectionists, Hodgskin rivaling even the best of the orthodox, with whom he often agreed. But their answer to the injustice of capital seizing much of labor's share of the wealth had no appeal to the landed or the rising mercantile classes. Thompson looked to Owenite communities and Hodgskin to no very clear solution, so deep was his hatred of government and his anarchist's faith in reason.[11] Not one of the advocates of the popular economy sat in Parliament. Orthodox political economy had no real rivals.

But was it not weak because so divided in opinion? Did not the economists differ on most questions? Did not profits rise when wages fell and fall when wages rose? Yes! said David Ricardo and his disciple J. R. McCulloch; no! replied Richard Jones and Mountifort Longfield, professors of political economy at King's College London and at Trinity College, Dublin. Did not the size of the wage fund in relation to population determine wages? Yes! said McCulloch and James and John Stuart Mill with Ricardian enthusiasm; no! replied the Whig economist Edward West and the Benthamite Thomas Perronet Thompson, the author of the renowned *Corn Law Catechism*.[12] Does the cost of labor determine the value of all commodities? Most assuredly it does, argued the giants in the field, Adam Smith, Ricardo, McCulloch, and the Mills; no! replied the lesser-known but sharper political economists Scrope, Colonel Torrens, and Mountifort Longfield.[13] And so the arguments multiplied, Perronet Thompson joining Longfield, Jones, and Scrope in denouncing Ricardo's theory of rent, Malthus calling Ricardo wrong in claiming depressions can never result from overproduction and gluts, and the younger economists, Scrope, John Rooke, Thomas Tooke, and Nassau Senior, denying the claims of their elders that the cost of food determines the level of wages.[14] By 1840, the whole of the Political Economy Club declared Malthus's law that population grew at a geometrical and food at an arithmetical rate "errone-ous," and in 1831, they announced that much of Ricardo was wrong. No won-der that Thomas De Quincy spoke of "this anarchy of opinion," the *Journal of the Statistical Society* of "conjectural results as wild as they are often contra-dictory," and the Tory *Standard* of "blunder to blunder."[15]

The political economists did disagree and did err. But that they differed on the wage fund and erred on the labor theory of value meant little to a public indifferent to such nuances. It was the core of political economy that mat-tered, those central propositions most relevant to society's problems and in-terests and those larger truths that gave clear and simple answers—larger truths on which the economists did agree. Four of the more relevant of these central propositions were (1) the principles of non-interference in the econ-omy, (2) free trade, (3) the need to discipline the poor, and (4) the supreme virtue of small government and low taxes.

The first proposition was far and away the most important. "The principle of non-interference . . . this great principle of political economy," proclaimed the liberal M.P. John Trelawny in the 1844 factory debate, "should be adopted by the state"[16] It was a principle, a fixed rule, that hardly a single economist opposed, since whenever they did favor interference—and on occasion they all did—it was invariably and distinctly an exception, a case of particular cir-cumstances. The principle of non-interference was, of course, older than Adam Smith and arose from interests and outlooks far broader than political economy. But the powerful, logical, and unbending arguments of the economists certainly strengthened this basic foundation stone of a laissez-faire society. Even if Ricardo was wrong on rents, had he not demonstrated with the rigor of a scientist the harm that government interference does to the natural identity of interests?

And did he not also prove the wisdom of free trade? That principle, of course, could also be subsumed under the principle of non-interference, but given the importance of international trade to England's economy and the overwhelming importance of the corn laws to English agriculture, the princi-ple of free trade assumed a paramountcy all its own. On the corn laws, the economists were largely in agreement. There were, to be sure, protectionist economists and elaborate protectionist arguments, just as there were mar-ginal differences between the orthodox—Ricardo, largely for political rea-sons, accepting a ten shilling fixed duty.[17] But these arguments and compro-mises counted for little in the face of the economists' formidable attack on the corn laws and the navigation acts. Who could deny the theory of com-parative costs, which proved that if each nation freely exported what it could most efficiently produce, all would be richer. It was of course far too recondite a theory for the public and was seldom used in Parliament and the press, although often with other economists. For the public, it was enough that tariffs, by increasing the cost of food, hurt the poor. Costly food also raised wages and cut into profits, thus weakening capital and depressing the economy. Tariffs also hurt the economy by limiting the foreigners' chance to earn and spend pounds on English goods. The economists also made it clear that the corn laws favored the landed over other classes.

Harmful, too, was the explosion of population and pauperism, a growing evil that demanded the disciplining of the poor. It was a need most dramatically proclaimed in Malthus's dire prediction that the multiplying poor would outrun the food supply, a prediction that led him to plead with the poor to be prudent in marrying; and prudent, too, added nearly all economists, by freeing themselves from the corruptions of the old poor laws and by becoming, under the discipline of the New Poor Law, sober, industrious, and provident.

The plea to be industrious and provident was no preserve of the economists. It was a moral argument centuries old, one that filled the writings and sermons of moralists of all persuasions. But by becoming an indelible part of political economy the plea to discipline the poor gained enormous strength. Three of the favorite theories of the economists gave it much greater weight: Malthus's law of population, Ricardo's theory of a subsistence wage, and his wage fund theory. A population multiplying faster than the supply of food demanded, of course, that the poor limit their numbers by prudent marriages. It was also evident that the poor's inexorable multiplication, given the law of supply and demand, would force wages down to the subsistence level, a fact even more evident because of the Ricardians' belief that the wage fund was fixed. That population did not, in fact, outrun food, that wage funds actually expanded, and that wages, even in the hungry 1840s, rose, made no difference. In 1848, J. S. Mill's *Political Economy* reaffirmed both Malthus's fear of population growth and Ricardo's wage fund, two theories that placed the old arguments of moralists on the sturdy foundation of economic theory.[18]

Also centuries old was the universal passion for low taxes and less government, a passion that welcomed the economists' argument that the lower the taxes the greater the capital for investment and prosperity. Many, then, were the reasons for political economy's triumph.

But not all was favorable to political economy. Its triumph evoked resistance and disapproval, suspicion and contempt. It was not only arid, abstract, and dogmatic but a theory based on a cold, calculating, and most unchristian plea to be selfish. It was, insisted the Tory *Leeds Intelligencer,* "as bad-eyed, cross-grained, pig-headed old beldame as ever snatched . . . bread from an infant."[19]

Hatred of political economy was widespread, ranging from Tory squires and High Churchmen to Chartists and Owenites, and including Christian reformers, much of literary London, and, as Disraeli said, thousands of "practical men." Political economy would not triumph easily, certainly not without a group of dedicated and determined apostles.

THE UTILITARIANS: APOSTLES OF POLITICAL ECONOMY

"I was," claimed Jeremy Bentham, "the spiritual father of James Mill, and Mill was the spiritual father of David Ricardo."[20] James Mill in turn was the actual as well as the spiritual father of John Stuart Mill, and the two Mills the inspirers of many others in this utilitarian apostolic laying on of hands. The power and extent of their economic writings soon identified the utilitarians with political economy and strongly shaped the outlook of the "philosophical radicals" of the 1820s, a group who included the economist Ricardo, the banker George Grote, Francis Place, tailor and reformer, and Charles and John Austin, professors of law at Cambridge and London Universities. Ricardo and Grote entered Parliament in the 1820s and joined Joseph Hume, William Ewart, Poulett Thomson, and Henry Warburton to form the "Philosophical Radicals," a party strengthened in the 1830s by Perronet Thompson, John Leader, John Arthur Roebuck, Edward Strutt, Charles Buller, William Molesworth, Charles Villiers, and Samuel Romilly's two sons John and Edward. All but Hume, Ewart and Roebuck came from Cambridge University, where George Pryme taught political economy and where William Paley's utilitarian doctrines were required reading. The attempt to form an independent political party in the 1830s failed, but most of the thirteen Philosophical Radicals remained to press forward their utilitarian ideas, ideas that gave great prominence to political economy.[21] Poulett Thomson told Parliament that "political economy served as a fixed line to guide him," while John Arthur Roebuck declared that "political economy's principles are great and shouldn't be violated," views with which John Bowring agreed when he called the law of supply and demand "inexorable" and warned the Commons against any "departure from the sound principles of political economy."[22]

They also expressed their laissez-faire convictions by their votes. None of the utilitarian M.P.'s opposed the New Poor Law until Bowring and Leader did so in 1842; and none supported the ten-hour day except Charles Buller in

1844 and William Ewart in 1847.[23] Neither did the utilitarians support bills for government protection of lace mill operatives, hosiery workers, London bakers, framework knitters, and those unloading coal in the port of London. None either ever urged legislative protection for the thousands of children exploited in England's myriad workshops.[24]

The utilitarians' greatest cause was, of course, free trade in corn. In 1835, two years before Manchester's Anti-Corn Law League, they organized the Anti-Corn Law Association. In the same year Charles Villiers initiated the annual motion for the Law's repeal. Its repeal in 1846 was political economy's greatest victory, a victory that owed much to the utilitarians, not only as M.P.'s but as journalists.

The utilitarians had a remarkable influence in the London press. Friends of Bentham and the Mills included five powerful editors, John Black of the *Morning Chronicle*, John Wilson of the *Globe*, Albany Fonblanque of the *Examiner*, Robert Rintoul of the *Spectator*, and W. E. Hickson of the *Westminster Review*, whose past editors included Perronet Thompson and John Stuart Mill.[25] Less close to Bentham and the Mills, but not less close to political economy, were editors or owners like H. G. Ward of the *Weekly Chronicle*, James Wilson of the *Economist*, G. H. Lewes at the *Leader*, Robert Bell of the *Atlas*, and "the old Benthamite" Charles Dilke of the *Athenaeum*, the author of *The Remedy of National Difficulties Deduced from the Principles of Political Economy*.[26]

For many apprentices in journalism, work on these papers provided an education that included the rudiments of political economy. William Wier, Dickens's secretary at the *Daily News*, and its future editor, was trained "in the famous school of Rintoul" at the *Spectator*; John Forster and Douglas Jerrold learned journalism at Fonblanque's *Examiner*, just as Fonblanque had earlier learned some of his economics at John Black's *Morning Chronicle*. The Benthamite Black, said the Scots journalist James Hedderick, exercised an "influence on shaping the destiny of the Empire." Also under Black were Charles Mackay, G. H. Lewes, and Eyre Crowe (all future editors) and two of Dickens's editorial writers, W. J. Fox and the economist Thomas Hodgskin.[27] Writing often for the *Morning Chronicle* were Charles Buller, James Wilson, Albany Fonblanque, and John Stuart Mill. Mill, author of the century's most widely read text on political economy—no fewer than twenty-two editions in fifty years—wrote 36 articles for the *Chronicle* and 225 for the *Examiner*. Mill also contributed to both the *Westminster* and *Edinburgh* reviews as did G. H. Lewes, W. E. Hickson, W. R. Greg, William Ellis, and John Austin, all part of London's utilitarian circle, all devout believers in political economy, and all active in expressing its truths in the London press.[28]

As seminal as were the economic writings of the utilitarians and as unrelenting as were its M.P.'s and editors in propagating their truths, they were too few to carry the day without the support of a major party. It found just such an ally in the Whigs.

THE WHIGS LEARN ECONOMICS

Political economy's conquest of the Whigs was slow but remorseless. It had many beginnings: Lords Russell, Palmerston, and Lansdowne had learned it in Edinburgh as students of Dugald Stewart; George Villiers and some fifteen M.P.'s, at the London lectures of the Whig economist J. R. McCulloch; the young Lord Morpeth and Sir Francis Baring, chancellor of the exchequer from 1839 to 1841, from much study at Oxford; and those at Whiggish Cambridge, from the lectures of George Pryme and Paley's *Moral and Political Philosophy*. For some Whigs, like Lord Howick, heir to the third Earl Grey, and Charles Villiers, the brother of Lord Clarendon, it was friendship with the Philosophical Radicals that led to an awareness of the new science, or perhaps membership in the Political Economy Club, over half of whom were Whigs.[29]

By the mid 1830s, however, most landed Whigs distrusted a science so favorable to a free trade in corn; Lord Russell pronounced it "an awful thing," and two-thirds of the Whigs in 1838 helped defeat a proposal to repeal the Corn Law, 361 to 172.[30] But while the country Whigs voted for the Corn Law, some Whig peers and most Whig intellectuals opposed it. At Nassau Senior's modest No. 25 Hyde Park, young Whigs debated the finer points of the labor theory of value. Senior's *Outline of Political Economy* of 1835, based on his Oxford lectures, made him, always a loyal Whig, the most distinguished publishing economist between J. R. McCulloch and John Stuart Mill, whose 1848 *Political Economy* helped fuse Radicals and Whigs into the Liberal Party of the 1850s.[31]

In partnership with the utilitarians, Whig believers in political economy also used the press to expound its truths. The Whig Lord Radnor helped finance the founding of the *Economist*, and James Wilson, its editor, prided himself on being a Whig and not a Radical. He was also proud to be a guest at Lord Lansdowne's Bowood, Lord Clarendon's Kent House, and Senior's Hyde Park Gate. A prolific writer, Wilson also supplied economic analyses for the *Examiner*, the *Morning Chronicle*, and the *Globe*, a paper that Harriet Martineau said taught her political economy and that the *Daily News* called "the devoted worshiper of political economy."[32]

The Whigs also brought that worship to the House of Lords. To the acute discomfort of many of its members, Whig lords lectured them interminably on the new science, Brougham stridently and endlessly for thirty-six years, Lansdowne philosophically and detachedly, Monteagle and Fitzwilliam trenchantly, Grey and Holland sparingly, and Radnor belligerently. Whig M.P.'s also lectured on economics in the Commons. For Lord Howick, it was a "beautiful system," based on Adam Smith's "immortal work," and for Sir John Trelawny, a system full of "principles they could not controvert, and deductions they could not refute."[33] Two good Whigs, Alderman Thompson and Sir Francis Baring opposed railway subsidies, Thompson because they were "contrary to the principles of political economy" and Baring because "he fell back on political economy." It was a political economy that, Scrope told the Commons, formed "the vivifying principle of commerce—the stimulus to all improvement—the mainspring of civilization."[34] Copious, of course, were references to the great economists, especially in the endless debates on the corn laws. Even Lord John Russell ceased to call political economy an awful thing. In preparation for the corn law debates, he read Smith, Malthus, Ricardo, McCulloch, and current pamphlets, coming out in 1841 for an eight shilling fixed duty, and in 1846 for total repeal.[35] Although not all Whigs were pleased with the economists' arguments, those that were prevailed, not only in parliamentary debates but on select committees, on royal commissions, and in high bureaucratic appointments. Many of those Whig commissions, so odious to the Tories, were packed with economists and their friends: the most odious of all, the Poor Law Commission of 1833, was headed by Nassau Senior. On it sat John Bird Sumner, bishop of Chester, whose *Records of Creation* married natural theology to political economy; Charles Blomfield, bishop of London; Edwin Chadwick, secretary to Jeremy Bentham; and Walter Coulson, also once an assistant to Bentham and now a member of the Political Economy Club. Some half of its assistant commissioners were also friends of Senior and political economy.[36]

Two of the four commissioners of the Royal Commission on Handloom Weavers were distinguished economists, Nassau Senior and the Reverend Richard Jones, and its message that government could do little more for the weavers than repeal the Corn Law was orthodox political economy at its purest and harshest. The economist Thomas Tooke joined two utilitarians, Edwin Chadwick and Southwood Smith, on the 1833 Factory Commission, which recommended excluding children under nine from factories and limiting those between nine and thirteen to eight hours, but denounced any regulation whatever of adult labor, male or female.[37]

Dominating the Tithe Commission were the Reverend Jones and his fellow economist and Whig William Blamire. Economists also sat on committees inquiring into railways, the merchant marine, charities, child labor in the workshops, Irish land tenure, burial grounds, enclosures, lighthouses, and copyhold tenure. There were few select committees free of the influence of political economists. Professor Frank Fetter has designated as "economists" thirty-two M.P.'s who were active for some or all of the two decades after 1830 and "on average, sat, during their Parliamentary career, on 88 select committees.[38]

In varying degrees, most factory, prison, and mining inspectors and most assistant poor law commissioners (mostly Whig appointees) were believers in political economy, as were school inspectors, to a surprising degree. These inspectors and commissioners flooded the country with powerful reports whose underlying assumptions were consonant with political economy. The bureaucrats also appeared often as witnesses before select committees. And no set of Whitehall bureaucrats was more convinced of the truths of political economy and more forceful as witnesses than those from the Board of Trade. In 1840, the president of the Board of Trade, Poulett Thomson, and four of its members, John Bowring, George Porter, Deacon Hume, and John MacGregor testified before the Committee on Imports of 1840. Their evidence, wrote J. R. McCulloch, "provided an arsenal of facts and arguments" against "the ruinous operations of restriction."[39]

No one welcomed those facts and the end of ruinous restrictions more than those allies of the Whigs who called themselves Liberals, Reformers, or Radicals. Like the utilitarians, who by the 1840s had abandoned dreams of a new party, they helped form part of that large party traditionally led by the Whigs and increasingly known as Liberal. It was a motley group representing various interests, but interests that were nevertheless gaining unity, a unity furthered by a common belief in political economy. It certainly tied Manchester Radicals like John Bright and Richard Cobden to a Whig leadership with whom on education, Church, and the franchise they differed. But they did not differ on the Corn Law, which political economy showed was ruinous—so at least argued the Anti-Corn Law League quite vehemently and with such recourse to economics that Disraeli referred to them as the Manchester school of economics. Although the Manchester school differed with Ricardian orthodoxy in arguing that profits and wages could rise together and would do so upon the repeal of the Corn Law, they did not differ on its larger assumptions or on those four central propositions—non-interference, free trade, a disciplined poor, and low taxes and small government.[40] The Manchester Radicals, men like Cobden, Bright, Mark Phillips, and Milner Gibson, and the great dailies of the north like the *Manchester Guardian* and the *Leeds Mercury* all opposed the ten-hour day, supported the New Poor Law, and championed repeal of all tariffs.[41] They represented a rising, powerful, mercantile class, whose economic interests had long led them to welcome the truths of political economy. In winning over many Radicals and all Liberals, political economy won the allegiance of that class. It only needed to win over some Tories to win the day, a most unexpected event, which occurred in 1846 when two-fifths of the Tories voted to repeal the Corn Law.

POLITICAL ECONOMY DIVIDES THE TORIES

Many of the two-fifths of the Tory Party who voted for repeal shared their leader's enthusiasm for political economy. Peel, who boasted of reading "all the gravest authorities on political economy," also compared their laws to "those governing the planets." He repeatedly cited Adam Smith, whom he compared to Newton and claimed, as far back as 1824, that the principles of free trade were "irrefragable." Peel believed in Adam Smith's arguments for free trade, Ricardo's wage fund, and Malthus's theory of population.[42] So also did his home secretary, Sir James Graham, author in 1824 of the Ricardian *Corn and Currency*, and Peel's young lieutenants, William Gladstone, Sydney Herbert, Edward Cardwell, and Lord Lincoln, all of whom had learned political economy on the job just as twenty years earlier. Tories like Viscount Sandon, John Stuart Wortley, and Lord Francis Egerton heard its truths expounded by William Huskisson. The younger Pitt was a proclaimed disciple of Adam Smith, as were Canning and Liverpool, who, along with Huskisson and Burke, made political economy part of Toryism. It thus surprised few to read in the *Times* in 1844 that Peel's Ministry was "infected with Political Economy."[43]

All of the above Tories, except Burke, attended Oxford University, renown as the home of archaic learning and lost causes. So thought the *Edinburgh Review* when it claimed in 1810 that political economy was unknown at Oxford. Edward Copleston of Oriel College replied that it was not unknown there, that it was much discussed by the professor of modern history, and that its "best works" were "in the hands of many students." Copleston promoted political economy by making his brilliant student, Richard Whately, a fellow of Oriel. Whately in turn helped make his brilliant student, Nassau Senior, Oxford's first professor of political economy in 1825 and then, in 1829, assumed that professorship himself. Cambridge, always more progressive than Oxford, had already appointed George Pryme its first professor of political economy in 1816.[44]

In 1831, Whately became archbishop of Dublin and published his *Lectures on Political Economy*. His successor at Oxford as professor of political economy was Herman Merivale, also a pupil of Copelston and a writer on political economy.[45] No young Peelite could have attended Oxford without realizing that the truths of Smith, Ricardo, and Malthus deserved nearly the same respect as that which Oxford had long accorded Aristotle.

The Peelites' conversion to repeal liberated their deeper economic convictions. After 1846, they spoke out far more freely and boldly for political economy and laissez-faire. It was a conviction that led William Gladstone, Sydney Herbert, Beresford Hope, and Lord Lincoln to purchase the *Morning Chronicle*, the once proud organ of the Philosophical Radicals.[46]

Since Gladstone, Hope, Herbert, and Lincoln were also paternalists, the cause of political economy seemed to face a significant loss. But political economy proved its toughness, respectability, and ability to fuse with other outlooks. After 1847, the *Morning Chronicle* opposed the ten-hour day and gave no support whatever to those urging legislative protection for exploited hosiery workers, London bakers, or Spitalfield weavers. The Peelite *Chronicle* also pronounced Malthus right "in the main," urged protectionists to read Adam Smith, invoked the authority of Ricardo, and praised John Stuart Mill's *Political Economy*.[47]

The editor of the *Morning Chronicle*, E. Douglas Cook, like his predecessor John Black of the radical *Morning Chronicle*, came from Scotland, home of Adam Smith and later of many of his followers who brought his teachings south of the border.

SCOTTISH AND OTHER MISSIONARIES

The Scotsmen who came South did not edit insignificant journals. Robert Rintoul edited the *Spectator*, James Wilson the *Economist*, Macvey Napier the *Edinburgh Review*, and John Lockhart the *Quarterly Review*. Also from north of the border came the editors of the *Morning Post*, the *Literary Gazette*, the *Mechanics Magazine*, the *Era*, the *British Banner*, the *Christian Witness*, the *Christian Examiner*, and, in the provinces, the *Leeds Times, Manchester Guardian, Newcastle Guardian*, and *Bradford Observer*.[48]

Scotland's parish schools, democratic universities, and intellectual Calvinism produced what England's two universities, crazy quilt of schools ranging from elegant Eton to wretched dame establishments, and latitudinarian Anglicanism could not, a literate, educated, ambitious class of journalists—journalists also learned in political economy. "The young" wrote the Scottish advocate Henry Cockburn, "were immersed . . . in political economy" and "lived upon Adam Smith." At Edinburgh University, Dugald Stewart lectured on political economy from 1800 to 1810. So great was his fame in 1807 that Oxford's Grillon Club traveled north to hear him. "Even his idle hearers," wrote Cockburn of his lectures on political economy, "retained a permanent taste for it."[49] Throughout the land of Adam Smith, political economy was king: at Dumferline, more than a thousand mechanics attended lectures on its truths; and in Edinburgh, noblemen, gentlemen, and merchants paid £10 to attend J. R. McCulloch's lectures, and in countless sermons Scotsmen and Scotswomen heard its truths proclaimed as nearly divine by Scotland's most eloquent minister, the Reverend Thomas Chalmers. McCulloch, Chalmers, Black, Mill Sr., Rintoul, and scores of journalists and pamphleteers came south, as did endless issues of the *Edinburgh Review, North British Review,* and *Chamber's Edinburgh Journal.* They brought the light of the new economic science to the uninitiated in England.[50] None of the journals reached more readers than *Chamber's Edinburgh Journal.* Its circulation was 60,000, and it was read by many more. It was, said the Owenite George Holyoake, "the favourite publication of the young person." There were, of course, English journalists quite as zealous to purvey economic truths to the populace. Charles Knight's *Penny Magazine* and the numerous tracts of the Society for the Diffusion of Useful Knowledge enjoyed, although not for as long, as much success as did *Chamber's.* Of one of its tracts, *The Results of Machinery* (1831), a Whig minister, Thomas Spring Rice, boldly asserted that it did "more good for the repression of outrage than a regiment of horse."[51]

Overly sanguine Spring Rice no doubt was, but overly sanguine too was the zeal of many to educate the workers in the salutary truths of political economy. Everywhere there were lectures on it—at mechanics institutes, athenaeums, literary societies, debating clubs, town halls, statistical societies, music halls, factories, chapels, coffee houses, schools, and colleges—even in the fields of Suffolk, where Squire Strutt said that he "harangued [his laborers] on capital and labor." "Almost sealed books a few years ago," declared the *North of England Magazine* in 1843, the axioms of political economy had "become the watchwords of popular assemblies of every class." It even penetrated the agricultural districts through the press. R. N. Bacon spend twenty-eight years as editor of the *Norwich Mercury* seeking to educate his readers in political economy, while Bacon's fellow provincial editors John Gibbs and Thomas Latimer brought its message weekly to readers in Buckinghamshire and Devonshire—Latimer so forcefully that he believed that "the people have mastered the laws of political economy."[52] Latimer's extravagant claim was no doubt an exaggeration. As extensive as were the conquests of political economy there were still powerful forces that were either ambivalent or hostile to the new science.

One powerful force was the literary world of London and its satellite cir-
cles in the provincial cities. Unable to earn a livelihood from their poems and
novels, these aspiring authors staffed a burgeoning press of no little influence
on public opinion. Bohemian in their tastes and lovers of the poetic and humane, of Wordsworth and Byron, they were not entranced with political
economy's grim reasoning and cold maxims. They delighted in Dickens's
satire of its harsh, unfeeling inhumanity in his portrait of Gradgrind in *Hard
Times,* just as they applauded when *Punch* called political economy the greatest of "humbug," the very opposite of the golden rule, and a science that justified noble lords in doing nothing while the Irish starved.[53] Douglas Jerrold
had no higher an estimate, condemning it as "the idolatry of mammon." Yet
Jerrold could not reject it out of hand. In a later issue of the *Douglas Jerrold
Magazine,* in a favorable review of McCulloch's *Political Economy,* he confessed it was very necessary for legislation. Douglas Jerrold was the most
popular and lovable of London Bohemian journalists, a man whose wit and
compassion for the poor won him a place on Dickens's *Daily News.* But he
couldn't handle complex economic and political questions and was dismissed
as "utterly inefficient in his attempts at leaders."[54]

Many London Bohemians, being equally ineffective on economic issues,
had to fall back, as Jerrold did, on the political economy that was winning
such widespread acceptance. John Forster found no viable answers to perplexing economic questions in his historical studies, and neither did Thomas
Hodgskin in Godwinian anarchism. All three of the chief editorial writers of
Dickens's *Daily News* turned to the same political economy that they had
learned either at the *Morning Chronicle* and *Examiner* or in earlier readings of
the sovereign masters.

Dickens, in choosing these editorial writers, must have known that he was
bringing political economy to the *Daily News.* Since he claimed to have read
and approved every leader, he must also have known that his newspaper
compared "the axioms of political economy with those of Newton's in his
Principia."[55]

Also powerful in the London press were the writers for influential religious
journals. If political economy was so hard-hearted, should it not be the task
of the disciples of a loving Christ to promote a different and more caring social philosophy? The devout of those journals felt it did, but only by a social
philosophy that did not contradict political economy.

The Church of England's three principal journals, the *Christian Remembrancer,* the *Christian Observer,* and the *Guardian* found the new science quite

compatible with Christianity. Political economy, wrote the *Remembrancer*, formed "the link between the physical and moral sciences." Every student of the ministry, urged the *Christian Observer*, "should read Adam Smith, [Mrs.] Marcet and the Mills." And socialism is wrong, concluded the *Guardian*, because it is in "defiance of . . . political economy."[56]

Nonconformists, with their deeply rooted individualism were even more enthusiastic. "Economic truth is no less divine," wrote the Congregationalists' *British Quarterly*, than astronomical truth, a view their brethren at the *Eclectic* shared in pronouncing political economy a "strictly natural science." The Unitarians' *Christian Teacher* pronounced the same principles "absolutely first rate," a conviction that the Baptist divine Edward Miall held so fervently that, in 1843, he founded the *Nonconformist*, a journal surpassed by none in devotion to the new science. At the Baptists' Wymondley Theological Institute, Miall and his fellow students "read Dugald Stewart and Adam Smith with close attention."[57]

How curious that Anglicans and Nonconformists should praise so highly doctrines based on an avowed selfishness and praise a system often productive of huge inequalities and widespread exploitation. For Christian socialists like Charles Kingsley, the new economics seemed, at first glance, intolerable. In 1850, in the *Christian Socialist*, he called political economy "absurd and imbecile humbug." But by the end of the very same article, Kingsley recommended that all should read "Bentham, Ricardo, and Mill," and should "pay attention to its known and proved laws." The *Christian Socialist*'s mélange of paternalist attitudes, philanthropic pleas, and cooperative schemes offered an alternative to political economy that was no more effective than that proposed by the humanitarians of the London literary world.[58]

The Tory paternalists, the most hostile of all to political economy, also lacked a viable alternative. "We must too," lamented Lord Ashley in the *Quarterly Review* as late as 1847, "have a political economy on our side."[59] Noble as was the trust of the paternalists' belief in property, Church, and locality, it was a trust that increasingly fell short both of meeting the many problems of urban and industrial England and of offering a full and clear explanation of the forces governing the economy. The disquisitions on social duties in R. B. Seely's, John Sandford's, and Arthur Helps's manuals contain little economic theory, a vacuum that the theoretically thin works of E. S. Cayley, Michael Sadler, and both Mathias and Thomas Attwood could not fill. They could in no way rival Adam Smith or David Ricardo, or even Robert Torrens, J. R. McCulloch, and Nassau Senior. In 1848, the paternalists virtually surrendered to John Stuart Mill's universally praised *Principles of Political Economy*. The French revolution of that same year unleashed a flood of attacks on socialism, attacks that also reflected a fear of an increasingly militant working class that demanded the Charter and economic justice. Political economy seemed a bulwark defending a property long considered inviolate. It is thus not surprising that two of the paternalists' great dailies, the *Times* and, after 1847, the *Morning Chronicle* embraced, its truths. Thomas Barnes, fierce enemy of political economy and editor of the *Times* in the 1830s, left it in 1841. Its owner, John Walter III, venomous in his hatred of the "economists'" New Poor Law, yielded control in the 1840s to the new editor, John T. Delane, and his Oxford friends. By 1853, the *Times* was denouncing as socialist the ten-hour day that it had once supported.[60] The *Morning Chronicle* meanwhile was proclaiming Malthus right, praising John Stuart Mill, and embracing laissez-faire and free trade.

In the great collision of contending social outlooks that worried Disraeli, political economy was gaining the ascendancy. Professor Longfield was telling his students at Trinity College, Dublin, that political economy was "everyday extending its empire," while Professor George Pryme was telling Cambridge students that "its principles are not only admitted by nearly every statesman . . . but have been carried out by repeated acts of legislation."[61] And in 1846, in the House of Commons, its arch enemy, the Tory Stafford O'Brien, exclaimed with exasperation that everyone was now "too apt to confound political economy with the science of legislation."[62] In the intellectual competition between the two great contending social philosophies, political economy had, by 1850, taken over first place. It was a victory that raises another question, what impact did that intellectual victory have on the social legislation of early Victorian England?

CHAPTER 5

The Impact of Political Economy

Ideas that enjoy great success do not necessarily have an equally great impact on legislation. Ideas often become popular because they meet the intellectual and psychological needs of a perplexed public, because they explain a bewildering world and justify dominant attitudes that other, more powerful forces, determine. That they satisfy and justify, of course, also helps determine the course of events. It is a complicated process, as is evident when one examines the impact of political economy on the three greatest legislative battles of the 1830s and 1840s, those over the corn, factory, and poor laws.

THE REPEAL OF THE CORN LAW

When the exasperated Stafford O'Brien charged, in 1846, that M.P.'s confused political economy with the science of legislation, he was, although not unmindful of the harsh Poor Law, most angry at the repeal of the Corn Law. It was the greatest event of the 1840s in Britain. No issue was argued more vehemently, more lengthily, and more bitterly, and no other issue so dominated parliamentary debates and the editorials of the press. And although the demands of the workers for the Charter produced many pamphlets, petitions, lectures, and huge demonstrations, they fell very short of the Anti–Corn Law League's press coverage, parliamentary oratory, and pamphlets, not to mention free trade lectures, bazaars, tea parties, fund raisers, voter registration, and a triumphant outcome.

Repeal was no mere economic issue, but one with powerful social, political and moral ramifications. At first, to be sure, it was presented to Parliament by a handful of Philosophical Radicals in economic terms. William Molesworth's 1837 denunciation of the Corn Law, a dry exercise in Ricardianism, fell flat before a perplexed Commons. The denunciation of that law by Charles Villiers in 1838 was livelier and plainer in argument. It broadened the attack by pointing to the "monstrous and palpable injustice" of taxing the bread of the poor to add to the fortunes of wealthy landlords. Yet still, at the heart of his attack, lay two cardinal doctrines of political economy: first, that only the freest application of each nation's capital and labor to that which it can most efficiently produce would promote the greatest prosperity, and, second, the more general claim that all restrictions distort those harmonious economic laws that so beautifully convert private gain to the public good.[1]

Villiers and Molesworth were of the landed class: Villiers was the brother of the earl of Clarendon, and Molesworth was from an old, wealthy landed Cornish family. They had few connections with manufacturers. Neither did their fellow Philosophical Radicals, John Arthur Roebuck, George Grote, Joseph Hume, Henry Warburton, and John Leader, M.P.'s who spoke often in the Commons in the distant hope of educating its 658 members of the truth of free trade economics. They were great admirers of Jeremy Bentham and the Mills, and their minds were steeped in political economy. Villiers had studied under Malthus and McCulloch. They also wrote about economics; many, like Molesworth, Roebuck, and Grote, contributed to the utilitarian *Westminster Review*. The owner of the *Review*, Perronet Thompson, was the author of the *Catechism on the Corn Laws* of 1826, one of the first salvos of the anti–Corn Law movement.[2] But this and other salvos were no more than damp squibs. The attempt of disinterested intellectuals to employ political economy to persuade a landed Parliament to repeal the Corn Law proved a failure. Ideas seldom seemed so impotent.

What the Philosophical Radicals lacked was a powerful constituency that would give political clout to their economic logic. Just such clout emerged in 1838 when the men of Manchester established the Anti–Corn Law League. At the heart of that League lay the wealth and power of the manufacturing north, although it soon broadened the movement to include the growing middle classes throughout Britain, classes full of resentment at the lordly privileges of the aristocracy.

The Anti–Corn Law League readily accepted the two cardinal doctrines of the Philosophical Radicals, that free trade by maximizing the efficiency of each nation maximized the wealth of all, and that, at home, untrammeled market forces best regulated distribution and best stimulated production. To these basic premises, the League added three specific economic claims, that the cheaper corn resulting from the repeal of the Corn Law would not lower wages, that repeal would substantially lower the price of bread, and that repeal would end distress.

That free trade in corn would not lower wages was a most un-Ricardian claim. Although most political economists would accept the argument of Richard Cobden and John Bright that by opening up and stimulating the economy, free trade would push up wages, they still felt that, with labor abundant, employers would lower wages if food prices fell. Was not this the wisdom of Ricardo and McCulloch and Senior? Most certainly. But then were Cobden and Bright that much inspired by the logic of political economy? Or even by the fragmentary data that wages did not always fall when food prices did? How could they, deeply anxious as they were to wean the working classes from Chartism to free trade, tell them about the Ricardian dictum that cheaper corn meant lower wages? Politics more than economic logic lay behind the first of their three claims.[3]

Politics and morality may well have also informed their second claim, that the Corn Law kept bread prices exorbitantly high. That in theory a Corn Law protected the price of corn from cheaper imports few contested. It was more debatable that the Corn Law, given the not inconsiderable costs of transportation and insurance and given that bad harvest often drove up European prices, prices that in most years remained high because of other costs. In 1838, Villiers claimed that the Corn Law made grain 24 percent more expensive and in 1848 Thomas Tooke estimated that if the Corn Law had not been repealed, grain would have been 41 percent more costly.[4] The Whig McCulloch and the Radical J. S. Mill had doubts about these claims, since both doubted whether, on the whole, the law had a significant effect,[5] doubts supported by D. C. Moore in the *Economic History Review* of 1965, but seriously questioned by Susan Fairlie in that journal in 1969. Fairlie insists that in years of bad English harvests, it did make a difference. Not mentioned by her, but sustaining her argument, is James Deacon Hume's estimate of 1840 that the Corn Law made bread 16 percent more expensive, and the fact that in the Channel Islands of Guernsey and Jersey, where there was no Corn Law, corn in the 1830s was nearly 20 percent cheaper.[6]

That grain was more expensive because of the Corn Law was not a negligible fact when, according to one estimate, flour made up 48 percent of a laborer's food bill and his food bill constituted 73 percent of his weekly budget.[7] Talk of a bread tax was not idle chatter. And although its exact economic impact was and is controversial, its moral dimensions, for many, were clear and compelling. Was it not a palpable injustice that the poor should pay extra pennies for bread so that dukes and earls could have extra pounds for balls and fetes? For some, these inequalities seemed to flout the injunction of the Lord's Prayer itself, "Give us this day our daily bread." The biblical morality of the evangelicals was one of the Anti–Corn Law League's most formidable weapons. It was the central theme of the great conference of 700 ministers, mostly Nonconformists, that met in 1841 in Manchester, and of scores of editorials in the Nonconformist press. Sir Valentine Blake even told the worldly House of Commons: "He who keepeth people from corn, him shall the people curse." The bishop of Oxford, Samuel Wilberforce, a late convert to repeal, also condemned the Corn Law. It violated "the providential laws," he said; "Would God ever allow the poor to buy food on the cheapest market?"[8] Taxing the poor's bread was as much an affront to the Enlightenment's sense of natural justice as to the evangelicals' biblical morality. The Whig Lord Howicke said that the Corn Law violated "the wise provisions of a merciful Providence." John Bright, after first citing the "laws of nature," quoted the Koran to the effect that "one hour of justice is worth seventy days of prayer."[9] In the innumerable editorials and speeches denouncing the Corn Law, the humanitarian outcry against taxing the bread of the poor was voiced far more than any theory from political economy. Without this righteous indignation against injustice, the second economic claim, the debatable one, that the Corn Law significantly raised the price of bread, would have fared badly.

The Manchester School's third economic claim, that the Corn Law caused the distress of the early 1840s rested on far shakier economic grounds than did the claim that the Corn Law significantly raised the price of bread. In 1954, R. C. O. Matthews, in *A Study in Trade Cycle History*, argued quite convincingly that the cause of the depression of 1841–42 lay, not with the Corn Law, but with a drastic fall in the once "excessive investment in railways, mines, shipping and textiles," a fall aggravated by bad harvests and a slump in the American economy. The economy collapsed, in part, from its own excesses.[10] Neither did most economists at the time argue that the Corn Law caused that depression. In theory, most economists agreed that a free trade in corn would allow French, Prussian, Polish, and other nations growing wheat to earn English pounds, which pounds they and their countrymen would spend on textiles and ironware lying unsold in English warehouses, all of which would stimulate the English economy. But in actuality few economists believed that the Corn Law had sufficient impact to have caused the serious depression of 1841–42. Indeed, most political economists, Malthus excepted, felt that there could be no extended depression and no extended overproduction and gluts. Economists critical of the Corn Law nevertheless did admit that it deepened the depression. Frustrated with the depth and length of a depression that should not have happened in a burgeoning capitalism, they, like the capitalists themselves and the politicians, needed an explanation.

Blaming distress on the hated Corn Law also satisfied their deep hostility toward those landed classes whose other monopolies in Church and state, Army and Navy, and public schools and universities had long angered them. It was a hostility that the landed classes and their press reciprocated. The distress of the working classes, said the Tory *Standard,* resulted from their sub-jection to machinery, from excessive competition, and from "the money power." Mill owners and capitalists, added the *Standard*, were rogues, knaves, and vultures, full of fraud, greed, and tyranny, and were entirely unlike land-owners.[11] *John Bull,* the *Morning Post,* and the *Morning Herald* agreed. For these Tory journals, distress was due both to the "rottenness" of a system based on millocrats and machinery and to the frauds and cheats "of grasping greedy manufacturers" whose "hearts are hardened," who made "bond slaves of the people."[12] While the *Herald* would have no regrets if "the whole enor-mous pile were levelled," the *Standard* concluded that England would be "as powerful and happy if the whole of the manufacturing towns were engulfed in ruin."[13]

The anti–Corn Law press was just as abusive. "The landed classes," de-clared the *Daily News,* then under Dickens, "have robbed their neighbours, ruined their tenants, starved their labourers, and trebled their rents." "Landlords," wrote the *Weekly Chronicle,* are still "feudal lords who treat their feudal villeins like animals." The great landed monopoly, wrote the *Morning Chronicle,* "can plunder openly on a large scale," since it "seizes greedily and keeps tenaciously what it can," a harsh indictment that the *Morning Advertiser* equaled in condemning the landed classes' "frightful mendacity" and "ma-rauding cupidity." While the *Globe* found landlords full of selfishness and iniquity, the *Sheffield Independent* found them "revelling in unwonted pomp and luxury [amid] a starving and miserable people."[14]

A deep and pervasive hostility between the landed and manufacturing classes also marked the debates in the House of Commons. In 1842, William Busby Ferrand, an intemperate Yorkshire squire, condemned the manufac-turing class as "gambling speculators" with an "insatiable thirst for wealth," a class whose skill in "artful villainy and swindling" had led to "tyranny, op-pression and plunder, committed on half starved operatives." And one of that class, Richard Cobden, ran his mills night and day.[15]

Although Cobden replied in a restrained and temperate manner, his de-piction of landlords as too stupid to make agricultural improvements was just as galling and just as full of class jealousy. It was a lecture full of advice on the use of manure and drainage, a speech that insisted that repeal would benefit England's farmers. It was a speech Sir Robert Peel said he could not answer, which is curious, since hardly one political economist agreed with Cobden that the abolition of a law that kept corn prices high would benefit farmers.[16] There was in fact little political economy in Cobden's lecture on manure and drainage. But then was the reasoning of political economists of much rele-vance to an Anti–Corn Law League that represented the power and wealth of a rising middle class that viewed the Corn Law largely as yet another privilege of a lordly, arrogant aristocracy that gloried in their exclusive privileges. Monopoly was the only right word for these exclusive privileges. There were the Church monopoly, the university monopoly, the Army monopoly, and the great political monopolies—the House of Lords, the county magistracy, the pocket boroughs, and the law. The Corn Law was not so much an economic error as a prime symbol of the dominance of the aristocracy.

Aggravating and complicating this deep and pervasive class jealousy was a widespread distress that resulted from the breakdown of capitalism. That from a quarter to a third of the textile workers in Paisley, Stockport, Bury, Oldham, and other mill towns were unemployed was profoundly disturbing to a mercantile class who believed that laissez-faire capitalism had no contradictions and no crises.[17] But there it was in shambles. An explanation was needed, and none was more readily available and persuasive than that it resulted from the Corn Law, the last great remnant of that protectionism and mercantilism whose evils the great Adam Smith had described. Evils of all sorts were ascribed to this unjust law. Why was the Poor Law's workhouse test so cruel? Why were wages too low and factory hours too long? Because of the Corn Law, answered the *Weekly Chronicle*. Why did Leeds have 20,000 paupers, why were its factory workers overworked, and why were its poor "half-naked" and living on "empty stomachs and in filthy habitations?" Because of the Corn Law, answered the *Weekly Dispatch*.[18] Why did lace makers employ three-year-olds? Because of the Corn Law, wrote the *Globe*, adding that "the spirit of monopoly has brought us to the verge of ruin," a judgment that the *Morning Chronicle* echoed in declaring "the Corn Monopoly the centre of the pestilence of pauperism."[19] And just as their frustrations over a widespread and inexplicable distress led them to blame all kinds of evils on the Corn Law, so their sanguine hopes of a brighter world led them to see in the end of that monopoly every possible good. Total free trade would bring high wages, well-fed, well-clothed, and well-housed workers, class harmony, social stability, political tranquility, the advance of reason, concord among nations, the new Jerusalem. The anti–Corn Law cause, proclaimed the *Leeds Mercury*, was "the dictate of Divine Providence itself. It is founded on perfect justice."[20]

There was not much political economy in the speeches of John Bright and Richard Cobden, nor in those of W. J. Fox, the greatest of the League's orators, nor in the League's many publications. There was instead a welter of ideas and attitudes, ranging from humanitarian pleas to pious quotations from the Bible, from the homespun poetry of Ebenezer Eliot, the Corn Law Rhymer, to the anti-Church voluntarism of Edward Miall's *NonConformist*, from Cobden's pacifist dream of international concord to the self-help morality of Samuel Smiles's *Leeds Times*. All these ideas and attitudes and much more filled the minds of the hundreds who spoke and wrote endlessly against the monstrous law, which offered both a reason for England's economic distress and the clearest evidence of the selfish and arrogant dominance of the landed classes. The cogency of the economic reasoning of the Manchester School has often been exaggerated. They were seldom original and perceptive, seldom systematic and comprehensive. They even weakened their best economic argument, that the Corn Law increased the price of bread, by vastly exaggerating the extent of that increase and by invariably accompanying it with the quite dubious claim that the Corn Law caused distress. They hardly ever quoted economists or employed economic theories. Economic logic also bowed to political rhetoric when Cobden weakened the central argument that repeal would make bread cheaper by arguing that repeal would not hurt farmers, whose returns depended on a high price for wheat. In all these arguments, the theories of the political economist played but a modest role.

Did political economy, then, have any impact at all on the repeal of the Corn Law? The answer is, yes; but, paradoxically, its effect was not so much on the minds of the law's long-standing critics as on those of those supporters who converted to repeal in 1846. Political economy had a decided impact on Sir Robert Peel and many of the 113 Peelites who abandoned their defense of the Corn Law in January 1846. Peel's conversion was surprising, perplexing, and crucial. The explanations of three contemporary observers are instructive. For the duke of Wellington, Peel's "alarm" at the potato blight and fear of its consequences was the reason; for John Wilson Croker, it was Peel's "original disposition to abstract free trade"; and Disraeli attributed it to a sharp turn against the Conservatives in the Lancashire and Yorkshire polls.[21]

Peel himself admitted fright at the potato blight. But might not that have been, in part, a rationalization? Not only had there been worse wheat harvests in the past and no thought of repeal, but free trade in wheat would do nothing for the potato-eating Irish, who were far too poor to buy any wheat at all. Furthermore, Peel could have temporarily suspended the Corn Law until the potato harvest was healthy. Croker was right: the reasons lay deep in "abstract thought," the abstract thought of political economy. Peel had long been a disciple of the new science. He had read it at Oxford, and in 1819, as chairman of the Committee on Currency, he immersed himself fully in its most arcane doctrines. In 1824, he called free trade an "irrefragable principle," and in 1834, he said that the Corn Law "diminished the sum of national wealth." He considered economic laws as certain as those "which determine the planets." And in his plea to end the Corn Law, he paid "homage . . . to the progress of reason and to truth."[22]

But what of the other 113 Tories who voted for repeal? Why did they convert? It could not have been their economic or class interests, since William Aydelotte of the University of Iowa has shown that these 113 were just as landed and aristocratic and just as involved with stocks and bonds and trade as the Protectionist Tories.[23] Their speeches, however, do give some clues. "Every eminent writer in the science of political economy," said Edward Cardwell, "was opposed on principle to protection"; "that first of all authorities, Adam Smith," announced Sir James Graham, "favored free trade in Corn"; "free trade," proclaimed Sydney Herbert, is "absolutely true"; "the leading doctrines of political economy," concluded Henry Barkly," were as true as the propositions of Euclid."[24] Such were the economic convictions of four Peelites, convictions also voiced by 19 other free trade Tories who made up the 23 Peelites who spoke often in debate. These 23 were, on the average, ten years younger than the 25 Tory M.P.'s who spoke most often for protectionism. Many, like Thomas Acland Jr., Lord Lincoln, Gladstone, Herbert, and Cardwell, went to Oxford when Richard Whately and Nassau Senior were exciting all with the inexorable truths of political economy. In Peel's government, older ministers—like Peel, Graham, and Lord Francis Egerton—who themselves had learned economics from David Ricardo and William Huskisson—passed its principles on to assistants at the Treasury and Board of Trade and to the members of the select committees on banking, finance, and railways.[25] The speeches of these Peelites, after repeal, are full of a vigor and enthusiasm for free trade that reflects a liberation of their real selves. Sir James Graham, author in 1824 of a free trade pamphlet, could now freely express his deepest economic convictions. Peelites could now employ the elegant and empirical arguments of Adam Smith, the iron logic of Ricardo, and the eloquently argued free trade doctrines in Edmund Burke's *Thoughts and Details on Scarcity*.[26] Political economists did differ on various questions, and some, like Ricardo and McCulloch, were for a moderate fixed duty on foreign corn as a compensation for tithes and taxes on land. Adam Smith, for reasons of national defense, even supported a navigation act.[27] But these were marginal compromises, made for political reasons, and were in no way used to deny the central truth that free trade would bring much greater prosperity than did a restrictive protectionism. The Protectionists were certainly aware of this fact. "The Government," complained Stafford O'Brien in 1846, "places political economy as its sole consideration." "Free traders," said John Colquhoun, "are the rigid disciples of political economy." Saddened by these developments, Disraeli proposed "a limbo for political economists and their sophistries." Disraeli would not have disagreed with the free trader Earl Grey that "the principles of this bill began 80 years ago with Adam Smith."[28]

The shrewd Disraeli also believed that Peel's conversion was furthered by the Conservative Party's decline in Yorkshire and Lancashire polls. Powerful economic and social forces as well as powerful ideas were at work in early Victorian England. The Anti–Corn Law League had mounted a furious drive in larger boroughs and more urbanized counties both to register voters and to create new voters by encouraging them to purchase 40-shilling freeholds.

Peel certainly knew that, given those voters, the Conservatives, in a time of blighted potatoes, costly wheat, and a massive agitation by the League and the Whig-Liberals, would be defeated. In Peel's mind, as in the minds of the 113 Peelites, these realities mingled with the free trade theories of the political economists. Although it is difficult to say which proved the most powerful, it is also difficult to dismiss the economists' theories as negligible. For all of England's commercial and manufacturing growth, members of Parliament were still predominantly from the landed class. And although some of the 113 Peelites did represent urban constituencies and reflected their interests, many did not. Indeed, some lost their seats by their vote for repeal. For these crucial Peelites and for crucial Whigs with landed estates and landed constituencies, it was not all economic interest, it was also the power of ideas, the power of economic theory, a fact also evident in their laissez-faire indifference to the exploitation of the working classes.

CONDITIONS OF WORK

Political economy, proclaimed its champions, was a great benefactor of mankind. Had it not freed Britain's economic energies, lowered prices, multiplied exports, and brought forth the justice of the free market? From the 1820s and the removal of the duties on manufactures to the 1840s and the repeal of the Corn Law, political economy, by checking selfish monopolies and removing barriers, had advanced the public good. That England, after 1842, entered three decades of unparalleled prosperity fulfilled every expectation of these free traders. They were proud, confident, and boastful and not surprised that their vision of a laissez-faire England was becoming ever more popular. Political economy not only freed men from the shackles of restrictive government but brought greater prosperity and cheaper bread. Could anyone doubt that the laws of political economy were synonymous with the laws of progress? After 1850, indeed, fewer and fewer did.

But some did. There were still those who agreed with Thomas Carlyle and

John Ruskin that political economy was cold, heartless and selfish. True, it removed government shackles on trade, but only to permit industry to impose heavier shackles on the workers.

Political economy was a powerful ideological force, both for good and evil. It was Janus-like, both benign and severe in countenance; and its various roles were as changeable as those of Dr. Jekyll and Mr. Hyde.

Twentieth-century historians, like the Victorians, have differed about political economy's cruel Hyde-like role far more than about its benign Dr. Jekyll aspect. That the laissez-faire policies of the economists made Britain's economy wealthier few doubted, but whether it did so without the cruel exploitation of the working classes is a much debated question.

There is also a debate whether the actual policies of the economists were as laissez-faire as its critics charge. Professors Lionel Robbins, Warren Samuels, and P. S. Atiyah have questioned not only how complete the laissez-faire outlook of the political economists was but how extensive were the actual laissez-faire conditions of the early Victorian economy.[29] Their claims have much substance. J. R. McCulloch wrote that although "laissez faire may be safely trusted on some things . . . on many more it is wholly inapplicable," and Nassau Senior insisted that the government should intervene wherever it was conducive to the welfare of the governed.[30] Adam Smith urged the government to promote education, manage costly public works like harbors, and, for Britain's defense, preserve the Navigation Act. It was an interventionism that was to flower in J. S. Mill's chapters "On Government" in successive editions of his *Political Economy.*[31]

The idea of laissez-faire, although central to political economy, never fully engulfed it.

Laissez-faire also failed, even after the repeal of the Corn Law and Navigation Act, to engulf the British economy. In 1843, observed McCulloch, more than 2,000 laws regulated British commerce and finance.[32] And although many of these laws were subsequently repealed, many more, such as countless railway acts and voluminous merchant marine acts, joined the many enclosure, copyhold, canal, and local improvement acts to pack the statute books with ever more government. And there were also banking, joint stock company, friendly society, medical, and food adulteration acts. Parliament even regulated London cabs. There was never a purely laissez-faire economy, and neither did the political economists have a purely laissez-faire outlook.

The key words, of course, are "entirely" and "purely." If one reads the statute books and the passages of the economists that Robbins, Samuels, and Atiyah select, government intervention looms large, but if one also reads the great parliamentary inquiries of the 1830s and 1840s on children's and women's labor in manufacturing and agriculture, and on the Law of Settlement, the health of towns, handloom weavers, game laws, landlord-tenant relations, Irish famines, and working-class housing, the laissez-faire aspect of Victorian thought and society looms very large. It is an aspect that journalists and statisticians also investigated, journalists like Henry Mayhew and Charles MacKay whose reports for the *Morning Chronicle* in 1849 and 1850 revealed a large world of suffering and exploitation that was almost completely neglected by government.

But it was not neglected by the assiduous investigators of Britain's new statistical societies. In article after article, the *Journal of the Royal Statistical Society* showed in painstaking detail that in housing, schooling, sanitation, working conditions, and medical care, English society was a laissez-faire, not a protective, society.[33] The Factory Acts of 1833 and 1847 did not touch that harsh laissez-faire world endured by the more than nine out of ten workers who were not employed in textiles. No laws limited their hours or demanded whitewashed walls, fenced in machinery, and schooling. There was instead an unchecked profusion of child labor, long hours, fatalities, broken limbs, fetid, overcrowded rooms, misery, and oppression. In a room seven feet by seven feet in Hemel Hempstead, eighteen girls, aged from four to fourteen, plaited straw for from twelve to fourteen hours a day, earning three to four shillings a week for work that the investigators called "painfully distressing." In Glasgow, boys aged from seven to twelve wound tobacco from 6 A.M. to 7 or 8 P.M. in workshops "saturated with black clammy juices," earning 1s. 2d. a week when young and 2s. 8d. when older. The inspector also reported "nakedness, hunger, shortness of stature, filth, scrofulous tumors" and the use of the strap. At ironworks in Wolverhampton, seven-, eight-, and nine-year-olds worked from twelve to thirteen hours for one to two shillings in "wretched workshops." In London, eleven-, twelve-, and thirteen-year-old dressmakers toiled until 10, 11, and 12 at night—once working twenty hours a day for three successive months. The inspector found all of them pale and sickly.[34]

In Staffordshire potteries, eight- to seventeen-year-olds worked twelve-hour days, and longer if there was a rush order. The drawers, who dipped, scoured, and threw the pots were "dull and cadaverous," the lead and arsenic of the glazing fluid reportedly producing asthma, consumption, and death.[35]

Not all trades were as cruel and oppressive. Some type foundries employed no one under nineteen, kept the shop clean, and paid adequately. Such enlightened workshops were not, however, the rule. Almost all manufacturers employed children at pitiful wages and worked them twelve hours a day or more in filthy, ill-ventilated, overcrowded workshops, where accidents and disease were well known.[36]

The story of the agricultural laborers and of their long hours, widespread use of children, and lowest of low wages makes it clear that more that nineteen out of twenty suffered from an economy that was purely laissez-faire.[37] Nearly as unregulated were areas of the economy and society revealed by other royal commissions and select committees, journalists and statistical societies, such as housing, transport, education, medicine, burials, sanitation, where, despite some statutes and codes and an inspector or two, railway magnates, tenement owners, builders, schoolmasters, and physicians and surgeons were free to do what they wished—as were the clergy who ran the burial grounds. In these areas, as with regard to working conditions, textiles excepted, laissez-faire did reign supreme and did permit a harsh exploitation of the working classes.[38]

The laissez-faire conditions of the early Victorian economy had roots far older and deeper than the tenets of political economy. Child labor and long hours had for centuries been the fate of the working classes. But although political economy certainly did not cause these evils, it likewise did little to remove them. With few exceptions, it vigorously denied that government had any role in the removal of such suffering.

It was not the subtle and elaborate axioms of political economy that opposed such intervention, but its simplest and most basic assumptions, the laissez-faire assumptions made popular in press and pamphlet and parliamentary speeches. Although economists differed about theories of value, population, wages, and rent, they did not differ that the laws of supply and demand—the invisible hand—translated private gain into public good, that "capital" was the great engine of prosperity, and that the individual was far wiser than government. A nearly religious belief in these axioms helps to explain why Parliament in the 1840s rejected the pleas of silk weavers, hosiery workers, lace makers, London bakers, and handloom weavers for some protection. It also helps explain why Parliament rejected out of hand legislation requiring that allotments be given to farm laborers, that tenants receive compensation for improvements, and that food be sold cheaply to the starving Irish. Each of these groups had stout advocates. The Tory Henry Halford was unflagging in defense of hosiery workers; the radical Thomas Duncombe energetically pleaded the lace makers' cause; Thomas Greene argued for both silk and handloom weavers; the Whig Lord Grosvenor was tireless for bakers; the evangelical William Cowper asked repeatedly for allotments; and the economist Poulett Scrope was unstinting in support of the tenants' rights. None, for all their vigor, won more than a handful of votes.[39] In the 1840s, the only victories for the government protection of workers were the Mining Act of 1842, the Print Work Act of 1845, and the Ten Hour Act of 1847, and each was declared an exception. Women and children in mines became totally un-acceptable when investigators discovered naked males, half-naked females, copulating couples, and overworked infants; the Print Work Act only com-pleted the exclusion of children from textiles, and the Ten Hour Act reflected particular, even exceptional, forces, the power of a concentrated workforce, the dramatic, humanitarian evoking images of satanic factories, and the wish of landed Tories, after the repeal of the Corn Law, to get even with the League and the manufacturers. Tories who were normally aghast at any interference between master and men nevertheless voted for the Ten Hour Act. The deep-est convictions of these Tories differed little from Sir Robert Peel's belief that "the general rule" was to leave "private enterprise undisturbed." Hardly a sin-gle Whig or Tory opposed that rule, and even those urging intervention be-gan by acknowledging it. "As a general principle," said William Gladstone, in urging the regulation of how London's coal whippers were paid, "the legisla-ture should not interfere with labour." Thomas Macaulay, George Muntz, and John Bright made the same solemn avowal as they nevertheless voted for the Ten Hour Act.[40] Few dogmas ran deeper than the conviction that gov-ernment interference in the economy was unwise. And though it was a senti-ment older than political economy, it nevertheless was greatly strengthened by the cogent arguments of Adam Smith, David Ricardo, and Thomas Malthus. Adam Smith, "the highest authority," declared H. G. Ward, M.P. and editor of the *Weekly Chronicle*, had demonstrated that "in the long run the interests of capital and labour are identical." "He adhered to the princi-ples of Adam Smith," added his fellow Whig M.P. Charles Wood, who joined Ward in opposing the Ten Hour Act.[41] Many who opposed that act invoked "the science of political economy," "every just doctrine of the economic sci-ence," and "that science which taught us how to legislate." Other opponents cited the "irrefragable rule" that "labour . . . should be left to . . . the operation of supply and demand," and the fact that "the moral and physical well-being of the operative classes was identical with [the interests of] the employers."[42]

These and many other invocations of political economy came from some 60 of the nearly 100 M.P.'s whose speeches in the 1840s reveal their social outlook. Of these 60, nearly half held these convictions, if not with flawless consistency, at least with intensity. Although Joseph Hume supported gov-ernment legislation for railways, mines, and merchant shipping, it in no way lessened his opposition to the Ten Hour Bill or mitigated his bold claim to "let one general and uniform principle of perfect liberty" pervade British leg-islation.[43] Joseph Hume had read, as most M.P.'s had, Adam Smith's elegant and reasoned disquisition on "the obvious and simple system of natural lib-erty," and of how supply and demand determined price, wages, and profits, and how these self-adjusting mechanisms harmonized private interests with the public good. No thinker was cited and praised more often in Parliament and the press than Adam Smith. Even the Tory *Morning Herald* noted that "the principles of Adam Smith are ones which no one now denies."[44] And among those principles, none was more popular than that of non-interference.

Almost as popular with some M.P.'s was David Ricardo on the miraculous powers of capital as the great engine propelling the economy. "In proportion to the increase of capital" wrote Ricardo in 1817, "will be the increase in the demand for labour," and, as a result, a rise in "the market price of labour." Wages, insisted J. R. McCulloch in 1843, depended on the proportion between capital and labor. For Nassau Senior, wages rose and fell according to the fund for the maintenance of labor, and for J. S. Mill, wages depended on the proportion between population and capital. An expanding capital not only sustained wages but the whole economy. So idolatrous were economists over capital's miraculous powers that Colonel Robert Torrens wrote of "a school of political economy who assume that capital possesses some occult quality or influence by which it creates for itself the field in which it is employed."[45]

Members of Parliament were also persuaded of its occult powers. That wages rose and fell with capital was an inexorable law, which no legislature could change. And also inexorable was the fact that wages would fall if workers worked fewer hours. Nassau Senior, in his *Letters on the Factory Act* of 1837, made the simple calculation that because a ten-hour day was one-sixth shorter than a twelve-hour day, it would produce one-sixth fewer goods. He also calculated that because expensive machinery that often needed replacement formed so large a part of capital costs, it needed to run every hour that it could. The cutting off of the last two hours of production would wipe out a firm's net profit.[46] All would be ruin as cheaper foreign goods flowed in and British capital flowed out. The Tory Home Secretary James Graham, the Whig spokesman Henry Labouchere, the Radical Joseph Hume, the prime minister, Sir Robert Peel, and many others used Senior's calculations to oppose the Ten Hour Act. And even Colonel Torrens, who cautioned about imputing occult qualities to capital, was still sufficiently persuaded by arithmetical laws to calculate that a ten-hour day would bring a 25 percent fall in wages and profits, a calculation that persuaded the Radical Thomas Duncombe to withhold support of the ten-hour day.[47]

These calculations, however, were not correct. The factory inspector Leonard Horner, a shrewd and doughty Scotsman, told Senior at a Political Economy Club meeting that his claim that profits depend on the last hour was untrue. And the club's secretary, Mr. Mallet, declared that Senior's insistence on "the accuracy of his minuteness" was part of the "coxcombry of the political economists."[48] Leonard Horner's factory report of 1845 showed that production in a Preston mill that ran for eleven instead of twelve hours did not decline. Lord John Manners also cited McCulloch's *Commercial Dictionary* to the effect that not only had every prediction of ruin made on the passage of earlier factory acts proved false, but that, quite to the contrary, greater productivity, profits, and wages had ensued.[49] It is doubtful whether most M.P.'s took these claims seriously; Duncombe for one did not allow Torrens's predicted 25 percent loss to prevent his conversion, in 1847, to the ten-hour cause. But although suspicious of every precise calculation, they did not doubt that the wage fund and the laws of supply and demand determined the rate of wages. It was a belief that persuaded M.P.'s to oppose, not only the ten-hour day, but all protection for handloom weavers, lace makers, and hosiery knitters. It was a belief enshrined in the often cited and influential report of the 1841 Handloom Weavers Commission, a report written by Nassau Senior, the preeminent expounder of the wage fund theory. For Senior, so inexorable was the fixed wage fund's role in defining wages that all legislation on wages, or on hours, would be as useless as defying the tides.[50]

To limit hours would also expand the role of the state and lessen that of the individual, in itself an evil, since political economy, and much else, had shown that economic man is far cannier and more energetic than cumbersome and blundering government. Adam Smith had laid it down that the state had three duties, to protect from violence, both external and internal, to administer justice, and to support public institutions that it was not in the interest of the individual to establish. And to fulfill these three duties, he added the raising of revenues. Beyond that, government interference was largely pernicious.[51]

The Whig Lord Chancellor, Henry Brougham, was even more severe concerning the role of government. An admirer of Adam Smith, he would limit government "to secure the rights of the people, the rights of property . . . [and] not to impede the end of laws." The Philosophical Radical John Arthur Roebuck would restrict the state just as severely. "All that a government can do," he argued, "is to protect life and property."[52] Although most M.P.'s had a broader view of government, most did accept that, on economic matters, individuals were more prudent and efficient than government. They agreed with H. G. Ward that "a well regulated self-interest is the great moving principle with the world" and with Sir Robert Peel that "it was precisely by the vigorous, judicious, steady pursuit of self-interest, that individuals and companies ultimately benefitted the public." Peel's praise of individual self-interest came in 1844 in a debate on railways. A year later, again on railways, he insisted that "nothing could do more harm, than that any government should interfere."[53] For Peel and most M.P.'s, government was vast, cumbersome, inefficient, and full of political appointees and mediocrity. Country Tories, like Colonel Sibthorp, hated all commissions, all patronage, all bureaucrats. Government was expensive, wasteful, and meddling.[54] Radicals like Roebuck, Hume, and Bright also hated government, believing it to be oppressive and arbitrary, the handmaid of the aristocracy and the enemy of the people. Moralistic Whigs and Peelites also found government interference, especially through a too generous Poor Law or regulation of wages and hours, as corrupting. "The ten hour bill is no kindness," asserted Thomas Gisborne, since it "would destroy their self-reliance." "To substitute legislative interference," said Peel, would "change materially the character of the people."[55] In talking of "self-reliance," and the "character of the people," Bright, Gisborne, and Peel left the axioms of political economy for the realm of morality. Other M.P.'s also departed from those axioms in opposing protection for weavers, knitters, and lace makers. Just as a belief in the laws of supply and demand and the invisible hand merged with a belief in a natural law and a providential harmony, so did a belief in the individual's superiority to government merge with a wider moral and political individualism. The teachings of political economy were by no means the weaker in Parliament for their consonance with supporting attitudes, but it does make it difficult to disentangle these many parallel forces that explain why Parliament did so little to check the exploitation of workers and why what they did do was so little and erratic.

On March 18, 1844, the House of Commons voted 179 to 170 for a ten-hour amendment to the factory bill, and on May 13, 56 days later, it reversed itself by voting 297 to 159 to defeat a ten-hour amendment. The act that passed placed no limitations on adult labor. But three years and a general election later, Parliament voted 153 to 88 for a ten-hour day.[56] The sudden reversal in 1844 occurred in large part because 80 Tory M.P.'s, absent on March 18, voted on May 13 against the ten-hour amendment. Only eight Tories actually changed their votes. Some 38 Tories who had favored the ten-hour day on March 18 also stayed away on May 13. Peel's use of the party whips and his threat to resign no doubt led to the sudden presence of the 80 Tories as opponents of a shorter workday and the absence of 38 of its friends.[57]

But it is also true that the pleas of Lord Ashley in March had failed to move those Tories who chose to be indifferently absent. The Tories were split on the ten-hour day. The more self-conscious and articulate paternalists, led by Young England and Lord Ashley, were for it; the Peelites, full of political economy, resolutely against; and the majority, both wedded to property rights and hostile to manufacturers, of divided mind. In the tirades of W. B. Ferrand and Lord John Manners, the landowning Tories expressed a virulent hatred of manufacturers, a hatred greatly intensified by the Anti–Corn Law League's attacks on the landed classes' sacred Corn Law, a hatred also of the League's allies, whether Liberals, Whigs, or economists.[58] In 1844, the *Manchester Times, Morning Advertiser, Morning Chronicle, Economist*, and *Sun* explained the Tories' March vote for a ten-hour day in terms of a vindictiveness toward manufacturers and the League, charges repeated in 1846 and 1847 by two M.P.'s, Milner Gibson and John Arthur Roebuck, and three journals, the *Carlisle Journal*, the *Scotsman*, and the Tory *Standard*. The *Standard* in 1847 stoutly denied the charge of vindictiveness but in doing so seems to have forgotten that on March 30, 1844, it had told the agricultural M.P.'s that they had "the League at their mercy, [and that] they may crush it into annihilation by supporting Ashley."[59]

How great a role such vindictiveness played in the 1847 passage of the Ten Hour Act is difficult to judge. It passed 153 to 58 in a House of Commons of 658. The departure from the Conservative Party of 114 Peelites introduced disarray into the forces favoring laissez-faire. It also heightened hostility to that traitor Peel. Of 241 Protectionists, 78 voted for the Ten Hour Bill and only 10 against. Of 114 Peelites, 16 voted against and only 8 for the Bill.[60] Most elusive in this crucial vote were the 163 absent Protectionists. Almost all would certainly have voted "no" to a ten-hour day if the Bill had included agricultural laborers. Instead, it only applied to textile factories, some of whose owners financed the Anti–Corn Law League. Even if many were not vindictive, what happened to textile mills was not their concern. Workers in mammoth factories, like women and children in mines, were exceptional and so required exceptional legislation. But for all other workers, the general rule should be non-interference. The fearful accident rate, the abominable housing, the disease, the payment of wages in pubs, and the drunkenness of thousands of railway workers, all revealed in the Select Committee on Railway Labourers, no more moved Parliament to action than the copious revelations of the grim labor of women and children in field and workshop. In the early Victorian economy, laissez-faire was king, a fact that owed much to the impact of political economy on the Victorian social conscience. Political economy was not the only source of a tolerance of the exploitation and wretchedness of the working classes, but in reinforcing older attitudes, it showed its Mr. Hyde, not its Dr. Jekyll visage. Many early Victorians felt that it was also just as Hyde-like in its support of the harsh New Poor Law.

THE POOR

For many early Victorians, the bitterest fruit of political economy was the New Poor Law of 1834. Critics denounced it as cruel, harsh, and mean. It was also unconstitutional, Malthusian, and destructive of local government. In calling it Malthusian, they erred. Malthus did not want a new law, but the abolition of the old. In 1817, Ricardo agreed, as did other, lesser economists, who feared that poor laws only encouraged the growth of population, joblessness, and pauperism. Escalating poor rates would destroy the wage fund, which alone could save the poor from utter destitution. A poor law, especially one that lavishly supplemented wages, was also a foolish interference in the labor market, which was best regulated by the laws of supply and demand. Although most economists were not for outright abolition, nearly all were severely critical of those old laws, much patched together, by which some 15,000 parishes administered relief in a bewildering variety of ways. Some did so extravagantly and some niggardly and, for its critics, far too few in accordance with Malthus's law of population or Ricardo's wage fund. And many a Tory who called the new law cruel still defended those settlement clauses that made it very difficult to obtain poor relief except in the parish of one's birth, thus denying laborers their rightful mobility.[61]

If, on April 17, 1834, when the Whig Lord Althorp introduced the New Poor Law Bill, M.P.'s expected to hear the economists' strictures on the old poor laws, they were soon disappointed. Although a member of the Political Economy Club and a devotee of that science, Lord Althorp mentioned neither economists nor axioms of political economy. Quite the opposite. He claimed that the New Poor Law was "contrary to the more strict principles of political economy." He did, to be sure, mention the threat of mounting poor rates to property, but he said not a word about mounting rates lessening the fund for wages, about a law of population, or about a poor law that did not tie laborers to their parishes. The brunt of his argument was moral. A lavish poor relief, Althorp argued, corrupted and degraded the laboring classes. It turned independent laborers into dependent paupers.[62]

It was a moral refrain that Althorp took from the 1834 Report of the Royal Commission on the Poor Laws. Although the largest part of that report was written by one of England's leading economists, Nassau Senior, it mentioned neither Adam Smith and Ricardo nor Malthus's law of population. It did touch on the wage fund and the labor market, but very slightly and in a most surprising way. Nassau Senior wrote, not of a lack of capital for wages because of high poor rates, but instead of "low interest and a profusion of capital," a capital that "overflowed in all channels of manufacturing and commerce" but avoided agriculture because it was so "ill managed" and its labor so demoralized that capital applied to it became "wasted capital."[63]

Senior is also surprisingly quiet on the laws of political economy when he castigates magistrates for attempting "to regulate the incomes of the industrious poor." In castigating them, he nowhere talks of a foolish intervention in the laws of supply and demand. Instead, Senior pronounces them hopelessly inept at distinguishing between the deserving and undeserving poor. Moral and administrative, not economic arguments, inform this 180-page report. Again and again, in anecdote, in dubious statistics, in psychological theorizing, in exhortations, one reads that extravagant and indiscriminate outdoor relief destroys a laborer's industry, providence, and independence, corrupts self-reliance, destroying the affections between parent and child, and begets every form of vice—idleness, dishonesty, drunkenness, poaching, smuggling, insolence, and disobedience. Not all parishes gave such corrupting relief and certainly not in the same manner. Those strict in granting relief, especially those granting the able-bodied no relief but in the workhouse, were presented as models to imitate. But far too many parishes, said the report, increased outdoor relief as more children were added to a family, thus causing parishes to become overpopulated. There was, it concluded, a steady, rapid descent into social decay and moral corruption, a descent accompanied by a large rise in poor rates, a rise that threatened property itself—a dubious claim, because poor rates had actually fallen in the past two decades.[64]

The report's picture was biased and its evidence selective. Rates were not bankrupting property and neither was the agricultural laborer of 1834 any more corrupt and idle than his parents and grandparents had been—they were only more numerous, because of a population growth that itself reflected an increase in prosperity. Yet the report did reflect some uncomfortable truths: attempts to relieve distress caused by bad harvests and trade depressions by means of allowances in aid of wages had proven, if not as corrupting as asserted, certainly messy and indiscriminate, and a possible encouragement to farmers to pay lower wages. There was also a need to distinguish the truly indigent from the fraudulent, and even to treat the various kinds of poor that lay between the two differently. There were serious faults with the old laws and urgent problems to solve. But in its diagnosis of and remedies for such problems, the report made few references to the principles of political economy.[65]

Neither did the parliamentary debates on the New Poor Law of the 1830s and 1840s refer to such principles. Not one speaker mentioned population, wage funds, or the labor market and its laws of supply and demand; nor did anyone mention Malthus or Ricardo. Adam Smith was never mentioned, not even in the debate on the parish settlement he so cogently criticized. A Parliament of landowners neglected the findings of political economy and kept the mode of settlement that tied the labourers to their parish. The landed classes, anxious to keep poor rates low, had long attempted to limit relief to the paupers of their own parish. They were very chary of granting settlement—and so relief—to the poor from adjoining parishes. By greatly reducing the mobility of the poor, the law of settlement greatly limited the freedom of the labor market. Nearly all political economists had condemned it, yet it was kept, with only a few modifications, in the New Poor Law, further evidence again that the ideas of political economy were far from omnipotent.[66]

The many and long debates on the New Poor Law focused largely on three matters: its centralization, its workhouse test, and its instances of cruelty. Attacks based on those concerns came largely from landed paternalists attached to the parish and urban radicals resentful of the poor law commissioners' encroachment on their towns' local autonomy and at its refusing the ablebodied any relief but that given in the workhouse.[67] Most of the supporters of the law, some 80 percent of M.P.'s—gave it a silent and approving vote. Why complain of a law that, from 1834 to 1836, reduced poor rates 23 percent? From 1836 on, parliamentarians continued to defend the law, and again largely with moral and administrative, not economic arguments. Did the ideas of political economy make no impact, then?[68]

Not quite. To deny any impact is to deny a consonance between the laissez-faire individualism of political economy and the self-reliant individualism of Victorian morality. It would also be to deny the deeper consonance between political economy's general rules, logical analyses, and rational planning and the general rules, logical analyses, and rational planning that lay behind the growth of the central government. Economists, however wedded to laissez-faire, still considered it to lie within their sphere to construct schemes of banking, currency, joint stock companies, enclosures, tithes, and poor laws. For those economists well versed in Bentham, there was no deep conflict between political economy and administrative centralization. John Austin, a friend of Bentham and the Mills, argued in the *Edinburgh Review* of 1847 that centralization and laissez-faire were quite compatible, since centralization did not mean big government, but a government—even a small one— that efficiently supervised its local authorities.[69]

The consonance between the individualism of political economy and the individualism of Victorian morality was no less explicit in the thought of two other friends of Bentham and the Mills. In the reports recording the triumph of the New Poor Law in 1838 and 1842 by James Kay-Shuttleworth and E .C. Tufnell, both assistant commissioners, the truths of political economy and of a self-reliant morality are combined as in few other reports. There is no silence about the wage fund, but its fullest application. In those Suffolk and Norfolk parishes that severely reduced outdoor relief, wages and employment rose dramatically. Tufnell claimed that distress in Kent had arisen from "the funds of the employers being so diminished [for poor rates] that they are unable to give the usual quantity of work." With the end of wasteful relief and high poor rates, wages would rise. Tufnell denounced all use of poor relief to raise wages above the market rate as "fruitless."[70]

The ending of outdoor relief would not only increase the fund for wages but make the poor more industrious and self-reliant. Political economy and Victorian morality thus meshed together to win for the New Poor Law the support of almost all political economists. In that meshing, the precise impact of the truths of political economy is difficult to judge. Who can tell which of two strong sailors pulling on a rope is the most decisive? It is again wisest to conclude that while the role of political economy should not be exaggerated, it did play a reinforcing role, and a reinforcing role that was at times marginally crucial. But it was also a role that on many issues—railways, canals, banking, water supply, and enclosure—was confusing, complex, and, given the simultaneous growth of laissez-faire attitudes and of government agencies, strikingly paradoxical.

CHAPTER 6

Sacred Property and Divine Providence

The Victorians' vision of a laissez-faire society sprang from many and varied sources. Political economy was not its sole source—and perhaps not even its principal one. Rivaling political economy in its insistence on a free society and economy were not only the emerging forces of Nonconformist individualism, voluntarism, and a radical hostility to government, but two older forces, a belief in the sacredness of property and a belief in a divinely ordered and harmonious society. These two old forces were much more powerful and pervasive than the newer forces since they were such an integral part of three realities, a de facto laissez-faire society that arose from the wreck of Stuart despotism, the triumph of capitalism, and a conservatism imbedded in the common law, in the writings of giants like William Blackstone, Edmund Burke, and William Paley, and in the theology of the Anglican Church.

At the heart of this conservatism and laissez-faire society lay a deep veneration for private property. That such property was sacred was an intense conviction with most Members of Parliament, one that found eloquent and passionate expression. "Civilization," the historian Macaulay told the House of Commons in 1842, "rests on security of property," for without it a "country will sink into barbarism." In the House of Lords, Brougham, well on his way from radicalism through Whiggery to conservatism, made the same claim, calling "the right of property . . . the line of demarcation which separated the savage from the civilized state of society." He also called it "the most sacred of all rights . . . the corner stone of the whole edifice, its fundamental principle." The leader of the Tory Lords, Lord Stanley, the future earl of Derby and prime minister, was equally enthusiastic, rejoicing in the "sacred, high and indefeasible right of landowners in the property of the soil." He elsewhere declared such rights "above all constitutional theories," since property and life "are the foundation, the bases, the main bond of all constitutions and all rights."[1] The House of Lords was inordinately fond of the rights of private property. For Lord Lansdowne, "the undoubted rights of property" were part of the laws of Divine Providence and formed "the great foundation in which all improvement must rest, . . . the foundation of all social advantage." The Lords were quick to invoke the sacred right of property whatever the cause: for Lord Londonderry, it justified working children in mines, for the earl of Malmesbury, using dogs to draw carts, and for the duke of Beaufort, the earl of Wicklow, and Lord Segrave, the employment of chimney sweeps. Beaufort knew that using chimney sweeps was "opposed to the dictates of humanity" but to outlaw them would be "very dangerous to property."[2] Few in the Commons—Tory or Whig or Radical—doubted the inviolable rights of property. That inveterate critic of all vested interests Thomas Wakely had called property "one of the first fruits of civilization," while all the Benthamites and other adherents of political economy realized how central it was to the theories of Adam Smith and David Ricardo.[3] Radical and Whig opponents of the Ten Hour Bill used the sacredness of private property to oppose it. A ten-hour limit, they argued, interfered with the only property a worker possessed, his right to labor. "The most sacred of all rights," argued the *Examiner*, "was the poor man's . . . freedom to work." Invoking the sacredness of property was an old and much employed tradition. Thomas Hobbes had used it two centuries earlier, as had Adam Smith when he invoked "the property which every man has in his own labour." It was also invoked by the Liberal Milner Gibson in 1844 and the Radical Joseph Hume in 1846.[4]

But although Whigs and Radicals never doubted the rights of property, their favorite rhetorical term was "capital," a term hated by Tories as the child of political economists and manufacturers. The Tory's favorite word, "property," was central to a creed hostile to an encroaching and centralizing government. No Tory expressed that creed more loudly than Colonel Sibthorp. No one, not the Radical Hume nor the Benthamite Roebuck, spoke and voted against the growth of government more consistently than this feisty, garrulous county M.P. from Nottinghamshire. "I hate all commissions," he exploded, "I hate all jobs, I suspect all government." He thus voted against the Poor Law, Railway Acts, Inclosure and Tithe Commissions, public works in Ireland, Drainage Loan Acts for English landlords, the regulation of London's hackney cabs, and every and all measures limiting a landlord's power over tenants or game birds, and in doing so, he invoked "what had always been held sacred, the rights of property."[5]

Most Tory M.P.'s from England, although steadfast in defense of property, usually did so in a silent way. But the M.P.'s from Ireland were not so discreet. From 1846 to 1850, they denounced almost every measure to alleviate the famine as an invasion of property. They formed an angry, loud chorus of dissent. Frederick Shaw, an M.P. from Dublin, proclaimed in 1846 that strengthening Ireland's not very effective poor law of 1838 would "absorb the whole property of the country," and in 1847 that it "would ruin the landlord." In that year, too, the Irish landlord Stafford O'Brien, a friend of Young England and worshipper of Wordsworth, said that a poor law would "swamp the property of Ireland," and Henry Thomas Corry, M.P. from Tyrone, predicted that it would cause "the confiscation of property," a deplorable event, since "a flourishing condition of property is as necessary to the welfare of the poor as of the rich."[6]

Any bills enhancing tenants' rights also threatened property: they infringed, said Viscount Bernard, on "the rights of property." And such infringements were unnecessary, added Joseph Napier, M.P. from Dublin University, because the "true interests of the tenants are identified with those of the landlords." Since even modest proposals to reform leasehold conversions brought shouts of "complete subjection of property," it is not surprising that the 1849 Bill for a uniform and supplementary poor rate of 6d. on the pound on all Irish property led Colonel Fitzstephen French, of Roscommon County, to complain loudly of the annihilation and confiscation of the property of Ireland.[7] By 1849, with the famine tragically persisting, the Whig government proposed a 6d. rate throughout Ireland in order to rescue the starving in the hard-hit and impoverished Western districts. The proposal led five Irish landlords in Parliament to protest that it would be "confiscatory of property," cause "the melting away" of "the whole of property," "end laws of real property," "destroy the security of property" and introduce the "communist doctrine."[8]

Talk of communism and socialism had greatly increased since the French revolution of 1848. The dissemination of the ideas of Fourier, Proudhon, and Louis Blanc only doubled the energies of the defenders of property. Bernal Osborne called the 6d. rate "legalized communism," while J. B. Walsh, an English landlord, feared that it and Scrope's plan to give wastelands to the landless would abrogate property and bring in the socialism of Proudhon and Louis Blanc.[9] The pressure of the Irish famine combined with fears evoked by socialist ideas and the French revolution of 1848 led Parliament to reaffirm as never before its devotion to the sacredness of property.

That devotion was all the greater because its roots lay in the writings of the giants of political thought and because of its wide popularity in current periodicals and works. The library of an English country gentleman commonly included nothing to disturb and much to reaffirm the sacredness of property. It would very likely contain the works of John Locke, William Blackstone, Edmund Burke, and William Paley. Although these much thumbed classics differed on the nature and origins of private property, they never questioned that property was indispensable.

John Locke's arguments, if, for some, a little out of date by the 1840s, had become with many a commonplace. Private property was legitimate because of the labor that had made it possible—the labor of clearing and draining and fencing fields, and of building corn mills and houses. Property as accumulated labor was part of the natural state of man. It was a natural right that preceded the state. "Man . . . hath by Nature a power," wrote Locke, "to preserve his property that is his Life." Man also "has Liberty and Estates [that] I call by the name of property." He has the right "to pass his accumulated labor on to his heirs, or to sell it to another for money." Money was itself a form of accumulated labor. Property, in short, could be free and alienable.[10] This strong emphasis on hard labor as the origins of the natural right of property not only won the approval of those improvers of agriculture and pioneers of manufactures who made eighteenth-century England a beehive of industry and wealth, but also influenced or reinforced the arguments of Adam Smith and David Ricardo that labor gave a commodity its value.

To the two main arguments that property was a rightful accumulation of labor and that it accorded with reason and natural law, Locke brought in others: property was useful as an incentive to labor, as a cement of society, as a way to avoid turbulence over possessions, as a way to discipline the lower classes.[11]

In 1765, William Blackstone published his *Commentaries on the Laws of England*, which soon became Holy Writ for all students of law and for many more. While Blackstone granted that "bodily labour . . . is universally allowed to give the fairest and most reasonable title" to property, he said little about it in his historical sketch of the rise of property from Abraham's claiming a well of water as his property through Cicero's insistence that "the place which any man has taken is for the time his own" to a realistic awareness of the role of the state and law as the real buttresses of private property. Property is thus a "right," which is all the more solid because ordained by law. But Blackstone draws back from making property solely the offspring of law. Since it both existed prior to government and is universally accepted by the common sentiments of mankind, it is a natural right and part of natural law. It is also, of course, eminently useful. Blackstone weaves in every possible argument in his defense of property, and if the argument is not flawlessly coherent, its erudition, sweep, and agreement with the assumptions of a landed society deepened the gentry's view that property, if not sacred, was at least solidly rational, useful, natural, and legal.[12] The countless members of Parliament who extolled property with such vigor must, if somewhat unconsciously, have brought Locke and Blackstone to Westminster. Most of them were probably Whigs and Liberals. Tories raised on Burke had doubts about property as a natural right and as accumulated labor. Burke, and others before him, saw the egalitarian ramifications of both. If labor is the basis, why do the hard-working receive so little and the leisurely so much, and should not that be rectified? And should not such a huge inequality also be rectified because property is a natural right of all men? The shrewd Burke saw that the best defense of property was prescription. "Our Constitution," wrote Burke, "is a prescriptive Constitution, it is a Constitution whose sole authority is that it existed time out of mind." "The foundation of property," he added, "is the old habitual, unmeaning prepossession in favor of historic right." Supporting the sacred rules of prescription, Burke believed, were natural law and utility, the one distantly and the other immediately. Property, like the state, the Church, law courts, magistracy, the parish, and constables had evolved because they met deep needs and were eminently useful; moreover, their abolition would lead to anarchy. Property was the linchpin of this salutary, even sacred, edifice.[13]

Members of Parliament quoted Burke much more often than Locke or Blackstone. His only rival was William Paley, a writer of clear, persuasive, eighteenth-century prose, a straightforward prose, far less complex than Burke's. Paley's view of property may well have strengthened many an M.P.'s conviction of the inviolability of property. Published in 1765, his *Principles of Moral and Political Philosophy* enjoyed its twenty-first edition in 1850. It was required reading at Cambridge and was found in many a rectory, manor house, and town residence. It had no involuted Burkian sentences. All was simple. "The real foundation of our right [to property] is the LAW OF THE LAND." That law is just both because it reflects divine law and because property is useful. Paley combines natural theology, common law, and utilitarianism to form a coherent defense of private property. As to its usefulness, he is specific: property incites people to "increase the produce of the earth" and to preserve and distribute that produce. It also prevents violent clashes over that produce and the land that creates it, leads to the division of labor, "improves conveniency of living," and prevents "wars, waste, [and] tumult." Property also is a historic right and rests on prescription.[14]

Although classical theories of the origin and nature of property differed and rested on some dubious assumptions in early Victorian England, no one except the Owenites, Fourierists, and a few extreme Chartists doubted that private property should form the basis of the economy. That property was accumulated labor some doubted; that it was a natural right originating in a state of nature, Jeremy Bentham pronounced a fiction, "the effusions of a hard heart operating a cloudy mind," and that prescription gave it imperishable rights meant little to those who found all institutions hoary and decrepit with age and in need of reform.[15] The crusty McCulloch showed his awareness of this discrepancy when he cautioned, "It does no good to look into theories of property [since] it seems to be sufficiently obvious," a view John Stuart Mill adopted, with a cryptic "we must leave out of consideration its actual origin."[16] Mill wrote a long defense of property in his *Political Economy*, but it was one haunted by a sense both of its unjust inequalities and dubious justifications.

The same is true of other critics. As Christian Socialists, Frederick Denison Maurice and Charles Kingsley condemned the great inequality in the distribution of property and the harshness of its use, as did Thomas Hodgskin and William Thompson and many Chartists. But none would declare for property in common. Maurice praised private property as "crucial" to society, a symbol "of personal distinction" and Hodgskin, who called "the right of labour" the true natural right, contended that "even the sacredness of the present right of property can not be too strenuously upheld against . . . the violations of government."[17] John Stuart Mill, deeply alarmed by French socialist ideas, also feared that property in common would destroy that "multi-form development of human nature that stimulates mental and moral progress." It would also end the independence and freedom and bring despotism.[18]

Private property was far too pervasive in Victorian society, far too active a part of its economy, and far too venerated for John Stuart Mill to become England's Proudhon or Fourier. Belief in private property cut across the whole spectrum of politics. Not only did Conservatives like Southey, Coleridge, and Sadler extol its virtues, but so did Whigs like Thomas Arnold and Lord Macaulay, all the Benthamites, the evangelicals led by Thomas Chalmers, and, with great learning, all the economists. Even the Radicals in the tradition of William Godwin and Thomas Paine gave it their blessing. The Chartist convention of 1839 declared "the rights of property are sacred and inviolable."[19]

Nowhere was this widespread popularity more evident than in the periodical press, particularly the Tory section. *Blackwood's* and *Fraser's*, the Tories' two great monthlies, and the distinguished *Quarterly Review* made it the centerpiece of their paternalism. The adage "Property has its duties as well as its rights" ends on rights. To Croly and Alison, *Blackwood's* leading writers, private property was "the primary purpose of society" and "the sole principle of progress," a view that John Croker of the *Quarterly Review* shared. *Blackwood's* Croly called Burke "the greatest of political philosophers," and the *Quarterly Review's* Croker insisted that Burke's "expansive and comprehensive power of intellect was superior to all." Burke's exaltation of property informs all of Croly's and Croker's denunciation of any government interference with railways, game laws, Church property, or landed estates.[20] A writer in *Fraser's* was quite explicit on how holding property sacred meant a pervasive laissez-faire. It is a "principle of our Constitution," he asserted, "that let his property consist of what it may, man may do what he likes with his own." "Do what he likes with his own" was one of three maxims that lay deep in the Tory mind, the other two being "Leave well enough alone" and "Live and let live," adages heard often at agricultural meetings and at the hustings. Michael Sadler called "Live and let live" a "noble English maxim" and the *Sussex Agricultural Express* pronounced it "a homely but very truthful saying." The Tory *Standard* also voiced this sentiment when, after citing Edmund Burke, it wrote, "The sacredness of the right of property must for ever prohibit the interference of the state."[21] The *Standard* hated political economy. So did *Fraser's*, the *Quarterly Review*, and *Blackwood's*, the latter's Thomas De Quincy denouncing its "cold indifference."[22] But since both economists and paternalists envisioned a laissez-faire society, what was the difference? The *Standard*, which constantly denounced capital, machinery, manufacturers, and new wealth, insisted that there was a big difference. "The rights of capital," it wrote in 1848, "is a different thing from the sacred right of property since the latter secures a man only that which he has; the former asserts his right to use what he has to the ruin of his neighbour." It was a flimsy and dubious distinction, especially coming from a paper that called railway legislation "a violation of sacred property."[23] Did not railways incarnate the evils of capital and new wealth as much as cotton mills? Yes, but it mattered not to the *Standard*. A cynic might observe that railway advertisements greatly enhanced the *Standard's* revenues, an observation that wise Burkians like Stanley Lees Giffard, its editor, would not mind, since for Burke, vested interests were part of the elaborate and beneficial edifice of property. That the *Railway Times* constantly invoked the rights of property to oppose government interference with railways was no more surprising than that the *Farmer's Magazine* insisted on "the absolute and uncontrolled right of the first owners of soil to do as they pleased with their own."[24] There is no gainsaying that the sacredness of property, quite as much as the invisible hand of the economists, appeared attractive to a host of vested interests for quite clearly material reasons. But it also had strength as rhetoric, as a vision, and as an ancient and helpful ideology. The Tory *Mirror* even called on all national schools to teach "the sacredness of property."[25]

Hugh Miller, editor of the *Witness*, also called for the sanctity of property to be taught in the schools. He was so persuaded of "the great natural law of property" that he called it an "institution of God . . . which no man or nation can set aside with impunity."[26] Nonconformist journals seemed second only to Tory paternalists in embracing property. For the *Eclectic,* "private property is the most powerful agent in the promotion of civilization"; for the *North British Review,* "the sacredness of property" was an ancient belief, long the basis of society; and for Edward Miall's *NonConformist,* it was a Lockean natural right, because "all property we take to be merely condensed and accumulated labour." The *NonConformist,* so often full of the laws of political economy, still disliked the "frigid calculations" of the "cold blooded economists."[27] Deep in the Nonconformist mentality lay a tough, puritan worship of work, and Locke's natural right of property as the fruit of industry seemed far less "frigid [a] calculation."

Locke's view was also a far older and far more popular and far simpler form of laissez-faire, a fact noted by more than one contemporary journal. W. E. Hickson, a discerning observer of public opinion, noted that "laissez faire is by no means the doctrine exclusively of political economists; it is the creed of a far more numerous section of the community." It was also a far older creed, as the Unitarians' *Prospective Review* realized when it wrote that the right of property was antecedent to and different from political economy.[28]

Older than political economy, more pervasive, more varied in appeal, and more varied in its ties to corporations, churches, land, capitalists, and a wide array of voluntary institutions, a belief in the sanctity of property certainly formed a major part of the early Victorian vision of a laissez-faire society. But what was its actual impact? Did it prevent crucial legislation? Was it much more than rhetoric?

At first glance, its impact seems great. A cry of property in danger seemed to meet every proposal for reform. For Lord Wynford in 1833, a proposed lunacy commission would be "too heavy a burden on property," and for Stuart Wortley in 1849, a measure to require Scottish railways to run on Sundays was "a direct infringement on the rights of private property." In the sixteen years between 1833 and 1849, property in danger was raised on more than thirty measures of reform.[29] It was invoked against bills to control dogs, chimney sweeps, mines, the New Poor Law, the ten-hour day, the Railway Board, the Public Health Act, and on both sides of the Corn Law debate. It was also used to oppose a bill on Scottish Church sites, the collection of agricultural statistics, and the reform of the Church living at Bishop Wearmouth.[30] The reforms of charities, cathedral chapters, enclosures, tithes, and metropolitan building also aroused tender feelings about property. There was often in enclosures, John Hill Burton concluded, "a fanatical spirit against all proposals importing an interference with property."[31] But did it matter? A great many of the measures denounced as an interference with property did pass. In many measures, there was also an ambiguity about property rights. The New Poor Law, for example, created a central commission that interfered with the rights of property, but it was also intended to defend property itself. "The old laws," said Lord Althorp in 1834, would have caused, "the destruction of all property."[32] This vastly exaggerated fear was countered by its opponents with the charge that the new law's three commissioners themselves infringed on the sacred rights of property. These protests, however, were of no avail, since landowners soon found out that the commissioners were successful in lowering rates, which explains the curious paradox that whereas Tory M.P.'s attacked the New Poor Law at the hustings during the general election of 1841, almost all later voted to renew it.[33] Invoking the sacred right of property always involved complexity and ambiguities, particularly since so many of the above measures were to the advantage of property because they brought an efficient and salutary order to the economy. There would have been far fewer railways without the compulsory purchase of property. The railways would also have been far more dangerous for many a property-owning traveler but for railway inspectors interfering with property. Cathedral prebends and canons, who did little, protested when some of their incomes went to curates who did much, often in working-class areas, but it made for a more efficient Church, and one no whit less rich in property. And so it went with banking, joint stock companies, metropolitan building, and numerous matters in which government interference, despite protests about property's sacred rights, did little harm and much good. The use of government to regulate property and improve its effective use even extended to land in the form of the Inclosure and Tithe Commissions and loans to improve drainage, but no further. Sir Robert Peel, who presided over much of the wise ordering of property—even against his own rhetoric—said in 1846, "On all these matters connected with the tenure of land and the relations of landlord and tenant he would uphold the rights of property."[34] Peel knew his Tory landowners well and their jealous regard for property rights. No one, not even captains of industry, enjoyed such extensive freedom from government interference as did England's landed gentlemen. Talk of ten-hour days or even of limiting the hours of child labor would be unthinkable of agricultural laborers. Nor was cruelty and exploitation and injustice any less in the countryside: farmers worked women and children long hours for scanty pay, and landlords tore down or failed to build or to repair cottages so as to avoid supporting the parish poor. Landlords also gave tenants, when evicted, no compensation for having built a barn or drained a field.[35] In Ireland, these cruelties and injustices were in good times far more distressing and during the famine unimaginably tragic. Although government commissions and select committees revealed all these grim realities, and bills were proposed to remedy them, nothing was effected. Just as some nineteen out of twenty workers in manufacturing knew no government protection, so in the English and Irish countryside agricultural laborers had no protection. They were subject to the arbitrary will of employers who enjoyed a freedom untouched by government, a freedom defended by appeals to the sacredness of property.

The ideologies of the paternalists and the economists never had a harsher impact than on legislation for Ireland during the famine, when the baleful influence of political economy has rightly been seen in the attitude of the Whig cabinet, notably Chancellor of the Exchequer Charles Wood and Secretary of the Treasury Charles Trevelyan.[36] But a closer scrutiny of the imperfect and ill-executed Public Works Acts, of the limited and meager poor laws, of the rejection of bills for compensating tenants, and of the denunciation of all thought of using wastelands or seriously reforming the land, all reveal the even more baleful influence of a dogmatic devotion to the sacred right of property.

Contemporaries and later historians have claimed that Irish land was too poor to support adequate measures, but Poulett Scrope noted that in 1848, the poor rate was only 1s. 11d. on the pound in Leinster and 2s. 7d. in Munster, with the landlord paying only half. Some of the areas in the West, to be sure, were too poor, too hard hit by famine, too engulfed in pauperism, to support their poor, but if all Irish property—estimated to be worth £16 million—were rated for all the Irish poor, a minimal subsistence might have been given.[37] The modest 6d. on the pound throughout Ireland in 1849 was a step in that direction, but it was a rate that the Irish and Tory M.P.'s denounced as an attack on their cherished local control and on their sacred right to property.

The poor rate might, of course, have been extended further. England, Wales, and Scotland belonged, like Ireland, to the "United Kingdom," and the king in Parliament was their sovereign. But that all Britain help Ireland was an idea never raised in Parliament or the press.

The sacred right of property was a far more powerful idea than political economy in the English and Irish countryside, more powerful because it not only enjoyed the support of a powerful intellectual tradition—that of Locke, Blackstone, Burke, Paley, and others—but because it was also tied intimately and directly to landed property itself, to its rents and profits, and because its votaries were dominant in the Parliament that ruled Britain. It was also powerful because it fused so perfectly with the even older, more pervasive, and deeply entrenched belief that society was made harmonious by a Divine Providence.

DIVINE PROVIDENCE

Sacred property, so crucial to a landlord's and a capitalist's vision of a laissez-faire society, was but part of a larger scheme, a scheme of Divine Providence. The Supreme Author of Our Being had ordained not only that property should be private and inviolable but that society should be unequal, that the poor should toil and the rich rule, that there be magistrates, bishops, and kings, that tithes be collected and taxes raised, and that famine punish the wicked and wealth reward the virtuous.

A belief in such a providential scheme ran deep and wide in the mentality of the early Victorians. Firmly rooted in traditional Anglicanism, it gained strength in the religious revivals of the evangelicals, the Nonconformists, and the Tractarians; and it persisted to a surprising extent in the natural law outlook of the Enlightenment. Its Anglican roots were evident in every parish church and every cathedral where its worshippers could read in the Book of Common Prayer of the wisdom and goodness of God's ways. The Bible itself, of course, so glorified God's sovereignty, majesty, and omnipotence that theologians from Augustine to Calvin argued that God not only predetermined the fate of every soul but also the path of every raindrop and the rise and fall of nations. And although eighteenth-century reasonableness weakened that severe determinism, it did not end the belief that God created, determined, and had fore-knowledge of even the most minute of events. Even the rationalist theologians of the late eighteenth century saw God in the smallest event. Abraham Tucker, in *The Light of Nature*, published in 1778, insisted that "not a hair is lost out of the number upon our head, not an atom stirs . . . nor a fancy start upon the imagination of any animal without the permission or appointment of our Heavenly Father."[38] Although *The Light of Nature* had a third edition in 1831, most early Victorians read of Tucker's ideas in William Paley's immensely popular *Natural Theology*. Paley also saw God's work everywhere, not only in "the web feet of the water fowl, the fang of the viper . . . and the abdomen of the silk worm," but in "the mite, the ugly spider, the filthy maggot."[39]

God's omnipotence governed the rise and fall of nations quite as much as did the stirring of atoms, and it was from just such rises and falls that pious Christians developed their classical view of a righteous and wrathful Providence. For the greatest of the evangelicals, William Wilberforce, it was "the fate of Sodom and Gomorrah," and the ruin of Babylon, of Tyre, of Nineveh, of Jerusalem "that loudly proclaims his moral government."[40]

In the 1840s, the pious of the Church of England still proclaimed God's awful vengeance on sinners. The Reverend Henry Bickersteth pronounced the cholera of 1830 a Divine Judgment. He published sixteen volumes on God's prophecies and warnings.[41] The bishop of Chichester, in a sermon on "God's Blessing, The Only Security Against National Want" invoked "God's great Sovereign Power and Awful Vengeance" to explain the Irish famine. It was a "Heavenly inflicted blow," a blow "chastising sin." "We had forgotten" he added, that God is "alone . . . the source of plenty and strength and goodness." Instead, we had exalted "our own wisdom into the place of His Providence." Science had produced "an ungodly and idiotic security" to the neglect of the fact that the "one end and purpose of His Superintending Providence" is our salvation.[42]

Similar sentiments echoed throughout England. To packed churches, Liverpool's most famous pastor, the Reverend Hugh M'Neil, preached on "Famine, A Rod of God." God, who "ordereth all things: and "personally directs all the affairs of the world," is "sovereign and awful to sinners and idolaters," but an "unwearied benefactor to the faithful," hence "it is only by the power of God himself that the calamity can be removed."[43] For M'Neil, God was the "only" remedy, and for the bishop of Chichester, God "alone" was "the source of plenty and strength." M'Neil's "only" and Chichester's "God alone" reflect an old-fashioned and deeply pious view of Divine Providence, one William Wilberforce would have endorsed, and one that never exalted "our wisdom into the place of Providence." It was a view that had informed John Foxe's *Book of Martyrs* in the sixteenth century and the pronouncements of the Puritans in the seventeenth century, a view that saw Providence suddenly and inexplicably intervening in human affairs; perhaps to save a martyr, perhaps to win a battle, but always unexpectedly, mysteriously, like a revelation. True, sinners usually suffered more than the faithful, but not always, since Providence was inscrutable. Famines and floods came, nations rose and fell, the good died young while the evil grew old, and the rain fell on the wicked and the virtuous alike in ways unknown to reason, but that did not diminish the all-powerful, all-knowing, infinitely wise, infinitely good nature of God. However arbitrary the ways of God on earth, all would be balanced out on the Day of Judgment. Such was the scheme of Divine Providence proclaimed by William Wilberforce, the Reverend Hugh M'Neil, the Reverend Henry Bickersteth, the bishop of Chichester and believed by thousands of pious evangelicals, High Churchmen, and Nonconformists.

Had this belief in a righteous but inscrutable God constituted the only view of Divine Providence, that doctrine would not have enjoyed the widespread acceptance that it did in early Victorian England. But with the rise of science and the spread of Enlightenment ideas, the idea of Divine Providence fused with the idea of a natural law that governed the universe. Providence now became a popular element in the world outlook of even the less pious early Victorians and thereby became an important part of their vision of a laissez-faire society. Hundreds of early Victorians owed to William Paley their belief that Divine Providence revealed itself through man's reason and through nature's laws. In his *Principles of Moral and Political Philosophy* (1785), Paley argued that "there are two methods of coming at the will of God, [by] scripture and [by] the light of nature."[44] The term "light of nature" was the title of Abraham Tucker's four-volume work, which Paley acknowledges had a great influence on him, a work describing how the Creator reveals his wisdom and goodness through his vast array of natural laws. For Tucker, these natural and moral laws constituted a chain "descending from the First Cause, which is God Omniscient." From their study, he asserted, we "improve our sense and knowledge of the economy of Providence."[45] There was, of course, nothing original in this idea. The Roman Stoics had preached it, and it was integral to the thinking of the Newtons, Boyles, and Lockes of the seventeenth century and to the Butlers and Shaftesburys of the eighteenth.

Many were the comparisons of God's moral law for man with those governing the orbit of the planets, an analogy informing the *Records of Creation,* a work first published in 1816 by John Bird Sumner, bishop of Chester. By the year 1848 and its third edition, Sumner was archbishop of Canterbury. In his *Records,* after citing Newton's grand principle of gravitation, Sumner celebrates a Deity that "by regulating, according to a general law, the state and condition of mankind . . . [reflects] the same comprehensive wisdom which is seen in the natural world."[46] Tucker's and Sumner's books ran to only three editions, but they were still often cited in the periodicals of the 1840s, although not nearly as often as Edmund Burke and William Paley.

In his *Thoughts on Scarcity* (1795), Burke referred to "the laws of commerce, which are the laws of nature and consequently the laws of God," a statement of the rationalist view of Providence so pithy that it adorned many review articles and parliamentary debates.[47] Paley's pronouncements were equally popular. By 1847, his *Natural Theology* was in its twenty-ninth edition and his *Moral and Political Philosophy* in its twenty-first, and parts of both were required reading at Cambridge University. Coleridge, to be sure, denounced them as shallow and was joined in his disapproval by De Quincy, Shelley, and Hazlitt. But far more frequent were praise of and quotations from this most successful popularizer of dominant intellectual trends. "His admirable good sense," wrote Charles Neave, rose "to the height of genius"; William Smith judged Paley sound and correct; and Samuel Warren argued that Paley proved "the unity of the Deity . . . [by] the uniformity of the plan observable in the system [of nature]."[48] Neave, Smith, and Warren all wrote for *Blackwood's* and helped Archibald Alison and George Croly bring to that Tory journal a distinctly providential view of society. So, too, although he was no Tory, did George Combe, another occasional reviewer, most fully in his *Constitution of Man* (1828) and *Lectures on Moral Philosophy* (1840). By 1850, the *Constitution* was in its ninth edition and the *Lectures* its third. Combe was a phrenologist who believed that the varying shapes and sizes of the skull revealed varying temperaments and character. He was a rationalist who declared that since the age of miracles was long past, "the key to Divine Government is a knowledge of our own nature, the nature of things, and beings around us, and the relations subsisting among them." Combe was skeptical that God caused epidemics and famines. When cholera swept over Europe in 1830, he praised Edinburgh's Board of Health for a wise reading of the ways of Providence and condemned the pope for a superstitious reading. The Board of Health, he asserted, had looked to natural laws, to "cleanliness, hospitals, and medicine," and the pope to a procession headed by "a black image of the virgin."[49] For rationalists like Combe, the Unitarian Dr. Southwood Smith, and the popularizers of political economy, natural law crowded out revelation, famines, and epidemics as the way of knowing Providence. But for most, as for those who clung on every word of the eloquent Scottish divine Thomas Chalmers, the voice of Providence spoke both in terms of natural law and through epidemics and famines. Chalmers, Edinburgh University's professor of moral philosophy, published over 100 works expounding the ways of God to man. Among them were *Church Revelations Viewed in Connexion with Modern Astronomy, On Political Economy,* and the *Institutes of Religion.* In the *Institutes,* he insists that God "ordained the purpose of every being and established the laws of nature," just as He "determines the progress of every planet, every particle, [and] every individual living creature."[50] Chalmers, as much read and quoted as Burke or Paley, never doubted the pervasive power of Providence. Neither did Coleridge and Carlyle, however shallow they found Paley. Coleridge through Kantian reason, and Carlyle through the great men and great events of history, felt that they could discern the workings of the Supreme Being.

Even minor figures joined the interpreters of God's way: moral philosophers like Jonathan Dymond, George Ramsay, Adam Sedgwick, Southwood Smith, and Samuel Spaulding.[51] They differed on metaphysics and theology but not on the existence of a Sovereign Providence. There was more than one version of Providence: there were Catholic and Protestant versions and liberal and conservative ones, as well as those of Tories and Whigs and paternalists and individualists—even those of phrenologists. A belief in Divine Providence was nearly universal. It was often invoked in Parliament and by no one more explicitly than Lord Lansdowne in his reference to "the general laws by which the dispensation of Divine Providence governs the actions and regulates the whole system of society."[52] So widespread was a belief in Providence that it raises the question, how did such a pervasive belief influence the social outlook of the early Victorians?

Of the many ways it did, four are prominent: first, that the institutions of society are ordained of God and should be accepted; secondly, that the schemes of Providence itself, so rich in nice harmonies and marvelous designs, are good and wise; thirdly, that evil, sin, poverty, and disease are an inevitable and inscrutable part of a larger scheme; and fourthly, that in the England of the 1840s, the best society is a laissez-faire society.

Most educated early Victorians were religious, many deeply so. An all-powerful and all-wise God was the Creator of all things, large and small, including the institutions of human society and the orbits of the planets. And whatever He ordained, He did so from His infinite wisdom. Mrs. Marcet told her many readers that "God in His goodness has contrived everything wisely to suit the purpose of everyone"[53] "Contrivances" was a favorite word with William Paley. All of God's contrivances, argued Paley, are good.

That the Supreme Being was not merely all powerful but all-wise and all-good was an ancient view, deriving from the early Church Fathers and medieval schoolmen. Moreover, it was expressed in English classics such as John Bunyan's *Pilgrim's Progress*, Richard Hooker's *Ecclesiastical Polity*, and Bishop Butler's *Analogy of Religion*. It became part of the eighteenth-century complacency articulated by Alexander Pope in his *Essay on Man* in the dictum "Whatever is, is right." And it was a view greatly reinforced by victory over Napoleon, the Industrial Revolution, the conquest of the second British empire, and the coming of Victorian peace and prosperity.

Among the wisely ordained contrivances was inequality. Scripture, man's reason, the order of nature, the whole of history, and prescription all testified that it was an integral part of the providential scheme. "The scheme of Providence" rejoiced the Unitarian *Christian Teacher*, is "that there should be many gradations in human life"; "social hierarchy," asserted the Catholic editor of *The Tablet* is "part of an order established by Divine Providence"; "inequalities of condition," exclaimed the Anglican Reverend John Sandford, "are not only natural but designed by God for the most wise and beneficent ends"; "God designs," concluded the Congregationalist Reverend Andrew Reed, "that inequalities are part of His own Providence."[54] And so went this refrain all across the board, Unitarians, Catholics, Anglicans, and Congregationalists. Even the utilitarian *Westminster Review* called "poverty part of the designs of Providence," and the rationalist *Athenaeum* said it was part of "the primal law of nature."[55]

Inequality is necessary, wrote Bishop Sumner in *Records of Creation*, "because God ordained it." He added that it was "also agreeable to the attribute of divine wisdom." The alternative, equality, was certainly not agreeable, either to divine or to Sumner's wisdom. Everywhere, wrote Sumner, it led to stagnation of the mind and "the lowest and most savage state." It had paralyzed Sparta, as it had, elsewhere, led to "careless ignorance and indifference to all improvement." Inequality, on the other hand, "exercises the natural powers of man" and provides "the foundation of civil society"—all views shared by Thomas Chalmers, who argued that "it is not by the abolition of rank, but by assigning to each rank its duties, that peace and friendship and order will be firmly established."[56]

The idea of "rank and station" formed an indispensable part of the belief in inequality. In the great chain of social being, from ducal palace to peasant cottage, it was by the performance of those duties appropriate to one's appointed sphere that one both created a civilized society and fulfilled God's will. That God ordained rank and station was as common a refrain as His establishment of inequality. The churches again took the lead. At the 1848 annual meeting of the New Connexion, the dutiful Methodist was told to be satisfied with "one's station in life to which God has seen fit to call him"—a message of obedience that youthful Anglicans learned when reading in the *Christian Penny Magazine* that "it is his Providence that furnishes the several stations we occupy."[57] As adult Anglicans, they also learned from the Reverend Walter Hook of Leeds that, not only was every providentially allotted station the best, but that "God had predetermined particular persons to particular offices." The Reverend Pye Smith, a Congregationalist who fought Hook on education, poor laws, and factory hours, was in complete accord with the truth that, in Pye Smith's words, "Providence has distributed talents in a wise diversity."[58]

"Talents" was a popular word in describing the power and wealth of those of high station, as was "stewardship." Both were biblical and full of scriptural and paternalistic overtones, and both reflected St. Paul's famous "For there is no power but of God: the powers that be are ordained of God" (Rom. 13:1), which William Paley combined with Peter 2:13, "Submit yourself to every ordinance of man for the Lord's sake," to justify the rule of civil magistrates.[59] The Victorian men of God also found it part of God's providential scheme that servants owed obedience to masters, children to parents, and wives to husbands. There were many stations, all ordained, all in a hierarchy of mutual dependencies and subordination, and each with its sphere, rights, and duties. For William Wilberforce in his *Practical View of the Religious System*, the obligation to fulfill the duties of ones own circle was as binding as the law of gravity. Both held together "the greatest and the least." Those of lower station should be "diligent, humble, patient," and aware "that their more lowly path has been allotted to them by the hand of God." The wealthy, on the other hand, should be full of Christian charity, charity being one of "the conditions on which that station is conferred."[60]

That station and rank were providential and had rights and duties suffused the paternalist outlook of Paley and Sumner, as it did that of the Tories William Sewell, Michael Sadler, Robert Southey, Coleridge, and the writers for the *Quarterly Review, Blackwood's,* and *Fraser's.* It was preached from every pulpit, informed the rural press, and was even used in Parliament to defend the employment of women in coal mines and children in factories.[61] That inequality and high station should exist simply because God had ordained them might satisfy the deeply pious and the deferential, but for many others, it was necessary that such gradations and spheres be part of a harmonious scheme in which power and wealth promotes the good of all, a scheme that Providence has happily designed through mutual dependencies and an identity of interests. That such was the case formed the second assumption of the early Victorians' belief in a Divine Providence.

That design and harmony defines the world followed logically from the belief in an all-powerful God who was also infinitely wise and good. If God is both omnipotent and benevolent how could the world not be good? The great expositors of Divine Providence never doubted this consequence: "The infinite benevolence of the Supreme Being," wrote William Wilberforce, "loudly proclaims the principles of his moral government"; "God is good," asserted Abraham Tucker, and "orders all things for the best"; "the general laws of our system," disclosed Bishop Sumner, "evince that regard for the happiness of mankind which we call goodness in the Deity"; God combines, Chalmers told his congregation, "the separate interests of every individual . . . into a harmonious system . . . "; and the most read of all, Paley, said: "It is the will of God that the happiness of human life be promoted."[62]

Firmly supporting a belief in God's harmonious universe was the proposition, drawn from science and philosophy, that the world of nature was of marvelous design. Even the most otherworldly and devout could not resist the grand analogy between the precisely ordered nature of science and the hierarchically ordered world of human society, both reflecting the laws of Providence. The evangelical Wilberforce and the High Church Sewell, the Presbyterian Chalmers and the orthodox Sumner all invoked the physical laws of the universe as evidence of the wondrous designs of Providence. So did the more rational and philosophical, the Tuckers and Paleys, the Priestleys and Godwins, and the Scottish moral philosophers—Hutcheson,

Stewart, Mackintosh, and Brown, and their popularizers, George Ramsay, Samuel Spalding, and Jonathan Dymond. They all saw God's beneficence both in the extraordinary contrivances and superfecundity of nature and in the rational constitution of man. For the always positive Paley, it was not just the planets in their orbits but such "ingenious contrivances" as the "web feet of the fowl." Nature overflowed in a "myriad of happy beings," fish "so happy they leapt out of the water" and cats whose purring reflects "happiness no less than the playful kitten." Most extraordinary of all was the human body—"the pivot upon which the head turns . . . the socket of the hip joint, the pulley or trochlear muscles of the eye." All in all, "It is a happy world . . . the air, the earth, the water teem with delighted existence."[63]

Paley's hymn to the human body was still sung in the 1840s, even by the tough-minded *Economist*. After praising "Dr. Paley's eloquent and popular description of the human frame . . . all regulated by self-acting laws," it concluded that "the moral frame of society is not less perfect, nor less provided with self-acting regulation." It was a society that contained "a perfect system of natural law." The *Economist* also quoted George Combe to the effect that "God governs the world . . . through the organs and faculties of man."[64]

That human nature reflected God's designs, and that it was good and rational, characterized not only the phrenologist Combe's sanguine view that bumps on the skull reveal organs of "Benevolence" and "Veneration," but also the much more popular and defensible argument of the Scottish moral philosophers that man possesses an innate guide to right and wrong. For Sir James Mackintosh, it consisted of "an innate moral faculty"; for William Hutcheson, of "the dictates of a moral sense"; and for Dugald Stewart, of a moral faculty distinguished by "kind affections that are accompanied with an agreeable feeling." Thomas Brown, although he agreed with Paley's view of a harmonious and providential universe, could not abide his utilitarian ethics. In his *Lectures on Ethics* (1819), he believed that he had demolished Paley's "Selfish System," in which the greatest happiness is the moral yardstick.[65] Brown's *Lectures* were not only republished in 1846 but were popularized in George Ramsay's *Inquiry into the Principles of Human Happiness and Human Duty*, Samuel Spalding's *The Philosophy of Christian Morals* (both published in 1843), and Jonathan Dymond's *Morality* (1828). For Spalding, who quoted Brown extensively, the design of Providence shows that "goodness . . . pervades the whole of God's moral administration"; while for Ramsay, who called Brown the "most acute of philosophers," "every faculty, every feeling, every desire perform useful purposes." For Brown himself, "Nature . . . the world of social harmony which God made" had conferred on man such "noble powers" and such "benevolence" that he "will be eager to relieve every form of personal suffering."[66]

Although moral philosophers debated fiercely whether utility or a moral faculty determined right and wrong, there was remarkable agreement that a wise, omnipotent Providence ruled, that it did so through uniform natural laws, and that enlightened man would pursue the good. Very few accepted the two cynical arguments of Bernard de Mandeville's 1750 *Fable of the Bees* that virtuous acts themselves were done for vain and selfish reasons and that the pursuit of "private vices" resulted in "public virtue." Adam Smith, in his *Theory of Moral Sentiments*, condemned Mandeville's system as "wholly pernicious," but he nonetheless says in the *Wealth of Nations* that "it is not from the benevolence of the butcher, the brewer and the baker that we expect our dinner, but from their own interest." But for Smith it is not unchecked selfishness that should rule but an awareness that an identity of interests promotes the well-being of all. This awareness also appears in both the utilitarian and intuitionist systems and in those Christian moralities that are based on revelation.[67] But they almost all qualify self-interest by the words "enlightened" or "benevolent." Some were visibly worried about the economists' grosser appeals to selfishness. George Combe, who never doubted that political economy was part of God's natural law, still considered that both the economists in their studies and the capitalists in the marketplace were blind to the truth "that the world is arranged on the principle of the supremacy of the moral sentiments and intellect," a criticism that the Baptist editor Edward Miall also voiced in the *NonConformist*, a journal rivaled only by the *Economist* in its devotion to laissez-faire principles. The Presbyterian Thomas Chalmers, also a staunch believer in political economy and its identity of interests, agreed with Combe and Miall when he insisted that the "world is so constituted" that we are "physically happy" only if "morally right." The devout Chalmers also agreed with the evangelical Wilberforce's claim that though the "precepts of Christianity . . . are coincident with worldly interest," the "general weal" follows only when "the desire and aim of every individual [is] to fill well his own proper circle."[68]

For Combe, Miall, and Chalmers, there were deeper, wider, more compelling moral and providential laws than those that Smith, Ricardo, and Mill had discovered in the marketplace. It was a truth particularly apparent in those who popularized political economy. Moral far more than economic axioms mark the elementary lessons of Mrs. Marcet and Harriet Martineau. Mrs. Marcet's opening premise is a theological one: "God in his goodness had contrived everything so wisely as to suit the purpose of everyone," and Martineau, after doubting that political economy is a science, granted that it did help establish, "the grand truth that social affairs proceed according to great general laws no less than natural phenomenon."[69] Thomas Hodgskin taught that the "moral laws of nature [are] as invariable and unalterable as her physical laws"; John Hill Burton praised the "unalterable laws of human nature"; and Poulett Scrope celebrated the "contrivances of a beneficent Creator." These authors reflected, as did Marcet and Martineau, a larger, older, more pervasive, and more profound, belief in a harmonious order than that presented by the economists.[70]

It is a belief that even informs the *Wealth of Nations*. Adam Smith was a Scottish moral philosopher before he was a founder of political economy, and it was in his *Theory of Moral Sentiments* (1759) that he first used the term "invisible hand," referring to the belief that "the advancement of the private person will be the advantage of the publick," a claim made as early as 1656 by the Reverend Joseph Lee. It was a claim that the Reverend R. W. Hamilton, Leeds's famous Congregationalist, proclaimed in the 1840s. "There is no more inconsistency of . . . self-love with universal good," wrote Hamilton, "than of the daily rotation of our earth with the annual revolution around the sun."[71]

Good did seem quite universal to prosperous Victorians who shared Hamilton's optimistic view of Providence. But it did not lead them to deny evil. Indeed, a belief that evil was inevitable, widespread, ordained, and an ineradicable part of man constituted the early Victorians' third assumption about Divine Providence. Embarrassing to admit, this unpalatable truth did follow from the first assumption, namely, that an omnipotent God had created and ordained every existing thing, the cruel, ugly, and harsh as well as the merciful, beautiful, and generous. For the literal providentialist who emphasized an omnipotent God's unlimited powers, evil was inevitable. Illness, infirmity, disease, famine, plagues, floods, and shipwrecks all came from the hand of God, just as surely as did toil, poverty, hunger, homelessness, crime, drunkenness, riots, and wars. For the rationalists, who saw Providence in the harmonious laws of nature, these prolific evils proved more perplexing. In reconciling ubiquitous evil with an all-powerful God, the strictly pious could cite three arguments: that God's ways are inscrutable, that the final reckoning comes in Heaven, and that the scriptures reveal evil. "O! how small a part of the universal creation of God," exclaimed William Wilberforce, "does He allow us to see." It makes us, he added, "wholly incompetent to judge of the scheme of his infinite wisdom." Abraham Tucker, in his long chapter on "Providence" shared this view. "We can not," he confessed, "penetrate into the secret purpose of God." But Tucker's diffidence did not discourage his search for the ways of Providence. In a lengthy argument, he showed that since God's "bounty flows alike upon all . . . there must be an exact equality of fortune," an argument he could complete only by asserting that "at some future time all will be balanced."[72] It was a view that many clergymen used to explain evil, just as they were also quick to cite God's incomprehensibility, the sinfulness of man, and the judgments of the Bible. To zealous evangelicals, devout High Churchmen, and the moderately orthodox, the Bible made it clear that evil came from sin. Their writings are full of allusions to "the curse of human nature," "our fallen race," "doomed man," "our fallen lot," "the sin of Adam," and "man's depravity"—full, too, of the Bible's solemn pronouncements: from Genesis, "In the sweat of his face he shall eat bread"; from Job, "the bread of adversity and the water of affliction"; from Proverbs, "for the drunkard and the glutton shall come poverty"; from St. Paul, "if he would not work, neither shall he eat"; and from Deuteronomy, and the most cited of all, "the poor shall never cease out of the land."[73] It formed a universal refrain that reveals how deep and wide was the conviction that poverty was inevitable. Surrounded by millions living in destitution, confronted by unprecedented population growth, aware of Malthus's gloomy prognosis, and utterly perplexed as to remedies, most members of the governing classes believed that poverty was truly ordained by God.

Some of those who saw poverty as inevitable felt, however, that it was not so evil. Were not the poor as happy as the rich, and was not poverty receding before an inexorable, providential progress? "A labourer with wages," the Reverend George Croly told readers of *Blackwood's*, "is virtually as rich as the owner of £100,000 a year." "They are happy," wrote the Reverend Legh Richmond in his very popular *The Dairyman's Daughter*, because they are "healthy and clean . . . [eat] the bread of honest industry," and surpass the rich by "true piety and grace . . . [and] Godliness and contentment." The poor, claimed William Wilberforce, facing fewer temptations than the rich and enjoying "food and raiment" are favored above others "by the blessings of Providence [and] true religion," a view that Thomas Chalmers shared when he insisted "that the humble life may be just as rich in moral grace and moral grandeur as the loftier places of society." Croly, Legh Richmond, Wilberforce, and Chalmers were all intensely religious and thus saw the poor as happy largely in terms of "true piety" and "moral grace."[74] Providentialists of a more secular turn also saw them quite as happy in worldly terms. William Paley, the inveterate optimist, was convinced that "happiness is pretty equally distributed," a view Adam Smith shared. Paley argued that laborers are happier than the rich, because they have no worries about placing their children in good positions. He also pointed out, in his *Natural Theology*, that they had nightly rest, daily bread, health, and the pleasure of the use of their limbs and senses. Their bread and cheese also gave as much pleasure as the dainties of the rich.[75] John Bird Sumner added that even distress is not so burdensome, since "habit and the elastic adaptation of the mind" made misfortunes less

onerous: it "equalizes the apparent qualities . . . and blunts the edge of imag-
ined hardship." It was a smug view that led to the even bolder claim that, not
only was evil less extensive than it appeared, but "evil itself was a necessary
part of Providence's grand scheme."[76] It was an old argument. In 1774, Tucker
had argued that evil was "so interwoven with good that one cannot be had
without the other." Paley explained how evil worked in his famous, to some
infamous, tale of the 100 pigeons. If 99 of them, he wrote, worked long and
hard picking corn, and received only chaff and refuse, "while an idle one, the
weakest, perhaps the worst" received the rest, and if also a hungry pigeon, for
stealing one grain, was torn apart, "you should see nothing more than what is
established among men." The realistic Paley then insisted that inequality of
property was "an evil," but "an evil . . . which follows from those rules concerning the acquisition . . . of property by which men are incited to industry
and by which the object of their industry is rendered secure."[77] John Bird
Sumner, who praised Paley's ingenious reconciliation of good and evil, carried it even further by the use of Malthus's law of population. Like Paley and
Tucker, Sumner found that evil formed a necessary trial, an invaluable
stimulant, and, befitting his Christian convictions, a chastening experience—
all of which formed character and excited industry and furthered virtue. Because of the "proneness of the mind to sink into languid indolence" and of
people to multiply mindlessly, God wisely brought forth the law of inexorable
population increase and from it "the division of property," both of which
stimulated industry, promoted the arts, and led to civilization, all part of
those natural laws by which Providence uses evil to produce good.[78]

That natural law was a part of the scheme of Providence even the most rational of moral philosophers accepted. The Unitarian Dr. Southwood Smith,
in *Divine Government,* assumed the existence of "an intelligent, all powerful,
wise and good Providence," for whom, "evil is the means of producing incalculable good," while Spalding, in *The Philosophy of Christian Morals,* saw in
physical suffering itself "the means by which divine benevolence accom-
plishes his purpose of goodness."[79] That evil should be accepted as a necessary
part of the scheme of Providence certainly did not encourage comprehensive
efforts at its removal. Such a belief, combined with the conviction that society's institutions were ordained by God and that the laws governing them
were harmonious and self-acting, could not but lead to the claim that England's existing laissez-faire society was itself providential.

That a laissez-faire society formed part of God's grand design was the
fourth widespread assumption about Providence. It was an assumption that
permeated the periodicals, sermons, and parliamentary debates of the 1840s,
as it did those classics by Burke, Paley, Sumner, Wilberforce, and Chalmers

that helped form the outlook of the early Victorians. It was a view of Providence that saw government as the protector of life and property and the guardian of order and morals, but not as an active, reforming, assuaging agent. That God had ordained all existing institutions and that such institutions were already part of a deeply-rooted laissez-faire society, one that rested, as Burke insisted, on hallowed prescriptions, only made such a laissez-faire society the more sacred, venerable, and inviolable. And that natural laws of divine origin identified private interests with the public good only made the intrusion of government less necessary, as did the belief that evil was an inevitable part of sinful man's destiny.

Burke and Paley certainly found in the designs of Providence few schemes for more government. The Burke who had invoked Providence's "unalterable relations" not only insisted that "it was not within the competence of government to supply the poor [with] those necessaries which it pleased Divine Providence . . . to withhold," but also demanded that "farmers, traders, speculators, factors, should be left to their free course," and that the poor should practice "patience, labour, frugality and religion." Paley was no more anxious for reform. He condemned "incessant, universal, indefatigable activity."[80] The sanguine Sumner, like the cheerful Paley, found in Providence such a "wonderful subserviency of appointed means to the accomplishment of some uniform design" that he even found the employment of eight- and nine-year-olds in cotton mills healthy and necessary, and in a chapter on "The Capabilities of Improvement," he saw in the voluntarism of friendly societies, Church of England schools, and savings banks the best possible remedy for poverty.[81] The somber Wilberforce would not have dissented. As pessimistic about inevitable evil as Sumner was optimistic about society's natural laws, he did agree that the answer to social grievances lay with the stewardship of the rich. Distrusting "the fabrications of man . . . [as] clumsy, weak and contradictory" when compared to "the work of the Supreme Being," he concluded that the general weal is best produced when each individual did his duties in "his proper circle." Thomas Chalmers carried further the idea of the stewardship of the rich with an even greater emphasis on the individual and locality and an even greater distrust of government—even urging the end of all compulsory poor relief. "The legislature and . . . her intermeddling," wrote Chalmers, "always mars and never mediates."[82] In Wilberforce and Chalmers, a deep belief in Providence did not mean inaction or even the more complacent acquiescence of Burke and Paley, but led, on the contrary, to strenuous activity, Wilberforce to end slavery and reform morals and Chalmers to lessen poverty in Glasgow and bring evangelical truth to England. Neither did Wilberforce disdain acts of Parliament against slavery as Chalmers did any law to redress poverty. Yet Wilberforce's wider distrust of "man's fabrications" and his faith in stewardship remained part of the evangelical tradition that, in trusting Christian virtue and the designs of Providence, distrusted government.

In the 1840s, the evangelical Hugh M'Neil said of the Irish famine, "it is only by the power of God himself that the calamity can be removed."[83] The sermons of the evangelicals were not alone in seeing the answers to social evils in God's designs and not in the government's interference. The High Church Reverend Francis Paget argued that "if the country is to be saved at all it will be saved by something different from . . . [either] Acts of Parliament or guinea subscriptions," a sentiment that the Reverend Arthur Martineau echoed when he concluded that "the only remedy [to social distress] under Providence . . . was that every man in his appointed station do his duty."[84]

Tories preached the same message in their periodicals and debates in Parliament. *Blackwood's*, the *Quarterly Review*, *Fraser's*, the *Leeds Intelligencer*, and the *Leeds Conservative Journal* were all Tory, all convinced of Providence's wisdom, and all distrustful of government. "With landlords," wrote *Fraser's* in discussing social distress, "much more than with government . . . rests the grave duty of devising some cure." "Do your best," it added, "and leave the rest to Providence," a view shared by the *Leeds Intelligencer* and the *Leeds Conservative Journal*. Since the cure of distress, wrote the *Intelligencer*, is "beyond the reach of human power," it is "to God alone we look for present relief." "There is in connexion with our manufacturing system a whole train of evils which," argued the *Conservative Journal*, "can only be averted by a special Providence." A week later, the *Journal* also said that many of these "evils which beset our manufacturing population [are] those legislation can neither grapple with, nor cure."[85]

In Parliament, distress both in Ireland and England evoked the same sentiments. "Providence had willed it," said the Irish M.P. Joseph Napier of the famine, a view that the home secretary, Sir George Grey, in urging, in 1847, a Day of National Fast, found "in accordance with the opinion of the present day." Not all, however, would go so far as the Irish landlord Augustus Stafford O'Brien, who, in 1849, concluded that "it was out of the power of the government to deal with so great a calamity." Indeed, legislation, said Stafford had only "aggravated" evils coming from "the visitation of Providence." God's hand was also seen in the country's blessings as well as in its calamities. For George Palmer, its bountiful crops were evidence of the "Providence of God" and as such dictated that man leave untouched those corn laws that protected them. To end those laws, or to pass any legislation, concluded the Tory Viscount Pollington, would "only touch the surface of social evil." Parliament, he added, should instead, "rely on other modes . . . thrown up by Providence."[86]

For most Tories, raised on Burke, those "other modes" seldom varied much from the British status quo, which was not only ordained by God but, unlike those in Austria or Russia, was relatively free of government intervention and had been so for some time. An actual laissez-faire (domestic order and foreign wars excepted) thus formed a traditional, customary, and not inconsiderable part of the early Victorian vision of a laissez-faire society.

There had, of course, long been government intervention through a national mercantilism and a local J.P. paternalism, but a mercantilism and paternalism designed to accommodate and favor the rights of property. It was also a mercantilism in decline before free trade and a paternalism that did not extend to Britain's burgeoning cities and towns. Contemporaries spoke, and spoke correctly, of two different "old" systems, that which regulated trade and morals, suppressed disorder, and fought wars, and that which protected property rights and English liberties—local, corporate, and individual. Each system faced new and challenging forces, whether from political economy's laissez-faire axioms or from the new protectionism of ten-hour acts and health boards. But although there were two differing "old" systems, most contemporaries judged property rights and English liberties to be the most entrenched and general. "Non-interference was the old system," announced Earl Fitzwilliam, one "which ought never have been departed from." The Whig Radical M.P. Charles Buller was for departing from it, since that old system had "contented itself with protecting property . . . [and had] shrunk from giving its protection to the poor." Tories, as well as Whigs, agreed that non-interference was the true "old" system. In 1839, Disraeli opposed both the Whig government's Police Bill and its education scheme. In a speech opposing the education scheme, after raising the horrors of Prussian despotism, he boasted that the "State in England had not formed a single road, made a single bridge, or dug a single canal" and declared that earlier statesmen "had always acted on a system diametrically opposed."[87] The "diametrically opposed" system was a product of that eighteenth century that saw the spread of a belief in laissez-faire doctrines and the growth of more latitudinarian attitudes. While Abraham Tucker was rejoicing that "happy Britain" had snapped short "the iron rod of despotic sway" and enjoyed "glorious liberty," the poet Oliver Goldsmith proclaimed "How small a part of their present weal and woe is the part which laws or kings can cure," a quintessential eighteenth-century aphorism that was often quoted in early Victorian periodicals. For Edmund Burke, it was the French, not the British monarchy that relied on a surfeit of laws and kings, a monarchy whose "leading vice" was a "restless desire of governing too much."[88]

For many Tories, those English liberties that contrasted so sharply with the despotisms of continental monarchies reflected a special dispensation of Providence, which had also ordained that property and rank should rule. While Tories insisted that God had, above all, ordained property and rank, Whigs and Liberals adopted a different view of Providence, one that emphasized those immutable and self-regulating natural laws by which the all-wise and all powerful Creator governed the physical and social worlds. It was a view expressed in Parliament quite as often and unreservedly as the Tory view, and it formed quite as sound a foundation for a laissez-faire society. To the Whig Viscount Howicke, free trade was "the order appointed by Providence" and was much wiser than "the clumsy contrivance of legislation." For Richard Cobden, the Corn Laws violated "the law of God and Nature," a phrase he took from Burke, and one that Sir James Graham also used after his conversion to free trade in corn.[89]

The same view of providentially established laws—rational, harmonious, benevolent, inviolable, and immutable—appeared in Unitarian and Congregational sermons, in liberal periodicals, and in the popular writings of Cobden's friend George Combe.

There was, of course, not a little of political economy in this rational view of Providence. But it was only a part, and that a subordinate one, of a larger philosophical concept of a universe governed by God's inexorable natural laws, a concept far older and far more widely held than political economy. It was an integral part of popular social attitudes in the 1840s. It even formed the wider framework of the economic writings of Mountifort Longfield, Richard Jones, Poulett Scrope, and Thomas Hodgskin (to name only a few of the economists).[90] It was a belief that, along with the more theological views of an inscrutable, arbitrary and intervening Providence, filled more sermons, more books, more pamphlets, and more periodicals than did the drier axioms of the economists. In its many ways it played a more pervasive role in forming the early Victorians' vision of laissez-faire society than did political economy. The only set of doctrines that was as widespread and popular were those moral precepts that defined the enormously popular doctrine of self-reliance.

CHAPTER 7

Self-Reliance

The early Victorians had considerable faith in political economy's invisible hand, in the harmonious workings of Divine Providence, and in the sacredness of property. But despite this faith, poverty and social misery refused to go away. Some even claimed that they increased as towns and manufactures increased, or as bad harvests, wars, and trade crises exercised their baleful influences. In the face of widespread poverty and social misery were not their hopes in a laissez-faire society overly optimistic? Most early Victorians thought not. Poverty, squalor, and wretchedness did abound, to be sure, and did reflect the shortcomings of their trust in political economy and of their faith in a Providence that was not always beneficent and a property that was not always just. But whatever those shortcomings, they believed that the social ills that did persist could still be better met by the self-reliant energies of the industrious and provident and by the benevolence of the well-off than by any action of an inept and meddling government.

The self-reliance of the poor would lessen poverty and squalor or mitigate its impact even more than the benevolence of the rich, since benevolence itself was so often corrupting. Because so much of poverty and misery resulted from the failings of individuals, would not the reform of those failings, rather than bungling legislation and corrupting charities, provide the best remedy? In early Victorian England, that opinion was nearly universal. The doctrines of self-reliance did not begin with the publication of Samuel Smiles's *Self Help* in 1859, and neither were they the sole preserve of Liberals and Radicals. They were also part and parcel of paternalist thought.

PATERNALISM AND SELF-RELIANCE

While the belief that the source of social evils lies in the individual and that its redress lies in the individual's reform did not form as prominent a part of the paternalist outlook as did a belief in the rights and duties of prop-

erty, it was still quite pervasive. Paternalist theorists, journalists, and clergymen never tired of ascribing destitution and distress to indolence and improvidence and of finding its answer in the industry and frugality of the
poor. For Oxford's William Sewell, the paternalists' most productive theo-
rist, the poor were "poor through folly and indolence and sin." Since "the
relief of the civil power is corrupting," since "the relief of promiscuous benevolence will only ruin the work," and since the apostle had said, "If they
will not work, neither let them eat," Sewell consigned "the indolent and
worthless . . . to jail houses of poverty."[1] *Blackwood's* George Croly was no
less preoccupied with individual failing. That employment was often "pre-
carious" only evoked his stern admonition that "men should be prudent and
be prepared for . . . precariousness." Since Croly judged a poor law a "direct
contradiction to the principle that man should be provident," his advice was
"less gin and tobacco, no improvident marriages, and fewer indulgences of
an idle life." "Reform yourself!" proclaimed *Blackwood's* a year later, citing
Thomas Carlyle, "and the nation will be reformed."[2]

Most journals of the paternalist persuasion agreed that individual failings
caused and individual reform lessened poverty and misery. Since "idleness
and incapacity are the roots of [poverty]," *Fraser's* argued, only "by cleanliness, sobriety, order, economies and careful and anxious foresight can the
workers' condition be improved." "Poverty, like most social evils," argued
the Tory *Morning Post,* "exists because men follow their brute instincts."
This fact led the *Post* to warn the poor not to "rely on the assistance of governments independently of their own exertions." That an economic depression caused poverty did not faze the editors of the Tory *Morning Herald,*
which argued that even the revival of trade "depends more upon the working
classes themselves than upon any measure which the legislature can take."[3]
The Peelite *Morning Chronicle* in 1849 was even pithier and more grandilo-
quent in placing responsibility on the individual. "The mass of poverty is inevitable," it announced, "until habits of industry, forethought, frugality,
[and] enlightened self-restraint shall regulate the conduct of the whole human race."[4]

Anglican clergymen also sought social betterment through individual reform. Convinced of the massiveness of Adam's curse, they sought social improvement in the individual's triumph over sin. After assuring his congregation that "the poor are, for the most part, answerable for their abject poverty," the Reverend Charles Girdelstone concluded: "Nothing can effectually
help them without their earnestly endeavoring to help themselves."[5] It was a
sentiment shared by the High Church Reverend William Gresley, the moderate Reverend Sydney Godolphin Osborne, and the Broad Church Henry

Melville. What, they asked, caused poverty? "Improvidence and want of self denial," said Gresley; "habits of waste and extravagance," asserted Osborne; "the bread of idleness," opined Melville. Although unable to agree on theology, the three joined the evangelical Reverend John Saunders in the belief that a poor man was "the architect of his own independence; and that by industry, sobriety, and providence . . . he may . . . ward off pauperism."[6]

None of these calls for the poor to be self-reliant disturbed their bishops, who also lived in a theological world and a propertied society in which individual sin and the faults of a brutish populace were perceived as underlying social evils. "Indigence is seldom experienced," said John Bird Sumner, bishop of Chester, "except as a consequence of vice," an opinion justifying the bishop of Norwich's insistence that "it is through Christian knowledge only that we can hope to see the social and political condition . . . purified and perfected." For those in poverty, insisted Richard Whatley, archbishop of Dublin, such a purification required "habits of forethought and frugality," and for the bishops of London, Ely, Chichester, and Ripon, "their own exertions," "early habits of order," "self-reform," "principles of industry, diligence, frugality, regularity and obedience," and "the training up of . . . all their children in the way they should go."[7] Not even the High Church *Christian Remembrancer* could find fault with these admonitions to self-help, which reflected the basic assumptions of most Anglicans, namely, that because "all human evil arises from human depravity, so the only searching remedy . . . is to cure the common root."

Ascribing social evils to depravity and bad habits had both a long history and a bright future: both seventeenth-century Puritans and twentieth-century Thatcherites told the poor that much of their poverty was due to their own shortcomings. But although the core of the doctrine of self-reliance possesses a centuries-long continuity, the extent to which it was carried out varied. Most eighteenth-century, but fewer Victorian, paternalists, shared Daniel Defoe's and Arthur Young's view that low wages were necessary in order to spur the poor to industry, while high wages only encouraged indolence and insubordination. The eighteenth century was more static and less wealthy than the nineteenth century; its hierarchies were more stable, its population (until the 1780s) was less expansive, and its urban growth (London excepted) was less dynamic. Its sterner paternalists distrusted the education of the masses and grand schemes of amelioration. The self-reliance that they felt necessary involved a stoical endurance of adversity. "Patience, labor, sobriety, frugality, and religion should be recommended to [the poor]," declared Edmund Burke, "all the rest is downright fraud."[8]

There were early Victorian paternalists who shared this static view of a working class that must be industrious, long-suffering, and patient. Thomas Moseley, the ardent Tractarian editor of the *British Critic*, judged the harsh lot of the poor to be "a necessary discipline." "Nothing but the deepest and bitterest poverty," he insisted, "will subdue the uneducated classes."[9] Although devout, Bible-reading Anglican clergymen were not alone in invoking St. Paul's injunction "If they will not work, neither let them eat," most paternalists much preferred more general formulations such as "The poor shall never cease out of the land" (Deut. 15:11) and "In the sweat of thy face shalt thou eat bread" (Gen. 3:19). Most Victorians would let even the laziest eat, if only the bread and gruel of the workhouse. Most also accepted, if only in theory, Adam Smith's argument that higher wages produced a more skilled and industrious working class. Economic growth had made eighteenth-century pessimism less fashionable. Tory paternalists like Robert Southey could now claim that when England adopted a system of national education, "poverty will be diminished, and want will disappear in proportion as the lower classes are instructed in their duties." For Southey, "a moral and religious education will induce habits of industry, just as the new savings banks would engender habits of frugality.[10]

Quite as enthusiastic for the integration of self-reliance with paternalism were two of the most widely read of Christian paternalists, the Reverend Thomas Chalmers and John Bird Sumner. Both broke with eighteenth-century attitudes, Chalmers by insisting on "the natural equality between man and man" and by urging that the poor be enlightened and Sumner by denying Dr. Johnson's claim that evil preponderates. He asserted instead that God works through "the medium of pleasure instead of the operation of pain." For Sumner, the Gospel "elevates the general character" of all. These two evangelicals saw in Christianity a reforming power that few in the eighteenth century would have held it to be. Chalmers praised "the transforming power of religious education," since it led "to self command . . . [and] habits of frugality and good conduct." For Sumner, man was "endowed with the noblest faculty . . . improvable reason." Sumner's *Records of Creation* (1818; 3d ed., 1840) is suffused, not only with a sense of the goodness of God and the harmony of His laws, but with a faith in savings banks and in that Madras system of schooling in which one teacher taught 150 pupils self-reliance. "An indefinite capacity of improvement," he announced, "opens before us." A similar optimism suffuses the description in Chalmer's *The Christian and Civic Economy* of his work at St. John's parish in Glasgow with its schools, chapels, elders, deacons, district visitors, lay helpers, and benefit societies, all voluntary, all reforming, all promoting self-reliance.[11]

The optimism of Chalmers, Sumner, and Southey had its limits—limits at times so exacting that they seem to contradict that optimism. Chalmers, a self-confessed Tory, did see in Christianity a transforming power. But as a Calvinist still not free from a belief in predestination, he never doubted man's sinfulness. For Chalmers, evil was as universal as the *viz inertia* of matter. For Sumner, poverty had its origins in "the curse pronounced upon the first transgressor," a curse that doomed the earth to "bring forth thorn and thistles" and man to eat bread by the sweat of his brow. Chalmers and Sumner were as ardent in their Malthusianism as they were in their evangelicalism, which only deepened the tension between their pessimism and optimism. Like the curse God had pronounced on Adam, Malthus's inexorable law doomed multiplying man to abject poverty. But not quite. Not if men heeded Malthus's exhortation to make fewer, later, and more provident marriages. In facing the curse of original sin and the specter of overpopulation, there could be no remedy that did not depend on the self-reliant individual.

That man was sinful and procreated abundantly also required that society be authoritarian, hierarchical, and propertied. Chalmers wanted "no great change in the external aspects of society," and Sumner never faltered in his belief that inequality was "an ordinance of Providence" and "the foundation of civilized society." Most paternalists in the 1840s shared only Chalmers's and Sumner's conservative assumptions. They were hesitant about encouraging self-reliance as a means of rising above one's sphere or of elevating an entire class. They saw no way to end poverty or to earn bread but by the sweat of the brow. They sought only the self-improvement that would make those appointed to sweat and poverty more industrious, law-abiding, and long enduring. Deference and respect were expected, not defiance and ambition. And if they occasionally urged independence, it was independence of the poor rates, not of their master.[12]

It was a confined view of self-reliance, one that found its plainest expression in the speeches at agricultural association dinners that accompanied the granting of prizes to virtuous, long-enduring farm laborers. In Wiltshire, the Reverend Mr. Austin gave forty-two prizes, many of them "for having brought up large families of children by their own exertion"; in Suffolk, the duke of Grafton gave two pounds to an eighty-two-year-old father of nine for never going on the rates "except when flour was dear"; and in Sussex, the duke of Richmond called such prizes a powerful "stimulus to honest industry." They encouraged, Richmond added, "sobriety, honesty and obedience." The marquis of Camden claimed that prizes "excited them to rely on their own resources for support and not to depend on others for relief."[13] All such prizes, concluded *Fraser's,* "improve habits of forethought."

The paternalist press and pulpit also promoted a formula of self-reliance that emphasized deference and obedience as well as frugality and industry. They exhorted the poor to practice "piety, morality, industry and obedience," "obedience to law, patient industry and quiet endurance of tribulation"; and "deference, obedience, duty, patient endurance, humbleness."[14]

To help the poor practice these deferential virtues, and so to eradicate the root cause of poverty and distress—the failings of the individual—paternalists promoted savings banks, benefit societies, clubs for clothing, coal, and blankets, and, most hopefully, allotments—all institutions aimed at encouraging the individual to be self-reliant. Saving banks would promote "habits of dignity, energy, and independence," proclaimed Dr. Duncan of the Scottish village of Ruthwell, who published an effusive account of the wondrous effect of his savings bank in 1816 and won great praise in the next three decades. Robert Southey extolled savings banks in his essays for the *Quarterly Review,* and the Reverend Legh Richmond gave them prominence in his *Dairyman's Daughter,* a portrait of paternal benevolence that ran to some twenty-four editions by 1866.[15] The Reverend Godolphin Osborne also championed savings banks, but not alone; in his *Hints to the Charitable* (1838), he urged the establishment of a parish coal club, a penny clothing club, a benefit club to help the ill—all of which would teach providence and frugality. And crowning all such efforts would be quarter-acre allotments to promote industry. For many, its impact would be miraculous.[16] "It can not help but call forth habits of prudence and forethought," exclaimed the *Sussex Agricultural Express*; "habits of privation and self-control—of prudence, foresight and frugality," added *Blackwood's;* "habits of industry," echoed the *Morning Herald,* and habits that kept men from public houses. It turned the "drunkard," declared the *Salisbury Journal,* "into a more steady worker.[17]

To the above institutions for developing self-reliance nearly all early Victorians added the parish Sunday school and the schools of the Church's National Society. But although less fearful of educating the people than their eighteenth-century forefathers, they still felt that education should be limited largely to instruction in reading, the catechism, and the morality of deference. They wished to encourage no undue ambition. They did not see in self-reliance a ladder upwards. They wanted a self-reliance that aimed at correcting sin, overcoming indolence, diminishing improvidence, stopping drunkenness, lessening extravagance, and checking imprudence—all those vices that led to dependence on poor relief and trouble in the parish. They believed that dependence on parish relief also further corrupted the poor, a supposed corruption that made paternalists and many others the enemies of the old Poor Law and the friends of the new one.

THE NEW POOR LAW

On May 16, 1834, on the second reading of the Poor Law Amendment Bill, the House of Commons voted favorably 319 to 20. It was an act that imposed a new system of central commissioners and poor law unions on the old system of magistrates and parishes. A more severe and uniform relief was also to replace the generous allowances and lax administration that many claimed turned the industrious poor into paupers. The famous report of the Royal Commission of 1832-34 urged the central commissioners to insist that throughout all England, no able-bodied man or woman was to receive relief unless he or she and their family entered a workhouse—there, it later ensued, to be separated, man from wife, children from parents. The New Poor Law also made it more difficult for mothers of bastards to have the putative father pay for the upkeep of the child, a severity adopted in order to teach young girls, whom it made responsible for the upkeep of the child, to guard their chastity. The New Poor Law of 1834 was not a mere amending act; it was a revolutionary one, one that established a new, centralized, structure and inspired a much sterner policy. Although it infringed on those local interests that defined paternalism and made the poor laws more severe, it passed overwhelmingly. Only two Tories opposed its second reading, and only one county member. And in 1842, when Peel's Tory government continued this Whig act, support was again overwhelming: 260 to 61, with Radicals more numerous than Tories in the 61. The vote cut across party lines; supporting it were Radicals like Roebuck, Grote, and Hume, Tories like Miles, Packington, and Knight, and Liberals like Ward, Philips, and Gisborne. Only Radicals deeply sympathetic to the working classes and relatively untouched by political economy, such as Fielden, Wakley, and Duncombe, and eccentric Tories, such as Sibthorp, voted consistently against it.[18] But such Radicals and Tories never had the numbers to significantly amend the New Poor Law. They could not even get Parliament to denounce the workhouse test, even though many local authorities had quietly and unobtrusively modified it.

One of the principal reasons for Parliament's overwhelming passage and continuance of the New Poor Law was the nearly unanimous belief that the poor must be self-reliant. "The principle of the new law," said the wisest of London's weeklies, the *Spectator*, "is to force self-reliance on the distressed by ... the meanest scale in a sort of prison."[19] There were, of course, other reasons: the ideas of political economy, fear of rural violence, a desire to replace administrative chaos with administrative order, and a desire for lower rates. To many a critic, the political economists were the villains. Malthus favored abolishing the Poor Law, although gradually, so great was his dread of a flood of paupers reducing all to misery. For some of Malthus's followers, that dread only led to a greater ardor for the workhouse test. The economists' wage fund was also invoked: all relief not requiring one to enter the workhouse squandered the limited fund of capital needed for wages. There was also a basic laissez-faire belief that individual enterprise and free markets, not paternalistic magistrates and meddling vestries, best governed society.[20]

Just as widespread as the veneration of political economy was a fear of rural disorder. The Captain Swing riots of 1830 and 1831 in the south and east were but the largest and most violent of a series of early nineteenth-century outbursts of an angry, exploited, discontented, rick-burning peasantry; a peasantry, many claimed, full of false expectations engendered by an easy, lax, overly generous Poor Law. Only a stern, efficient, disciplining law, said the Whig ministers Melbourne, Althorp, Lansdowne, and Richmond, could grapple with mounting rural violence. Many in Parliament and on county benches agreed, hence the New Poor Law.[21]

Other critics saw chaos in the countryside but less in riots and rick burnings than in a hopelessly anarchic system based on 15,553 parishes and a vast multitude of parish officers and magistrates, each with his own privileges, prejudices, and inconsistencies. It was a system full of abuses, not just of overly generous allowances, but of graft, peculation, cruelty, favoritism, arbitrariness, irresponsibility, and confused accounts, or no accounts at all—a system not only abhorrent to the well-ordered minds of Benthamites but to all those who sought the more rational and ordered society that economic progress, political reform, and the march of mind all promised. It was a social and intellectual force that expressed itself in many local poor law experiments and in a flood of pamphlets, a progressive force that led the Reformed Parliament, elected in 1832, to pass prison, factory, municipal, lunacy, education, tithes, enclosures, and ecclesiastical reforms.[22]

Another reason—perhaps the most important—for the passing of the New Poor Law was simply the desire for lower rates. "Landowners in Parliament" observed the *Manchester Guardian* in 1842, "have refused to repeal the Poor Law Amendment Act as it saves them £2,000,000 in poor rates a year."[23] Many dressed up the bluntly selfish cry for lower rates in the apparently disinterested cry "Property endangered," and so, of course, civilized society itself.[24]

Although the above forces played distinct roles in the passage and continuance of the New Poor Law, none was as frequently expressed as the moral argument that the old laws corrupted and the New Law would reform the pauper. The frequency of that argument is abundantly evident not only in the report of the Royal Commission of 1832-34 and in parliamentary debates but in the annual reports of the poor law commissioners, in the press's endless accounts, and in the testimony of seven assistant poor law commissioners appearing before the Select Committee on the Poor Law of 1837 and 1838. As one of them, D. G. Adey, told the committee, before the New Poor Law, there was "constant idleness" and after it "never . . . idling about."[25]

In these many reports, debates, editorials, and hearings the ideas of the economists are not very prominent. Malthus was, in fact, never mentioned in the Commons, and only once, by Lord Brougham, in the Lords. It was a brief mention, one quite buried in his larger moral argument that the old laws encouraged "idleness, vice, and profligacy."[26] No other member of Parliament mentioned Malthus or his law of population, nor did any of the 187 witnesses before the Select Committee, or, strangely enough, any of the three poor law commissioners or their assistants and hundreds of local officials.

Ricardo's theory of a wage fund did little better than Malthus on population—only one assistant commissioner, E. C. Tufnell, in 1838, uses it and then only briefly before a lengthy disquisition on the moral corruptions of beer shops and the great need for the "improvement of character."[27] Not specific doctrines so much as a general belief in a free market for free laborers characterizes the economists' contribution; a contribution whereby a deep belief in self-reliance strengthened the early Victorians' vision of a laissez-faire society.

A fear of rural violence and a passion for administrative order are also weakly expressed in the debates, editorials, hearings, and reports in support of the New Poor Law. The very cabinet that supposedly feared rural riots— Melbourne, Althorp, Lansdowne, and Richmond—never pushed forward the bill, drawn up for them in 1832, that called for a provincial police, a measure certain to arouse Parliament's hostility, as in fact it did when a watered-down version of it came up in 1839. Neither witnesses before the Select Committee nor editors of provincial papers expressed a fear of riots as their principal reason for supporting the New Poor Law. Far more compelling was their anxiety to end the moral corruption of individual paupers. The same conclusion also holds for the desire for a centralized, orderly, rational administration. It was certainly an important concern to those who constituted the Royal Commission and most particularly to the Benthamite Edwin Chadwick and the Whig economist Nassau Senior, the actual authors of the 1834 report. Not political economy, writes Nassau Senior's biographer, Marian Bowley, but the "ideal of individual freedom and responsibility" led to the New Poor Law.[28] Once established, the centralization aspect of the Poor Law was, in the press and Parliament, far more often condemned than praised. But although verbally abused, it was also quietly accepted, since it did save ratepayers £2,000,000 a year.

Many, of course, did speak for the New Poor Law and most often because it was morally good for the poor. Although the suspicion remains that such moral concerns were in part a rationalization of a desire for lower rates, it is still a fact that no reason for the passage and for the continuance of the New Poor Law can compare in frequency and urgency of utterance with the conviction that the poor must be disciplined, improved, and reformed—in short, made self-reliant.

Of the 20 who opposed the second reading of the New Poor Law in 1834, only two were Tories; of the 61 who opposed its renewal in 1842, only 27 came from the some 355 Tories who dominated the Commons.[29] Peel and Graham and the front bench were its stout defenders. Peel was convinced that "indiscriminant relief has the lamentable effect of destroying habits of self-reliance and of discouraging industry" and Graham that the law's renewal was necessary so that the poor may be "rendered . . . a moral . . . industrious and provident labourer in contradistinction from the idle and improvident."[30]

The front bench were Peelites not a little steeped in political economy. But what of the back benchers, many of whom detested the "dismal science"? They too, although largely in silence, voted for the severe law. The model paternalist, Sir John Packington, told the Commons that "while the Old Poor Law demoralized," the New Law "promoted the welfare of the working classes." Even his fellow ultra Tory George Bankes, who condemned the law's centralization, would not "deny the general principle," a principle that another ultra, Gally Knight, admired, since it meant training "the poor to habits of providence, sobriety and independence."[31]

The moral conviction that the old laws corrupted the poor and that the new law would lessen that corruption kept theorists of paternalism and the Tory press alike from a full-scale denunciation of a law whose centralization they detested. Michael Sadler called the old laws "a great demoralizer," and his biographer, R. H. Seely, considered the imposition of the workhouse test on vagrants "quite right."[32] *Fraser's* shared Sadler's dislike of the old law, "whereby pauperism and vice, indolence and imposition were encouraged." The Tory *John Bull* approved of the New Poor Law for refusing to place the idle and improvident . . . on the same footing with the industrious and frugal."[33] *Blackwood's*, reflecting its Scottish home base, would have no poor law at all, since such laws not only "extinguish discipline" but "[take] from the drunkard, the idler and the profligate that only human guard against their vices." And finally the Tory *Quarterly Review*, in 1835 greeted the New Poor Law with an enthusiastic account by Sir Francis Bond Head, an assistant poor law commissioner, describing the wonders that it worked in promoting a more self-reliant laboring class.[34]

That Parliament's view of the poor and the New Poor Law was couched so often in moral terms and in terms of individual failings was as evident in its debates over Ireland as in its debates on the New Poor Law. To many M.P.'s, an ample poor law for Ireland, by destroying self-reliance, would bring ruin. To the marquis of Granby in 1849 a larger "relief from tax money . . . would destroy the spirit of self-reliance" and, in the same year, Edward Horsman opposed an Exchequer grant of £50,000, since such a grant, "in removing all feeling of self-reliance . . . demoralized the whole population"—a view that won both Disraeli's and Peel's assent, although Peel added that having already destroyed "habits of self-reliance" by public works and loans, such grants must be continued.[35] Tories were not very generous to the Irish poor. Lord Stanley, the future earl of Derby and prime minister, argued that tenants, not landlords, should pay the poor rates, otherwise it "would annihilate and deaden all exertion."[36]

Irish landlords were particularly wary of a corrupting poor law whose rates they would pay. When famine struck Ireland in 1846 its limited poor law relieved only 37,000 of some 2.3 million, and workhouses were too few. For these reasons the government, a year later, proposed a moderate expansion of a very modest outdoor relief that would be given the pauper in return for his labor.[37] Irish M.P.'s immediately objected. "Every motive of independence and self-reliance," retorted Frederick Shaw, would be destroyed. "Outdoor relief is demoralizing," added Henry Corry, and "would corrupt as people are lazy," a sentiment shared by Sir William Gregory, who insisted that only a workhouse test would teach "habits of self-reliance." In 1847, the government abandoned public works and special relief for a more complete Irish Poor Law. It thus fell to Irish poor law unions to take care of hundreds of thousands of famine victims. This was a task they could not do, and so, in 1849, because so many unions in the west of Ireland were bankrupt, Parliament proposed a bill that would require every union in Ireland to collect an additional sixpence on a pound of rateable value, the proceeds to help the most distressed areas. The 6d. additional rate again evoked from Irish M.P.'s the classic twin response: it endangered property and it corrupted morals. It was, said Colonel Fitzstephen French, part of the Poor Law that "had destroyed all the self-reliance of the people." To Sir Lucius O'Brien, it would simply "paralyse industry," while for Lord Hamilton it would check "prudence, improvement, enterprise and self-reliance."[38]

These hard judgments on the Irish peasantry, along with equally severe ones made about the poor by supporters of England's New Poor Law, reflect the sentiment, widespread among the governing classes, that poverty had its source in the failings of the individual and that a too generous relief only increased those failings. It was one of the most pervasive of sentiments, because it was deeply rooted in the growth of both an earnest Victorian morality and an individualistic, capitalist social outlook. Nassau Senior, co-author with Edwin Chadwick of the *Poor Law Report of 1834*, declared in an article in the *Edinburgh Review* of July 1843 that there are "clear scientific truths in moral science as in economics." For Senior, as for Ricardo and John Stuart Mill, political economy dealt with the production and distribution of wealth, not with morals, a subject that belonged to another set of scientific truths and natural laws.

One of those "laws of nature," wrote Senior in the 1834 *Poor Law Report*, determined that "the effects of each man's improvidence or misconduct are borne by himself and his family."[39] It was a natural law that led the moralist in Senior to expound at length on the corrupting faults of the old laws, laws that were not only too often overly generous with relief given outside the work-house, but overly generous in giving outdoor relief to those already earning a wage. Senior also wrote at length on the reforming merits of the new law, giving a psychological disquisition far clearer and more incisive than his confused disquisition on the relation of capital to the Poor Law.

It was a moral disquisition that would have pleased the two bishops who sat on the Royal Commission on the Poor Law. Charles James Blomfield, bishop of London, strongly supported the *Report,* because, as he wrote in his *Memoirs*, the law it envisioned "would tend to discourage immorality" and "raise the social position of the laboring class by promoting a feeling of independence," a moral stance quite appealing to his colleague on the commission, John Bird Sumner, bishop of Chester. This famous author of *Records of Creation* pronounced "indigence the punishment which the moral government of God inflicts upon thoughtless and guilty extravagance." For Sumner, nine-tenths of the world's misery was due to sin.[40] Although Sumner was the only Malthusian on the Commission, it did not prevent him from supporting a *Report* that fell far short of Malthus's wish to abolish all poor laws. The moral conviction that a stern law would promote virtue was far stronger than his belief in a remorseless law of population.

Moral concerns more than economic laws defined the New Poor Law. In 1831, the year the Political Economy Club voted unanimously that Malthus was wrong, economists were more divided over the Poor Law than were the bishops. McCulloch, Poulett Scrope, and Colonel Robert Torrens found the new law too harsh, while only three of the twenty-six bishops voted against it.[41]

The parish clergy were nearly as unanimous for the new law. On its behalf, they wrote pamphlets, gave sermons, acted as poor law guardians, appeared as witnesses before select committees and edited and wrote articles for religious journals. The Reverend Thomas Spencer was the most indefatigable of pamphleteers. He published seven of them. To Spencer, the old laws favored "the profligate and abandoned" and promoted "idleness and licentiousness." "The best way of doing good to the poor," he concluded, "is not making them easy in poverty, but . . . driving them out of it." Spencer did not consider his moralistic view new but traced it to Bishop Butler's claim in his *Analogy* that "all of which we enjoy and a great part of what we suffer, is put into our own power"[42] For Thomas Spencer, who was for many years an assistant poor law commissioner, St. Paul's injunction that those who "would not work should not eat" was a "very plain direction for the exclusion of the idle and profligate from . . . the Church's alms."

Such a harsh policy should certainly have appalled Christian Socialists like Charles Kingsley, yet even this Broad Church clergyman could not escape the intense moralism of early Victorian England. Although Kingsley would excuse the deserving poor from the New Poor Law's insistence on no relief but in the workhouse, he would not excuse the "idle, heartless and shrewd."[43]

To a quite remarkable degree, the Church of England clergy were active poor law guardians and enthusiastic witnesses to the law's wondrous effects. No less than ten of them from Sussex filled many pages of the 1836 *Annual Report* with testimony of its miraculous workings: idlers put to work; "moral and religious improvement"; "greater savings," "less beer shops, less improvident marriages, less bastardy"; "more respectful and civil towards their superiors"; "discontent and insubordination subsiding"; "greater attendance at Sunday School and penny clothing societies"; "fewer in beer shops"; a closer union between master and servant; "paupers . . . under best possible control"; and lower poor rates.[44]

None of the ten spoke of Poor Law schools, agricultural training, or the elevation of the poor. "Best possible control" and "respectful to superiors" reflected their sense of a self-reliance stronger in patience and perseverance than in independence and ambition. Self-reliance had two versions, the limited, controlled form based on inevitable poverty, sinful man, and a rigid social hierarchy, and an expansive, reformist form based on progress, equality, and independence. Champions of both versions supported the New Poor Law, all hoping to make the poor sober, provident, industrious, and independent.

Independence was the quality most esteemed by the Nonconformists, especially those who were the least theologically conservative. Thus, as Nonconformity grew enormously in numbers, wealth, and liberalism, so self-reliance as a doctrine came to mean far more than simply independence from the Poor Law. It also meant an independence from the establishment, Anglicanism, and paternalism. It was an independence that rested on a Nonconformist self-reliance, which was stubbornly individualistic and puritan.

THE NONCONFORMIST CONSCIENCE

In 1851, for the first and the last time in British history, there was an official census of religious worship on a given Sunday. It discovered that Nonconformist church attendance numbered 4,536,264 and Roman Catholic attendance 383,006, together nearly equaling the 5,292,551 who attended Anglican services. They also discovered that the church buildings and seatings of the Nonconformists equaled those of the Established Church. Most, but not all, of England was astonished.[45]

Among those not astonished were the many Methodists, Baptists, and Congregationalists long proud of their multiplying numbers. From 1800 to 1841, the Baptists and Congregationalists experienced a threefold and the Methodists a ninefold expansion of church buildings and sittings, while the Presbyterians, who at the turn of the century had seen hundreds of their churches turn Congregational and Unitarian, regrouped and revived. In 1850, they had 848 places of worship and 58,678 communicants, a solid figure, but exceeded by the Congregationalists, whose 808 chapels in 1812 had increased to 1,853 by 1841—part of the "vital and irrepressible energy of our system." The Congregationalists, along with the Baptists and Presbyterians, were part of the reinvigoration of Old Dissent.

The Unitarians gained little after 1800 and the Quakers even declined, but only in numbers. In wealth and influence, Unitarians and Quakers formed the aristocracy of Dissent. By 1850, wealth and influence also graced many a Congregationalist and some Baptists and Methodists. Over sixty Nonconformists sat in the House of Commons after 1847, certainly not in proportion to the voting power of their adherents, but a great increase over the handful in 1830.[46] In municipal governments, they were a power: from 1835 to 1845, all the mayors of Leeds and half of those in Hull were Nonconformists, and of Leicester's forty-two councillors and fourteen alderman in 1835, only sixteen were Anglican.[47] Nonconformists dominated the new industries and won a larger role in the press. The *Liverpool Times, Bradford Observer, Sheffield Independent, Manchester Guardian,* and *Leeds Mercury* were but a few of the burgeoning newspapers edited by Dissenters. From 1801 to 1890, under the redoubtable Congregationalists Edward Baines Sr. and Jr., the *Leeds Mercury* enjoyed one of the largest circulations in the north of England.[48]

There were also innumerable publications of the Nonconformist churches themselves. They ranged from the Congregationalists' intellectually distinguished *Eclectic Review* to the *Baptist Guardian*, "undertaken . . . in entire dependence upon Him who has all things at His command." By 1840, more than two million boys and girls attended Sunday schools, 55 percent at Nonconformist ones.[49]

These millions of Nonconformists—industrialists, bankers, editors, ministers, Sunday school teachers, shopkeepers, and artisans—constituted a growing and powerful force, which helped define the early Victorians' vision of a laissez-faire society. While not indifferent to the truths of political economy, the sacredness of property and a wise Providence, it was self-reliance—a sturdy, individualistic, resolute self-reliance—that formed the core of their social conscience. The only way to achieve the godly society was to create godly individuals, and that only by a religious awakening, a moral seriousness, a righteous life. It was a conviction based on two powerful experiences common to most Nonconformists, conversion and social mobility.

The experience of conversion was the most central. In the history of English Protestantism, an emphasis on conversion began with the sixteenth-century doctrines of Luther and Calvin, blossomed in English Puritanism, lost out to the *via media* of late Stuart Anglicanism, and retreated to the confines of a persecuted Nonconformity, only to emerge in the evangelical revival that created Methodism, revived the faith of lukewarm Baptists and Congregationalists, and won over a third of the Anglicans.

John Wesley above all saw conversion as fundamental. He exhorted humble, religiously starved miners, artisans, clerks, and shopkeepers to acknowledge their sinful ways, to open themselves to faith in Christ, to the workings of the Holy Spirit, to a grace free for all, to conversion. Bristol's Bishop Butler was aghast, as were most Anglicans, fearful of the emotionalism of the humble. But in those conversions lay an explosive power. It turned lions into lambs, declared Wesley, and "drunkards into the exemplary sober." All was anxiety and gloom, wrote John Ashworth, a young printer's apprentice of the 1830s, then came conversion, the end of gloom, "the unspeakable love of God," success in business, and one more Methodist memoir among scores that testify to the power of conversion.[50]

Conversion, the fruit of an individual conscience struggling for godliness, was a very personal matter, and one that greatly enhanced a belief in the right of private judgment. "We began our religious life," argued the *Baptist Magazine* in 1842, "with an assertion of independence . . . we must act for ourselves." It was a view that squared with tradition. Had not the Westminster Divines of 1644, asked the *Baptist Magazine*, insisted on the "necessity of individual and voluntary assent"? It was a conviction that, in 1849, led the Reverend Baptist Wriothesley Noel, chaplain to the queen, brother of an earl, and most popular of preachers, to totally immerse himself, at age fifty, and before

2,500 worshippers. Converted and duly baptized, he thus became a member of the Baptist Church. Noel believed that "each is bound to do God's will as he sees it, individually and independently."[51]

"Individually" and "independently," no two words lay closer to the heart of early Victorian Nonconformity or more definitely underlined its vision of a laissez-faire society. For Congregationalists, they were the *summum bonum.* "All religion," pronounced the Congregationalist Reverend James Evans, "consists of individuality. Religion is a personal thing." Few felt this truth more intensely than Edward Miall, a merchant's son, who at eighteen years of age "solemnly dedicated" himself "soul and body unto the Lord." He became a Congregational minister in Leicester, but only briefly. Dismayed at the su-pineness of the Congregationalists toward a persecuting Church and state, he founded and edited the *NonConformist*, a weekly that translated the individu-ality and independence arising from conversion and private conscience into a social outlook. "What is Dissent?" asked Miall, and answered, "It is a mind asserting its native claim to independence." It was an answer with which even the Congregationalists' less truculent *Patriot* could agree. "The grand peculi-arities of Dissent," it declared, "are the absolute personality of man inde-pendent of every other man and the right of private judgment."[52]

The Congregationalists' intense individualism even led to doubts about the paternalists' favorite metaphor, the organic. Just as jewelers value individ-ual diamonds, wrote the *Christian Penny Magazine*, so Christians value "humanity not as an organic whole but as a community of souls." A good Christian also disliked the use of the term "masses," wrote the Reverend R. W. Hamilton of Leeds in the *Congregational Magazine*, "as each is an individ-ual."[53] Although conversion, private conscience, and independence were cen-tral to all Dissenting churches, there were many theological and social differ-ences. The Baptists had split into five branches, the Methodists into seven, and the Presbyterians into three. The Congregationalists never split, there be-ing no need to do so, since each congregation was already sovereign. Wesley-an Methodists had a centralized church organization and had inherited Tory political and social attitudes from an Anglicanism that would not resent or-ganic metaphors. The Baptists divided over predestination, as did Congrega-tionalists and Presbyterians.[54] Unitarians and Quakers, following reason and the "Inner Light," were far removed from the polemics on atonement and original sin that burdened Old Dissent's struggle to be free of the more severe doctrine of Calvinism.

There were even differences in social thought. The Methodists' preoccu-pation with personal salvation and with the life of chapels, classes, bands, and Sunday schools expressed an otherworldliness and a group fellowship that distinguished them from the highly individualistic and increasingly political Congregationalists, Unitarians, Quakers, Presbyterians, and Baptists. Yet for all of their differences—and they should not be underestimated—none of them seriously weakened the individualistic and self-reliant nature of the Dissenters' relation to God and society. There is no real evidence that believers in predestination were any less self-reliant than believers in a grace open to all.

There was, however, one important theological change, the gradual move from a conservative, fundamentalist theology and an otherworldly concern for salvation to a liberal, rational theology and a worldly concern for the moral improvement of man and society, a change that increased the Nonconformists' focus on a society of self-reliant citizens. Many Wesleyans and Baptists in the 1840s were slow to make this change. "We must trace the cause of evil," declared the Wesleyan's *Watchman* in 1843, "to the sins of the people." The disorders that afflict society, echoed the *Baptist Examiner,* "are all the consequences of sin." Methodists and Baptists cared deeply for sinful people, but it was a concern for their Godliness, their salvation, their eternity, far more than for their release from poverty. "Our sin," warned the Wesleyan Reverend James Bourne in 1842, "is the cause of our being covered with thick darkness."[55]

For some Congregationalists and Baptists, that darkness was neither so thick nor the sin so ineradicable. Even the self-styled Calvinist Dr. R. W. Hamilton, one of Leeds's most learned and popular of ministers, confessed that because "each individual man is the subject of atonement," he has "the remains of greatness . . . [and the] pledge of restoration to that greatness." The Reverend Thomas Binney, as popular among London Congregationalists as Hamilton was at Leeds, told his congregation that "the most obvious distinction of human nature is its capacity for improvement." The Congregationalist Reverend John Ely, like Binney, was moving away from Calvinism. Ely told his congregation at Leeds's Salem Chapel that "there is a latent power among us adequate . . . for the world's restoration." The future was bright, because man was good. The *Congregational Magazine* felt no inhibition in praise of "the dignity and perfectibility of human nature," and neither did the *Baptist Examiner* in arguing in an article on "The Dignity of Man" that man's fall was little compared to the "elevating influence of the Gospel" and the soul's "vast capabilities for action."[56]

Hamilton, Binney, Ely, and the two journals reflect the power of the Enlightenment as it wove itself around those solid Protestant traditions that were indeed not absent at the Enlightenment's birth. In the 1840s, Enlightenment ideas inspired Nonconformists to a greater faith in man and in his individuality and independence. In 1844, the *Congregational Magazine,* after

praising the Swiss educator J.-H. Pestalozzi as a great expounder of Enlightenment ideas, concluded that there is "no real good that may not be expected
from an enlightened community." In Birmingham the Reverend George
Dawson preached an "earnest and heart stirring religion" that would go beyond evangelical preaching to "beautify and animate the world" and would
produce "a manly reliance on individual conviction." For his zealous efforts
to elevate man as a moral, social and intellectual being he was, in 1845, given
100 guineas; and for his broad views on infant baptism and open communion, he was dismissed from Mt. Zion Chapel—only to win greater fame in
another one. He was a deep admirer of Thomas Carlyle, from whom he
learned that "it is useless to clamour about government reform without there
be reform within."[57]

For many Nonconformists at midcentury, for those, for example, who had
Dawson fired, Enlightenment ideas of noble, perfectible men and a perfectible society were heretical; for others, the fusion of the two only enriched their
faith in a laissez-faire society of perfected individuals. For both, however,
those theological and philosophical convictions that enshrined individuality
and independence were powerfully reinforced by the upward mobility of the
generality of the Nonconformists.

In 1800, the population of Great Britain was around 10 million, and in 1850
around 21 million. In 1750, the middle classes constituted only 4 percent of
the population; by 1867, they made up some 12 percent—even larger if the
middle classes are defined with greater elasticity. In the same period, the proportion who were in the lower middle classes rose from 9 percent to 20 percent and the skilled working classes from 12 percent to 35 percent. In 1850,
Britain's industrial product was forty-three times greater than in 1811. In 1801,
Leeds had 50,000 and Liverpool 82,000 inhabitants; a mere two decades later,
in 1831, the figures were 123,000 and 202,000.[58] Neither Britain nor any other
country in world history had ever expanded like this. It is not known how
many of the 4.5 million who attended Nonconformist services in 1851 belonged to the enlarged middle and skilled classes, but Alan D. Gilbert estimates that all but 8.6 percent of their strength came from that 67 percent of
society lying between the professions and the unskilled laborer, a not unin-
telligent guess if by profession Gilbert means physicians, barristers, and the
clergy and not land agents, warehouse supervisors, and clerks, and if the 67
percent includes the manufacturers, merchants, and shopkeepers, both opulent and modest, who crowded into Baptist, Congregationalist, and Methodist chapels. According to David Thompson, the Congregationalists did well
among wealthy manufacturers, Baptists as smaller men of business, Wesley-

ans as shopkeepers and small manufacturers, and Primitive Methodists and the New Connexion as artisans and craftsmen.[59]

The Nonconformists were unashamed in confessing that their religion led to success. "Godliness" announced the Reverend Dr. J. W. Massie in the *Congregational Year Book*, "is profitableness in all things." And because of that fact, "multitudes from the humblest origin . . . have reached the most honored eminence." *The Congregational Year Book's* favorite illustrations of Congregationalists rising in the social scale were found in its memoirs and obituaries of distinguished preachers. These careers truly exemplify self-reliance: poverty was defied, vicissitudes conquered, disadvantages overcome, and success won. The Congregationalist Reverend William Sylvester was in youth neglected, uneducated, vicious, and doomed to farm labor until he experienced a conversion; then, "from new industry and faithfulness" came success in business, six years of study, and a ministry in which he fought "irreligion and godlessness." *The Baptist Magazine* was also replete with memoirs of self-educated, self-made ministers, ministers like the Reverend Christmas Evans. His father, a shoemaker, was too poor to educate Christmas or keep him from "utter neglect," and at nine, he was put to work on a farm. Later, six men would have beaten him to death but for his crying out "Jesus save me." Saved, converted, and self-educated, he became a Baptist preacher.[60] Not all Baptist and Congregational ministers rose from poverty, since many came from the educated middle classes. But in the early nineteenth century, far more of them, and of their upwardly mobile followers, could look back on fathers who were stocking makers, weavers, farm laborers, farmers, coach builders, upholsters, dyers, printers, and booksellers. Only a handful could look back on fathers who were barristers, army officers, or bankers. And the Baptists and Congregationalists, along with the Unitarians and Quakers, were the best educated of Nonconformist ministers. In the 1840s, Primitive Methodists, Bible Christians, and Reformed Methodists were still mostly self-educated.[61] Almost all these ministers, and many of their followers, experienced a significant upward mobility, which owed much to the tough, stubborn, puritan independence of mind that defined the Nonconformist conscience and the content of thousands of sermons.

The same conscience, although perhaps less austerely, defined the lives of their congregations. Memoirs and social statistics speak to this upward mobility. In a population that had, in one generation, nearly doubled, the middle class had quadrupled. At the top of that class, the splendid monuments of success won by self-reliance, were distinguished Nonconformist families: the Unitarian Rathbones and Roscoes of Liverpool; the Cadburys and Rowntrees,

Quaker chocolate kings of Birmingham and York; the Barclays and Lloyds, Quaker bankers of London; and the Congregationalist City merchant Samuel Morley. Nonconformists were not only giants of industry and commerce but, as with the Congregationalist Edward Baines Sr. and the Unitarian John Edward Taylor, giants of the newspaper world. Baines presided over the *Leeds Mercury* and Taylor over the *Manchester Guardian*. The careers and memoirs of these self-made men celebrated the fact that godliness was profitable.[62]

Beneath these giants were a myriad of Congregational, Baptist, Unitarian, and Wesleyan small manufacturers, wholesalers, and shopkeepers, and beneath them, craftsmen of all sorts and, in a belt running from Devon to Essex and up into East Anglia, successful farmers. Innumerable Nonconformists experienced careers of solid but modest success. The many memoirs of these self-made men tell of how the chapel and the Sunday school and their own passion for self-education and self-help made them increasingly prominent in England's manufacturing and commercial centers, centers themselves increasingly active in electing Parliament. The *Baptist Guardian* in 1845 could not hide its sense of newly won power: "The Baptist denomination" it boasted, "occupies a most important and promising position at the present time. It is fast rising in intelligence and influence."[63]

That influence expanded in every direction. It expressed itself in stones and mortar as well as in votes for mayors and M.P.'s. It also expressed itself in imposing chapels, burgeoning schools (Sunday, day, and evening), Dissenting academies, Dissent-dominated Mechanics Institutes, and Home Missions, all of which gave evidence of an irrepressible vitality and newly won wealth. In Leeds, in 1841, finding their famous Salem Chapel too small, the Congregationalists built the East Parade Chapel, "one of the most spacious, substantial and complete . . . in the kingdom," in the classical Doric style, with "a noble portico of six fluted columns, resting on colossal steps." Crowned with an "enriched entablature and pediment," it was both "grave and grand," and attached to it were "school rooms, a separate lecture room, class rooms, committee rooms, vestries and a chapel keepers home."[64]

To conquer oneself through conversion and godliness and then to conquer the world through industry, prudence, and frugality gave one the confidence to preach the virtue of self-help; and such preaching in Nonconformist pulpits, publications, and Sunday schools was uninhibited. It was a law, declared the Reverend Thomas Binney, that "industry, probity, intelligence, uprightness, activity, labour, prudence, discretion" would bring success, just as "folly, vice, idleness, vanity, expensive habits, neglect of business, disobedience to parents will bring failure." "Act as a man," commanded the *Christian Pioneer,* "not as a serf or slave." Be "active, never idle," since "idleness always brings its own punishment," preached the *Baptist Pioneer*. Young Congregationalists would find in the *Christian Penny Magazine* (circulation 35,000) an article on "Industry Necessary to Success," which proclaimed, "never intemperance, never self-indulgence, never the public house, and always frugality, always manly dignity." Manliness was emerging in all its Victorian robustness. The Unitarians' *Christian Teacher* urged that "a manly independence replace public charity" since people must "rely on their own resources."[65]

The commandment to "act as a man," not a slave or serf, struck at that deference so integral to paternalism. It was not the socialists or even the Chartists who first declared war on paternalism, but Nonconformists determined on independence. Deference to God, yes, and certainly to lawful authority and earned social distinctions, but not to unjust establishments and exclusive privileges. The *Congregational Magazine* called "a spirit of dependence on fellow creatures" an "unmixed evil." "Hence the great object," it added, "is to encourage a spirit of independence." The Unitarian *Prospective Review* had only ridicule for what it called a "feudalism" in which the poor "are to be fed, washed, dressed, housed, taught, park-ed, amused, churched." For society to provide for a person's needs, it said earlier, was "to keep him a perpetual child."

Few could exceed Edward Miall's acute sense of the battle between paternalism and self-reliance, which informed nearly every issue of the *NonConformist*, leading him in 1845 to urge the working classes to raise themselves to that "position of self-reliance and self-respect which feudalism will hereafter find it impossible to subvert."[66] But what of the myriad social problems—of poverty, ignorance, disease, overcrowding, crime, unemployment, depressions, vagrancy, prostitution, and homelessness? For the leading Nonconformists, the answer was self-help and the help of others universalized into a Christian laissez-faire. "Christianity," the Reverend Thomas Binney assured his hearers, "certainly contains exactly those things which if they were . . . generally carried out would cure all the disorders . . . and make society everywhere virtuous and healthy." It was a formula that Binney's friend in Leeds, the Reverend John Ely, expanded on in a most sanguine manner: "If we can . . . elevate the individual . . . we have only to calculate on its universal application and its universal social and moral elevation will be secured." "The workshop," continued the rhapsodic Ely, "shall be the scene of profitable industry; the market a mart of honorable exchange," and as a result "the triumph of righteousness and purity and goodness and mercy." In an article denouncing socialism, the *Eclectic* was so persuaded that since "past improvements have been the result of the improvement of individuals . . . the exertion of each leads to the social progress of all." And for the archconservative Wesleyan

Reverend Robert Newton, "the only thing to effect a radical reform in all classes of society" is "the revival and extension of pure and undefiled religion."[67]

The Nonconformist vision of a Christian laissez-faire society, one rooted in individual conversion and private conscience, was for many in the 1840s still narrowly bound by a singular concentration on eternal salvation and original sin. The reports of Baptist and Wesleyan home missionaries (and even of Congregational ones) speak far more of saving souls and preaching piety and holiness than of assuaging poverty, improving slums, or educating the poor. Quite different were the Unitarians and Quakers, and increasingly the Dawsons and Binneys among Baptists and Congregationalists.

In between these conservative and liberal theologies lay most Nonconformists, in various positions of ambivalence, still persuaded of man's wickedness and still concerned with eternity, but also aware that man, once touched by grace and reason, could be improved, that society could be made freer and more just, and that a new Jerusalem could be created here and now. It was a position tense with differences but one in which an inner religious individualism begot an outward independence of mind, an independence of mind that in the more liberal Nonconformists approached that fullness and great optimism of the true believers in self-reliance, the true believers who saw in education the great panacea.

EDUCATION: THE GREAT PANACEA

For true believers in the reformed individual as the fundamental building block of a laissez-faire society, education was the grand remedy. It promoted self-reliance, and self-reliance promoted political stability and economic progress. Many in the 1840s shared a belief in education, although not all with the zeal of the true believers. Some still feared it, but they were far fewer than a generation earlier, when the French Revolution, Painite radicalism, Luddite riots, and demagogic oratory led to a pervasive fear of education, a fear enhanced by Tory rhetoric. In those tense days, many in the upper classes believed that schooling only made laborers dissatisfied with their lot, seditious in politics, and insolent in their self-reliance.

In the 1840s, some—in the rural areas many—still feared education. "Many object to the education of the working class," said Sussex's Reverend C. M. Klavert in 1841, because it makes "the humble classes dissatisfied with their station." Some even in manufacturing areas, said the education inspector, Alexander Thirtell, viewed education "with suspicion."[68]

These fears should not be exaggerated. Although divided on how religious and how secular education should be and to what extent education was a Church or public matter, no M.P. and no periodical openly opposed its expansion. A sound education made laborers industrious, provident, skilled, sober, respectful, and self-reliant—and, if not all of these, at least less likely to be truculent or to go on the poor rates.

Most early Victorians wished the humbler classes to be better educated and more self-reliant, but they differed as to the extent of that education, the degree to which self-reliance should be encouraged, and on what the consequences would be. They did not divide for and against education, but instead on how much, what kind, in what faith, and how great their expectations. Their views formed a spectrum. At the violet end were cool, hesitant High Churchmen and ultra Tories; at the red end, true believers. Between the two, listing toward the violet, were ordinary Tories, Peelites, conservative Whigs, High Church Anglicans, and the Establishment, and listing toward the red, Nonconformists, liberal Whigs, Broad Churchmen, and the towns of the north.

For High Church Anglicans, education was fine if it taught the poor self-denial, obedience, frugality, and prudence, indispensable virtues, said the Reverend William Gresley, since "the sufferings of the poor are caused by their own improvidence and want of self-denial." But Gresley wanted no overeducation. A clever Chartist, he wrote, shows that "education only makes him more mischievous." Furthermore, "independence and perfect equality are not good for man." Much better were the Church's catechism and the simple moral lessons of Mrs. Hippisley Tuckfield's popular *Education for the People* in "habits of regular industry and self-control; of kindness and forbearance, of personal and domestic cleanliness . . . [and] simplicity, humbleness, virtue." After extolling field and workshop for boys, and knitting and sewing for girls, Mrs. Tuckfield warned against "the incalculable mischief" of overteaching.[69]

Evangelical Anglicans all heartily agreed that the Church should teach obedience, patience, and self-denial, but many doubted whether independence was unsuitable to a man struggling for righteousness in a society sunk in worldliness. Nor did they worry unduly about overeducation. On the education spectrum, many had moved toward those Nonconformists who saw conversion and independence as central, and all education to that end as helpful. Nonconformists also varied greatly, as did Anglicans—or Tories and Whigs—in their enthusiasm and their hesitancies over education. The self-educated Joseph Barker of the New Connexion Methodists had an expansive belief in education, including the teaching of writing in Sunday schools, a position his own New Connexion denounced. Many theologically conservative

Wesleyans, Congregationalists, and Baptists focused so narrowly on the chapel and the salvation of souls that their educational horizons barely extended beyond Sunday schools and the teaching of Scriptures, and then only, in the words of the Congregationalist Reverend James Griffin, if they made "for patience and contentment."[70] More liberal Congregationalists, like Thomas Binney and Andrew Reed, and the more enlightened Baptists, like George Dawson and J. B. Mursell, had moved across the spectrum toward the true believers' enthusiasm for the power of knowledge. So had liberal Whigs, such as George Poulett Scrope, Charles Villiers, and R. A. Slaney, members, along with Liberal and Radicals, of the Central Society of Education, established in 1839 to promote a national system of education.

These liberal Whigs, liberal Nonconformists, and Broad Churchmen shared with Liberals and Radicals both the Enlightenment's assumptions about improvable man and reformable society and a greater sensitivity to the demands of the emerging middle and working classes. The expectations of these true believers in popular education and the advance of knowledge were enormous. For them, human ignorance was the leading cause of pauperism, crime, drunkenness, insanity, fever, destitution, despotism, and riots. To the *Leeds Mercury,* "human ignorance," along with human depravity, was "the grand source of human misery;" to the education inspector J. D. Morell, ignorance created a "great mass of evils" including "exploited needlewomen," the "squalor of back streets" and "the death struggle of mere material existence;" and to the Whigs' Lord Morpeth, "the evils of ignorance are still more mischievous and still more fatal than those evils of destitution, of fever, of mortality."[71]

In removing the causes of these evils, an education designed for self-help and self-reliance became the great panacea. "Education . . . is the one step," asserted the *Athenaeum,* "which alone leads to the amendment of society." The *Westminster Review* said that it was "almost impossible for even the imagination to exaggerate" the benefits of education. W. R. Greg, a former cotton manufacturer turned social essayist, was no less sanguine. For Greg, the only plan for the end of destitution was "to provide instruction among the masses by every means in our power and then leave them to work out their salvation." Even the staid *Edinburgh Review* could not resist the charms of this sovereign remedy. "We found our chief hope for the redemption of our country," it declared in 1848, "on the increase of intelligence, education, morals, and religion." "Nothing else," it added, "will extricate us," an optimism surpassed by the *Morning Chronicle's* boast that a comprehensive education could "in the course of a single generation reduce crime and imprudence and the misery . . . which attends them."[72]

As powerful as the steam engine and as revolutionary as the railroads, such were the comparisons applied to education made by the early Victorians, whose intoxication with the miracles of the industrial revolution carried over to the power of knowledge. For Lady Byron, whose school for the poor at Ealing won countless admirers, education on Pestalozzian lines would cause "a moral revolution" that would produce "morality, religion and national wealth . . . with as much speed as by railroads." Education was good for all. It was an integral part, wrote Samuel Smiles in 1842, of "the great idea of this age—the grand idea of man," especially since it "will teach those who suffer how to remove the cause of their suffering."[73]

The millennium was truly at hand. "If destitute children were educated," a buoyant *Chambers' Edinburgh Journal* predicted, "prison and police officers might almost shut up." If learning were "generally diffused," wrote Thomas Bailey of the *Nottingham Mercury*, "progress was inevitable and civilization knew no bonds"—and, most gloriously, "all would live three times longer." That education would end crime, said the *Edinburgh Review* was "almost a law of nature." That it would end pauperism was the declared belief of Whig poor law inspectors, the Tory Robert Southey, and Jelinger Symons, the education inspector who founded the *Law Magazine*. "If one half of the poor rates were spent on education," declared Symons, "there would be no need of any poor rates at all." For the *Quarterly Review* in 1845, it was the "sole hope for Ireland." Little wonder that Symons also judged education "identical with the greatest good and the primary temporal agent of human welfare." Chartists also shared this exhilarating vision. Education, wrote their leader in London, William Lovett, would cause "every latent seed of mind . . . to spring into useful life," which would in turn "enlighten ignorance, remove misery, and banish vice." Lovett was not alone in seeing misery evaporate before knowledge. Writing in *The Social System*, the Owenite John Gray declared "we shall have the millennium at once."[74]

One of the most powerful forces increasing the early Victorians' belief in education as the grand remedy was the belief that man is capable of great improvement. It was an old idea, found in Francis Bacon's "Knowledge is power," and in Thomas Hobbes and the Cambridge Platonists. And it was an idea elaborately analyzed and developed in John Locke's *Essay on Human Understanding* (1690) and *Thoughts on Education* (1693; eighteen editions by 1836). It was part of the growth of rationalism that gradually and pervasively defined the eighteenth century's enlightened view of man as noble, rational, and free of hopeless sin, a view that suffered some setbacks during the evangelical revival and Tory repression of the 1790s and after. Yet during those years, the Priestleys, Benthams, Godwins, Owenses, and Millses not only sustained but furthered the Enlightenment's rational and optimistic view. It was indeed a view that played a role in the outlook of some evangelicals.

In the 1830s and 1840s, the Enlightenment view that a correct and well-designed education could teach the lower orders the virtues of self-reliance and so promote a laissez-faire society spread far and wide. The central assumption of that view was John Locke's argument that at birth the mind is a tabula rasa, a blank sheet, and that how it develops depends on what is written on it by one's sensations and by the proper (rather than improper) associations of those sensations. Out of the British empirical tradition—Bacon, Hobbes, and Locke—came the theory of association, a theory that David Hartley expounded by arguing that sensations and their sequence of associations fully determined one's thought and feelings. Hartley's *Observation on Man* of 1749 influenced Jeremy Bentham, James Mill, Robert Owen, William Godwin, Harriet Martineau, and many others—including the young Coleridge. For Bentham, it meant that the individual was so malleable that by education he could become rational and good, and that poverty and crime would then diminish.

Not all who gloried in the march of mind believed that all knowledge and feelings began with sensations imposed on a tabula rasa. The great Scottish moral philosophers—Thomas Reid, Adam Smith, Francis Hutcheson, Sir James Mackintosh, Dugald Steward, and Thomas Brown—all argued that everyone had an innate moral faculty, a conscience. Also innate is a rational faculty. Although philosophers presented cogent arguments both for and against such innate faculties, they differed much less in their belief in the improvability of man. Education could "mold" the moral and rational faculties, just as they could order sensations and associations. Indeed, for some belief in a moral faculty was quite compatible with belief in associations. "We form our sentiments of virtue and duty," wrote that staunch defender of the moral faculty Sir James Mackintosh, "by means of the association of ideas."[75]

There was not one single channel of Enlightenment ideas but many branches and estuaries. To the empirical and utilitarian channel may be added those of the Scottish moral philosophers, the English Unitarians, the liberal Nonconformists, Whig rationalists, Broad Churchmen like F. D. Maurice, the Oxford rationalists of Oriel—Richard Whatley, Thomas Arnold, and Nassau Senior—and, at Cambridge, the philosophical William Whewell and Henry Sidgwick. Nor can one overlook the many branches of the rise of rationalism among the new historians, the groundbreaking scientists, and intellectuals of every kind. Broad and diverse was the advance of knowledge and the growth of rationalism, both of which promoted the idea that education, by creating well-trained, industrious, disciplined, and self-reliant workers could remove many of the miseries afflicting the lower orders.

The utilitarians had long thought that such an education would create the greatest happiness for the greatest number. James Mill, in his famous article on education in the *Encyclopedia Britannica* of 1818, wrote so exuberantly that an education based on the theory of association would transform the whole human race that his son later confessed that his father had found in "the universal principle of association . . . the unlimited possibility of improving the moral and intellectual condition of mankind." The son was scarcely less sanguine about the power of education. "Ignorance and want of culture" he wrote, were "the primary and perennial source of all social evils."[76]

In the 1840s, the young Mill and Bentham's friends, John Black at the *Morning Chronicle,* William Ellis at the *Westminster Review,* and Charles Dilke at the *Athenaeum* carried forward the utilitarian faith in the generative powers of education. Because "we consider education as lying at the basis of our social improvement," asserted the *Morning Chronicle* in 1843, it should be our great object "to fashion and mould men." "Education," said Ellis, "is the first as well as the most powerful of the instruments . . . for the promotion of well being," a view that the *Athenaeum* never tired of propounding. Although aware of crime, the handloom weavers' wretchedness, sanitary evils, and "vices of all sort," the *Athenaeum* turned not so much to legislation (of which it once said there was "too much") for a remedy as to "the improved and extended education of the masses," to the "diffusion of knowledge," and to the abolition of "the most potent source" of these evils, "ignorance." Little wonder that the *Athenaeum* concluded that "education is the best surety for human progress."[77]

The *Westminster* and the *Athenaeum* also promoted the educational philosophy of Pestalozzi and his disciple P. E. de Fellenberg. The key terms in their philosophy were not "sensation" or "association" but "faculties," "habits," "reason," and "nature." Education is not the rote memory of facts but the development of every faculty of mind and body, all of which—moral, intellectual, and physical—form an organic whole. Successful instruction must promote those powers of observation, intellectual development, and habits of conduct that resist vice and promote virtue and happiness.[78]

Although Pestalozzi praised Locke, it was Rousseau's ideas of a naturally good and educable man that inspired his optimism. He saw in man's benevolence, the power of love, and sentiments of beauty and order, all virtues that too often society distorted, but ideas that were inherent in nature itself. Doughty Benthamites might be uncomfortable with talk of ideas inherent in nature, but they were far more popular in the 1840s than talk of "association." They certainly inspired enthusiasm for education in some Unitarians.

Unitarians, of course, did not all think alike. J. H. Thom and J. R. Beard of Liverpool and the *Christian Teacher* (after 1845 the *Prospective Review*) were rivaled by few in their defense of the middle class, laissez-faire, and the New Poor Law, a defense also made, but with less rigor by William and Mary Howitt, W. J. Fox and Southwood Smith in *Howitt's Journal* and the *Peoples' Journal*. All were, above all, ardent for an education that would allow the workers to improve themselves. A larger education was needed, said the *Christian Teacher*, an education that would exercise "the faculties and virtues of the mind." In his *Spiritual Blindness*, J. H. Thom, co-editor of the *Christian Teacher*, told his readers of the "mightiest of all influences, the wisdom, holiness and refining grace of individual minds"—minds in living communion with the Divine.[79]

The Unitarians' extraordinary faith in social progress through the education of the individual reflected an optimism not only about the noble, divine-touching faculties of reason and goodness but about the natural laws, progress, and harmonies of a rational universe. The writings of Southwood Smith and W. J. Fox, along with those of the visiting American William Ellery Channing, fused this optimism about man and nature so exuberantly that the millennium seemed at hand. To attain it, men need only be taught what Fox called "the eternal principles of morality," Smith, the "simple laws of nature and science" and Channing, "the Eternal All-comprehending Mind."[80] Because both man and the universe were rational and divine, because "knowledge and virtue are so entirely the same," because the "mind's capacity [for] ... illimitable improvement" is a "law of nature," early education can "bring the faculties of mind to perfection." Such were the buoyant hopes of Southwood Smith, hopes not much different from Fox's belief that because "all vice has been traced to ignorance," ignorance will fade before the "Great Law of Progress" and a science that "pours forth a flood of glory over the globe," thus releasing a "self-dependence that generates ... the power of exercising the reasoning faculties."

An uninhibited confidence in the reasoning faculties also informed Channing's widely read essays "Self-Culture" and "Elevation of the Working Classes." It was Channing's hope that educators who "understood the perfection of human nature" would concentrate on developing "the self-forming power," the "divine powers of the soul," and the "harmonious action of all its faculties." If such an effort were made, and above all by the working classes, it would "work a fundamental revolution in society."[81]

Each of Channing's two essays had five English editions between 1838 and

1852. W. J. Fox not only wrote for the *Morning Chronicle*, the *Daily News*, the *Examiner*, the *Weekly Dispatch*, the *Retrospective Review*, the *Monthly Review*, the *Westminster Review*, and the *League*, but at South Place Chapel, Finsbury, he gave sermons to overflowing crowds on "The Education of Workers" and "The Morality of Poverty," which quickly found their way into print. Southwood Smith, author of *A Discourse on the Human Mind* (1818), *Illustrations of Divine Government* (1826), and *Philosophy of Health* (three editions by 1847), won fame as a sanitary reformer and member of many government commissions. Few exceeded the zeal of the Unitarians for the education of the self-reliant individual. In the late eighteenth century, they pioneered Sunday schools, night schools, libraries, and scientific and literary societies. In the early nineteenth century, Southwood Smith helped establish the Society for the Diffusion of Useful Knowledge and Harriet Martineau was the indefatigable author of elementary moral and economic lessons. Unitarians gave unstinted support to the establishment of mechanics institutes throughout England, and it was Unitarian manufacturers who were the most likely to have good factory schools. At Hazelwood school, outside Birmingham, and at Bruce Castle in London, the remarkable Hill family ran famous experimental schools for the middle and upper classes. The Unitarian Mary Carpenter in 1850 helped establish reform schools that began a movement that promised to reduce crime through education. Meanwhile, periodicals and a flood of publications also carried the message that education was the great remedy.

If few exceeded the Unitarians in zeal for education, few also exceeded their zeal for a laissez-faire society. W. J. Fox's editorials in 1846 denounced the Ten Hour Bill; Harriet Martineau in 1851 directed a fiery blast against the new home secretary, Lord Palmerston, for ordering dangerous machinery fenced; the Unitarians at Manchester College in 1843 voted to oppose government support of education; and the *Christian Teacher* and its editor J. H. Thom denounced corrupting charities and poor laws as no real answer to that "improvidence, illness, and drunkenness" that were "the bane of the working classes." "Man" insisted the *Christian Teacher*, "should be largely left to himself," since for the state to assume "his cares and responsibilities" is to "keep him a perpetual child" and deny "the fullest development of his mental and moral individuality."

It was the concept of "moral individuality" that formed the core of the Unitarians' laissez-faire outlook. Neither political economy nor private property was much mentioned, except by Harriet Martineau. "Manly independence," "habits of steady sustained application," "self-reliance," and "the development of all the faculties" are the bright promises that inform the *Christian Teacher's* vision of a laissez-faire society and that led Thom to conclude that "the mightiest of all influences [is] the wisdom, holiness, and refining grace of individual minds."[82]

The vision of a laissez-faire society based on reformed, self-reliant individuals extended far beyond the Unitarians. It was held by liberal Nonconformists, Scottish journalists, advanced Whigs, and even that new class of reformers, the government's inspectors of schools, prisons, factories, and insane asylums, a class who, having confronted social evil more directly than most, also turned to education as the grand remedy.

One of that new breed was J. D. Morell, one of Her Majesty's inspectors of schools. In 1833, Morell attended the Congregationalist Homerton College, where he learned of original sin and eternal punishment. Further study at Glasgow and Bonn, a stint as a Congregational minister, and the publication of A History of Philosophy led to his appointment as the government's inspector of the schools of the British and Foreign School Society. Morell no longer believed that man was cursed with sin and doomed to eternal punishment. On the contrary, "God has given us all faculties capable of indefinite improvement, an entire nature evidently destined for illimitable expansion and progress." Morell was thus for "popular education without stint . . . for all classes," education requiring the "development and improvement of the whole man" and that would "prompt them [the poor] to advance themselves." Morell's yearly reports reflected this hopeful outlook. Education, he wrote in a Pestalozzian vein, should not be a "mere technical instruction . . . hitherto the evil of primary education" but the comprehension of "the real things themselves as concrete realities." Such an education "for the whole life" would so "strengthen purpose and self-reliance" and "habits of morality, industry, and piety that poverty and ignorance will pass away."[83]

None of the Anglican clergy who inspected Church of England schools dared speak of poverty passing away or illimitable progress. The world of these clergymen was more traditional and fixed, as were the National Society schools that they inspected. Education, wrote the Reverend Henry Bellairs, should teach the child "to conduct himself piously, honestly, soberly, and industriously" so that he would "fit properly for his situation." In all schools, the Reverend J. D. Norris wrote, "the pupils must be taught habits of forecast and self-control." The New Poor Law is admirable, added the Reverend Henry Moseley, for lowering rates and bringing "orderliness and cleanliness." And most admirable of all, concluded the Reverend Frederick Watkins, are devout teachers who assure a "Christian upbringing of immoral creatures for time and for eternity." A sound Anglican education was a social necessity more than a grand remedy for transforming the lower classes.[84]

Morell's only allies at the Committee on Education for such a transformation were the other two inspectors of British schools, Hugh Tremenheere and Joseph Fletcher, two of the inspectors of Poor Law schools, E. C. Tufnell and Jelinger Symons, and the secretary of the committee, James Kay-Shuttleworth. All five came from affluent families, enjoyed a good education, and believed in political economy, private property, and a social hierarchy. None wished a radical change in society, only a radical improvement in its lower orders. All but Kay-Shuttleworth had read law at the Inns of Court. Neither Nonconformist nor Radical, these men of the Establishment yielded to few in their zeal for education as the sovereign remedy. Although they were always careful to call for a religious and moral education, their faith in reason, social and moral laws, and man's improvability reflected a secular outlook. It was an outlook that led Jelinger Symons to insist that "selfishness is identical with ignorance" and that "education is identical with our greatest good."

In varying degrees, the other four agreed. Education, reported Tremenheere, will lessen "temptations to vice and improvidence [and] occasional distress and permanent suffering." For Tufnell, education "infallibly depauperizes," and for Fletcher, "ending their ignorance and improvidence" and strengthening "all the faculties of body and mind" is the great remedy. The four inspectors would also have agreed with Kay-Shuttleworth that "education is to be regarded as one of the most important means of eradicating the germ of pauperism."[85]

Kay-Shuttleworth wrote the above claim in 1838 to the Poor Law Commission. E. C. Tufnell, also an assistant commissioner of the Poor Law, sent in similar memos. Both were true believers in the New Poor Law, its workhouse test, and the moral assumptions on which it rested. Their enthusiastic reports of the 1830s spoke of more jobs, higher wages, less bastardy, less immorality, and greater self-reliance. For a while jobs and wages did rise, and bastardy and immorality seemed to abate, but the depression of the early 1840s brought a quick end to these optimistic reports, although not to their belief in self-reliance. Self-reliance remained the key to the new Jerusalem. Unhappily, according to Tufnell and Kay-Shuttleworth, it too often fell prey to ignorance. The two assistant commissioners thus became the tireless campaigners for pauper education, for better workhouse and district schools, for industrial training (spade husbandry for the boys and sewing and knitting for the girls) and, for all, religious and moral instruction.[86] Had not Pestalozzi and de Fellenberg shown in their much visited schools at Yverdon and Hofyl in Switzerland that an education that developed all the faculties, mental, moral and physical, was just what the poor required? And had not Mr. Aubin at his school at Norwood in London showed how homeless urchins could be made self-reliant? In the late 1830s, the Poor Law Commission appointed Tufnell and Kay-Shuttleworth to inquire into pauper education, and in 1839, the Whigs made Kay-Shuttleworth secretary to the Committee in Council on Education. By 1860, that Committee employed thirty-four inspectors and dispensed £723,115 in grants, while Tufnell and three other inspectors worked both to create first-rate district poor law schools and to greatly improve the existing workhouse schools.[87]

A new orthodoxy had joined political economy at the heart of Her Majesty's government: the belief that education would create a trained, provident, industrious, sober, and intelligent working class—a self-reliant working class. It was an orthodoxy also held by prison and factory inspectors. Frederick Hill, Whitworth Russell, and William Crawford, three of the more prominent prison inspectors, all listed ignorance as a principal cause of crime. Since crime so visibly rose with economic distress and fell with prosperity, they also included destitution as a cause. But when it came to the remedies of crime, they all favored the end of ignorance. "The most effectual . . . remedy," wrote Russell and Crawford in 1847, is "to render education as cheap, attractive and efficient as possible." "Good mental, moral and religious education" said Frederick Hill is "the great preventive." For the sanguine Crawford and Russell, the criminal's "lamentable ignorance" could be replaced by "habits of order, cheerfulness, alacrity, industry, modesty . . . truth and honesty."[88]

Factory inspectors also sang the praises of education and constantly complained that factory owners failed to establish the required factory schools. The dean of these inspectors, Leonard Horner, believed that if schools improved "the natural faculties of the working class," wealth and prosperity would increase, Chartism, trade unions, and violence decrease, and everywhere there would be "useful and orderly citizens," the consequence of "religious and moral training and habits of order."[89]

By the end of the 1840s, a belief in education as the grand panacea had spread far beyond its early pioneers. Even the Church of England, which received the lion's share of the government's education grants, spoke enthusiastically of its miraculous effects. All of England, it seemed, realized that a laissez-faire society required its people to be educated. This nearly universal belief in the benefits arising from the intellectual and moral instruction of the people reflects three powerful social facts: that education's advance was inevitable, that the viable remedies for social remedies were few, and that a public education based on sound theory had yet to be tried. Given England's growth in wealth, towns, and all manner of cheap publications, and given her tradition of self-education and her religious zeal for the Gospel, no sluice gate in the world could hold back a flood of literacy and learning. Not even the bishops could stop the self-taught from reading Tom Paine or prevent Dis-

sent from establishing Sunday schools. So galling was it for Charles Blomfield, bishop of London, to see the Unitarians take the lead in Sunday schools
that he redoubled his own efforts to have the Church of England be the nation's schoolmaster. And for the High Tory John Kaye, bishop of Lincoln,
"the very existence of the Established Church rested on instructing the rising
generations in her principles."[90]

Kaye not only feared Dissent, he also feared the violence and disorders
spawned by mounting social evils, evils for which he and his colleagues had
few if any remedies. Deeply averse to government interference, not happy
with corrupting poor laws, even hostile to any sanitary reform that lessened
the Church's burial ground fees and privileges, churchmen felt even more
impelled to place their hopes in the education of self-reliant individuals.

That remedy was all the more hopeful because it was so new and untried.
Unlike a late twentieth-century public grown skeptical after many educational failures, the ebullient early nineteenth century knew only the promise
of the new and untried. England had, to be sure, its Etons and Oxfords, its
Lockes and Wollstonecrafts on education, and a myriad schools, but it had
never had a public school system for all nor theories as comprehensive and
progressive as those of Pestalozzi and de Fellenberg. Having never actually
experienced a public system nor extensively tested the new pedagogy, and
being deeply anxious for a remedy to hugely perplexing evils, the early Victorians turned with vigor and alacrity to the education of the self-reliant individual—and did so with a powerful mixture of illusions and realities.

ILLUSIONS AND REALITIES

In the early Victorians' vision of a laissez-faire society, few convictions
were as widespread as the belief that the individual and not government was
responsible for his or her condition in life. Political economy's invisible hand
was too recondite a concept for the multitude, which in any case did not possess enough private property and sufficient income to hold property sacred
and the world divinely providential. But nearly all, from duke to costermon-
ger, from archbishop to Methodist Sunday school teacher, believed that the
condition of most depended largely on their own prudence, industry, sobriety, providence, and skills. Even the working classes themselves espoused self-
reliance far more than socialism.

That the self-help philosophy should be so widely held is a curious, even a
paradoxical, fact. It is paradoxical in the sense that it reflects two illusions and
one reality. The illusions concerned the causes of destitution and the power
of self-reliance to remove it, the reality concerned how an individual could

best grapple with poverty. In prosperous times, self-reliance worked well, as thousands proved by bettering themselves through industry and frugality; but in times of depression or cholera, many of the industrious and frugal became destitute or sick or both, belying the *Spectator*'s claim that "every man's happiness depends upon his own exertions."[91] That claim, although based on eminently wise and useful admonitions, faltered in the face of economic vicissitudes and the tragedy of disease. Yet the *Spectator*'s advice was nonetheless salutary, because even in depressed times, the most industrious fared the least badly. The advocates of self-help did give sagacious advice. Yet the stern moralists who gave that advice often based it on illusions, on the illusion that outdoor relief corrupted and a workhouse test reformed the poor.

One of the more prominent upper-class illusions was that by means of sermons, tracts, domestic missions, edifying stories, penny magazines, mechanics institutes, lyceums, schools, and exhortations, one could indoctrinate the working classes in the virtues of self-help.

Few believed more fervently in such efforts than the women authors of edifying tales. From the High Church Sara Trimmer in the 1790s to the Unitarian Harriet Martineau in the 1830s, and including in between the evangelical Hannah More, the rationalist Maria Edgeworth and the popularizer of political economy Miss Jane Marcet. These authors played a remarkable role in efforts to refashion the humbler orders. Their moral tales sold very well, Hannah More's in the thousands through the Church's Cheap Repository Tracts. Miss Marcet's 1816 *Conversations on Political Economy* enjoyed six editions by 1839, only to be outdone by Miss Martineau's opening sale of 5,000 copies of *Poor Law Tales*.

Trimmer was an enthusiast for almsgiving, catechism readings, and Anglican truth; More wrestled with sin and corruption and looked to the fruits of conversion; Edgeworth expounded a progressive, rational view of a broad education, and Marcet and Martineau found self-reforming truths in political economy. The Unitarian Martineau was also far less paternalistic than the four Anglicans. Instead of being content with their places, her exemplars of virtue and political economy grow rich and independent. "The first requisite to advancement," she wrote, "is the self-reliance which results from self-discipline." Class advancement was never the goal of Trimmer, More, or Marcet.

But although they differed on much, they certainly shared a common morality and clung to some excessive hopes and illusions about it. More might look to God, conversion and faith and Martineau and Marcet to the law of population and Malthus, but underneath these views runs the real message, as it does with Trimmer and Edgeworth—one's salvation, earthly or heavenly, lies in virtue and good conduct. The three greatest and most invoked of the social virtues—industry, sobriety, and frugality—are fundamental to all these writers, as they were to most early Victorian moralists. Marcet and Martineau do invoke the most elementary maxims of political economy, as Trimmer and More do the elementary maxims of Christianity, but most urgent of all is to tell the poor to work harder, never depend on poor relief, avoid drink, and be frugal. Marcet's favorite character, Mrs. B, would not teach political economy to the laboring classes, but "industry . . . prudence and forethought," without which there can be "no amelioration of the poor," a view not unlike Martineau's glorification of "indefatigable industry and frugality."[92]

The moral tales of More, Marcet and Martineau sold in the thousands, but the people of England numbered in the millions. And many of these moral tales, paid for by the Church's Cheap Repository Tract Society or the Society for the Diffusion of Useful Knowledge, ended up in the hands of middle-class readers. Nor was the promise that industry and providence would bring well-being less than illusory to hard-working agricultural laborers whose weekly wage of eight or nine shillings allowed no savings for long winter layoffs.

But those concerns did not bother Henry Brougham and the Society for the Diffusion of Useful Knowledge. The brilliant but erratic Brougham, Scotsman, educational reformer, and avid Whig, had helped establish the Society in 1826, just two years after he, George Birkbeck, John Robertson, and Thomas Hodgskin founded the London Mechanics Institute.[93]

In its twenty years of existence, the S.D.U.K. published many cheap works and periodicals, including Harriet Martineau's. Its publisher and the author of some of its works was the Windsor newspaper owner and publisher Charles Knight, who was convinced, as a man of the Enlightenment, that "what sharpens the intellect ought, undoubtedly to elevate the morals." Knight's firm supplied England's burgeoning mechanics institutes with elevating knowledge of all sorts—at sixpence a book, two books a week. By 1850, there were 550 mechanics institutes in Britain. Liverpool's institute cost £15,000 and had 3,300 members, 850 pupils in three day schools, and 600 in evening classes. Leeds's institute was not quite as resplendent or well attended, but nonetheless enjoyed steady support and moderate attendance, its support coming from the town's new self-made elite, who managed it for the 900 members.[94] Its president in 1845 was Edward Baines Jr., the editor of the *Leeds Mercury*. That mechanics institutes were "multiplying on every side" meant, said the *Mercury*, that "the reign of ignorance will be at an end and society will live under a brighter, milder, happier sway of knowledge and truth." In these institutes, Baines told the Leeds membership, they would learn "habits and character" that would elevate "the condition of the many." The Whig peer Lord Morpeth, the great engineer George Stephenson, the novelist Charles Dickens, and the factory and prison inspectors Leonard Horner and Frederick Hill all visited the Leeds Mechanics Institute and held out the same vision of advancing knowledge and an improved and self-reliant working class.[95] It was another mix of illusion and reality. The reality was that mechanics institutes did educate clerks and small shopkeepers of the lower middle class and some skilled artisans of the working class; the illusion was that it elevated an entire working class, when in fact only a small number of that class ever attended its sessions, in which talk of religion or politics was not allowed. The members were also excluded from governing the institutes, a role that sometimes fell to Nonconformist clergymen, who presided as presidents, enforced temperance, and viewed these institutes, according to the *Leeds Mercury*, as "the auxiliary of the Temperance Society." That kind of virtue did not suit most workers. The workers did not support the great instrument of their salvation. Of York's population of 28,000, only 150 joined the institute.[96]

Successes the mechanics institutes did have, as did the tracts of Trimmer, More, Marcet, and Martineau and the works of the S.D.U.K., but largely with the upwardly mobile workers and with a middle class resolved to promote the values by which it had succeeded. But none of these efforts won worker readership as did William and Robert Chambers's *Chambers' Edinburgh Journal*. First published in 1832, its circulation rose to 60,000 in the first year, continued to rise thereafter, and it became, said the *Scotsman*, as popular as Dickens. Although the circulation of Charles Knight's *Penny Magazine* exceeded that of *Chambers'* for a while, the former publication failed in 1846, while *Chambers'* won a devoted and long-lasting readership among ambitious and literate workers. Samuel Smiles also won great popularity as editor of the *Leeds Times*, lecturer at the Leeds Mechanics Institute, and author of the classic *Self Help* (1859).[97]

Chambers' Edinburgh Journal was no less hopeful of social progress through reformed individuals than the tracts of Charles Knight and the speeches at the Leeds Mechanics Institute, but it expressed its belief in self-improvement in terms less condescending and paternalist and more independent and resolute. In an article "Self-Doing and Being Done For," *Chambers'* pronounced "the energy evoked by habits of self-dependence" as a "great force in human affairs," which would make "men of all classes . . . independent of each other," and, above all, end the "constant pretendings from one class to be taking care of another, providing for it, flannel-petticoating it, cottage and gardening it." Man ought not to be beholden to man, it concluded, but "self-dependent."[98]

Far less assertive of self-dependence were the speeches at the Leeds Mechanics Institute and Charles Knight's stories in his 1831 *Worker's Companion*. In 1842, Edward Baines Jr. told his Leeds audience that education was needed "for social order [and] the prosperity of their manufactures and commerce" and stressed in his *Leeds Mercury* how supremely important these institutes were in cultivating "a kindly union between the middle and working classes . . . a union in which the envy of the workers would be lessened" by the rich stooping "in order to raise up his inferiors."[99]

Charles Knight would have applauded Baines's condescending benevolence. He too saw education as a force for order and tranquility. "There was but one golden secret of happiness," he wrote, "BE INNOCENT AND BE CONTENT." Knight's belief in the "Great Wisdom and Providence of the Almighty" and the laws of political economy led to such an inordinate praise of capital, machinery, factories, and strike breakers, that the London Radical Francis Place warned him that it would alienate the workers.[100]

Far less alienating was the realism of the Chambers brothers and Samuel Smiles. Smiles advocated a far less deferential role for the working class than Baines and Knight. In his *Education of the Working Classes* (1842), Smiles exulted in the "grand idea of man, of the importance of man as man . . . with noble faculties to cultivate, great rights to assert, a vast destiny to accomplish." The "great rights" and "vast destiny" included not only efforts "to remove the cause of suffering" but the "elevating and improving of the whole class." As editor, from 1838 to 1842, of the *Leeds Times,* Smiles promoted that destiny by condemning the New Poor Law for branding poverty as a crime, championing universal suffrage, and lamenting the fact that "the working classes [were] the slaves of property and capital."[101]

Smiles and the Chambers brothers were Scots. So were nearly one in five newspaper editors throughout England and Scotland, even though Scots made up only 10 percent of Britain's population.[102] The Scots, famously self-reliant, were also preeminently upwardly mobile. A tradition of free parish schools, four accessible universities, and a Calvinist heritage led to such skills, energy, ambition, and independence of mind that they never doubted the self-help ethos. It gave to their self-reliance a tougher, more defiant, fiber than that encouraged in an England with a powerful Establishment and a more pervasive deference. Robert Chambers confessed as much to another self-made, resolutely independent Scot, Hugh Miller, editor of Edinburgh's *Witness.* "My years of direct hardship," Chambers told Miller, had led him by the age of sixteen to a "stern and burning defiance" and a "defying, self-relying spirit." It was a spirit shared by many a self-made artisan and reader of *Chambers' Edinburgh Journal.*[103]

One of the most radical newspapers in England and one widely read by the working classes, the *English Chartist Circular*, also expressed a defiant and assertive self-reliance. It hated paternalism, distrusted government, and knew little of socialism beyond Robert Owen's vision—itself not free from both a strong individualism and a distrust of government. The *Chartist Circular*, after quoting Tom Paine that "government, in its mildest form, is an evil," denounced "the infamous and demoralizing dependence which now exists between rich and poor." The answer to the social evils that afflicted the English, it said, lay in "individual improvement," in "education," and in "the formation of early character." The same suspicion of government and the same faith in education informed G. J. Holyoake's spirited monthly, *The Movement*. Unjustly jailed for blasphemy at Cheltenham in 1847, Holyoake was hardly confident that government would set things right. Neither, he asserted, would the Church's national schools, those "hotbeds of superstition," nor politicians full of "the cant of social reform." Instead, he was convinced that "the great fountain of prosperity and happiness . . . must ever be the principles of human nature . . . guiding the action of individuals," a sentiment echoed in G. A. Fleming's *The Union* in an article denying that a general wellbeing could be promoted by "external laws or coercive forces." Instead wellbeing would come only when "each individual would be gifted with a self-restraining and guiding power," when "each man is a huge colossus." And in reviewing Samuel Smiles's book on *The Education of the Working Class*, Fleming had only praise for that "self-dependence which ennobles man."[104]

Most Chartist leaders were self-educated. Indeed, self-education had saved from poverty leaders such as William Lovett, Henry Hetherington, John Cleave, Julian Harney, and the later recruits Thomas Cooper and Henry Vincent. For them, universal education was the grand remedy. Radicalism had long flourished on self-education and faith in education. It was integral to the corresponding societies of the 1790s and to the great war to free newspapers from the four-shilling stamp tax—that prohibitive tax on knowledge. The flourishing of an unstamped and cheap press itself was, in an England destitute of public education, a part of the working classes' self-education, as were the proliferating coffeehouses where the radical press was read and discussed. The Radicals' faith in education and in self-reliance ran deep, both in the Paine-Godwin gospel of natural rights and in their actual experience of upward mobility—an experience they shared not only with the early Nonconformist ministers but with most early Victorian newspaper editors.

Research has shown that the fathers of 128 newspaper editors came from more than 60 different employments. None of their fathers was a peer, baronet, knight, or bishop, and only five came from the gentry. Of the 128 fathers, 13 were farmers, 8 booksellers, 7 newspaper editors, 10 merchants, 5 printers, and 4 smaller manufacturers, and dozens more in similar middle- and lower-middle-class callings. Hailing from the working class were fathers who were stone cutters, seamen, coopers, weavers, glaziers, porters, carpenters, dyers, saddlers, farm laborers, and mole catchers. Of families about whose father's calling nothing is known, many were recorded as "in narrow circumstances." And quite overwhelming in obituaries and memoirs of these editors are accounts of their self-education, which led men like Thomas Latimer, editor of the *Western Times*, to "visualize . . . the world as consisting of individuals self-sufficient like himself."[105]

It is a vision that the leading moral-force Chartist, William Lovett, fully shared. "Education," he wrote, "will cause every latent seed of mind . . . to spring into useful life" and so will "alleviate misfortune, remove misery, and banish vice." Misery and vice persisted, but in Chartist lecturers, Owenite Halls of Science, Sunday schools, and countless improvement societies, self-education nonetheless flourished. In Leicester, Thomas Cooper, a self-educated Methodist turned Chartist, told adults in his Chartist Sunday school to read William Channing's *Self Culture* (a book also recommended by the Chartist Henry Vincent). Later in 1851, after Chartism had failed, in *Eight Letters to Young Men in the Working Class,* Cooper cautioned his readers, "Do not direct your poor brother to the rich man for help if you have the slightest power to help him yourself." He also warned against "improvidence and ignorance."[106]

Of the many institutions teaching self-reliance, few were closer to the working class than those Sunday schools and teetotal societies where working-class men and women taught reading and writing and lectured on the evil of drink. They did so with a reality and effectiveness far exceeding the condescending platitudes of Hannah More or Jane Marcet. Thomas Laqueur has shown in *Religion and Respectability: Sunday Schools and Working Class Culture* (1976) both how numerous and effective Britain's Sunday schools were and how much they had became part of working-class culture by the 1840s. More than 20,000 Sunday schools taught nearly two million pupils. Classes lasted four and more hours a Sunday, and the average child attended for three, four, or five years, learning to read, write, and do some arithmetic. Their teachers in the 1840s came from the same working class as the pupils. The paternal supervision of Anglican and Nonconformist clergy, so crucial to Sunday schools of the late eighteenth century, was much eroded, but not the morality of self-improvement. "Sunday schools with their accoutrements of reading clubs, libraries, and improvement societies," writes Laqueur, "offered a road to the twin ends of self-help and respectability." Self-help, he adds, was "replacing. . . older views of deference." Workers were appropriating the self-reliant ethic that they saw brought success—a success recorded not only in a rising literacy but in scores of memoirs and biographies. For some, the ladder upwards also involved membership in a temperance society.[107]

The temperance movement, while smaller than the Sunday school movement, had much in common with it: both originated in upper-class, church-centered efforts to improve the morals of the lower orders, both increasingly slipped into the control of the workers themselves, and both saw the workers appropriate the self-help morality. As Brian Harrison concludes in *Drink and the Victorians* (1971), the nineteenth-century temperance movement was "the movement, par excellence, of the self-made man . . . against a corrupt paternalism." In the British and Foreign Temperance Society, established in 1831, bishops, peers, and distinguished evangelicals hoped to wean all classes from the heady intoxication of spirits. Beer and wine in moderation were parts of civilized life, wine of the communion itself, but gin and whiskey and brandy were evil.[108] This London-based, upper-class, paternalist attempt at a moderate reform of drunkenness never worked. It erred in not seeing what Joseph Livesey, a cheese factor in Preston, Lancashire, saw so clearly, namely, that beer and wine were just as harmful, especially beer, to the working class. Livesey was an entirely self-made man. He spent seven years of his youth in a cellar weaving for long hours for a pittance and educating himself in the brief intervals. In 1832, as a strict Baptist, sturdy Radical, and leader of an adult school, he persuaded six other workers to sign the total abstinence pledge and thus began the Total Abstinence Society, which enjoyed a vigorous growth in the north of England, unaided by the British and Foreign Temperance Society. It taught self-help, said a weaver who rose to be mayor of Chester, which, he added, "is the best of all help, the best because it brings with it manly satisfaction." Lilian Shiman, in *Crusade Against Drink in Victorian England,* describes the huge impact of the teetotal movement on those of the working class most determined on self-improvement. At Bradford in Yorkshire, 2,000 joined, 500 of them being reclaimed drunkards. Teetotal societies built halls, established improvement societies and Sunday schools, ran endless tea parties, sent missionaries all over England, and in 1848 held a meeting of 180 men of the cloth, 151 of whom were Nonconformists.[109]

In one temperance meeting after another, abstinence was seen by the workers themselves as the first and greatest step in the reform of the individual—the only reform, said Livesey, that really counted. Most workers, of course, liked their beer more than abstinence, and most were not heroic in pursuit of frugality, industry, and sobriety. But many did realize that some education, some skills, even if acquired at dame and day schools or in the streets of London, would prove useful.

In the hugely varied patchwork of English education, thousands of private schools, often labeled "common day" or "dame" schools, accommodated more than a third of the children of the working class, charging about nine-pence a week. For Anglican promoters of National Society schools and for rationalist and Dissenting supporters of nonsectarian British and Foreign Society schools (both aided and inspected by government) these day and dame schools were "inferior," "worthless," "dens of ignorance," "nurseries of inaccuracy and superficiality." They were taught by untrained men and women who could earn a living no other way, who knew nothing of "correct method" and utterly neglected morals and religion.

The critics of dame and day schools were correct that the teachers came from the working class, that classes often met in kitchens or living rooms, that teachers taught little religion and only a few moral rules, knew no methods, and preached little self-help. But in these small classes, they nevertheless taught much reading, some writing, and a little arithmetic, and taught them to children who could attend at hours and days suitable to their part-time work. Rudiments, practical rudiments, were learned, and beyond that, according to those benefiting from these schools, self-education might take over. Dame and day schools were, like Sunday schools and temperance halls, part of working-class culture, as were improvement societies and halls of science. They were popular because they taught the reading and writing and ciphering needed for later skills. In 1861, more working-class children went to dame or day schools than attended National and British Society schools, the ratio remaining much what it had been in 1831.[110]

An unaided self-reliance also characterized the street people and laborers of London. In 1849, Henry Mayhew began an investigation of their condition, which he published in 1861–62. He discovered many astonishing things, not the least being how at the bottom of the social scale, often from sheer necessity, the very poorest adopted the philosophy of self-help. Mayhew was no romantic idealizer of the working classes. He was a realist who, in his collective portrait of London's 45,000 street people, did not overlook their faults— their cheating on sales, love of drink, thefts, fraud, and bouts of idleness. But far more common are the stoical virtues involved in their survival. Distress, misfortune, illness, misery, and homelessness afflicted these fallen gentlemen, jobless mechanics, redundant artisans, orphans, widows, cripples, drunkards and ex-paupers, who became costermongers, herring hawkers, onion sellers, shrimp sellers, balladeers, patterers, water carriers, bone grubbers, scavengers, sweeps, and rat catchers. They did just about anything rather than beg or steal or go on parish relief. They responded, reports Mayhew, with "fortitude and courage and perseverance," "general sagacity," "precocious sharpness," "stubborn self will," and "an honorable pride—even in privation." "The heroism of the unknown poor" left Mayhew in awe of the inner resources, the patience, and the good conduct of London's poorest, a class that many an upper-class moralist insisted were poor because they lacked self-reliance.[111]

For the London poor, self-reliance was, in fact, a necessity in the struggle for existence. Mayhew admitted that some of their misfortunes were "brought on by their own imprudence or sluggishness," but he also saw that they were often caused "by a series of misfortunes . . . beyond their control." But, for whatever reason, the surmounting of these misfortunes depended not on society or government but on the skill and energy and resolve of the individual. For London's street folk and casual laborers, as for those who escaped poverty through Sunday, dame, and day schools, or temperance halls and improvement societies, industry, sobriety, and providence were essential for survival.

So powerful was that reality for those who succeeded that it obscured the fact that the self-reliant did not always prosper. Great numbers of the industrious, provident, and sober not only did not prosper but suffered much destitution and exploitation. The refusal to admit this fact constituted the great illusion involved in the early Victorians' belief in self-help. From 1839 through 1842, and briefly in 1847 and 1848, economic depression threw millions out of work. Samuel Smiles, who in *Self Help* argued that "great social evils will for the most part be found to be only the outgrowth of our own personal life," was editor of the *Leeds Times* in 1841. That year, his paper noted, "of 19,936 individuals, only 3780 persons were at work and they at an average of only 11 and 1/2d a week." They were "willing to work, but with no work to do." Half of Stockport's and Oldham's mill hands were jobless, and two-thirds of London tailors. In Bolton 60 percent of mill workers, 84 percent of carpenters, and 97 percent of bricklayers looked for work in vain. In Newcastle and Leeds, J. G. Kohl, a German visitor, found many beggars whose "respectability, industry and order" showed that their plight arose from some deeply rooted evil in the social system and not from their own fault—a fact that the Leeds Society for the Suppression of Mendicity confirmed. Of 1,233 cases of distress investigated in 1842, 960 occurred from want of employment, 96 from sickness, 64 from loss of relatives and only 6 from "want of character."[112]

Economic depression was not new in 1839. Distress had swept Britain in 1801, 1811, 1816, and 1826. The depression that ran from 1839 to 1842 should not have appeared so exceptional and perplexing, yet it did.[113] The nearly complete closing of textile mills in Paisley in Scotland greatly perplexed Sir Robert Peel but left him publicly unmoved. In 1836, Peel had insisted "that when industry was combined with good moral character there was a certainty of [the workers] providing for their own subsistence." In 1842, despite mass unemployment in Paisley, which, being in Scotland, had no compulsory poor law, Peel opposed any government relief, because "the poor of that town will be taught to look . . . to the legislature, which can not apply any effective aid."[114]

Low wages, as much as depressions, made calls for self-help empty. The Reverend Sydney Godolphin Osborne at first did not admit this fact. In 1838, he opposed all injudicious charity, since "poverty arises from habits of waste and extravagance." A good paternalist, he urged landowners to sponsor penny clothing funds, coal funds, and benefit clubs so that waste and extravagance would yield to frugality and providence. In 1844, after helping the government investigate women and children in agriculture, he published *A View of the Low Moral and Physical Condition of Agricultural Labour.* He found the wages of laborers were 6s. 6d. to 8s. a week in Dorset, with most below 8s., and with single men at 6s. a week. Hopes of clothing and coal funds quickly evaporated, and "a very large proportion of the agricultural labourers have it not in their power to rear their families in the common, decent habits of civilized society." Indeed, he could not understand how they even existed.[115]

Godolphin Osborne's awareness of the actual plight of the agricultural poor led to doubts about the New Poor Law's basic assumption that easy relief had corrupted the poor—an assumption at the core of many an early Victorian's illusion about self-reliance. Two M.P.'s who were skeptical were John Fielden and Thomas Wakley, both of whom sat on the Select Committee of 1837 and 1838 on the New Poor Law. Witnesses who airily talked of the corruption that would result from demanding that those seeking relief perform some labor, rather than enter a workhouse, were asked to name names, to give examples. When a witness failed to do so, Fielden expostulated, "If you can name not one what good [are your claims]?" The contention that outdoor relief corrupted seldom survived close examination. Fielden's fellow Radical Thomas Wakley asked the Commons in 1846 why if, from 1837 to 1844, outdoor relief to the able-bodied had far exceeded relief given them in the workhouse, it had not demoralized the poor?[116] Edinburgh's sagacious Dr. W.P. Alison had long pondered the question. Scottish self-help philosophers, led by the popular Thomas Chalmers—who was happy Scotland had no compulsory poor law—never tired of claiming that poor laws led to idleness and improvidence. "The facts," wrote Alison in 1846, "distinctly refute this since . . . the nations most celebrated for industry have long had poor laws." When there was no demand for employment, he added, destitution was not due to "misconduct of any kind."[117]

These observations in no way dented Chalmer's opposition to a compulsory poor law, a position he also applied to Ireland, and one that elicited an indignant response from the bishop of Kildaire. To Chalmers's claim that aid to the aged would undermine thrift, the bishop replied that Ireland's "enormous deep, wide misery made such moralism a mockery."[118]

Chalmers was not alone in moralizing about Irish laziness and improvidence. Scores of M.P.'s and editors discoursed on the corrupt character of the Irish at the very moment when the fault lay with diseased potatoes. That all poverty came from a lack of self-reliance had become a grand illusion, an illusion applied not only to Irish peasants, of whom the M.P.'s and editors knew little, but to the English poor, whose stoical self-reliance only a few like Henry Mayhew had explored.

There are many reasons why the propertied classes indulged in such illusions. They wished, of course, to avoid the expense of caring for the destitute. But powerful in justifying that avoidance was the eminent usefulness of the self-help ethic in the lives of countless men and women. It really had worked for millions. Among the reasons for holding an illusory views of self-reliance's great powers, one struck Hugo Reid as especially revealing. In his 1848 pamphlet *What Should Be Done For The People,* he wrote that "It is a common opinion of those who by superior energy and talent or fortunate chance, have made their way in the world . . . that all may do as they have done." It was an assumption that led to the belief "that those who do not at least maintain themselves have themselves to blame, deserve to suffer and ought to be sharply dealt with as a terror to evil doers." It was a harsh doctrine, since there are "thousands, hundreds of thousand, in deplorable circumstances . . . [who have] no possible chance."[119]

To these charges, many an early Victorian would have replied that those in deplorable circumstances would not suffer excessively, since hospitals and charities would help them. The admirable outpouring of altruism, energy, and charity that was part of the larger, more diverse, many-sided, and pervasive movement called voluntarism was just as crucial as the belief in self-reliance to the early Victorians' vision of a laissez-faire society.

CHAPTER 8

Voluntarism

A basic assumption that defined the early Victorian vision of a laissez-faire society was voluntarism, especially in its charities, a safety net for the destitute. It was invoked when paternalism was found wanting and when the harmonious working of the invisible hand, Divine Providence, and inviolable property broke down, and self-reliance itself could not meet adversity. It was also invoked in defense of religious liberty. It took many forms and had various definitions. "The word 'voluntary,'" exclaimed Alderman Luccock to the Leeds Town Council, "does not convey . . . a very clear idea." It did not, said Edward Miall, England's most enthusiastic voluntarist, because "the deviations from it in practice [have] so misled the public as to its true nature." Its true nature was of course religious, a fact that Miall's fellow Congregationalists at the *Patriot* were quick to observe. "The voluntary principle," they noted, "is a vague expression . . . [except] as applied to religion."[1]

That all churches should be entirely free of the state constituted the purest and most intense form of voluntarism. Since government was worldly and churches spiritual, the state should never interfere with religion. "Corruption" pronounced the *Baptist Magazine*, "comes into government schemes but not voluntary schemes." For the more radical among Dissenters that meant that the Church of England should be disestablished, a proposition that became the aim of the British Anti-State Church Association, which was founded in 1844.

In the first meeting of the Anti-State Church Association, the Reverend Joseph Fox declared "the unhallowed and adulterous union of church and state as the greatest evil that ever affected Christianity." At a quite different meeting in 1849, at a meeting of the Church of England's National Society, the Reverend George Denison announced that "the conflict between the church and the world is a perpetual conflict admitting of no armistice." Both Fox and Denison also condemned state aid to schools, institutions that should be entirely religious and entirely voluntary.[2] Fox was a Congregationalist and Denison a High Church Anglican. Both detested that Erastian secu-larized Church of England whose ruling bishops were appointed, after 1830, by worldly and latitudinarian Whigs. In 1833, Whig ministers had persuaded Parliament to reduce the number of bishops in the established Protestant Church of Ireland, bishops shunned by a Catholic majority in Ireland. The act also created an ecclesiastical commission to make more efficient use of the bishops' revenues.

Later Whig governments established another ecclesiastical commission to reform the Church of England. Acts of Parliament also ended the Church's monopoly over registering births, performing marriages, and presiding over burials, created a commission to commute Church tithes, and even tried, unsuccessfully, to excuse Dissenters from paying Church rates for the main-tenance of parish churches. Finally, in 1839, the Whigs not only proposed that government inspectors visit Church schools but urged the establishment of a teachers' training college with nonsectarian religious instruction. Such meddling in and reforming of the venerable Church of England by such known rationalists as the Whig Lords Melbourne, Russell, Palmerston, and Lansdowne proved too much for High Churchmen.[3] In 1833, Oxford's John Keble, in a sermon on "National Apostasy," expressed alarm over the Whigs' abolition of some Irish bishoprics, their creation of an ecclesiastical commis-sion, and the commission's plan to divert cathedral incomes to needy urban livings. The sermon marked the beginning of the Oxford, or Tractarian, Movement, which, in its dread of a secularized, government-influenced Church, listed toward voluntarism. In 1838, one of its more enthusiastic fol-lowers, Richard Hurrel Froude, urged that a disestablished Church of Eng-land rest on its own resources. By 1845, the High Church *Christian Remem-brancer* insisted that all schooling be Church of England schooling and be based "on that voluntary agency, the free gift of private men."[4] Having found as much "mischief" as "advantage" in the union of Church and state, the editors of the High Church *Oxford and Cambridge Review* declared in 1845 that "they were not among those called Establishmentarians." Furious at an Erastian Establishment full of Broad Church and evangelical bishops, the Tractarians talked boldly of voluntarism. But the always perceptive *Spectator* was, in 1845, quite dubious of the "High Churchmen saying that they prefer voluntarism to general endowment . . . [since they] are all for one Church endowment." Government grants to the Church of England, yes; to any other church, no! The *Oxford and Cambridge Review* in 1845 revealed the same ambivalence by denying that it was Establishmentarian, yet still prais-ing the union of Church and state because such a union made it clear that the Anglican faith was right and the Dissenters' faith wrong.[5]

The only consistent, unvarying voice for a pure religious voluntarism came from the radical section of Dissent. That Dissent gave rise to the most vigorous expression of religious voluntarism is not surprising. The Dissenters' theology was highly individualistic; their experience of persecution long, harassing, and ever present; their veneration of the Bible and the early Christians' voluntarism deep and intense; and, most important, their early nineteenth-century growth through voluntarism quite astonishing.

For Congregationalists and Baptists, the most militant of voluntarists, religion came not from the sacraments of an Established Church but from within. It was by the "regeneration from fallen man and sin through grace," as the Reverend R. W. Hamilton told his Leeds congregation, that man became "voluntary" and so "morally responsible."[6] If not voluntary, then not truly godly. There was "little vital Godliness" said the dean of Congregationalist theologians, Dr. Pye Smith, in a state Church. "Let civil government keep to its own provinces, [and] let religion be left to its own energy," especially since such a religion, one that lay "in the hearts and conscience of men," became "a system of divine benevolence."[7]

Many an Anglican evangelical, while finding religion and benevolence in the "hearts and conscience of men," could agree neither that the state Church lacked godliness nor that the union of state and Church was "adulterous," and that the Church was a "painted harlot," "a wen on the body politic."[8] Devout Anglicans had not experienced a past full of persecution, of exclusion from Parliament, town councils, and universities, and of their marriages and burials being performed by alien priests. The Dissenters' liberties, to be sure, had improved with the repeal in 1828 of the Test and Corporation Acts and the passage in 1836 of two acts that allowed marriages to be performed and registered in Dissenting chapels and civil, not just Church, authorities to register births. But Dissenting pastors still could not read burial services in parish cemeteries, and young Dissenters could not win degrees from Oxford and Cambridge. In the countryside, Anglican landlords ejected Dissenting tenants and refused to buy from Dissenting tradesmen. Most vexing of all was the fact that Dissenters had to pay Church rates for the upkeep of Anglican churches. In 1839 and 1840, a Chelmsford shoemaker, John Thorogood, and a Leicester shopkeeper, William Baines, refused to pay the rate. Both were imprisoned, a fate other martyrs also suffered, although to the applause of an expanding world of Nonconformist periodicals, which never tired of telling their readers of the coercive tyranny of a Church that was not based on the voluntary principle.[9]

The fact that most of the Dissenters' grievances were not, by the 1840s, of great magnitude, made little difference. The Dissenters were now powerful and they were now proud, and they found Church rates and exclusion from the universities insulting. A new force, a voluntarist force, had risen to confront the Establishment. The Census of 1851 revealed that Dissenters constituted nearly half of all churchgoers. The more than 8,000 churches that the Dissenters attended had all been paid for by voluntary contributions, as were thousands of Sunday schools, scores of academies, divinity schools, temperance halls, and periodicals. These voluntary institutions, said the *Leeds Mercury*, constituted "The Glory and Hope of England." "The principle of religious zeal," added its editor, Edward Baines Sr., "had done everything in Leeds." For his fellow Congregationalist Edward Miall, editor of the *Non-Conformist*, the principle of voluntarism lay at the heart of Christianity, so much so that he confessed, "I would give up Christianity itself if it is to be compulsory."[10]

Not all Dissenters felt so strongly. Some even preferred to work closely in philanthropic societies with Anglican evangelicals who believed with Burke in the value of an Established Church and with William Wilberforce and Thomas Chalmers in the power of both voluntary societies and an Established Church. Chalmers thought that education should be the task of a state Church and poor relief voluntary. As the High Church Oxford Movement became stronger within the Church of England, evangelicals became more ambivalent about the idea of an Established Church and tended increasingly to voluntarism.

The evangelicals' ambivalence deepened and their voluntarism grew stronger when a Scottish court of law determined that not the congregations of the Church of Scotland but the lords who were the patrons of the parish churches had the final say on the appointment of ministers. In 1843, the quarrel over the appointment of ministers led nearly one-third of the Scottish clergy, including Thomas Chalmers, once strong for the Establishment, to secede and form the Voluntary Secessionist Church of Scotland. This had been the aim of Sir Culling Eardley Smith, M.P. and many other Anglican evangelicals when they formed the Voluntary Church Association in 1839.[11] They were, however, a minority. The power, influence, wealth, prestige, and venerable history of the Church of England kept most evangelicals, as it did most High Churchmen, within its comfortable and wealthy confines.

But for those, whether the Congregationalist Miall or the High Church Froude, of a deep, intense, all encompassing and dogmatic faith, a faith that a state Church might corrupt, the answer was a voluntary church. How else could error and heresy be excluded? It was in such religious experiences that the first and most powerful form of early Victorian voluntarism had its roots.

Not as dramatic or intense was a second, less obtrusive, although quite pervasive form of voluntarism, a political one, which proposed to answer the evils of a laissez-faire capitalism not by laws but by voluntary arrangements. The Radicals Joseph Hume and John Bright were for a shorter workday for bakers and mill hands, if "voluntarily" arranged; Bingham Escott and Thomas Wakley were for allotments, but on the "voluntary" principle; Lord Lincoln and Colonel Sibthorp were for tenants' rights, but only if "voluntarily" accepted; Lord Grey was for emigration and the duke of Buccleuch for better sanitation, but not if compulsory; and the bishop of Exeter condemned prostitution and Charles Adderly the cruelties of the game laws, but opposed any laws against these evils whose removal must be by "voluntary" action. And surpassing all in a faith in voluntarism was Sir Robert Peel, who applied it to emigration, allotments, education, game laws, and Scottish and Irish poor relief.[12]

The press also liked the voluntary, not the coercive, principle. *John Bull* would leave sanitary reform, emigration, and a shorter working day to private efforts, and the *Economist*, whose laissez-faire outlook only Miall's *NonConformist* could rival, added to the economists' harmonious laws the wisdom of voluntarism, which it called "the good old English custom of managing our own affairs." It was a custom so widespread that it ran from the staunchly paternalist *John Bull* to the Unitarians' staunchly individualistic *Christian Teacher*. For the "knottier problems," said the *Christian Teacher*, the "remedy is still voluntarism."[13]

A third form of voluntarism, a most idealistic one, was that of individual benevolence. If neighborly benevolence were universal, it would do much to assuage the evils of excessive self-interest. There would be a laissez-faire of kindliness; or, as the *Patriot* put it in 1848, "a free trade in kindly feelings and human offices," which it hoped would render poor laws unnecessary. The *North British Review* and the *Eclectic* agreed, looking for the just society in "the general and earnest application of the Gospel to our dealings with each other" and in the working of "the highest moral and spiritual elements into all arrangements of society." The *North British Review* even saw in "voluntary benevolence" a "check and corrective to self-interest."[14]

Neither the *Patriot, North British Review*, nor *Eclectic* were Anglican, and all reflected, in preaching self-reliance and voluntary benevolence, the keen individualism of Nonconformity. But such benevolence was also extolled by the earl of Chichester in the Tory *Sussex Agricultural Express* and by the Owenites in the *New Moral World*. We must rely, said Chichester, "on our private capacities to promote religion and virtue" and look to the "individual efforts of good men for the suppression of crime." The *New Moral World* insisted that progress would arise from man's "nobler properties" and those "affections that lead to attachment to others."[15] Be manly, said Carlyle, repeatedly; do good and be virtuous, said Coleridge, as did the sermons of hundreds of clergymen of every faith, who all hoped that voluntary kindness in the fields and workshops and markets would create a truly Christian society.

Yet there would still be epidemics, ill health, orphans, penniless widows, and the aged and destitute, and since sin is original and ineradicable, so would there be prostitution, theft, blasphemy, vagrancy, and a host of crimes and immoralities. To meet these many inevitable evils, a fourth form of voluntarism arose, the philanthropic society. Individual acts of kindness were not enough. Those blessed with wealth, power, position, learning, and Christian faith must organize to remove or alleviate the distress and misery of the down-and-out, the lost, and the bereft. When Queen Victoria ascended the throne in 1837, the age of philanthropic societies was in full swing, and they already constituted a most pervasive form of voluntarism, one that expanded its efforts beyond a jealous defense of religion, beyond the mitigation of capitalist exploitation, and beyond the promotion of individual kindness. It expressed itself in hospitals, dispensaries, soup kitchens, home missions, sisters of charity, visiting societies, model lodging houses, orphanages, mechanics institutes, athenaeums, ragged schools, industrial schools, baths and washhouses, female emigration societies, houses of refuge, temperance halls, libraries, and many more such societies, all private, all voluntary, and all expressive of the principle of association.

If the upper class could employ the principle of association to mitigate misery, why could not the working class do likewise? In the rapid growth of benefit and friendly societies and cooperatives and unions, the workers answered, yes, we can, and their answer pleased many in the upper class. How admirable that a few pence a week to a society would guard the poor against illness and unemployment and would pay for burials. But less pleasing to the upper class was the workers' enthusiasm for associations that sought to control shops and workplaces or build socialist communities and cooperatives. Such efforts constituted a fifth form of voluntarism—that of working-class associationism.

In an England deeply hostile to government, voluntarism, as Miall said, took "many deviations." This contributed to its spreading widely and becoming one of the most powerful forces underlying the early Victorian quest for a laissez-faire society. Voluntarism inspired powerful elements both of the Church of England and of Dissent to oppose state education, for example, although at different times and in different ways. Just as the United States and European nations were creating systems of public education, England became entangled in an inept and inadequate compromise between a voluntary and a public system.

THE BATTLE OVER EDUCATION

In 1839, the Whig government proposed to give £30,000 in grants to elementary schools that belonged to the Church of England's National Society and the nondenominational, but Protestant, British and Foreign School Society. The government also created a committee in council on education, appointed two inspectors of schools to supervise the grants, and established a normal school to train teachers. Although this went beyond the £20,000 that Parliament had in 1833 granted the two societies to build schools, it certainly did not envision a national system of rate-supported schools. But some system was needed. The chaos of private, Church, and charity schools fell far short of educating the young. More than half of those aged between five and fifteen attended no school at all, and the education of those who did was lamentably deficient because they spent only a few years at school, and the schools taught little more than reading and a bit of writing—and that not very well because classes were huge and teachers untrained.

Despite the profound need for a system of public education and the modesty of the Whig proposal, the Church of England nevertheless denounced the scheme. Behind the denunciations lay a mix of Establishmentarianism and voluntarism. The High Church part of the mix was the most avowedly voluntarist. High Churchmen had no fear of that word. Britain did not need a "colossal system of state education," declared the *British Critic* in 1837, but rather "education voluntary and unfettered." In 1838, it praised voluntarism in education, and in 1839, it called the idea of a public system of education "unEnglish and Prussian." Oxford University's Thomas Mozeley was editor of the *Christian Remembrancer* in 1846, when it too came out for voluntarism in education. After insisting that no government, Whig or Tory, should apply public money to education, Moseley argued that education belonged to "that voluntary agency, the free gift of private men . . . the only channel from which these things can come." The concept of the Church as a "voluntary agency" was not new, said William Sewell, in his classic statement of paternalism, *Christian Politics*; it had always been "recognized and maintained by the Catholic Church."[16]

In Parliament in 1839, Young England, Disraeli's knights errant in the cause of High Church ideals, condemned the education scheme. A government that "had not formed a single road, made a single bridge or dug a single canal," argued Disraeli, could certainly not educate. Education should be left, not to government, which should be weak, but to the individual, who should be strong. It was a sentiment his fellow Young Englander John Manners echoed when he warned that government schemes of education would supersede that "system of private munificence" on which Church and charities were founded.[17]

Endowments were central to High Church voluntarism. The centuries-old Anglo-Catholic Church had been built by the private munificence of voluntary gifts, a sacred endowment that neither bureaucrats in Whitehall nor radicals in parish vestries should endanger. The government might, of course, increase it. No meticulous consistency ruled out such grants. "The voluntary principle" wrote William Sewell, "touches not the question of tithes . . . nor Church rates"; nor was it inconsistent with a grant of public funds to the Church.[18] The idea that such a Church-centered system, one resting not only on private munificence but also on compulsory tithes, Church rates, and Treasury grants for Church extension could be voluntary would certainly have left both militant Dissenters and political radicals dumbfounded.

Even Anglican evangelicals were astonished. They, too, had a strong strain of voluntarism, one centered not on endowments but on voluntary societies. In 1839, the evangelicals also denounced the government's education scheme.[19] They possessed great confidence in that outpouring of voluntary energies and wealth that had founded and sustained the Pastoral Aid Society, the Bible Society, the Religious Tract Society, and the District Visiting Society. In 1838, much enthusiasm and energy—and not just from evangelicals—went into the Church of England's National Society for the promotion of education. It led to the creation of twenty-six diocesan and subdiocesan boards of education, the appointment of Anglican school inspectors, and the establishment of teacher training colleges and many schools whose instruction centered largely on reading the Bible and committing to memory the catechism and related doctrines. The National Society wished to prevent the government from creating schools with an undue amount of secular learning and any religious instruction not purely Anglican.[20]

William Howley, archbishop of Canterbury, and Charles Blomfield, bishop of London—neither of them either an evangelical or a High Churchman—led the attack on the Education Minute of 1839. They succeeded in killing the normal school because its nonsectarian religious instruction was anathema to those devout Anglicans who were utterly convinced that only Anglican instruction, doctrine, and catechism could provide a truly religious and so safe education. But they did accept grants to National Society schools and their inspection—although not before gaining great—some felt dominant—influence on the appointment and control of the government's inspectors of national schools.[21]

To many Anglicans, the compromise involved in this "concordat" only furthered voluntarism. The *Christian Observer* expressed the cheerful hope that government grants would allow the Church to promote religious education "upon the principle of voluntarism." But the purer voluntarists, the *Times* included, saw in the Whig scheme only the baleful hand of despotic government.[22] For Blomfield and Howley, the Church of England was the Established Church of all Her Majesty's subjects. It represented voluntary zeal, even though it possessed rights to tithes, Church rates, Treasury grants, political privileges, and legal jurisdictions. If the Church no longer enjoyed that monopoly of political and military offices that it had enjoyed before the 1828 repeal of the Test and Corporation Acts and the Catholic Emancipation Act of 1829, it was nevertheless still a power—although not a power wealthy enough to educate all. It needed both government money and independence in its use in order to ensure an exclusive education in Anglican doctrines. It thus entered into the concordat. It negotiated a compromise, a settlement reflecting the blend of voluntarism and establishmentarianism that had long been the genius of the Anglican via media.

It was a blend Sir Robert Peel supported. Peel often expressed a decided liking for the voluntarist answer to social problems, to distress and emigration, and to railways and education. In 1841, having become prime minister, he announced that in education, "it is on local voluntary exertion that the great reliance must be placed."[23] Two years later, however, Peel reversed himself. In 1843, he accepted a bill put forward by his home secretary, Sir James Graham, for rate-supported factory schools in which there would be Anglican religious instruction, but with a conscience clause exempting Dissenters, if they chose to use it. The bill created local school boards of seven trustees chaired by an eighth, ex-officio trustee, always the local clergyman. Since two of the trustees had to be church wardens, two appointed by magistrates, two mill owners, and one the donor of the site, the probability was overwhelming that Anglicans would dominate the board. It was a domination made more certain in that the local bishop had to approve all schoolmasters and religious instruction had to be Anglican. Dissenters could opt out only if their parents were bold and informed enough to request exemption.[24]

The bill was too much for the Dissenters. Even the quiet Quakers, aloof Unitarians, and Tory Wesleyans petitioned against it. Leeds's leading Unitarian, Homer Stansfield, claimed that it would create "conflict . . . between voluntary principle . . . which admits . . . all the power the Creator has blessed us with, and the protective principle, which by shackling and counteracting those powers, wars on Deity." Confronted with 15,873 petitions and 2.6 million signatures, Peel withdrew the bill. Not only were all Dissenters furious against it, but the *Times* and many bishops opposed it, including the bishop of Ripon, who concluded that the Church must now depend "chiefly on her own resources and voluntary contributions."[25]

James Kay-Shuttleworth, the secretary of the Committee on Education that supervised Treasury grants, knew that the still formidable Church of England would not abide a national system of rate-supported schools imparting nonsectarian religious instruction. He also knew that a rising, wealthy, numerous Dissent would not abide a national system of Anglican rate-supported schools. The only alternative was government grants to those Anglican and Dissenting (and in 1847 Catholic) schools that in fact reflected the pervasiveness of voluntarism among all classes and in all walks of life. Kay-Shuttleworth hoped that the marriage of government grants and inspection with local voluntarism would be England's unique way of educating her people. Under Peel, Parliament did little to further this compromise, because 1839's meager £30,000 in grants had become only £40,000 by 1844.[26]

Not until the return of the Whigs in 1846 and grants totaling £150,000 did the fusing of government grants and voluntary giving and management receive a fair trial. The minutes of the Committee in Council on Education of December 21, 1846, proposed to give government grants of from £10 to £20 a year to pupil teachers. The best of these apprentices would receive yearly scholarships of £20 or £25 for further training at a normal school. Government grants would also enhance the salaries of those teachers whose certificate of merit qualified them to supervise the pupil teachers or to attend normal schools. Government money would also finance pensions for retired teachers. It was a proposal that substantially increased the role of government in education.[27]

When, on February 5, 1847, the government announced this increased role, militant Dissent and political Radicalism erupted in anger. It was unconstitutional! Despotic! Prussian! It undermined voluntarism and so chilled benevolence. It created a monstrous bureaucracy. Its proposed 80,000 pupil teachers would form an army of government hirelings, part of the proliferation of Whig patronage. And the increasingly Tractarian Church of England, which received nearly seventeen out of every eighteen grants, would reign supreme.

The leading organs of Dissent, the *Eclectic*, the *Patriot*, the *Christian Witness*, the *Baptist Magazine*, and the *NonConformist* were unequivocal in condemning the minutes of 1846 and 1847, as were the *Leeds Mercury*, *Manchester Times*, *Economist*, *Sheffield Independent*, *Cheltenham Free Press*, *Plymouth and Devonport Journal*, *Evangelical Magazine*, and other journals wedded to voluntarism.[28]

Not all Dissenters shared this militant voluntarism. Dissent split on the question of public education. Quakers and Unitarians either resumed a quiet neutrality or a quiet support of the government scheme.[29] The Wesleyans signed on—for a paltry 1½ percent of the grants, complained critics, with 88 percent going to Church of England schools. And most disturbing of all, the London Congregationalists under Robert Vaughan and Thomas Binney supported the government, while some Lancashire Dissenters helped form the Lancashire [later National] Public Schools Association in order to demand the establishment of local, rate-supported, nondenominational schools.[30] But although the Dissenters did divide, the periodicals, debates, meetings, and pamphlets of the time make it clear that militant Dissent was the most vocal, active opponent, its meetings and petitions the most numerous, and its pure voluntarism the most intense and complete.

Three powerful emotions lay behind this intense outburst of voluntarism: fear, pride, and piety. Fear of a state Church was nourished not only by memories of past persecution but by knowledge of present harassments. Baptist and Congregational periodicals, in particular, never relaxed their vigilance. The *Baptist Pioneer* painted the story of Anglican landlords refusing to license a Dissenting chapel in the harshest colors, and the *Congregational Magazine* told of a Puseyite clergy who insisted on compulsory baptisms and refused workers not attending Church of England services the right to an allotment. To the *Baptist Guardian,* the greatest threat came from "a multiform priestcraft" that constituted "the hydra of persecution," while to the *Baptist Magazine,* the proposed pupil teachers meant only "a system of spiritual despotism."[31]

The *Baptist Magazine* also invoked our "forefathers' struggle for a free conscience." Dissent of every persuasion was proud of its past struggles and past achievements—and most particularly of its cherished voluntary principle. "Nothing in history can be compared to it," exclaimed the *Leeds Mercury,* "for furthering religious and benevolent ends." It was, it added, "one of the splendid discoveries of modern times." It was so splendid, asserted the *Congregational Magazine* in 1842 because of its "vital and irrepressible energy," which since 1835 had built 528 chapels. Voluntarism, reported the *Congregational Yearbook* in 1851, had "wrought the most miraculous change in human society ever recorded—it is competent to meet all spiritual exigencies." Certainly, the Christian education of the young was a spiritual task easily accomplished by voluntarism, which had not only built chapels and Sunday schools, formed myriad societies, and spread learning, but produced world-famous Manchester, Liverpool, and Leeds and many of their great inventors, industrialists, traders, and philanthropists? Who would doubt that such a voluntarism could educate a nation? Certainly not Leeds's Reverend John Ely, who told his congregation, "Oh there is a latent power amongst us . . . for the world's renovation."[32]

Pious Dissenters also had no doubt that all education should be religious—and religious according to the Gospel! These devout Dissenters believed deeply in their form of Protestant truth. Like their High Church counterparts, they were trapped in a simple syllogism: education should accord with their religious truth, government schools would never teach that truth, ergo, churches not government must educate. It was a logic that drove the deeply devout, whether Anglican or Dissent, to believe in voluntarism.

Also promoting voluntarism was the parallel emergence of a laissez-faire economics and a growing hostility toward all monopolies. Few expressed this general exhilaration in advancing freedom more than the Congregationalist Reverend Andrew Reed: "We ask, in short, that we shall be free; in labour, free; in trade, free; in action, free; in thought, free; in speech, free; in religion, free—perfectly free."[33] If the agitation against the Corn Law monopoly could win out in 1846, why couldn't the attack on the Church's threatened education monopoly?

For all its enormous energy, hundreds of meetings, flood of periodicals and pamphlets, and petitions signed by thousands, the voluntarists' attack failed. Government grants increased, pupil teachers and certificated masters multiplied, training colleges expanded, and the number of Her Majesty's inspectors of schools rose from two in 1839 to eighteen in 1849. The main reason for the failure of the Dissenters' attack was the inherent weakness of the voluntary principle. People simply would not give to build and run schools as they did to build and run chapels and churches. The Wesleyans and Congregationalists did not even establish boards of education until 1839 and 1843, and the Baptists did not create a national school society until 1848.[34] In 1844, the Congregationalists raised £70,000 from 1,000 churches, a paltry £70 per church. In 1846, they sent out 1,159 education questionnaires. Only 671 were returned, and 532 of them reported that the local Congregationalists had done nothing. In Leeds, the Congregationalists had only one public day school, and the much vaunted Leeds Sunday School Union in 1845 had a total budget of £170. It could teach nearly 10,000 only because its teachers taught without pay.[35]

The battle over the 1846 and 1847 educational minutes did galvanize greater efforts, but they soon subsided. "The voluntary principle," concluded the Westminster Review, "is fickle"; "desultory, uncertain, irregular and sporadic," added the Leeds Intelligencer; "sporadic and spasmodic," said the Athenaeum.[36]

Even those voluntary efforts that government grants hoped to encourage proved inadequate. Anglicans were no more inclined than Dissenters to pay for schools. Only £50 was given to the schools in a district with a population of 10,000, of whom the twenty-five wealthiest had £50,000 a year in net income; the average income of each of the 105 schools in another district was a meager £81 14s., one out of four teachers was untrained, and the average number of pupils per teacher was over 100; and in a third district, the trustees of only 33 out of its 136 schools met to examine what progress was being made. These dismal reports came from two of Her Majesty's inspectors of schools, Henry Moseley and Frederick Watkins. Moseley admitted that the public "has little faith [and] no money" for education, and Watkins that "liberality among the lay is rare." Little wonder, then, that the Oxford Diocesan School Board reported in 1846 that "at no time has the lay agency been less effective."[37] The result of such apathy was that the expansion of education by the combination of government grants and voluntarism failed to keep abreast of the growth of population. Between 1839 and 1856, although Church of England schools were built for some 495,000 pupils, the number of children of school age—that is, between five and fifteen years old—rose by nearly a million. Since Dissenters built far fewer schools, it is clear that England's voluntary efforts were not keeping up with population. Even Lord John Russell, the co-author of the schemes of 1839, 1846, and 1847, was disappointed—although not sufficiently disappointed to support W. J. Fox's bill for a national system of rate-supported schools. Like Arthur Roebuck's and Thomas Wyse's scheme in the 1830s, Fox's bill garnered only a handful of votes in Parliament.[38] Although voluntarism had fallen far short of its educational goals, it was still preferred to a larger government role in education, and not just by Dissenters and High Churchmen, but by quite a few Radicals. Following William Godwin and Joseph Priestley, Radicals like Cobbett, Hetherington, Hodgskin, Lovett, and Collins so feared the despotism of government that they sought to promote education, which they believed in ardently, by Owenite halls of science, Chartist schools, people's colleges, and, in Lovett's vision, a national association of district halls with schools, field gardens, workshops, museums, and baths.[39]

Middle-class Radicals and Liberals like Samuel Smiles, William and Mary Howitt, and Birmingham's Reverend George Dawson were also ardent for an educational system independent of government. In 1847, *Howitt's Journal* championed a national, not a government, system since government education would "mould the people to a patient acquiescence," whereas education needs "perfect freedom." It also urged the people to take the question of education into their own hands and establish a people's college in London, an idea that Samuel Smiles saw enshrined in the Sheffield People's College and that the Reverend George Dawson said promised "a manly reliance on individual conviction." For Mary Leman Gillies, a frequent contributor to *Howitt's*, such colleges presented the "collective self-culture doing its work."[40]

In Smiles, Dawson, and Gillies, a strong voluntarism was interwoven with an equally strong belief in self-reliance, just as the economists' idea of free trade was woven into the voluntarism of the Reverend Andrew Reed and other Nonconformist ministers. Indeed all three—voluntarism, self-reliance, and free trade—combined to block the development of a system of public education. Great was the enthusiasm for education on the part of Whigs, Liberals, and Radicals, but their advocacy of a viable scheme was tepid. The *Edinburgh* and *Westminster* reviews and the *Athenaeum, Spectator, Morning Chronicle*, and *Weekly Chronicle* were all eloquent on the need, but silent on the means, of educating the working class.[41]

The religious difficulties, of course, were formidable. In 1849, although it was clear that nearly nine-tenths of government grants had gone to National Society schools, the High Churchmen John Keble, Henry Manning, Archdeacon Sinclair, and the bishop of Salisbury, led by the crusading George Denison, archdeacon of Taunton, demanded, at the annual meeting of the National Society, that the management agreements that gave Anglican laymen dominance on most school committees be replaced in the smaller parishes by agreements giving that dominance to the clergy. When defeated, they again raised the cry for an entirely voluntarist scheme of Church education. Although the pure voluntarism of these High Churchmen was defeated as decisively as was the voluntarism of militant Dissent, the quasi-voluntarism of the moderates was not. It was, for example, voluntarists, pure and quasi, who defeated the 1852 Manchester and Salford Public School Bill, a bill for financing church schools from local rates, with schools of each faith offering their own religious instruction. In 1853, voluntarists also defeated a bill for local, nondenominational rate-supported schools offering comprehensive religious instruction; and 1855 saw five bills for some form of public education collapse.[42] The 1853 bill was the product of that National Public Schools Association, founded in Lancashire in 1847, largely by Dissenters. The wiser among the Dissenters perceived that if education remained largely voluntary, the wealthiest would predominate, and the wealthiest of all were Anglicans backed by the Established Church and the government. A nonsectarian, scripture-based religious instruction, the only one suitable for rate-supported public schools, also better fitted the Dissenters' Bible-based faith. It was, however, anathema to Anglican divines.

A truly public system of public education was not to be until 1870. Although religious jealousies were the primary reason for this delay, widespread faith in voluntarism was also a powerful cause. It was a faith nourished in part by the Whig schemes of 1839 and 1847, schemes whose marginal grants covered up the profound inadequacies of voluntary giving.

There was also much confusion and inconsistency, if not cynicism, in the various positions taken. In 1838, Edward Baines Sr. told the House of Commons, "Education ought to be attended to by the state." However, in 1847, in his *Leeds Mercury*, he condemned all government education as unconstitutional, despotic, and unchristian. Nor was Peel any more consistent. After being explicitly voluntarist in 1841, he went on to propose rate-supported factory schools in 1843. Peel was a voluntarist on many issues, but when John Bright asked that Church rates be voluntary, he replied, "Never!"[43] Voluntarism was often a rhetorical garb that was assumed whenever a sacred institution, especially a religious one, was threatened.

For many among the truly Christian, of course, voluntarism was also the best means of helping the poor. Had not Christ commanded his followers to visit the poor, feed the hungry, and clothe the naked? To carry out that command, voluntarism created home missions and district visitors and entered into the very hovels of the poor.

VISITING THE POOR

Each week in the 1830s and 1840s, thousands of British men and women visited the poor as members of dozens of societies anxious to help the sick and distressed, the erring and the lost. Many were part of the home mission societies of Baptist, Congregational and Presbyterian churches; others were part of the Unitarian domestic missions in Liverpool and Bristol and other large towns. The greatest of them all was the interdenominational, evangelically inspired, London City Mission. There were also district visiting societies in Cheltenham, Norwich, Birmingham, and many other towns, part of that General Society for the Promotion of District Visiting that Anglicans and Dissenters established in 1828. The variety of voluntary organizations visiting the poor was prodigious. Visitors from the Indigent Blind Visiting Society read the Bible to the physically blind, while agents of the Bible Society, Religious Tract Society, Christian Knowledge Society, and the Church of England's Reading Association exhorted the spiritually blind. The Stranger's Friend Society in Leeds and London and elsewhere helped the worthy poor who fell ill, while visitors from the Society for the Repression of Mendicity gave to the deserving and refused the undeserving.[44] Just as numerous and energetic as any of these visitors were those from temperance societies; and rivaling them were those who helped prostitutes or were active in forming clothing and blanket clubs.

Visiting the poor, that is, their own poor, was a solemn duty for Methodists. Their pastors, deacons, class leaders, Sunday school teachers, and all believing members formed a grand family, whose mission, said the *Wesleyan Times* in 1849 was to spread godliness.[45] It meant much visitation, even by the barely literate and nearly poor, a fact that greatly disturbed the Church of England.

For most Anglican clergymen, Christ's injunction to visit the poor was a duty incumbent not so much on the layman as on those ordained of God. It was a manageable duty in small rural parishes and a key element of rural paternalism. But what of a parish nearly the size of Leeds? Its vicar, the Reverend W. F. Hook asked Parliament to divide it into seventeen subparishes, each with a curate, who could visit the poor. The High Church Hook denounced the evangelicals' Church Missionary Society, Bible Society, and Pastoral Aid Society for bypassing the rule that only those ordained of God should give spiritual help. All High Churchmen and many other Anglicans agreed. But, by 1839, the Church Pastoral Aid Society had declined to five curates and three laymen, and the regular clergy did little about the half of England that lived in godlessness or wretchedness or both.[46]

Meanwhile, great were the boasts of London's City Mission and Leeds's Town Mission Societies and the Baptists' and Congregationalists' home missions. The London City Mission in 1850 employed 340 missionaries, each visiting more than 500 families a month. By 1855, it had grown even larger, and they made 1.5 million visits and distributed 2 million tracts. In Leeds, in 1848, the Town Mission, largely supported by Baptists, Congregationalists, and Wesleyans, made 80,915 visits and distributed 254,593 tracts. The Baptist Home Mission had 100 agents and 300 subordinates, and the Congregationalists had 130 agents preaching in 624 villages and towns. The Stranger's Friend Societies in London and Leeds also performed a division of labor with the home missions by caring for the temporal wants of those among the worthy poor who fell ill. In London, in 1840, the Stranger's Friends distributed £2,500 to the sick and distressed, and in 1847, they visited 2,100 cases and spent £480 to relieve 1,600 of the poor in Leeds; in both cities, this was done only after careful investigation.[47]

Evangelical Anglicans and Dissenters had much more success with their town missions and district visitors than did High Churchmen and strictly orthodox Anglicans who bridled when they heard of laymen who were not ordained by a bishop preaching the Gospel. But the High Church and orthodox also believed in visiting the poor both to console them in their inevitable lot and to make those marginal improvements allowed to sinful man. High Churchmen like John Keble, Edward Pusey, and Lord John Manners hoped, as did Robert Southey, that sisters of mercy would visit the poor, with Pusey adding the idea of celibate priests penetrating mines and mills. Devout, crusading Anglicans, like Harry Inglis, M.P., also wanted parliamentary grants for more churches and more clergy.[48]

The visitation of the poor was immensely popular. It covered the entire spectrum from the Unitarians' domestic missions to the Tractarians' sisters of mercy. It was a popularity that reflected the age's earnest religious belief. Rationalism had yet to assert its most eroding effects. Both Anglicans and Dissenters still hoped to convert each other: the *Oxford and Cambridge Review* foresaw a time when Dissent would be no more and the Church would "again 'fold the nation.'"[49] Conversion was central to visiting the poor. Also important were three basic assumptions that defined the outlook of these home missionaries and district visitors: that man is sinful, that Christianity reforms and renews, and that Christ demands that the rich help the poor.

That man is ineradicably sinful was, except for Unitarians and Quakers and some advanced Congregationalists and Broad Church Anglicans, a commonplace among early Victorian Christians. It was also widely accepted that sin underlay social evils. It formed part of the political philosophy of Burke and Coleridge and was fundamental to two of the most read of religious writers, the evangelicals J. P Sumner and Thomas Chalmers. It also permeated Dissent. The *Watchman*, in commenting on the physical suffering in cities, concluded that "we must trace the cause of evil to the sins of the people." "The disorders that afflict society," affirmed the *Baptist Examiner,* "are all the consequence of sin." Sin also, of course, imperiled one's soul for all eternity.[50]

But there was hope in Christianity, not only for eternity, but in terms of assuaging social evils. Although they differed in theology, church organization, and who should preach to the poor, all the churches, each in its own way, developed a laissez-faire social vision, more pervasive than that of the economists, based on a belief that sinners could be redeemed by Christianity operating through the voluntary exertions of individual Christians. And since social evil arose from sin, social good would surely flow from Christian grace. Social evils could be purged "by Christian truth," the *Baptist Examiner* said; they could be removed, in the *Christian Remembrancer's* words, by "the holiness which Christianity produces."[51] Inspired by Christian holiness, truly Christian individuals would feed the hungry, clothe the naked, visit the poor, and lessen those social evils that legislation and government could only make worse.

It was a vision developed in the 1820s by Thomas Chalmers in *A Christian and Civic Economy*, a detailed account of his work in St. John's parish, Glasgow, which offered a blueprint on how pastors, deacons, elders, and wealthy Christians should visit the poor, teach them self-reliance, bring them to godliness, teach respect for the Sabbath, urge the children to attend school, and inculcate a Christian neighborliness, all of which would lessen poverty and ignorance and crime. Visitation would spread the reforming power of the Gospel.[52]

By the 1840s, this vision of individual Christians voluntarily remaking and defining society had spread widely. In 1844, Chalmers was still preaching it in the *North British Review,* although in an even more voluntarist form since he had left the Established Church of Scotland and joined the Secessionist Church. More than ever, he believed that the "Christianity of the people is the sovereign cure for all social and all political disorders." His colleagues on the *North British Review,* Edward Maitland and Lord Moncrieff, spelled out how that "sovereign cure" would solve society's social problems. Christianity, argued Maitland, would become an all-pervading principle of human life. Believers would constitute a distinct religious society, with a government of its own and social duties and responsibilities incumbent on its members. The result would be a "vast physical amelioration." His colleague Moncrieff, who saw religion as "the great regenerator of society, the grand reformer, the instrument of redressing every social evil," was just as sanguine.[53]

The evangelicals of the Secessionist Church of Scotland were not alone in seeing in the visitation of the poor one key to social reform. No theologies were so far apart as the Unitarians and the Tractarians, yet both saw in their domestic missions and sisters of mercy and celibate priests answers to the misery and destitution of the poor. J. H. Thom, editor of the *Prospective Review,* saw in "the wisdom, holiness and refining grace of individual minds . . . the mightiest of all influences." And by its work "in the relations of society . . . all the woes of man" shall be relieved.[54] In Liverpool, Bristol, and Manchester, the Unitarians' domestic missions carried out their "individualistic" mode of preaching self-reliance, just as in Leeds celibate priests and in Plymouth, Devonport, and London sisters of mercy carried out their "corporate" mode of bringing "wisdom, holiness and reforming grace" to the poor.[55] Both High Churchmen and Unitarians confronted the ills of society with the transforming power of religion, as did, on a larger scale, Baptists, Congregationalists, Methodists, and evangelical Anglicans.

The Congregationalists' belief in the transforming power of the Gospel was spelled out at great length in Dr. Campbell's spirited *Jethro.* "Everywhere Godlessness! everywhere drunkenness and crime! everywhere destitution!" he exclaimed, and so little done. The answer: the Home Mission Society and its lay missionaries. "Lay power," declared Dr. Campbell, "may be likened to

steam power." The Home Mission Society was indeed high on the Congregationalists' agenda. It brought evangelical truth to the multitude, and such
truth, said the Reverend J. W. Massie, "improves the personal, the social and
oft times the domestic position of its recipients." By it, he added, society will
be "regenerated from the roots."[56] Both the Methodist Reverend James Dixon
and the Anglican bishop of Chester shared Massie's grand hope. "The solution awaiting the social and political world is," said Dixon, "the acceptance of
the Gospel as the basis of society." The Gospel, which "elevates men," said the
Bishop of Chester in 1841, was the "only remedy of that spiritual destitution
which is the cause of the temporal," just as "Christian charity" is the remedy
for moral and physical evils.[57]

That Christianity could transform individual lives and so lessen society's
worst evils only heightened the sense of a mission commanded in the Sermon
on the Mount. Visit the poor, said Jesus; feed the hungry and clothe the naked. Taken literally, it was an embarrassment to all, whether Unitarian, Tractarian, or evangelical. It was embarrassing because they believed that giving
meat to the hungry or clothing to the naked could corrupt the poor. "Giving
to beggars" said Archbishop Whatley, "leads them to live in idleness and
filth." "Public charities," insisted the Unitarians' *Christian Teacher*, "are
bounties to indolence and imprudence." And according to the *Eclectic*, "alms
corrupt and pauperize."[58] The leading evangelical journal, the *Record* and the
greatest of the visiting societies, the London City Mission, following Chalmers, opposed the distribution of relief. The fear was fraud practiced by the
poor and corruption flowing from charity.[59] The only answer, since Christ did
command the feeding and clothing of the poor, was to visit them and distinguish between the deserving and undeserving.

Feeding and clothing was also by no means the main aim of visiting the
poor. The voluntarists' true zeal was to save souls. As the governing committee of the London City Mission announced, "Its greatest design is to SAVE THE
SOUL." For most home missions, the great evil was irreligion. To the *Baptist
Magazine*, "infidelity will prove the hydra-headed monster." The great evil for
the *North British Review* was "ungodliness," and for the *Congregational Magazine*, "false religion, indifference, intemperance, and irreligion."[60] The journals and memoirs of Methodist preachers are obsessed with the overriding
need to save lost souls. It was a powerful obsession, one that also informs the
literature of the Bible Society, Religious Tract Society, and Christian Knowledge Society. High Church priests and sisters of charity, while speaking little
of conversion, were no less persuaded of the paramount necessity of spreading the saving grace of a sacramental Christianity.

A second goal was to console, comfort, and counsel the afflicted, to give them sympathy and so assuage their earthly woes. The sick and dying, above all, deserved consolation, as did poor widows and all those pitiable cases that could persuade every Christian to be his brother's keeper. The Stranger's Friend Society, in particular, gave solid if modest material help to those of the destitute who fell ill. In fact, many of the poor were so desperately destitute that the *Congregational Magazine* urged its missionaries to "minister to them food, cordials and clothes," and many Church of England district visitors helped with coal and clothing clubs.[61]

Emerging as a third and most compelling goal was the moral reform of the lower orders. While the saving of souls for eternity remained the summum bonum of home missions and district visitors, their reports increasingly reflected their moral conviction that the basis of a better society lay in individual reform. For Unitarians, whose recognition of eternity was not obsessive, their domestic missions became instruments of social reform. The third report of the Liverpool Domestic Mission Society urged its visitors to set up savings banks as a check on "recklessness and improvidence" and create juvenile gardens to encourage "habits of forethought, religion, industry . . . [and] love of nature." The Bristol Mission urged its visitors to teach "self-improvement as the means of bettering their condition." Since the Unitarians' *Prospective Review* condemned public charities and generous poor relief as corrupting, it urged that Unitarians' own voluntarist activities promote self-reliance. Their domestic missionaries insisted on the education of both children and parents. "The age of reason" declared Leeds's leading Unitarian minister, the Reverend Charles Wickstead, "must come to them."[62] Although the arrival of the age of reason was not an idea that the *Oxford and Cambridge Review* welcomed, its editors did consider that it was the function of those visiting the poor to instruct them "to fear God, honour the Queen and to love thy neighbour as thyself." Moral instruction writ large emerged as the grand object of the visitations. "Instruct his mind," enjoined the *Baptist Examiner*; "open their eyes, renovate their hearts," declared the *Congregational Magazine*; teach them, urged the *Wesleyan*, that "every man ought to be . . . his brother's keeper." Instruct, reform, foster independence, and make the poor self-reliant, such moral injunctions year after year were joined to the otherworldly goal of saving souls. "We must," said the *Congregational Magazine*, whose concern for moral reformation increasingly rivaled its concerns for salvation, "encourage a spirit of independence."[63] Many and various, of course, were the motives and goals of myriad home missionaries and district visitors. Besides their concern for eternal salvation and for the consolation and reform of the poor, there was a desire for social order, for a more integrated society, for secure property, and for closer-knit families.

The results of these great efforts were mixed. At first glance, they were paltry—paltry because of want of funds and paltry because the gulf between rich and poor was so great and the number of poor so vast. In 1861, Henry Mayhew pronounced the religious, moral, and intellectual degradation of London's poor to be "positively appalling"—and this after decades of dedicated work by the London City Mission and many others.[64] But dedication was no substitute for funds. In 1845, for their mission and visiting work, the Baptists of England raised only £5,000 and the Congregationalists only £7,000. In the wealthy West Riding of Yorkshire, the home mission raised a meager £900. A London drive to help the General Visiting Society netted only £250, a scandalously low figure, declared the famous evangelical Reverend Edward Bickersteth, compared to the £3.5 and £8.2 million collected from the taxes on tobacco and spirits.[65]

Home missionary efforts also fell far short of converting the multitudes. In 1840, at a large meeting, the Leeds Town Mission could boast of 32,632 visits, "2,000 meetings for reading and exhortation," and visits to workhouses and prisons, but only 100 conversions; and in 1846, "after 56,258 visits, 39,593 tracts, and 2,301 meetings attended by 79,000," only 84 joined a church. There was a superficiality to these visits, even those by the Stranger's Friend Society. To aid 1,600 worthy poor who fell ill in 1843, the Society spent £482, or about 3s. 7d. per person, certainly a distinct help, but not for an illness of any length.[66] However grim the ordeal of applying to the Poor Law authorities for medical relief, it at least had the resources to continue its aid. Voluntary benevolence, although often more sensitive and personal than bureaucratic relief, suffered in its visitations to the poor what voluntarists suffered in managing schools, a want of funds.

A want of funds, a reflection of early Victorian niggardliness, and the failure to win converts should not obscure the psychological value of many a visit, although this is difficult to measure. Some at least of the thousands who answered the knocks at the door must have felt their world was a little less dark, a little less friendless. The utilitarian *Westminster Review*, although intellectually removed from the largely evangelical visitors of the poor, was still full of praise for their work. "The present age," it declared, "may be called an age of religious sectarianism." Evangelicals now had much influence, especially among the lower orders. "They have gone to them in their . . . abodes of poverty, distress, and disease . . . and made the lower orders decent, sober and orderly." And, it added, "sects are now more liberal."[67]

The morality of the utilitarian was as filled with self-reliance and self-improvement as was the morality of the sects. Both also valued the voluntary efforts of private individuals and associations in furthering that morality.

Mayhew's general observation does not provide the best measure of the impact of the thousands of visits—an impact measured far better by the minority whom they had helped, if only a bit, to climb into the artisan and lower middle classes, there to become part of a huge sea of voluntary societies.

A SEA OF VOLUNTARIES

In 1851, a London barrister, Sampson Low, published *The Charities of London*. It presented both a familiar and an astonishing picture: familiar because it described old and widely known charities, astonishing because of their great numbers and variety. Low described nearly 600 in London alone. They ranged from charities providing drinking fountains to those providing lifeboats.[68] Although a few charities received supplementary aid from the government and more than a few existed on endowments from the past, the greatest number existed by yearly voluntary subscriptions. It was, as the battle over education and the story of home missions and district visitors has shown, the heyday of the voluntary society. The paternalism of landed estates and rural parishes had few remedies for the evils faced by mushrooming towns and cities, while a government "in itself evil" was still considered too dangerous as a solver of social ills. The great solver of social ills thus became, from 1840 into the 1860s, voluntarism. "Every improvement that is really valuable," declared *Bentley's Miscellany* in 1840, "must be voluntary." There was little it could not cover. "A new belief has arisen" announced the *Athenaeum* in 1847, "hence baths and washhouses . . . education, literature for all the people."[69] The High Church alone disagreed—but only for a while. As true paternalists, they feared that voluntary societies endangered the Church's paramountcy. "The several offices of the Church," warned the *British Critic,* "are all usurped by self-constituted bodies," bodies like the temperance and district visiting societies, bodies that deists joined, "discordant agencies" constituting "a quagmire." It was a quagmire that the *Christian Remembrancer* could not abide. "All schemes . . . of charity, allotment, emigration . . . are like quack medicine . . . ; education even, which is another of the panaceas that do very little good."[70] Other High Church journals agreed: for the *Englishman's Magazine* voluntary associations were "dangerous" because they engendered "feelings of independence"; for the *Quarterly Review's* High Church reviewer, the Reverend John Armstrong, because "Churchmen are everywhere heard to reprobate and condemn the voluntary system"; and for the Tory *Standard,* simply because "We abhor voluntarism." Henry Phillpotts, bishop of Exeter, expressed his abhorrence by making no Christmas gift to Plymouth's charities.[71] Yet voluntarism was too pervasive, and for the moment too appealing, to be totally dismissed by High Churchmen, particularly since they also distrusted the Whig government. One, the Reverend William Gresley, admitted that "some voluntary associations are better than others." For Pusey, Newman, W. F. Hook, and the *Christian Remembrancer,* the better were the sisters of mercy, the Incorporated Society for Church Building, and the celibate priests who plunged into the slums of Leeds. Some reviewers—not High Church—were also strong voluntarists. In 1846 and 1847, the *Quarterly Review* had one of the giants of that species, Lord Ashley, write on behalf of ragged schools and model housing for the working classes.[72] The wave upon wave of voluntarism could not, in fact, be checked. It flooded Britain, creating a veritable ocean of societies. They came in every form and size and kind. But great as was their variety, they were enough alike to fit into six classifications.

The first and wealthiest were the religious societies that sought to save souls; the second were the educational and religious institutions that sought moral reform. The British and Foreign Bible Society and the Religious Tract Society are examples of societies that concentrated on saving souls, and Sunday schools and temperance societies of institutions that focused on the moral reform. The Bible Society had 2,500 local associations, an income of over £100,000 and over 10,000 agents. The Bible Society did not stand alone in believing that infidelity was the great evil and Christian conversion the great good. It was joined by the Christian Instruction, Christian Knowledge, Scriptural Readers, and Tract societies, as well as by visiting and home mission societies. In 1861, Sampson Low listed eighty-one Bible and home and foreign missionary societies in London. He also listed thirty-one charities aiding schools, twenty for "maintaining and educating children," fourteen for orphans, twenty-two houses for penitent prostitutes, and sixteen reformatories and refuge institutions.[73] Moral reform now rivaled the saving of souls in the vast world of voluntary societies. Indeed, by 1861—since Low omitted mechanics institutes, athenaeums, and improvement societies—societies to promote moral reform no doubt exceeded societies to save souls. Evangelical home missionaries and Tractarian sisters of mercy would deny that saving souls excluded moral reform. Tractarians, for example, poured much selfless energy into Magdalen houses for penitent prostitutes. So did the evangelicals. In 1850, London had nearly thirty penitential homes, and such homes also graced the larger towns in the provinces. The passion to save and to reform sinners and potential sinners ran deep in Victorian piety and led to ragged schools for the near savage children of the destitute, industrial schools for youth on the edge of crime, reformatories for those falling over the edge, and even charities for discharged prisoners.[74]

Convinced Christians, like Lord Ashley and the Glaswegian Congregationalist Reverend Ralph Wardlaw, saw no clear-cut line dividing theological truth from moral reform and moral reform from social improvement. Yet insensibly, the theological gave way to the moral and social. Lord Ashley's orthodoxy was impeccable, but it plays no explicit role in his moving article on the need for ragged schools. The 1846 article, which appeared in the same *Quarterly Review* that had in 1840 criticized voluntarism, opens by praising "the efficacious virtues of the voluntary principle" and closes on the need to civilize "these wild colts of the pampas." In the entire article, there is not a word about the soul's eternal life. The Reverend Ralph Wardlaw's *Lecture on Female Prostitution* of 1842, although strictly puritan and full of dubious statistics, does provide a moral and sociological study unencumbered by concerns for eternity. It ends with a plea for the voluntary support of houses of refuge, a plea as moving as Ashley's for ragged schools.[75] If the orthodox Ashleys and the devout Wardlaws found their voluntarism enveloped in the earnest morality of the early Victorians, what of founders of industrial schools and reformatories like the rationalist Matthew Davenport Hill, the Unitarian Mary Carpenter, the Quaker William Allen, and the progressive Lady Noel Byron, in all of whom morality constituted an even larger part of their religion?[76]

That morality, in addition to the advances of science, also greatly increased a third type of voluntary societies—those caring for the ill and handicapped. They too enjoyed an exuberant growth. Foremost in that growth were voluntary hospitals and infirmaries, many founded in the eighteenth century, which flourished not only in London but in the larger towns. In 1863, they numbered 117 and had more than three times as many beds as they had had in 1800. Most of them also had dispensaries for outpatients, dispensaries that, along with those that were independent of hospitals, probably did more good than the hospitals. They dressed wounds, mended limbs, gave drugs, taught hygiene, and generally buoyed up the spirits. In 1838, while 17,000 became inpatients in Britain's twenty-one provincial hospitals, 50,000 were outpatients, and even more received treatment in London's dispensaries and hospitals.[77]

Specialized hospitals also emerged to treat the frequently excluded: lying-in hospitals for pregnant mothers, houses of recovery for fever patients, lock hospitals for those with venereal diseases, eye and ear hospitals, lunatic asylums, and schools for the blind and deaf and dumb. Almost all of these hospitals, infirmaries, and dispensaries were supported by the annual donations of subscribers, who could vote for the trustees, attend annual meetings, and give out tickets of admission to the deserving poor.[78]

From 1850 to 1860, no other form of charity grew so rapidly. Like Bible societies seeking conversion and institutions promoting moral reform, hospitals and dispensaries did not corrupt one's morals. "Charities lead to drunkenness and idleness," said the *Metropolitan Magazine* in 1834, "but not hospitals and dispensaries." The sentiment was echoed by John Hamilton Thom, who, after noting that "almsgiving charities create the very evil they profess to cure," went on to say that "hospitals and dispensaries are fountains of healing . . . producers of wealth." For Henry Melville, infirmaries and dispensaries "encourage industry by renovating health."[79] Thom was a Unitarian, Melville an Anglican, and both saw a real danger in generous relief to the poor. So did Congregationalists, Methodists, economists, Whigs, utilitarians, and paternalists. "Certain charities," said the Congregationalist Wardlaw, fostered "the idle and lazy . . . and dissolute." "Charities," declared the Methodist Benjamin Love, "in some instances induce improvidence." The economist John Burton said that charities had "a virulent effect on independence . . . industry, energy and self-restraint." "Pauperized and demoralized . . . London," argued the Whig secretary of the Treasury, Charles Trevelyan, was "due to charities." "Charity only hurts" added the utilitarian *Westminster Review*; and the paternalist Arthur Helps insisted that "philanthropy and charity" were too often "unthinking and indiscriminant."[80]

It was only "certain" and "some" charities that corrupted—the indiscriminate kind—not hospitals or Magdalen houses or orphanages. It was above all material aid, especially money, that worried the voluntarist. For the Wesleyan *Watchman,* it posed the dilemma that, although the warning that charity corrupts was everywhere voiced, the Bible commands it.[81] It was a dilemma that helped lead to a fourth classification of charities, those seeking to relieve immediate and dire want. Christian Victorians could not let the destitute starve, hence soup kitchens, night asylums, relief committees, strangers' friends societies, societies to suppress mendicity, and metropolitan visiting and relief associations. Soup kitchens were easily the most popular way to solve the dilemma. Soup, it seems, did not make the poor idle and improvident. It kept them alive during depressions and other dire emergencies. When the market for textiles collapsed and joblessness mushroomed, the Manchester Society of Friends distributed, from January to September of 1842 over 160,000 gallons of soup and rice to some 4,000 of the destitute at a cost of £3,500. The Church of England's Manchester and Salford Charity also distributed soup, paid for by contributions from London evoked by a Queen's Letter. In Leeds, affairs were more ecumenical and modest: the Congregationalist Edward Baines Sr. moved that the High Church Reverend W. F. Hook preside over the General Committee for Relief, which in the grimmest months of 1842 issued 16,000 tickets a week for 16,000 quarts of soup.[82]

In 1847, soup kitchens in the Highlands won from the *Scotsman*—a declared enemy of corrupting charity—the terse judgment that they were "among the best devises . . . for the temporary relief of the needy." The Irish famine, of course, dwarfed all other crises. The Society of Friends once again opened soup kitchens, but because the desperately hungry far exceeded its resources, it turned the kitchens over to the government. In 1847, the government spent £1.7 million on them and then abandoned the program.[83]

Relief, if the emergency was desperate and temporary, was allowable, but only if given in kind. Hence to soup kitchens were added night asylums, vagrant shelters, and refuges, all temporary accommodations for the homeless. Allowable too, for some, was aid to the deserving poor, to whom clothing or bedding or coal might be given. Manchester's District Provident Society, after examining 889 cases, found only 379 deserving of tickets of relief.[84] Relief of sorts also came to the dirtiest of the poor in the bath and washhouse movement of the 1840s and 1850s. Baths and washhouses were also a civic improvement—as were cleaner Londoners and Mancunians. Baths and washhouses thus fall into a fifth classification of voluntary societies, those flattering the pride and aiming at the well-being of towns, such as those that sponsored parks, walkways, museums, athenaeums, music halls, symphony orchestras, recreation grounds, and drinking fountains. Joseph Strutt won renown for giving Derby public walks and a splendid arboretum, a munificence the duke of Norfolk emulated for Sheffield. As Peter Bailey shows in *Leisure and Class in Victorian England*, however, such benefactions were not very numerous before 1860.[85]

Proud as early Victorians were, however, of these societies for saving souls, reforming character, improving health, relieving the starving, and promoting civic amenities, it was the sixth kind of voluntary institution that held out the greatest promise. Provident societies, which are discussed in the next section, combined the virtues of self-reliance and voluntarism, and the early Victorians saw in them the perfect answer to social ills.

There were, of course, more than six kinds of voluntary societies. There were also cricket clubs and political economy clubs, peace societies and committees to emancipate slaves, and societies for retired clergy and jobless governesses. But these did not grapple directly with the formidable problems of irreligion and destitution, homelessness and ignorance, vagrancy and crime that came with the dramatic urbanization that, along with increasing prosperity and growing moral and religious seriousness, was one of the three most important wellsprings that fed the ocean of voluntarism.

That urbanization led to a flood of voluntary societies is almost axiomatic. Many and serious urban evils presented challenges that demanded answers, and a vigorous growth of urban wealth and an urban and learned class provided the means. And since government was distrusted, what better means than voluntary societies, societies most acceptable to early Victorians whose moral earnestness had been heightened by the great religious revivals of the evangelical and High Church movements. Broad Churchmen, too, contributed, as did rationalists of every persuasion, whose mechanics institutes, halls of science, and farm and industrial schools constituted a vigorous, though to many dangerous, part of the flood of voluntarism. Scientific advances, the spread of literacy, and the rise and spread of rationalism must therefore be added to urbanization, religious revival, and the growth of wealth as forces that made the voluntary society the Victorians' favorite panacea.

But was it a panacea? Although oceanlike in its vastness, buoyant in its hopes, and prodigious in energy, did voluntarism, in fact, substantially lessen the wretchedness of the poor and the myriad evils plaguing British cities and towns? No, the *Spectator* said. "Charitable societies grow like mushrooms," it observed in 1843, "yet misery in the squalid rooms of the poor continues."[86] That the mushrooming charities did not reduce the numbers of the able-bodied poor was, as already noted, in part because of the formidable barrier to their work constituted by the ubiquitous fear that charity, like outdoor poor relief, was corrupting.

Few voluntary societies, of course, even thought of attacking destitution and squalor head-on; their aim was to mitigate poverty's harshest blows, to bandage its worst wounds, to assuage, to ameliorate, and to provide the young some prevention through education. The goal of night asylums, soup kitchens, orphanages, hospitals and dispensaries, and ragged schools and reformatories was not to end destitution but soften its harshest edges.

But even in that restricted field, the results were disappointing. The voluntary hospitals, so lavishly extolled in charity sermons and annual banquets, fell far short of offering adequate medical care to the poor. In no city in Britain was voluntarism praised more enthusiastically than in Leeds, yet its voluntary hospitals and dispensaries offered free medical care to only 2.2 percent of its population. That the Poor Law gave medical care to another 4.5 percent certainly helped, although that left 93.3 percent to fend for themselves. Manchester and Liverpool did much better, their medical charities covering 20 to 23 percent of their citizens—the highest percentage, indeed, in all Britain. Lincoln covered only 1.8 percent, Bradford, 3 percent, and Carlisle the lowest percentage. Dr. H. W. Rumsey told the 1844 Select Committee on Medical Relief "that most towns ought to provide not less than 3/5 of the population with medical care, but in fact most fell far short." He also found overcrowded, dirty, and poorly ventilated hospitals, hurried, two-minute examinations, and not a little illegality.[87]

It was a grim report, but it in no way dampened the festivity of balls held to raise money for hospitals and infirmaries. At Chichester, the ball on behalf of the infirmary was "crammed with the fashion and elegance of the neighbourhood," and a ball on behalf of the dispensary held in the Assembly Room of the Royal Hotel, Wigan, in Lancashire, was attended by "the nobility of the countryside and gentry of the town . . . [with] the ladies richly attired."[88]

The management of voluntary societies often left much to be desired. Some could not even spend their funds. The Metropolitan Visiting and Relief Association raised £21,000 for its Christmas fund of 1843 but despite the Yuletide work of its 1,000 visitors, left £14,000 unspent, a ratio not unlike the Highland Destitution Fund, which raised £117,000 but left £7,000 unspent. Mismanagement had, of course, also plagued endowed charities, which although not dependent on annual subscriptions were nevertheless a part of, and often an embarrassing part of, the world of voluntarism.[89] Endowments to ransom the captives of Barbary pirates or to toll St. Sepulchre's bells before an execution at Newgate were the work of private munificence, just as were the some 300 endowed schools in London, many of which had atrophied by 1850.[90]

While not remotely as anachronistic or mismanaged as endowed charities, the most promising of the new voluntary societies still fell far short of their goals. According to Mary Carpenter, an ardent advocate of industrial schools and reformatories, Lord Ashley's ragged schools, although numerous, popular, and well intentioned, were "utterly ineffective." Their statistics, as was frequent with voluntary societies, were impressive: from 1844 on, the Ragged School Union had established 85 ragged schools in London, employed 1,392 voluntary teachers to instruct 5,353 evening pupils and 10,439 on Sundays. The goal was admirable, but the actual education was meager.

The need was certainly great. Lord Ashley told the readers of the *Quarterly Review* in 1846 that of 1,600 pupils, 162 had been in prison, 253 lived by begging, 249 had never slept in beds, 101 had no body linen, 170 came from lodging houses, and 68 were the children of convicts. They constituted "a wild and lawless race," too ragged and uncouth for regular schools. But their teachers were untrained and unpaid, their curriculum consisted mostly of the Bible and *Pilgrim's Progress*, and the attendance of over three-quarters of them, in itself exceedingly irregular, was restricted either to Sundays or to one or two evenings a week.[91] And the singular reward for sticking it out for five years was a one-way trip to the colonies.

Meager, too, were the results of another of Lord Ashley's noble efforts, the scheme to provide the homeless with model lodgings. From 1844 to 1853, he and Prince Albert, Charles Dickens, Angela Burdett Coutts, and a host of wealthy and distinguished Victorians contributed to these working-class houses. Again statistics were paraded forth. We have spent, Lord Ashley told the Commons in 1851, £20,750 on new buildings and £2,250 renovating old ones, all at a return of 5½ percent; and in the same *Quarterly Review* where he earlier had praised the "efficacious virtues of the voluntary principle," he now promised that his model lodging houses would not be based on "eleemosynary principles" but on profit to investors. In fact, both investment and donations played a role in the erection in 1846 of three buildings and the renovation of a fourth. The four served 20 families and 30 single men. In 1847, another lodging house was built to hold 104 men. In 1851, the five-story Streatham building, offering 47 apartments was completed, along with a common lodging house at Drury Lane accommodating some 100 male transients for a night or two. While, from 1846 to 1851, the buildings erected by Lord Ashley and his friends housed 600 of London's homeless, London's population increased by some 30,000 a year, and thousands remained without housing.[92]

The Achilles heel of the voluntary societies was the eternal "want of funds." In Manchester, in the midst of a depression, the soup kitchen closed "from want of funds." In Exeter, the dispensary treated a third fewer patients because of "want of funds." In Leeds, when "inadequate giving" left the dispensary in debt, "a renewed appeal seemed hopeless"; it was therefore cancelled, and the soup kitchen was "nearly paralyzed from want of funds." In Ireland, the Friends turned the soup kitchens over to the government, and a year later the government closed them because the Irish, who were to pay for them, had "want of funds." "When the poor are left to voluntary charity," wrote Scotland's Dr. William Alison, "they are miserably neglected." And most tragic was the want of funds that allowed more than a million Irish to die of famine.[93]

A most appealing and often necessary means to overcome a want of funds was to make the society in part self-supporting. When the Manchester Lying-in Hospital found its funds low, it charged a fee. That the number of patients fell by one-quarter was regrettable, but not too regrettable, said the proposers of the fee, since fee-paying encouraged providence and forethought. Such morale-building fees in fact made up—in the form of the school pence—a greater part of the funds of most voluntary schools than the donations of the rich. Pupils also earned money. Two of the most admired schools for the poor—Mrs. Davies Gilbert's at Wallington, Sussex, and Richard Dawe's at King's Somborne, used their workshops and fields not only to educate in skills but, from the sale of their produce, to pay the bill.[94] But of all the self-supporting voluntary societies, the most promising of a world free of pauperism and destitution were the provident and friendly societies and savings banks and building societies that brilliantly combined self-reliance and voluntarism.

SELF-HELP VOLUNTARISM

Self-reliance and voluntarism were two of the most important attitudes defining the early Victorians' vision of a laissez-faire society. How solid, then, would institutions be that rested on both of those attitudes; institutions that encouraged thrift, forethought, and the avoidance of poor relief, and did so freely in associations of working men where all gave mutual support to one another. Such an institution was the friendly society, sometimes also called a benefit or benevolent or provident society. It was a society in which all its members paid a weekly fee of four or five or six pence into a fund from which, if they fell sick, they received 10s. a week and, if they died, £10 was provided for a respectable burial. Some societies even gave a modest sum to tide them over a period of unemployment. It was not a negligible institution. The best-informed guesses in 1848 estimated that there were over 25,000 friendly societies in Britain, with over a million members. Also numerous were its cousins, the burial, the collecting, and building societies and the savings banks—the latter, in 1844, with 999,543 depositors and £27.6 million in deposits.[95] Yet although the self-help and voluntarist pedigree of the friendly society was beyond question and its extent significant, it does not loom large in the editorials, sermons, pamphlets, and speeches that in the 1840s defined the social conscience of the Victorian governing classes. The middle and upper classes in fact took an ambivalent position toward this most authentic of working-class responses.

That journals of a paternalist outlook were silent is somewhat paradoxical, since friendly societies were not only nearly as old and traditional as rural paternalism, but many paternalists had, from 1780 to 1850 encouraged them. It was in the seventeenth century that laborers began to pay a few pennies a week for relief when ill and burial when they died. By 1800, there were over 7,000 friendly societies, with some 700,000 members, and the hope even spread among the clergy and gentry that these self-help societies would teach the laborers such ways of thrift and providence that poor relief would be greatly reduced, even abolished.[96] Friendly societies in the first third of the nineteenth century became part of the paternalist program. The Reverend Legh Richmond urged clergy and gentry to establish such, although he insisted that they never meet in public houses. The Reverend Godolphin Osborne urged that "benefit clubs" for illness and burials be established alongside clothing funds and coal clubs. The Reverend John Saunders in *Parochialia* urged that all "benevolent persons should promote benefit societies." The Reverend Charles Girdlestone urged the same, and "with no drink allowed." And the Reverend Thomas Dale encouraged clothing funds, savings banks, and provident societies.[97] Landowners also established county friendly societies, including Mr. T. H. S. Sotheran in Wiltshire and Charles Adderly in Staffordshire. Both clergy and gentry helped form county societies in Essex in 1818, Hampshire in 1825, and Kent in 1828—with more following in the 1830s as the New Poor Law compelled laborers to be more provident. These county societies, as the smaller ones under a clergyman or landowner, had "honorable members," those among the wealthy who both ran the society and who contributed the funds needed to make a society of laborers earning eight or nine shillings a week solvent.[98]

But despite the role of the gentry and clergy in many rural benefit societies, the great Tory newspapers in the 1840s devoted scarcely a single editorial to their support. Neither the *Morning Herald, Standard, Morning Post, John Bull*, nor the Peelite *Morning Chronicle* devoted editorials to working-class societies that promoted voluntarism and self-help. The Christian Socialists' *Politics of the People*, a journal more paternalist than socialist, said little of the people's most participatory institution; nor did the Michael Sadler and R. B. Seely school of paternalism highlight friendly societies. A *Morning Post* editorial might offer a clue for this want of enthusiasm. After noting the "offensive strain in the poor's demand for independence," it concluded that "the best system for the poor is a system of protection."[99] Girdlestone's Wiltshire society no doubt provided such protection, but not those competing friendly societies that ranged from small ones that innkeepers established in order to increase business or by societies formed by the workers themselves to increase camaraderie at public houses. More effective were the large affiliated orders such as the Manchester Unity of Odd Fellows, with its 4,200 lodges, and the Order of Foresters, which was especially strong in rural areas. By the 1840s, most friendly societies in the countryside and almost all in towns were established and run by the workers themselves. By 1848, the Odd Fellows had a membership of 260,000. "We are in every town," said their grand master, "and almost every village." Yet in the agricultural areas, the Foresters outdid both the Odd Fellows and the county societies of clergy and gentry, hardly a palatable fact to the paternalist press.[100]

It also seemed of no great interest to the more individualistic, Whiggish, Liberal and Radical press. How curious that these great preachers of thrift, perseverance, and self-help were as silent on the virtues of friendly societies as was the paternalist press. Throughout the 1840s, the *NonConformist, Eclectic, Congregational Magazine*, and *Baptist Magazine* showed no more enthusiasm for friendly societies than did the Whiggish *Globe* and *Edinburgh Review*. The *Leeds Mercury*, unstinting in its admiration of voluntarism, lists under its editorial on "The Glory and Hope of England" Bible societies, hospitals, colleges, Sunday schools, and temperance and missionary societies, but not friendly societies.[101]

Three failings, said the middle and upper classes, disfigured the friendly societies: secret rituals, financial instability, and too much conviviality and drink. Tory paternalists, while admitting the societies' loyalties, saw in the secret rituals of 26,000 Odd Fellows and in those of thousands of the Foresters and smaller societies, a potential for subversive activities. Why secret passwords, handshakes, and ritualistic initiation? Why so many lectures and graveside orations?—lectures possibly subversive and orations that took the place of a clergyman's blessing. And all these ominous doings from organizations run by workingmen! Such were the questions asked by peers of the realm in the Lords Select Committee of 1848 on Friendly Societies.[102]

The committee also asked about the financial instability of those myriad societies ranging from the giant Odd Fellows to a handful of men in a pub. Could their weekly contributions of five or six pence cover, as many societies promised, 10s. a week for three months of illness and 5s. a week thereafter if the illness persisted? And could they also cover a £6 or £10 burial? The best actuaries told the Lords and the Commons select committees that they could not. Hundreds of small societies did, in fact, collapse, either from inadequate fees or bad management or fraud. The witnesses for the Odd Fellows and Foresters denied the charge and showed themselves abreast of the best actuarial studies, which, while not so mistaken about the incidence of illness, had yet to create correct tables for mortality, old age payments, or unemployment relief. Critics also found it financially and morally harmful to spend money on club nights, annual banquets, and drink. The societies answered that donations and expenditures for conviviality were increasingly kept in a separate fund, and that without such gregarious evenings, few would join.[103]

Not a little of the criticism of bad finances overlaid a deeper moral disapproval of drink and banquets. It led Nonconformists and political economists to prefer savings banks as voluntary self-help institutions. The Congregationalists' *Eclectic*, the Unitarians' *Christian Teacher*, and the Scottish Free Church's *Christian Witness* and *North British Review* all joined the *Leeds Mercury* to praise the savings bank. Such banks, wrote the *Christian Teacher*, increased habits of self-help," and they provided, said the *North British Review*, "the means of the most "perfect independence."[104] Savings banks for laborers became a popular idea at the end of the eighteenth and beginning of the nineteenth centuries. Mrs. Priscilla Wakefield founded one at Tottenham in 1798, and the Reverend Henry Duncan one in Ruthwell, Dumfriesshire, in 1810. George Rose adopted the idea for the Society for Bettering the Condition of the Poor, Robert Southey praised it in the *Quarterly*, and the S.D.U.K.

pronounced it "character building." Bentham, who found friendly societies actuarially unsound, outlined an elaborate set of plans for "Frugality Banks." The great idea was to save in good times so as to need no poor relief in bad times. More than one advocate, including Malthus, hoped savings banks would even replace the poor law.[105] And since the decision to open a savings account was a very individual one, it appealed to the individualism of Nonconformists and political economists.

The much-heralded savings banks were neither as wholly self-help nor as independent and successful as were the friendly societies. Middle- and upper-class trustees, not laborers, ran the show. At Ruthwell, Duncan even fined those who, having enrolled, did not regularly deposit. The government also helped. The National Debt Commission paid a subsidized rate of interest on savings bank funds invested with them. The rate was ½ percent above the market rate. It was a good bargain. But very few workers became depositors, except some servants whose free board and room allowed modest deposits. Of the nation's 999,000 depositors, most were tradesmen, clerks, or well-off craftsmen. "Operatives don't save in such banks" reported Manchester's Benjamin Love; and only a small percentage of artisans did so, added Sheffield's Dr. Calvert Holland. A considerable amount of the £27 million deposited did, however, come from laborers, but only through their friendly societies, and it was not enough to keep the savings banks growing after the financial crisis of 1847.[106]

Laborers also formed only a small part of building societies, although at their inception, they formed a rather larger part of these self-help societies. From the eighteenth century on, workers formed clubs of twenty or so subscribers, clubs whose pooled resources, along with some loans, enabled them to buy land and build houses. A ballot was used to determine who obtained the first house. After all had received their houses the society was disbanded. Although many building societies failed, by the 1840s, they were quite extensive. But then, after 1850, the more solid and middle-class permanent building societies replaced the working man's building clubs. The permanent building societies did not build houses but received deposits, gave loans for the building of houses, and paid interest. A few workers participated in the election of the trustees of the Leeds Permanent Building Society, but its trustees mostly served both that "class . . . slightly superior in station" to the workers and the solid middle ranks.[107]

Friendly societies, more than savings banks or even building societies, were genuinely of the working classes, a fact that the Radical press celebrated. *Howitt's Journal,* the *People's Journal,* and the *Manchester Times* praised this most authentic of workers' self-help societies. At the White Horse Inn, according to the *Manchester Times*, the chairman of the meeting proudly announced to more than 200 Odd Fellows: "We . . . nourish and cherish all our sick, succor and assist all our poor members, render . . . assistance to all our artisan brethren who . . . travel to seek employment; [and] allow ample funds to our deceased brethren." They also cared for their widows and orphans. With one-fifth of all adult males in Manchester belonging to the Odd Fellows and another fifth to the Foresters, Druids, or Rechabites, such aid and succor was no little thing. Indeed, for *Howitt's Journal*, the Odd Fellows was "one of those self-helping societies, exclusively . . . supported by the working class, which marks the advancing spirit of the age," one of "self-help, independence, mutual aid and cooperation." Even Tory journals vouchsafed them some praise. The *Mirror* devoted four articles to societies that "raise the labour population . . . to a degree of independence they have never known."[108]

The spirit of self-help was very much alive in Leeds. "By far the best part of what is doing for the people in Leeds," wrote Samuel Smiles in the *People's Journal*, "is being done by themselves." The people, he added, through their own mutual assurance societies contributed no less than £15,000 a year to their brethren. Smiles himself joined both the Odd Fellows and Foresters as an "honorable member," as did many of the middle classes, who contributed without requiring payments in return—contributions that could prove the margin of the order's solvency. A Scotsman, a doctor, and an editor, Smiles knew his working class, knew how deeply they feared weeks of poverty-stricken illness or a pauper's burial, and knew too the value of camaraderie and a pint of ale to lives of hard, grinding work. In 1875, in *Thrift*, Smiles doubted friendly societies would have endured had they not offered ale and fellowship.[109] To fellowship and security, these friendly societies added a feeling of pride and independence. In 1831, a Glamorgan farm laborer and friendly society member announced: "Poor as I am, I am obliged to no man for a farthing, and therefore I consider myself as independent as any gentleman." Although less immodest in tone, such independence of mind marks the testimony of many of the witnesses who in 1848 and 1849 testified before the select committees on friendly societies. Exceedingly well informed and sensible, these actuaries, grand masters, and secretaries put to rest fears of secret oaths and sedition, or of gross fraud and extravagant drunkenness. Instead, they advertised the workers' skill and competence, pride and independence. We infuse, said the Grand Master of the Odd Fellows, "Feelings of Self-Respect" and "a Certain Degree of Pride." Drunkenness was fined, temperance was common, accounts were very sound, there were no oaths, many clergy belonged, management costs were limited, and the best actuarial tables were used; such were the responses of the Grand Master, culminating in the audacious, we meet in pubs in order to be more independent and "are better managed without the influence of the gentry."[110]

Better managed without the gentry! The press of the governing class had good reason to grow silent about an institution some of them had once patronized as an alternative to a poor law. Like Sunday schools, the friendly societies had, on reaching maturity, declared their independence. The working classes found in these many societies of mutual assurance, from the smallest village club begun by a publican to the grand affiliated order of Odd Fellows and Foresters, an answer to immediate, practical needs, and an answer that depended entirely on themselves and not on patronizing superiors. Like Sunday and dame and day schools, people's colleges, and many temperance and improvement societies, the friendly societies were constituted of, by, and for the workers.

Some workers hoped that cooperative stores and workshops and socialist communities—in partnership with middle-class progressives, and all based on self-reliant voluntarism and the principle of association—could not only better their lives but remake society. Voluntarism, too, had its formula for utopia.

THE PRINCIPLE OF ASSOCIATION

It is a measure of the remarkable pervasiveness of voluntarism that it could envelop socialism. It was not, of course, the socialism of the twentieth century. It was not the socialism of government planning, government welfare, and government ownership, three features that would have appalled those socialists of early Victorian England, to whom government was hateful and fearsome, the handmaiden of the propertied class.

Not a tyrannical, corrupt government, but free, voluntary, collective self-help was the basis of their socialism. Not the triad of government planning, welfare and ownership, but the triad of village communities, producers' workshops, and cooperative stores—all voluntary—defined early Victorian socialism. The new principle was "association," a term used far more often than "socialism," a principle that meant mutual cooperation and sharing, not ruthless competition and profit, a principle embodied most purely in socialist communities, producer-owned workshops, and cooperative stores, but a principle also embodied in charities, schools, mechanics institutes, joint stock companies, and dock and canal companies—all associations, all voluntary.

The principle of association enjoyed a broad popularity. Infidel Radicals and pious Christians both praised it. In 1847, scores of churchmen, "many powerful and distinguished Tories," filled Exeter Hall, the temple of the evangelicals, to hear John Minter Morgan expound his scheme of Church of England villages organized according to the principle of association. In his *Revolt of the Bees* (1826), *Colloquies* (1837), and *Christian Commonwealth* (1845), Morgan had already described his communities of 400 families working together cooperatively, not competitively, on 1,000 acres.[111]

A far different meeting was held in May 1840 at the Music Salon on South Parade Street, Leeds. Hundred of Owenite socialists gathered at their annual conference to raise a fund to help purchase 530 acres in Hampshire for the founding of Queenswood, a community based on the cooperative principle.[112]

Between the devout of Exeter Hall and the rationalists of South Parade lay many greatly different versions of the widely held principle of association. It flourished in the Chartist Julian Harney's *Democratic Review* and *Red Republican*, journals full of extracts from Louis Blanc on "the associative system," praise of the great Robert Owen, and Harney's exuberant "good speed to every association"—the favorite idea of social reformers. The progressives, along with the Conservatives were, according to the journalist Hepworth Dixon, divided between "the Economists and the Associationists." Dixon added that while the economists were in the ascendant, "the profoundest minds of the age are deeply impressed with the principle of associationism." In 1850, there was a *Journal of Association* and a Society for Promoting Working Men's Association.[113]

Association was not solely an English idea. From France in the 1820s and 1830s came Charles Fourier's idea of *phalansteries,* where, despite keeping property private and a hierarchy of four classes, communities would be formed on the principle of mutuality, sharing, and harmonious association. Also from France came Claude-Henri de Saint-Simon's idea of a universal association extending throughout the world, one in which women would be equal with men, one's status a reflection of one's capabilities, one's rewards a function of one's work, no inheritance, the rule of the most educated, and cooperation replacing competition. There would also be a revived rational Christianity, with Saint-Simon its second Christ. Fourierism led in the 1840s to a London paper, *The Morning Star,* and to Hugh Doherty's organization of Fourierists, while Saint-Simonian missionaries influenced not a few intellectuals, including the paternalist Thomas Carlyle, the utilitarian John Stuart Mill, and the Christian Socialist Vansittart Neale. Carlyle soon became disillusioned, as in a lesser way did Mill, although later, in his *Autobiography,* he confessed that Saint-Simonian ideas more than any other, brought him "a new mode of political thinking." His friendship with Harriet Taylor furthered that new mode, a mode most distinctly associationist, a mode that made him a friend of cooperatives, both consumer and producer, and ardent for employer-employee partnership and profit sharing—all without government interference, all voluntary.[114] William Thompson, friend and disciple of Bentham, appalled both by the ruthlessness of capitalism and the tyranny of government, joined Mill as another utilitarian straying from economic orthodoxy toward cooperative associations. In his *Labour Rewarded* (1827), he "sought total change in the present *principle* of society" through an "association" of "capitalist-labourers" that would manage the entire economy. The Owenite John Bray believed that this associationism was perfectly embodied in the joint stock principle, whereby "the united working class could [command] the work, the commodities, the child care, the health—in a word the happiness" of the nation.[115]

Most Radicals, zealous for associationism, were not utilitarians—at least not strictly so. The *People's Journal* and *Howitt's Journal* were their main platforms. Some of their contributors, like Dr. F. R. Lees and Goodwin Barmby, were Owenites; some, like Hugh Doherty, Fourierists; others, like Samuel Smiles, apostles of self-help; and the Howitts, William and Mary, were Quakers.[116]

In Britain, the largest number of believers in the principle of association were followers of Robert Owen. "Owenism is at present," said the *Westminster Review* in 1839, "in one form or another, the actual creed of a great proportion of the working class." Robert Owen, in 1839, at the age of sixty-eight, the grand patriarch of British socialism, had made a fortune in his cotton mill at New Lanark, Scotland, the largest in Britain. He also made New Lanark a model factory, published an account of its grand principles, and welcomed 2,000 visitors including the tsar of Russia. The children were well schooled, the workers well-housed and well-paid, the conditions clean and safe, and, if more paternalist than cooperative, it was still a first step toward a rational society, one in which a correct education, free of superstition, would so form the next generation's character that people could live in harmony in those communities where cooperation and kindness and not competition and selfishness ruled. In these communities of from 500 to 1,500, all property would be held in common. In the 1830s and 1840s, 250 Owenite societies talked hopefully of this utopia, 50,000 attended Owenite halls of science, and even more read some dozen of its periodicals. Like their periodicals, however, the Owenite communities lasted but a short time.[117]

These failures did not lessen the early Victorians' fascination with the principle of association. In 1848 and 1849, Frederick Maurice, professor of theology at King's College, London, Charles Kingsley, writer, clergyman and journalist, and John Ludlow, an English writer raised in Paris on Fourierism, joined with Thomas Hughes, a favorite pupil of Thomas Arnold, and Vansittart Neale, a wealthy businessman, to form the Christian Socialists. All were disturbed by the selfish competitiveness of capitalism and the wretchedness of the workers. The Christian Socialists established two periodicals, *Politics of the People* and the *Christian Socialist,* and were indefatigable in publishing tracts, lecturing, and organizing workers' associations. In 1850, the *Christian Socialist* announced that "a new idea" and "a new force" had "gone abroad into the world," the new idea being "socialism" and the new force "association," a force "which combined the interests of producers and consumers by fair price and equality of exchange."[118]

Among the developments that explain the popularity of this new idea and new force, three were most prominent: (1) the actual existence of innumerable associations, (2) a moral revulsion at capitalism's harshness and political economy's selfishness, and (3) an entrenched voluntarist distrust of government. The first of these developments, the existence of so many associations, raises doubts on just how "new" that force was. John Stuart Mill found it far too extensive to be new. "The country is covered with associations," he wrote in 1836, citing only those among the working class as a "novelty." Later, in his *Political Economy* (1848), he added the American clipper ships and Cornish mines as examples of "profit-sharing companies." In 1849, the *Westminster Review* found "the principle of association" in proprietary schools, mechanics institutes, sick clubs, building societies, and "joint interests in a ship or mine or canal." *Howitt's Journal* added natural history societies, reading rooms, and libraries, and the *People's Journal,* railways, banks, assurance companies, infirmaries, industrial schools, and night asylums. To this list, John Ludlow added Bible, missionary, and tract societies, while James Hole of Leeds's Redemption Society included friendly, educational, and mutual improvement societies—all part of a "host of voluntary activities . . . to further the elevation of the people."[119]

The principle of association was remarkably comprehensive and elastic. Cotton mills and landed estates run on paternalist lines were nonetheless associations of men and women that owed nothing to government, and such paternalist mills and estates had a powerful impact, not only on the communities and cooperatives of John Minter Morgan and the Christian Socialists but also on the Owenites' Queenswood, a paternalist-run community that had neither property in common nor practiced full democracy and equality.[120]

The second reason for the popularity of associationism was its moral superiority to capitalism. Victorian capitalism, so remarkably productive, could be cruel, just as political economy, so remarkable in advancing knowledge, could be heartless. Such cruelties and heartlessness led many morally sensitive Victorians, from Coleridge and Arnold to Carlyle and Ruskin, to condemn capitalist exploitation. Their ethical revulsion against capitalism and political economy, combined with a bewilderment as to any viable alternative, led them to look both to the moral improvement of the individual and to a society in which sharing would replace selfishness.

The Christian Socialists and the followers of John Minter Morgan, in particular, saw in a new morality the basis of a better society. "Socialism," wrote James Hole in the *Christian Socialist*, is the "attempt to introduce kindness and justice into social relations." Owenites, of course, envisioned more revolutionary changes toward a society without private property and inequalities, but they nonetheless sought progress through the reform of character. "Disinterested benevolence," declared the *New Moral World*, "will become the master spring of society."[121]

The new world of associationism—the world of cooperative stores, producers' workshops, and village communities—preserved that individualism dear to many early Victorians, even a self-reliance that was no less sturdy for being collective. Cooperative policy, wrote George Jacob Holyoake, "has a distinctly English character, which means ... self-help not state help." It was such a spirit of self-help that Christian Socialists expected would inspire their producer cooperatives of tailors, shoemakers, bakers, and printers to work hard, balance their books, repay loans, and share equally. Self-reliance, like paternalism, wove its powerful way into working-class associations. "The people would remain miserable," William Howitt told the Cooperative League in 1847, "until they had learned to help themselves."

It was a sentiment that would have pleased John Stuart Mill. Few Victorians wrote more powerfully on behalf of individuality, yet few were more enthusiastic for associations, two views that were not really inconsistent, because for early Victorians the principle of association implied a loose, voluntary, free, very private, and personal arrangement.[122]

That self-help associations were always voluntary is the third reason for the popularity of the principle of association. Whether a producer's workshop, a cooperative store, or a village community, they demanded nothing from government but the same protection of their finances as friendly societies and joint stock companies enjoyed—a protection they won in the Friendly Societies Act of 1852. Christian Socialists such as Frederick Maurice and Owenite socialists such as George Jacob Holyoake would have little to do with government. Maurice in 1839 even opposed the government inspection of schools, while Holyoake found Karl Marx's 1848 socialism "disfigured by ... a pernicious State point sticking through them." For Holyoake, government "in the province of doing evil," was "almost omnipotent."[123]

In an England full of associations that worked, and full also of the hope that such associations would both replace vicious capitalism and be free of despotic government, the principle of association was bound to have thousands of adherents, many of whom looked with the greatest favor on one or more of three particular forms of association, village communities, producers' workshops, and cooperative stores. Of the three, it was the village community—free, self-supporting, voluntary, and with equality for all—that excited the greatest zeal. It promised an utopia. It promised freedom from the claims of greed and competition. It promised, said the *People's Journal*, "self-supporting societies in which the selfish principles which produce devotion to private property and the unsocial and unchristian competition will be unknown." It was a promise that led the Quaker philanthropist William Allen, not only to outline a scheme for "the voluntary association of benevolent persons" in his *Colonies at Home* (1827), but also to purchase a few acres near Brighton and start a village community of twelve cottages, a bakehouse, a piggery, and washhouse—later a school on Pestalozzi principles.[124] Zeal for such communities burned even more intensely in Leeds in 1848, when James Hole persuaded the Leeds Redemption Society to purchase land in Wales for a "self-supporting village society." Houses and workshops were built, and fourteen people moved in. The Chartist Thomas Cooper was also enthusiastic for communities. Praising Fourier for his "theory of association," he declared himself a fervent believer in "the free and voluntary association of hands, lands, and capital."[125]

Robert Owen, of course, had long and tirelessly preached the gospel of "villages of cooperation" and helped establish them from Sussex to Indiana. "For nearly 30 years," writes John Harrison in his *The New Moral World,* "a steady succession of Owenite communities spread over England, Scotland, Ireland and Wales." At Orbiston, near Glasgow, in 1823, Owenites turned a five-story stone building into a place of communal living and communal work; at Ralahine, in Ireland, in 1831, fifty Owenites combined agriculture and manufactures in their desire to create a self-supporting community; and at Wisbech, in Cambridgeshire, Owenites created Manea Fen, a grand experiment in mutual self-help. All failed. But failure seldom extinguishes the utopian zeal of true believers. In 1841, Owen himself, as president, joined other investors in purchasing many acres and many impressive buildings for the creation of Queenswood, a community that also failed.[126]

The main reason for these failures was their excessively optimistic expectations of an easy and superabundant productivity, expectations encouraged by an equally optimistic view of scientific and technological advances. A second reason was their ambivalence about authority and property and class. John Minter Morgan's scheme in *Christian Commonwealth* was undisguisedly paternalist, hierarchical, and Anglican, which explains why it was never attempted. Owenites preached instead the abolition of private property, class, and Church, but, in practice, at Queenswood, they kept property, kept classes, and even sought to transform rationalism into a religion.[127]

To believe that 500 to 1,000 could live in these free associations, and that thousands of such associations could constitute a nation, was to be extraordinarily sanguine about the viability of the principle of association. The term "association" implies a loose grouping, a free and voluntary coming together, a relationship of trust and mutuality and not authority and discipline. It was a principle perhaps better suited to small producer workshops.

John Stuart Mill certainly held this view. So did most of the Christian Socialists. Based in London, which was full of exploited tailors, shoemakers, bakers, printers, and builders, they looked to the cooperative workshop as the means of substituting Christian sharing for capitalist exploitation. In 1850, the Christian Socialists established the Society for Promoting Workingmen's Associations, which in turn helped set up twelve workers' associations of bakers, builders, printers, tailors, smiths, piano makers, and other trades. Two decades earlier, Owenites had encouraged both "union shops"—those set up by craft unions or benefit societies—and the workshops of cooperative societies, both of whose products could be exchanged at labor exchanges for other goods or for Labor notes, a proposed currency based on units of labor.[128]

Workers' associations were briefly in vogue. In the *Edinburgh Review* in 1845, John Stuart Mill urged that employers and employees either be partners or that the employees themselves run the business. In his *Principles of Political Economy* (1848), Mill looked ahead to the time when, through "profit sharing" and the "co-operative or joint stock principle," "the workmen and capitalists would shade into each other," and in 1850, he told a committee of the House of Commons that the laws should give these workers' associations the same limited liability and legal protection enjoyed by friendly societies and joint stock companies. "There is no way," he added, "that the working class can make so beneficial a use of their savings . . . as by the formulation of associations to carry on the business with which they are acquainted." Robert Slaney, chairman of the Select Committee was as strong for such associations as was Charles Babbage, the inventor of the first calculating machine, who made highly explicit proposals for sharing profits, a practice already customary among some fishermen on the south coast and Cornish miners, and in a few New England mills and the People's Mill of Leeds.[129]

Few workers' associations for the cooperative production of goods lasted long. The ruthless competition they sought to replace was too ruthless for them. An ambivalence about authority also plagued them—especially with those associations fostered by the Christian Socialists, in which investing promoters insisted on control. Endless wrangling and considerable arbitrariness ended with the Christian Socialists dissolving the entire program. To the acerbic Chartist George Julian Harney, the entire effort was pathetic. How could a handful of small cooperative workshops with only twenty or thirty workers prevent the exploitation of millions of miserably paid and overworked workers?[130]

Millions miserable? Yes, admitted Mill and many social reformers, but later, more and more would be less miserable if morally improved by such voluntary self-help organizations as producers' and consumers' cooperatives. Mill told a Commons committee that although producers' cooperatives did not greatly lower prices, they did elevate the workers by giving them responsibilities. Furthermore, the consumers' cooperatives would make significant savings, Mill said, because the profits of England's many layers of distributors were extravagant. In 1844, twenty-eight citizens of Rochdale in Lancashire won fame by establishing the most significant and lasting of the three forms of cooperative associations, the cooperative store. The Rochdale cooperative was founded on the principle that all profits would be divided among the consumers in proportion to the amount of their purchases. The consumers were also the owners and, through an elected committee, the managers. It was a voluntary and collective form of self-help.[131]

Consumers' cooperatives arose from both economic distress and political disappointment. The severe depression of the early 1840s so drastically reduced the incomes of the poor that they found the high prices and extravagant profits of stores—particularly company owned stores—intolerable. They were also disappointed in the failures of both village communities and producer workshops. Half of the twenty-eight founders of the Rochdale cooperative were Owenites who had not only read of the debacles of Orbiston, Ralahine, and Queenswood but knew that Robert Owen, seeing the millennium at hand, was quite uninterested in small cooperative stores. The founding of the most successful and lasting of the three forms of cooperatives sprang, as did Sunday, day, and dame schools, and friendly, building, and mutual improvement societies, from the working class, and for eminently practical purposes. In 1876, the Rochdale store showed a profit of £50,668, and those in Halifax and Leeds profits of £19,820 and £34,510 respectively. Cooperative stores in time spread throughout Britain and the world. They were, as their stoutest champion and first historian, George Holyoake, said, all "self-created, self-fed, self-sustained, self-growing and daily growing," and without, "a light of charity or paternal support . . . but a luminous, inextinguishable, independent light."[132] The principle of association, so disappointing when embodied in village communities and producers' workshops, thus finally had a measure of success. The results of associationism, like the results of voluntarism, present a very mixed picture, one in which successes and failures intermingle, perhaps with the latter prevailing. The principle of association would provide no miraculous cure for Britain's many and deep and painful social problems.

PART III

Basic Attitudes

CHAPTER 9

Philanthropy

The early Victorians took an ambivalent view of philanthropy. Some were ardent devotees, some scathing critics, and some—perhaps most—of mixed mind. Quite unmixed, though, was recognition of its vigor and ubiquitousness. With its hundreds of societies, myriad committees, and thousands of visitors, fund raisers, organizers, and contributors, it displayed an unparalleled zeal in attacking every evil—social, moral, and religious. Leading philanthropists, such as William Wilberforce, Elizabeth Fry, Thomas Fowell Buxton, and Lord Ashley, became the heroes of the age. Had they not ended slavery, reformed prisons, relieved Spitalfield weavers, and freed children in factory and mine? And innumerable were the lesser heroes who saw in philanthropic societies the only hope for the removal or amelioration of the frightful evils of an urban, manufacturing and capitalist society. Paternalism had not penetrated inchoate Manchester, Leeds, and London; capitalism had not brought the general and lasting prosperity it promised; self-help, so wondrous to the upwardly mobile, did little for the downtrodden; and almost all saw government as evil.

Having found paternalism, capitalism, self-help, and government unable to redress the evils of industrial society, early Victorians thus turned with zeal to philanthropy, which was, in many respects, the other side of the voluntarist coin of self-reliance. Philanthropic societies of every kind were established: societies to help penitent prostitutes, penniless governesses, distressed widows, oppressed chimney sweeps, the homeless, vagrants, drunkards, orphans, the imprisoned, and, if deserving, the destitute.

Beyond these philanthropic societies lay two equally vast spheres for doing good, the area of religion, where a multitude of societies preached the Gospel to the lost, and the area of education, where a large variety of institutions, ranging from ragged schools for London urchins to Oxford and Cambridge for the privileged, attempted to enlighten the nation. And then, most practical, most desired, and most alive and expanding, there were also medical charities of all kinds: hospitals, dispensaries, infirmaries, and asylums for the insane. It was, as the historian Thomas Babington Macaulay said in 1823 and the barrister Sir James Stephen in 1846, "the Age of Societies." There were societies "for the redress of every oppression," Stephens told the readers of the *Edinburgh Review*, "there is a public meeting . . . for the diffusion of every blessing [and] . . . a committee."[1] Bright and radiant were the hopes that philanthropy would be the grand social remedy. "Thank God," said the Methodist *Watchman*, that philanthropic societies were "increasingly so numerous." Even the stern *Economist* rejoiced that "benevolence and philanthropy have now taken the place of bigotry and class love."[2] And from the evangelical pulpit there was unending enthusiasm: the Reverend Henry Melville called philanthropy "the very perfection of the social system"; the Reverend R. W. Hamilton praised its "vast capacity"; and the Reverend William Stowell rejoiced in its power "to check the ravages of society."[3]

Given such bright hopes and so many actual good works, why did so many treat the idea of philanthropy so unkindly? Why, for example, did Britain's leading novelist, Charles Dickens, and its sternest prophet, Thomas Carlyle, satirize and denounce it?

In "The Ladies' Societies" and "Public Dinners," two of his *Sketches by Boz* (1838), Dickens recounts the bitter rivalry between "the ladies' bible and prayer-book circulation society" and "the ladies' childbed-linen monthly loan society" and describes a lavish and indulgent banquet held by the "Indigent Orphans' Friends' Benevolent Institution." Both sketches are loving and amiable in tone, although, in the end, the foolish vanities of the ladies and the vulgar pomposity of the banqueters leave a picture of philanthropists just as self-involved and vainglorious as those Dickens caricatures in *Bleak House* (1850). Mrs Jellyby and Mrs. Pardiggle in *Bleak House* are parodies of noisy, pretentious, self-righteous do-gooders; Jellyby is so absorbed with Africa's Borrioboula-Gha tribe and her vast correspondence that she leaves her family "in a devil of a state," while Mrs. Pardiggle is an indefatigable visitor of the poor whose "volubility—on the unruly habits of the poor" is unrivaled. Both inhabit a world where benevolence is "spasmodic" and charity "restless and vain in action, servile . . . to the great." Dickens's final parody of philanthropy occurs in *Our Mutual Friend* (1865) with its caustic portrait of a ragged school in "a miserable loft—oppressive and disagreeable—crowded, noisy and confusing," packed by "a hotbed of flushed and exhausted infants," whose instruction amounts to only a "lamentable jumble" and a "monotonous droning."

Ragged schools, banquets for orphans, ladies' prayer-book circulating societies, and foreign missionary societies all had their faults, as well as their virtues. Nowhere in Dickens's novels are the virtues underscored, everywhere the faults are magnified, a curious fact, since Dickens was not only an ally of Miss Angela Burdett-Couts in managing Uranus, a home for reclaimed prostitutes, but, as Norris Pope has shown, was active all his life in a vast number of philanthropies.[4] In fact, it seems, Dickens, like so many early Victorians, was ambivalent about philanthropy.

So was Thomas Carlyle, although not in his chapter on "Model Prisons" in *Latter Day Pamphlets* (1850), where he calls philanthropists a dangerous breed. "Most sick am I, friends," he writes, "of this sugary disastrous jargon of philanthropy." He could not endure "this universal syllabub of philanthropic twaddle . . . a phantasm . . . fashioned out of extinct cants and modern sentimentalism." Such sentimentalism was part of "a blind loquacious prurience of indiscriminant philanthropy," substituting itself "for the silent divinely awful sense of Right and Wrong."[5]

Dickens's parodies and Carlyle's fulminations were part of a much wider disquietude with philanthropy. In using the term, the periodicals of the 1840s often surrounded it more with negatives than positives. A reading of some 100 periodicals of the 1840s reveals a motley list of pejoratives: they call it feigned, quixotic, blind, saccharine, morbid, unctuous, false, luxurious, clamorous, dreamy, claptrap, misdirected, blundering, fussy, bustling, prying, noisy, stealthy, selfish, vainglorious, indiscriminant, utopian, passive, intolerant, pernicious, virulent, dangerous, raw, sanguine, quackery, and petticoated. Flattering terms also occur: enlightened, sound, practical, true, real, Christian, comprehensive, genuine, enlarged, benign, warm, earnest, zealous, pure, exalted, judicious, and enterprising. In number and frequency, however, the negatives quite outdo the positives, especially when the three most common pejoratives, pseudo, spurious, and specious, are added to the list, adjectives that contrasted with the three most frequent positive ones, true, genuine, and Christian, a contrast reflecting a deep ambivalence. The early Victorians were skeptical of philanthropy, especially of charities and societies that were too pretentious and pontificating. Their ambivalence was in a sense discriminating, since many were aware that philanthropies did in fact come in all sizes and kinds and varieties, with the genuine jostling with the spurious.

VARIETIES OF PHILANTHROPY

Of the seven different definitions of 'philanthropist' in the *Oxford English Dictionary*, three are particularly revealing. One, taken from the Tory *Anti-Jacobin Review* of 1791, simply cites in illustration: "Tom Paine, the Philanthropist." One from 1829 quotes Isaac Taylor on "the spirit that should actu-

ate a Christian philanthropist." By 1878, however, a philanthropist had become one who has "astonished the world by giving a large sum of money."[6]
The three definitions point to three prominent species of philanthropist, the
reforming rationalist, the earnest evangelical, and the wealthy benefactor.

The reforming rationalists were steeped in the eighteenth century's belief
in universal benevolence, the triumph of truth and virtue, the limitless power
of education, and the liberation of mankind. Although many shared Paine's
assumptions, the heroes of most radical reformers, after 1800, were William
Godwin and Percy Bysshe Shelley. A few might even have supported Shelley's
"Association of Philanthropists" proposed in 1812. For Shelley, as for Godwin,
the philanthropist was one who loved all mankind, all fellow creatures. The
aim of the "Philanthropic Association," proclaimed Shelley, was "a radical
reform of moral and political evil . . . by diffusing virtue and knowledge, by
promoting human happiness," a hope not unlike Godwin's promise that the
"advance in science and useful institutions" would so fuse "individual will
with abstract justice" that there would be "general happiness."[7]

Although only a few turn-of-the-century rationalists agreed with the Utopian and anarchical visions of Shelley and Godwin, most of them agreed in
varying degrees that reason and knowledge did lead to virtue and the public
good, that the public good should encompass all mankind, and that it could
do so because man was either innately good or could be greatly improved by
education. Godwin saw in man a permanent "disposition to promote the
benefit of another." Jeremy Bentham, occasionally called a philanthropist,
saw in self-interest a far more basic and pervasive disposition, but he does, in
his *Deontology* (1834), emphasize "effective benevolence," "extra-regarding
prudence," "universal benevolence," and "a beneficence [that] consists in
contributing to the comforts of our fellow creatures." "To do evil for its own
sake," he added is not "in the nature of man."[8]

These optimistic views also occur in the Scottish moralists, in Dugald
Stewart, Sir James MacIntosh, and Thomas Brown, and formed a foundation
for a rationalist philanthropy. "The general principle of benevolence," wrote
Dugald Stewart, "disposes us to promote the happiness of others . . . [and] to
relieve their distress." Stewart's fellow Scotsman Thomas Brown was even
more ebullient, quoting Erasmus Darwin's enthusiastic verse: "And now,
philanthropy, thy / rays divine / dart around the Globe."

Erasmus Darwin's vision was reiterated in the 1788 report of the recently
established Philanthropic Society, with its "plan which has a common and
universal claim upon all men . . . [that will] produce beneficial effects on the
community at large," a plan the editor called "full, rational and forcible . . .
and in the spirit of philanthropy."[9]

The French Revolution, the rise of large towns, the emergence of proletariats and the coming of religious revivals not only made the sanguine visions of a Shelley and Godwin, or even the more moderate hopes of a Bentham, seem fanciful and shallow but threw doubt on the rational philanthropists' belief in the goodness of man and the power of reason and knowledge. But however deep the Tory repression and however pervasive religious revivals, a rationalist philanthropy persisted. In the 1840s, it was anything but routed. "The spirit of the age," said the *English Chartist Circular* in 1842, "is emphatically philanthropic, knowledge and benevolence are inseparable." "The goal . . . of the more enlightened and warm hearted philanthropy," concluded the Owenite *New Moral World,* is "the removal of MOST of the evils . . . in the social state of man and the mitigation of all."[10] R. H. Horne in his *Spirit of the Age* insisted that "philanthropic principles" influenced "the first intellects of the time." No evangelicals made Horne's list, a list headed by intellects such as Dickens, Southwood Smith, Alfred Tennyson, Harriet Martineau, and Thomas Carlyle.[11] In 1844, a new journal, *The Provident Philanthropist,* said its aim was to promote a union for benevolence, and in 1842, the newly formed "National Philanthropic Association" resolved to promote "Social and Salutiferous improvements"—which meant bath- and washhouses, model lodgings, soup kitchens, and sanitary reform.[12] Owen and Bentham were still popular. There was no more "genuine philanthropist," proclaimed the *People's Journal,* than Robert Owen, while *Howitt's Journal* praised Bentham for opening up a "limitless field for the exercise of philanthropic philosophy."[13] The rationalist George Holyoake found in Owenite communities "the philanthropy of these reconstructors of the world."[14] Owenite communities proved ephemeral, but not so Bentham's "philanthropic philosophy," which embodied itself in endless rational reforms of all kinds, all based on the greatest happiness principle, a principle universal in its application. Yet, in fact, in the 1840s, Bentham's philanthropy was largely limited to law, prisons, and educational reforms, and even in these areas, his ideas were part of a crowded scene. Rationalist philanthropists were many and diverse. In law, the great Italian criminologist César de Beccaria was the most widely cited, and on prisons and reformatories, the authorities were Gibbon Wakefield, Frederick Hill, and Captain Maconochie. When it came to education, they were innumerable, including Joseph Lancaster, founder in 1809 of the Royal Lancastrian Association (later called the British and Foreign School Society); George Birkbeck, who in 1812 established the first of many mechanics institutes; Thomas Hill, founder in 1812 of Hazelwood, one of the first progressive schools in England; and Samuel Wilderspin, founder after 1819 of countless infant schools. Following their pioneering efforts came Lady Noël Byron, William Allen, and many others who began farm and industrial schools, as well as the numerous unnamed founders of Owenite halls of science and experimental schools of all kinds. It was a movement that was supported by a flood of writings, ranging from Maria Edgworth's didactic tales and James Mills's definitive *Essay on Education* to Lady Byron's *What De Fellenberg Has Done for Education* and Thomas Hodgskin's *Popular Political Economy.*[15] Rationalist philanthropists dominated the advance of popular education in the early nineteenth century, a domination that led the seriously religious to redouble their efforts—and all in that voluntary spirit, free of government, that fit the philanthropic spirit.

It was not, of course, all rationalism. William Allen, who ran a farm school, was a Quaker, as were Joseph Lancaster and Thomas Clarkson, the most ardent of philanthropists . All three reflected a blend of rationalism and pietism. Allen, who edited the *Philanthropist* from 1810 to 1811, was secretary to the Lancastrian society for education and worked closely with James Mill and Henry Brougham in the Society for the Promotion of Useful Knowledge.[16] Education was the rationalists' preeminent field of philanthropy, a field wherein their belief that knowledge leads to virtue and virtue to social betterment made them far more zealous for popular education than the evangelicals, with their belief in original sin and a divinely ordained poverty.

The Unitarians, the sect that most doubted original sin and most rejoiced in reason, greatly strengthened the ranks of rational philanthropists. Mary Carpenter, of Bristol, and Thomas Hill's son Matthew, of Birmingham, both raised as Unitarians and both educated by fathers who admired Priestley and Hartley, were the two most active philanthropists in laying the basis for the reformatory movement. Mary Carpenter established ragged schools and reformatories, and in Birmingham in 1851 and 1853, Matthew Hill, the city's recorder, organized the two national conferences that led to the Juvenile Offender Act, which allowed the government to give grants to voluntarily run reformatories.[17] In their zeal for education, the Unitarians even discovered philanthropy in a poor law's assistant commissioners' report. In 1840, the Unitarian *Christian Teacher* praised the education report of Kay-Shuttleworth and Tufnell for its "judicious, enterprising philanthropy."[18]

A rationalist philanthropy had its opponents and rivals. The *Eclectic, Blackwood's,* and *Quarterly Review* all warned their readers against it. Beware, said the *Eclectic,* of "those philanthropists who see in the progress of civilization . . . the solving of political and social evils"; do not be beguiled, cautioned *Blackwood's,* with "visionary consequences pursued by the humane and philanthropic"; and, said the *Quarterly Review,* shun Bentham's "philosophico-philofelon-philanthropy."[19] The *Quarterly Review*'s political writer, John Croker, later confessed, "I have done with theoretical benevolence and

philanthropy," a view the Tory *Mirror* shared when it denounced the philanthropy of the rationalists as an "idle dream" that "vanishes in barren specula-
tion [and] universal sympathy" and "terminates in visionary schemes,"
schemes that the *Leeds Intelligencer* called "selfish" and full of the "ecstacy
[*sic*] of universal philanthropy."[20] These Tory papers would certainly have
agreed with the *Christian Remembrancer* that "the sympathy of your universal
philanthropy is gloriously obscure, indefinite, impractical and cheap."[21] The
Remembrancer was High Church, but High Churchmen were not the only
ones suspicious of a rationalist philanthropy. "Do not be deceived," warned
the Reverend John Giles, a Baptist, by the socialists' philanthropy.[22]

The right system for Giles was the philanthropy of the evangelicals, whose
two giants, William Wilberforce and Thomas Chalmers, realized that the
philanthropy of the rationalists was a rival to their own. Wilberforce told his
readers to avoid "the greatest stir about general philanthropy," since it promoted acts that arise "from worldly motives," acts that were "very neglectful
of those close to them." The imperious Chalmers simply dismissed out of
hand the "universal schemes" and "designs of magnificence" of the "raw and
sanguine philanthropists."[23] Both Chalmers and Wilberforce realized that
philanthropists of a rationalist outlook were their rivals. But both also felt
that, seductive as were the rationalists' philanthropic schemes, they would
weigh little against that far more formidable force, a triumphant evangelical
philanthropy.

THE PHILANTHROPY OF THE EVANGELICALS

So formidable was philanthropy of the evangelicals that it led David Owen
in his *English Philanthropy* of 1964 to conjecture that "in the public mind the
world 'philanthropist' became all but synonymous with 'evangelical.'" It was
a conjecture with which many early Victorians would concur. Even R. W.
Church, a member of the Oxford Movement, and its later historian, admits
that "the evangelical religion which led Howard and Fry, to assail the brutalities of the prisons . . . and Clarkson and Wilberforce to overthrow slavery . . .
[provided] an impetus to countless philanthropic schemes." It provided such
an impetus, said Thomas Gisborne, one of the evangelicals' favorite philosophers, because Christ's essential message was a "universal benevolence" that
was part of a "genuine and benign philanthropy."[24] For the evangelical Reverend Thomas Dale, "Philanthropy without religion is just talk," and the *Christian Observer* pronounced "the religious philanthropist . . . the best benefactor of his species." The Congregationalists, no friends of the hidebound
Christian Observer, but still evangelical, agreed, since "to the direct or indirect

influence of Christianity all the genuine philanthropy in our world may be traced."[25] However dubious it might be that all genuine philanthropy in the world derived from Christianity, few doubted that in Cheltenham, all philanthropy derived from the evangelicalism of the incumbent Reverend Francis Close and the corps of evangelical curates who presided over the many churches and schools that he had built in a thirty-year reign that began in 1830. Close was omnipresent and omnipotent. There was not a charity whose meetings he did not chair, not a Christian cause he did not espouse, not a Whig or Dissenter he did not denounce, not a Puseyite he did not condemn, not a theater he did not close, nor a school to whose piety he did not attend. He was a sabbatarian, an enemy of horse racing, and a foe of strong spirits— but no teetotaler. Loudly compassionate about the poor, he nonetheless excoriated Chartists, socialists, and trade unionists and preached obedience. As great as was his zeal for African colonization, the Church Missionary and the Newfoundland societies, so was the energy he poured forth into the Christian Knowledge, Church Pastoral, and Church of England Reading societies. His proprietary appetite was all inclusive. He boasted of "our charitable societies, our Hospitals, our Orphan asylums, our District Visiting societies, our schools, and various benevolent institutions."[26] His "our" like the "our" of many evangelicals, reflected an attempt to corner the market in philanthropy. To make all philanthropy "Christian philanthropy" in Cheltenham was one thing, but to do so for all England was quite another. Yet Ford K. Brown, in *Fathers of the Victorians,* presents a powerful case that, led by William Wilberforce and the group of Low Church social reformers known as the Clapham Saints, the evangelicals made such an attempt. Brown not only lists 345 societies in which the evangelicals were active but enumerates ninety-one wealthy and titled evangelicals who each belonged to fifteen or more philanthropic societies.[27] Equally impressive are those great achievements that ranged from the freeing of slaves to the rescue of children from factory and mine and including the spread of the Gospel abroad and at home.

The Quakers, who were themselves not untouched by evangelicalism, were among the evangelicals' greatest and most productive allies in the emergence of a Christian philanthropy. Few would rival the zeal and effectiveness of Joseph Lancaster in education, Thomas Clarkson on slavery and merchant seamen, Elizabeth Fry and Sarah Martin with prisons, Joseph Gurney on slavery, capital punishment, and distress, Joseph Sturge on temperance, William Allen on slavery, law reform, and education, Samuel Hoare on factory children, and Thomas Fowell Buxton on slavery and law reform and the destitute. All were Quakers—even Buxton and Clarkson, who were also members of the Church of England—and all devout Christians.

But although devout and touched with evangelicalism, they were also heirs to the Enlightenment. William Allen, chemist, lecturer on science, intimate of James Mill, Henry Brougham, and Robert Owen, was founder of the *Philanthropist*, a journal whose "sole object" was not to spread the Gospel but "to stimulate to virtue and active benevolence . . . and [to] render material assistance in ameliorating the condition of man." Convinced that the "prodigious" advance of knowledge had promoted "the happiness of our species," Allen established a farm school in Sussex, worked for the British and Foreign School Society, and urged that American Indians be taught that "the Great Spirit of Infinite Power" is "goodness itself." In his *Memoirs,* he says not a word about original sin, conversion, or atonement, but speaks only of the "Divine Good" and "Supreme Source of Good." The religion of Wilberforce's Clapham Sect was not Allen's religion, so it is not surprising to find Allen's Quaker friend Richard Reynolds writing him about "the ignorance of Wilberforce of [the Quakers'] principles as a religious society."[28]

The *Christian Observer*, once the Clapham Sect's main organ, felt the same way about Elizabeth Fry, Joseph Gurney's sister. They praised her good works but had great doubts about her religious principles. And although the American Quaker evangelical William Savery awakened the twenty-year-old Elizabeth Gurney to "a state of enthusiasm" and the "blessing of immortality," she had made her revealing confession "I love to feel for the sorrows of others, to pour wine and oil into the wounds of the afflicted" three years earlier, not long after what she called her "Deistical phase."[29] Neither do her *Memoirs* speak of original sin, atonement, or conversion.

Thomas Fowell Buxton also had deep ethical impulses. His favorite passage from the Scriptures was "Except your righteousness exceed the righteousness of the scribe and pharisees ye shall in no case enter the kingdom of heaven." Buxton's yearning for righteousness occurred before he encountered the evangelicalism of the Reverend Joseph Spratt, and before the illness at the age of twenty-four that marked his "ascendancy to religion." Although he had been baptized as an Anglican, his father's death when he was six meant that he had a Quaker mother, a Quaker school, and a Quaker wife, a Gurney and Elizabeth Fry's sister. He, too, was more than a little touched by Enlightenment ideas, ideas that fitted well with Quaker beliefs that an inner light dwelt in all, a belief that Joseph Gurney, the leading religious thinker among the early Victorian Quakers, compared to Wesley's belief in inner grace. Historians have called Gurney a Quaker evangelical, which, in some ways, he, Fry and Buxton were, but not entirely nor even largely. What evangelical would have written of sinful man, as Gurney did, that "in the midst of his ruin by the fall, he is visited with a ray of heavenly light independently of any outward revelation."[30] It was a belief that would have pleased Thomas Clarkson, who wanted religion to be "open to free inquiry" and "free of all superstitious shackles." In 1780, Clarkson was the leading opponent of the slave trade, and in 1840, he championed oppressed merchant seamen. When Coleridge asked him whether he ever thought of the next world, he replied: "How can I? I think only of the slaves in Barbados." Clarkson believed that true Christianity lay "in the lives and actions of its professors." Although formally an Anglican, he confessed his Christianity was "nine parts pure Quakerism."[31] It was also part Enlightenment, and part a piety that was, although different in theology, as deep as that of the evangelicals. It was not, however, as the *Christian Observer* and Richard Reynolds insisted, the otherworldly salvation-centered evangelicalism of a Wilberforce or Chalmers. Evangelicalism was not of one piece, and neither did it constitute the whole of the religious revival that, along with Enlightenment ideas and economic and social developments, led to the flowering of philanthropy. James Stephen even noted that William Wilberforce was not evangelical in "the blunt and uncompromising tone of his immediate predecessors." In his *Practical View*, Wilberforce argued that "Christian morality provides . . . proofs of its divine origins."[32] It was an idea that was to expand and give a larger emphasis to morality as the basis of Christian faith. Not a few Nonconformist divines welcomed this development. In the sermons of the Congregationalist Thomas Binney and Edward Miall and the Baptist George Dawson, morality not only crowded out any notion of predestination but nearly crowded out any references to the soul's fate on Judgment Day. For these modernists, the great Christian duty was to do good, and the more philanthropic the better. For Wesleyan Methodists and Anglican premillenarian evangelicals, conversion and eternal salvation still loomed large. For the premillenarians, Christ's Second Coming would occur before the millennium because so sinful is man and so omnipotent is God that Christ is needed to usher in that millennium when all will be judged. God was constantly interfering with plagues and misfortunes and arbitrariness. Man could do little and must look instead to eternity. In the memoirs of many Wesleyan ministers and in the sermons of premillenarian evangelical Anglicans, the concern for social problems is slight. This helps to explain the surprising and revealing observation in Lord Ashley's diary that he could not rely on "evangelical religionists" in causes that were "called Humanity."[33]

The premillenarian Anglicans and the otherworldly Wesleyans had, of course, their favorite form of philanthropy, one in keeping with the Reverend Rowland Hill's admonition, "How preferable is that bread which endureth to everlasting life, to that which perisheth."[34] Conservative evangelicals were exceedingly active in Bible and tract societies, foreign and home missions, and the district visiting societies that entered the hovels of the poor to bring the glad tidings of everlasting life. And for postmillenarians who believed that Christ's Second Coming would occur only after a truly Christian people had, by creating the new Jerusalem, brought about the millennium, it was their philanthropic duty to work for the improvement of Christian life, as well as the salvation of souls—hence a concern to care for the worldly needs of their flocks, to organize clothing and coal clubs and establish schools and benevolent societies. Some pious clergymen of the postmillenarian persuasion— among them the Reverend William Champneys of Bethnal Green, the Reverend Hugh Stowell of Manchester, and Wesleyans anxious to care for the worldly needs of their flocks—also organized clothing and coal clubs and benevolent societies.[35] There were philanthropies for every faith and every shade of faith: High Church sisters of charity and brotherhoods of young men, Baptist temperance societies, Unitarian schools, and secular philanthropies established and run by civic leaders, such as local hospitals, dispensaries, asylums, bathhouses, and soup kitchens, which everyone could support.

In 1847, the *Athenaeum* announced that a "new belief . . . has arisen amongst us . . . hence we have parks for the people—baths and wash houses for the people—model dwellings and lodging houses, and sanatory [*sic*] regulations."[36] A year later, *Fraser's* announced that this new belief constituted "the New Philanthropy and its spirit was found in the Model Lodging House, the Bath and Wash house, and the Ragged schools."[37] Samuel Smiles declared in 1846, "Ours is the Age of real practical purpose, of high philanthropic aims," one that in Leeds reflected "an earnest desire for improving." It was a pragmatic outlook shared by the *Decorator's Assistant*, which insisted that "the philanthropist can do nothing better than to build houses for the poor" and praised the building of model lodging houses, baths, and washhouses, the creation of public gardens, and the Health of Towns Association. Civic leaders of all persuasions promoted these urban improvements. "Baths and wash houses," suggested the *Athenaeum*, "are too vulgar and lowly for the echoes of an Exeter Hall."[38] Vulgar, perhaps, but eminently useful, even greatly necessary. The vision of rationalists might inspire Owenite communities and societies to amend the laws, and the zeal of evangelicals might promote Bible and tract societies, but it was the growth of large towns and their multiplying problems that evoked the new philanthropy. It was up to philanthropy, wrote the reformer George Boole in 1847, to remove "the darker features in our large cities."[39]

Darker features had long existed in the eighteenth century in the form of disease. Before evangelicalism invaded the upper classes, and while rationalists dreamed of utopias, practical citizens in Britain's burgeoning towns had established hospitals, dispensaries, infirmaries, houses of recovery for fever victims, lock hospitals for those suffering from venereal disease, and asylums for the blind, the deaf, idiots, and the insane. When the explosion of population and manufacturing in the early nineteenth century produced not only rapid growth and great wealth but severe economic fluctuations and grim social conditions, practical philanthropists established night asylums, strangers' friend societies, soup kitchens, infant societies, savings banks, and benevolent associations of all kinds. And after 1848, when prosperity replaced depression, public baths and washhouses, parks, gardens, colleges, and art galleries followed. A general and practical benevolence and civic pride, not the utopian schemes of rationalists or the Bible and tract societies of evangelicals, now defined the nature of philanthropy.

"For nine out of ten," conjectured Edward Copelston, bishop of Llandaff, "benevolence and philanthropy might be used as synonyms," with both words meaning "actions of kindness, mercy, humanity." But he quickly added that to use them in that way was "the main error of illiterates, the error of being indiscriminate."[40]

If philanthropy meant simply benevolence or humanity, what better philanthropist than Charles Dickens, with his kindly Brownlows and Cheerybles rescuing wretched Olivers and harassed Nickelbys? Did not R. H. Horne say that Dickens expressed the spirit of philanthropy? The radical *Westminster Review* and the Tory *Blackwood's* also called Dickens a philanthropist, but neither meant it as a compliment. *Blackwood's* Sam Phillips called Dickens one of those "philanthropists" who "teach the loveliness of all that lies in the hovel and the hatefulness of all that dwells in the palace," while W. R. Greg, in the *Westminster*, condemned Dickens for letting his "feelings warp his judgement." So, also, added Greg, did Mrs. Norton in *The Child of the Islands*, by making her "philanthropy ... somewhat indiscriminating" but not Mrs. Barrett's "Cry of the Children," in which "the sympathy of the philanthropists [finds] its most powerful form."[41] That philanthropists came in various forms was the opening theme of *John Bull's* "Ode to Philanthropy of 1841," namely, that "One scarce can tell what shape you'll next appear in; / Sir Fowell Buxton, Owen, Mrs. Fry, / [or] Chadwick (in Poor Law high authority)." To that motley list, some would have added Dickens, Mrs. Barrett, and others such as the Wiltshire gentry and clergy whom the *Devizes and Wiltshire Gazette* called "the best friends and true benefactors" so dear to "every philanthropic mind."[42] In an article in the *Edinburgh Review*, John Stuart Mill also identified the paternalism of squire and parson with philanthropy, and, to the confusion of not a few readers, dated the origins of the philanthropic movement to Malthus's *Essay on Population*. Even manufacturers could be philanthropic, as Alexander Ure makes clear in his 1835 *Philosophy of Manufactures*.[43] The list grows ever more diverse, and the view that nine out of ten early Victorians saw philanthropy as synonymous with benevolence grew ever more persuasive; in fact, many early Victorians did just that, identifying benevolence of every kind with philanthropy. But many meant something different by philanthropy—they meant a zeal for Christian benevolence, the Gospel, and moral reform as determinedly asserted in a society or an association. It was such philanthropy, often evangelical, that often evoked charges of being spurious, hypocritical, and pernicious, charges that came above all from those periodicals and pulpits that championed paternalism.

PATERNALISM AND PHILANTHROPY

Six Tory periodicals denounced philanthropy in the 1840s: *Blackwood's*, *John Bull*, the *Quarterly Review*, the *British Critic*, the *Englishman's Magazine*, and the *English Review*. *Blackwood's* and *John Bull* were the most caustic and snarling. "Philanthropy is a luxurious creature," wrote Samuel Philips in *Blackwood's*, "she does not work, she talks. Her disciples . . . sit at home in satin dressing gowns . . . feeding on turtles." But not all reclined in satin gowns. Those from "Puffington Hall," said another *Blackwood's* author, preached to Eskimos and Africans of the "wonders of tracts and the woes of new rum." *John Bull* was no more flattering. It not only accused the "Exeter Hall Saints" of confining their labors to love of talking, grunting, and groaning, and to tickling the ladies, but spoke of "a morbid and spurious philanthropy" that indulged in a "large amount of eloquent braying."[44] Although the *Quarterly Review* was more restrained, it too condemned both universal philanthropy, which was "gloriously obscure," and the philanthropy that could be indulged in while in an easy chair. Its editor, John Lockhart, advised Fowell Buxton to confine his labors to Spitalfields, advice that would have delighted three other *Quarterly Review* authors, William Sewell, John Armstrong, and John Sterling: Sewell because he hated "indiscriminate philanthropy," Armstrong because only Church soldiers should enter "the very strongholds of profligacy and sin," and Sterling because Exeter Hall, so often Buxton's podium, flowed with the "unctuous silkiness of the professional . . . [and] dismal obscurantism and raving folly."[45] The *British Critic*, *Englishman's Magazine*, and *English Review* hoped that High Church soldiers would replace unctuous philanthropists, the *Critic* because "bazaars, shilling and six pence subscriptions and balls, dinners . . . all blunt our consciousness"; the *Englishman's Magazine* because "the multiplication of clubs and associations had been a sign of decay"; and the *English Review* because "raising money by public subscription and printed lists" constituted one of the "saddest records of faint energies and fickle zeal."[46]

The principal reason so many Tories were hostile to philanthropy was their attachment to the Church of England as the main agency of social policy. There were, to be sure, secular reasons for opposing philanthropy. Great philanthropic movements to end the slave trade and slavery, to prohibit the employment of women and children in mines, and to limit hours in factories threatened vested interests and led to dangerous changes. To Tory peers, ranging from Lords Eldon and Sidmouth to Lords Wellington and Londonderry, all change was subversive of a prescriptive and divinely ordained order. For Eldon, all philanthropists were men "pretending to humanity but brimful of intolerance and swollen with malignity"[47] To a moderate voluntarist like Peel, the secular fear of such malignity had, by the 1840s, diminished, but not the ecclesiastical hostility.

The High Church was at war with the evangelicals, not only in defense of the efficacy of sacraments as the way to salvation but also in defense of the offertory, alms, clergymen, deacons and deaconesses, and Anglican schoolmasters as the principal means of mitigating the poor's misery and teaching Christian truth and social obedience. High Churchmen could not abide evangelical devices and societies. "Spurious," "extorted," and "questionable" declared the Reverend John Sandford of "charity sales, . . . balls and bazaars"; such balls and bazaars, proclaimed the Reverend F. G. Hopgood, "endanger the principle of Christian charity"; and for the Reverend T. J. Hussey, balls and bazaars arose from "the delusive complacencies of a selfish and vainglorious philanthropy."[48] The Reverend Frances Paget told his parishioners that the evangelicals' "penny subscriptions, missionary boxes and such like trumpery" were a "pandering to personal vanity." For the Reverend J. E. N. Molesworth, the error of philanthropists ran even deeper than the trumpery of balls and bazaars, since "half the miseries of the world arose from misdirected attempts to relieve them."[49]

The views of these paternalistic High Church clergy were not all negative. Indeed, their negative strictures arose from a positive vision of a truly national Church meeting the nation's social needs, a dream not unlike Coleridge's idea of a clerisy. At the center of that vision were the altar, the offertory, and alms. Charity's "fittest mode," proclaimed the Reverend William Gresley, "is by offering alms at the altar of the Lord previously to the partaking of the holy sacrament of the Lord's Supper." Gresley's colleague Sandford wanted to revive the offertory, because alms are nobler than "the scanty dole . . . extorted from an ill concealed reluctance by questionable expedients," and Paget because the offertory gives "less scope for hypocrisy and ostentation."[50] With the abundant alms of the offertory (and ample tithes and endowments), a truly national Church would create parochial and diocesan institutions to handle every social problem. They would include churches and chapels, schools of all kinds that required the catechism and Anglican masters, collegiate chapters for young priests, sisters of charity, almshouses, hospitals, asylums, and at the center, the bishop.[51]

High Churchmen were not the only ones to dream of a clerisy or to expound the virtues of parochial and diocesan institutions. The Broad Church also had glorious but unrealistic dreams of such institutions, although they would, to the horror of High Churchmen, welcome Dissenters. The evangelicals had their own formula for fusing parochial and voluntary institutions. "A resident clergy in every district of the parish" was the Reverend Thomas Dale's vision, "the center within his own allotted sphere of all those philanthropic and pious institutions which the influence of the parochial system calls into operation." Evangelicals were proud of the term "philanthropic," a term seldom used by High Churchmen—certainly not by Gresley, the evangelicals' archenemy. Frances Close's "benevolent societies," insisted Gresley, arose from "unworthy motives."[52] From Robert Southey to the bishop of Exeter, from Oxford's William Sewell to Parliament's Sydney Herbert, a passionate allegiance to an Apostolic Church of England led to deep suspicions of the proliferating philanthropies that encroached on the Church's holy work. "Self-founded communities like temperance societies," protested the *British Critic* have "wrested from [the Church] its manifest attributes [while] several offices of the Church are usurped by self-constituted bodies."[53] To the extent that Tories and High Churchmen believed that the Church of England should be the dominant social institution in a clearly defined and contained paternalist society, they held the proliferating and varied world of philanthropy, with its temperance societies, mechanics institutes, and Dissenters' visiting societies, to be a dangerous enemy.

Many a London humanitarian also saw philanthropy as an enemy. They could not abide the philanthropists' self-righteousness any more than they could endure the arrogance of paternalism; nor did Chartists and Short Time men like the philanthropists' condescending soup-kitchen mentality. Self-help moralists also doubted some of the philanthropists' generous views of charity. Diverse and many were the critics of philanthropy.

A CHORUS OF CRITICISM

Two events flourished in early Victorian England, the growth of philanthropy and the growth of its critics. While praise of a general philanthropy was tepid, particular philanthropists were exuberantly praised; and most praised of all was Lord Ashley. Lesser philanthropists, however, were also esteemed, like the Reverend Andrew Reed, builder of orphanages, Angela Burdett Coutts, rescuer of prostitutes, and Elizabeth Fry, comforter of prisoners. Carlyle's righteous thunder and Dickens's cutting satire could abuse and parody philanthropy, but not its leaders—again more ambivalence.

Criticism came from all sides. Liberal individualists as well as Tory paternalists had great doubts about philanthropy. Five weaknesses in particular bothered its various critics: it was ineffective, it corrupted, it looked abroad instead of at home, it warped judgment, and its rhetoric and cant hid unworthy motives.

That it was ineffective in dealing with poverty was the radicals' cry. For William Cobbett, philanthropy offered the poor only a "basin of carrion soup," on the one hand, and a "halter on the other," an old view, echoed in the 1840s by the working-class poet William Thom and the radical journalist Douglas Jerrold. "Hospital charities for devastated homes!" expostulated Thom, "Laugh! Give me a wage." "Benevolence," declared Douglas Jerrold, "very often, like a dog, runs around with her tongue out, yet somehow forgets to show her heart." By the 1850s, even the staid *Times* saw that philanthropy was often ineffective because it flowed in "so many and partial channels that few reached the objects desired and many ran dry."[54]

Liberal and Radical periodicals ascribed much of philanthropy's ineffectiveness to the impracticality of philanthropic schemes. The *Weekly Chronicle* found Lord Ashley's joint stock company scheme for building houses for the poor hypocritical. The idea that substantial dividends could be paid by building "semi-palaces for the poor," it called "humbug" and a "delusion." The *Daily News* took a similar view when it called Ashley's society to aid seamstresses just another of his "benevolent contrivances." The *Westminster Review* felt the same about Thomas Fowell Buxton's hope, in *Remedies of the Slave Trade*, that pattern farms, schools, missionaries, and agricultural and benevolent societies would lead Africans to oppose the slave trade. It simply would not happen. Neither, said *Bentley's Miscellany*, would desultory benevolence end England's lack of education.[55]

Philanthropy was not only ineffective because impractical and desultory but it dealt with symptoms, not causes. Such was the view of that prolific journalist and eloquent free trader W. J. Fox, for whom philanthropy "penetrates little below the surface," and Robert Vaughan, of the *British Quarterly*, who argued that "no charity can be compared with free trade," since before the enormous wretchedness of the lower orders, "the philanthropy of a whole nations of Howards and Clarksons would sink abashed and confounded."[56]

Philanthropy was not only superficial but, far worse, in the form of charity, it corrupted the poor, which bothered many a political economist, most particularly its popularizers, Mrs. Marcet, in *Rich and Poor;* Harriet Martineau, in *Poor Law and Pauper;* John Hill Burton, in *Political and Social Economy;* and Poulett Scrope, in *Principles of Political Economy.* For Martineau, charity both corrupted the poor and lessened the wage fund. Scrope was less severe, but like many early Victorians, he saw in "the clamorous imposter charity's main beneficiary." Mrs. Marcet agreed, concluding that "the more is given the more beggars there are." Burton insisted that "schemes of philanthropy can be dangerous, "since charity has so virulent an effect on independence of character, industry, energy and self-reliance . . . that it often produces frightful moral devastation."[57] Unitarians and Tories also feared the devastation wreaked by charity. In both his sermons and in his *Christian Teacher,* the Unitarian J. H. Thom raised the fear that a charity formed "only a palliative that multiplies distress," while the Tory Dr. Calvert Holland of Sheffield warned of the "incalculable mischief from . . . zealous philanthropic exertions."[58]

Nothing seemed more indiscriminant than lavishing Bibles and tracts on Africans abroad while the English starved at home. The *Weekly Dispatch,* *Daily News,* and *Spectator* all had doubts about faraway missions. The *Dispatch* wondered why "enormous sums . . . [went] to Africa, Asia, and America in order to impart instruction to savages that cannot receive it." The *Daily News* felt it knew why: it was "much more agreeable to give abroad [since] no self reproach is associated with the suffering." For the *Spectator,* it was the abstract nature of the "African" that led to uncritical giving. For the astute Edward Edwards, pioneer of public libraries, the remoter the area, the greater the philanthropy, which might explain why the London Missionary Society had begun with the South Sea Islanders.[59]

Criticism of benevolence abroad and neglect at home was not, however, widespread. In the deeply religious 1840s, few doubted Jesus' command to go forth and preach the Gospel. Far more widespread was the fourth of the charges, the charge that the philanthropic impulse too often warped one's judgment. It led to "mawkish sensibility," "foolish benevolence" to the poor by "humanity mongers who seek to build a reputation," "utopianism," "maudlin sentimentalism," "a blind and therefore false philanthropic impulse," and, in the case of Dickens, "feelings" that warped his judgement— such were the views of *Bentley's Miscellany,* the *Spectator,* the *Sunday Times,* the pamphlets of Toulmin Smith, the *Athenaeum,* and the *Westminster Review.*[60]

For many, the movement led by Lord Ashley to limit the hours of factory labor most clearly showed how feelings could distort judgement. But other causes also elicited that charge: full of sentimentalism and deficient in tough-mindedness were ardent free traders, amenders of the criminal code, reformers of the game law, and advocates of a more generous poor law. The *Economist* said in 1854 that Lord Palmerston lacked "great penetration or judgment," because he was "easily led by philanthropic notions." Palmerston's folly was to urge the renewal of the General Board of Health. Nine years earlier, the *Economist* had insisted that "charity is the national error of Englishmen, generally a very mischievous and very ostentatious one."[61]

The mention of "ostentation" always rang a bell with those suspicious of the motives of philanthropists. It was not Carlyle alone who shouted "cant"; the *Durham Chronicle* in 1847 announced that "the cant of philanthropy" was "rapidly becoming what all cants should be—supremely ridiculous."[62] The cant in question was Thomas Duncombe's motion for a parliamentary inquiry into mining accidents. Francis Place had much earlier charged that the Quakers were benevolent "principally from a love of distinction," reflecting the Radical's suspicion of power and wealth, which by 1860 led Henry Mayhew to claim that philanthropy "rose from love of power."[63] "A love of lucre and respect for rank," said the *Athenaeum,* too often lay behind the philanthropist. For the *Eclectic,* their sin was "a selfish desire to win approval," one that encouraged a "semblance of beneficence."[64]

Some worldly motives for philanthropy were not hidden at all but openly advertised—hence balls, bazaars, banquets, and concerts, with their lists of patrons. Concerts in particular evoked *Punch's* mirth. "How cheering to the philanthropist," it wrote, willing to help "the wretched widow and orphan [by listening to] the very best music." Arousing *Fraser's* satirical fancy were philanthropists as busybodies—"Committees of Gentlemen and Committees of Ladies," whose "rivalries and jealousies, yea enmity itself, work for the sick and maimed."[65]

There were, of course, more than five reasons to fault the philanthropist. From William Cobbett's "Halter for the poor" to Douglas Jerrold's "'slavery, the Only Remedy,' by a Philanthropist," radicals saw in philanthropy a threat to liberty. Philanthropists could not, said the *Sun,* resist "undue meddling." "A spurious charity," declared the self-help moralist Thomas Beggs, taught "contentment instead of high ambition."[66]

Some of the vast and varied criticisms of philanthropy came from its admirers and participants themselves, criticisms that reflected the deep ambivalence of the early Victorians toward philanthropy. A pervasive sense of "pseudo" as against "genuine" philanthropy underlay a perplexing picture of weaknesses and strengths.

David Owen in his magisterial *English Philanthropy, 1660-1960* and Frank Prochaska in two perceptive studies, *Women and Philanthropy in Nineteenth-Century England* and *The Voluntary Impulse,* have strongly underlined the hugeness, diversity and dynamism of early Victorian philanthropy.[67] There was little, said its supporters, that it could not do. If there were homeless in the cities, let them turn to London's Charitable Night Refuge or to the homes of the Stranger's Friend Societies in Leeds, Manchester, and Liverpool; if unruly vagrants were a problem, let the Society for the Repression of Mendicity feed, shelter, and work them hard in the stone yards, as they did in London from 1830 to 1850, with half a million meals provided and countless stones crushed; if girls were being lost to prostitution, let Magdalen houses or the less theological Rescue Society of London rehabilitate them; if criminal laws were too harsh, join the Law Amendment Society and urge their mitigation; if thousands were facing starvation as capitalism broke down, open soup kitchens—soup kitchens that, David Owen notes, became a permanent feature of towns that suffered economic distress; if factory workers labored for long hours, form Short Time Committees; and if women in prison, workhouses, asylums, and slums were friendless, godless, and despairing, send good Christian women to visit them, because in consoling, advising, and caring, Victorians felt, women far surpass men. The list goes on and on, so vast and many were the social problems in early Victorian England and so vast and many the societies for their mitigation. It was indeed the first and most manifest strength of philanthropy that it was so flexible and adaptable, so far-ranging and so purposeful, that it could address problems far different in nature and context.

Philanthropy did much good, for example, in the world of medicine. By 1840, the provinces had 114 hospitals, as against the 38 of 1800, and in those thirty years, London added 14 hospitals as well. They were also much improved hospitals, not a little owing to the philanthropists who had helped establish the medical schools associated with both London and provincial hospitals. Great advances were made, not only in the study of anatomy, the status and skill of surgeons, and the care of patients with fever, but in the development of effective anesthesia and the use of antiseptics, improvements that lowered mortality in hospitals, according to John Williams, to an average of 4 percent. Dispensaries and infirmaries served the many who could not afford or did not need hospitals—some 6,000 were "on the books" of London's Charing Cross dispensary. Nearly a third of those treated at Sheffield's dispensary had fractures set, burns salved, cuts bandaged, and other treatment.[68] Philanthropy was not mere cant to these laborers or to the 23,490 Manchester destitute who found lodging in 1842 in the Night Asylum. According to the German visitor J. G. Kohl and the ardent Methodist Benjamin Love, a flexible, wide-ranging philanthropy took the hard edge off grim, dirty, depression-ridden Manchester. To the Night Asylum, innumerable churches, eighty-six Sunday schools, and a full array of medical charities, ranging from the Royal Infirmary to the Eye Institute, Manchester's philanthropists added yet more charities: for the deserving poor, tickets from the Provident Society and blankets and sheets from the Loyal Fund; for all the hungry, soup kitchens, and for those reported dying, a Humane Society. There were also, as part of the march of mind, two Lyceums, an Athenaeum, a statistical society, a mechanics institute, a zoological collection, an art gallery; and, as part of advancing self-reliance, 500 friendly societies serving some 8,000, a school of the Royal Lancastrian Association, two National Schools, a Jubilee school for the affluent, a Blue Coat Hospital school for the less affluent, and an industrial school for the delinquent. Countless Bible, religious tract, and church building societies promoted Christian faith, as did a most remarkable institution, the Town Mission, whose "60 agents visited the miserable haunts of the poor."[69]

It was the peculiar strength of philanthropy to have a voracious appetite. No problem was beyond its wide-ranging desire to ameliorate. Juvenile crime, distressed needlewomen, the loneliness of the jobless, alienated governesses, and the filthy dwellings of the lower orders all evoked compassion. For children on the verge of crime, the enlightened instruction and healthy work at farm schools run by Lady Byron, Mrs. Davies Gilbert, William Allen, and Lord King, Sheriff Watson's famed industrial school in Aberdeen, and industrial schools in Manchester, Liverpool, and Glasgow all offered reform and an escape from a career of wretchedness and misery. And for juvenile offenders, there were the reformatories of the Philanthropic Society's Red Hill, Mary Carpenter's Kingswood, and the magistrates of Warwickshire's Stretton-on-Dunsmoor.[70] To these children, philanthropy was neither spurious nor pseudo. Nor was it such to the distressed needlewomen and jobless governesses whom philanthropists helped go to the colonies and a new career.

In 1847, Mary Chisholm established the Family Colonization Society, and in 1849, Mary Jane Kinnard started the British Ladies Female Emigrant Society. The establishment of these societies and a proliferation of further emigration societies at midcentury reflected the widely held conviction that emigration was the great panacea for destitution. That it barely scratched at the extent and depth of destitution meant little to those needlewomen and governesses who did escape the thralldom of pitiful wages or a lonely, jobless alienation. Not so dramatic, but still salutary were the baths and washhouses of Hull, which offered cleanliness to the grimy and filthy, the result of the broadest of philanthropic efforts. "Not a single name of eminence" said the *Hull Adventurer* in 1840 of the meeting to build the baths, "was missing."[71]

Emigration societies and baths and washhouses that did their modest good, paled into insignificance in the eyes of most early Victorians compared to that Christian philanthropy that made paramount the soul's eternal welfare. "The most important of all charities, the charity to the soul," proclaimed the Reverend Edward Bickersteth, "is the soul of charity." A resolve to save souls sent Anglican and Dissenting evangelicals to the furthest corners of the globe and to the most squalid slums at home.[72] Samuel Low's *Charities of London* lists eighty-one home and foreign missionary societies. The greatest of these was the British and Foreign Bible Society, which in 1829 had over 2,500 local associations and 10,000 agents (mostly women), and distributed one and a half million Bibles and two million tracts.[73] To an age still concerned with eternity, a central purpose of philanthropy was the salvation of the soul. But the men and women of these societies valued just as highly the moral reformation of the lax and wicked and the consolation of the sick and dying and imprisoned. They also sought to console and reform the destitute in their hovels, the pauper in the workhouse, and prostitutes in penitentiaries. Women once again admirably manifested the strength of this Christian philanthropy. Elizabeth Fry and her lady visitors brought the blessings of the Gospel to prison upon prison; workhouse visitors brought cheer into these grim barracks; and temperance ladies rescued drunkards. Drunkards, declared the *Congregational Magazine*, are "one of the special provinces of Christian philanthropy."[74]

It could have added prostitutes, criminals, and juvenile delinquents. Toward these sinners, many philanthropists poured forth much compassion, often a compassion exceeding that shown to those many who were destitute through no fault of their own. Very few were the evangelicals who did not support the harsh New Poor Law. Sin absorbed the evangelicals. The curse of Adam left an indelible stain of sin, which only Christ's merits and sacrifice could remove. The best of Christian philanthropists condemned sin but not the sinner. The resulting compassion toward all sorts of sinners certainly forms one of the most impressive strengths on the asset side in any balance sheet of philanthropy.

Kindness to sinners and to the less sinful as well, ranging from orphans to the insane, also lessened many a philanthropist's anxiety about his or her own sinful soul. Middle-class women in particular, who played such an active role in philanthropy, gained significance in a life otherwise constricted. And for all the charitable, there was the happiness that, said the Reverend Hugh M'Neil, arose from "an active service of brotherly kindness and widespreading benevolence." Many in that age of religious anxiety lessened their doubts by making morality the buttress of their faith.[75]

"Visiting" lay at the core of Christian philanthropy's hope for the moral reform of society. Not only would it bring the Gospel to infidels and heathens and console prisoners and prostitutes, but through the District Visiting Society and Home and Town Missions, it addressed the festering problems of an industrial and urban age. In 1845, the First Report of the Young Men's Society for Aiding Missions praised "that Gospel which alone can elevate the minds and thus alleviate the moral miseries of our countrymen." For the Reverend Edward Bickersteth, "systematic visiting" was the best means for "aiding and relieving the necessities of the poor." In 1850, the London City Mission had 340 paid workers systematically visiting the poor; the Congregational Union boasted of 120 Home Missionaries "proclaiming the Gospel to 60,000"; 214 of 250 Church of England parishes in London had visitors; the General District Visiting Society had 573 volunteers; and at Leeds, the Town Mission visited 56,258 "cottages of the poor" and delivered tracts to every house.[76] To the message of Christ's saving grace was added the morality of self-help, of frugality, industry, providence, and sobriety, as the philanthropic and the self-reliant outlooks merged to help define the social conscience of the early Victorians.

Flexible, widespread philanthropy could merge not only with a self-reliant voluntarism but with reliance on law and government. At first glance, to be sure, philanthropy often appears to be identical with voluntarism, but it could depart from that allegiance. Although it did fuse nicely and extensively with voluntarism, it also embraced reform by act of Parliament. It did much good through factory, mining, and sanitary measures, a good that definitely belongs on the asset side of the balance sheet.

Philanthropy's two greatest moments were in fact the acts of Parliament of 1807 and 1833 that ended the slave trade and slavery. The early giants of the great liberation and of the world of philanthropy, Wilberforce, Clarkson, Buxton, and Allen never hesitated in using government to do good or in forming societies to force it to do so. Among their successors who kept that tradition alive, none exceeded Lord Ashley with his tireless advocacy in Parliament for a ten-hour factory day, an end to child labor in mines and factories, healthier towns, more humane insane asylums, and emigration.

To Ashley's supporters and enemies, these were acts of philanthropy. The *Sun* celebrated the Ten Hour Factory Act of 1847 as "a triumph of philanthropy," while the *Sunday Times* ascribed it to "the utopian dreams of philanthropists"[77] The sanitary reformers were also praised and abused as philanthropists, as were education reformers and advocates of the humane treatment of animals.[78]

Even free traders and defenders of the Corn Law were called philanthropists. J. O'Connell told the Commons that "true philanthropists were those who by unshackling commerce gave industry employment," while the *Sussex Agricultural Express* called the Corn Law a part of "Christian philanthropy." There was, indeed, as W. R. Greg noted in the *Edinburgh Review*, "plenty of floating philanthropy at work."[79]

Of this "floating philanthropy," none obsessed its critics more than prison and law reformers. Had not Carlyle singled them out for his vituperation? And did not the *Quarterly Review* denounce the "extravagance" of a "philanthropy" that would abolish capital punishment altogether? Since the 1820s, the death penalty had been ended for some 600 offenses, a reform that constituted another great monument to the early giants of philanthropy, to Sir Samuel Romily, Sir James MacIntosh, William Allen, Fowell Buxton, and Elizabeth Fry.[80] In parliamentary reforms, as in the creation of voluntary infirmaries and soup kitchens and farm schools, there was indeed plenty of floating philanthropy. The good it did was far-reaching, vastly diverse and, in precise terms, incalculable; in its prodigious variety and extraordinary earnestness, it greatly strengthens the positive side of the philanthropic ledger.

Few are more appreciative of these strengths than David Owen and Frank Prochaska, and yet both are uneasy about philanthropy's overall record. After describing the admirable work of the Metropolitan Visiting Relief Association, Owen confesses that there was still "a huge gulf between rich and poor," while Prochaska admits the philanthropists were never free from an embarrassing "persistence of poverty" and occasions of "confusion and muddle."[81] In terms of bustling activity, inexhaustible energy, and countless societies and associations, early Victorian philanthropy seems awesome, but in terms of results, it is often less impressive.

THE BALANCE SHEET; WEAKNESSES

The ledger on philanthropy also has its debit side, its weaknesses. There were, for example, too few really active philanthropists, and too many who were apathetic. Too few! When philanthropy was so vast and wide-ranging? Yet such was the judgment of Lord Ashley. Most philanthropic work was done, Ashley claimed, by "a small knot of chosen persons, whose names you will find repeated in the catalogue of every charity," a verdict David Owen also gives in noting that certain names, "Gurney, Hoare, Buxton, and Thornton, not to mention the omni-present Ashley . . . occur again and again, often constituting interlocking directorates."[82] The dedication of an Elizabeth Fry, a Fowell Buxton, or the seamstress Sarah Martin, with her indefatigable visits to console Yarmouth gaol prisoners, was, in fact, in an England of sixteen million, singular and exceptional. An anonymous pamphlet on destitution in Edinburgh observed that relief efforts were the work of "a few practical philanthropists," while among the others there reigned "a surprising amount of apathy," a condition the reforming Edinburgh doctor W. P. Alison confirmed by noting that during the acute distress of 1842, only 1,348 citizens gave more than a pound to the relief committee. It was a stinginess Londoners could emulate: three of the wealthier trade associations, the grocers, the goldsmiths, and the merchant tailors, gave only twelve shillings each to the British Female Penitents Refuge.[83]

If perhaps a penitential refuge was too negligible, certainly the work of the all-important London City Mission and its visits to the destitute were not—and yet, in 1845, it received only £3,484 from all sources.[84] In 1849, according to the Reverend Henry Worsley, sixteen million English gave, if hospitals and schools were excluded, less than one million pounds a year to the country's charitable and philanthropic institutions.[85] If Worsley is at all accurate, and if foreign missions were, as the evidence suggests, one of the first priorities of the evangelicals, then not much was left for grappling with the social evils of an urban and industrial society. Although there is no way of measuring what was actually spent in philanthropy, much must have been left undone. In Chapter 8, on "Voluntarism," efforts to improve the housing and health of the poor were shown to be decidedly defective. "In spite of efforts of statesmen and philanthropists," observed the Times in 1854, "those classes who form the substructure of society deteriorate, while all around them advance."[86] Most worthy philanthropic endeavors gave more the appearance than the reality of progress. Although hundreds read of Elizabeth Fry's visits to Newgate, of the work of the Philanthropic Society's school for juvenile delinquents, of the farm schools of William Allen, Lady Byron, and Mrs. Davies Gilbert, and of Joseph Strutt's magnificent gift of an arboretum to Derby, far fewer realized that except for the women's ward, Newgate, not to mention England's other wretched prisons, went largely unreformed; that Strutt's arboretum elicited few emulators; that in 1849, the Philanthropic Institute's school took in only fifty boys; that the enrollment in the farm schools mentioned above was thirteen, eighty, and twenty-one respectively; and that attendance at Mrs. Gilbert's school lasted only a few years. How minuscule compared to the thousands of juveniles sent to prisons in the 1840s, where hardened adults taught them crime.[87]

The annual reports of philanthropic societies boasted often and at length of great endeavors. None did so more vigorously than those of the London City Mission and the District Visiting Society, with their imposing statistics on the thousands of visits and tracts delivered, and yet poverty, disease, overcrowding, slums, ignorance, hopelessness, and crime continued unabated, as, indeed, did working-class indifference to religion. To the weakness of too few active philanthropists and too much apathy can be added another weakness, that of the Christian philanthropists' narrow concern with salvation.

The clearest manifestation of that narrow concern lay in England's passion for foreign missions. No other philanthropy received larger funds. Although it distorts history to claim that evangelicals were so busy saving souls abroad that they neglected suffering at home, it would also distort history to say that suffering at home enjoyed an equal emphasis. Nor is it true that for workers in Home Missions, material want enjoyed an equal emphasis with the salvation of the soul. An otherworldliness characterized Christian philanthropists of all faiths except the Quakers and Unitarians: for Frederick Lucas, the Roman Catholic editor of the *Tablet*, "the interests . . . of the soul were paramount over all political and worldly considerations whatsoever"; for Samuel Wilberforce, bishop of Oxford, the clergy's "one work is to win souls to Christ, not [the] amendment of society"; and for the evangelical *Christian Observer,* "the soul is of more value than the body."[88] Leeds's venerable Congregationalist Reverend John Ely, whose favorite cause was foreign missions, declared that, compared to the salvation of souls, "how little are our manufactures, our commerce, our politics, our empire . . . mere baubles, mere shifting shams."[89] For the great Dr. Chalmers, the "great monuments of philanthropy . . . [had] their eyes full on eternity."

Many with eyes on eternity still saw in the consoling of the dying or the cheering up of the imprisoned the greater part of the Gospel's blessing. The Congregationalist Dr. Campbell, a great admirer of Chalmers, and convinced that the power of "lay visitations" would prove comparable to "the power of steam," urged, in his *Jethro: A System of Lay Agency* (1839) that visitors console the dying peasant, "bring cheer to the prison cell," and dispel "the darkness of an island"—but not once, in 336 pages, does he mention material assistance. It was a spiritual view in keeping with the London City Mission's decision to prohibit its agents from distributing charity. The City Mission also declared that "ITS GREAT DESIGN IS TO SAVE THE SOUL."[90]

The Christian philanthropists were not always agreed on how to save the soul. Some Anglicans had doubts of the effectiveness of the London City Mission, since it had "no articles, no tests." The bishop of London, aghast that the City Mission was "a hot bed of dissent and schism," helped form the Church of England's exclusive Scriptural Readers Association, whose laymen could do nothing more than read the Bible to those they visited.[91] Sectarian jealousies, enmities, and quarrels over otherworldly truths weakened philanthropic efforts already narrowly focused on the soul and obsessed with Christ's Second Coming. Edward Bickersteth, Thomas Birks, Hugh Montague Villiers, Hugh M'Neil, and James Haldane Stewart, all evangelical clergymen, either helped establish or were active in the Prophesy Investigation Society and preached that after Christ's Second Coming, which was imminent, there would be a thousand years of peace and then the final judgment.[92] Evangelicals, who esteemed Bickersteth second only to Chalmers, would find in his sixteen volumes much on the Book of Daniel, on prophesies, and on the poisonous nature of Catholicism, and only rare comments on how to solve poverty or any other social problems. The same is true of the sermons of Hugh M'Neil and Thomas Birks. Awaiting the Second Coming was not conducive to organizing for the removal of social miseries.[93]

Many otherworldly evangelicals, even premillenarians, did relieve the destitute and did work for cleaner towns and more civilized prisons and asylums. Birmingham's Reverend William Marsh, although awaiting the Second Coming, did establish schools, shoe, clothing and blanket clubs, and provident societies. But Marsh's efforts were not typical of Birmingham's evangelical clergy. More typical was the Reverend John George Breay, who every fortnight left a tract at each house and had his agents urge those visited to read the Bible, give their children a Christian education, and observe the Sabbath.[94]

Whether promoting clothing clubs or Bible reading, Marsh and Breay would have agreed on the importance of a self-reliant morality, a doctrine second only to the importance of the soul's salvation among Christian philanthropists. Their self-reliant morality could be harsh, as it was in the evangelicals' favorite social philosopher, Thomas Chalmers. The Malthusian Chalmers told the poor not to marry and the Scots not to adopt a compulsory poor law. Nor was Chalmers the only one with harsh attitudes, attitudes that formed another weakness of the philanthropists: there were tough-minded prison philanthropists, insensitive proponents of compulsory child emigration, pleasure-denying Sabbatarians, Magdalene house despots, advocates of a harsh poor law, and those in the Society for the Suppression of Mendicity who were quick to send a vagrant to the stone yard. Even the humane Elizabeth Fry had either a harsh streak or myopia; she praised both the Parkhurst prison for juveniles and the old Coldbath Fields prison, even though Parkhust manacled its errant boys and imposed four months of separate confinement on every new inmate, while Coldbath Fields used the treadwheel, whipping, and, in place of separate confinement, the hated silent system, in which no prisoner was ever to speak to another. Mrs. Fry also had card games and novels banished at Newgate, shades of the moral severities of Wilberforce's Society for the Suppression of Vice.[95]

Fry and Buxton were the more humane of prison philanthropists; far more severe were evangelicals like John Field, John Clay, George Heaton, Whitworth Russell, and William Crawford (the last two also being prison inspectors). They were all evangelicals and all proponents of separate confinement, a form of solitary confinement relieved only by infrequent visits of a chaplain or turnkey. It was a prison discipline that William Wilberforce supported, believing that it would help "restore . . . [the] mind to a sense of shame and repentance." The separate system that these prison philanthropists imposed proved so cruel and damaging to mental health that it was, except for a few fundamentalists, abandoned or greatly modified.[96]

Good intentions also led other philanthropists to severe measures. The promoters of the Children's Friend Society rescued juvenile vagrants from the cruel streets of London, only to ship them to servile work in South Africa, and did so at the very time that many denounced transportation of convicts to Australia as inhumane. In 1839, the *Times* condemned the society's "secret and harsh ways" and its forced emigration. Nevertheless, it not only continued the practice but the greatest philanthropist of the age, Lord Ashley, urged that the products of his beloved ragged schools be sent to the colonies. It would be for their own good, said Ashley, a rationale that covered a legion of severities, including Magdalene houses that insisted on shaving off a prostitute's hair in order to increase her penitence.[97]

Among the legion of severities, none was more pervasive and more harmful than a neglect of the destitute. Many a tireless visitor to the squalid hovels of the poor would deny such neglect, and many justly so, since their many visits and occasional gifts reflect a genuine compassion. But for most of the destitute, there were either no visits or visits that helped very little. Often there was only the grim workhouse, the product of that harsh New Poor Law, which most Christian philanthropists supported. Very few of the evangelical M.P.'s voted to make the law more generous. According to Thomas Chalmers, whom so many evangelicals read for guidance, poor relief was not, as Paley argued, an inherent right, but should flow spontaneously from Christian benevolence—a theory that led Chalmers to an adamant opposition to a state poor law for Scotland. It was a theory that fitted well with the evangelicals' heroic attempt to have Christian philanthropy fill the urban void that neither the paternalism of property nor the intervention of government filled. It was a beautiful vision, if charity flowed freely and generously. But not too freely, not too generously, declared Chalmers. "Give as little as possible," he told his followers, or "nothing at all." He also declared that "a poor man who is ungenerous in desires is worse than a rich man ungenerous in doings." Such a poor man does "a far wider mischief," since "his rapacity [and] raven-ous gripe" mark him as "the arch-oppressor of his brethren." The poor men's "gall of bitterness" and "low sordidness" makes them like those "harpies . . . deadlier than baronial tyrants." The embittered poor spread "a cruel and ex-tended blight over the fair region of philanthropy."[98] The bitterness of this outburst helps explain why Chalmers preferred a voluntary to a compulsory poor law, a preference unfazed by the discovery of W. P. Alison and others that the voluntary system left the Scottish poor not only far more destitute than the English poor but just as idle and profligate. Although not many Christian philanthropists in England shared Chalmers's harshest views, he remained their favorite and won effusive praise from the *Christian Observer* and the *Record*. Prompted by fear of opening "the floodgates of pauperism," the *Christian Observer* in 1841 found no reason to object to Chalmers's *Christian and Civic Economy*, with its insistence that generous charity corrupts. In the grim depression of 1842, the *Christian Observer* not only insisted that poor relief belonged to the Church, not the state, but praised Scotland's voluntary system of relieving the poor. For England, the *Christian Observer* supported the New Poor Law, as it supported the Corn Law, separate confinement, capital punishment, and the belief that "the religious philanthropist is the best benefactor of his species." The *Record* differed little from the *Christian Observer*. It too stood stoutly by the Corn Law and the New Poor Law. While the old poor laws encouraged "idleness, improvidence and vice" and "women living in immorality," the new law was a "constant stimulus to . . . industri-ousness . . . [and] sober and moral habits." Neither the *Christian Observer* nor the *Record* ever criticized the separation of husband and wife in the work-house. In February 1847, the *Record* also pronounced "admirably good" Eng-land's policy toward Ireland, a policy that had the month before closed down its public works only to await until late spring to establish soup kitchens. And only in the autumn did the government establish a poor law—one that was barely adequate, and that the Irish, not the English, would pay for.[99]

It is paradoxical that a Christian philanthropy at whose very heart lay charity was so uncharitable. How could J. B. Sumner, bishop of Chester, who published twenty-three sermons entitled *Christian Charity*, one of which called charity "The Surest Mode of Benefitting the Poor," have played an ac-tive role on the commission that laid the basis for the New Poor Law and its uncharitable workhouse test? A possible clue to the paradox is the Reverend Henry Melville's insistence that "we estimate the worth of charitable institutions by their tendency to check pauperism." Christian philanthropy by mid-century had outgrown the mere command of Jesus to visit the poor, feed the hungry, and clothe the naked; it had instead grown into a narrowly moralistic outlook. "Christianity is the basis," said the Reverend Samuel Green, "of our asylums for age and infirmity, our hospitals for sickness and our alms-houses for maimed poverty and helplessness."[100] In this vision, charity became increasingly institutionalized. The philanthropy of Howard and Wilberforce and Romilly reflected a more diffuse humanitarianism; the philanthropy of the early Victorians was less diffuse, more focused on promoting moral reform, and less humanitarian. The evangelicals made of philanthropy something more than humanitarianism, because they organized and shaped it around a purpose, a moralistic and religious cause, one that it pursued in a sustained, even severe, manner.

The great visiting societies and home missions saw charity as more than kindness. It was also, said Bishop Sumner, a "preventive of evil," and, as Henry Melville said, a "check on pauperism." Christian philanthropy did seek to remedy the great social problems of Victorian England, and to do so by reforming the individual. But in doing so, it both acted from doubtful assumptions and attempted far more than it could handle. "Charity, itself," observed *Blackwood's* in 1844, "is repelled by the hopelessness of all attempts to relieve the stupendous mass of destitution," with the result that "philanthropy seeks in vain for virtue amidst thousands and tens of thousands of unknown names."[101]

The two greatest causes of the rise of Christian philanthropy, the growth of urbanization and of evangelicalism, posed insurmountable problems to its success, urbanization because of the massive scale of social ills and evangelicalism because of its narrow otherworldliness and its erroneous belief that humane relief would corrupt the poor, beliefs that were partly due to a theology anchored in a belief in man's innate depravity and partly to a conviction that property, authority, and inequality were divinely ordained. And given the fact that active philanthropists were only "a small knot" of men and women, and that public support was often stingy and evanescent, it became clear that for all the praiseworthy good that it did, Christian philanthropy could never be the great remedy of social evils that so many expected. Perhaps only a widening, expanding, contagious, and even indiscriminately compassionate humanitarianism could reach into all the slums and prisons and wretched cottages where destitution and crime and misery were stubbornly entrenched.

CHAPTER 10

Humanitarianism

A compassion for those who suffered unmerited pain and distress formed a distinct part of the early Victorians' social conscience. Like its cousin, philanthropy, it had roots in the eighteenth century and blossomed in the nineteenth. It was a development that escaped few educated Victorians. "There is," wrote John Stuart Mill in 1836, "a great increase in humanity." "We are awakening," proclaimed the *Journal of the Leeds Polytechnic Exhibition* in 1845, to "deeper and hitherto dormant sympathies with humanity."[1]

It was an awakening that delighted the London press. *The Athenaeum* rejoiced in the "newly awakened benevolence now so nobly and unceasingly at work," while the *People's Journal* rejoiced that "a moral" had replaced an "iron age," one distinguished by "the claims of the heart."[2] The liberal *Morning Chronicle* and the Tory *Standard* also welcomed "the spirit of humanity" and "the great movement of humanity," while the *Morning Herald* praised Lord Ashley for having "humanized an age."[3]

Even poetry fell under its domain—a poetry, said the *Westminster Review*, that "every day becomes more human, more true to the heart."[4] Diffuse, pervasive, and elusive in definition, humanitarianism was still strong enough to persuade the *Spectator* and *Punch* that it could form the basis of a new politics. In 1844, the *Spectator* proclaimed its hope for a new party, one based on a "New Faith," which would arise from a "rebellion of sentiment" against laissez-faire. And *Punch* saw both Whigs and Tories declining before a party "vindicating the sympathy, affections, and common rights of humanity."[5]

No such party was ever formed, but humanitarianism nevertheless invaded the House of Commons. A score of differing issues called forth appeals to follow "the dictates of humanity;" and, in response, opponents of such measures denounced "meddling humanity." Lords Chancellor and lordly mine owners were irate at its inexorable advance. Lord Londonderry, the greatest mine owner in England, denounced the "hypocritical humanity" that "reigned so much at present." It was the 1842 bill to remove women and children from coal mines that led the noble lord to denounce the current "humanity mania," a feeling that Lord Chancellor Brougham seconded in his warning not to be "led astray by feelings of humanity."[6]

Many of the foes of a generous poor law and the Ten Hour Bill refused to allow their opponents a monopoly on "humanity." "I will yield to no man," exclaimed the eccentric Tory Colonel Sibthorp as he denounced a more adequate poor law for Ireland, "in humanity." Henry Drummond took the same position in the same debate, with the admonition that the Commons should not "presume that all humanity was on one side." Numerous opponents of the Ten Hour Bill felt the same: "The best humanity," said the Whig F. T. Baring, is to "leave people to care for themselves," a sentiment that dovetailed exactly with the radical Charles Hindley's insistence that "the doctrines of political economy were not opposed to the principles of humanity."[7] Most M.P.'s, however, did not buy either Sibthorp's and Drummond's argument that humanity favors severe poor laws or Baring's and Hindley's marriage of humanity to political economy. Opponents of generous poor laws and of factory and mine acts, like opponents of reduced capital punishment, reformatories for young offenders, or a fairer game law, much preferred to see humanity as the enemy. It was, of course, a "meddling humanity," or one that was "mistaken," "sentimental," or "hypocritical," that they denounced.

Philanthropy, too, was often judged meddling, mistaken, or hypocritical and appeared to many M.P.'s and journalists not to differ greatly from humanitarianism. When Sir Joshua Walmsey, M.P. for Leicester, told his electors that "philanthropy and humanity . . . demanded that [the aged] be relieved," both he and most of them probably saw little difference between the words "philanthropy" and "humanity." Nine out of ten people, Bishop Copleston said, considered philanthropy and humanitarianism synonymous. Among those who did so were Leigh Hunt, who praised the poet Thomas Hood's "principles of philanthropy" and his "generous and humane feeling" as one and the same, and the *Mirror,* which praised the prison inspectors William Crawford and the Reverend Whitworth Russell as "humane and truly philanthropic."[8] But that Crawford, Russell, and many philanthropists urged the adoption of separate confinement and hard labor at the treadwheel, which humanitarians increasingly called cruel, suggests that philanthropy and humanitarianism did not always coincide.

The factory reformer Richard Oastler, one of the most passionate humanitarians, certainly realized this. He wrote in 1847 of the children in factories: "You were suffering but the prejudices of habit and custom . . . closed the ear of philanthropists to our cry."[9] The ears of Charles Dickens's Mrs. Pardiggle and Mrs. Jellyby were also closed to the cry of the children of England, so wrapped up were they in their Christian philanthropies in Africa. Dickens, the greatest of humanitarian novelists, could not endure Exeter Hall and its sanctimonious evangelical philanthropists. Neither could two other humanitarians, Douglas Jerrold, *Punch*'s most scathing satirist, and Henry Mayhew, the Victorians' most compassionate investigator. Jerrold pictured philanthropists as "purveyors of humbug," and Mayhew ridiculed them in his *Comic Annual* of 1851.[10] London was full of humanitarians who were not among the nine in ten who viewed humanitarianism and philanthropy as alike.

Neither did the leading philanthropists see them as alike. They suspected the humanitarians' diffuse and undisciplined feelings. The evangelical James Stephen praised the Clapham Sect's "philanthropy" because it did not "degenerate into a mere ballet of tender attitudes and sentimental pirouettes."[11] Tender sympathies and sentimental pirouettes abound in Dickens's humanitarianism and won censure from the Tory and religious press. *Blackwood's* denounced his *The Chimes* as full of "trashy" assertions and of "cockney sentimentalism," while the evangelical *North British Review* condemned Dickens's "full luxury of benevolence." John Anster, another *North British* reviewer, called instead for an "inflexible philanthropy."[12] For the High Church *Christian Remembrancer,* Dickens was too full of "sickly sentimentalities"; what was needed, in the words of Arthur Helps, the author of *Claims of Labour,* was not "sentimental benevolences" but "earnest philanthropy."[13]

At the heart of humanitarianism lay much direct and spontaneous compassion for the suffering of the exploited and the oppressed. Such a compassion was not entirely absent in great philanthropists like Wilberforce and Ashley. But the philanthropists added to compassion for the suffering a devout concern for their conversion, their moral reform, and their soul's eternal life. The humanitarians' compassion for the helpless seamstress or overworked child was uncomplicated and largely unchecked by that passion for moral reform and the soul's salvation that diverted many a Christian philanthropist's compassion. For many of them, an inviolate Sabbath was more important than feeding the hungry. The evangelical philanthropists of Liverpool, for example, refused to distribute relief on Sundays to the starving Irish who had fled the famine, while the evangelical *North British Review*, which boasted of its "philanthropic ethics," denounced poor laws, emigration and cottage allotments as no real remedies for social evils.[14] Evangelical hostility to theatergoing, novel reading, and assorted pleasures alienated many of the middle class, just as evangelists' hostility to beer shops, radical coffeehouses, and trade unions alienated the working class, driving both to the humanitarianism of *Punch*, the *Weekly Dispatch,* or the *People's Journal.* It was largely humanitarians, not philanthropists, who condemned the severities of the New Poor Law. Certainly, it was not the Wesleyans who did so; they, George Jacob Holyoake would later write, cared for "spirituality not humanity." The Congregationalist Reverend Robert Vaughan similarly observed, in his *Religious Parties in England* (1839), that there was "something in evangelical religion hostile to . . . humanity."[15] Basing one's social morality on the dictates or feelings of the heart, and not the commands of God, also alarmed the Christian philanthropist. The evangelical *Record* scarcely ever mentions "the dictates of" or the "principles of" humanity—or indeed the word "humanity" itself; and neither did the *Wesleyan*, although it proudly ran a weekly column entitled "Philanthropy." In the sermons of the evangelical Reverends Henry Melville, Edward Bickersteth, and Hugh M'Neil there is likewise hardly a single reference to humanity, but rather a scripturally correct emphasis on charity as a Christian duty and God's commands, an emphasis also found in the sermons of those Anglican clergy who were not evangelicals.

Conservatives, religious and political, feared the humanitarians' undue reliance on the "feelings of the heart." Humanitarians were not ashamed of such feelings. The *Westminster Review* rejoiced that Dickens was a "man with a heart," while *Douglas Jerrold's Shilling Magazine* invoked the "universality of the human heart."[16] In the House of Commons, there were also M.P.'s like Thomas Wakley, the unrivaled defender of the downtrodden pauper, the miserably insane, the overworked child and the wretched slum dweller, who was praised for his "kindness of heart."

Humanitarianism was not a theory. It possessed no axioms, as did political economy, none of the historical learning behind private property or the theology behind philanthropy. It was instead a simple, powerful feeling. "I learned to feel for the poor," said the temperance reformer, Joseph Livesey, "to acquire the first lesson of humanity."[17] The objects of such feelings were usually the suffering and helpless, and they were most powerfully evoked by concrete images: a boy "trapper" in a narrow coal seam; infants endlessly tending spinning machines; manacled, chained naked lunatics; young thieves facing the hangman's noose; cholera victims in filthy, disease-ridden courtyards. It was such concrete and graphic evils that evoked a widespread compassion and that made humanitarianism far more universal than the paternalists' duties of property and the philanthropists' Christian injunctions. Active humanitarians, in fact, outnumbered active philanthropists, who, Lord Ashley confessed, were few in number. Humanitarian newspaper editors, such as Robert Rintoul of the *Spectator,* and M.P.'s, such as Joseph Brotherton, were seldom called philanthropists; nor were humanitarian poets, painters, and novelists such as Thomas Hood, Richard Redgrave, and Charles

Dickens. The humanitarian movement was of a wider scope and more diffuse than philanthropy. To be a philanthropist was to join a society, to raise funds, to attend meetings, to serve in a sustained and organized manner; one could, on the other hand, be a humanitarian on the spur of the moment. To rise suddenly in Parliament and denounce capital punishment, to impulsively write a crushing editorial against child labor, or to plead with a fellow poor law guardian to allow workhouse inmates tea with sugar and milk were moments of humanity that did not constitute philanthropy but that occurred daily and weekly throughout England—though most fully and intensely in the great metropolis.

HUMANITARIAN LONDON

Impulsive, restless, classless, and pervasive, humanitarianism as an eruption of feeling was most powerfully centered in London, a response of the city's many writers and artists to its concentration of social evils. Few evils seemed more intolerable than the plight of the seamstresses, especially when made vivid by Thomas Hood's poem *The Song of the Shirt* and Richard Redgrave's painting *The Sempstress*. To be sure the Children's Employment Commission of 1843 had detailed the wretched existence of these 15,000 London girls. During the London season, April through July and October through December, they worked from eighteen to twenty hours at a stretch in overcrowded, fetid rooms, inadequately fed and even more inadequately paid. It is also true that the *Times* and the *Pictorial Times* had earlier protested the exploitation of these seamstresses. But not until 1843, when *Punch* published *The Song of the Shirt,* and 1844, when the Royal Academy hung *The Sempstress,* did the image of the seamstress shock the world of London and make its indelible impression.[18] It would quickly become, along with that of boys and girls dragging coal carts in mines, one of the most prevalent and vivid images of economic oppression.

Thomas Hood's *Song of the Shirt* caught the monotony and weariness and pain of the seamstress' ordeal in a simple, sentimental, and compelling manner. Its repeated phrases, "stitch, stitch, stitch, work, work, work" and "seam and gusset and band / band and gusset and seam," recreated the tedious misery of endless stitching, which in conjunction with "poverty, hunger, and dirt" and "a bed of straw, a crust of bread and rags," makes understandable the shirt maker's response to death: "I hardly fear her terrible shape / it seems so like my own."[19]

The poignancy in Richard Redgrave's painting *The Sempstress* is less harsh, less realistic. There are no rags, straws, or crusts; and in place of death's "terrible shape," a dawn and a church tower promise a better afterlife. Although the seamstress here occupies no wretched garret, her eyes and visage communicate a sadness nicely designed to evoke pity and sympathy from the middle-class viewers at the Royal Academy. "She is not a low born drudge," reported the *Art Union*. The *Times* found it an "ultimately unforgettable" painting, one that addressed the "best feelings of the human heart."[20]

Also ultimately unforgettable for many London journalists, novelists, and artists were the *Song of the Shirt* and the actual plight of the seamstresses. The *Mirror* called Hood's poem "a just condemnation . . . [of] the toil and suffering of slaves," and the *Morning Chronicle* called it a "protest against the world's heartless idolatry of cheapness." Leigh Hunt in the *Edinburgh Review* praised it for protesting a "heartlessness . . . to the evils of humanity," and W. J. Fox in the *People's Journal* said it gave "a distinct voice . . . to the moaning of misery."[21] The novelists were just as indignant and even more graphic and affecting in their depiction of the suffering seamstresses. Charles Dickens led the way in 1844 with *The Chimes*, a tale of destitute poor and heartless authorities. One of the destitute poor is Meg, a seamstress doomed to "so many hours, so many days, so many long nights of hopeless, cheerless never ending work . . . [all] to earn bare bread," an intolerable plight ending in suicide.[22] "Cheerless, never ending work" is also the fate of Ruth Hilton in Mrs. Gaskell's *Ruth*, of Virginia Mordaire in G. B. W. Reynolds's *The Seamstress*, of Camilla Toulmin's *The Orphan Milliner*, and of the heroine of Mark Lemon's play *The Sempstress*.[23] Almost as widely read as *The Chimes*, and as moving, was Douglas Jerrold's *The Story of the Feather*. "In an almost empty garret, through whose broken pane comes a gust of wind," Patty Butler sews away at two A.M. with "swollen eyes," "lean fingers of want," and "a wasted face." It is a "world of wretchedness . . . of want and suffering and all the sad and wicked inequalities of human life."[24]

Painters and caricaturists deplored the shameful exploitation of seamstresses quite as much as did journalists and novelists, and none more so than *Punch*'s usually jocular John Leech. His 1849 engraving for *Punch* of a careworn, anxious, needlewoman in a shabby room with broken plates and bare poverty was much more powerful, although no less poignant, than his tiny 1844 engraving of Meg in Dickens's *The Chimes*. Much more grief-stricken was George F. Watt's *Sempstress*, and much more savage and bitter was George Cruickshank's caricature *A Tremendous Sacrifice*, in which wealthy shopkeepers exploit poor seamstresses.[25] The contrast between exploiter and exploited also led Richard Redgrave to paint *A Fashion's Slave* in which a wealthy and haughty lady of fashion scolds a humble and abject milliner.[26]

Obsessed though London artists and writers were with the suffering seamstresses, there were many others among the destitute and outcasts of the heartless metropolis who evoked pity. Thomas Hood's *Bridge of Sighs* and George Frederick Watts's painting *Found Drowned* movingly depict the despair in the face of remorseless poverty and want that tempted destitute mothers with babies to commit both suicide and infanticide. George Cruickshank, as a reformed heavy drinker, powerfully chronicled the evils of drink in his eight designs *The Bottle*, while the novelists Edward Bulwer-Lytton, William Ainsworth, Dickens, and Jerrold all tried their hand at understanding the criminal.[27] Many were the London journalists who described with great pathos the cruelties of the New Poor Law and the sufferings of the destitute. These journalists, poets, novelists, painters, and engravers numbered well over a hundred in the 1840s, defining the world of London journalism, literature, and art that constituted England's clearest, strongest, and purest voice of humanitarianism. It was a compassionate, satirical, and at times angry voice, one far less inhibited than were the voices of paternalism, political economy, property, religion, and a reforming philanthropy. It formed the most compassionate part of the Victorians' social conscience and one centered in the world of London journalism.

Of the editors of London's great journals, the religious press excepted, only James Grant of the *Morning Advertiser* was an ardent evangelical, and only John Black of the *Morning Chronicle* and Albany Fonblanque of the *Examiner* were ardent Benthamites.[28] An examination of the backgrounds of some thirty of these editors reveals no great influence of a Coleridge or Bentham, or of a Dugald Stewart or Thomas Chalmers, and neither did these and other great luminaries loom large in the backgrounds of London's many writers and artists. But London itself had a great impact on them. Nearly two-thirds of a sample group of seventy London writers and artists had known the city from boyhood, and many of the remaining third had arrived in their youth. Thomas Wakley arrived at the age of nineteen, soon to edit the *Lancet*; Eyre Evans Crowe, a dropout from Trinity College, Dublin, had immersed himself in the world of London journalism and novel writing by the age of twenty; William Jerdan came down from Scotland at nineteen, eventually to edit the *Literary Gazette*; and *Punch*'s Mark Lemon arrived in London at seventeen.[29] Others from outside also went to school in London, like William Thackeray, who attended Charterhouse.[30] Many, too, were the young artists attending London's art schools—although Richard Redgrave, George Frederick Watts, Dante Gabriel Rossetti, Augustus Egg, George Cruickshank, and John Leech were seasoned native-born Londoners.[31] Charles Dickens, Thomas Hood, George Reynolds, Henry Mayhew and his two literary brothers, Horace and Augustus, as well as Gilbert À Beckett at the *Times*, Anthony

Fonblanque of the *Examiner,* and a long list of journalists, were also born and bred in London.[32] Arriving in London during boyhood were Charles Mackay, editor of the *Illustrated London News,* the novelist Douglas Jerrold, editor of many journals, and many others.[33] For all of these natives and young immigrants, London was an indelible experience.

London influenced them in two distinct ways, first as the center of the prosperous and varied middle classes that produced, nourished, and supported an impressive number of writers and artists and secondly as a vast sea of crying evils that evoked compassion and pity. The growth of the literate middle classes was the product of that wealth, population, literacy, and new technologies of printing and engraving that arose in the world's greatest center of trade and finance. It allowed, not just the *Times* and the *Morning Chronicle,* but *Punch,* the *People's Journal,* and the *Illustrated London News* to prosper, and at their editorial offices and at local cafes to plan their slashing editorials and cutting satires. It was a bohemian world, a world of drink and merriment, a bohemian world in the English not the French sense, since promiscuity took the form not so much of mistresses as of fly-by-night periodicals, raucous dramas, melodramatic stories, and much drink. Gilbert À Beckett, who was with Henry Mayhew at Westminster school and at *Punch,* edited three different periodicals, *Figaro, Wag,* and *Squib.* He also wrote fifty plays.[34] But À Beckett was not all frivolity. He was also a barrister and leader writer for the *Times* and *Morning Herald.* The London bohemians, being both industrious and talented, had a widespread impact: Jerrold edited the *Illuminated Magazine, Lloyd's Weekly Newspaper, Punch,* and *Douglas Jerrold's Shilling Magazine,* which he established. He also helped edit the *Examiner* and the *Ballot,* wrote leaders for Dickens's *Daily News,* published fifty plays, four novels, and many stories, and made *Punch* a radical force in the 1840s. Dickens reported for the *Morning Chronicle,* contributed to the *Examiner* and established the *Daily News* and *Household Words,* Bulwer-Lytton edited the *New Monthly Review,* Thackeray wrote for *Punch* and *Fraser's,* Ainsworth established and edited *Ainsworth's Magazine,* G. W. Reynolds edited the *London Journal* and *Reynolds's Newspaper,* Cruickshank established his own magazine, *The Omnibus* and issued an annual *Almanac,* while the poet Thomas Hood established and ran *Hood's Monthly Magazine* and Charles Mackay edited the *Illustrated London News* and wrote for numerous newspapers.[35] With the pulpit about to lose its ascendancy and radio and TV far off, the world of journalism became ascendant; and few were more active in it than those poets, novelists, and illustrators whose humanitarianism was the product of their London experience.

Experiencing London could be overwhelming. Wordsworth found it a "huge fermenting mass of human kind," and Tennyson wrote "I loathe the squares and streets and the faces that one meets."[36] Wordsworth retreated to the Lake District and the poetry of nature, while Tennyson wrote of medieval chivalry and loss of faith. Londoners like Jerrold, Dickens, Henry Mayhew, and Leigh Hunt could do neither. The giant metropolis was too much a part of them. "I have heard," said Jerrold, "the wailing voices of tens of thousands." Into London, wrote Dickens in *Dombey and Sons*, there comes "a weary, endless procession of paupers . . . swallowed up in its immensities." Little had changed by 1850, when Henry Mayhew found London, "[a] vast bricken multitude, a strange chaos of wealth and want . . . of the brightest charity and the darkest crime." It was a chaos of want and crime that increased awareness, William Empson argued in the 1847 *Edinburgh Review*, of its wretchedness.[37]

It is "a peculiar advantage of great cities," declared *Fraser's* that "the electric properties of benevolence and sympathy . . . are drawn out." Great cities also drew out a lively, shrewd, impious, and satirical street intelligence. "The wisdom that crieth from the street," said Walter Jerrold, "belonged to Douglas Jerrold." Dickens possessed it and made it incarnate in Pickwick's staunch Cockney friend Sam Weller. Cruickshank had it abundantly. His "life school," said a friend, "was in the streets," and it made him "the most masterly delineator of poverty, vice and the vulgarity of London."[38] Although meager in its attention to religion or economic and moral theories, humanitarianism was anything but meager in its sympathies and feelings. The results were not only novels, poems, prints, and paintings of great compassion, but a London press that was distinctly and self-consciously humanitarian. "Our politics," announced the *Illustrated London News* in 1842, "are, irrespective of all party, the politics of humanity." *Douglas Jerrold's Shilling Magazine* was dedicated, declared its editor, to "the social wants and rightful claims of the PEOPLE [and] . . . shall appeal to the hearts of the masses."[39] Jerrold had already fused that spirit into *Punch*, which denounced the cruel Poor Law, the unjust Corn Law, hanging, flogging, fagging, and dueling, satirized pompous paternalism and sanctimonious philanthropy, and championed the ten-hour day, prison and law reforms, and in all things justice and kindness.[40] It was a record not unlike that of Charles Mackay's *Illustrated London News*, which enlisted many from *Punch* on its staff, including Mark Lemon, the Mayhew brothers, and Jerrold. Mackay was the author of a collection of poems called *Voices from the Crowd*, one of which lamented the city's "alleys full of wretched life and odious pestilence."[41] Mackay's paper also denounced "the execrable tyranny of the New Poor Law [and] degrading thraldom of our factory toilers."[42] The harsh workhouse test and grim slums were two bêtes noires of the London press, denunciations of which, along with explicit appeals to humanity, make a portion of the London press different from the provincial press. Before 1841, of course, many a provincial Tory paper attacked the New Poor Law as a Whig measure and praised the ten-hour day, so distasteful to liberal manufacturers, but when Peel became prime minister, Tory attacks on the Poor Law and praise of the ten-hour day diminished. While many provincial Whig-Liberal newspapers, like the *Leeds Mercury*, *Manchester Guardian*, and *Newcastle Chronicle* agreed with Peel on these issues, in London, the *Weekly Dispatch*, *Sun*, *Morning Advertiser*, *Lloyd's Weekly*, *Pictorial Times*, *Illuminated Magazine*, *Spectator*, *Punch*, *People's Journal*, *Douglas Jerrold's Shilling Magazine*, and *Times* attacked the New Poor Law and urged a ten-hour day.[43] All of the above papers, except the *Morning Advertiser* and *Spectator*, were edited by Londoners—and the *Spectator's* chief political writer, Thornton Hunt, was the son of the Londoner Leigh Hunt, and the *Advertiser's* editor, James Grant, was so enmeshed in London life that he published *Lights and Shadows of London Life*.[44]

Thomas Barnes, editor of the *Times* from 1819 to 1841, was born and raised in London; he was an exuberant bohemian and one whose heart, it was said, was "quickly touched by the pain of others." It was above all the pain of the destitute, doomed either to starvation or the cruel workhouse, that moved Barnes to denounce the New Poor Law with an unrivaled fierceness and constancy. Also moved by the cruelty of separate confinement, child labor, dueling, hanging and the sending of boys to adult prisons, he supported prisons without separate confinement, fewer hours of factory work, a civilized law code, the end of dueling, and the advent of reformatories. The heart of his successor, John Delane, was less easily touched. In 1841, down from Oriel and surrounded by Oxford and Cambridge men, Delane tempered Barnes's humanitarianism with High Church and Establishment orthodoxies. Criticism of the New Poor Law abated, the ten-hour day became "socialism," and separate confinement became acceptable if well administered. Yet humanitarianism was only tempered: the *Times* still condemned dueling, urged reformatories and law reform, demanded the more humane treatment of merchant sailors and miners, and insisted on the end of transportation and flogging "on the grounds of humanity."[45] The *Times* was still touched by a London humanitarianism.

Three characteristics of the writings, paintings, and prints of these Londoners made them a powerful part of an expanding spirit of humanity: a talent for the vivid depiction of suffering, an uninhibited flow of sympathy and pathos, and a brilliantly satirical treatment of the stupidity and cruelty of the wealthy and powerful.

The vivid depiction of suffering was the first step in arousing the humane feeling of the Victorians, and its greatest master was Charles Dickens. Few were the readers not moved by the picture of little Oliver in the workhouse, "badged and ticketed," "half-starved" and in "old calico robes," as he asks the cruel beadle, "Please Sir, I want more." But Dickens was not alone in depicting the suffering of a hero or heroine. Bulwer-Lytton's *Paul Clifford*, Ainsworth's *Jack Sheppard,* and Jerrold's Patty Butler in *The Story of the Feather* all begin with scenes of squalor. In a "low and dingy" building near the Thames, writes Bulwer-Lytton, where a "farthing candle gives a sort of grimness and menace" and the wind "makes easy impress though many a chink and cranny," the boy Paul Clifford, in "garb . . . tattered and discoloured . . . trembled violently" as his mother expires. Ainsworth's story of Jack Sheppard begins in "sordid tenements and squalid courts," in a garret that is "old and dilapidated . . . the very picture of desolation," while Jerrold's Patty Butler, "in a pestilent and fever breathing alley," finds her "unwholesome garret" a "world of want and suffering."[46] Vivid, too, are the innumerable graphic accounts in the London press of misery, a not surprising fact since more than half of seventy London journalists of the 1840s about whom there is information were also poets, novelists, playwrights, painters, and caricaturists. They ranged from Thackeray, Dickens, and Jerrold, through the prolific novelists G. W. M. Reynolds, Captain Frederick Marryat, and Theodore Hook, to the barely known Thomas Gaspey, Thomas Holt, and John Saunders and included Henry Mayhew, author of six novels.[47] No wonder that sharply etched pictures of suffering were the hallmark of the reformist press. *Lloyd's Weekly* in "The Might of Mammon" told its readers of a seventy-year-old pauper hauled to a workhouse "in a cart across a cold and frozen county . . . his limbs rigid." The *Mirror* depicted a "starving female, as she drags herself by the rich man's door, [and] sickens from the steams from the kitchen," and *Howitt's Journal* described London outcasts "wandering half naked, diseased and friendless."[48] Few journals could rival the *Times* in vivid accounts of the cruel Poor Law: some 290 between 1837 and 1842. *Punch*, of course, had illustrations. No *Times* leader made suffering more vivid and compelling than *Punch*'s images of tired, worn needlewomen; of the wretched who were jailed only because they could not pay a fine; of famished Irish peasants, "given broth without bread and whipped"; of workhouse mothers, their children torn from them; and of a starving man whose only friend is death, dressed in a black cape and skull. Death appears again in cape and skull rowing on a polluted Thames full of dead animals. In the 1830s, revolutionary advances in wood engraving opened the way not only for *Punch*'s sketches of misery but for the *Pictorial Times*'s and the *Illustrated London News*'s pictures of ragged, famished, evicted Irish peasants, and for John Leech's poignant drawings of overworked, underpaid tailors as cross-legged skeletons.[49] Never before had graphic images of the suffering of the oppressed and outcast been so widespread.

The genre of narrative painting also flourished and with a greater focus on social evils. Richard Redgrave's portraits of lovely, unwanted, ill-paid governesses and teachers stirred a humanitarian response quite as much as did his famous *Sempstress*. So did Charles West Cope's *Poor Law Guardians*, a painting that the *Times* said revealed "hardness of heart and uncharitableness" and the *Art Union* called a fine lesson for legislators and an "emphatic teacher of humanity." George Frederick Watts's paintings of a suicide victim and of a homeless woman in *Found Drowned* and *Under a Dry Arch* also provided a lesson for humanity, although a "lesson so revealing of a terrible London evil as to leave the viewer in despair."[50]

It was however the emotion of pathos, not despair, that moved most London writers and artists and that constituted a second main characteristic of their work. That the unquestioned master of pathos was Dickens, his contemporaries had no doubt. "Wonderfully great," said the utilitarian M.P. Charles Buller, was his "capacity of pathetic description"; he was a man "with a heart in his bosom," wrote the *Westminster Review*; his tendency was "to excite our sympathy," declared the *Edinburgh Review*; to which Richard Horne in the *New Spirit of the Age* added, "his tenderness and pathos" evokes the "heart felt tears of tens of thousands."[51] Thousands did in fact drop a tear over the abandoned, mistreated Oliver, over the frail, stunted, and much tyrannized Smike in *Nicholas Nickleby*, over little Nell, buffeted about in a hostile world until death took her up, over *The Chimes*'s seamstress Meg ending her life in a canal, over the slowly dying young Paul Dombey, over the young, guileless Barnaby Rudge, wrongfully put in Newgate, and over a host of other weak, helpless, defenseless victims of cruelty, oppression, and heartlessness.

As the Tory *Oxford and Cambridge Review* noted, however, Dickens's "feeling of true pathos" was representative of "the whole modern school of novelists."[52] It might have added poets, painters, artists, and journalists. Not only did novelists like Jerrold, Bulwer-Lytton, and Ainsworth—and even the more cynical Thackeray—evoke the sympathy and compassion of the reader, but so too did poets like Thomas Hood, Charles Mackay, Mary Howitt, and Elizabeth Barrett Browning, painters like Redgrave, Cope, and Watts, caricaturists like Leech and Cruickshank, and journals like *Punch*, *Lancet*, and *Lloyd's Weekly*. They all shared with Dickens an uninhibited sympathy with and pity for the neglected, outcast, and suffering, unchecked by the evangelicals' moral censoriousness or the utilitarians' zeal to educate and improve.

They also shared with Dickens a strong tendency to focus their pathos on the defenseless and frail. The objects of their compassion were thus far more likely to be children, women, and the aged, especially the orphaned, widowed, or ailing, than able-bodied men. Thomas Hood's two most compassionate poems, *The Song of the Shirt* and *Bridge of Sighs,* shed tears over unprotected and destitute young women; John Leech's most poignant picture of destitution is in his *Children of Poverty*; while Redgrave and Watts painted lovely, neglected women, and Cope's family begging for charity consists of a widow and four children.[53] Newspaper stories of Poor Law cruelties—and they easily exceeded in number all other forms of pathos—generally follow Cope's formula of women and children only. The same formula in fact underlay the great humanitarian factory and mine reform legislation, which was limited to women and children. The humanitarians' pity extended to adult men only if they were insane or about to be hanged, and very guardedly to those in prison.

There were, however, exceptions. Bulwer-Lytton, Ainsworth, and Jerrold extended their compassion to the adult Paul Clifford, Jack Sheppard, and St. Giles, arguing that the wretched conditions of their characters' upbringing determined their criminal careers. "I came into this world," confesses Paul Clifford, "friendless and poor . . . its laws hostile to me." Falsely arrested and sent to a prison that corrupts him, he has no more chance to take the straight path than Jack Sheppard, who is born into poverty and vice and ill usage in London's Southwark, a district "infected by every description of vagabond and miscreant." Jerrold's St. Giles is "an infant pauper . . . the grand receptacle of the superfluous villainy of the metropolis . . . a human waif of dirt and darkness . . . cradled in misery and vice" and "born slave of penury and want."[54] All three were what Bulwer-Lytton in 1848 called "the victim of circumstances."

Though Dickens did not consider his two most famous criminals, Fagan and Bill Sykes, victims of circumstances and though, after abandoning his opposition to capital punishment, he argued that criminals were from early on inclined to crime, he did, in *The Chimes*, have the able-bodied laborer and rick burner Will Fern give a powerful speech on how pitiful wages, harsh laws, and unjust jailing have made him what he is.[55] Thomas Hood also evokes pity for the able-bodied male in his picture of the jobless, destitute, hopeless hero of *The Lay of the Labourer*.[56] But these were exceptional.

By no means exceptional, but indeed frequent and deeply rooted, was the London humanitarians' delight in satire, especially that aimed at the follies, pretensions, and cruelties of the rich and mighty. Few were the institutions or authorities of the Establishment that escaped the satirical barbs of the London bohemians. The law, Parliament, Church, aristocracy, and military could no more avoid its sharp attacks than could London's mayors, aldermen, Poor Law commissioners, sabbatarians, speculators, physicians, paternalists and philanthropists—or the practice of flogging and dueling. A majestic law that imprisoned children and employed incompetent judges was a favorite of Cruickshank, Dickens, Jerrold, and Leech. Cruickshank's engraving *A Farce Performed in Every Session* (1828) satirizes the Old Bailey criminal court for trying two children for stealing a penny pudding, and in 1834, he lampooned the infamous Judge Gasilee (whom Dickens ridicules as Judge Stareleigh in the *Pickwick Papers*) as pretending to write much (although without ink) and shutting his eyes to create an impression of profundity. Dickens never tired of satirizing the law: in *Barnaby Rudge*, he depicts Dennis the hangman, who is dedicated to "preserving the Old Bailey in all its purity and the gallows in all its pristine usefulness and moral grandeur." In *David Copperfield*, he finds the ecclesiastical lawyers of the court called "Doctors Commons" playing "all sorts of tricks with obsolete, old monsters of Acts of Parliament." And in *Bleak House*, he is merciless on the hopeless, endless delays and delays of a Chancery Court whose archaic proceedings are as "thick and impenetrable as the London fog."[57] Leech and Jerrold also lampooned the law, Leech in a hilarious drawing for *Punch* of drunken, overfed, smug judges, entitled *Old Bailey Justice after Dinner*, and Jerrold in his portrait of Mr. Montecute Cawley, a barrister in *The History of St. Giles and St. James* (1851), who argues any cause, however bad, at the nod of an aristocratic head and by tear-evoking histrionics proves guilty the innocent and innocent the guilty.[58]

Punch's favorite targets were dukes, bishops, evangelicals, philanthropists, and bureaucrats. The dukes of Richmond and Norfolk were particularly attractive objects of parody, Richmond for his grand beneficence in giving agricultural prizes to a laborer for never asking for poor relief after fifty years' service at eight shillings a week, and Norfolk for his grand wisdom in telling such laborers to assuage their hunger with a pinch of curry.[59] The dukes and their brother aristocrats felt the full brunt of *Punch*'s grave irony in articles on "The Lovely Game Laws," the "Milk of Poor Law Kindness," and the "Wisdom of the Philanthropist," while their military cousins became the objects of mordant comments on flogging and dueling. It was also open season on the bishop of London, for urging the clergy "to vindicate the humanity of their faith . . . by co-mingling with their fellow creatures," and on the bishop of Exeter, for urging famine be met by "every man [taking] up his staff and making a pilgrimage to the benighted area." Evangelicals who urged a "Day of Fast" and sabbatarians who wanted to end Sunday trading and travel were also ridiculed; especially John Plumptre, M.P., who, it was charged, wanted the Thames to stop running on Sundays.[60]

That the impulse to satire in a Jerrold or a Dickens was irrepressible poses a problem. It means that they ridiculed those with solutions as well as those who abused. Some solutions, of course, deserved ridicule, like the Malthusian solution, attacked by Dickens in *The Chimes* and most savagely of all by Thomas Hood's *Ode To Mr. Malthus*, a poem that starts with, "Oh! Mr. Malthus I agree . . . the world . . . wants a deal of thinning out" and ends, "I understand the thing you mean / we ought to import the *cholerus morbis.*"[61]

Dickens satirized paternalism in *The Chimes*, philanthropy in *Sketches by Boz, Bleak House, David Copperfield*, and *Edwin Drood*, utilitarianism in *Hard Times,* and teachers of England in Mr. Creakle of *David Copperfield*, Dr. Blummer of *Dombey and Son*, Squeers in *Nicholas Nickleby*, and M'Choakumchild in *Hard Times*. So severe were his caricatures that the *Educational Times* compared his "cutting and slashing the poor teachers" to Creakle's "cutting and slashing" of David Copperfield.[62]

There was, at times, a levity and hilarity in the London humanitarians' parodying of overly earnest reformers that was irresponsible. It may help explain the curious fact that though the London artists and writers gave the clearest, liveliest, and purest voice to humanitarian ideals, and spoke most directly to the heart, they were not the most effective in remedying social evils. For all their moving paintings, poems, and novels about the sad plight of seamstresses, for example, they could not lessen their exploitation. Seamstresses continued to be grossly overworked and underpaid. The law, so ridiculed by *Punch* and the novelists, still remained largely unreformed, except for the creation of county courts in 1841. The refusal to relieve the destitute able-bodied except in the workhouse, so roundly denounced by London writers and artists, continued, and, despite pervasive resistance at the grass roots, was actually revived in the 1860s and 1870s.[63] Education, which the London humanitarians were for, despite ridiculing many a teacher, made no decisive gains against a rising population of the undereducated until the Education Act of 1870. Imprisonment for debt, so movingly depicted in Dickens's *Pickwick Papers* (1837), decreased very little until late in the century. Game laws, flogging, fagging, and separate confinement and the crank and treadmill in prisons continued harsh and cruel, as did that authoritarian paternalism that humanitarians loved to satirize.

It was paradoxical: dominant in the world of London journalism, publishing, galleries, and academies, and increasingly dominant in English society and the public's eye, the artists and writers, the most humanitarian of all in their ideals, were ineffective at social reform. Superb in rhetoric, masters of pathos, of the most delightful wit, unrivaled in storytelling, it seemed not to add up to much more than a sad tear for a seamstress and angry indignation at the stupidity of bishops and the cruelty of landlords. One reason that the London artists and writers did not carry the day in social reform was that they were very much of the middle classes. The painter Redgrave, a successful member of the Royal Academy, certainly was, a fact that T. J. Edelstein realizes in her perceptive analysis of Redgrave's *Sempstress*. Redgrave, she notes, "softened realities" by omitting the "bed of straw, crust of bread, rags, shattered roof" and by presenting a well-dressed, neat, pretty, even pleasant young women with a dawn and church steeple in the background promising better in a future hereafter. Redgrave's successors in the affluent 1850s continued to soften the harsher realities.[64] The 1850s saw the economy take off, the middle classes prosper, and *Punch*, under Thackeray's editorship, drop its earlier radicalism.

But even that radicalism had underlying bourgeois loyalties. *Punch*, like Dickens's *Daily News*, never supported the working class's favorite cause, the ten-hour day, and it was quick to join shopkeepers and professionals in denouncing the income tax that could have reduced the indirect taxes that rested so heavily on the lower classes. Even Henry Mayhew, closest of all London humanitarians to outcast London, would accept trade unions only if they never bargained or struck for higher wages. Nor did Mayhew urge government regulation of the hours of work. In fact, he had no effective solution.[65]

The absence of a solution is a second reason for the ineffectiveness of London's artists and writers—an absence furthered by their deep distrust of government. The greatest of them, Dickens, certainly did not have a remedy. In *The Chimes*, his most radical work, the most radical speech is Will Fern's anguished protest against the oppression of agricultural laborers, just as one of the most satirical is his parody of paternalism in the form of the comic Sir Joseph Bowley; yet Will Fern's speech ends with a paternalistic plea: "Gentlemen, give us, in mercy, better homes . . . better food . . . kindlier laws."[66]

A third reason for ineffectiveness at social reform may lie in the very nature of the humanitarian sentiment, especially as expressed in paintings, poetry, and novels. William Lecky raised doubts that sentiment led to action. "Sentimentality over a novel can be an indulgence of a hard heart that is actually indifferent." This is hard to prove, but the possibility, if not probability, still looms large that the levity of many of *Punch*'s satires, the gentle delicacy of Redgrave's sentiment, the comedy of Leech, and the genius of Dickens's incomparable stories of sorrow and suffering ending in happiness led far more often to indulgence in feelings and a general show of pity than to support for more generous (and costly) relief for the poor. Support for a generous poor law would also have meant opposition to the moralistic preaching of Christian philanthropists, the laws of political economy and, most pervasive of all, the belief in self-reliance. These ideologies were far tougher and seemingly more cogent than the humanitarians' impulsive, subjective, and often evanescent sympathies.

Humanitarianism was, however, far from being absent in the passage of social reform, a humanitarianism far wider and more instinctive than that expressed by London's writers and artists. Had not the spirit of humanity gloriously ended slavery? And did it not exclude women and children from mines, limit their hours in mills, win factory workers the ten-hour day, humanize lunatic asylums, bring reformatory treatment to juvenile offenders—five achievements that reflect the impact of humanitarianism.

THE IMPACT OF HUMANITARIANISM

On June 7, 1842, Lord Ashley presented a bill that would exclude women and children under thirteen from employment in British mines. On August 7, 1842, amended by the Lords to exclude only children under ten, the bill passed Parliament. The unprecedented speed of its passage and by a nearly unanimous vote reflected humanitarianism in its purest form. "Abhorrent to every feeling of humanity," said the *Westminster Review* of children in mines; "an act of pure humanity" proclaimed the *Watchman*; "required by humanity," declared the *Leeds Mercury*; "part of the common feelings of humanity," concluded the *Morning Advertiser*. Even Sir James Graham, whose laissez-faire rigor few could rival, was "delighted at this unanimity for the 'cause of humanity.'"[67] For the *Eclectic,* this unanimity was understandable because of "the plain fact" of these "enormities," poignantly described in the drawings and words of the *Report of the Children's Employment Commission.* It told of three-year-olds brought into the pits to hold candles, of six-year-old boys in complete darkness and solitude opening and closing ventilation doors, of young girls, girdled and harnessed, pulling coal carts through dark and narrow seams, of women naked to the waist and men entirely naked, and some occasionally profligate. To sheer cruelty was added that immorality, which for straightlaced Victorians was the greatest evil.[68]

Not so purely humanitarian and not nearly as expeditious or unanimous in passage were the Factory Acts of 1833 and 1847. The former excluded children under nine and limited children aged nine to thirteen to eight hours' work a day; the latter limited the hours worked by women and young persons to ten a day, a limitation that promised a ten-hour day for all. The first move to exclude children occurred in Sir Robert Peel Sr.'s Factory Act of 1803, but it, like John Cam Hobhouse's act of 1825, proved ineffective. Not until the 1833 act established factory inspectors was child labor mitigated. And, despite the 1847 act, it was not until the Factory Act of 1853 declared illegal the use of relays of the young to run a mill for twelve or more hours that a true ten-hour day was won, thus ending half a century of struggle, one couched often and vigorously in humanitarian terms.

To the early Victorians, the greatest triumph of humanitarianism was the abolition of the slave trade in 1807 and slavery in the colonies in 1833. As a world historical event of unprecedented humanity, it was the pre-Victorians' bequest to their heirs. If the legislature "interposed . . . on behalf of the slave," Thomas Lennard told the Commons in the 1833 debate on the Factory Bill, it surely should "interfere on behalf of the helpless child." Such was also the view in that debate of Sir Samuel Whatley, who cited Dr. William Farr's view that "the labour of the slave's work was far less injurious than the slaves in English factories," and Daniel O'Connell, who wryly noted that legislation limited the hours of negro apprentices, but not factory workers, to ten hours.[69]

It would be difficult to exaggerate the enormous impact of the movement to emancipate the slave on the growth of humanitarianism. "Negro emancipation," said the *Spectator* in 1844, "set all political economy at defiance" and entered into a "higher and better region, that of humanity and benevolence."[70] Was emancipation not as appropriate to infant labor in cotton as to slave labor in sugar? Accounts of five- and six-year-olds working twelve-, fourteen-, or sixteen-hour days, and of their stunted and sickly growth and brutalized life, could not but evoke the compassion and sympathy that lay at the heart of humanitarianism. The 1833 bill reducing such evils easily passed. Even one of political economy's most ardent devotees, Joseph Hume, announced that "the case of the children was the exception to the rule."[71]

Protecting children was one thing, limiting the hours of adults quite another, as Lord Ashley found out in 1844 when he moved to amend the government's Factory Bill to limit young people and women to ten hours' work. Although on March 18, his ten-hour amendment won 179 to 170, the victory so upset Sir Robert Peel that he had his whips round up the backbenchers. On May 13, Tory backbenchers, most of whom held property sacred and hard labor to be the poor's lot, joined Peelites steeped in political economy to defeat a ten-hour amendment 295 to 159.[72] The debates in 1844 and again in 1847 were long, passionate, and dramatic and cast political economy against humanity. It was a conflict that tormented individual M.P.'s. After telling his constituents in West Surrey that "the Ten Hour Act was wrong in principle," W. J. Denison confessed that he had voted for it, because "humanity got the better of me."[73] The Whig Lord Morpeth was also at odds with himself, since his widely recognized humanity clashed not only with his political economy but with the pecuniary interests of West Riding mill owners, whose political support he needed.[74] It was another example of what the *Sun*, in commenting on the 1844 ten-hour debate, characterized as a clash "between the claims of humanity . . . and the claims of the breeches pocket."[75]

The impact of humanitarianism on factory legislation, although substantial, was not as great as it was on mining, lunacy, and animal legislation. Four other forces furthered factory legislation: the self-interest of workers, the calculations of the great mill owners, the reports of factory inspectors, and Tory anger at manufactures who attacked the Corn Law and the aristocracy.

The self-interest of the workers, although weak in Parliament, was strong in the towns of the north. Textile operatives and their trade unions constituted a loud, marching, demonstrating, petitioning, agitating force. When combined in the 1830s and 1840s with the anti-Poor Law and Chartist movements, it had an impact that cannot be neglected, and in 1847, it helped elect a House of Commons whose 60 votes against the Ten Hour Act were a far cry from the 297 largely Tory votes against the bill in 1844.

The calculations of some great mill owners also helped shrink the opposition. A few of them, having discovered that they could produce as much in eleven hours as in twelve, did not mind further restrictions, which would also hurt their smaller, more marginal competitors. The owners of large spinning mills in Manchester, said Edwin Chadwick to the Political Economy Club, were in favor of reducing hours. The fact that the government's factory inspectors also argued that factories could produce as much in eleven as in twelve hours and that shorter hours were morally preferable also had an effect, and might explain the fact that, according to Lord Ashley, some 300 mill owners in 1847 supported the Ten Hour Bill.[76]

Some 300, however, counted little among some 5,000 mill owners. A more powerful force was needed to explain why the opposition fell from 279 to 60. That force was one that emerged with Peel's fall from power, which released an ever-deepening Tory hostility toward manufactures, economists, and those who had repealed the Corn Law. That such a hostility played a role was the view of the *Standard*, *Lloyd's Weekly*, *Sun*, *Economist*, *Morning Chronicle*, *Manchester Times*, and *Scotsman*.[77]

Historians from Karl Marx to today's J. T. Ward and Robert Gray have concurred.[78] Of the twenty-five leading rural Tory squires, seventeen voted for and none against the Ten Hour Act in 1847, votes in keeping with the hostility to manufactures voiced by Southey and Coleridge and pervading *Blackwood's* and the *Quarterly Review*. That hostility, combined with the conversion to the ten-hour cause of Whigs such as Russell, Grey, and Macaulay, suggests that many and varied were the forces leading to factory reform. Humanitarianism, a compassion for the suffering of the helpless, inspired the efforts to relieve both the hardships of seamstresses and those of factory operatives, but the operatives alone succeeded. Efforts on behalf of the seamstresses did not enjoy nonhumanitarian forces, namely, the organized, agitating workers, the large efficient mill owners unafraid of a ten-hour day, and, above all, Tory anger at those usurping, upstart manufacturers who had repealed the Corn Law and destroyed rural felicity.

Another triumph of humanitarianism was the advent of a less brutal and more civilized treatment of the insane. It was a smaller, less dramatic, and more disparate movement than factory reform, one at first glance more purely humanitarian. Many of the early revelations of abuse and cruelty came from seven parliamentary committees investigating the care of the insane from 1805 to 1844. It mattered not whether they investigated the great St. Mary of Bethlehem (called Bedlam) and St. Luke asylums in London, the nine hospitals that the more prosperous counties had built by 1828, or the more than 100 private, unregulated madhouses, since in all of them they found the same dark, airless, crowded, filthy rooms and the same chains, cribs, and manacles. No better were the backrooms and outhouses of the workhouses where some 8,000 of England's 20,000 insane were kept in 1844.[79] In 1815, in the recesses of Bedlam, a parliamentary committee found eight naked men chained to a table, and, in another cell, a man named William Norris who was so constrained by heavy chains, chains never taken off in nine years, that he could neither lie flat nor stand erect. In York Asylum, in a series of eight-by-eight-foot cells, whose walls and one small hole to the outside were caked with excrement, huddled a group of wretched women. In 1827, in a private madhouse, another parliamentary committee discovered cribs to which the patients were chained from Saturday to Monday, after which they were washed down in the courtyard. The committee also found a woman chained to a damp stone floor in a workhouse, with only a little straw, and that dirty, who was allowed no water to wash herself.[80] Although these lurid stories are exceptional, they do reflect a larger world of leg-locks, manacles, hobbles, straw beds, and cold, damp, stone cells, a world not without nakedness, beatings, and wrongful detention. Cure was not expected unless by bleeding, vomiting, and enemas.[81]

There is a second, parallel story of the care of the insane. It begins with the Quaker William Tuke and his establishment of the York Retreat in 1792 and culminates in the proud claim of the lunacy commissioners in 1854 that the abolition of all forms of physical restraint, of all chains and manacles, had become the practical rule. In that story, the work and writings of Dr. Edward Charlesworth and Dr. Robert Gardiner Hill for the complete removal of physical restraint at Lincoln Asylum looms large, as do the work and writings of Dr. John Conolly in ending restraint at Hanwell. Also of importance was the work of the metropolitan commissioners of lunacy from 1828 to 1844 and of their successors as lunacy commissioners for all England after 1845. In place of chains, straw, bleeding and flogging these humane reformers brought to the York Retreat, Lincoln, and Hanwell solid material comforts: clean, healthy surroundings, warm baths, clean clothes, freedom of movement, and a kindness and attentiveness that made mechanical restraints unnecessary. The managers of the Retreat, Hanwell, and Lincoln believed that by an attentive moral management that used work and activity, games and amusements, music and reading, walks and gardening, sound and virtuous habits would be formed that lay at the basis of sanity.[82]

In 1844, the *Quarterly Review* claimed that "these great improvements of half-a-century" were based on "the ordinary principles of humanity." The Scottish Whig Fox Maule, in 1845, praised a Parliament that had established the lunacy commissioners and required counties to build asylums, for acting on "the broad basis of humanity"[83]

That in the second half of the century, however, county asylums grew large and prisonlike, a few doctors carried out a severe moral management in a self-aggrandizing manner, too few attendants forced a partial return to physical restraint, and far too many of the pauper insane suffered in miserable workhouses may, to a degree, justify the skepticism that Andrew Scull in *Madhouses, Mad Doctors, and Madness* and Michel Foucault in *Madness and Civilization* show toward the lunacy reformers' humanitarianism. But these later developments should not blind one to the remarkable progress achieved from the 1820s to the 1850s. In those years, asylums moved from dark, stone cells and dirty straw beds, bleeding and emetics, beatings and abuse, and nakedness and chains to the decent accommodations, warm clothing, clean bedding, healthy food, absence of physical restrain, good medical care, and varied healthy activities of the improved asylum.[84]

Not humanitarianism, say historians like Andrew Scull, so much as economic and social forces—capitalism, industrialism, urbanization—explain reforms in the care of the insane. Despite the appeal of their grand sociological sweep, these claims are nevertheless open to doubt. Capitalism, which emerged in the seventeenth century and blossomed in the eighteenth, brought no lunacy reform in either century. The industrial revolution of the late eighteenth and early nineteenth centuries was centered in Manchester, Birmingham, Leeds, and other cloth and iron towns, none of which witnessed decisive improvements in the care of the insane. That these towns were great urban centers says little for urbanization as an inspiration for lunacy reform—any more than does the fact that London, the giant of cities, was the site of the unreformed and unreformable Bedlam and St. Luke asylums. Advances in the care of the insane occurred first in the York Retreat, Lincoln Asylum, and Hanwell, located respectively in a rural part of Yorkshire, an ecclesiastical town in rural Lincolnshire, and the fields of Middlesex. These fields, to be sure, were near London, but Hanwell's ruling body were county magistrates. The first six county asylums were established from 1812 to 1823 at Bedford, Stafford, Gloucester, Nottingham, Wakefield, and Lancaster, hardly either strongholds of King Cotton or Captain Iron or great megapolises.[85]

It is also unlikely that the propertied classes' passion for social control inspired lunacy reform. Lunatics could, no doubt, be annoying, and if too obstreperous, they were summarily put away as part of a normal, age-old, insistence on public order, one that could be equally satisfied by sending the lunatic to a workhouse shed or an unreformed asylum like Bedlam. Lunacy was no threat to social order. There were in 1841, only 23,000 of unsound mind in institutions, and of these 18,000 were discreetly but firmly placed in the back rooms, cellars, and outhouses of workhouses or in the workhouse itself.[86]

An examination of the writings and achievements of John Conolly, E. P. Charlesworth, Robert Gardiner Hill, James Cowles Prichard, and William and Samuel Tuke reveals no concern with industrialism, urbanization, or social control. Their work was also allied with no powerful political or economic movement, no organized workers' agitation, no vengeful Tories. Lunacy reform, however, was not as purely instinctive as the humanitarian response to the scandalous treatment of children in the coal mines. The early treatment of lunacy had its vivid scandals, which evoked compassion and led to reform. But that compassion and zeal for reform was also part and parcel of the advance in knowledge and science that helped define early Victorian England and that was closely and pervasively intertwined not only with lunacy reform but the growth of humanitarianism in general.[87]

Intellectual developments intertwining with humanitarianism also underlay the abolition of capital punishment for all crimes except murder and treason. In 1820, murder was but one of 220 offenses (600 according to *Blackwood's*) punishable by death.[88] From 1813 to 1833, the government hanged by the neck 1,547 English men and women, some for the most paltry of thefts.[89] But by the 1850s, only a handful were hanged, and all for murder. England's criminal code, the "bloody code," as many called it, had become much more humane.

The persistent agitation of the earliest reformers, like Sir Samuel Romilly and Sir James MacIntosh, failed in the 1810s to effect reform, but they, and their Whig and Radical allies, pressured Sir Robert Peel to begin the reform of the jumble of outdated, irrational, inconsistent, and cruel statutes that made up England's criminal code. Although the tidy and efficient Peel did, in the 1820s, consolidate and straighten out some of the chaotic and hopeless complexities of that jumble, he only touched on its draconian use of the gallows: one was still hanged if one stole goods worth more than £5 or if one broke into and robbed a church. In 1824, before Peel's reforms, forty-nine persons were hanged, in 1830, after the reforms, forty-six. Peel's small changes led the *Morning Herald* to judge his reforms as "almost entirely consolidation and arrangement."[90]

From 1832 to 1841, radical M.P.'s and Whig ministers almost abolished the "bloody code." In 1832, the Radical M.P. William Ewart introduced bills to abolish capital punishment for stealing horses, sheep, and cattle and for stealing goods from dwelling houses to the value of £5. He also urged the end of the death penalty for rape, administering poison, and for intent to murder, goals that he achieved by 1841. In 1837, Lord John Russell, as home secretary, proposed and passed, with no debate, seven bills removing the gallows as the punishment for all remaining offenses against property and for all offenses against persons "if no grievous bodily harm." Russell's hope to stop at that point was in vain. By 1841, only murder, treason, sodomy, attempted murder, arson to a dwelling with persons inside, and robbing with a threat to kill were kept as capital offenses, although in fact only murderers were hanged.[91] From 1837 to 1856, William Ewart, supported by 50 to 60 M.P.'s, moved the entire abolition of the death penalty. In 1837, their motion lost by one vote; in 1856, by 94, and the movement fell into abeyance.[92]

Humanitarianism played a pervasive, powerful, but not wholly dominant role in the near abolition of the death penalty. But if not wholly dominant, much too dominant, said opponents of abolition. There was, they insisted, entirely too much "mawkish sympathy," "morbid sentimentality," and "the maudlin humanity of the present day." Not a maudlin but a healthy humanitarianism was invoked by many critics of the death penalty. Its end was called for, said the great Irish leader Daniel O'Connell to the Commons, by "the spirit of humanity that distinguished the present day." "In place of harsh codes," wrote William Empson in the *Edinburgh Review*, "we need words of humanity and reason."[93] In the Commons, Joseph Brotherton said that capital punishment violated "the principle of humanity, justice and mercy," and Ewart that it violated "facts and figures as well as humanity." For John Bowring and Sergeant Talford, the abolition of hanging was a vote for "humanity" and "in accordance with the enlightened dictates of humanity." No wonder that the *Northampton Mercury* concluded that "increased humanity had ended capital punishment except for murder."[94]

The *Mercury* was perhaps too exuberant. Capital punishment's leading critic, William Ewart, sensing the distrust of a maudlin humanity, emphasized, as did Lord John Russell in 1837 and the Criminal Law Commissioners in 1836, the practical and efficient as well as the humanitarian. There were no vivid, compassionate pictures of the condemned criminal on the gallows as there were of chained lunatics and overworked seamstresses. There was instead a concern for making the illogical, inconsistent, and inefficient mazelike confusion of criminal law more rational and effective. Russell, Ewart, and the criminal law commissioners offered two central arguments: that hanging did not deter crime, and that hanging did deter prosecutors, juries, witnesses, and judges from proceeding against criminals or judging them guilty. Russell used both in 1837 when passing his seven bills ending capital punishment on nearly 500 offenses. By removing the death penalty, he told the Commons, the conviction rate would go up, as it had for forgery, from 58 to 71 percent. A higher rate of conviction and a greater certainty of punishment would in turn deter crime.[95] That from 1823 to 1834, only one in twenty convicted of a capital offense was executed made unreliable the promises of a deterrent criminal law.[96] It was a lottery, full of inequalities and injustice and often favorable to the criminal.

The draconian severity of hanging also, according to the Criminal Law Commission, deterred private parties from prosecuting, witnesses from testifying, juries from convicting, and a few judges from imposing the maximum punishment. A powerful reason that Parliament abolished capital punishment on most offenses was a desire for an effective, law-and-order criminal code, one that would not let the criminal go free. It was no "false commiseration for the sufferers," said Dr. Charles Lushington, M.P., an inveterate opponent of the death penalty, but "the interests and feelings of the population," that persuaded him to urge its abolition.[97]

The criminal code had, as V. A. C. Gatrell argues, "a structural problem." The rise in crime led to such an excess of death sentences that four a day would have had to be hanged. To avoid such carnage, pardons became abundant, rising to 90 percent of capital convictions. The criminal code had become a lottery, exceedingly irrational, and increasingly dysfunctional.

Although the ministers and M.P.'s who dismantled the "bloody code" after 1832 sought above all to put their judicial house in working order and to make sensible that which was illogical, compassion for the criminal did play a broad, far-reaching role. It played no little role in the fact that jurors increasingly said not guilty and private parties chose not to prosecute and judges were lenient and that nineteen out of twenty judged guilty of capital offenses were not hanged. Although it was often imperfect and inconstant, there was a widespread, unspoken humanitarianism at work.

Persuaded that knowledge is power, the early Victorians found it very persuasive in the increasingly fashionable form of statistics. Knowledge not available half a century earlier played an important role in the reduction of capital punishment. Statistics on its effect raised doubts that hanging deterred crime. They came from ten different countries, including England, and showed that reductions in the death penalty had not led to any great increase in crime. Although some of these statistics were by no means incontrovertible, they were, as a whole, strongly suggestive that hanging did not deter. And given that better police records, a rising population, and economic depressions tended to increase, not lessen, the amount of crime, the absence of a marked rise in those crimes for which capital punishment was ended makes even more formidable the view that hanging was not a necessary deterrent. Not logic but biblical texts in favor of the death penalty, vivid depictions of dreadful murders, and a passion for retribution marked the pleas to keep capital punishment. Ironically, concrete, vivid images (e.g., of seamstresses, boy coal trappers, and infant textile workers), which so often evoked humanitarianism, now evoked its opposite in the form of depictions of cold-blooded, brutal murder. The image of the evil murderer impinged on the social conscience of early Victorians far more vividly than that of innocent men hanged, which, said Sir Fitzroy Kelly in 1848, had occurred forty-one times over the past fifty years.[98]

Not so lightly set aside was another image that humanitarians imposed on the late 1840s and early 1850s, the image of boys guilty of trifling thefts sent to the grimmest of adult prisons. Before the 1840s, that fact hardly bothered the governing classes. In 1777, John Howard had warned that adult prisons corrupted the youthful offender, and the warning was often repeated, but in 1853, magistrates still sent most of the 13,000 convicted juveniles to prisons for adult criminals.[99] In the 1840s, these prisons varied from small, unsupervised, overcrowded houses of correction, as full of profligacy and contamination as they were destitute of moral and religious instruction, to huge penitentiaries like Newgate in whose crowded wards there were chaos, corruption, beatings, and schooling in crime, "a veritable hotbed of vice." Some juvenile criminals were in fact segregated from adults, but only in miserable, filthy, overcrowded, unventilated hulks. From 1825 to 1845, 2,500 boys aged fourteen and under were crowded onto these old docked ships, given no instruction, locked between the decks for hours, and kept at hard labor by the cat-o'-nine-tails.[100] No less free of labor and the cat were those transported to the colonies.

An Australian magistrate told an 1837 Select Committee on Transportation if a juvenile were put among adult convicts, "nothing could save his being corrupted, every species of vice they glory in."[101] Appalling as were the fates of these juveniles, magistrates, in the very decade that saw women and children freed from the mines and the mentally ill gain legislative protection, nonetheless sent children to prisons that most knew to be nurseries of crime. Where was the humanitarian spirit of the age?

Just awakening, was the answer of Charles Dickens's *Daily News*. "It is within the last two years," insisted the *News* in an 1847 article on juvenile delinquency, that "the hand of humanity stirred the mud . . . round the basement of London life."[102] The hand of humanity was found in the ragged schools, and great were the expectations of philanthropists that in these burgeoning institutions, the teaching of religion and morality would reduce juvenile crime. Great, too, were the hopes placed in the less prolific but more effective farm, industrial, and reform schools: the Philanthropic Society's Redhill, the Birmingham Justices' Stretton-on-Dunsmore in Warwickshire, Sheriff Watson's much-heralded industrial school in Aberdeen, the Reverend Grantham York's Free Industrial School, and in Birmingham Charles Adderley's Saltey Reformatory.[103] There were also a score more of such institutions, all voluntary and many evangelical. It was the philanthropists' hand of humanity.

But the philanthropists' hand of humanity had a short reach. Redhill had around 100 boys, Stretton-on-Dunsmore only 12 to 20, and the others accommodated similar numbers, which were minuscule compared to the 13,000 juveniles annually convicted.[104]

In 1847, the response appeared so inadequate that Lord Brougham obtained a select committee of the House of Lords to investigate juvenile offenders. A House of Commons committee to investigate prisons also decided to examine the treatment of juvenile criminals. Neither reflected the hand of humanity stirring with any great vigor the pestilent mud of juvenile crime. The sheriff of Midlothian in Scotland told Brougham's committee that public opinion was not keen on reform. "It is commonly believed," he insisted, "that when a boy is sent to prison he must be incorrigible, and he is shunned ever after." If incorrigible, if wicked, asked a public largely convinced of original sin, of what use were reformatories? In 1850, the Select Committee on Prisons—although all witnesses said prisons were unsuitable for juveniles—could only conclude, lamely, that the committee "had not received sufficient evidence."[105]

Yet four years later, in 1854, Parliament passed the Youthful Offenders Act, which encouraged magistrates to send those under sixteen who had been convicted of a crime to reformatories run by voluntary societies, which would henceforth receive government grants and inspection. It was far from a perfect system and still had harsh aspects—such as first serving fourteen days in an adult prison—but it was far more humanitarian than what it replaced.

Among the many reasons for this fourth important impact of humanitarianism, three are prominent: the failure of the old system, the successes of voluntary reformatories, and a more humane view of the "incorrigible."

In the 1840s, the early Victorians were greatly bothered by both the remorseless rise of crime and the increasing proportion of crimes committed by juveniles.[106] Their two attempts to reverse these trends both failed: the establishment in 1838 of Parkhurst and the 1847 Youthful Offenders Act. Parkhurst, a large, forbidding penitentiary for juveniles, neither reformed nor deterred. It reflected the effort of evangelical philanthropists, two of whom drew up its rules, which aimed to combine moral reform and deterrent principles. At the very outset, the young boys would face four months of separate confinement. Thereafter, manacled, they worked in groups in strict silence; if not silent, they went back to separate confinement. Although Parkhurst won the praise of Elizabeth Fry, it had by the mid 1840s abandoned any claim to be reformatory.[107]

The Juvenile Offenders Act, which allowed magistrates to substitute whipping for prison sentences for felons under fourteen, did no better. Whipping was the favorite of the paternalists, as meditative solitary confinement was of the Christian philanthropists. Crime, especially juvenile crime, rose and rose. In press and pamphlets, in Parliament, before select committees, and at the Home Office, it became increasingly clear that the prisons to which some 13,000 youths were sent were schools of crime. As Matthew Baines, the president of the Poor Law Board, told the Commons, "imprisonment in gaol was perfectly inefficacious." Not just humanitarian compassion but also efficiency and society's need for law and order moved M.P.'s toward the idea of reformatories.[108]

That many reformatories at home and abroad did succeed was a crucial part of the movement to establish them. For those anxious to reduce crime, the fact that John Williams, one of the prison inspectors, could pronounce the Philanthropy Society's Redhill "very successful . . . [with] few recommittals" was as promising as the fact that France's famous agricultural reform school at Mettray reformed 85 percent of its young offenders. Mettray, in particular, won great attention in press, pamphlets, and Parliament. Its agricultural and industrial training, enlightened pedagogy, Christian kindness, and familylike life won it much acclaim. Equally positive was the response to reform schools in Belgium, Switzerland, and America, as well as those in

England and Scotland.[109] An expanding knowledge of a better way to treat juvenile offenders played a not inconsiderable role in the passage of the 1854 Juvenile Offenders Act.

The advocates of reformatories held, in varying degrees, the belief, common among humanitarians, that juvenile offenders were intrinsically not so much wicked as the products of unfortunate circumstances, circumstances so miserable and so powerful that they must rule out any retribution.

Two Unitarians who held this view, and who were the two most active advocates of reformatories, were Mary Carpenter, founder of schools for young delinquents and outcasts, and Matthew Hill, recorder of Birmingham and long an ardent champion of juvenile reform. For Mary Carpenter, youthful offenders were so decidedly the victims of circumstances that, as she told a select committee in 1852, society "absolutely owed them reparation." Matthew Hill also perceived the adverse influence of parental neglect, poverty, slums, and want of schooling, and he also criticized those who demanded retribution against juveniles perceived as incorrigible. "Tenacity of retribution," Hill told the Peelite M.P. Charles Adderley, "is the real source of error."[110] Adderley, who was deeply religious and a model paternalist, helped Lord Palmerston draw up the Youthful Offenders Act of 1854, which passed with scarcely any debate and without a division. It is only in the editorials and pamphlets leading to its passage that one sees emerging the view that, to a considerable extent, juvenile offenders were the victims of circumstances. The pamphlets and editorials vary when discussing the causes of juvenile crime, variously emphasizing drink, immorality, and vice, along with poverty, parental neglect, want of schooling, slums, and disease, but all implied a social determinism that led to a more humanitarian outlook.[111]

Humanitarianism was more a pervasive attitude than a focused force. Its strength lay more in its wide diffusion and compassion than in its political clout. Although its rhetoric was universally appealing, in battle it proved fragile. It was found everywhere, but everywhere weak. It declaimed against harsh game laws, denounced cruelty to animals, condemned flogging, declared dueling uncivilized, and called school birching and school fags barbarous.[112] It exposed the fearful mortality on emigrant ships and in coal mines, urged the abolition of window taxes and imprisonment for debt, urged the protection of women from seduction and breach of promise, demanded an end to the use of chimney sweeps, and insisted on eliminating the vexations, costliness, delays, and rank injustice of a legal system that did not even allow decisions in criminal law, however erroneous, to be appealed to a higher court.[113] The dictates of humanity also condemned, although largely in vain, the exploitation of handloom weavers, stocking frame workers, and London bakers. Equally in vain were efforts to end the exploitation of children as London seamstresses, Sheffield metal grinders, Birmingham wire pullers, and Gloucester lace makers. All of these efforts and more reflect humanitarianism's ever-extending public voice of sympathy and compassion for the suffering and helpless.

Even more pervasive was the humanitarian's private voice, which could even be heard in the most inhumane of edifices, in Newgate, Bedlam, and workhouses, where the kindness of a turnkey, the helpfulness of an attendant, or a matron's small favors did much to mitigate the institution's harshness. It also is reflected in the observation, made by the Manchester Methodist Benjamin Love, London's Henry Mayhew, and many more, that the poor themselves were the most generous to the poor.[114]

But varied and extensive as was humanitarianism, it proved brittle before powerful interests and institutions and deep-seated fears, prejudices, and avarice. Early Victorian humanitarianism could not, for example, end England's love of flogging and birching. In 1836, five M.P.'s, led by Joseph Hume and Colonel De Lacy Evans, told the Royal Commission on Military Punishment that flogging in the Army and Navy was a needless cruelty, that it encouraged rather than discouraged the mutinous spirit, and that companies with no corporal punishment had better discipline. These arguments were of no avail. Neither were the protests of General Charles Napier in his *Remarks on Military Law and the Punishment of Flogging* (1837), of John Gardner in his *On the Inhuman and Disgraceful Punishment of Flogging in the Army and Navy* (1832), and eight of London's humanitarian journals.[115] In Parliament, De Lacy Evans in the 1830s and Hume in the 1840s, repeatedly denounced this savage form of discipline, which was practiced by only a few European armies. Again to no avail. In 1861, the Navy still flogged erring sailors.[116] In the 1860s, birching and fagging also continued at England's great public schools, as did those laws that gave landlords a monopoly on game and made criminals of poachers.[117] The game laws were cruel on three counts: the lure of game made poachers and criminals of the spirited young and needy poor, the hunting and the preservation of hares ravaged the farmer's fields, and the wholesale slaughter of pheasants and grouse pained lovers of birds.[118] Nevertheless, nothing was done. Like the Army, Navy, and public schools, landed estates were far too deeply rooted in tradition and sacred to the Establishment to yield to humanitarian sentiment, however widespread. Property as such was sacred, which thwarted humanitarian protests against imprisoning debtors, employing chimney sweeps, and the overcrowding of filthy, ill-supplied, unsafe emigrant ships. In 1840, Lord Beaufort told the House of Lords that he used small boys to clean his chimneys, that he knew it was against the "dictates of humanity," but that not to use them would "be even more injurious to property." Beaufort, the Lords, and property lost the vote in 1840, and a second law entered the books outlawing chimney sweeps, followed by a third. All three, concludes the historian P. W. I. Bartrip, were "largely ineffective." The 1842 act to protect emigrants from disease-ridden, accident-prone, over-crowded passenger ships sailing to North America, ships with an unbelievably high rate of mortality, was also, contends Oliver MacDonagh, largely ineffective. Failure also characterized acts to prevent the imprisonment of debtors. Thousands of debtors, according to G. R. Rubin, continued to be imprisoned as the new county courts enforced other laws disciplining debtors.[119] One should treat with skepticism the statutes of the realm as a record of humanitarian effectiveness. Statutes against imprisoning debtors, for example, failed to end that practice, just as statutes against dueling failed. Despite laws prohibiting duels, the earl of Cardigan fought one quite openly in 1841. The *Standard* defended him, the Lords took no action, and the arrogant earl went unpunished.[120]

Equally in defiance of statutes in the 1840s was the continued cruelty to animals. From seventeenth-century divines and eighteenth-century philosophers to nineteenth-century evangelicals, a humane sympathy for animals slowly expanded among the governing classes. It led to an 1822 act against the cruel treatment of horses and cattle, an 1835 act outlawing bull baiting and cockfighting, and an 1839 act prohibiting dog carts. But despite these acts, cruelties to horses, cattle, cocks, dogs, and other animals continued. In 1849, another act imposed a £5 fine on anyone who "shall cruelly beat, ill treat, overdrive, abuse or torture" any animal or take part "in the management of any place for the purpose of fighting or baiting bull, bear, badger, dog, cock, or any other kind of animal." Bull baiting and other "blood sports," Peter Bailey notes in *Leisure and Class in Victorian England*, nevertheless "flourished clandestinely." In the mid nineteenth century, writes Harriet Ritvo in her *The Animal Estate*, the earl of Derby in Lancashire and local authorities in Newcastle openly patronized cockfighting, and Stamford officials sponsored bull runnings. The fact that acts of Parliament could not end cockfighting, dueling, the use of boy chimney sweeps, and wretched emigrant ships, and that agitation to end flogging, birching, and imprisonment for debt failed, does not mean that humanitarianism had no effect. Although it did not "completely" end these abuses, many of these cruelties were reduced, and some, like dueling and cruelty to animals, considerably reduced. Humanitarians may have lost many a battle with powerful interests and prejudices, but humanitarianism grew, slowly and incrementally, like a coral reef. More and more people came to share William Wollaston's view, expressed in 1731, that there is "something in human nature which makes the pain of others obnoxious to us."[121]

Since feeling the obnoxiousness of pain is most strongly evoked by vivid images of the suffering of the helpless, it played a lesser role in the more abstract and theoretical discussions of the education question, the Corn Law, and Public Health. But it nonetheless played a role. Many a free trader drew graphic pictures of the hunger that costly bread imposed on the poor. In Parliament, free traders, such as Charles Villiers and Joseph Brotherton, evoked much compassion with their vivid depictions of suffering; but so did protectionists such as Edmund Wodehouse, Lord Lincoln, and Lord John Manners, with their vivid depictions of farms ruined and peasants jobless and hungry as foreign corn flooded England. "Corn laws are not at odds with the interests of humanity," the Tory *Leeds Intelligencer* said.[122] As the debate grew fiercer, humanitarianism receded before class animosity, vested interests, economic theories, and paternalist and individualistic philosophies. Just as the clash of interests, classes, and outlooks lessened and confused the humanitarian dimensions of the Corn Law debate, so fierce religious conflicts, different views of education, and varying fears and hopes of change crowded out a simple compassion for children denied any schooling. It is remarkable how seldom the word "humanitarian" occurs in the hundreds of pamphlets, sermons, and speeches on education. The greatest obsession was over whether the Church of England, the state, or Nonconformists and Catholic societies would control education. Church, Dissenters, Catholics, and secularists also clashed over the ends of education. The Church wanted to train obedient, deferential and not overeducated Christians; Dissenters to prepare Christians for conversion, righteousness, and individual growth; Catholics to preserve the true faith, and the secularists to create virtuous and enlightened citizens. In their bitter quarrels over the ends and means of education, there was not much room for compassionate pictures of woefully ignorant Bethnal Green waifs or Norfolk farm boys.

The disease-ridden waifs of Bethnal Green were also surprisingly not very prominent in the debate over the 1848 Public Health Act. Statistics of diseases and mortality and appeals to society's larger self-interest drowned out images of individual suffering. There were vivid images, but of filthy sewers, polluted rivers, malodorous graveyards, and foul slaughterhouses. Many a humanitarian was, of course, ardent for the Public Health Act. When it came to love for humanity, few could rival Southwood Smith, Lord Ashley, and Lord Morpeth, who, with Edwin Chadwick at the helm, made up the General Board of Health. Distinguished humanitarians also supported education, but since they were divided in their advocacy of Church, state, and voluntary schools, they checkmated one another quite as much as did those humanitarians who were for and against the Corn Law. On the question of public health, although scarcely any humanitarian opposed that cause, its most powerful leader, Edwin Chadwick, cast its appeal largely in terms of society's self-interest. He disclaimed appeals to benevolence. And so did Lord Morpeth, always so effusively benevolent, in his two lengthy speeches introducing the Public Health Bills of 1847 and 1848, speeches in which he never appealed to the dictates of humanity, but rather to the self-interest of all England in ending fearsome evils that led to disease and death in fashionable Belgravia as well as in Bethnal Green. Chadwick appealed even more openly to self-interest when he argued that private companies could make a profit from selling sewerage as manure to outlying farms and that sanitary improvements by reducing disease, a great cause of pauperism, would reduce rates.[123] Many were dubious of Chadwick's claim, but few doubted cholera's deadly reach. Along with the usual yearly tolls of typhus, pneumonia, and consumption, outbreaks of cholera in England in 1830–31 and 1848–49 did more than humanitarian sentiment to bring sanitary reform. There were, in fact, many motives for sanitary reform besides warding off disease—among them civic pride, better streets, purer, cheaper water, and an end both to pervasive stenches and corrupt, expensive, and inept local authorities. Compassion for the dwellers of wretched urban slums and rural hovels did not rate very high amid these motives.

No issue—not the Corn Law, not education, not health—evoked louder protests against man's inhumanity to man than did the New Poor Law of 1834. Humanitarians of every kind, Tory, Radical, Whig, Chartist, London bohemian, and romantic, protested against its harshness. The workhouse test "acted against humanity," said John Fielden, Radical member for Todmorden, a town that, for a while, successfully defied the New Poor Law. Its separation of husband and wife, added the reformer H. B. Yorke, violated "the humane feeling of the house." Joseph Brotherton, one of Parliament's staunchest humanitarians, said that it pitted "cold, abstract, calculating" political economy against the "principles of humanity." For the Radical Major Beauclerk, the New Law was simply "harrowing to the feelings of humanity."[124]

In the election of 1841, not a few Tories took up the cry of humanity. "Disgraceful to humanity" and "repugnant to the humane feelings of the country," proclaimed Young England's Lord John Manners and Baillie Cochrane. In the 1841 election, the Tory Monckton Milne, a friend of Manners and Cochrane and almost a Young Englander, declared his opposition to the New Poor Law in keeping "with the humanity of common life."[125] In that election, the Tory *Standard*, *Morning Herald*, *Morning Post*, and for a while the Tory *Times*, joined the radical *Sun, Weekly Dispatch, Howitt's Journal, Illustrated London News*, and Wakley's *Lancet* in denouncing the Poor Law Commission's insistence that relief be given to the able-bodied destitute only in the workhouse. The destitute, said the *Weekly Dispatch*, had a "positive right [to relief] by the laws of humanity"[126] The new voice of humanity, in countless publications, told of workhouse horrors and the near starvation of those too proud to enter these "bastilles."

There were, however, some who claimed that the workhouses were humane. The New Poor Law was humane, declared the Whig home secretary, Lord Althorp, in 1834, because it abolished that easy relief, which corrupted the poor. It was a view shared by R. A. Slaney and George Grote, a Whig and a Philosophical Radical, who were as humanitarian on education, public health, law reform, and juvenile delinquency as any critic of the New Poor Law. The humanitarians had again divided.[127] The *Spectator*, whose humane outlook few journals could rival, nonetheless condemned as "humanity mongers" those whose hostility to the New Poor Law arose from "unreasoning opposition of sentiment and sympathy." "Large doles," declared the *Spectator,* are not "humane but corrupting." Most certainly corrupting, echoed the *Economist*, a journal that saw the issue as a perpetual battle between feeling and reason, one in which reason should prevail. The *Westminster Review* agreed, lamenting that of late it had been "the fashion to decry the truth of political economy" in preference to "the weakness of the heart."[128]

The impact of humanitarianism in the battle over the New Poor Law was a complicated one. It was ambiguous, first, because the agitation against the law was by no means purely humanitarian, and, secondly, because the New Poor Law was not without humane ideals. A genuine compassion for the destitute did, of course, move many of its strongest opponents in Parliament, M.P.'s such as Joseph Brotherton, Thomas Wakley, and John Fielden, as well as Thomas Barnes of the *Times*, Charles Mackay of the *Illustrated London News*, and Stanley Lees Giffard of the *Standard*. Compassion also moved not a few local poor law officials, who knew the plight of the destitute intimately, officials who defied the Poor Law Commission and gave outdoor relief, allowed husbands to live with wives, and served beef and pudding at Christmas.[129] A measure of their defiance is the fact that in the 1840s and 1850s, most of those receiving relief received it outside the workhouse: around 70 percent in East Anglia, writes Ann Digby, 78 percent in Lancashire, says Michael Rose, and 88 percent in the West Riding of Yorkshire, according to David Ashworth. Digby claims that the Norfolk guardians treated the poor "far more humanely" than the "stereotypical view," a finding similar to Michael Rose's claim that the "humanity" of the local guardians was one of the two motives for resisting the workhouse test. Outdoor relief, however, was not always very humane; certainly not when, as Lynn Lees points out, the Chelsea guardians gave only 1s. or 1s. 6d. a week to female-headed households.[130]

The second motive, according to Rose, was to keep rates low, a motive that was probably greater than compassion for the poor. Parsimonious farmer guardians, notes Digby, actually took over East Anglia's rural unions, dispensing a meager dole that was far less costly than relief in an expensive workhouse. This fact also held true in the urban parts of Lancashire and the West Riding, where a pauper cost £5 10s. a year in a workhouse but only £3 11s. 5d. out of it.[131] A large, general, mixed, commodious workhouse, the kind the commission insisted on, was expensive to build, too expensive for the northern guardians, who simply leased an old, small, run-down parish poorhouse, even though it was a wretched place for sick, aged, insane, orphaned, and vagrant paupers who needed institutional care. In the Bolton workhouse, in 1843, "the aged and young were covered with vermin; infants, patients from scarlet fever—and children free from disease were all cooped up in . . . confined rooms," while in Huddersfield in the 1848 typhus epidemic, children slept up to ten in a bed." The Leeds workhouse was no better. "A disgrace to a civilized country," declared an assistant poor law commissioner.[132] Such scandalous conditions arose far more often from local jealousy, parsimony, and negligence than from the commission's orders, much of it often arising from those loudest in their humanitarian protest against the New Poor Law.

Partisan politics, civic pride, fear of high rates, hatred of centralization, entrenched interests, control of patronage, and Tory paternalism merged with a humane concern for the poor and an awareness that the workhouse test was cruel to constitute a formidable resistance to the hateful New Poor Law and its three despised commissioners. There is no doubt that these commissioners did push the workhouse test and did issue petty, niggling, harsh regulations—no milk and sugar for tea, no beef and pudding at Christmas, no leaving the workhouse for Sunday walks.[133] Assistant Commissioner Kay-Shuttleworth, who believed that easy relief caused indolence, profligacy, and malingering, could be very hard on the poor, denouncing excessive diets and the provision of beer, and his colleague E. C. Tufnell warned that "too much and not too little relief" was "the great danger." But both fought local guardians far more often for better conditions, for better medical care, warmer and cleaner quarters, no birchings of children, and, above all, an education in the skills and self-reliance that would permit an escape from pauperism. Kay-Shuttleworth and Tufnell were in their way humanitarians. Kay-Shuttleworth, as secretary of the Committee on Education, devoted his life to the cause of education, as did Tufnell, who provided from his own income the initial support of the Battersea School for training teachers.[134] Even their severe view that easy relief corrupted was part of a belief—however mistaken—that fitted their idealistic hope of liberating the pauper.

Paupers, and the poor in general, were also liberated by better health, which was promoted by the 1838 report of the Poor Law Commission's Dr. Southwood Smith and the 1842 *Sanitary Report* of Edwin Chadwick. Most assistant poor law commissioners fought for better medical relief. On education, health, and the care of the aged and orphaned, local guardians were more negligent and tight-fisted than the commissioners and their assistants.[135] The same was true of education where, after twenty years, local poor law authorities had established only a handful of district schools, while leaving their workhouse schools in dismal shape. A report on the Gilbert unions— locally autonomous and unsupervised by the Poor Law Commission— revealed that they treated their old and orphaned much more harshly than unions under the Commission. M. A. Crowther observes in her study *The Workhouse System* that the commissioners were more humane on workhouse management than local guardians.[136]

In fact, the Poor Law Commission was occasionally more humane than local authorities in granting relief. Peter Dunkley in his article on the Durham Poor Law Union finds that in the 1842 depression, the guardians defied the commissioner's order to substitute outdoor labor for a workhouse test. When local miners struck, the guardians refused to give any relief at all.[137] Resistance to the New Poor Law should never be automatically equated with humanitarian responses to that law, any more than reports on education and sanitation by a Kay-Shuttleworth or a Southwood Smith and the work of other assistant commissioners to mitigate local harshness and negligence should excuse the three commissioners from their inhumane insistence that husbands and wives live separately, and that the severe and sometimes cruel workhouse test remain their summum bonum. Measuring the impact of humanitarianism is a complicated matter, since it expresses itself in so many different ways, a fact especially true in the debate over prison discipline.

At first glance, the new humanitarianism appears to have had an impact on prison reform. Had not the great philanthropist John Howard exposed the inhumanities practiced in prisons and pointed the way to their removal? Had not Howard and his many followers worked to end the worst abuses, abuses of criminals associating with criminals in dismal, filthy, wards that were cold and damp and full of vice? Often run for the profits of the governor and staff, institutions countenanced drunkenness and extortion, intimidation and prostitution.[138] By 1835, many of these glaring abuses had been reduced in some of the new county prisons, which were cleaner, more commodious, better ventilated, warmer, and capable of proper classification—distinguishing the young from the old, the untried from the convicted, the minor from the serious offenders—with individual cells, and without drunkenness and corruption. Incarceration and control were certainly much stricter and freedoms fewer, but as the Reverend Sydney Smith claimed, "inspection and supervision are the parents of humanity." He added: "A system of humanity is now established in gaols."[139]

The Reverend Sydney Smith's "humanity is now established" was far too sanguine a judgment. Parliament had, to be sure, passed progressive acts, and a few counties had reformed their prisons, but the result was a hodge-podge of permissive acts, most of them unenforced, and of local prisons that remained quite unreformed. To rectify this state, the Commons in 1835 formed the Select Committee on Prison Discipline, passed a prison act, and established five Home Office prison inspectors.[140] The committee and the inspectors found not only that the condition of most local gaols was still dismal but that their discipline did nothing to deter or reform the criminal. With crime rising at four times the rate of the population, the discovery of some method of deterrence or reform had become ever more urgent.

Perplexed and unsure about the correct prison discipline and hesitant to defy powerful local authorities, the government appointed inspectors of differing views. In the 1840s, they represented four of the more important prison disciplines. Captain Donatus O'Brien pursued the stern, orthodox view that reform was an illusion and that the wicked deserved a severe incarceration. The Home District inspectors, the Reverend Whitworth Russell and William Crawford, believed that the substitution of separate confinement, religious instruction, and work at individual treadmills, in place of a contaminating association, would both deter and reform. Captain John Williams favored a third way, association at work and chapel but in absolute silence. And the most humanitarian of the five, Frederick Hill, brother of Matthew and Rowland, began as a believer in separate confinement, but then grew critical of it, urged its drastic reduction, and argued for the adoption of industrial training, education, kind treatment, and reform.[141] There was little humanitarianism in O'Brien's view, a view also common to the House of Lords and the Tory press, a view based on retribution. There was, in the 1830s, considerable humanitarianism in Crawford's and Russell's boundless faith in separate confinement, a philanthropic humanitarianism, one that sought the reform of prisoners. In the solitude of the cell, the prisoner would reflect on his wickedness, would feel shame and remorse, would repent of his sins, and by religious instruction, see the ways of righteousness. By the mid 1840s, mounting evidence showed that separate confinement not only did not reform but damaged the mind. Separate confinement appeared anything but humanitarian. Charles Dickens, having seen in Philadelphia's Eastern Penitentiary the cruelty of separate confinement, denounced it in his 1842 *American Notes.*[142]

Cruel, too, was the silent system. Frederick Hill pronounced it pernicious since it warred on our natural impulses.[143] It was separate confinement, not the silent system, that became the ascendant doctrine, the doctrine of what the *Gloucester Journal* called "that philanthropy" that deals with "the abandoned and depraved." It was also the doctrine of Archbishop Whatley and Fowell Buxton, whom the *Eclectic* called "prison philanthropists."[144] Prison reform was a favorite part of the evangelicals' philanthropy. It offered a way of dealing with hardened sinners. The best way, of course, was to separate a sinner from other sinners and to confine him to a lonely cell where he could feel remorse and learn contrition. Separate confinement was pioneered by the evangelical George Onesiphorus Paul, Gloucester's famous prison reformer, and was blessed by the evangelicals William Wilberforce and James Hannay. By the 1840s, separate confinement enjoyed the powerful support of the prison inspectors Whitworth Russell and William Crawford, the prison chaplains Daniel Nihil, John Clay, and J. C. Field, the home secretary, Sir George Grey, the *Christian Observer,* and the *North British Review*—all evangelical.[145]

Many humanitarians, however, had doubts about separate confinement, which further separated them from the Christian philanthropists. Jeremy Bentham opposed it, and in the 1840s, Frederick and Matthew Hill and Captain Alexander Maconochie (like Bentham full of the Enlightenment's belief in the educability of man) became its critics. Frederick Hill urged, in his reports, such useful labor as weaving and tailoring in place of the useless treadmill. Prisoners, said Hill, "must be treated as rational beings with ordinary feelings of humanity." In his 1845 report, Hill praised Captain Maconochie for using "the best prompting of your nature . . . those proceeding from the Christian spirit of love . . . and the most profound principle of philosophy."[146]

Maconochie, governor in the early 1830s of Australia's Van Diemen Prison and of the Birmingham borough prison in 1851–53, was the enemy of separate confinement and the originator of the so-called mark system, in which, by good behavior and industry, prisoners could earn marks that would enable them to purchase amenities in prison and to shorten their stay. It provided positive and reforming, not negative and deterring, reinforcements, and it worked.[147]

Although Frederick Hill's reforms—useful labor, industrial training, and never the treadmill or solitary—worked in Scotland and Captain Maconochie's mark system on Norfolk Island, they did not define Britain's prison policy. Nine months of separate confinement, the crank or treadmill, and a harsh regimen became the policy of the new penitentiaries that, with transportation being phased out, constituted the government's policy in convict prisons. The county and borough gaols and lockups continued a patchwork of abuses, improvement, and widely differing disciplines. In 1853, scandals at Birmingham and Leicester, both on the separate system and the crank, revealed how little humanitarianism had dented the cruelty of prison life. At Birmingham, a sadistic governor not only imposed "the crank machine *ad libidum*," reported the *Times*, but denied the recalcitrant "bread, water, sleep and society"; while at Leicester, it was 14,400 turns of the crank or less food, and if still intransigent, a flogging—cruelties that prompted the *Times* to warn all to "keep a watch on the prison philanthropists."[148]

Humanitarian protests did help end the vile hulks and, in widely diffused, individual and small ways, did mitigate the harshness of prison life, but they had only a modest impact on official policy. That humanitarianism that led to factory and mine acts, improved mental hospitals, and the advent of juvenile reformatories rested heavily on images of helpless children and the mentally ill, but in the case of the Poor Law and prisons, the large forbidding image of adult paupers corrupted by easy relief and dangerous, wicked adult criminals shut out that compassion and sympathy that the image of the pathetic and abused child so often evoked.

Strong economic and institutional interests and deep prejudices could also thwart that compassion and sympathy. As a result, the impact of humanitarianism presented a mixed picture. In five areas, mines, factories, care of the insane, capital punishment, and juvenile offenders, humanitarianism had a decided impact, although not without disappointments—not without asylums and reformatories grown far too large, grim, and impersonal, capital punishment not fully abolished, ten-year-old boys still in mines, and children worked in every manufacture in Britain but textile mills. On the great issues of the Corn Law, public health, and education, humanitarianism did play a role, but an ambiguous, varied, and confused one, as it did in the debate over the New Poor Law. The reformers finally found that their humanitarian hopes in the workhouse test and separate confinement proved anything but humanitarian.

The new humanitarianism also helped pass laws against dueling, the use of chimney sweeps, death-dealing emigrant ships, and cruelty to animals—but all too often they were not enforced. But however disappointing, confused, and ambiguous its results, however weak before powerful interests and prejudices, humanitarianism still steadily advanced, making up a larger and larger part of the early Victorians' social conscience, a steady advance that raises the question of the sources of its strength.

CHAPTER 11

The Sources of Humanitarianism

For many historians, it is not the dialectic of ideas but economic and social forces that best explain the rise of humanitarianism. Historians of nineteenth-century England have long regarded the most prominent of such forces to be those released by the industrial revolution. Did not infant slavery in satanic mills evoke one of the earliest and most sustained of humanitarian protests? Did it not lead to select committees, royal commissions, a flood of articles and pamphlets, fierce and endless debates, and, from 1802 to 1853, to seven acts of Parliament? And was not infant labor but one of many, proliferating evils brought by the industrial revolution? These evils were, to be sure, by no means the only ones that evoked the compassion and sympathy of the early Victorians. The industrial revolution had little to do with the mistreatment of lunatics, debtors, chimney sweeps, seamstresses, and tailors, capital punishment, juvenile delinquency, flogging, dueling, cruelty to animals, or game laws. And as a spur to and an expression of humanitarianism, it certainly had to share the honors with, if not yield in point of time to, the ending of the slave trade and slavery. Because the steam engine was used increasingly in mining, the cruel exploitation of women and children in mines could be ascribed to the industrial revolution, but only in part, since such abuses long antedated the use of steam—as did the exploitation of merchant marine sailors. The abuses of the industrial revolution thus form only a part, and not the larger part, of the cruelties that helped evoke a widespread compassion for suffering.

The cruelties and brutalities of urbanization also aroused a sympathy for the exploited and abused. No social development left a more indelible mark on the early Victorians than the growth of towns and cities, which both aroused their fears and broadened their outlook and feelings. "Towns," said William Empson in 1847 in the *Edinburgh Review*, "have great advantage and specific evils." There is "so much more humanity and so much misery" that its "terrible contrasts [demand] enlarging the views of some and stirring the feelings of others."[1] Both the lordly *Times* and the Chartist poet Thomas Cooper observed the same contrasts. London was, for the *Times,* "the most self-inconsistent place . . . a place where extremes meet . . . both enlightenment morality . . . and a whole population of mendicants." For Cooper, cities contained "huge tombs of squalor," along with "knowledge, freedom, moral growth."[2] The Congregationalist *Eclectic Review* agreed with the *Times* on the cities' enlightenment. "Great cities are conducive to the expansion of the mind," it declared in a review of the *Age of the Great Cities* by the Congregationalist Reverend Robert Vaughan, for whom great cities brought light after years of feudal darkness. In 1843, the *Edinburgh Review* praised Vaughan's work; three years earlier, it had published John Stuart Mill's praise of the intelligence "almost universal in populous towns."[3]

But in towns and cities, there were also thieves, beggars, prostitutes, street people of every kind, the destitute, and the homeless, as well as much disease, squalor, crime, crass exploitation, and infinite misery, all in striking contrast to the prosperous lords and gentry in their clubs and town houses and the capitalists in their suburban villas.

No other feature of city life haunted the periodicals of the day more than the immense contrast between wealth and poverty. It was also the grand theme of the novels of Dickens, Jerrold, Bulwer-Lytton, Ainsworth, and Disraeli, and of many a poem and painting. These glaring inequalities and glaring evils even evoked humanitarian responses from the not strikingly compassionate *Blackwood's, Quarterly Review,* and *Fraser's.* Few articles in *Blackwood's* expressed more sympathy with the poor than John Murray's series on London life, and the *Quarterly Review's* most humane moments came in Lord Ashley's articles on London's ragged schools and model lodging houses. The articles in *Fraser's* reflect a growing involvement with London: Torylike in 1830 in its ridiculing of all reform, by 1850, it was an eager champion of reform, with many articles on London's problems. A major contributor of the late 1840s, the Reverend Robert Lamb, after asking his readers "to consider the numbers that have gathered into our crowded towns," noted that the "heaving behemoth has startled many a stout heart."[4]

Urbanization, powerful as it was in startling stout hearts, had and still has its limits as an explanation of humanitarianism. A fairly urbanized early eighteenth-century Britain did little to protest brutal asylums, wretched prisons, frequent dueling, child labor, cruelty to animals, many hangings, and much flogging, and early nineteenth-century Germany and France, which were no more urbanized than early eighteenth-century Britain, had powerful humanitarian movements.

Large cities could also be inhumane. London, giant of cities, boasted the unreformed Bedlam and St. Luke's asylums, and advances in the care of the insane first occurred in the York Retreat and Lincoln Asylum, which belonged to rural not industrial England. Insanity was not a strictly urban problem, and neither was the overworking of children, the most egregious examples often occurring in those mines and small manufacturers located in the countryside. Urbanization, however short it falls as a sufficient cause, was still a dominant force in the growth of humanitarianism. Not only did it create, concentrate, and make visible evils that human nature found intolerable, but it provided a home for the rising middle class, which, along with the industrial revolution and urbanization, forms part of the classic triad so beloved by social historians.

For Coleridge, the rising middle class was part of the growing overbalance of the commercial and its "blind practices" and speculations. For Carlyle, the middle class was part of a cold, calculating cash nexus, and for many a Tory editor and M.P., it had a grasping, avaricious spirit. The novelists of the period also paint a less than flattering picture of the middle class, but it is not simply a homogeneous middle class that they depict so much as varied, many-layered "middling classes." Dickens pictures these classes as running from the wealthy and powerful merchant Dombey Sr. to the humble, penurious clerk Tom Cratchit, with much in between.

These middling classes were also not homogeneous in compassion and sympathy. Not a few urged a more severe poor law and a tougher criminal code, exploited seamstresses, turned beggars away, became wealthy as slum landlords, opposed sanitary improvements, and constituted a vast array of selfish interests. Many of the rising middle classes did not further but undermined humanitarianism. Many, of course, among the middling classes also championed humane reforms. But they had no monopoly in urging such causes. The working classes and their journals agitated and demonstrated for humane reforms, while many of the landed classes presided over humanitarian causes: Lords Littleton, Harrowby, Norton, and Houghton all spoke at the 1853 and 1854 conferences on juvenile delinquency, as did baronets like Sir John Pakington.[5] Lords Nugent, Winchelsea, Lushington, and Suffield championed the end of capital punishment, and Lord Morpeth, sanitary reform, while Lord Ashley was the most indefatigable of all in working for lunacy, juvenile, factory, and sanitary reform.[6]

It was not the rise of the middle classes that simply explains humanitarianism, so much as the growing power within that most pluralistic and expanding of classes of such groups as medical men, journalists, educators, bureaucrats, lawyers, and actuaries. Medical men above all were active in promoting humanitarian reform, men like Dr. W. P. Alison with his probing exposure of poverty and disease in Scottish cities, Dr. James Kay-Shuttleworth with his exposure of poverty and disease in Manchester, Dr. John Conolly, Dr. Robert Gardiner Hill, and Dr. Edward Charlesworth in their fight for more civilized treatment of the insane, and Dr. Thomas Southwood Smith in his long struggle to make all towns healthier places in which to live.[7]

Many of these doctors were also bureaucrats, and bureaucrats played a crucial role. Captain Maconochie, Frederick Hill, and M. D. Hill were all public servants when they led in the reform of prisons and the treatment of juveniles. The education inspectors Seymour Tremenheere and Joseph Fletcher, the poor law assistants E. C. Tufnell and Dr. Neil Arnott, and the factory inspectors Leonard Horner and Robert Saunders spoke out for reforms in education, the care of the poor, and factories. Even the military produced such opponents of flogging as Admiral Charles Napier and Colonel De Lacy Evans.[8]

That critics of flogging formed a tiny minority of the military is true—and it is true, too, that the rich Quakers and Unitarians who took such a prominent role in humane reforms constituted but a minority of the wealthy and of the churchgoers who dominated the middle classes, but as those classes grew larger, the growing minority voice of humanitarianism grew louder and more insistent.

These groups were not only a part of the growing middle classes but also part of a society increasingly defined by new social institutions and advances. Queen Victoria's subjects in 1840 were, for example, far more literate than King George III's subjects had been. Between two-thirds and three-quarters of the working classes could read, a tribute to the crazy quilt of schools— dame, day, Anglican, Nonconformist, endowed grammar, elite public, Owenite, farm, and industrial—some of which outlawed corporal punishment and placed humane discipline at the heart of their pedagogy.[9] The resulting literate British could in 1830 choose from 153 provincial newspapers, where their ancestors in 1780 had had only 27.[10] Churches and chapels also proliferated. The churches grew more unified and held district and national conferences. Meetings for causes of every sort proliferated among the more morally earnest of the varied middle classes. Secular institutions also proliferated. The great towns gloried in their philanthropic institutions—hospitals, infirmaries, and dispensaries—and their proud array of societies, learned, artistic, botanical, statistical, and reformist.[11] After the 1835 Municipal Reform Act, there were also 178 new town councils, the scene of many a humanitarian exhortation.[12] On the national level, the 1840s saw, as the 1760s did not, a British Association for the Advancement of Science, the British Institute, statistical societies, mechanics institutes, and lecture halls of every kind, ranging from

Owenite halls of science to the evangelicals' famous Exeter Hall on the Strand in London.[13]

The early nineteenth century also witnessed the growth of a large, more active, less aristocratic national government. Between 1800 and 1832, Parliament created sixty royal commissions, a fact that would have astonished the parliamentarians of the eighteenth century; and from 1811 to 1834, 543 select committees reported to Parliament, most of those in the later years.[14] By the 1840s, such commissions and committees were even more numerous, as were government departments and bureaucrats drawn from the middle classes. They formed a part of the proliferating social and political institutions that were increasingly part of a more industrialized, urbanized, and middle-class Britain and that helped further humanitarianism. But are social and economic forces alone sufficient as an explanation of the rise of the spirit of humanity? Does not the rise of a spirit of humanity in less industrialized and less urbanized France and Germany suggest that ideas are also important?

THE IDEAS OF THE GREAT THINKERS

John Stuart Mill said that the two seminal minds of the early nineteenth century were Jeremy Bentham and Samuel Taylor Coleridge. Certainly, these great sages must have furthered humanitarianism? They did indeed, although in varying degrees and not nearly as much as their later admirers claimed. Coleridge's influence, for example, was great on the Cambridge Apostles of the 1820s and 1830s, men such as Julius Hare, John Sterling, and Frederick Maurice. He also influenced, in those same decades, the brilliant scholars of Oxford's Oriel College—men such as John Hampden, Edward Copleston, and Archbishop Whatley. All six were clergymen, all Broad Church, and all scholars who found Coleridge helpful to their theological and philosophical developments.[15] None won fame for championing humanitarian causes except possibly Frederick Maurice, although his idealistic Christian Socialism was vague and ineffectual. Coleridge himself did little for humanitarian reforms, a not surprising fact, since he declared that he "had no great faith in Act of Parliament reform" and that "nothing more could be asked of the state than to withhold . . . all extrinsic and artificial aids to an injurious system." The older Coleridge could be severe, denouncing mechanics institutes and Lancastrian schools and defending the burning in Calvin's Geneva of the sixteenth-century unitarian Michael Servetus. For Coleridge, the remedy for social evils lay in becoming better people, a phrase echoed by Frederick Maurice's belief that "right human relationships" provided the basis of the kingdom of heaven on earth—views Maurice's colleague in Christian Socialism found "visionary." Although some of Coleridge's ideas were more acute and specific, John Colmer contends that he "failed to communicate them."[16] Although capable of compassion for overworked factory children and full of Christian benevolence, Coleridge was hardly a great inspirer of humanitarian causes. Perhaps that title belongs to that other seminal mind, Jeremy Bentham.

Not entirely, say many of his critics. Gertrude Himmelfarb, Michael Ignatieff, and Michel Foucault argue that Bentham's proposed plan for a Panopticon raises great doubts about his humanitarianism. For Himmelfarb, used as a prison, this huge, six-storied, ringlike building, with every cell open to unremitting inspection from a central tower, would have been a place of constant spying, enhanced terror, absolute solitude, deprived diets, and punishment. She quotes Bentham's own words that it was to be a place "of barbarous perfection" and "labour . . . the hardest and most severe." Labor not so severe but long and hard and including children was part of a variant plan if the Panopticon were used as a National Charity Company, a company Bentham hoped would earn 300 percent profits. Ignatieff sees the projected Panopticon, which was to be outfitted with whipping machinery, as an authoritarian institution of "constant inspection." Foucault calls it a "cruel ingenuous cage," "a design of subtle coercion," and, since it could serve as factory, hospital, school, or asylum, "a perfect disciplinary institution."[17]

The above criticisms are not without foundation. Bentham's mind had a decidedly authoritarian and regimenting cast, and he could be cruel, as when he urged that rapists be castrated. But he had, nevertheless, an even larger humanitarian cast to his mind. His pauper management scheme was not all regimentation; there was also much attention to physical comforts, to clothing that was warm, if inexpensive, to diets that were healthy, if plain, to "domestic ties strengthened," and to good schooling, music, gardening, and useful labor—none unhealthy or excessive. His scheme provided security against every want, and its sole object was the maximum of happiness. Bentham also abandoned, as Himmelfarb rightly notes, solitary confinement and urged association both in the cells and at work—productive useful work, not the treadmill and crank. Bentham declared that punishment in "whatsoever a shape . . . is an evil," that it should never be based on wrath or vengeance, that it should not only deter but aim at "amendment or reformation," and that it should "promote the social good [and] meet the offenders' needs." Bentham also opposed whipping, mutilation, and all capital punishment except in the case of "murder when accompanied with circumstances of aggravation," views that made him, Leon Radzinowicz writes, "the most advanced in ending capital punishment." His great life work, to make England's barbarous law code civilized and humane, like his endless schemes of human betterment, is suffused with a benevolence often in abeyance in his Panopticon schemes. The severe side of Bentham reflects both an eighteenth century that was itself severe and Bentham's overly mechanistic approach, one marked by a naive optimism that the deterrence of pain and the encouragement of pleasure can, if nicely calculated and nicely mixed, be powerfully effective on the plastic human nature of a pauper or criminal. But both the eighteenth-century context and Bentham's mechanistic outlook yielded to his sanguine and benevolent temperament and his great belief that reason can lead to the improvement of man and of society, most particularly if guided by the greatest happiness principle. The shadow of the Panopticon should not obscure the Bentham who denounced cruelty to animals, condemned the holding of women in "perpetual wardship," and in his *Deontology* defined humanity as "effective benevolence . . . directed at a particular case of suffering [and] the removal of some positive and weighty evil."[18]

For all his harsher aspects, Bentham was a dedicated humanitarian. But did he inspire others to be so? Yes, but not in great numbers. Even though his *Works* appeared in 1843, he was seldom mentioned in the 1840s either in Parliament or in the press. The *British Critic* was convinced that Bentham was "rapidly becoming more contemptible and contemned," while Abraham Hayward of the *Times* confessed that "the greater part of respectable society" looked on Bentham with "horror and indignation."

These judgments came from sources hostile to Bentham. Friendly sources, however, also saw no major impact. Bentham made "little progress" with public opinion, claimed Charles Dilke's *Athenaeum*. "Bentham is neglected," said his friend Sir Rowland Hill, "by a great part of his countrymen."[19] Bentham's later writing became increasingly technical, full of jargon, and forbidding in detail and in proliferating classifications. He was largely unread. He was also seldom heard. "Only James Mill and Dumont," said John Stuart Mill, "have the opportunity of learning much from his lips," and he added elsewhere that the notion "that Bentham was surrounded by a band of disciples who received their opinions from his lips is a fable."[20]

It was neither Coleridge nor Bentham who excited the British press of the 1840s but Thomas Carlyle, whose 1839 *Chartism* raised the "Condition of England Question" and called for great action. But the great action consisted only of emigration and education, on both of which he was vague. Carlyle's call to action in his 1843 *Past and Present* was largely for a medieval type of paternalism, and his 1850 *Latter Day Pamphlets,* with its furious attacks on philanthropy and all humane prison reform, reflected an increasingly angry and harsh Carlyle and one whom the press constantly criticized. He was "ridiculously erroneous" said the *Manchester Guardian*; full of "moonshine" declared the *Eclectic Review*; "full of rage and hatred," charged the *North British Review*. The *Spectator* found him "exceedingly one sided," "far from satisfactory on remedies," and full of "mystical verboseness."[21] The *Edinburgh Review, Christian Teacher,* and *Athenaeum* were no kinder. James Grant, editor of the *Morning Advertiser,* noted that none of Carlyle's works had enjoyed an extensive sale.[22]

Wordsworth, who enjoyed a much greater popularity and esteem than did Carlyle, was also disappointing as an advocate of humanitarian reforms. His long poem *The Excursion* was certainly full of sensitivity and sympathy, but for nature, the Church, and, briefly, in book 8, for the factory child. The wider world of the exploited and oppressed escaped his purview. There was a coolness in the older Wordsworth that turned to coldness in his sonnets in praise of capital punishment, sonnets that the critic R. H. Horne called "the tomb of his prophet-title." It made him, Horne added, "the prophet of the past."[23]

Far more esteemed and cited by politicians and journalists than Carlyle and Wordsworth were two professors of Edinburgh University, Dugald Stewart and Thomas Chalmers. Dugald Stewart was, for Henry Cockburn, "the greatest of didactic orators," one who "exalted the character of his country and generation."[24] His reputation drew many eminent men to Edinburgh to learn from him: Whigs like Lords Palmerston (who lived with Stewart), Lansdowne, Russell, Minto, Lauderdale, and Webb Seymour; intellectuals like Sir James Mackintosh, James Mill, Thomas Brown, Henry Brougham, and Macvey Napier; and Tory M.P.'s such as Sir Thomas Acland and Sir Robert Inglis.[25]

Thomas Chalmers, one of Stewart's students, evoked even greater veneration from his students. He was a "second Luther," declared Patrick Dove, and Sydney Smith called him "not one man but a thousand." Wordsworth wrote that "all the world [was] wild about him."[26] Popular, admired, and influential as both Scotsmen were, their severe laissez-faire views kept them from being the ardent inspirers of humanitarian causes. Chalmers, in particular, was too Calvinist on sinful paupers and criminals and too convinced that social evils were providentially ordained to inspire a vigorous humanitarianism. Nor did Dugald Stewart, for all his celebration of the benevolence that arises from an "innate perception of rectitude" and the pity that arises "in every heart," move beyond a Scottish paternalism that, although it praised allotments and parish schools, insisted that solitary confinement did "honor to the enlightened benevolence of the age" and called "anything approaching to a compulsory maintenance of the poor a glaring absurdity."[27]

Stewart's Enlightenment assumption that man can be taught the good by reason promoted a broader, more rational, more optimistic outlook than Chalmers's Calvinism, but, like William Paley's moderate, prudential morality, it nonetheless embodied a deep satisfaction with things as they were. Paley's utilitarian *Principles of Moral and Political Philosophy* was far more widely read than Bentham. It was required at Cambridge University, and its many editions populated the shelves of many a member of the gentry. Paley's opposition to torture, slavery, dueling, and the slave trade revealed a humanitarian streak, but a weak one compared to the sternness that led to his defense of England's fierce criminal code, a defense that led Dugald Stewart to denounce his "reckless inhumanity." Stewart, full of the Scottish moral philosophers' belief in an innate moral sense, could not abide Paley's utilitarianism, which Stewart called "sophistry."[28] But however they differed on the greatest happiness principle of the utilitarians or an innate conscience as the criterion of the good, both adopted a moderate and secular Whiggish morality that prudently accommodated itself to existing institutions and customary ways. Although the great philosophical debate of the 1840s involved the utilitarians' happiness principle versus the Scottish philosophers' innate moral sense, its vast literature deals little with humanitarian causes.

It was not so much learned and subtle discussions of utility or a moral sense, or even the ideas of a Carlyle, Coleridge, or Bentham, that furthered the rise of humanitarianism but ideas and attitudes that stemmed from a host of thinkers and from intellectual developments far broader and more diffuse than the doctrines of a few seminal minds.

HUMANITARIANISM AND THE RELIGIOUS REVIVAL

For many early Victorians, quite the most momentous fact in their lives was their religious faith. For many of the educated, a revival of serious religion had replaced the latitudinarianism of the eighteenth century, and for many of the uneducated, a prevailing ignorance and indifference. Whether Anglican, Nonconformist, or Catholic, High Church or Broad, religious convictions of various kinds gained a powerful hold on early Victorians' hearts and minds. It must surely have had an impact on the growth of humanitarianism.

It did, but in a diffuse, ambiguous, and limited manner. It made less impact in the 1840s on new humanitarian causes than it did on traditional paternalist and philanthropic activities. It added vitality to the local clergy and Christian laity, made parishes alive with good works, and gave energy to a host of societies. The story of that reawakening has been told in George Kitson Clark's *Churchmen and the Condition of England*, Diana McClatchey's *Oxfordshire Clergy*, David Mole's *The Church of England and Society in Birmingham*, Kathleen Heasman's *Evangelicals in Action*, and Donald Lewis's *Lighten Their Darkness.* Its heroes were the clergymen who performed humane services for parishioners or formed societies that served the poor. George Kitson Clark describes such a hero in William Champneys of Whitechapel, who built three churches, established a boys' and a girls' school, a providential society, a shoe-black brigade, and a refuge and industrial home for boys. Diana McClatchey discovers such benevolence in George Herbert, priest of a rural Oxfordshire parish, who supervised the local charities, taught the children to read, lectured at the mechanics institute, gave the sick his home-brewed medicine, and saw that the really sick went to the hospital. David Mole admires William Marsh of Birmingham, a parson busy managing district-visiting programs, day and Sunday schools, and shoe, clothing, blanket, and coal clubs. For Kathleen Heasman, the heroic clergyman is the Congregationalist Andrew Reed, founder of orphanages, and for Donald Lewis, Baptist Noel, who helped found the London City Mission.[29] It was through such activities that a broad, diffuse humanitarianism made paternalism and philanthropy more active, sensitive, and benevolent. It was the "humanity" said Charles Blomfield, bishop of London, "of the true philanthropist."[30]

It would be quite unfair to overlook such a broad humanity, often so selfless and sacrificing at the individual, local, and traditional levels, when observing how limited the religious revival often was in defining the humanitarianism of great causes, the humanitarianism that the Tory M.P. Peter Borthwick had in mind when (quite forgetful of Wilberforce and slavery), he praised Lord Ashley for being the first "to introduce into the legislature . . . the principle of humanity."[31] Two facts prevented the humanity of the paternalists and philanthropists from embracing great causes—and indeed blunted their own efforts—an intense parochialism and a religious and social conservatism. High Churchmen were particularly parochial in their love of the parish church and the diocesan cathedral, love even of its very altars, offertories and sacred almsgiving. Nothing was to be done beyond the orbit of the Church; visiting the poor, that sacred commandment of the Scriptures, was to be done by the clergy, and if not by them, then by sisterhoods and brotherhoods who had taken vows. Thus circumscribed, it was not very likely that High Churchmen would lead movements opposing capital punishment or child labor or for the better treatment of debtors or the insane.

Anglican evangelicals also loved the parish, and Nonconformists loved the chapel and its faithful. But they added to them the philanthropic society, although for many Anglicans only if, as the bishop of London demanded, the society were exclusively Anglican. The effort in the 1840s of Nonconformist evangelicals to win the cooperation of the Church of England in their visiting societies ran into the deep hostility of most Anglican evangelicals. Absent in the 1840s was the ecumenical spirit of the anti-slavery movement. Instead, as Kitson Clark laments, the evangelicals' intolerance nullified much of the good that they did. And the good that they did do remained largely local; E. R. Norman concludes, in *Church and Society in England,* that most of the Church's work remained largely "at the parish level."[32]

Their conservative religious and social views also limited their promotion of larger humanitarian causes. An examination of some fifty charges to the clergy by bishops and archdeacons and hundreds of sermons by Anglican ministers—High, Broad, and Low churchmen alike—finds no great enthusiasm for any national crusade. Also very rare are any references to the dictates or principles of humanity, phrases that might rival appeals to God's biblical commands. The charges and sermons deal with no large humanitarian movement except education, and on that subject, they largely insist that it be exclusively under the Church of England.[33] None of the charges and scarcely any of the sermons (besides those of a few radicals like the Reverend G. S. Bull) mention the plight of women and children in factories and mines, a confirmation of Lord Ashley's claim that the clergy gave less support to factory bills than did mill owners or doctors. There were also no great pleas in support of the sanitary movement, although there were many references to cholera as a Divine visitation.[34] Liverpool's most popular evangelical, the Reverend Hugh M'Neil, judged "plagues, pestilence, famine" to be "punishment for our national sins," as did London's most popular Tractarian, the Reverend W. J. E. Bennett. For Bennett, "prayer would be of great help," while for M'Neil, as he contemplated the Irish famine, "it is only [by] the power of God that the calamity can be removed." M'Neil was a premillenarian who expected Christ's Second Coming so immediately that he abandoned efforts to promote Christian unity, which the Savior would bring.[35] That God both caused and remedied pestilence and famine was a far greater formula for repentance and prayer than for organizing and legislating. It is thus not surprising that Lord Ashley, at the General Board of Health, was saddened by the apathy of the clergy and the inaction of the churchwardens in the fight to contain cholera.[36]

The Providence that punished sin was nevertheless a good Providence, much praised in the charges and sermons for designing a hierarchical world, one that ran, said the Reverend Henry Melville, from palace to cottage, and in which everyone had a divinely ordained place. "Poverty," proclaimed the Reverend Samuel Green, "is His infliction. Wealth is His gift. The gradation of society is His appointment." One's "final rewards," he assured the reader, "would be won in heaven."[37] It was an optimistic message for the wealthy, although tempered by a deeply rooted belief in original sin. "The evil passions" and the "destructive career of man" were part, announced the evangelical *Christian Observer*, of a human nature "corrupted by the fall."[38]

For the High Church Reverend William Gresley, "the cause of crime is the evil heart," and for the evangelical John Breay, "poverty and sickness . . . [were] the consequence of the fall." Such a sense of sin dampened the optimism that inspires great movements, especially when combined with the claim that the "principal cause of temporal evils is spiritual destitution." Such was the belief of J. B. Sumner, bishop of Chester, one that led to his insistence that the only remedy lay in a greater moral and spiritual instruction.[39] An otherworldliness that placed the salvation of souls above the removal of temporal evils heightened even more the evangelicals' concentration on conversion and the High Church's concentration on the saving grace of the Church's sacraments.

Their concentration on salvation of souls still left room, however, for the moral reform of the individual, which was for many a plea to be sober, provident, industrious, self-reliant, and long-suffering. Poverty for the Anglican clergy, many of whom as poor law guardians administered the New Poor Law, lay in the failings of the individual: for the Reverend Thomas Stevens, "wicked and abandoned habits," for the Reverend Charles Girdlestone, "grievous errors and gross misconduct," and for the Reverend William Gresley, "improvidence and want of self denial."[40] With poverty thus rooted in moral failings, London's most popular minister, the evangelical Henry Melville, promised "to end destitution," not by any act of Parliament, but "by a mighty regeneration" that would "make every inhabitant independent."[41] For Melville, self-reliance was not a blueprint for a new society, as it became for the theologically liberal Nonconformists. For Nonconformists who were not liberal, the blueprint was still found in salvation of the soul. The Congregationalist Reverend James Davies of Sherborne, Dorset, told future ministers that they should teach that repentance, faith, and holiness prepared one for "a blessed immortality," while the son of the Congregationalist James Evans of London noted of his father's sermons, "No time was wasted . . . on any other subjects than . . . the salvation of souls." There was nothing in the sermons of Davies and Evans about social questions; nor in the sermons of Rotherham's William Stowell, who insisted that a "concern for the soul must be paramount," "that the great business of life is to prepare for a better," and that our "wellbeing is to be found in the gracious presence of our Lord and Saviour," which would "tranquilize your conscience and soothe your heart."[42]

The giants of Methodism, the Reverend Jabez Bunting and the Reverend Thomas Jackson, were equally orthodox and otherworldly and had no trouble following the Wesleyan Association's rule to avoid politics. "The no politics rule," said the Primitive Methodist Reverend Hugh Bourne, "was the controlling element in the Methodist attitude towards society." Mavericks, like the Reverend John Raynor Stephens and the Reverend Joseph Barker, who championed factory and poor law reform, soon departed from the Wesleyan Methodists. Toward their own flock, the Methodist ministers were full of a stern humanity, but a humanity limited by parochialism and religious conservatism. Methodists, said Bourne, were silent on the reform bill—as indeed on most social questions except education. Wesleyans, said George Jacob Holyoake, "prided themselves on Spirituality not Humanity."[43]

Quite different from these orthodox and evangelical Nonconformists were the liberals among them, ministers such as the famous Congregationalist Reverend Thomas Binney, of the City's Weigh House Chapel; J. B. Mursell, a Baptist of Leicester; and the Reverend George Dawson, famous at first as Birmingham's most eloquent Baptist and then, after dismissal, as its most eloquent ex-Baptist. In their sermons, predestination, original sin, God's visitations, and Christ's imminent Second Coming are notably absent; in their place, we find Binney's "large and inexhaustible humanity," Mursell's "breadth and humanity" (as expressed in his denunciation of flogging), and Dawson's buoyant faith that ending capital punishment would "smooth the highway along which the great car of humanity will roll."[44] The emergence of a sturdy morality in place of theological doctrine as the raison d'être of Christianity opened the door for many, including both Broad Churchmen like Thomas Arnold and liberal Nonconformists like George Dawson, to a larger humanity.

But the door was not fully opened. The sturdy morality was a self-reliant one, highly individualistic, and in the case of the Nonconformists, full both of a deep hostility to a state that had persecuted them and of a great zeal for the voluntarism that fitted neatly with their faith's love of independence. The sermons of Thomas Binney, with their "large and inexhaustible humanity," mention no humanitarian causes. Binney never took part in politics and seldom appeared on a platform. Instead, he aroused his audiences with sermons on the "Righteousness that Exalteth a Nation" distinguished by "its temperance and industry, its invigorating habits, its intelligence and skill." Dawson and Mursell, theologically liberal and more active politically, were nonetheless inhibited by a jealousy of the state and an optimistic belief that the answer to social evils lay in an educated, self-reliant people.

It was the mission of the Christian ministry to exalt righteousness and of

Christian laymen to fashion laws that would blend that righteousness with the dictates of humanity. And among that laity, it fell to the most seriously religious among the members of Parliament to carry out those dictates. The following analysis of the votes and speeches of twenty-five of the most seriously religious M.P.'s is only a sample. It does not suggest that others lacked faith, but only that these twenty-five were more avowedly religious, or at least seen to be so by contemporaries and later historians. Some were evangelicals, some High Church, and some simply deeply Anglican, and all sat in the Commons at one time or another in the 1840s.

Their votes and speeches in the 1840s, with the exception of the speeches of Lord Ashley and their votes on factory legislation, do not link them very strongly to the rise of humanitarianism. The twenty-five more deeply Christian did, to be sure, vote in four divisions sixty-one times in favor of and twenty-one times against a ten-hour day.[45] It was a vote in keeping with Coleridge's claim that the state should regulate manufactures but not commerce and agriculture, since these seriously religious M.P.'s voted twelve to none to kill a bill guaranteeing Irish tenants compensation for the value of their improvements.[46] They were not indifferent to landed property, voting forty-nine times to five for a Corn Law that supported a high price for grain, and twenty-three to one for a New Poor Law that had tightened up on relief and lowered poor rates.[47] They would, of course, have insisted that their goal was not low rates but the end of pauperism. That ending pauperism involved the harsh workhouse test was, for them, as necessary as the whipping of juvenile offenders and the hanging of murderers: they voted thirty-four times to four against abolishing capital punishment and nine times to zero for the whipping—up to six times a year—of juvenile offenders.[48]

Harsh punishments bothered few of them, only two compared to fifteen Rationalists protesting the flogging of soldiers and sailors and none of them the severities of separate confinement and the game laws. In two divisions, the seriously religious voted seventeen to two against abolishing flogging in the military, a practice abandoned throughout most of Europe. Five evangelicals—Sir George Grey, Robert Palmer, Henry Halford, Sir John Packington, and Charles Adderley—spoke for and none against separate confinement.[49] They opposed by fourteen to thirteen a sixpenny rate on all Irish property to help the worst famine-stricken areas, and they voted four to none (there were always abstentions, often in considerable numbers) in favor of denying relief to anyone, however destitute, with a quarter of an acre of land.[50] A vote of four to zero is a small one, but it shows that not one of the twenty-five came to the rescue of Irish cottagers, however destitute, who occupied a quarter-acre plot.

There was, however, one among the twenty-five who did believe in rescuing the destitute, an evangelical whose humanitarianism none could equal. Lord Ashley, who sat in the Commons from 1831 to 1851 (except for the fifteen months after April 1846), was unstinting in his efforts to protect the weak and oppressed, the ill and abused. His many bills and his many compassionate speeches on mines, factories, print works, lunacy, the health of towns, ragged schools, and juvenile delinquency make him a towering figure of humanity, and often lonely figure. He was, said Lord Francis Egerton, "the paragon of humanity."[51] There were, to be sure, other devout M.P.'s who promoted humanitarian reforms. Among such reforms promoted by evangelicals were Henry Halford's bill to protect hosiery workers, Robert Grosvenor's effort to free London bakers from all-night labor, William Cowper's effort to make compulsory the provision of allotments to the laboring poor, and Charles Adderley's Reformatory Bill. One High Churchman, William Gladstone, sponsored a bill to regulate the payment of London coal whippers who unloaded barges.[52] Of the above bills, only Gladstone's passed, and that over the protests of a noted Whig evangelical, F. T. Baring, who insisted that there was "nothing in the world so meddling as humanity."[53] Most evangelicals also gave no support to Halford's and Grosvenor's meddling. Thus, to a remarkable extent, the linking, after the great anti-slavery successes, of the religious revival with humanitarian causes rests rather heavily on the prodigious work of Lord Ashley, not just as M.P., but on the Lunacy Commission and at the General Board of Health. Take Lord Ashley away, and the link weakens— even on the factory question. The slavery abolitionists (who were in great numbers evangelical), complained the Tory Radical Richard Oastler and the Reverend G. S. Bull, either gave the Ten Hour Bill little support or opposed it, one of the many facts that perhaps led Boyd Hilton, in his *Age of Atonement*, to conclude that "the evangelicals as a body opposed the movement for factory reform."[54] Certainly, the religious periodicals—the evangelical *Christian Observer*, *Record*, and *North British Review*, the High Church *British Critic*, *Christian Remembrancer*, and *Oxford and Cambridge Review*, and the Broad Church *British and Foreign Review*—reveal no great humanitarian zeal, unless for an educational system run exclusively by the Church, although even this cause divided more than it united, limiting what slow expansion did occur. Not even evangelicalism—to Owen Chadwick, "the strongest force" in early Victorian England—could remain united. "As a united political force," writes Boyd Hilton, "evangelicalism was broken by . . . bitter divisions."[55]

In the growth of humanitarianism, the religious revival played a very widespread role in infusing a greater compassion into traditional paternalist and philanthropic activities and greater energy into the preaching of a self-reliant morality, and the seriously religious occasionally took part in humanitarian movements. But all too often, the seriously religious were either inactive or hostile to these movements. The growth of rationalism is thus a more probable source of the humanitarian movements that promised to end cruelty of all kinds and to protect the weak and abused everywhere.

THE GROWTH OF RATIONALISM
AND HUMANITARIANISM

A wide variety of commentators noted the growth of rationalism. Improved manners and less cruelty to animals, declared *Chambers' Edinburgh Journal*, were "due to the spread of intelligence." The *Decorator's Assistant* discovered that "the more the enlightenment the less the cruelty," a claim the *English Chartist Circular* also made: "the moment enlightenment enters the heart, superstition, bigotry, and cruelty leave it."[56] "Barbarous means of punishment," insisted the conservative *Magistrate*, "are alien to the improved intelligence of the age." "The collision of intellect," argued the evangelical prison inspector Whitworth Russell, "had illumined the world and improved it." And the *Eclectic Review* rejoiced in the triumph "of truth over falsehood and of virtue over vice."[57]

Humanitarian reformers agreed. "Reason must take over," Sir Charles Napier declared in his book attacking flogging in the Army and Navy; and in his denunciation of capital punishment, Sydney Taylor similarly called for "chain[ing] the passions to commanding reason."[58] In the fight for humanitarian causes, reason was invoked more often than religion. It was the progressive schools of the rationalists, not Church of England schools, that abolished corporal punishment. It was also neither High Churchmen nor evangelicals who opposed the crank and the treadmill, but enlightened critics, from Jeremy Bentham to Frederick Hill and Captain Maconochie. Nor did men of the cloth lead the fight against diseased towns as vigorously as engineers and doctors trained in science. The *Westminster Review*, the *Spectator*, *Punch*, *Douglas Jerrold's Shilling Magazine*, *Howitt's Journal*, and the *Weekly Dispatch*, not the religious journals (the *Eclectic Review* excepted), were the publications that invoked compassion for those who suffered from enclosures, game laws, eviction, famine, flogging, imprisonment for debt, and the barbarities of the hulks.

In Parliament, too, it was M.P.'s of a rational bent who opposed capital punishment, flogging, the imprisonment of debtors, and enclosures that robbed the poor, just as it was the same M.P.'s who supported reformatories, not prisons, for juvenile offenders, a poor law for Scotland, safer mines and passenger ships, and the abolition of the barbarous hulks. A sample of twenty-five M.P.'s of a strong rationalist outlook selected as a counterpart to the twenty-five deeply religious M.P.'s, shows them voting in the various divisions on capital punishment twenty-four times to abolish and only ten times to continue.[59] They also voted sixteen to two in favor of more generous relief to the famine-stricken Irish compared to the religious M.P.'s fourteen against and thirteen for. The rationalists, however, were just barely kinder to Irish tenants and the destitute occupying a quarter of an acre. Only three times did they vote to compensate tenants for their improvements, with seven opposing, and only two wished to help the quarter-acre destitute, with two opposing.[60] While the religious M.P.'s supported flogging in the military seventeen times to two against, the rationalists urged its abolition with fifteen votes for to seven against.[61] The twenty-five rationalist M.P.'s were no more cut from the same rationalist cloth, however, than the twenty-five religious M.P.'s were from the same religious cloth. The rationalism of Russell and Palmerston, and other Whigs (all good churchmen) not only reflected the Whig intellectual tradition, stemming from John Locke, but the teachings of the Scottish moral philosophers and William Paley's Cambridge. The utilitarians reflected Cambridge, too, but also the writings of Bentham and James Mill. Some utilitarians had a Calvinist background; others were influenced by the romantic radicalism of Shelley and Byron. There were also M.P.'s who had been raised neither as Whigs nor as Benthamites, such as Thomas Wakley, who had had a medical education, and William Ewart, whose background was in Liverpool commerce and Oxford Aristotelianism.[62] All the rationalists were religious, too, in their way, but religion was not nearly as influential as rationalism in defining their social outlooks.

But were these rationalists really more humane and benevolent than the evangelicals? On issues of hanging or flogging, yes, but what of their views on the New Poor Law and the protection of factory labor? While in various divisions on the New Poor Law, the seriously religious M.P.'s voted thirty-four to continue and only two for change, the rationalist M.P.'s voted fifteen to keep and nine to reform. And on a Ten Hour Day that saw the religious M.P.'s vote sixty-one times for and twenty-one times against, the rationalists, forgetting for the moment the dictates of political economy, voted thirty-four for and eighteen against. They were not so generous to hosiery, framework, and lace workers, or to Irish tenants. On no bill to protect these exploited laborers could they muster more than two votes.[63] The Benthamites in the Commons, William Molesworth, John Roebuck, Joseph Hume, John Bowring, and George Grote, and, in the Lords, Lord Brougham, all brimming with political economy, led in the opposition to the Ten Hour Bill. Were not these utilitarians the heartless Gradgrinds and Bounderbys of Charles Dickens's *Hard Times?* F. R. and Q. D. Leavis certainly believe so. They called *Hard Times* "a comprehensive vision in which the inhumanities of a Victorian civilization are seen as fostered and hardened by a hard philosophy—an inhuman spirit." It was the spirit of utilitarianism.[64] That rationalism had a cruel and inhuman edge, that it was an instrument both of social control and middle-class hegemony, has been a frequent theme in recent histories. A. P. Donajgrodzki, in *Social Control in Nineteenth Century Britain,* finds the rationalists' passion for social control powerfully expressed in that most Benthamite of bureaucrats, Edwin Chadwick. Chadwick not only worked unstintingly for the universal use of the severe workhouse test but urged the establishment of a state police that would suppress trade unions and punish vagrants, beggars, and other deviants. A social police, declares Donajgrodzki, "is part of Benthamite thinking."[65]

A similar Benthamite authoritarianism, Ruth Richardson argues, in *Death, Dissection and the Destitute,* led Henry Warburton to help pass the Anatomy Act of 1832, which forced many paupers to forgo that Christian burial so dear to them for medical dissection, which was abhorrent. Masters at manipulation and duplicity, says Ruth Richardson, the Benthamites represented the "Reason" that Roger Cooter claims made "artisans its victims" in order "to safeguard the Reasonable bourgeois world."[66]

Benthamites were not alone in displaying reason's stern visage. Both Michel Foucault and Andrew Scull argue that the doctors who reformed the treatment of the insane were also zealous to manipulate and discipline, so intent were they to control deviants. Lunatics, claims Scull, were to be "transformed," "remodelled," and "made over in the image of bourgeois rationality . . . so that they could compete in the market place." The making over was no longer by chains and emetics and frigid cells, but by a severe internalization of guilt, one assisted by "environmental manipulation."[67] Foucault places the "birth of remorse" in the nineteenth-century asylum and declares remorse more cruel than chains. Reason for Foucault, whether of the classical seventeenth century, the enlightened eighteenth, or the positivist nineteenth, had, in various ways, mastered madness, "by disciplining and brutalizing"; by submission, confinement, and punishment; and, in the new asylums, by transforming the lunatic "into a minor."[68]

The rationalism of English prison reformers, argue Michael Ignatieff, in *A Just Measure of Pain,* and Michel Foucault, in *Discipline and Punish: The Birth of the Prison,* also sought to control deviancy through harsh discipline and confinement. For Ignatieff, the new, massive, grim penitentiary with its solitary confinement, treadmill, crank, and bread-and-water diets was not only part of "the tightening up of social control" due to mounting social crises but also a reflection of that "imperative to control, to dominate or to subdue [that] is written deep into the structure of those ways of thinking we call the human sciences," a way of thinking that began in the eighteenth century.[69] The desire to control and subdue, says Martin Wiener in *Reconstructing the Criminal*, characterized even the most humane of reformers, Mary Carpenter, the champion of enlightened reformatories, who said that "the chief object of punishment" was "reform by means of severity."[70]

Educational reformers also, claim recent historians, reflect the rationalists' desire for social control. Their campaign for a truly national education, Richard Johnson says, in "Educating the Educators: Experts and the State," can only be analyzed in terms of hegemony . . . a necessary compromise of a faction of the dominant class so as to get order." Even the animal rights movement, claims Harriet Ritvo, involves "the manipulation of people."[71]

There is some truth to the claims that rationalist reformers could be severe and coercive. Whig rationalism certainly appears harsh and coercive in the *Edinburgh Review*. It condemned the Tories for supporting the Ten Hour Bill, strongly supported the New Poor Law, praised separate confinement, supported capital punishment, denounced allotments, opposed greater relief for famine-stricken Ireland in 1848, and, in discussing child labor, decried the fact that "the spirit of humanity is too roaming and restless."[72] The article on Ireland was written by Sir Charles Trevelyan, assistant secretary to the Treasury, educated at the Hailebury of Thomas Malthus, of an old Whig family, steeped in political economy, and proud to be eminently "rational." All three articles praising the New Poor Law were by Nassau Senior, the co-author, with Edwin Chadwick, of that law. Senior, a friend of the Whigs and a leading political economist, had been Richard Whatley's pupil at Oxford. W. R. Greg, a former mill owner, a prolific essayist, and a Unitarian, lament the amount of "busy, prying, laborious benevolence in England" in an article on the Ten Hour Act.[73] Greg could have cited the factory inspector Leonard Horner on the dangers of a ten-hour day, and Senior and the poor law assistant commissioners Kay-Shuttleworth and E. C. Tufnell on the need of the workhouse test to combat pauperism. He could also cite both Trevelyan and Whatley to the effect that the 1844 and 1847 Irish poor laws were ruinous, and that an ampler one would be worse.[74] The new social bureaucrats prided themselves on reason, logic, and firmness. The more rational of the education inspectors were not averse to social control; Joseph Fletcher praised the regimenting monitorial system, and Seymour Tremenheere condemned not only the workers' "wish to dictate terms" and "excitability" but the "moral contamination" that spawned the pernicious trade unions.[75] Doctors who treated the insane also had despotic urges and grew angry when the courts told them that if mental patients were not dangerous and did not desire treatment, they could not be forcefully incarcerated.[76] There is certainly considerable evidence that reformers of a rationalist disposition could be coercive and anxious for social control.

But the rationalists' concern for social control should be placed in a wider context, one that not only emphasizes the fact that all societies in their normal functioning need some coercive and disciplinary measures but points out that Victorian society had inherited from earlier centuries many harsh and severe customs, institutions, and attitudes. The rapid growth of cities, an emerging proletariat, rising crime, and recurrent economic crises also demanded social control. These facts should not be forgotten when estimating the role of rationalist ideas in making social reform more authoritarian.

But neither should it be forgotten that the rationalists themselves often heightened an existing authoritarianism by their idealistic belief that by the right education, by the inculcation of correct habits, and by the use of pain as a deterrent, they could reform the deviant and improve the erring. Thus for Tufnell and Kay-Shuttleworth, the New Poor Law was a reforming effort, the workhouse deterring paupers from evil ways and the schoolroom inculcating virtuous habits. In a similar vein, prison reformers and lunacy doctors hoped to mold character by a mix of sternness and benevolence. That the stern and deterring part of their reform schemes did, on occasion, lead a Mary Carpenter, a Frederick Hill, or a James Kay-Shuttleworth to demand discipline and punishment should not obscure the fact that they and their fellow reformers sought to improve far more than to repress and to elevate far more than to punish the lower classes.

These rationalists were idealists. Tufnell gave much of his own income and time to establish Battersea College, one of the first schools for training teachers. Kay-Shuttleworth, as secretary to the Privy Council's Committee on Education, exhausted himself in efforts to square the circle of religious jealousy and public need of a national system of education. Leonard Horner dedicated enormous energies to making factories safer, ending child labor, educating the young, and promoting an eleven-hour day. And Archbishop Whatley, although foe of too-easy an Irish poor law, gave £8,000 to famine relief.[77] The belief that individuals could be improved and whole classes elevated through self-reliance owed its origins in part to the powerful hold that British empiricism had on the minds of the early Victorian rationalists. The greatest philosopher of that tradition was John Locke, whose greatest work, the *Essay Concerning Human Understanding* (1690), had appeared in over thirty editions by 1850. It was required reading at Cambridge, and it inspired many Oxford students, especially those at Oriel College, of which the logician Richard

Whatley was a fellow.[78] In his essay, Locke compared the mind at birth to a blank slate, a tabula rasa, on which sensations were inscribed. Reason in turn used these sensations and not innate ideas to mold our understanding and our conscience. Great, then, were the possibilities of fashioning wiser and better humans, especially since, as David Hartley showed in *Observations on Man* (1749), virtuous actions could be associated with pleasurable consequences and evil ones with pain. Since character could be fashioned, one could make something of man.[79] "Make men diligent," wrote the prison reformer John Howard, "and they will be honest." Robert Owen, half a century, later believed that by correct social organization "we can materially command those circumstances which influence character." James Mill was just as optimistic. A good education and a good diet, he announced, would give the working class an "unlimited possibility of improving their minds."[80]

Locke's and Hartley's ideas were developed further in the writings of Joseph Priestley, William Godwin, Jeremy Bentham, James and John Stuart Mill, and many others and won a large following in early Victorian England. These ideas also crossed the channel, influencing Helvetius, Condorcet, Condillac, Rousseau, and Pestalozzi, and the works of these *philosophes* in turn influenced English readers.

Empiricism also underlay the more humane treatment of the insane and animals. Insanity began, declared the most humane of reforming doctors, John Conolly, with disturbances in the chain of faculties, "beginning in sensation and ending in reason," a disturbance caused by "false perceptions . . . and too vivid an imagination."[81] Animals also had sensations and feelings and could suffer pain. Two great empiricists, David Hume and Jeremy Bentham, urged kindness to animals, Hume because it was a "law of humanity," Bentham because animals were sentient beings who had feelings and could suffer. Many others also considered that animals, being subject to the sensation of pain, could suffer. "The emphasis on sensation," concludes Keith Thomas, "thus became basic to those who crusaded on behalf of animals."[82] Two other assumptions basic to rationalism also furthered the rise of humanitarianism: that reason, not authority, is the principal arbiter of the good, and, from British empiricism, that one's character and behavior reflect those circumstances, both good and evil, that so powerfully influence one's life. Reason became sovereign, writes John Stuart Mill, with the Reform Act of 1832, which finally made it "the recognized standard of authority."[83] No longer would the Bible, Burke's prescriptions from history, and the oracular pronouncements of Church divines rule the world of legislation and morals, but reason.

A rational, not a theological, rule, argued the *Eclectic Review*, must provide the test for the discussion of capital punishment, a test William Ewart also adapted when he told the House of Commons that he would use "practical," not religious, arguments.[84] Supporters of hanging had the Old Testament on their side: did not Leviticus (24:17) say, "He that killeth any man shall surely be put to death"? Those demanding the abolition of hanging occasionally invoked the New Testament, but dealt far more copiously in reasoned arguments.

The opposition between the Bible and reason was less pronounced on other humanitarian issues where reason was opposed by the authority of a sacred common law, by customs held time out of mind, and by old, venerable, sacrosanct institutions.

That reason was becoming the new standard found its fullest expression in Bentham's sovereign utilitarian rule, the greatest happiness of the greatest number, a rule as widely debated by moral philosophers as was the existence of innate ideas or the value of a priori reasoning. Two Cambridge moral philosophers, Adam Sedgwick and William Whewell, chastised John Stuart Mill for denying innate ideas. Mill in return denounced innate ideas and a priori reasoning for their support of "false doctrines and bad institutions" and "all deep seated prejudices"[85]

The disputes over innate ideas and the greatest happiness principle that obsessed Victorian moral philosophers had far less impact on press and Parliament. Much more significant to the growth of humanitarianism were two key doctrines of British empiricism: first, that powerful circumstances mold character, and if altered can improve that character and so society, and, second, that there are not only physical laws of nature but mental and moral ones, all harmonious, all discoverable by observation and reason, and all promising progress toward a just and prosperous society.

The belief that one could fashion character by controlling circumstances promised great things: the cure of the demented, the education of children to virtue, the reform of young criminals, and the reduction of pauperism and of disease in towns.

Although only the most sanguine thought men and women innately good, many found it quite wondrous what a kind upbringing and correct education could do. Although man "is what the circumstances make him," declared Southwood Smith, he has a "capacity for illimitable improvement." It was an improvement Southwood Smith ascribed to increasing knowledge, an increase that the phrenologist George Combe said would end those sufferings of humanity once considered inevitable and would bring "numberless enjoyments . . . avoid thousands of miseries," raise "happiness to an incalculably higher pitch," and bring about "the millennium." J. D. Morell, author of a *History of Philosophy*, was equally sanguine. "Has not every man," he asked, "the germs of boundless faculties—unlimited improvement." Southwood Smith, an educational and sanitary reformer, Combe, a phrenologist who influenced those who reformed the treatment of juveniles, prisoners, and the insane, and Morell, one of the most progressive of the school inspectors, were all active humanitarians and all boundless in their schemes for improving society.[86]

Although many humanitarians could not share a belief in the "illimitable" and "boundless" and the "millennium," most of them did accept the basic assumption that men and women are improvable. Henry Moseley, an Anglican clergyman and inspector of schools, was convinced that a child's early impressions form his or her character as certainly as "metal takes the form of the mould into which it is poured."[87] The belief that by the correct circumstances one could define character took many forms: for Dr. John Conolly, the insane were curable; for Captain Maconochie, the character of prisoners could be modified; and for the Whig M.P. Robert Slaney, good schools and healthy towns could elevate the working classes. Maconochie was the most deterministic. "If we were similarly born, educated and tempted," he argued, "we would be criminals." But also part of that deterministic belief was a conviction that it is "certain that the impulse to crime can be reduced by the laws of kindness."[88] From its most extreme form, Robert Owen's "your character is made for you not by you," to the Anglican educators' biblical "train up a child in the ways he should go and he will not depart from it," the belief grew widespread that old evils once seen as inevitable would yield to new and altered circumstances. It was a part, wrote John Stuart Mill in his *System of Logic* (1843), of "the universal laws of the Formation of Character," laws demanding that "our characters follow from our organization, our education, and our circumstances."[89]

Reason could discover not only Mill's laws of character but the laws defining society. Reason had already led to parliamentary, municipal, administrative, and legal reforms. In doing so, it had cleared out many past obstructions to the triumph of knowledge and intelligence. The way was now open to the discovery of society's laws and limitless progress. Never before had the English possessed such optimism, enjoyed such high expectations.

"Our social evils," rejoiced one of the most rationalist of journals, the *Westminster Review*, "are wholly removable or greatly mitigable."[90] Society itself seemed a tabula rasa onto which any scheme could be inscribed; and the schemes were many. There were the visionary utopias ranging from the Deist Robert Owen's parallelograms to the Anglican John Minton Morgan's Christian communism, schemes condemned by rationalists of a more practical bent. But these practical rationalists had their own hopeful schemes, their own Mark system (to make criminals virtuous by positive rewards), monitorial arrangements, workhouses, separate confinements, panopticons, asylums without chains, reformatories without vengeance, schools of industry, and a society free of capital punishment. There would be "new principles of government," principles that required, said the utilitarian M.P. Charles Buller, "a new social state".[91] Separate confinement did not reform, free trade was not a panacea, asylums did not cure all lunatics, and workhouses did not reform or end pauperism. But in the 1830s and 1840s, in a period not yet strewn with wrecked schemes, many rationalists were convinced that man and society formed tabulae rasae on which a new world could be inscribed. An exuberant optimism, more than a concern for social control arising from fear of disorder, led to experiments that were humanitarian in their aims, if occasionally inhumane in means and results.

The belief that evil circumstances had corrupted the helpless and disadvantaged was the other side of the coin of British empiricism's doctrine that improved circumstances would improve the individual and so reform society. Criminals were no longer seen as inherently evil but as the products of an evil society. One no longer believed, with *Blackwood's*, that crime arose from a "desperately wicked" heart or, with *John Bull*, that reform and education could "never utterly eradicate sin."[92] The poachers and paupers, juvenile and adult offenders, mendicants and destitute, the insane and the drunkards, were the products of a cruel upbringing and a harsh society; and none of them more so than juvenile delinquents, who, since but children, were clearly less responsible. Innumerable pamphlets and articles traced the erring ways of criminals and juvenile delinquents to parental neglect or depravity, filthy, overcrowded hovels, vicious neighborhoods, destitution, an appalling lack of schooling, and the corruption of time in prison. There were also the great cities with their prostitutes, beer houses, bawdy amusements, and the breakdown of paternal authority. These many evils were so formidable and corrupting that Mary Carpenter insisted that society "absolutely owes them [juvenile offenders] reparation."[93]

Although Victorians viewed adult offenders as more responsible than juvenile ones, the most humanitarian among them nonetheless observed that the same circumstances were at work. That crime went up in the economically depressed years of 1839 to 1842 and down in the prosperous years from 1843 to 1845 multiplied those who considered poverty and want of work a mitigating circumstance. Thus, for Humphrey Woolrych, a champion of prison reform, the incidence of arson rose with the price of corn and as wages fell.[94] Even the assistant poor law commissioners, those stalwart defenders of self-reliance, ran headlong into mitigating circumstances. In their 1842 reports on massive unemployment in Nottingham, Stockport, Paisley, and other manufacturing centers, they admitted that the causes of destitution lay in want of work, not want of virtue, and so temporarily abandoned the workhouse test.[95]

Want of health was also a cause of destitution, a fact powerfully and compassionately laid out by Edwin Chadwick in his famous Sanitary Report of 1842. It was illness and disease more than indolence and improvidence that created pauperism. It was an astonishing report. Self-reliance hardly showed itself; instead, all was material environment. Foul air, water, and refuse combined with overcrowding in wretched slums to create conditions that spawned all sorts of disease—conditions that demanded not moral censure of the diseased but humanitarian sympathy.[96]

The more that problems were closely examined on their own and not in the rhetorical terms of political economy, self-reliance, or a providential order, the larger mitigating circumstances loomed. This was particularly the case with those imbued with British empiricism's sense of the power of circumstances, a sense reinforced by the science of Newton, Davy, and Lyell, with its array of material forces. The materialism of medicine, whether of insanity or of cholera, made it difficult to ascribe someone's misfortunes to sin or immorality. If it was a damaged brain or polluted water, then the lunatic or diseased pauper deserved only humane sympathy; and there were many doctors convinced it was a damaged brain. "All mental illness," wrote the surgeon W. A. F. Browne in 1837 "is traceable to the brain." By 1851, Dr. Henry Munro found no reason to differ, saying, "Insanity is wholly and primarily of bodily origin . . . the brain acting imperfectly."[97] John Conolly and William Ellis, two other medical experts, might have balked at Browne's "all" and Munro's "wholly," but their view of insanity also had a largely materialistic base, as did that of George Combe, whose Constitution of Man sold 80,500 copies from 1835 to 1847. Conolly, Ellis, and Browne admired Combe and shared both his faith in material forces and belief in universal natural and moral laws, which, Roger Cooter argues, not only made humanitarianism a distinctive feature of The Constitution of Man but helped inspire the "reformed humanitarian treatment of the insane."[98] Enlightenment rationalism had long taught that if only the fixed, certain, and harmonious natural laws governing man and society were followed, it would produce a more moral, juster, and happier world. "Vice and misery," proclaimed Combe, would not diminish if "natural laws are too much overlooked."[99]

Combe's belief in the perfectibility of man and society, if only reason apprehended the natural laws governing man, arose far less from empirical research than from his idealized vision of a more rational, humane, and juster world, a vision just as full of feeling and passion and of reason glorified as were those of the romantic radicals, whose embrace of the most ardent of feelings included the exaltation of reason. In 1812, Shelley, deep into Godwin's *Political Justice*, wrote its author and his future father-in-law thanking him for making him both "think and feel."[100] Charles Dilke, the editor of the *Athenaeum*, which campaigned against numerous social evils, confessed that although he could not agree with most of Godwin's *Political Justice*, "it made a powerful impression on me." The Unitarian barrister, essayist, and diarist Henry Crabbe Robinson also could not share Godwin's anarchist views but had to admit that "it made me feel more generously" and "directed the whole course of my life."[101] Impressive as was Godwin's grand intellectual system, with reason at its center and knowledge leading to virtue and harmony, Dilke, Robinson and Shelley were moved more by his transparent, earnest compassion and his plea for "universal benevolence" and "love of mankind." Shelley especially in turn inspired many others to feel ardently for humanity. "We can not know," declared that most compassionate of weeklies, *Howitt's Journal*, in 1847, "too much of Shelley." Shelley's feeling ran along two lines, one, an ardent love of mankind, of sympathy and compassion for the oppressed, and, secondly, a bright hopefulness in a perfectible mankind, once reason and justice had supplanted kings and priests. Lord Byron, a romantic poet greatly different in style, was, in his brilliant satire of obscurantism and prejudice a rationalist, a rationalist also full of anger at tyrants and oppressors. Many were the ways and forms in which a growing rationalism fused with romantic feeling and even with religion itself to promote humanitarianism. Even the utilitarians, so often denounced as desiccated intellects devoid of emotion, had far more feeling than their critics allowed. Charles Buller, a utilitarian himself, claimed that Benthamites had very good hearts but wanted intellect.[102] Although overstated for dramatic effect, Buller's pronouncement carries some truth, especially about their hearts. The *Westminster Review* of the 1840s defended downtrodden needlewomen, whose "wail melts us to pity," and it defended the hungry made hungrier by the Corn Law, whose "cry of want and woe" cannot be denied.[103] It attacked the game laws and the massacre of defenseless birds and, more than any other periodical, graphically depicted the cruel treatment of the insane, in four articles in the 1840s.[104] It rejoiced that poetry had become "truer to the heart" and praised Dickens's "great sympathy," Hood's "Song of the Shirt," and the "heartfelt sympathy" of the working-class poets William Thom and Ebenezer Eliot.[105] Unrelenting, too, were its attacks on the cruelty of capital punishment and flogging.[106] Alexander Bain, a biographer of James Mill and a utilitarian, argued that "Humanity is the voluntary outgrowth of our sympathetic nature."[107] Utili-

tarian M.P.'s like Joseph Hume and John Bowring cared deeply about individual suffering, whose elimination Bentham called the object of humanity.[108]
For Joseph Hume, the individual cases were many that brought forth his
protests. He lamented that a Mr. Dean had to spend four months in prison
for selling four pheasants, decried a Mr. Larkin's month in prison for inability
to pay a poor rate of a few shillings, and condemned the acquittal of Captain
Stoddard, one of the army's great floggers, who had had a soldier whipped to
death at Hounslow because he refused to mount a horse. The Hounslow flogging also led John Bowring to confess, "he could not restrain his feelings . . .
at this horrid system at which humanity recoiled."[109] Bentham himself was no
dry, arid, cold rationalist, but full of warm and passionate likes and dislikes, a
lover of animals, books, and music, and a hater of unnecessary pain. His
posthumous *Deontology* (1834) is distinguished by a warm, hopeful benevolence. There was a mixture of feeling and reason in his character. The same
was true of his fellow utilitarians. The growth of rationalism was a far more
complex development than it seems at first sight, a growth that promoted
humanitarianism, not through the advance of a pure, undiluted reason, but
by the fusion of reason with other parts of human nature, with empathy and
sympathy, and very often with religious convictions. Such a fusion occurred
with particular forcefulness in the case of Unitarians and Quakers.

There were in the England of 1851 only some 37,000 Unitarians and 14,000
Quakers, yet their humanitarian achievements were out of all proportion to
these numbers.[110] The Unitarians could boast of many great humanitarians:
Lant Carpenter, a campaigner against slavery, and his daughter Mary, second
to no one in bringing juvenile reformatories to England; Thomas Hill, founder of the Hazelwood progressive school, where there were no religious tests
or corporal punishment; John Bowring, an inveterate opponent of capital
punishment and flogging; John Fielden, second only to Lord Ashley as a factory reformer; Dr. John Conolly, a convert from Anglicanism and pioneer in
the humane treatment of the insane; the brothers Matthew and Frederick
Hill, law, juvenile justice, and prison reformers; and Dr. Southwood Smith,
that most compassionate of humanitarians, who was active in factory, education, and sanitary reform.[111] The author of *The Principles of the Human Mind*
and of *The Divine Government,* Southwood Smith espoused the empiricism
and associationism of Locke, Hartley, and the Unitarian Joseph Priestley.

The Quakers, although fewer, were no less active. Thomas Clarkson, who
in 1786 exposed the horrors of slavery, was in the 1840s busy revealing the
horrors suffered by merchant seamen. In between these battles, he campaigned against capital punishment, for juvenile reform, and for an ampler
relief to the poor.[112] His friend and fellow Quaker William Allen was just as

prolific in humanitarian activities, attacking not only slavery abroad but, along with the Quaker Samuel Hoare, child slavery in British factories. Allen also established the first society opposing capital punishment, urged improved prisons, favored better treatment of juvenile offenders, and sought a humane and progressive education for all. Working with Allen and Clarkson were Joseph Sturge and Thomas Fowell Buxton. Buxton also won prominence for exposing the suffering of the Spitalfield weavers, his desire to make prison discipline reformatory, and his relentless war on capital punishment.[113] Quaker humanity was found everywhere, in William Tuke's York Retreat for the mentally ill, in promoting animal rights, in attacks on the game laws, in relieving Irish famine victims, in Elizabeth Fry's visits to Newgate prison, and in the writing of Mary and William Howitt and their *Howitt's Journal.*[114]

The above achievements—and many more—reflect the fusion in the Quaker outlook of religion and reason, a fusion quite evident both in William Allen's research in chemistry, with its scientific regard for fact and logic, and in his life of devotion, with its daily prayer and doing of good. The Quakers' "light from within" presented an open window to the bright rays of the Enlightenment, allowing Thomas Clarkson to base his opposition to slavery not only on the "revealed voice of God" but on "reason, justice and nature." It also allowed the devout Christian Buxton to invoke "reason and equity" and Christian compassion in his condemnation of capital punishment, just as it allowed Elizabeth Fry to insist that "the holy mind is like the beams of the sun."[115] Both Fry and Buxton were steeped in the Enlightenment before being touched by evangelicalism, a fusion astonishingly productive of humanitarian efforts. The inner light could merge with the evangelicals' conscience as well as reflect the rational truths of nature just as Scripture and God's commandments could enhance the dictates of humanity.[116]

The Unitarians, less pietistic and more rational than the Quakers, achieved a less balanced fusion of reason and faith. The rational outlook of Locke and Priestley, not the mysticism of George Fox, was their inspiration, an inspiration that informed Southwood's Smith's writings. God, Southwood Smith wrote, is "a Being . . . infinite in wisdom, power and goodness" who has designed a harmonious world of universal benevolence, awaiting only the advance of knowledge and the progressive improvement of man. To this rational appeal to God's "plan of a wondrous order" and to the laws of nature, Southwood Smith added the wisdom of the Scriptures and the genuine feelings of the heart. Others were also eclectic. In her *Meditations* (1845), the eminently reasonable and empirical Mary Carpenter expressed a near mystical holiness, and in his crusade for the ten-hour day, John Fielden drew on a piety dating from his Quaker upbringing and Methodist days, which he fused with a rationalistic Unitarianism that, says his biographer, gave him "an innate faith in man's goodness" and a "commitment to freedom, to toleration . . . [and] social and political reform."[117]

Quakers and Unitarians had no monopoly on an eclectic mix of a revived religion and a growing rationalism. The radical M.P. Joseph Brotherton, a Bible Christian and vegetarian, whose humanitarianism few could rival, and Lord Morpeth and Robert Slaney, the most ardent among Whig M.P.'s for the poor and oppressed, all represented the fusion of faith and reason. Brotherton's religious convictions in no way hindered his championing of scientific education and belief in the rational truth of the laws of political economy.[118] The cheerful, amiable Lord Morpeth, who seldom missed Sunday church and often attended twice, was also at home at free-thinking Holland House. The author of *Criminals and Their Reformation*, he won respect for his humane rule of Ireland and was vigorous for juvenile reformatories, education, and laws against child labor. He opposed the Corn Law as against both "reason" and the "highest sanctions of the Supreme Being." In his educational philosophy, he sought to combine "humanizing science" with "the fear and love of God."[119] Robert Slaney, a Shropshire squire, although conventional in his Anglicanism, paternalism, and political economy, was unconventional in his consuming passion to improve the condition of the poor. In pamphlets, in his many, long and compassionate speeches, and in his arduous work on select committees and committees of the Health of Towns Association, he urged a Christian benevolence, but one that "must take the means which reflection and reason point out." And reflection and reason taught that one should not consider the reckless and improvident at fault, for they are "the children of circumstances."[120]

Reason and faith have coexisted and interacted in all ages, although in different ways at different times. In the middle of the eighteenth century, the latitudinarian rationalism of an uninspiring, arid Anglicanism met neither the psychological nor the social needs of a considerable portion of the population, needs soon met by a challenging evangelical religious revival, the success of which brought a different balance in the fusion of faith and reason. But by the 1840s, evangelicalism itself had for many become arid and uninspiring, rigid and narrow, unable to meet psychological and social needs. The pervasive growth of rationalism among Unitarians, Quakers, liberal and radical Dissenters, and liberal Anglicans brought about a fusion that, by combining a rationalism that saw human nature as infinitely improvable with the Christian belief that benevolence was God's command, greatly promoted humanitarianism. But with the advance of biblical criticism, comparative religion, and archaeology, as well as the skeptical questioning of every doctrine from atonement to baptismal regeneration, rationalism attacked the theological base of a revealed religion. More and more, Victorians began to see the essence of Christianity in Jesus' inspiring morality, a tendency that itself often promoted a more humanitarian stance. Humanitarianism also arose in some from a need to strengthen faith and dissipate doubt.

The ebb and flow of religion and rationalism and their interaction are subtle and complex. That humanitarianism assuaged religious doubt or that a strengthened morality reflected a weakened theology are risky conjectures, perhaps merely intelligent guesses. The impact on a growing humanitarianism of the accumulation of fact, of the advance of knowledge, is more demonstrable and measurable.

THE ADVANCE OF KNOWLEDGE

In 1788, the newly established Philanthropic Society for the Prevention of Crime announced that it would "collect facts" and also "appeal to reason." And collect facts and appeal to reason they did, as did their successors among the early Victorians.[121] Knowledge advanced on all fronts, in education, literacy, science, and scholarship, as well as by travel and travel books, cheap printing, and an avalanche of inexpensive periodicals and books. Scarcely a day went by, declared *Chambers' Edinburgh Journal* in 1847, without "social progress . . . especially mental improvement, hired lectures, libraries, mutual improvement societies." The Victorians from 1800 to 1900 began an estimated 125,000 different periodicals, thousands of them before midcentury. Book titles were also unprecedented in numbers, and the price of books fell on average between 1828 and 1853 from 16s. to 8s. 4d.[122] "The spirit of the age," declared the Reverend Richard Hamilton of Leeds, "is the spirit of knowledge."[123]

Science and technology led the way in the advance of knowledge. The discoveries of the scientific revolution and the constant work of multitudes of eighteenth-century and early nineteenth-century scientists and inventors astonished the Victorians. Was there anything reason, observation, and experiment could not do? Was there any field, social, economic, moral, legal, or political, that would not yield to advancing knowledge? Hardly any, replied the enthusiasts of science. Full of Bacon's faith that the inherent order in observed facts would lead to an ever-expanding knowledge, they had no doubt that the social sciences would yield discoveries as revealing as the physical sciences—that is, if only enough solid facts were collected.

The Philanthropic Society was not alone in collecting facts and reasoning upon them. In 1810, the Home Office began systematically to compile statistics on crime, and social investigators such as Patrick Colquhoun made statistical studies of Britain. The government created the Statistical Department of the Board of Trade in 1833 and the General Registry Office in 1837, with its 88 employees and 2,189 local registrars collecting facts on births, marriages, and deaths. Its chief compiler of statistics, William Farr, became, because of his shrewd and judicious handling of figures, the age's outstanding statistician.

Statistical societies also burgeoned: Manchester's was founded in 1833 and London's in 1834, quickly followed by a dozen others. The London society established the *Journal of the Statistical Society of London* in 1838.[124] Meanwhile, the volumes of papers and reports presented to Parliament grew from seven in 1802 to fifty-eight in 1850, volumes replete with facts and figures, many of which showed up in parliamentary debates, where they joined facts and figures gleaned from the press and pamphlets, facts often compiled with no great statistical sophistication. Such was the case, said critics, then and now, of the statistics concerning two conflicts central to the rise of humanitarianism, the conflict over the consequences of ending capital punishment and that over the role of ignorance as a cause of crime.

In the first of these conflicts, the effect of ending capital punishment, the proponents of its abolition presented two sets of statistics: first, that ending capital punishment for a host of offenses—horse stealing, burglary, sheep and cattle theft, rape, forgery, arson, and attempted murder—had led to no increase in such crimes; and, second, that the substantial reduction in or the total abolition of capital punishment at different times in Bombay, Tuscany, Russia, Austria, Norway, the duchy of Lucca, ancient Rome, Baden, and Prussia had led to no increase in crime.[125]

The opponents of abolition countered with statistics showing that the ending of capital punishment often led to an increase in crime. Both sets of statistics had some truth to them, because the abolitionists often ended their series showing a decrease in crime before the depression of 1841–43, while those in favor of retaining hanging often ran their series through that severe crisis, which so decisively increased crimes against property. Despite the discrepancy, it was clear that the poverty and joblessness from 1841 to 1843 had fostered crime. Poverty as a cause of crime became increasingly part of the knowledge of the early Victorians, as did the fact that hanging thieves did not deter theft.[126]

Nor did hanging murderers stop murder. When, for a period of seven years, Sir James MacIntosh ended capital punishment in Bombay, the murder rate fell by nearly two-thirds, and when the number of murderers who were hanged in England fell by 60 percent after 1836, the murder rate fell by 50 percent.[127] Similar results were reported for some eight other countries, and although these statistics fell far short of today's standards, they did increase the already growing doubt that capital punishment had a deterrent effect.

That the science of statistics was imperfect and rudimentary and often dangerously speculative, its practitioners admitted. In the first volume, in 1838, of the *Journal of the Statistical Society*, Samuel Redgrave of the Home Office declared that the statistics on crime were "very imperfect" and the source of "fallacy." Even more speculative were guesses at the number of prostitutes, juvenile delinquents, or preventable deaths in England.[128] Parliament, nevertheless, whether on the Corn Law, Ireland, or public health, couldn't get enough of statistics. "Statistics are," claimed the home secretary, Sir George Grey, in 1847, "the element of party warfare." Grey had just countered William Ewart's claim that whatever the offense for which capital punishment was ended, the number committing that offense declined. It did just the opposite, said Grey, with respect to rape, arson, and burglary. In 1849, after Ewart exposed the weakness of his statistics, Grey announced, "I did not profess to rest the case on statistical arguments."[129]

Statistics did not always support the liberals' position, not even their most cherished belief that ignorance was a cause of crime and education its remedy. Conservative journals, such as *Blackwood's* and the *Oxford and Cambridge Review*, challenged the liberals by claiming that ignorance was not a principal cause of crime,[130] a challenge made more formidable when Joseph Fletcher, in 1843, and G. P. Niesen, in 1846, noted in the *Journal of the Statistical Society* that the level of reading and writing skills of criminals was no lower than that of the general population. Their lack of education could not, therefore, be the determining factor. But by 1848, Joseph Fletcher kept the liberals' cherished belief alive by distinguishing between mere instruction in reading and writing, which was not determinative, and a moral and religious education of quality, which was.[131]

Statistics, if indecisive on ignorance as a cause of crime, were increasingly less so on poverty as a cause, and, behind poverty, disease, or even insanity. The statistical correlation of social forces grew clearer as knowledge advanced, creating a tension between the old assured morality that individuals were responsible for their actions and the new environmentalism that taught that the individual could be the victim of wretched circumstances. Poverty now assumed for many a larger role than did ignorance as a cause of crime.

The increasing knowledge of social interconnections that often strengthened the humanitarian outlook owed more to doctors than to any other group. The number of physicians and surgeons—soon to be called doctors—increased greatly in the early nineteenth century. In Scottish and foreign universities and in London's teaching hospitals, they received an improved education, a scientific one that, however limited by today's standards, taught them to search beneath the symptoms of illness for its underlying causes. They carried this same search for causes into their work in slums, workhouses, prisons, asylums, and unsanitary towns. The knowledge that medical advances brought forth elated them. For R. D. Grainger, a professor of anatomy and a Board of Health inspector, it was a knowledge that would banish "misconceptions and errors" and that was of "paramount importance," especially since it "ended the most profound evils." W. A. F. Browne, in his work on lunatic asylums, claimed that everywhere "knowledge is beginning to diffuse its cheerful light."[132]

The knowledge that so elated the doctors was often more practical than theoretical. True, they held some underlying philosophical assumptions in common. Most shared the convictions of the Board of Health's Dr. John Sutherland that it was an established truth of science that one's well-being and the duration of one's life were "connected with the laws of the universe." Many doctors also developed theories, some as fanciful as phrenology. Dr. Southwood Smith regarded it as an established truth that the cause of cholera and typhus lay in a local atmosphere full of a poisonous effluvium, a view no sounder than Henry Munro's belief that one cause of insanity was the "abnormal exhaustibility of the vital powers of the sensorium." Some theories of insanity, to be sure, did not seem so fanciful. That mental illness often took the form of "moral insanity" was a popular belief in an age increasingly earnest in its morality. "Moral insanity" was not marked by the traditional derangement of the understanding but by a derangement of the emotions, will, and morals. Popular, too, was its remedy, that a cure lay in moral management that emphasized the will's firm control, by sound habits, of the emotions.[133]

In the long run, it was not theories that promoted humanitarianism so much as practical advances that made towns cleaner and asylums more humane. Dr. Robert Gardiner Hill, in an 1839 lecture describing his successes in ending all mechanical restraint at Lincoln Asylum, told his audience that "no technical terms are needed, nothing beyond . . . good sense and benevolent feeling."[134]

Good sense and benevolence, in fact, defined the work of the leading doctors of lunacy in their respective asylums: Jepson at the York Retreat, Hill at Lincoln, Conolly at Hanwell, Ellis at the Hull Refuge, and Prichard at Northampton. It was not learned tomes on the causes of insanity that improved its treatment but the ending of chains, nakedness, and brutality, and the advent of comfortable quarters, warm clothing, nutritious food, open air exercise, amusements, libraries, and above all, said W. A. F. Browne, warm baths, which made "ferocious maniacs peaceful." Hill wanted "carpets and featherbeds," and Conolly, "every soothing comfort."[135]

Also practical in their findings, and also promoting cleanliness, good ventilation, and nutritious foods, were the doctors of the sanitary movement, who intuitively grasped that local unsanitary conditions were connected with disease. In 1797, Dr. Currie of Liverpool found typhus where ventilation was bad; in 1809, Dr. Robertson of Edinburgh found disease to be common where housing was wretched; and by 1839, Dr. Richard Howard had established illness where scarcity and distress were the greatest.[136] After William Farr, the registrar general, began compiling statistics of death, parish by parish, the connection between disease and unsanitary condition grew firmer. With the publication of Thomas Southwood Smith, Neil Arnott, and James Kay-Shuttleworth's 1838 *Report on Fever in the East End,* and Edwin Chadwick's monumental *Sanitary Report of 1842,* the fact that filthy, foul, unsanitary conditions caused disease and premature death became part of the early Victorians' expanded knowledge.[137] Doctors were active everywhere, not only at the General Board of Health, which was created in 1848, but in the more than 180 localities where the board made inquiries: at Lancaster, it was Dr. Johnston the honorary secretary of the local board of health; at Derby, the "indefatigable labours for sanitary reform" of a local surgeon; at Edmonton, "the cordial cooperation" of Mr. Hammond, "a medical man"; and at Birmingham, "many doctors."[138] Few were more forward than doctors "in promoting sanitary improvement," said Inspector William Lee; no one, said Inspector Robert Rawlinson, better knew "the utter wretchedness and want of sanitary regulation."[139] The findings and views of these doctors, along with the views of the engineers who conducted the inquiries, were widely disseminated in some 32,000 copies of local reports, 1,500 copies of the report on cholera, 6,000 on burials, and 11,000 on pipe drainage, all part of the information revolution of the early nineteenth century.[140]

Doctors sought to cure society of its illness in every nook and cranny of the realm, even in those prisons and workhouses where vengeance and parsimony and an absence of clear-cut answers made it difficult to find remedies that the public would accept. That doctors viewed the world more humanely was evident in the views of the two doctors who were prison inspectors, the surgeon John Perry and the physician Bisset Hawkins. What a contrast between their reports and those of the two army captains, Donatus O'Brien and John Williams, who also inspected prisons: the captains emphasized deterrence, the doctors reform; the captains favored keeping juvenile offenders in prisons, while the doctors urged sending them to reformatories; the doctors were against corporal punishment, and the captains were for it—O'Brien personally ordering thirty-six lashes for an errant prisoner. O'Brien and Williams praised the crank and treadmill, and Hawkins and Perry useful labor. Hawkins saw crime arising from licentious parents and poverty, O'Brien from "idle habits" and "the propensity to do evil." The doctors saw crime as a disease arising from environmental causes; the captains saw it as the wickedness of evil men.[141] In varying degrees, medical officers of many prisons shared these views, as in a different context did the medical officers of many poor law unions.

Ruth Hodgkinson, in her massive study of the medical services of the New Poor Law, describes how local medical officers throughout England fought for more ample medical relief and better accommodations for the sick, while a spokesman for the Provincial Medical and Surgical Association told parliamentary committees that since the New Poor Law, the condition of the poor, with their miserable housing, diets of potatoes and bread, and fevers of every kind, had greatly worsened. Denying that medical relief led to pauperism, they urged it be separated from the Poor Law. Orchestrating these protests in the Commons was Dr. Thomas Wakley, surgeon and editor of the medical journal *Lancet*, who was unrivaled in his denunciations of the New Poor Law and one of the most active humanitarians in Parliament.[142]

The views of the reforming doctors on prisons and the New Poor Law did not prevail, as they did, although only partially, with respect to lunacy and public health. There were no clearly successful experiments, no advance in knowledge, that could reform criminals and end pauperism, no Hanwells or Lincolns, no pure water helping to prevent cholera. The practical knowledge that arose from experience, far more than grand theories, promoted humanitarianism. Such experiences were also not limited to reforming doctors. Investigators from various professions revealed abuses and exposed social evils, just as they discovered and urged social remedies. Exposing abuse did not, of course, begin in the nineteenth century, although it occurred to an unprecedented extent. With no convincing remedy at hand, however, even such extensive revelations of suffering did not necessarily lead to reforms. Descriptions of flogging moved the emotions but ran afoul of the military's claim that it was necessary; the corruption of juvenile offenders in prisons for adults excited indignation, but for years no action; and that nearly 800 miners a year died from mining accidents made the humanitarian T. S. Duncombe, M.P., furious, but left most of his colleagues unmoved. Yet in the 1840s, flogging was greatly reduced; in 1850, the government established inspectors to make mines safer; and after 1854, juvenile offenders were sent to reformatories. Why the changes? Partly, no doubt, owing to constant, ever-increasing revelations of barbaric floggings, corrupted juveniles, and dead miners, but also in part because of the knowledge, based on experience, that these abuses could be remedied. Regiments that practiced no flogging, a select committee learned in 1835, had better discipline than those that flogged, just as, said the M.P. Captain Bernal Osborne in 1842, the Irish Constabulary and the Indian Army under William Bentinck proved very efficient, although entirely free of flogging.[143]

The success of juvenile reformatories and schools of industry also encouraged humanitarian reforms. Many and triumphant were the accounts of reformed juvenile offenders at the progressive schools at Mettray and Hofyl on the Continent, the Aberdeen School for Industry in Scotland, and in England the Philanthropic Institution, the Saltey Reformatory, and many progressive farm and industrial schools.[144] There was no easy way of avoiding successful experiments, no easy way of denying that improved ventilation and wider airways reduced a mine's explosions. The death rate in mines fell by nearly a half from 1851 to 1861. It was a humanitarian advance that Oliver Macdonagh attributed to "protracted field work, observation and comparison," particularly in those reports of the mining inspectors that "prepared educated opinion for further changes."[145] Advances in technology also diminished railway accidents, smoke pollution in cities, and losses of ships at sea.

Pervasive as was the role of advancing knowledge, one should be cautious not to imbibe the early Victorians' uncritical enthusiasm for its promises and power. Some of that knowledge was dubious or highly selective. Presumptuous, dogmatic, and disputable were the statistics on both sides in the debate on the Corn Law, Poor Law, and Ireland. One should also be cautious not to fall prey to the Whig historians' belief in the constant, progressive, and liberating advance of knowledge or the naive Baconianism that sees knowledge as springing entirely from mere observation and experiment. But one also should not react so strongly against naive Whiggism and naive Baconianism that one overlooks the dramatic growth of practical knowledge, with its myriad social revelations, its vast collections of fact, its increasingly correct use of statistics, its deeper understanding of social interconnections, and its many informing experiences, which were full of promising remedies. This dramatic growth, no less than urbanization or rising middle classes, was part of the emergence of a stronger humanitarianism.

It was, however, not always powerful enough to overcome the reigning orthodoxies of a paternalism jealously protecting its local power, a laissez-faire political economy fearful of government, and the universal worship of property. Also checking its growth were an equally universal belief in self-reliant morality and the virtues of voluntarism. Above all, it bowed to the sovereign power of vested, class, and self-interest, which also formed a very large part of the early Victorians' social conscience.

CHAPTER 12

Vested, Class, and Self-Interest

Many early Victorians feared that the ideals that inspired their social out-look were being undermined by powerful material interests: paternalists saw their ideal of property doing its duties overwhelmed by property's appetite for profits; the political economists' vision of a harmonious laissez-faire economy foundered on an unharmonious persistence of exploitation, eco-nomic crises, and poverty; and believers in the nobility of self-help found so-ciety anything but noble in providing the education so necessary for the first step. The philanthropists' ardent desire for moral reformation and the hu-manitarians' compassionate desire to remove suffering ran afoul of pervasive selfishness, deeply entrenched vested interests, and jealous and bitter class feelings.

There were more than a few Jeremiahs in the 1840s who believed that ma-terial interests had so corrupted the early Victorians as to reduce the ideals defining their social conscience to the hollow platitudes of a Pecksniff, who boasted of virtues he never practiced, or the smooth words of a Uriah Heep, whose unction covered a deep hypocrisy. Mere pretension, too, from a peo-ple whom the *Examiner* called "the most mammon worshipping people on the face of the earth."[1]

It is a charge that many journalists, M.P.'s, clergymen and novelists made, the charge that a permeating self-interest, a growing selfishness, was corrupt-ing England.

SELF-INTEREST, A SELF-INDICTMENT

The radical press led the way. "Mammon," declared the *Northern Star* in 1842, "is the God of England, Mammon is exalted on our altars and enshrined within our palaces." It was all part of what *Lloyd's Weekly* in 1847 called "The Mighty Mammon," a might that made money more powerful in England than anywhere—a place where "almost everything can be bought and sold."

In the England of 1842, announced the *Leeds Times*, "an intense spirit of self-ishness . . . pervades the entire system of society."[2]

It is not surprising that papers speaking for the unenfranchised and poor should have cried out against the inexorable workings of self-interest. The Tory press could be just as indignant. The wealthy, claimed the Tory *Fraser's*, had been "hardened" by "systematic selfishness and Mammon worship,"—so much so that the high Tory *Morning Post* found selfishness "the predominant element of our system."[3] *Fraser's* and the *Post* found this selfishness, as did *Blackwood's* and the *Quarterly Review*, largely among manufacturers and traders and in the capital of mammon itself, London.[4] But all elements, including peers with their town houses and gentry wives bargaining for cheaper millinery, made up the London that, argued John Murray of *Blackwood's*, was "Everyman for himself . . . and devil take the hindmost." But mammon, noted the *Oxford and Cambridge Review*, had also penetrated the countryside, where cottage-destroying landlords denied that they were "their brother's keepers."[5]

The Whig and Liberal press joined the Radical and Tory papers to make nearly universal the age's condemnation of inordinate self-interest: the *Edinburgh Review* denounced the "haughtiness" of the rich for "treating the poor as slaves," the *Sussex Advertiser*, the "selfishness which predominates in our legislature as well as our social arrangements," and the *Educational Times* those upper classes who, it said, were "growing every year more selfish."[6]

Members of Parliament, since they represented particular constituencies, were more particular in their charges. Rural M.P.'s condemned the grasping, mercenary, rapacious spirit of trade and manufacturing, while urban M.P.'s denounced the arrogant, domineering, heartlessness of landlords. Some Radicals did broaden their indictment by accusing the rich as a whole of oppressing the poor: the many customs and excise taxes hit the poor harder than the rich, enclosures robbed them of their rights, the Poor Law treated them "worse than dogs," and Irish landlords, after exacting every last farthing, drove them from their homes. These and many other injustices to the poor led the utilitarian Charles Buller to conclude that in Parliament, "selfish wealth had always showed its indifference to the wellbeing of the poor." It also led Robert Grosvenor to see in Parliament "the prevailing selfishness with which human nature is afflicted."[7]

As a devout evangelical, Grosvenor knew that original sin was human nature's great affliction, the source of the age's evils and corruptions. Years earlier, William Wilberforce had found not only that the rich were steeped in corruption and profligacy but so were "the whole body of the people." In Grosvenor's own time, the greatest of evangelicals, Thomas Chalmers, lamented over the "desolate tide of selfishness."[8] It is not surprising that the early Victorians' indictment of self-interest rang out from many a pulpit. The premillenarian Reverend Edward Bickersteth declared that the age was sunk in "hard heartedness and odious selfishness," while Liverpool's leading evangelical, the Reverend Hugh M'Neil, announced that "covetousness was the ruling sin of England."[9]

High Churchmen also chastised the rich. "Selfishness in all its forms," announced Henry Phillpotts, bishop of Exeter, "has usurped the empire of our heart." His fellow Tractarian the Reverend Francis Paget, in his novel of moral edification, *The Pageant,* pictures a society whose poor law is "hard-hearted," whose manufactures are "worldly-minded" and in whose "Guilty City . . . Mammon has stamped his mark on every brow."[10]

The sermons of the Nonconformists are less obsessed with the excesses of self-interest. "I have no wish," announced the Reverend Thomas Binney of the City's King's Weigh House Chapel, "to see rich men stripping themselves of their estates." Binney never declaimed against riches or self-interest in themselves, pleading that they served God's purpose, a sentiment shared by Binney's fellow Congregationalist the Reverend R. W. Hamilton of Leeds. Our lives should be governed, insisted Hamilton, by a "self-love" that is "consistent with our intellectual existence and the universal good."[11] Neither Binney nor Hamilton, nor the ministers of other Dissenting churches serving an urban and upwardly mobile middle class pictured those classes as displaying an odious and ubiquitous selfishness. But some Nonconformists, writing anonymously in the *NonConformist* and *Eclectic Review,* did broaden their indictments. In 1844, the *NonConformist* pronounced avarice "the curse of this country," and in 1848, the *Eclectic Review* angrily attacked the "selfishness which makes the earth barren, selfishness which starves the millions" and the "selfishness which dethrones the conscience."[12]

Although less persuaded of original sin than the devoutly religious, early Victorian novelists were even more graphic in their picture of a world made evil by the excesses of self-interest. Their stories abound in rogues and scoundrels and the evils of a selfish, moneyed world. Few, of course, were more masterful in exposing these miscreants than Charles Dickens in *Nicholas Nickleby, Dombey and Son, Martin Chuzzlewit,* and *Little Dorrit.* Brilliant are the portraits of the hard-hearted Ralph Nickleby, who has "no appetite except for pounds, shillings and pence," and in pursuit of them "he's greedy as a wolf"; of the cold, self-absorbed, and remote Mr. Dombey; and of the brutal materialism of Jonas Chuzzlewit, whose education began with a lesson on how to spell, first, "gain," and, second, "money." Many are the minor characters devoted to money-getting by any means, fraudulent or not, men like Twigg, the crafty director of the Anglo-Bengalee Disinterested Loan and Life Assurance Co., or *Little Dorritt's* Mr. Merdle, whose self-seeking speculations, like a plague, infect all around him.[13]

Dickens also has his benevolent characters—his Brownlows and Cheerybles—as spotlessly virtuous as his miscreants are indelibly black, but somehow they seem less vivid, less convincing, than the miscreants, which is true also of the virtuous and evil characters in the novels of Douglas Jerrald, Edward Bulwer-Lytton, W. Harrison Ainsworth, Benjamin Disraeli, Charlotte Gore, and C. P. R. James. And in the more realistic novels of Thackeray, the virtuous are few and not spotless at all. *Vanity Fair* paints an unflattering picture of the upper classes, classes vitiated by snobbery, worldliness, social ambition, and self-interest, and not even aware of the poor. Its leading character, the ambitious, crafty, dissimulating Becky Sharp is introduced as one "never known to have done a good action," while her more innocent well-intentioned friend, Amelia, neglects her friends "as such selfish people commonly do." Both are part of that "naughty London" so full of "vanity-fairians . . . of the most selfish disposition."[14]

It is perhaps less in their characters than in their backgrounds and narratives that the novelists paint a society riven by avarice. It is such a society that forms the grim backdrop for Dickens's *Oliver Twist, Bleak House,* and *Little Dorrit.* There seems no evil that does not befall Oliver as he moves from a cruel workhouse through the miserly clutches of the undertaker Sowberry to Fagan's world of crime; neither is there any manner of injustice that the fee-hungry lawyers will not commit in order to defend antiquated courts where "moneyed might [has] the means of wearing out the right." By 1857 and *Little Dorrit,* Dickens's world has grown darker, a world dominated by a passion for gain, and a world that has no Brownlows and Cheerybles.

Very few institutions escaped the early Victorian novelists' indictment of self-interest: certainly not the law, whose iniquities are exposed by most of them, nor such evils as rack-renting and evicting landlords. Douglas Jerrold, in his stage play *Black-Eyed Susan,* and David Wilkie, in his painting *Rent-Day,* show that dramatists and painters as well as novelists could expose villainy. Bulwer-Lytton in *Paul Clifford,* after denouncing "parsons who rob the poor, lawyers who do mischief, and courtiers who obtain sinecures," confesses that he is sickened by a society where men "lie and cheat and defraud and peculate." It is a society not wholly at odds with the world of Disraeli's *Sybil.*

The backdrop to *Sybil* is a catalogue of evils gleaned from government reports: child labor in mines, near-starvation wages of seven or eight shillings, filthy, fever-ridden tenements, wretched weavers, cruel game laws, and company stores that cheat the laborers. There are also manufacturers full of "avarice, meanness, cunning and hypocrisy," a part of the larger class of whom Charlotte Gore cynically observed, "the richer, the more they take account of their money." Mrs. Gore, the most popular of the silver fork school of novelists, added, with an even greater cynicism, that education did them little good, since "public schools and college life do their best to cauterize their hearts."[15]

The novelists' picture of society is not, to be sure, entirely evil; benevolence and kindness, honesty and uprightness, win out in the end. But though the virtuous often triumph, they do so only after overcoming deeply rooted evils, evils that the press, the pulpit, and M.P.'s were also denouncing—evils like the great contrast between the hugely rich and the desperately poor or wealth's profound ignorance of the life of the poor, two evils so frequently commented on that they became a cliché part of the early Victorians' indictment of the pervasive self-interest that so disfigured society.

It was an indictment that surprisingly few contested. Where was triumphant political economy? Where was Adam Smith's celebration of the fact that the self-interest, not the benevolence, of the butcher, baker, and brewer, brought meat, bread, and beer to the table? Certainly not with the age's sages. Coleridge could not abide the "new rich men" who threatened "spoilation." Carlyle lamented that "with the triumph of cash, a changed time has entered." Southey denounced the" grinding rents" of landlords and the "greedy spirit" of commerce and manufactures. Thomas Arnold called "monstrous" and "unparalleled" a society with a "population poor, miserable and degraded." John Stuart Mill judged the large profits that capital took as "unjust," and the "immense amounts" going to wholesalers and retailers "extravagant." For Mill, nothing was more universal than "the desire for wealth."[16] The indictment was massive. Self-interest was seen as a great evil—an active, damaging, sinful, ubiquitous evil. But was that indictment justified?

SELF-INTEREST AT WORK

Severe though the many indictments of it, the triumphs of self-interest in the late eighteenth and early nineteenth centuries were great. Britain's economy grew by leaps and bounds. In 1801, the country's gross national product was £138 million; by 1851, it was £491 million. The population had, of course, grown too, and prices had risen. Still, in constant prices, the per capita GNP rose from £12/9s. in 1801 to £23/7s. in 1851. Never had England known such productivity, never so many gallons of ale, joints of beef, and loaves of bread, and, as Adam Smith noted, not by the benevolence of the brewer, butcher, and baker, but by their self- interest. The national pie had tripled in size.

But was the pie divided more equally? Were the ale and beef more fairly shared? Here, there was less to boast of. Inequality rose sharply in Britain from the 1820s to the 1830s, notes the Harvard economist Jeffrey Williamson, who estimates, on the basis of the window tax returns, that in 1851, England's top 5 percent received 48.38 percent of the national income, and the top 10 percent, 56.53 percent. Williamson is properly modest about the precise accuracy of estimates based on an imperfect set of returns, but quite confident that England experienced "a surging inequality," which is also attested to by the findings of the economists Simon Kuznets and Phyllis Dean and the historians Harold Perkins and Eric Hobsbawm.[17]

Exactly how the larger pie was sliced is difficult to know. After much controversy over the question of whether British workers' standard of living rose or fell during the industrial revolution, there is some agreement that it did rise, if not by 1840, then by 1850. But the working class was huge, varied, and heterogeneous: some did well, others poorly, with not a few falling into pauperism, then climbing out as the economy lurched from crisis to prosperity and back to crisis, or as harvests failed or farmers, as winter came, sacked laborers. Unevenness was the rule, whole sections verging on starvation while others grew richer and richer, creating that great contrast of wealth and poverty that not only evoked much criticism but challenged the basic assumptions of the Victorian social conscience. Was there not, at the very roots of society, a self-interest that was corrosive of its social ideals, a self-interest at work in those thousands of individual decisions to keep wages low, working conditions harsh, and rents high, a self-interest also quick to oppose taxes for poor relief, sanitary improvements, and relief for famine-stricken Ireland?

WAGES AND CONDITIONS OF WORK

Self-interest certainly kept the earnings of agricultural laborers low. In 1827, according to Williamson, their wages were 49 percent of the average earnings of working people in general, but in 1851, they were only 38 percent of the average worker's wage. The average itself of course had gone up, but not enough, according to K. D. M. Snell, to prevent the agricultural wages in the south from falling. By 1850, Snell calculates, the wages of farmworkers in twenty southern counties fell, on average, by 21 percent. Farm wages in the north were 37 percent higher than those in the south in 1850; those in Lancashire were a robust fifteen shillings a week, compared to Wiltshire's six shillings, a difference owed less to the relative returns to the landowners than to the greater demand for laborers in a north bustling with manufactures and money. Lower wages were not the only change that hurt the farm laborer. Also greatly reduced were employment by the year, boarding with the farmer, apprenticeships, close relations with landlord and farmer, and the use of the commons; instead, there were weekly hirings, dismissals in winter, a harsher poor law, lost commons, remote landlords, and farmers who were, said a laborer, "a close fisted, hard set of fellows."[18]

The farm laborer was not alone in suffering low wages and harsh conditions. Weekly wages for adult male farmworkers that ranged from 6s. to 9s. in Wiltshire and Dorset shocked many, but so did wages of 3s. or 4s. for young women putting in a twelve-to-fourteen-hour day at straw plaiting or lace making. Even harsher was the 1s. 2d. to 3s. a week paid to boys in Glasgow's shoemaking and tobacco-spinning trades. Kitchen and housemaids made 3s. or 4s. a week, plus their room and board and uniforms, but slavelike subservience was expected of them and they endured much abuse.[19]

Conditions of work—long hours, grim workshops, tyrannical masters—were, in fact, often more oppressive than the low wages paid. Wages often rose with an industry's growing demand for workers. Navvies building the new railways could make 22s. a week, miners in some areas earned 25s., and pottery workers were paid much more than farm laborers. But railway navvies, although paid well, were exploited in other ways. Paid monthly, not weekly, and in pubs, the navvies drank and spent, fell into debt, and took loan-tickets at 20 to 30 percent annual interest, the tickets being good at a company store—the tommy shops—that overcharged and cheated. They were also housed in dismal temporary huts, notable for overcrowding, promiscuity and filth. Work was hard and dangerous. Accidents, a select committee heard in 1846, were "formidable and distressing." The same committee heard that though the majority of accidents were not the workers' fault, not a penny was ever given in compensation.[20] Sheffield grinders also received no compensation for the disease that the dust from grinding steel inevitably brought. Dry grinders, who began at fourteen years of age, had difficulty breathing by the time they were twenty and seldom lasted beyond thirty-five. Powerful fans and dust flues, which cost no more than £2, proved helpful but were used only by a few employers.[21]

Miners also suffered lung diseases, a far greater cause of death than the explosions and cave-ins that made mine work so dangerous. Dangerous, too, was the work of potters, who were exposed to lead and arsenic.[22] Parliamentary investigations not only revealed these dangers but made two things clear, first, that most employers were reluctant to improve safety if it involved higher costs, and, second, that nearly all employers opposed, and opposed successfully (because of the state of the law) paying any compensation to injured workers. Parliamentary investigations also revealed that except in mining and textiles, both regulated by acts of Parliament, child labor and long hours were as rife as ever. Some textile mills, after the Ten Hour Act of 1847, even worked children aged nine to thirteen in relays in order to work adults longer than a ten-hour day. In 1859, after thirty-six years as a factory inspector, Leonard Hornmer complained of the "systematic violation of the Factory Act." The Chimney Sweeps Act, which prohibited children from cleaning chimneys, was even less enforced, and despite the Mines Act of 1850, the *Mining Journal* in 1855 could call the working conditions in mines a "public disgrace."[23]

The power of self-interest among early Victorians was not, however, limited to a passion for low wages and high profits and an indifference to the health and safety of laborers. For countless landlords, it took the form of a desire for high rents.

RENTS

The owners of land, houses, and rent-earning property of all kinds did not fail to get an adequate slice of the expanding income. From 5.3 percent in 1801, their share had, by 1841, increased to a gratifying 8.2 percent. From 1770 to 1850, farm rents rose 100 percent. Rents, however, were not everywhere the same. According to James Caird, a survey taken in 1850 showed that rent was a "very capricious thing, often more regulated by the character of the landlord or his agent and the customs of the neighborhood than by the value of the soil or the commodities it produces." Rents, like wages, thus varied greatly. It was not always economic necessity that led to exorbitant rents and abysmal wages, but the landlords' or farmers' disposition. Tenant farmers, like laborers, often faced landlords who were "closed fisted" and a "hard set."[24] A Lincolnshire tenant farmer told the 1848 Select Committee on Agricultural Customs that his landlord "wished to have all the rent he could get," and another witness insisted that "the present state of the law favours the bad landlord." It did so by giving the tenant, if his lease was not renewed, not one penny of compensation for permanent improvements that he had made to the property.[25] To these complaints about high rents and no compensation for improvements, the witnesses added a third: yearly leases, which discouraged improvements. Other government inquiries revealed landlord self-interest at work: the 1846 inquiry into the game laws revealed how their love of hunting hares ruined many a farmer's fields, and the 1844 inquiry into enclosures showed how their engrossing of the commons and wastelands deprived villagers of their customary rights to graze a cow or a pig on the com-mons, to collect fuel from wastelands, and perhaps to cultivate a small plot.[26]

Both Edwin Chadwick's *Sanitary Report* of 1842 and the 1843 inquiry into women and children in agriculture showed rural landlords charging high rents for miserable cottages. The cottages in "nine villages out of ten," de-clared the Reverend Sydney Godolphin Osborne, were "still nothing but slightly improved hovels." Osborne was speaking of Dorset, but others re-ported on hovels that often had only one or two rooms, mud walls, and earth floors, some of which rented at £3 a year or more, a sum that cut deeply into a laborer's scanty wage.[27]

Conditions were no better for the lowest class of town dwellers. Urban rents were higher than rural and took a larger share of the workers' income, a share that seemed always to increase. In the 1790s, in Leeds, the dismal back-to-back houses took 5 percent of the workers' incomes, and by the 1830s, 10 to 20 percent. The landlords' returns on London tenements were increased by subdivision of a tenement, which allowed more and more renters to crowd in a single rental. In 1841, in the slums of St. Giles, noted the *Journal of the Sta-tistical Society*, there had been twenty-four tenants to a house, but by 1851, it was forty-six.[28] Housing, rural and urban, in an era of unprecedented popula-tion growth presented complex problems, problems not without extenuating circumstances. Difficulties in collecting rent from defaulting tenants and ten-ants who abused property can help explain, said Edwin Chadwick, the 20 per-cent return on urban housing.[29] But some landlords seemed not to face this problem. Lord Lansdowne in Wiltshire, for example, charged only half the prevailing yearly rent of £3 to £4 and provided three-room cottages with gar-dens, while in Norfolk the Reverend E. Benyon provided even better cottages, four rooms, two up and two down, and a pantry, for about £4/9s. a year.[30] The manufacturer Titus Salt provided model housing not for a 20 percent but a 4 percent return, and the duke of Norfolk supplied fine dwellings at 15 percent below the going rate. These are just a few of many examples that led profes-sional men to tell Chadwick that good housing could be provided at less cost.[31]

In an England where per capita income had doubled, where the rich were richer, where technology advanced by strides, and where inadequate wages and exorbitant rents were often not an economic necessity, there is no doubt that the self-interest of the wealthy could be grievously harmful to the lower 30 or 40 percent of society.

That same self-interest also fueled Britain's promethean economy, multi-plying its wealth, clothing, feeding, and housing its burgeoning population, and bringing wonderful inventions and amenities to its ever-more-civilized life. Self-interest thus showed itself profoundly paradoxical. A force for so much good and so much evil, it posed a formidable challenge to the Victorian social conscience, a challenge that not only faced thousands when deciding about wages, working conditions, and rents, but also the thousands who as M.P.'s or local officials, or those who elected them, would determine whether taxes and rates were lowered or raised, taxes and rates and laws that might soften the harsher face of self-interest.

TAXES AND RATES

Perhaps no passion is more universal in world history than a deeply imbedded hatred of taxes. In Britain, in the nineteenth century, at the local level, this took the form of a hatred of those local taxes on property called rates. The largest of these was the rate for the relief of the poor. In 1813, this came to 16s. 5d. a year per capita, a sum that caused a mounting chorus of protest about property being endangered and morals corrupted, a protest which remained oddly undiminished in 1831, despite the fact that the rate had by then fallen to 11s. 9d. The 1830–35 average yearly expenditure on the poor rate, given the increase of wealth, was, as a percentage of the national income, only half as great as the average for 1815–20.[32] Nevertheless, in 1834, Parliament passed the New Poor Law, partly in hope of reducing rates, and by 1847, the poor rate had fallen to 6s. ½d. Edwin Chadwick in 1849 proudly and correctly boasted that the New Poor Law, in its first 15 years, had saved English property £30 million. The *Standard* in 1842 accused the Whig government of robbing the poor of £4 million.[33] There were also loud protests by some Tories in the election of 1841 and at all times by some Radicals, but in both cases not so much against lower rates and stingier relief as against its centralization, corrupting patronage, attack on the parish, and cruel workhouses—very expensive workhouses, some said, which increased rates. In fact, the New Poor Law did lower rates, and it therefore won the support of most Tories, Whigs, and Liberals, as well as a portion of the Radicals. It became for the wealthy, declared Suffolk's John Glyde in 1852, "one of the most popular measures ever passed."[34] £30 million in savings! But what of the poor? Greatly improved in morals and paid better wages was the immediate answer of the government and much of the press. Yet farm wages did not rise, the depression of 1841–42 made thousands jobless, and there was no marked improvement—assuming there had ever been a marked decline—in morality.

The research of Ann Digby, Michael Rose, Rhodes Boysen, and David Ashworth has shown that never in the 1840s did relief given in the workhouse even approximate that given as outdoor relief, which usually constituted some 85 percent of poor law expenditure.[35] Local authorities, far more than the commissioners in London, called the tune. But local defiance of the commissioners did not necessarily mean generous relief. The local ratepayers and those that they elected were often as stingy as the commissioners. The great Andover workhouse scandal of 1846, where sparse diets led paupers to eat the marrow of the bones that they crushed for fertilizer, was but the most famous of scores of scandals whose cruelties and neglect lay far more with parsimonious guardians than the tyrannical commissioners.[36] In 1843, at Durham, parsimonious guardians, although faced with great unemployment, defied the commissioners' order to grant outdoor relief in return for a day's labor. At critical moments, they also even denied workhouse relief unless forced to provide it. Outright refusal, however, was rare. More often it was cost-cutting in every possible way: reducing allowances to the aged from 3s. 6d. to 1s. 2d.; making it harder to obtain nonresident relief in parishes not of one's settlement; hiring fewer relieving and medical officers, paying them less, giving them larger districts, and curtailing the amount of relief they could give; refusing to hire a chaplain or to support an adequate school; and, finally, implementing the commissioners' decision that there should be no sugar and milk for tea and no beef for Christmas dinner.[37] But the greatest of all cost-cutting policies was the threat of no relief unless in the workhouse. At first glance, the fact that most relief took the form of outdoor allowances suggests that the workhouse test was not so widely enforced.[38] But in fact able-bodied men constituted only a small part of those receiving outdoor allowances—a much larger share went to those widows and dependent children also listed as able-bodied. In fact, the New Poor Law increasingly relieved a smaller and smaller percentage of the jobless. The workhouse did deter![39] By 1870, four in five poor law unions had large, menacing new workhouses that frightened the poor. "The poor dread the workhouse," reported a laborer to the 1837 Select Committee on the Poor Law, "as a prison." "I'd rather be shot," added another. Henry Mayhew's vast world of London's underclass felt the same way; it was a world of widespread and often acute poverty but one with little recourse to the Poor Law. After a few months in the workhouse, a hawker told Mayhew, "Oh I hate it, I'd rather live on a penny loaf a day." Little wonder that so few able-bodied male workers received relief. Before 1834, the Poor Law had relieved more than 100,000 destitute able-bodied men annually, but in the 1840s, with a larger and wealthier population, it relieved only, writes Karel Williams, a "negligible" number.[40] Neither were the poor law authorities liberal in other ways to the jobless. Although in 1858, with trade union statistics showing unemployment at 12 percent, only 12,000 of the able-bodied jobless received outdoor relief—and in normal years only 5,300, a fraction of the unemployed so small that it justifies Karel Williams in concluding that "in the 20 years after 1834 a line of exclusion was drawn against able-bodied men."[41] •

Poor Law guardians were also resolved to limit outdoor allowances and guard against extravagant medical relief. The "parsimony" of urban guardians, writes David Ashworth, "was pervasive," a parsimony that Anne Digby also found among farmer guardians in rural East Anglia, who were vigorous for low rates.[42]

The wealthy were no less resolved to avoid high rates. Most successful in avoiding them were the one, two, or three landlords who owned an entire parish, a parish thus called "closed." Many of them either destroyed or would not build or repair cottages, since the fewer the cottages, the fewer the laborers who might become paupers and so be chargeable to their closed parish. The laborers therefore had to live miles away in "open" parishes, which had to pay for their relief if they became destitute. How widely were cottages in closed parishes demolished or left unrepaired or unbuilt? "Very much indeed," in "a great many parishes," "a great tendency," "in many small parishes," "extensively," such are the reports of five witnesses in 1847 to the Select Committee on Settlement. "The great majority of the owners of land," declared the *Oxford and Cambridge Review*, "have deliberately done all in their power to diminish their [cottages'] number."[43]

The majority of the wealthy also evaded high rates by having the smaller property owner assessed. Three-fourths of Leeds's assessment and two-thirds of Sheffield's fell on property worth £5 or less, and in Bradford, the figure was over 70 percent. The poor rate often hit the poor as hard as or harder than the rich.[44] With the national income doubling, with "inequality surging," with the rich growing richer, how did the guardians of the Victorian social conscience justify their harshness to the poor? How did the rhetoric of paternalism, philanthropy, self-help, voluntarism, and humanitarianism confront this injustice? The answer, in no little part, was to blame the poor. Outdoor relief corrupted them, made them lazy, tempted them to vice, made them surly and rebellious. Less and less prominent were political economy's wage fund and population theories, and more prominent was the need to promote self-reliance, thrift, sobriety, and industry.

The blame was almost always general and rhetorical. Inquiries that focused directly on the cause of poverty found them not in laziness but in unemployment, sickness, abysmal wages, high rents, economic crises, winter layoffs, declining craft industries, and a profound lack of education and training in skills. This was certainly the finding of government inquiries into the depressions in Stockport, Rochdale, Paisley, Nottingham, and Bolton, and into the condition of handloom weavers and agricultural laborers. It even came out in the 1837 and 1838 select committee hearings on the New Poor Law. These hearings reveal a curious juxtaposition of sweeping claims of improved morals with painful details of the poor's struggles with poverty. In their final report, the select committee nevertheless judged the New Poor Law a success, as, on the whole, did Parliament, and, increasingly, a press that had once been critical of the law.[45] The more stringent the wealthy became in relieving the poor, the more they persuaded themselves it was necessary for the moral health of the poor. "An excuse for neglect," declared Dr. W. P. Alison in 1840, was found in the widespread view that "relief corrupts." Fears of a poor law for Scotland, he called "fundamentally and absolutely erroneous," since Holland, Hamburg, and Venice all provided generous relief and had industrious populations. And were not English workers far more provident and industrious than those in Ireland and Scotland, with their more severe policies? G. W. Perry, in the *Peasantry of England,* shared Alison's skepticism of the moralistic preachments of the affluent. "Most gentry and all farmers," he quoted a laborer as saying, "think that every unfortunate creature must be a bad man." When such a sentiment became a prejudice, he observed, it "forms an insuperable barrier to its removal."[46]

Such a prejudice certainly helped inform the outlook of those M.P.'s who in 1847 opposed a more effective poor law for Ireland and in 1849 denounced an additional 6d. rate on all Irish poor law unions to assist the twenty-seven hardest-hit unions in the west of Ireland. In 1846 and 1847, the government had spent over £8 million on various well-intentioned but ill-planned programs in Ireland: public works, aid to landlords for drainage, relief committees, soup kitchens, loans to fever hospitals—all done in a faltering and often ineffective manner.[47]

In 1847, Parliament decided to make Ireland, and Ireland alone, care for its own poor and to do so by a more effective poor law. In 1849, because the poorer unions in the west of Ireland suffered the worst devastations of the famine, the government proposed to help them by means of a Treasury grant of £50,000 and an additional 6d. rate on property in all Irish poor law unions. The 6d. rate infuriated Irish M.P.'s. Ruinous and corrupting, they protested: "it would end self-reliance," was "a bonus on idleness," would "demoralize the people," "ruins character," would "dampen the spirit of the people," "weaken self-independence," and "destroy[s] self-reliance and places a bonus on idleness."[48]

English M.P.'s with estates in Ireland echoed the views of these half dozen Irish M.P.'s: Sir John Walsh declared the "industry was paralyzed," and Viscount Jocelyn that the expanded relief "discouraged exertion and self-reliance." August Stafford O'Brien concluded by issuing an appeal "for the twentieth and thirtieth time to the great principle of self-dependence." Disraeli also opposed the bill, saying it "taught the people to rely on other energies than their own," a sternly moral view that, in 1848 and 1849, led five evangelicals—Sir George Grey, Thomas Fowell Buxton, John Plumptre, Richard Spooner, and Henry Drummond—to oppose a more effective poor law for famine-stricken Ireland.[49]

It was in the self-interest of Irish landlords to keep rates low and of English taxpayers to have Ireland care for its own, a self-interest that made a mockery of Irish paternalism and English humanitarianism. It was, of course, a mixed picture. There were extenuating circumstances and there were a few caring landlords; there were poor law unions in the west of Ireland too impoverished to support the flood of destitute. But there were also better-off unions adamant against an additional 6d. rate and landlords who drove the poor from their cottages—in Kilrush Union in one year driving 1,500 from their homes, many to die. In 1847, six landlords with rents totaling £23,600 gave only £55 to the local relief committee. Exports of grain, cattle, and dairy products—the mainstay of rents—declined very little during the famine. In 1847, Irish property was still worth some £16 million, and the average poor rate was only 6s. ¼d. on the pound. Wales, with a quarter the population, spent more on its poor than did Ireland.[50]

The obsession with low rates did not only affect relief of the poor; it also inspired local opposition to sanitary improvements. "A strange and undefined dread of expense," observed the Board of Health's Inspector Robert Rawlinson in 1851, "led Macclesfield rate payers to oppose improvements." It even touched education: the Manchester Town Council voted in 1850 against a measure to establish publicly financed schools partly because it would "operate oppressively on rate payers."[51]

A passion for low rates was universal and relentless. Now clamorous and now silent, boasting of the virtues of frugality and self-help, proud of its defiance of a tyrannical centralization, and viewing low rates quite as sacrosanct as private property, it constituted a form of self-interest that insinuated itself into the early Victorian's social conscience quite as much as that more visible, collusive, and dramatic form of avarice called "vested interests."

VESTED INTERESTS

Many of those with vested interests based on their membership in a particular group or profession, in their great desire for gain, differed little from avaricious landlords and employers. It was, however, a collective, not an individual, expression, a collective expression that often transformed a seemingly private and selfish desire for gain into a public act for the good of a larger group. A vestryman opposing sanitary reform could invoke a generous regard for the local rights of fellow parishioners, while a member of the National Association of Factory Occupiers appeared to have an altruistic concern for his fellow mill owners in bravely defending their rights against the dangerous meddling of a tyrannical government. And if the vested interest was the College of Surgeons or the Church of England, their defense of their privileges and powers could become a moral crusade on behalf of the physical and spiritual health of the nation. In their collectivity, in their larger aims, in their greater power and moral appeals, and in their extraordinary numbers and kinds, vested interests exerted a powerful and pervasive influence and defined as perhaps no other force did the social conscience of the early Victorians.

That vested interests were powerful and pervasive was a widely accepted fact. M.P.'s of all parties often referred to them; the Radical Joseph Hume complaining that the landed proprietors and their interests controlled Parliament, and the Tory Gally Knight that the Whigs warred against "three great interests, the agricultural, the colonial, and the shipping."[52] Reference to rapacious landlords and greedy manufacturers were common in a Parliament that fought over corn laws and ten-hour days. For the realists, such as the Irish Liberal Richard Lalor Sheil, it was all a fact of life. "I do not blame men," he told the Commons, "for consulting their interests." He then cited landlords defending the Corn Law, manufacturers opposing the Ten Hour Bill and the West Indian planters championing a tariff on slave-grown sugar. For Coleridge, they constituted a "barbarous tumult of inimical interests."[53]

On the hustings, M.P.'s were especially frank. The Tory E. C. Cayley told his North Riding rural constituents, "I am a friend of the landed interests," while in Newcastle, where there was a hat industry, the Liberal Samuel Christie promised, "He should be anxious to forward the interests of that trade."[54] The numbers and kinds of vested interests were many, and their influence was great. They ranged from the various associations of the captains of industry and the lords of broad acres to vestrymen, apothecaries, and sextons anxious about their burial fees. "Tanners, bone boilers, brewers, saw-mills, flour mills, distilleries, engineers, and wealthy proprietors," announced the *Times* in 1852, combined to oppose sanitary reform. Earlier, it had also listed "town clerks, city solicitors, attorneys for local improvement acts, turnpike acts . . . [and] surveyors and contractors . . . pecuniarily interested."[55] These, and other, vested interests united in 1854 to destroy the General Board of Health, leading the *Liverpool Chronicle* to lament, "It is painful to witness the interference which self-interest has on the legislation of the country."[56] As widespread and potent as individual selfishness was, the selfishness of vested interests was, like all selfishness, a far more insinuating and influential force on the early Victorian social conscience than the more abstract and rhetorical appeals to class. In the words of Leed's leading manufacturer, John Marshall, "Everywhere there is a dismal civil war of clashing and selfish interests."[57]

Diverse and assorted as were these "clashing and selfish interests," the more important ones can be classified into three groups, those of the world of business, of the world of local government and local institutions, and of the world of the Establishment and its professions.

For many, the power and influence of economic enterprises, whether agricultural or mercantile, was nearly synonymous with vested interests. It was its classic form. The "battle" over the Corn Law, claimed the *Guardian* in 1846, was between the country's "two great interests," a view shared by the *Morning Post*, which pitched the "agricultural interests" against "the money jobbers who rule the House of Commons." That money ruled the Commons was also the view of *Blackwood's*. "Two-thirds of the Commons," it argued, were "in the power of the shopkeepers," a curious claim, given that 38 percent of the M.P.'s were either Irish or Scottish peers, baronets, or closely related to peers of England, Ireland, and Scotland; and that another 34 percent were gentry, making 72 percent of the House of the landed class.[58] Journals of a paternalistic outlook were not averse to an economic interpretation of society, especially since its picture of many and various interests fitted its view of a diverse, hierarchical, and propertied world of different spheres. It was natural that the owners of land, mines, ships, factories, houses, and shops should exert their full rights of property.

Economic interests were indeed powerful and more often than not did prevail. But not always. The West Indian planters, one of the most powerful of the eighteenth-century vested interests, lost in 1807 the right to trade in slaves, and in 1833 the right to own slaves. In the 1840s, they also lost the rights of extended apprenticeships and of a protected market. The factory owners, whom the *Westminster Review* called a "sinister interest," had to accept a ten-hour day in 1853. Owners of ships and mines had to yield to more than one statute regulating their industry.[59] Metropolitan builders and expanding railways, wealthier than ever, also bowed to acts of Parliament, as did the greatest of all interests, the landed, when Parliament repealed the Corn Law.

The above defeats, however, did not always go deep; nor did the power of these vested interests cease. Factory owners used relays to evade the first Ten Hour Act, that of 1847, and many mine owners took so little heed of an 1850 Mines Act that the *Mining Journal* found it "defective . . . in almost every clause." Neither did the General Shipowners' Association, a powerful vested interest, find the passenger acts particularly bothersome; nor did mild sanitary laws hurt slum landlords or builders.[60] All of these interests continued powerful and prosperous, although none as dramatically as the railway interest.

In 1845, the English went mad over railways. By October, they had invested in 813 schemes registered with Parliament and in scores more not yet registered. Each scheme was submitted to a private bill committee both in the Commons and the Lords, in the hope that it would become an act of Parliament giving the company the power to acquire land and to manage its new railway largely unchecked by government. There would be no government planning or supervision as on the Continent. So indifferently did the various private bill committees treat the Railway Department's review of each scheme that Peel, undiminished in his faith in laissez-faire, had the reviews discontinued.[61] The field was now wide open for the uncontested rule of vested interests.

Although the result was a British railway system with many glorious features, its financing and construction were chaotic and not without considerable pain and much dishonesty and fraud. Most acute was the pain caused by the panic of October 1845. The bubble had burst. By December, 549 of the 813 registered schemes had collapsed. Many more would follow. At every level, an insatiable greed had been exploited on a grand scale by amoral lawyers, cunning financiers, and swindling adventurers. Thousands of the duped lost their life savings; many went bankrupt and some to the debtors' gaol. Ruined financiers fled abroad or committed suicide. Many of the middle classes now suffered the harshness of capitalism so often experienced by the lower classes.[62]

A second consequence of the uncontested rule of vested interests was the persistence of those private bill committees that made railway promotion costly, corrupt, inefficient, chaotic, the prey of vested interests, and the subject of prolonged battles. The act creating the Great Northern Railway, which passed on the same day that the Corn Law was repealed (and which was for many more important), constituted the most prolonged and costly battle in railway history. The committee promoting the scheme included ten peers, thirty-two M.P.'s, and powerful local men, and was chaired by Edmund Denison, M.P. for the West Riding of Yorkshire. The cost of promoting the act was £432,620.[63] Offers of money, shares, and sham directorships won the support of landowners, capitalists, and local politicians, many of whom testified before the private bill committees, men who, according to the *Railway Times*, showed "no fixed principles" in supporting a report "generally at variance with common sense, equity, and justice." Still angry five months later, the *Railway Times* denounced these committees as "incompetent" and "the seat of every species of illegitimate influence."[64] It was a judgment sustained by knowledgeable contemporaries; to Gladstone at the Board of Trade, they were "lavish, extravagant and discreditable." But the criticism availed little against share-holding M.P.'s and peers or with M.P.'s, like Edmund Denison, Charles Russell, and George Hudson, who were chairmen of railway companies. Hudson, in fact, managed four railways. "He wielded," observed a contemporary "an influence in England unparalleled and unprecedented."[65]

The consequences of a system of clashing vested interests were not always happy. It meant, for one thing, that the Great Western Railway laid down its rails seven feet apart and the other companies in what became the standard gauge of four feet eight and a half inches, an anomaly later corrected at great cost. Costly, too, was the passage of railway acts—if contested, they never cost less than £100,000. By 1860, English railway companies had spent £30 million on parliamentary business.[66] It left them starved of capital for the actual building of railways and made English railways far more costly than those of Belgium, France, or the Germanies. It left George Hudson so heavily in debt that he resorted to unwise and illegal speculations, falsifications of accounts, and payment of dividends from capital, all of which spelled ruin.[67]

Once established, these railways became one of the most powerful of vested interests, successful in weakening and evading government regulations. There were railway acts as there were factory, mining, prison, lunacy and passenger shipping acts, but all of these acts were exceedingly chary with powers of enforcement. Gladstone's attempt in 1844 to check exorbitant fares and profits was made impotent by amendments that struck out over half of the bill's clauses, a defeat that Gladstone attributed to railway "engineers, directors, solicitors and agents who filled the lobbies soliciting members' votes." M.P.'s did succumb, said *Fraser's*, noting that "the RAILWAY INTERESTS can whip up 300 M.P.'s." In 1852, the *Times* declared that the railway directors' "pecuniary interests . . . [had] entirely severed them from the rest of the community," and in 1853, it found railway services "extremely defective" and fares "exorbitantly large."[68]

The railway interests were not alone in lobbying Parliament. In 1850, the *Liverpool Chronicle* announced that "all existing interests opposed the Merchant Marine Bill," and it cited shipowners, captains, mates and the Liverpool Chamber of Commerce.[69] An act was passed, but a weak one. The early Victorians were far more alive to social abuse than their forefathers and far more willing to legislate. But in legislating, they retained a deep faith both in the power of persuasion and suggestion and in the merits of a large area reserved for laissez-faire and voluntarism. It was a faith not yet shaken by repeated failures to make improvements. Reformers were not yet fully aware of the power of the vested interests both of business and of local government and local institutions.

LOCALISM

Of infinite variety and with deep roots in both the past and people's affections, local governments and local institutions formed some of the most ubiquitous and influential of vested interests. To more than 15,000 parishes, 5,000 J.P.'s, some 200 chartered towns, and 53 counties, all with their thousands of vestrymen, overseers, church wardens, constables, mayors, aldermen, councilmen, and bailiffs, were added 1,800 local act authorities—improvement commissions, paving, lighting, cleansing and watching boards, highway and turnpike trusts, and sewer commissions. Many were the local residents honored by an appointment to these august boards: in Dover, 105 citizens became pavement commissioners; in Great Yarmouth, 113 became improvement commissioners; and in the metropolis 1,015 would-be solons sat, speechified, voted, and banqueted on eight commissions of sewers. The average highway trust numbered around 100.[70] These were honors and dignities not to be lightly given up or subordinated to central control.

They also gave one power, although often more to resist change than to reform. At first sight, the many acts that created prison, lunacy, poor law, education, health, and charity inspectors, and that gave them some power to advise local governments, appeared relatively effective, but in fact many were so circumscribed that the local authorities retained their essential sovereignty. Indeed, these acts often strengthened local government: 550 new poor law unions and 182 new local boards of health added more, not fewer, powers to local government. In the 1850s, boards of guardians were still defying the Poor Law Commission. And local visiting justices of prisons and of asylums were often just as defiant of prison inspectors and lunacy commissioners from London. Local jealousy, wrote the prison inspector John Perry, was so widespread that despite the entreaties of the inspectors, no prison would unite with another, each fearing the loss of its precious patronage.[71]

The multitude of local authorities formed a labyrinth of confusing and conflicting jurisdictions, some of little use, many extravagant, and almost all opposed to any consolidated plan for improvement. Such problems certainly plagued efforts to achieve a cleaner, less diseased England. For each service—drainage, paving, cleansing, nuisance removal—there was a separate authority. Three hundred boards ruled the metropolis. One parish had five paving commissions and three lighting and cleansing boards.[72] Despite much patronage, many jobs, and long meetings, they did little to reduce England's scandalous death rate.

From 1811–20 to 1831–40, the death rate increased nearly 10 percent nationally, and in Bristol, Leeds, Birmingham, Manchester, and Liverpool it rose 50 percent.[73] Although the sanitary reformers mistakenly thought that a polluted atmosphere, not polluted water, was the main cause of disease, they did include polluted water among the conditions that made a locality unhealthy. Purer water in fact helped in the distinct improvement in the public health made by the 182 new local boards of health. In some of the unhealthiest working-class areas, these boards reduced a yearly death rate of 30 in every 1,000 to 20.9 in every 1,000. If all England had experienced the same reduction, 70,000 lives a year would have been saved and the average lifespan would have been 48, not 29.[74]

But it was not to be. In 1854, responding to an array of vested interests far more formidable than the humanitarianism that underlay the sanitary movement, Parliament abolished the General Board of Health, amid a chorus of abuse of centralization and praise of local government.

Many of the hostile interests were at base economic. Private water, gas, and cemetery companies and their directors, employees, and shareholders wanted no interference in their affairs and no limits on their profits. Landlords, large and small, wanted no improvements that would raise rates or cost them money. Many, too, were the polluting trades—the tanneries, brewers, and distilleries listed by the *Times*—who were adamantly against all regulations; and builders were just as firmly wedded to laissez-faire. These companies, landlords, and builders employed and contracted for services of engineers, surveyors, lawyers, architects, and parliamentary agents, all of whom they enlisted in their battles.

Also enlisting jobbers, engineers, and lawyers in their battles were local authorities, the sewer, paving, and improvement commissioners; the vestrymen of the parish; town mayors, aldermen, and councillors; county J.P.'s, poor law guardians, turnpike trustees, and many others. In numbers and influence, they were potent; and even more so when allied with the Church of England and myriad voluntary institutions. This alliance proved strong enough, when joined to economic interest, to overwhelm the General Board of Health and to occupy a large place in the social conscience of the early Victorians.

Samuel Finer and R. A. Lewis, in their biographies of Edwin Chadwick, and Royston Lambert, in his study of Sir John Simon, spell out in convincing detail how these vested interests defeated the metropolitan water, burial, and sewerage improvements planned by the General Board of Health and then abolished the board itself. In 1852, a disconcerted Lord Harrowby told the Commons that "the vested interests were in the ascendant." Lord Derby, the leader of the Tories, did not deny it. "Existing interests," he confessed, "had to be taken into account." Lord Derby and the Tories, briefly in power in

1852, had passed a weak act that allowed London's privately owned water companies to continue their monopolies. The companies continued to fail to provide a constantly flowing supply of pure water at reasonable prices.[75] Although economic interests largely undid the board's water schemes, it was the pride and jealousy of the local authorities that undid the board's plans to cleanse England and fight cholera.

Local pride and jealousy also proved the bane of the Poor Law Commission and the Home Office. Great was the enjoyment of office, power, and status of local officials, even the most petty. It was an enjoyment shared by many, and one that, when fused with a powerful and deeply rooted local patriotism, could even override the passion for low rates. Some towns preferred their own improvement commission, one created by a local act of Parliament that was far more expensive than a local board created by an order in council of the General Board of Health. And compounding their extravagance were the actual works done by their local commission, works far costlier than if done under the supervision of the General Board of Health's engineers.[76]

A jealous regard for independence certainly defined the City of London, that square mile of financial wealth, sanitary squalor, and medieval government. With a revenue the envy of all England, with handsomely paid officials, and with a Common Hall, a Court of Aldermen, and a Common Council distinguished by endless oratory, elaborate ceremonies and celebratory banquets, its participants felt themselves the apotheosis of local virtue and honor. That the City's mortality was well above the national average, that its overcrowded graveyards, open cesspools and piles of refuse smelled of putrefaction, and that its foul water spread cholera, in no way inhibited the City's mission as the leading defender of local government and leading foe of centralization.[77]

Just as furious against centralization as the City were the Tory squires in Parliament. Since they represented rural areas and were less involved with sanitary evils, not to mention water companies and slum landlords, their localism was more purely political. But the Tory squires' hatred for Whig commissions and boards was not therefore less entrenched. He "hated central commissioners," announced Oxfordshire's Joseph Henley; he was "opposed to every kind of commission," insisted Devonshire's Lewis Buck; and Lincolnshire's R. A. Christopher declared that "centralization is the greatest evil," a sentiment the irascible Colonel Sibthorp, his fellow Lincolnshire M.P., concurred in, denouncing commission after commission, since he "much preferred the old system." For the Henleys and Sibthorps, the old system was the "parochial system," from which they should never have departed.[78]

Support of the parochial system meant opposition to the Public Health

Act, which not one Tory squire among the twenty-four most vocal in the debates of the 1840s supported. They believed that an expanding central government threatened those spheres that were indissolubly a part of a paternalist hierarchy.[79] So did the paternalist press, the most vocal of all against centralization. In 1834, the New Poor Law had evoked from the *Albion, Courier, John Bull, Standard,* and *Morning Herald* angry denunciations of centralization, and thirteen years later, the last three were still unrelenting in defending local government from the same evil. The *Standard,* after calling the Public Health Act quackery, asked, "How much farther are we to go with this centralization?" "We are for corporations against bureaus," announced *John Bull,* condemning the Public Health Act for striking at "that local vitality which [made] England and Englishmen what they are."[80]

Paternalists of an ecclesiastical bent in particular saw the tightly knit parish, whose self-contained, proud, inward-looking mentality gave rise to the term "parochial," as the centerpiece of society. A Christian bulwark against secular and centralizing forces, the parish taught morals, ministered to its parishioners, and improved society. It was a mentality that also infused those charities, visiting societies, hospitals, and schools so integral to the voluntarists' outlook. The advocates of nearly 30,000 charities—archaic, anomalous, and often grossly inefficient and corrupt—defeated centralizing bill after centralizing bill, settling in 1853 for a watered-down act that created charity commissioners with inadequate powers.[81] Great too was the clamor against "centralization" by Nonconformist voluntarists in 1847 as the Committee in Council on Education gave out larger and larger grants—over four-fifths of them—to Church of England schools. High Churchmen wedded to their parish schools joined in the outcry against this "Prussian" centralization, a cry that also opposed any suggestion of a national, rate-supported system of education.[82]

Localism found a fertile soil not only in the paternalist and voluntarist outlooks but in the civic pride of growing towns, where the laissez-faire and self-reliant outlooks flourished. Lord Palmerston who as foreign secretary made the sovereigns of Europe bow to his will, had in 1854, as home secretary, to bow before delegations from Liverpool, Manchester, and York. He withdrew a police bill that would have increased the Home Office supervision of borough police forces. The bill was too centralizing, as were proposals in 1839 that would compel counties and large boroughs to establish police forces under Home Office supervision. All that could be passed in 1839 was a permissive act authorizing the establishment of county police forces, whose regulations and chief constables need be approved by the home secretary only if the county so desired. There were no great economic interests involved, or even, as with resistance to the Poor Law, much jobbing and party factionalism, but there was much civic pride. John Bright of Rochdale observed that he had "a very excusable attachment to the old forms of local government." It was a sentiment as deeply rooted as hatred of higher rates and underlay the power of localism as a vested interest.[83]

Hostility to centralization came in many forms and harbored both sins and virtues; it left much undone but also did much that was admirable. Centralization also meant different things to different people. The clearest definition came from John Austin, professor of jurisprudence at the University of London, in the January 1847 *Edinburgh Review*. Centralization was not excessive government, proclaimed this Benthamite, still fearful of government, but only government whose local and central authorities are better coordinated. Austin's was a lonesome voice. Far more popular was the view of the unrelenting opponent of the General Board of Health, Lord Seymour, who said in 1854 that centralization was "the interfering with everything and everybody."[84] That was the fear of thousands, a fear exploited by the London barrister and antiquarian Joshua Toulmin Smith, whose many pamphlets in the 1840s and 1850s denounced centralization, exalted local government, and expounded a constitutional theory underlining both. There was, Toulmin Smith argued, a law of local self-government, part of a "fundamental law that was superior to Acts of Parliament," a law dating from the Old English folkmoot, or popular assembly, of King Alfred's day and reaffirmed by Magna Carta and the Petition of Right. Whig commissions and central boards and inspectors not only violated that fundamental law but undermined the local self-government that was all that stood between English liberty and Continental despotism. Toulmin Smith hated above all the General Board of Health, the pure embodiment of centralization, which was only "communism in another form."[85] Full of fictitious history and gross distortions, his arguments fitted John Stuart Mill's claim that centralization was a subject of "unreasoning prejudice." Yet Toulmin Smith was published and praised in the Peelite *Morning Chronicle,* and his pamphlets were distributed by the City of London.

Fear of centralization could also, J. S. Mill added, be the subject of "rational disapprobation."[86] Mill's own rational disapprobation was furthered by reading de Tocqueville's *Democracy in America* and expressed itself in an article in the April 1836 *London and Westminster Review*. Many visits to France and much study of European monarchies had persuaded Mill that highly centralized governments blunted the vigor and intelligence of citizens. In his *Political Economy* of 1848, he found that "in proportion as all real initiative and direction resides in government, there is a perpetual tutelage." Toulmin Smith was quick to use both judgments in his pamphlets.[87]

In Toulmin Smith, John Stuart Mill, and many Englishmen, the question of centralization blended confusedly with a fear of overgovernment. For many, centralization meant too much government, as in Lord Seymour's "interfering with everything and everybody." It was an association that often overlooked the meddling of local authorities.

But were local authorities "government"? For the most passionate lovers of local authority, not really, not truly. For them, government meant central agencies and Whitehall bureaucrats. Parishes and towns, county J.P.'s and improvement commissions were all part of that world of local institutions, like hospitals and schools, and almshouses, that had deeply entwined themselves into the affections of the people. As *John Bull* said, "We prefer corporations to bureaus."[88]

Such local corporations when allied, as they often were, with local economic interests, formed a vast and bewildering array of vested interests, all powerfully influencing the early Victorians' social conscience. Different in kind but no less a vested interest was the national Establishment, whose institutions—Church, law, Parliament, the military, universities, public schools, and professions—had long and powerfully defined social attitudes.

THE ESTABLISHMENT

Jeremy Bentham wrote often of "Judge and Company" and their baleful influence on English law. In his *Church-of-Englandism and Its Catechism Examined* (1817), he also considered the Church an entrenched part of the Establishment. Lawyers and clergy were among the "sinister influences" that Bentham found so harmful. So, in 1842, did *Punch,* which caricatured "the o'er fatted Bishop [and] the Croesus of costs, the lawyer . . . each a social evil doer." Army and naval officers were also part of the Establishment—eighty-three of them sat in the Commons.[89] Even the fellows of the Royal College of Physicians, all of whom had to be graduates of Oxford or Cambridge, prided themselves, as did university dons and professors, as being part of the respectable professions, professions that constituted a vested interest of no little influence.

These various members of the Establishment had three characteristics in common, (1) they belonged to exclusive and privileged hierarchies, (2) in performance they had striking shortcomings, and (3) they were generally hostile to reform.

That the Church and military were exclusive and privileged hierarchies both proudly confessed. "We are," said the bishop of Chester, "a distinct order of men, a peculiar people, set apart." Lord Cardigan, lieutenant colonel of the Fifteenth Hussars, felt the same, although only of officers of aristocratic background and high rank.[90] From bishops to curates, from generals to corporals, everyone knew his place, just as solicitors did when serving barristers, who could alone argue cases in court, or apothecaries when they met one of the 168 fellows of the College of Physicians or a member of the powerful College of Surgeons, who, along with physicians, monopolized the crucial positions in London's ten teaching hospitals. Some 5,230 curates, whose average pay was £81 a year, did most of the visiting and much of the preaching for rectors and vicars who received far more and many of whom were nonresident. Fellows and licentiates of the College of Physicians, only 5 percent of the medical men, made far more than apothecaries, who made up three-quarters of those practicing medicine.[91] And although solicitors on occasion did well, as in the railway mania, they never, on the average, equaled the incomes of barristers. In only a few short years, exclaimed *Douglas Jerrold's Shilling Magazine*, they earned three-quarters of a million pounds![92]

Entry into the exclusive realms of clergy, law, physicians, and commissioned officers went to the privileged and well-connected, not necessarily the ablest and best-educated. To become a barrister, one needed only to join one of the four Inns of Court, eat a certain number of dinners, and sit at the feet of a barrister, for whom they did some work. Graduation from Oxford and Cambridge, where no medicine and little theology were taught, plus some elementary questions answered in Latin, led to both the clergy and to the College of Physicians, while a lieutenant colonelcy in the cavalry went not to the skilled and experienced but to aristocrats wealthy enough to purchase a commission. "The officers were," writes Gwyn Jenkins in *The Army and Victorian Society*, "part of the ruling class . . . closely linked to . . . that class through ties of kinship, shared educational experiences . . . and a mutual wish to preserve the status quo."[93]

Once in their profession, the clergy, barristers, officers, and physicians could and did learn their respective arts, although by no means always fully and well. Almost all, however, did enjoy the fruits of a closed, privileged world. Even solicitors, because of the arcane and mystifying nature of the law, could join "Judge and Company," just as thousands of clergymen—the poorest curates excepted—did enjoy either the incomes, tithes, fees, and pew rents of 10,540 benefices and the ease of scores of cathedral appointments. Such was not the fate of regimental officers, those men of no connection but much experience, who actually trained and led the army, but who saw aristocrats of no real abilities gain through purchase and favor promotions and decorations that they were denied.

The second characteristic of these privileged professions, a striking shortcoming in performance, flowed in part from a lack of rigorous requirements for entry. "The defect of the enacted law and the failure of many solicitors," concludes the legal historian William Holdsworth, "is a reflection of an imperfect system of legal education."[94] The same could be said of the clergy, physicians, surgeons, and officers in the Army and Navy. The Army, which was to prove its bravery more than its skill in the Crimea, was ill-managed and ill-directed. Lord Worsley, looking back on the Crimean forces, judged them "completely ignorant of the art of war" and served by an "incompetent staff of officers." To *Punch,* the Army was "the most enormous job" and its officers "selfish, brutal and busy fighting duels and seducing women."[95]

The medical world, despite the conscientious work of many general practitioners, was not free of quackery. There was, according to the *Lancet,* "a whole army of quacks and high quackery." In an age when medicine was developing a scientific basis, such quackery, along with ignorance and incompetence, could have been reduced by strict examinations and licensing. But such did not exist. There were also no government regulations, no one to check the monopoly practices and high fees of the College of Physicians and College of Surgeons. Surgeons and physicians who made as much as £8,000 and £10,000 a year would, to the outrage of the *Lancet,* collect another £5,000 to £6,000 from struggling apprentices as payment for four or five years of hospital supervision.[96]

High fees and high costs—cannibal costs to *Punch*—were, of course, the hallmark of the lawyer and a principal reason for lawyers' unpopularity. "No other institution," confessed the *Law Magazine,* was more often blamed for "pecuniary injury." But high fees were, the *Law Magazine* added, necessary. The public, it said, simply did not understand how complicated and difficult the law was. The public's doubts were not allayed, and the law was denounced for its endless delays, useless technicalities, confusion of jurisdictions, and archaic practices, such as granting a few sergeants-at-law a monopoly in arguing cases before the Court of Common Pleas.[97] From Bentham's view that lawyers were full of "sharp-sighted artifice" to Dickens's picture of Dodson and Fogg in *Pickwick Papers* as "the sharpest of the sharp," the literature of the day pictured no profession more corrupted by self-interest—unless one turns to the highest dignitaries of the Church.[98]

One of the favorite targets was Henry Phillpotts, bishop of Exeter, who, having spent thousands to move his palace a hundred yards, then spent £3,000 for further improvements. He had in his cathedral, said the *Western Times,* "a pew twice as big as his state coach while the poor stood in the back." Other bishops also spent thousands on their palaces, using money, as Exeter had, from the very Ecclesiastical Commission that was supposed to distribute the Church's wealth more fairly. But according to Joseph Hume, in 1850, that Commission gave £128,000 to bishops and only £93,000 to the rest of the clergy.[99] To the public, the payment of tithes, fees of all sorts, pew rents, and Church rates to a Church already wealthy in endowments and property revealed a mercenary Church, a view heightened by stories of corruption in ecclesiastical courts and charitable foundations.

The shortcomings of the Church, law, military, and medicine were colorful and dramatic and enlivened the press and literature of the day, as they have many histories since. But they should not obscure the day-to-day useful work of an average clergyman, lawyer, doctor, and officer—nor those whose conscientiousness and talents brought distinction to these professions, often of a selfless and idealistic nature. There were doctors who attended to victims of cholera, law-reforming barristers, curates dedicated to the poor, and able, self-taught colonels. But admirable as was their work, they could not prevent these Establishment professions from forming a vested interest largely inimical to reform—the third characteristic.

Military officers' opposition to reform was unwavering. An Army that made no effort to abolish flogging, end the purchase of commissions, develop professionalism, and improve the dreadful lot of the common soldier also had the power and the friends to defeat any effort at reform from Parliament. The Navy was no better. William Williams told the Commons in 1847 that sailors were "the most oppressed and worst treated body of Her Majesty's subjects . . . and treated with a degree of cruelty unequalled in any other country."[100]

The College of Physicians and the College of Surgeons also made little effort to adopt that system of education, examination, and licensing that would end quackery. They also blocked parliamentary efforts at reform. From 1840 to 1856, 17 reforming bills fell prey to these proud, unreformable physicians and surgeons.[101]

The lawyers did better, but only marginally. The solicitors' Law Society created lectureships and examinations, while many judges and barristers did help Parliament reform some parts of the law, but the reforms were small and piecemeal. Not until the 1875 Judicature Act did the Victorians substantially reform their costly and cumbersome machinery of justice and its archaic procedures.[102] The *Law Magazine* in 1840 both realized the need for and yet feared reform. It criticized the high fees and monopoly privileges of the sergeants-at-law, found the arrears of the Queen's Bench appalling, denounced useless sinecures, and wished the law more simply stated. But in 1841, it also judged "bad" the past five years of law reform, defended the game laws, found fault with Lord Campbell's bill for Chancery reform, condemned the bankruptcy reforms, because they threatened the role of lawyers, and called the 1841 Local Courts Bill "the result of grievance mongers." It declared that the Chancery, the estate-swallowing monstrosity of Dickens's *Bleak House*, was for some purposes, "the most effective tribunal . . . it is possible to devise." The *Law Magazine* in 1849 was quite candid as to the cause of its mixed responses: "It is one thing to determine what reforms of the law ought to be and another to ascertain what reforms are practical."[103] A greater candor would have persuaded the editors to add "and reforms that left vested interests untouched." Never, it announced, should Parliament encroach on the powers of J.P.'s or force the Inns of Court to give examinations.[104]

The men of the law, like the men of the cloth, thought of themselves as "men set apart." They, too, had their ideals of fairness and justice, and they deeply believed that they served the public good, which some did. Service to the public good and pursuit of their vested interests became so mixed that the latter took on a more attractive attire, one more immune from criticism.

A mix of public good and private interests was certainly true of the clergy's resolve to be the teacher of the nation. It was both a selfless and self-aggrandizing effort; selfless, certainly, in that outpouring of energy and money needed to be the nation's teacher; but self-aggrandizing in the eyes of Nonconformists, Catholics, and rationalists. The ideal way, according to ardent Anglicans, for the Church of England to become the schoolmaster of the people was for the state to provide it with the necessary money, but with no, or very few, strings attached. The Factory Education Bill of 1843, with its Church-dominated but rate-supported schools, was an approximation of this ideal. But its defeat before a flood of hostile petitions, editorials, speeches, and pamphlets made it clear that in an England half of whose worshipers were non-Anglican, it was not a feasible ideal.

A second option, a pure voluntarism with no role for the state, formed the ideal of a large proportion of the Nonconformists and a significant number of High Churchmen. But unable to raise even a sliver of the needed money, the second option floundered on that nemesis of voluntarism, want of funds. A third option was a partnership of state and Church, one that was established in 1839 and 1840, in which the state helped with modest grants accompanied by modest strings, the strings being a Committee in Council on Education whose inspectors could visit and report on those schools receiving aid. The Church drove a hard bargain. It won for the archbishop of Canterbury the right of consulting on, and if necessary, vetoing, the appointment of inspectors of Church schools. It also won the right to issue religious, and to confirm all general, instructions. The Church also insisted that grants go only to schools that could raise an equal amount of money, a requirement that excluded the poorer districts with the greatest need. The Church made its own catechism the core of its religious instruction and religion the core of its modest secular instruction: reading (and even geography) was taught by the Bible.[105] It was the best approximation to the ideal of the Church as teacher of a nation that could be won. It was an option that became entrenched in the 1840s and 1850s as larger and more numerous grants strengthened the Church's role, but it was an option that failed to educate the nation.

Even though the government after 1847 gave large grants to supplement the salaries of schoolteachers and to train pupil teachers, the Church's National Society schools fell short of providing an adequate education to those requiring it. "The National Society," declared the Reverend Richard Dawes, founder of the excellent King's Somborne school, "has been a national deception . . . retarding the cause of education rather than advancing it." The voluntary system had been tried, announced the Reverend W. F. Hook in his 1846 pamphlet *On the Means of Rendering More Efficient the Education of the People*, "and has failed."[106] The reports of the Anglican education inspectors support both Dawes and Hook. Their reports emanate gloom: "deplorable teachers," the average stay at school only one and a half to two years, only one in six can read correctly, "dirty and squalid," "apathy of the country gentlemen," and, above all, "great deficiency of funds," "the rich don't give," and "want of funds growing worse and worse."[107] Hook in his pamphlet urged rate-supported schools with religious instruction given separately according to one's faith. Hardly any Churchmen supported Hook's plan, nor did they support W. J. Fox's 1850 Bill that advocated a similar plan. Only 58 M.P.'s voted for Fox's bill to 287 against.[108] The Church of England could command far more votes than any other vested interest. It would, of course, deny that an ancient and national Church established by law was a vested interest. Yet with nearly half of churchgoers on Census Sunday in 1851 non-Anglican, with much of the working class indifferent or alienated, and with freethinkers of all sorts multiplying, Anglican believers were not a majority. They had become a vested interest, a fact that made their insistence on being the nation's teacher an insuperable barrier to any effective solution to the education problem.

The Church even obstructed part of the sanitary movement. In London and northern cities, the Church still buried corpse after corpse in parish graveyards that were already overcrowded. In Leeds, in 1842, the Reverend W. F. Hook declared the parish graveyard full. In 1844, the town council opened a new suburban cemetery, with 22,000 of its plots set aside for the Church of England. Anglicans, but not Dissenters, were to pay the Church what they wished. But Hook wanted a shilling for every burial, Anglican or not, and continued burying 2,000 a year in a parish graveyard already overflowing and did so until he won higher fees. The Church in London was no less resolute in defense of burial fees, even though its graveyards were no less full, a fact that led Lord Palmerston in 1853 to call them "a disgrace to a civilized community."[109]

Vested interests whose goals were idealistic and made sacred and hallowed by tradition and religion were quite as insinuating and compelling as the material ones. What Anglican could deny the injunctions of the Church's ordained bishops? What Dissenter could challenge the pastor's invoking of infallible scripture? Certainly not William Gladstone, Lord Ashley, or John Bright. Gladstone and Ashley, Victorian earnestness and humanity personified, could rise above the most powerful of material interests—a mercantile Gladstone taking on the railway interests, a landed Ashley opposing the Corn Law—but both were in the 1840s unwavering in their insistence that the Church of England be the teacher of the nation. From the Quaker John Bright, in 1847, arose a loud cry against any education that was not purely voluntary. More than two decades later, Bright's and Gladstone's Liberal Government established a ratepayer system of primary education. The difficulty had been religious, Bright remembered, and arose not from the public but from "ministers of religion, not with any wrong intention, but because their eye was directed so much to . . . one great object."[110]

A parochial loyalty to a particular faith moved leading Anglicans and Dissenters. It constituted an idealistic vested interest far more subtle and persuasive than the lobbying of railway companies or protection societies. The Church of England, of course, being unrivaled in wealth, power, and privileges, had the greatest influence.

Soon engineers, architects and other emerging professions also joined the Establishment, each with its jealous regard for their learning, privileges, and petty powers, each willing to oppose reforms that encroached on its interests and all able, with considerable dexterity, to interweave their own concerns with the age's emerging feelings of class, feelings that Karl Marx, having just moved to Soho, saw as the main determinant of a society's social consciousness.

CLASS INTERESTS

For Marxists, a society's dominant ideologies are a reflection of the interests of its dominant classes, and the classes in turn a reflection of its modes of production. It is a model that Marxists and some non-Marxists have applied to the England of the nineteenth century. After three centuries of urban and capitalist growth and political and intellectual changes, the diverse ranks and orders of society began to coalesce into upper, middle and working classes, each with its own identity and consciousness. By the 1840s, E. P. Thompson, Asa Briggs, and Harold Perkin have argued, a working and a middle class had emerged to confront the landed or upper class.[111]

But the Victorians themselves did not quite see it in so Marxist a way. The Victorians held neither a simple nor a consistent view of "class" but views that were complex and varying. There were, however, amid these different views, three rough-hewn models that won considerable support: (1) that there were many and various classes, (2) that there were the rich and the poor (or propertied and unpropertied), and (3) that there were roughly three classes, lower, middle, and upper. The first two were inheritances from the eighteenth century, the third somewhat new, not well formed, and usually referred to by the plural as the "middle classes" and the "working classes."

The first view, that there were many and various classes, was the most widely held. From the Radical W. J. Fox's references to the "various classes," which included journalists, the military, the law, and the clergy, to the Tory Sir James Colquhoun's "the various classes and interests," most M.P.'s and journalists, like most of the English, saw a multitude of classes. The *Economist* even considered both West Indian planters and anti-slave philanthropists as classes. It was a pluralistic world, as the world of the eighteenth century had been, and like the latter, it was hierarchical, although rather less so. The "orders" and "ranks" of the eighteenth century had become the various classes and interests of the Victorian age. George Porter's "every class touches on that below . . . the tradesman the journeyman" is not unlike the Reverend Robert Vaughan's "the gradations of society are nicely marked."[112]

That these various gradations were no longer as linked to one another formed the lament of the paternalists. Lord John Manners, at a Young England gathering, decried the fact that the separate classes were not as in the past united. They constituted instead a multiplicity of "interests."[113] Few terms occurred more frequently in parliamentary debates and political editorials than "class interest," a term that reflects a very widespread identification of class with interests making the analysis of class overlap that of vested interests. But as universal and powerful as was this model, it sometimes yielded to the simpler, although just as old, model of rich and poor. It certainly did in the endless sermons of the day, as well as in editorials decrying both the growing gulf between rich and poor and the failure of the rich to help and to know the poor. It also underlay a popular economic interpretation of politics, namely, as Lord Grey declared, that there was one law for the rich and another for the poor, or as the *York Herald* argued, that "the rich too often legislate for themselves." Thomas Arnold declared that the rich and the poor formed "two distinct classes" and that the distinction constituted England's "real plague spot."[114]

In 1842, the *Spectator* spoke of three classes, the higher, the middle, and manual laborers. The concept is not often seen in eighteenth-century periodicals, but for Victorians, it was increasingly familiar. The Whig Sir William Clay told the Commons of the upper, middle, and "humbler classes"; the Peelite William MacKinnon of the upper and middle classes and "the poor"; and the Tory Philip Bennet of the "three great classes."[115] *The Spectator*, Clay, and MacKinnon all spoke of the middle and upper (or higher) classes, but none of them of a working class as such. Nassau Senior declared that society was divided into "three classes, labourer, capitalists, and proprietors of natural agents,"[116] and the triumph of political economy, with its economic triad of labor, capital, and land, did much to promote the concept of three classes.

But even more important was the actual increase in the numbers, power, and consciousness of the middle classes. "We are all aware," wrote Thomas Arnold, "of the middling classes." "We are far more middle class," declared the *Congregational Year Book*, "than a century ago"; and the *Edinburgh Review* said that "the real characteristic of English society is the extent, wealth, and power of the MIDDLE CLASSES."[117] A pride in the middle classes grew with their numbers and powers, a pride greatly promoted by the growing strength of Nonconformity. "The middle classes are more intelligent and educated than ever," wrote the Congregationalist Robert Vaughan, delighted that "no country in history had a larger middle class." From the Nonconformist *Patriot* and from the *Leeds Mercury*, edited by the Congregationalist Baines, came a view of the middle classes as "the most influential part of the community" and the source of "the domestic virtues—economy, forethought and the spirit of association."[118]

Strong in numbers, increased literacy, and activity, the working classes also made themselves felt, but not as effectively or self-consciously. The emergence of powerful and self-conscious working classes in Victorian England would ultimately lead, however, to the winning of the vote in 1867, the full development of trade unions, and the founding in 1900 of the Labour Party, whose roots lay in the process that E. P. Thompson so brilliantly describes in *The Making of the English Working Class*, but whose maturity came later than he asserts. Early Victorian England was the age when the middle classes emerged to claim partnership with the aristocracy, an age of 1832 Reform Acts, Corn Law repeals, a self-reliant ethos, and an uncontested capitalism.

There were, to be sure, some in the 1840s who spoke of the "working classes." In the Commons, they came from all parties: the Tory Edward Cayley, the Whig Robert Slaney, the free traders George Villiers and Mark

Philips, and the Radical Joseph Hume. Outside the Commons, *Blackwood's* and *Fraser's* used the term, but infrequently, and most of the press not very often.[119] W. F. Hook used it at a meeting on the ten-hour day, but seldom if ever in a sermon, nor did other Anglican divines. John Stuart Mill in 1836 praised the "working classes" for their advancing intelligence, but not many shared that optimism or used that term.[120] The workers themselves began to use the term, however, a sign of a growing working-class consciousness. The four decades of economic crises and political repression after the outbreak of the French Revolution increased their bitterness, a bitterness all the greater when high stamp taxes shut down their newspapers. In 1831, during the Reform Bill agitation, radical workers formed the "National Union of the Working Classes," and in 1834, many trade unions marched in support of the Tolpuddle farm laborers unjustly transported to Australia. That the Reform Act denied them the vote, the 1833 Factory Act the ten-hour day, and the New Poor Law outdoor relief only fueled an anger that erupted in Chartism. Chartists such as Ernest Jones, Bronterre O'Brien, and Julian Harney preached class struggle, while Feargus O'Connor in the *Northern Star* addressed "Letters to the Working Classes."[121]

The term "middle classes" had also emerged. But oddly enough, it was not very prominent, even in the Corn Law debates, although it did dramatically appear when Richard Cobden asked Sir Robert Peel in 1846 to govern through the "*bonafide* representatives of the middle class." Outside Parliament, writers such as Lord Brougham, John Stuart Mill, William MacKinnon, Edward Bulwer-Lytton and the Reverend Ralph Wardlaw, a Congregationalist from Glasgow, saw in the middle classes the center of intelligence and conscience.[122]

But for others the middle classes merged with the concept of the "higher," the "upper" classes, that large, many-layered category most often called the "rich" or "wealthy." The model of society that informed many educated early Victorians was not the triad of working, middle, and upper classes but a society of rich and poor, and, within that dualism, a multiplicity of gradations. Talk was less of class than of the people, the landlords, the farmers, the laborers, servants, and paupers, or of manufacturers, shopkeepers, operatives, and the destitute. The Bible itself and the many who preached its messages, spoke endlessly of the rich and the poor, as did M.P.'s and editors of every persuasion, and the latter did so far more often than they did of classes, working, middle, or upper. Such class terms are not only strikingly absent in the speeches and writings of the three greatest champions of factory reform, Lord Ashley, Richard Oastler, and John Fielden, but also absent in the speeches of the Radicals Thomas Wakley and Joseph Brotherton and the Chartists' friend Thomas Duncombe.[123] "Working classes" is also a term absent from the reports of select committees concerned with those who built railways, dug coal, and unloaded that coal in London, that is, of workers who thought of themselves as "navvies," "pitmen," and "coal whippers." Radicals like William Cobbett, William Lovett, and Jacob Holyoake made little use of the term "class," since their battle was with landlords, cotton masters, a corrupt and repressive government, a privileged Church and law, and fundholders and the moneyed men—a battle fought on behalf of the many, the people, the poor and distressed, the farm laborer and handloom weaver, overworked children and women in mines, paupers, and oppressed taxpayers, all of whom were denied their God-given rights as free-born English.[124] Few had a precise sense of class. The Chartist Feargus O'Connor certainly did not. In the *Northern Star,* he wrote on "The Industrious Poor of the Middling Classes," including therein tradesmen, although later he spoke of shopkeepers as "another class."[125]

O'Connor was not alone in his confusions; many early Victorians did not have a clear view of the classes that were emerging in a society in transition. The old hierarchical ranks and orders, whether in a landed community or a mercantile town, had not yet yielded to the horizontal groupings of distinct working, middle, and upper classes. As a result, the early Victorians enjoyed neither the more definite hierarchies of the eighteenth century nor the working-middle-upper triad of Edwardian England. Although there was no widespread sense of three distinct classes, there was much talk of "class legislation," of a law for the rich and a law for the poor, and even of a class-ridden society. Disraeli pronounced it "an age when all social evils are ascribed to the operation of class interests."[126] The *Northern Star* declared that the "greatest evil is class legislation." Even the Tory *Fraser's* and *Standard* declared that the "greatest evil is class legislation," and that when men act "as classes [they] act selfishly." The response of the *Leeds Times* was more vigorous; it called "the system of class legislation monstrous."[127]

Those who condemned class legislation were not always specific, but when they were, they pointed to game laws, enclosures, settlement acts and the Corn Law, all products of a landlord-dominated Parliament.[128] That enclosure gave landlords new land, that a parish settlement kept rates low, that the Corn Law kept rents high, and that game laws gratified the landed were part of their "class interest." But powerful as the rural landlords were, they were still one of many classes. Manufacturers were another class, and they pushed their legislation, as did shipowners or London bankers. It was still a pluralistic world, one filled with many classes. It fitted Sir Stafford O'Brien's paternalist world in which, on the new railways, all classes, "peers and peasants travelled together." It also suited the *Times,* which wrote of "those classes which form the substructure of society."[129] Among those many classes, the *Standard* singled out hosiery workers as "yet another class subjected to the money power," while the *Spectator* talked of the "helpless classes," that is, "rural agricultural labourers, milliners, shirtmakers, domestic servants, and oppressed governesses." For *Chambers' Edinburgh Journal* these workers add up, not to a working class, but to "the miserable classes." For Henry Mayhew, who rarely used the term "working class," workers constituted a vast and vastly various world of costermongers, crossing sweepers, bargemen, coal heavers, vagrants, street artists, and many, many other groups of striking diversity.[130] The *Christian Teacher* called juvenile delinquents "this neglected class," and Lord Ashley described lunatics as "this unhappy class." There were, said the *Patriot*, "different classes of clergymen," just as there were, for Disraeli, "those various classes that form what is called the agricultural interests." All were part of a diverse world of many classes, each with a particular interest.[131]

These diverse interests collided with each other, bitterly and often. The early Victorians knew class conflict, plenty of it. But it was less a conflict between a self-conscious working class and a well-defined middle class, or even between these two classes and an aristocratic class, than between particular interests, interests at times called "classes," as if the terms were interchangeable. "New interests have sprung up," wrote the *North British Review*, and "new classes of men."[132] Cotton operatives fought the cotton lords for shorter hours, the farmer fought the landlord for lower rents, the northern pitmen fought the mine owners for the right to form a trade union, and the costermongers the police for the right to sell on the street. England was a myriad of class struggles, struggles so often lost by the "helpless" and "miserable" classes that to speak of "the oppression of various classes" would be more accurate than to use the term "class struggle." Shirt makers and agricultural laborers could no more take on flinty contractors and tight-fisted farmers than navvies or women and children in lace making, straw plaiting, and a host of other small trades could overcome their all-powerful employers.

The early Victorians not only had a sense of many different class conflicts but, before Marx, their own sense of the importance of the mode of production, modes they knew as "interests." In the epic debate on the Corn Law, references to the landed and manufacturing interests, to landlords, farmers, agricultural laborers, and factory operatives predominate. And quite popular was the simple "cotton versus corn." Such references far outnumber those to a middle or working class. Neither, in the 1840s, did economic debates in Parliament deal so much with classes as with bankers, shippers, railway companies, joint stock enterprises, handloom weavers, frame knitters, hop pickers, London bakers, and many other particular modes of production, the basis of what the flax king John Marshall called a "war of clashing selfish interests." "Great," announced James Grant in his *Newspaper Press* "are the number of weeklies which are the organs of class interests"; and he then cited *The Railway Record, The Builder,* and *The Farmer.*

Was it not, then, the self- and vested interests of individuals and economic groups—of ratepayers for lower rates, millocrats for lower wages, and landlords for higher rents—and not the loyalties and values of landed, middle, and working classes that defined the early Victorian social conscience? At first glance, yes. But a deeper look reveals that, as many early Victorians knew, there was, at least, a rather homogeneous landed class, an elite, an elite often loosely called the aristocracy. As Thomas Arnold made plain, "when I speak of aristocracy I always mean the whole class of gentlemen and not the nobility."[133] It was a landed elite, many of whose younger sons, as gentlemen, had no rents to defend, no lands to enclose, and no game to preserve, but who nevertheless stoutly defended game laws, high rents, and enclosures, and did so from a sense of loyalty to and shared values of their own class. These loyalties and values, along with aristocracy's long history of social superiority, its wealth, and its dominant privileges gave it a cohesiveness other classes lacked. A privileged boyhood on a large estate, spartan years at a public school, and then Oxford, Cambridge, or the Army were the common molds for the shaping of a landed governing class that many held in awe and that made up two-thirds of the Commons and nearly the entirety of the Lords. Their class outlook formed a dominant part of the Victorian social conscience. It was preeminently a paternalist outlook, one first learned on the estate, at gatherings of the tenants, at occasions of hospitality, perhaps with acts of kindness to the poor—building good cottages, granting allotments, providing Christmas beef and ale. Paternalism was also learned from a father who as J.P. concerned himself with crime, prisons, highways, and poor laws. The estate was a small kingdom, hierarchical, deferential, based on a mystical sense of land's superiority and full of affecting ceremonies. Its paternal duties and virtues were preached from the pulpit, extolled in novels, and bred into the young heirs of England's broad acres.

Upbringing in the Church and in Anglican schools and universities only furthered in young gentlemen both a superiority and authoritarianism that bordered on the callous and a conservatism rooted in an undying attachment to the Establishment. The authoritarianism of the landed classes could be formidable, at times cruel. The duke of Richmond, in so many ways a model paternalist, had a severe side. As postmaster general, he insisted on capital punishment for those who stole letters, and as a commissioner of Pentonville Prison, he insisted on separate confinement and the treadmill. As a landlord, he dismissed laborers who frequented beer shops. The earl of Cardigan, in no way a model landlord, flogged and court-martialed his men and dueled with rivals for the most trivial reasons. And although exposed in the press, denounced in the Commons, and tried in the Lords for killing a man in a duel, he was nonetheless declared innocent by fellow members of his landed class. The earl of Lucan evicted hundreds from his Irish estates, the duke of Sutherland thousands from his Scottish ones, and numerous lesser landlords a great many for various and many reasons.[134]

None of western Europe's landed classes (except Russia's) countenanced so much flogging and birching, but then none had public schools in which both masters and student prefects birched pupils and bullied underclassmen. It was a system that not only bred much violence but furthered an authoritarianism first bred on the landed estate.

It is not surprising that the landed in both the Commons and Lords urged separate confinement and the treadmill or crank labor. Even the benign Whig Lord Lansdowne pled in the Lords for a punishment that would deter by "a degree of severity short of absolute cruelty." In the 1844 debate on prison discipline, not one peer was critical of separate confinement. Neither, in the 1840s, did any peer besides the earl of Stanhope criticize the severity of the New Poor Law's workhouse test.[135]

Also deeply ingrained in the outlook of the landed class was a conservatism whose love of the status quo underscored its indifference to social abuses. In the 1840s, the House of Lords initiated not a single social reform. Neither did most of the country gentlemen representing the rural counties. A suspicion of legislative action permeated the House of Lords. "One can not legislate," exclaimed the bishop of Exeter in 1844, "on the evil of prostitution." "There can be no legislation on sanitary matters," announced the duke of Buccleuch, since there "is not yet sufficient evidence." For Lord Melbourne, it was not only skepticism of legislation but, says his biographer David Cecil, the fact that social reform "bored him."[136] For a generation raised on Burke and Coleridge, act of Parliament reform was suspect. The Tory Lord Londonderry even pronounced the 1842 Mines Act excluding women and children from mines, a "rash and hasty alteration."[137] The Lords then forced the Commons to lower the age for excluding boys from fourteen to ten years of age. The Lords also killed bills prohibiting the use of boys as chimney sweeps and dogs as pullers of carts, as well as a bill guaranteeing tenants compensation for improvements. "They are utterly destroying," declared the Hull Advertiser of the Lords in 1847, "the Irish Poor Law Bill." The Lords also "expunged," complained Thomas Wakley, the clause in the Inclosure Bill compensating the poor who lost their cottages. They were quick to expunge, as they did the provisions for financing education in both the 1833 Factory Act and the New Poor Law. With twenty-six bishops in their midst, the peers, almost all good Anglicans and friends of an exclusive Church education, voted 222 to 118 against a Whig plan in 1839 to create an Education Committee, thereby forcing the Whigs to create it by an Order in Council.[138]

In the Commons, county members were no keener for social reform than the Lords; they too desired harsh prison discipline, defended military flogging and capital punishment, wanted no compensation for tenants or evicted cottagers, opposed any education that was not Anglican, and had doubts about the sanitary movement, attitudes that for many of them did not reflect their self-interests so much as the views of their class, views groomed in their estates and schools and furthered at an Oxford and Cambridge where, observed Lord Normanby, a dull and empty classical education drove them to "sport and dissipation." The only general rule of action that they learned, Normanby added, was "rank in society, the respect of our fellows."[139]

There was, of course, a new seriousness in the 1820s and 1830s at Oxford with the Noetics at Oriel and the Tractarian Movement and at Cambridge with the "Apostles," but none of its devotees, the Noetics' Thomas Arnold and the Apostles' Frederick Maurice excepted, dedicated themselves to the removal of social evils. Religious truth and error was their preoccupation. A few did learn from Nassau Senior at Oxford and George Pryme at Cambridge about political economy. "The young tyro who comes fresh from Mr. Senior's excellent lectures on political economy," declared Lord Ashburton, "carries all before him in the House of Commons."[140] Political economy's intellectually rigorous laissez-faire doctrines thus dovetailed with a deeper, laxer, live-and-let-live rural laissez-faire to underscore the landed class's conservatism and indifference to social reform.

The outlook, style and dispositions of the landed class, a class nurtured at university, school, and estate and anchored in an Establishment that included Church, law, the Army, and Parliament, encompassed many more characteristics than noted above. In its preoccupation with rank and its love of "sport and dissipation," it developed its own code, its own way of dress, its distinct gradations, even such niceties as the proper way to address a letter. It was a code and outlook that gave the landed class a greater unity than the more diverse middle and working classes.

For a while, during the great Corn Law debate, the middle class did assert an identity, not so much in reference to itself as in its attack on the aristocracy, an attack full of class bitterness, a bitterness with wider roots than mere vested interests. Both sides, of course, claimed that the other side acted from self-interest; a desire for cheap bread and low wages inspiring the manufacturers, and a desire for high corn prices and high rents the landlords. But in fact wages did not fall because of repeal, and neither did rents collapse; nor was it actual self-interest, so much as class enmities, that informed their grand meetings, thundering editorials and endless, bitter debates. The Anti-Corn Law League's collapse after repeal, wrote F. M. L. Thompson, the historian of England's nineteenth-century landed society, showed that there was no longer "any prospect of a middle class elite peddling a general bourgeois ethic." Instead, sufficient numbers from the middle classes were seduced into the aristocrat's "charmed circle" to prevent any challenge to the landed class from "a counter-elite." It was a seduction, wrote Lord Normanby, that many wanted. "The inferior ranks," he observed, "rush onward to mingle and confound amongst the first . . . all are pervaded by the same aristocratic feeling."[141] A large segment of the middle classes aped the manners and outlook of the landed elite, including its Toryism. "The English nation," wrote Lord Campbell in 1841, was "determinedly Tory, not only the peerage, the Church and the land . . . but the commercial and professional men."[142]

There was considerable truth in the Whig Lord Campbell's lament, but it was not the whole truth. Some of the new wealth did go Tory, seeking gentility in the purchase of a coat of arms and a country house, but significant as such parvenus were in the aristocracy's co-option of the ranks below them, they constituted only a part, and the lesser part, of that diverse, sprawling, heterogeneous mass of journalists, solicitors, clerks, shopkeepers, actors, innkeepers, manufacturers, East Indian merchants, bankers, Dissenting ministers, schoolteachers, and a hundred more callings, that lay between the landed elite and the lower orders. There was no common mold, no common experience of landed estates, public schools, and universities to shape the outlook of these various groups. They varied in every way, even regionally. The puritan ethic of the industrial towns bore no great resemblance to the bohemian world of London journalists, artists, victuallers and nouveaux riches. Charles Dickens, whose novels map London's many-layered middling classes as precisely as Henry Mayhew does London's lower classes, seldom, if ever, refers (as Mayhew also does not) to a middle or a working class.

Quite different from London's middle classes were those of the industrial towns of the north, less sprawling and multifarious, with fewer classes, but nonetheless classes that were varied and complex. The classic and oversimplified picture is of a proud middle class, its wealth gained from industry, its religion Nonconformist, its politics Whig-Liberal, in conflict with an oppressed, radical working class. But recent historians, like Anthony Howe, Patrick Joyce, John Garrard, Richard T. Trainor, and G. R. Serle have shown a more complex picture. Many industrialists, for example, in such Lancashire towns as Preston, Bolton, Blackburn, and Bury were connected with landed families and were Tory in politics and Anglican in religion.[143] Birmingham also knew substantial Tory, Anglican, and gentry influence, as, to a lesser extent did Bradford. Other West Riding textile towns, like Leeds, on the other hand, were Whig-Liberal, Nonconformist, and fairly independent of the landed interest. Religion was a divisive force; being Anglican or Nonconformist was often more important than one's class. Yet in these northern towns, industrial wealth did lead to the creation of urban elites, which dominated the towns' politics, culture, and philanthropies. Almost all the M.P.'s from Lancashire came from the middle classes.[144]

Although, in the 1840s, these urban elites differed in many ways from London's multifarious middle classes, and from the middle classes in the ports and the watering places of the south, there were three experiences that, in different degrees, they all shared and that had a somewhat similar impact on the early Victorian social conscience: first, they all confronted the privileged and sometimes arrogant aristocracy; second, they experienced more intensely than did the aristocracy the religious and moral revivals; and, third, by frugality, forethought, and industry, many of them had achieved considerable success, an experience that deepened their belief in self-reliance.

Some emulated the ways of the landed elite and yearned to join the ranks of gentility, but many more resented the landed elite's overbearing, arrogant, and importunate ways. In the Commons' debates on game laws, military flogging, chimney sweeps, law reform, the Law of Settlement, Irish famine, and the Corn Law one finds in the speeches of middle-class M.P.'s a compassion for the distressed that is joined to a resentment of the aristocratic authors of that distress—a class jealousy that inspired stern lectures on virtue from the northern press and jocular satires in London's *Punch*.[145]

The many ranks of the various middle classes read religious and moralistic periodicals, many evangelical, but some Broad Church, Unitarian, or Quaker. This was largely a movement of the middle classes, although one that impinged on the aristocracy and challenged it to become more respectable and moral. The morality of the religious revivals could, however, be as hard on prisoners and paupers and as indifferent to the overworked and underpaid as it was charitable in its visiting societies and philanthropies.

The third experience, success through virtuous industry, made the social consciences of many of them harsh and demanding. Their own (or their father's) hard-won success and elevation in society simply strengthened their belief in a rigorous self-help individualism. It is in such ways that these similar experiences of the middle classes had a "class" influence on the early Victorian social conscience.

The equally many-layered and regionally diverse working classes also had some experiences in common. They ranged from suffering miserable wages, long hours, and economic crises to the endurance of a severe paternalism and political oppression. Many also experienced an upward mobility and a hard-won respectability, experiences that helped bring workers together, although neither as firmly as the Chartists claimed nor nearly as firmly as the cohesion that occurred within the elites of industrial towns or among the merchant princes of the City of London. Still, the working classes were a reality, in multiplying numbers and huge concentrations, in an increased sense of its own identity, in large meetings and mass petitions, and in a radical press and societies for self-improvement and self-help. But workers were largely voteless in parliamentary and most local elections and barely represented in the most influential periodicals, in Church or chapel, or in the world of philanthropy. After the fall of Chartism, they withdrew to their friendly societies, new model trade unions, Owenite communities, newspaper rooms, working-men's colleges, temperance societies, and local protests against the New Poor Law and long hours.

In the 1840s, many felt that the working classes posed a threat. In April 1848, after Paris, Vienna, and Berlin had fallen, talk of revolution increased, rising to a pitch before May 10, the day of the mammoth Chartist meeting at Kennington Common. But after a cloudburst washed away the meeting, the landed and middle classes resumed a complacency that was disturbed neither by the continuation of the harsh Poor Law, which saved millions in rates, nor by the exploitation of women and children throughout agriculture and in all manufacturing except textiles.

No great impact could also come from working classes that still largely saw government as the great evil, a government supposedly full of spies, and sine-curists, guided by priestcraft, determined on repression, and dedicated to high taxes and profligate spending. Hardly any saw in education grants, industrial regulations, law reforms, sanitary legislation, and even the Poor Law's educational and medical programs, the beginning of a welfare state. Neither did the other classes urge the expansion of such a state. They also considered government an evil. It was the great paradox, the great riddle of the early Victorian social conscience, that the very growth of a government that lessened social evils more than did paternalism or philanthropy was so vigorously opposed.

PART IV

The Role of Government

CHAPTER 13

Government a Vast Evil

Nothing improved the well-being of the early Victorians more than Britain's vigorous capitalism. The political economists' invisible hand—the self-interest of brewers, butchers, and bakers, among others—had bettered the lives of millions; and no advice was wiser than that of practicing a vigorous self-reliance. But as prodigious as was capitalism's creation of wealth and as wise as were the admonitions of self-help, painful and widespread social grievances—many the offspring of capitalism itself—refused to go away. Paternalism and philanthropy did, to be sure, mitigate these evils, but however generous and successful their efforts, the grievances remained stubbornly widespread, a nagging and persistent blot on the early Victorian social conscience.

A capitalism not always benevolent, a self-help unable to cope with economic crises not of its making, a paternalism mostly rural, patchy, and often ineffective, a philanthropy more zealous and diffuse than focused and lasting, and a humanitarianism often more compassionate in poems and paintings than in effective legislation, all this left unsolved and persistent the worst social evils. Bewildered and disconcerted, more and more early Victorians saw few solutions for these unrelenting social ills other than the intervention of the government, which greatly displeased the many who found "government itself a vast evil."

There were few indeed who saw much good in government. For its milder critics, it was vexatious, mischievous, bungling, and too prone to meddle; for tight-fisted critics who held fast to their pocket books, it was costly, extravagant, wasteful, and rapacious; for lovers of English liberties, it was despotic, tyrannical, and dictatorial, as well as crafty, corrupting, and priest-ridden; and for the deeply pious, it was a government of near infidels. Their complaints formed a compendium of the evils of government that can be divided into three categories: (1) oppressive and unjust, (2) costly and corrupting, and (3) inept and unwise.

GOVERNMENT AS OPPRESSIVE AND UNJUST

It was the working class who suffered the most from an oppressive and unjust government, and it was their spokesmen—Chartists and Owenites—who complained most bitterly. Government's "crafty, dishonest acts," declared William Carpenter in the *English Chartist Circular*, lead to "oppression and extortion" and prove Tom Paine's dictum that "government in its mildest form is evil," a sentiment also expressed by Julian Harney in his *London Democrat*. Harney attacked "blood stained kings . . . tyrant aristocrats, . . . persecuting priests . . . and monstrous poor laws," all part of a government he later described as all barracks, bastilles, police, and enclosures. What constitutes history, asks Thomas Cooper in the Chartist epic poem *The Purgatory of Suicides*, but a constant struggle for liberty against despots and their hirelings, base priests, corrupt judges, and war-mongering generals?[1] It was a struggle, proclaimed England's leading Chartist, Feargus O'Connor, between freedom and despotism, and against a government of the "grasping, selfish and unprincipled," of men who substantiated Paine's famous claim that "government is the art of conquering at home." So deep ran O'Connor's hatred of government that he called the Education Committee a "miserable abortion," opposed the income tax as "a monstrous injustice," and denounced rural police, Whig centralization, and "all regulation of the hours of adult labour." That an income tax on the rich would relieve the burdensome indirect taxes on the poor, and that an education committee, the regulation of labor, and a good police would greatly benefit the working class, meant little to O'Connor, so deep was his obsession with an oppressive and unjust government.[2]

Owenite socialists shared, if more mildly, O'Connor's obsession. Owen himself had little faith in any government beyond a paternalist rule within a village community.[3] Neither did his disciples, although they were often more severe in their criticisms. George Holyoake, for example, in the *Movement*, condemned England's paternal government as "most degrading"—a tyranny composed of a "well flogged" Army, a "semi-savage" Navy, "brutal" revenue officers, and "a vast system of demoralization," a view shared by the Chartist Goodwin Barmby, who in his *Prometheus* lamented "the persistence of despotism and tyranny, the result of kings and class legislation."[4] The radical economist and journalist Thomas Hodgskin added that government was "profligate, poisonous, corrupt and rapacious," all part of "the shackles of paternalism." Hodgskin condemned government and called the system of taxation "monstrous."[5]

Popular Radicals had every reason to see government as oppressive. It formed an indelible part of their experience, both personal and from reading and hearing of past oppressions. It was an experience of countless unfair indirect taxes that weighed heavily on the people, of a brutal military, foul jails, workhouses, and asylums, and law courts and magistrates that were lenient to the rich and harsh to the poor. Forgetful that England was the freest of countries, working-class Radicals exaggerated these evils, but not by much. Owenites were imprisoned for blasphemy, Chartists for sedition, trade unionists for organizing and editors for selling unstamped newspapers. Magistrates imprisoned for the slightest offence, for playing cricket on Sunday, for not going to Church, and for begging. A huge war debt made heavier by the 1819 return to gold (whereby good pounds repaid the loan of inflated ones) was paid for, as the popular William Cobbett never wearied of proclaiming, by taxing articles consumed by workers and not by taxing the incomes of the rich. Nearly three-quarters of the revenue came from customs and excise taxes on such items as bread, soap, candles, windows, sugar, tea, and coffee.[6]

There were also the martyrs of a persecuting Church, part and parcel of an oppressive and unjust government. In 1842, the Baptist John Thorogood of Leicester and William Baines of Braintree sat in jail for their refusal to pay a Church rate for the repair of Anglican churches in which they never worshipped, while scores of others endured and resented the Church of England's appetite for tithes, property, fees for pews, burials, and a host of services, as well as fines imposed by ecclesiastical courts for a host of minor offenses.[7] And vivid and melancholy to witness were the brutalities in the Army and Navy—with their press gangs and floggings—and the wretchedness of prisons and workhouses, brutalities, which led Thomas Hodgskin, Douglas Jerrold, and many others to resolve to make war on an oppressive government.[8]

It was a war made harder to wage through the press because government imposed stamp taxes that made newspapers too expensive for most workers. Courageous Radical publishers such as Henry Hetherington and William Carpenter nevertheless published cheap, unstamped newspapers and were imprisoned for their efforts, leading one Radical to denounce the "brute force of government."[9]

The brute force of government had deep roots in the memory of working-class Radicals, memories of repressive laws and persecuting trials during the period of the French Revolution and during the postwar economic crises that followed. Working-class Radicals remembered the Peterloo massacre, the "Six Acts" against sedition, persecuting trials, acts outlawing public meetings, and acts declaring their publications seditious or blasphemous.[10] Most difficult would it be for a working-class radicalism formed in this period not to see government as anything but oppressive and unjust.

It was also difficult for the Radicals of the 1840s not to view the nearly sovereign rule of England's more than 5,000 J.P.'s as oppressive and unjust. Thousands endured squalid jails for poaching, vagrancy, begging, drunkenness, blasphemy, and other trifling offenses. The penalty was typically only a fine, but inability to pay it brought jail. Some 12,000 debtors also languished in prison. No wonder the *Weekly Dispatch* denounced the "oppression and injustice" caused by the "great unpaid."[11]

The bitter experiences of repressive authorities not only persuaded Radicals that government was oppressive and unjust but shaped their conception of socialism. The socialism that they developed was a socialism without a strong central government, a socialism whose government was limited to the community. Owenites even differed on the government of communities, Christian Owenites like John Minter Morgan desired the paternal rule of deacons, the economist William Thompson looked to a vast series of capital-labor associations, Abraham Combe preferred the rule of agricultural villagers, and Goodwin Barmby wanted "home colonies" financed by parliamentary loans. Ricardian socialists like Hodgskin—a socialist largely because he believed labor created all wealth while capitalists appropriated most of it unjustly—were more anarchist than socialist. A Godwinian who valued private property and hated government, Hodgskin ended up as an assistant editor of the *Economist*, England's leading advocate of laissez-faire. Mainstream Chartists, the followers of Feargus O'Connor, looked to private property, land companies, and local government while denouncing centralized poor laws and police.[12] There was little talk of nationalization of land, and it was in papers that few read. "Land must be made national property" through "an association of which the workers will be the only lords," Harney said, condemning the "unholy faction [that] perpetuates tyranny."[13]

An ingrained hatred of government as oppressive and unjust not only limited Chartists and Owenites to land schemes, village communities, and cooperative societies, but also blunted the social vision of other Radical and liberal friends of the workers. They were a varied group, including Benthamites like J. A. Roebuck, the Manchester School's John Bright, Radicals of Painite-Cobbett persuasion like Thomas Wakley, old Whigs grown radical like Sir George Strickland, proud urban localists like Captain George Pechell, the Irish nationalist Sharman Crawford, and the retired admiral Sir Charles Napier, the friend of the oppressed and the flogged. They differed on much, but not in their common hatred of an oppressive and unjust government. All agreed that a Corn Law that enhanced landlord rents by enhancing the price of bread for the poor was unjust. From 1837 to 1846, no other issue was debated so often and so fiercely. For many its injustice ran so deep and wide that its repeal would bring such prosperity that Parliament could pass ten-hour acts, abolish the inquisitorial income tax, and ease the stern Poor Law.

Many Radicals and Liberals believed that the New Poor Law was cruel and oppressive, though not all of them. The Benthamites Charles Buller and Edward Strutt supported it, although their fellow Benthamites John Leader, John Bowring, and, by 1842, Joseph Hume condemned it. Localists and humanitarians like W. T. Egerton and Thomas Wakley denounced its centralization and its cruelties. Even Richard Cobden opposed it.[14]

An analysis of the twenty to thirty M.P.'s who voted against the law shows a curious alliance of Radicals—Thomas Wakley, Thomas Duncombe, John Fielden, Williams Williams, and Joseph Brotherton—and a hard core of Tory paternalists—Colonel Charles Sibthorp, William Ferrand, Joseph Henley, Henry Halford, and Lewis Buck.[15] Centralization was its great evil for the Tories, easily government's most oppressive feature. For the Radicals, the great evil lay in the cruel incarceration of paupers in grim and oppressive workhouses. The Tory M.P.'s were part of the Establishment and so found themselves supporting repressive measures like the Master and Servant Act, which allowed J.P.'s to imprison insubordinate servants, enclosure acts whereby landowners ended the rights of the poor to the commons, game laws that imprisoned thousands, penal laws that preserved capital punishment, acts enabling magistrates to whip erring juveniles, laws closing pubs and railways on Sundays. These measures and the use of Home Office spies were part of what Thomas Duncombe called a "most insidious, oppressive, arbitrary, iniquitous and tyrannical attempt to oppress the working classes."[16] Except for the Ten Hour Act and acts to repeal repressive Tory acts, the Radicals proposed few significant social reforms calling for an active government; and they not only divided on ten-hour bills but many who were for a ten-hour bill wanted no inspectors to enforce it. Also, those who opposed it did so less on grounds of political economy than to preserve the "rights" of labor. The Radicals sought more to abolish repressive laws than to pass positive laws.

In 1847, the Radical John Fielden, who wanted a ten-hour act without inspectors, denounced "centralization in every form," since from it came "loss of liberty." Roebuck, a Benthamite, also proposed few social reforms to his Bath electors, but only the end of unjust taxes, bad laws, and tithes.[17] Numerous speeches at the hustings highlighted the faults, not the virtues, of government.

The middle-class Radical and Liberal press was also unhappy with an oppressive government. The hostility of the Liberal press, of the *Daily News*, *Weekly Chronicle*, *Economist*, *Punch*, *Examiner*, and *Sunday Times*, ran almost as deep as that of the Radical *Sun, Dispatch, Lloyd's Weekly, Howitt's Journal, Douglas Jerrold's Weekly*, and *People's Journal*. Most oppressive of all laws, of course, was that which taxed bread and brought economic crises. Remove the infamous Corn Law, they proclaimed, and famine, pauperism, and over-worked seamstresses would be things of the past.

For many, but not all of these periodicals, the New Poor Law was nearly as unjust. "Pernicious" and "brutal," declared *Howitt's Journal* of a law that the *Weekly Dispatch* called infamous, the *Sunday Times*, "iniquitous and cruel," and *Douglas Jerrold's Weekly*, "one dead weight."[18] The columns of the *Times* and the pages of G. R. W. Baxter's *The Book of the Bastilles* (1841) formed a vast and vivid catalogue of its cruelties. For many, these and innumerable other hateful laws came from a landlord-dominated Parliament. "So un-bending is the law," said Dickens's *Daily News*, that "the wonder is that the landowning-legislature has not done more mischief." The mischief was great: unjust game laws, laws excusing bankrupts while imprisoning poor debtors, confusing libel laws, ecclesiastical laws randomly enforced, and a huge crimi-nal law code, vexatious, costly, slow, mystifying in its technicalities and com-plexity, and brutal in its treadmills and hulks.[19] They all lent support to the *Economist's* claim that governments are far more powerful for mischief than good, a claim the *Leeds Mercury* was quick to use in its Nonconformist jeal-ousy of a government that supported a persecuting Established Church. The *Leeds Times* was just as severe in its condemnation of the government's "coercive system," with its many "soldiers, police, gaolers and hangmen."[20]

The *Leeds Times* omitted the justices of the peace from the "coercive sys-tem." The Radical and Liberal press, however, kept a vigilant watch on their harshness and injustices. From Exeter's *Western Times* and London's *Punch* and *Weekly Chronicle* came tales of a year in prison for a man who had stolen five fowls, of prison for three boys for taking some peas, of a woman impris-oned for taking some dried sticks, and of a woman fined 38s. for loud talk at a market, a woman sent to the lockup because she couldn't pay the fine.[21] Harsh sentences for trifles and prison for those unable to pay fines were not the only way the justices of the peace oppressed the poor: they also adminis-tered prisons, asylums, and workhouses with such indifference, parsimony, and cruelty that the *Spectator* declared that the justice done by the great un-paid was full of "enormities . . . that offend against justice," and *Punch* that the law was full of "iniquity" and "tyranny." The *Examiner* devoted a regular column to the "Justices' Injustices." One-fourth of the J.P.'s committals, an-nounced the *Economist*, were "unjust," part of a government vast in evil.[22]

A belief that government was evil even persuaded some Radicals to doubt whether government should limit a laborer's hours to ten or educate the people, two reforms most beneficial to the working classes. The *Sun, Weekly Dispatch*, and *Lloyd's Weekly*, all three friends of the workers and of humanitarian causes, all opposed the further regulation of factory labor: it was "vexatious and disastrous," wrote the *Sun* in 1842; it was "a direct blow at liberty," argued *Lloyd's* in 1844, and for the *Dispatch* in the same year, it was a denial of the workers' "undoubted right to dispose of their labour." A surge of humanity—or of the clamor of the workers—led the *Dispatch* and the *Sun* to reverse course, however, and, in 1847, they declared for the Ten Hour Act.[23]

Lloyd's could not reverse its course. The Ten Hour Act remained "a blow at liberty" and the ""subversion of every principle of self-dependence." To *Lloyd's*, government was still evil, as it was to *Howitt's*, and the *People's Journal*, which were both keenly humanitarian and opposed to government education. "We are," proclaimed *Howitt's*, for a "national and not a government system of education." Government education, it added, would "mold the people to patient acquiescence," a view not unlike that of John Stuart Mill, who, except for elementary education, preferred schooling by "voluntary societies." If education were managed by a "government corporation," it would mean "political despotism," since "a government which can mould the opinion and sentiments of the people from their youth upward can do with them what it pleases." Perhaps it was best, argued Samuel Smiles in the *People's Journal*, that the government do nothing for education, since "a government half school teachers and half policemen" would be "far more despotic than one with an army."[24] *Howitt's* and the *People's Journal* also gave no support to the Ten Hour Act. It is astonishing how suspicious these radical journals—the voice of the people—were of factory and educational reforms. The *Westminster Review* alone realized one of the reasons for this paradox. It was, it speculated in 1840, the "fateful legacy" of the impact of "mischievous and often wicked legislation on the public mind," one that continued "long after the government ceased to do evil . . . leaving it powerless to do good."[25]

Wicked laws did leave a fatal legacy, but a legacy left to a public mind receptive to it, a mind confident in the Enlightenment's faith that progress was inevitable once men freed themselves from perverse government and became wiser and more rational, a dream never more buoyantly expressed than in the writings of William Godwin and his followers, all of whom saw government as a vast evil. Among his admirers were Douglas Jerrold, Thomas Hodgskin, W. J. Fox, William Carpenter, Charles Dilke, and Edward Gibbon Wakefield, the owners, editors, and contributors of a score of journals, including the *Athenaeum, Daily News, Punch, Economist, Weekly Dispatch* (top among weeklies in circulation), and, until 1847, the *Morning Chronicle*.[26] Dickens chose three of them—Fox, Hodgskin, and Jerrold—as leader writers for the *Daily News*.

Francis Place knew Godwin, as did Robert Owen, who would argue little with Godwin's indictment that government "aggravates inequality . . . fosters injurious passions and . . . robbery and fraud." No wonder Godwin told his son-in-law Shelley not to push for social reform. Shelley did not. Instead, he denounced kings and priests, tyrants, and every form of oppressive government.[27]

Nonconformists also saw government as oppressive, but not entirely. They shuddered at Godwin's anarchism, although not at his scathing attack on priestcraft. By 1843, Dissenters, who could now hold office, and enjoy the civil registration of births, marriages, and burials, grew more moderate. Although compulsory church rates, exclusion from Oxford and Cambridge, ecclesiastical courts and burial fees still irritated them, government seemed less a vast evil. Then came the Tories' bill to establish factory schools managed and taught by Anglicans and inculcating the catechism and creed, schools that would be paid for by the ratepayers, many of whom were Nonconformists in factory towns. An aggressive, monopolizing Church of England aroused vivid memories of a persecuting Church and of unjust laws. The Nonconformists' fury was so enormous that Peel withdrew the Education Bill. In 1847, that fury was again aroused when a Whig government voted £100,000 for teachers and pupil teachers, four-fifths of which went to Church of England schools. Nonconformists found it intolerable that they had to pay taxes that helped propagate catechisms and creeds that they thought downright popish. Government was indeed oppressive and unjust.

"Iniquitous," "despotic," "plundering," "ungodly," and "tyrannical" were only a few of the invectives hurled at this unconstitutional "Prussian" scheme to pay "hordes of hirelings" to impose ecclesiasticism on England. That the Committee on Education intended to give greater aid to Dissenting schools did little to allay their fears. London's most popular Congregationalist, the Reverend Thomas Binney, called the Established Church a "great national evil," and that it should be "the teacher of the nation" was intolerable to most Nonconformists, who denounced the Education Bill as "a monstrous step towards bureaucratic despotism." Kay-Shuttleworth, secretary to the Committee on Education, a good Anglican and a judicious observer, admitted that under the Tories, that committee had become "nearly an engine of the worst despotism." The individualism and the independent-mindedness of the Nonconformist conscience could not abide such an evil, and its protests rang out in the pages of the *Eclectic, Patriot, Baptist Magazine, NonConformist,* and *Congregational Magazine,* as well as in the *Leeds Mercury* and *Sheffield Independent.*[28]

The Education Committee was not the only face of government oppression. There were also the Corn and Game Laws, the injustices perpetrated by J.P.'s (who were full of "oppression, chicanery and fraud," said the *NonCon-*

formist), ecclesiastical courts (which to the *Baptist Guardian* were "grinding and destructive), the infamous Poor Law, the oppressive and unconstitutional Metropolitan Building Act, and the General Board of Health (for the *Patriot* "despotic, absurd and audacious"). The besetting sin of the age, declared the *NonConformist*, was centralization, which is "despotism practicalized."[29] Nonconformity yielded little to Radicals in viewing government as oppressive and unjust.

Neither did some Tory backbenchers. Loud and persistent was their condemnation of centralization. Not only the New Poor Law, the Education Order, and the Public Health Act were condemned, but highway, police, burial, enclosure, and tithe bills. "I hate all commissioners," exclaimed Sibthorp, an antipathy shared by another county member, Lewis Buck, who denounced "every kind of commission" as "most unconstitutional."[30] There were good reasons, said Sir Henry Halford, for their antipathy: "officious functionaries" would bring an "army of strangers" and an "administrative despotism, odious and inquisitional."[31] For Disraeli, centralization was fatal to liberty, and for David Urquhart, it was "destructive of local government."[32]

Evangelicals such as Lord Ashley and High Churchmen such as Gladstone also condemned the Committee on Education as unconstitutional. High Churchmen deeply feared Erastianism—the doctrine that placed the state in control of the Church—and that fear increased as the Whigs moved to reform the Church.[33] It was a view furthered by much of the Tory press and its war on centralization. The *Times* led the way. Its hatred of the despotic New Poor Law spilled over into a hatred of a central police, "fashioned to keep people subservient," an anger at sanitary measures that were "inquisitorial and expensive," and a deep suspicion of a Metropolitan Building Act, disfigured by its "monstrous machinery." Highway acts, charity commissions, enclosure and railway bills and allotment schemes also formed part of the centralization that the *Times* saw as oppressive and unjust.[34] The Tory *Standard* and *John Bull* found no reason to disagree. For the *Standard*, the centralized Poor Law was, in 1834, worse than Turkish despotism. Fourteen years later, the Public Health Act evoked the lament, "have we not heard enough of the effect of centralization." *John Bull* had not. It found that the centralized Poor Law "degrades the gentry and clergy," and that the Public Health Act was a "positive evil" in its "oppressive interference."[35]

For Tories, the government was not oppressive and unjust in the same way as it was for Radicals. Government did not mean unjust prison sentences, laws against strikes, taxes restricting the press, and enclosure acts ending the rights of the poor, but rather laws oppressive to magistrates, town councillors, sheriffs, and myriad local officials who had long acted under the sway of a gentry and clergy who ruled the localities.[36] Government was oppressive to old ways, but perhaps not unjust, certainly not unjust, in Tory opinion, to those who suffered from the vagaries, capriciousness, neglect, and arbitrariness of a petty officialdom that was also often costly and corrupting, two characteristics many also imputed to all government.

GOVERNMENT AS COSTLY AND CORRUUPTING

Sir Robert Peel, in 1842, told the Commons that although the government needed £50 million to govern and protect Britain, its revenues barely exceeded £48 million. He therefore proposed a 2½ percent tax on incomes over £150 a year. The country exploded in anger. More hateful taxes for a more profligate, costly government. The hostility to taxes and to extravagant government had deep roots, not only in human nature, but in several specific factors: (1) the eighteenth-century British political system of influence and favoritism, of pensions, sinecures, and placemen; (2) the huge war debt run up starting in the 1790s; and (3) a system of taxation that was easy on the rich and hard on the middling and lower orders.

John Wade, in his *The Extraordinary Black Book* (1831), described in great and revealing detail the "Old Corruption," the system of the ruling oligarchy that not only dominated government itself, but the Church, the military, land, the county, the Bank of England, and the East India Company; in short, it was a wealthy, powerful, and very costly Establishment. Royalty itself, in 1831, cost £1.4 million pounds, roughly one-third the amount spent on the nation's two million paupers. Privy councillors, most of them already independently wealthy, cost £650,640, and the bishops cost £220,000. Six thousand idle half-pay army officers each received a generous stipend, not to mention 200 admirals, only 10 of whom were active. The civil service was filled with incompetents chosen for reason of family, friendships, and political favor. Then there was the law, a large, varied, and sprawling system of redundant and overlapping courts, thin on justice and fat on fees—as Dickens was to relate and Bentham to lament. There was finally the annual charge on the debt—in 1842, over £25,500,000, a sum constituting 59 percent of government expenditure.[37]

So revealing of these abuses, and of sinecures, pensioners and placemen, were the reports of the 1807 Select Committee and subsequent investigations that Bentham was persuaded that "everywhere the whole official establishment is a corruptive establishment: to possess the sinister benefits of corruption, is the universal wish." And, he concluded tersely, "government is in itself one vast evil."[38]

After 1815, four-fifths of the heavy taxes that paid for this costly, extravagant, and often wasteful government came from excise and custom duties on bread, bacon, butter, soap, candles, and more than a thousand other items. These duties weighed heavily on the lower classes.[39] In 1819, the Tories also returned the pound to the gold standard and so paid back to many creditors pounds of more value than the pounds loaned, thus enriching the wealthy at the cost of the many and raising debt payments to 59 percent of the budget—an injustice that William Cobbett and other Radicals never let the public forget. A costly and corrupt government thus became part of government as a vast evil.

Many in Parliament certainly thought so. In 1833, it led William Cobbett to oppose a £20,000 education grant. "Not one single farthing," he declared, "in the way of taxes."[40] In the 1840s, with Cobbett gone, Wakley, Fielden, and Duncombe kept up the protests against heavy taxes and a burdensome debt, Wakley against the debt, taxes and "profligate expenditure," Fielden over excessive taxation and the contracted currency of 1819, and Duncombe, in 1847, over the cost of ever-increasing patronage.[41] They demanded retrenchment, but not as persistently as its unrivaled champion, Joseph Hume. For four decades, he condemned sinecures and pensioners, bloated budgets, and profligate expenditure and preached the severest economy. It was a message that Cobden and the Manchester School never wearied of delivering. "Extravagance in your Imperial legislature," argued Cobden, "is the cause of the growth of pauperism and crime."[42] *Punch* satirized the bishops' need for tens of thousands of pounds, and the £70,000 spent on the Queen's stables. The *Westminster Review* asked angrily why London pageants cost £2,000. And why, asked the *Weekly Dispatch*, should the government spend £45,000 on royal palaces?[43]

Nonconformists also had their complaints. The *Eclectic Review* spoke out against "pensionary hordes" and the "mischievous race of placemen"; the *Baptist Examiner* against the "defiling patronage" and profligacy "of men of no religion"; and the *NonConformist* against "extravagant pensions" lavished on favorites. Even the government's working servants angered the *Patriot*, especially the "army of commissioners, surveyors and state stipendaries" that were part of a "place creating, all centralizing corrupting policy, borrowed from [France's "citizen-king"] Louis Philippe."[44]

The *Patriot*, in one sense, was the most accurate. The new extravagance (if extravagance it was) came from newly created commissioners and inspectors, not sinecures and placemen, a once common species now on the way to oblivion. The Tories of the 1820s and the Whigs of the 1830s had abolished most sinecures and pensions and placemen. What now angered Tories was that new species, expensive Whig commissioners.

In 1849, the Tories Joseph Henley and Henry Drummond attacked high government salaries, Drummond so boldly that he won the praise of Hume and Roebuck, those staunch champions of retrenchment. The Tory George Hudson, the railway king, joined Drummond and Henley in calling for the reduction of huge government salaries, unnecessary palaces, and high taxes.[45]

County Tories in particular demanded low taxes and cheap government. "All taxation is injurious," announced Henry Willoughby, and Somerset's William Miles and Lincolnshire's Sir John Trollope pleaded with Peel to allow no increases in the county rate. Devonshire's John Buller promised his electors that he would "through the greatest economy . . . end the burden of taxation," and Worcestershire's Sir John Packington promised "rates . . . as low as possible."[46]

In 1844, no tax was more unpopular than Peel's proposed income tax. Odious and inquisitional was the universal refrain from Whig, Liberal, and Radical M.P.'s, and even Tory ones when liberated from Peel's whips. But it was not odious. At less than 2.5 percent, and only applied to incomes over £150, it allowed Peel to reduce some of the indirect taxes so burdensome to the poor. Of the Radical and Whig papers, only the *Westminster Review* supported it. "A monstrous injustice," "unjust and odious," and "an enormous and unnecessary evil" were the angry retorts of the *Northern Star*, the *Examiner,* and the *Weekly Dispatch*, and to the *Leeds Times*, it was "a nuisance perfectly intolerable."[47]

It was most difficult for the Radical and Liberal press to see any tax as just. For decades, arbitrary and capricious taxes—stamps on newspapers, taxes on windows, the infamous Corn Law, unending excise duties, and innumerable legal and ecclesiastical fees—had persuaded them that taxation, like the profligate government it paid for, was part of an evil government.

That a costly, profligate government was seen as evil was not limited to London's M.P.'s and newspapers; it also pervaded local town councils, boards of guardians, improvement commissioners, highway boards, and those who elected them, as well as the justices who visited prisons and asylums and were ex officio poor law guardians. The same opinion was also dominant at the Treasury, which kept a tight rein on all Whitehall budgets and blunted the central government's efforts to end social abuses. Whatever the department, there were always too few inspectors and assistant commissioners. Fear of burdening the English taxpayer even led the Treasury, after 1847, to urge, and the government to accept, drastic cuts in aid to famine-stricken Ireland, and the same fear led justices, in county after county, to tolerate ageing and over-crowded prisons and asylums, guardians to neglect the poor, and town councils to do little about disease-ridden towns. Costly government was everywhere abhorred.

Abhorrent also was patronage, not only because costly, but because corrupt and corrupting, a legacy of the eighteenth-century world of placemen and pensioners, of jobbery and favoritism, and of appointments not by merit but by politics and friendship. Patronage led to a local and national civil service that was incompetent, torpid, and prey to special interests. The Nonconformists' *Eclectic Review* complained of "pensionary hordes and mischievous placemen," especially after 1847, when these hordes were Church of England teachers and pupil teachers paid for by the taxpayers. For the Radical Thomas Wakley, patronage made boards of guardians a "political instrument . . . [of] designing men," and for High Tories, patronage meant hordes of commissioners who were the favorites of Whig peers and the product of Whig jobbery.[48] For Toulmin Smith, it was all part of a "universal jobbery and universal corruption."[49] There was much patronage in early Victorian England, but it only led to some petty jobbery and malfeasance in the localities and a rare scandal in a central department. The *Eclectic Review*, Wakley, and Toulmin Smith were mistaken; there were no hordes of placemen, guardians with designs, and universal corruption. Patronage, to be sure, continued, but it was transformed. Although friendship and politics more than merit determined appointments until the civil service reforms of the late 1850s, both Whig and Tory ministers chose men of ability and honesty, in many cases a necessity, since such men were needed for the delicate and difficult tasks facing factory, education, and health inspectors, or railway, poor law and enclosure commissioners. But although the English government was not corrupt, placemen and pensions were fast disappearing, and patronage was responsibly used, protests against it persisted. Deeply etched memories and fears from an older age continued to persuade the early Victorians that government was evil because corrupt. Also deeply etched, and also largely in error, was a remarkably pervasive belief that government itself was corrupting.

The belief that a generous poor law corrupted was widespread. From the Whig Lord Brougham in 1834 to the Tory marquis of Granby in 1849, M.P.'s condemned poor laws, English and Irish, for encouraging idleness.[50] The Radical John Bright insisted that by encouraging idleness, poor laws increased pauperism, and the evangelicals Edward Horsman and Henry Drummond lamented that they "destroyed the character of the poor," and "would further pauperism." Young England's Augustus Stafford O'Brien insisted that they increased "misery and poverty."[51] The two evangelicals and Stafford were speaking of the Irish Poor Laws of 1847 and 1849, laws that persuaded Irish landlords in the Commons (Napier, French, Herbert, and Bourke) that an increase in poor relief would ruin Ireland. In 1843, *Fraser's* considered poor laws ruinous, saying that such laws "always have destroyed and always will destroy more lives than they save."[52]

The Irish M.P.'s also worried that an Irish poor law would "paralyse the exertion of the landed gentry," a worry that Peel shared when viewing the depression-ridden Scottish town of Paisley. Government interference, said Peel, would discourage local exertion.[53] Burke, and many paternalists and philanthropists after him, warned that government interference would dampen private benevolence. The eloquent Chalmers declared that it discouraged giving, and the voluble Henry Drummond that it "dried up all source of private charity."[54]

The High Church Edmund Denison said no to government education because it would dampen the flow of giving, while the liberal Baptist George Dawson said no to grants to Ireland because it "checked the flow of private benevolence."[55] Churches of all persuasions had a vested (although altruistic) interest in Christian benevolence, just as they had in a Christian education, a field in which all government interference was seen as an evil. It would "corrupt society," declared the Dissenters' Reverend Pye Smith; it would "debauch the public mind," concluded his fellow Congregationalist the Reverend Thomas Binney. Nonconformists feared that hundreds of government-paid Church of England teachers—many of Puseyite leanings—would propagate religious error, a fear Puseyites themselves had of teachers paid for and supervised by an infidel Whig government. The High Church *English Review* denounced the government's Battersea Training College for its state-controlled latitudinarian education and condemned the Reverend W. F. Hook's plan for schools supported by the ratepayers (with excused time for religious education in a faith of one's choice) as promising "a race of infidels."[56]

For many, the corruption brought by government education schemes and poor laws only proved that legislation in general was an evil. Legislation, said the *Leeds Mercury*, "spoils whatever it touches." The *Leeds Times* was even more severe: "Laws themselves are the greatest propagators of crime," since they "debase, demoralize and brutalize."[57] In Parliament, in 1848, Joseph Napier blamed Ireland's troubles on excessive legislation. The *North British Review* found no reason to disagree, saying that the "late legislation . . . had utterly and entirely demoralized the people."[58] These declarations are from Radicals, Irishmen, High Churchmen, Nonconformists, and High Tories, each often in opposition to new schemes and each with their own special angers. But even the Whig *Edinburgh Review* feared a government that corrupted. Three of its key writers, Nassau Senior, George C. Lewis, and Thomas Spring Rice believed that a generous poor law corrupted. Senior also warned in 1841 that morals should never be at the mercy of a legislature "capable of injury from rash interference," and in 1848, he declared that the greatest objection to government was its "tendency to keep people in leading strings." The warning that it was dangerous for government to keep people in leading strings came from John Stuart Mill's *Political Economy*, a book Senior also praised for its warning of the evils of centralization.[59] Mill's view of government was large and many-sided and often ambivalent. He saw its reality and necessity but also its dangers. He had read de Tocqueville (perhaps too enthusiastically), studied deeply the evils of Continental autocracies, and learned from his father and others of earlier repressive Tory governments. He also had at the core of his outlook a powerful belief in the sovereign virtues of individuality. There is thus in his writings a recurring anxiety about government: "Poor laws are generally injurious," "an income tax is inquisitional," "government is harmful to spontaneous action," and "people who habitually look to their government . . . have their faculties only half developed."[60] That Prussia's and France's centralized school systems, which were decidedly superior to England's, left their citizens' faculties less developed is most unlikely. Although Mill's fears of a corrupting government are part of a larger more favorable estimate of it, it was his warnings of the evil of government and his ardent belief in a self-reliant individuality that *Blackwood's*, the *Spectator*, the *Edinburgh Review*, the *Christian Remembrancer*, and most other journals, underscored in their reviews. Britain's most strident localist, Toulmin Smith, was as quick to use Mill's warning that dependence on government left faculties half developed as he was to adopt Mill's strictures on a corrupting centralization.[61]

GOVERNMENT AS INEPT AND UNWISE

A large number of early Victorians saw government as inept and unwise more than oppressive and corrupting, the latter indictments coming more often from angry Radicals, persecuted Dissenters, and Tory backbenchers irate at centralization. All, of course, saw government as costly, although with a growing prosperity, that objection came more from county magistrates, town councillors, and boards of guardians than from members of Parliament. With the government becoming less corrupt and many injustices remedied, the public found government less oppressive, although many still saw it as both inept and unwise.

Economists had long judged government interference to be ignorant and

meddlesome. Few were the educated who had not read Adam Smith's catalogue of the folly of allowing mercantilist laws to regulate the economy. Far
wiser was it to trust in the laws of the marketplace and individuals' decisions,
which were far more intelligent than those of government. None of the leading economists of the 1840s—Senior, McCulloch, Torrens, Mill—doubted
the superiority of the laws of the market and the decisions of individuals to
government interference. The economists, however, also had their lists of exceptions, which were by no means modest ones. But these exceptions were
quite overshadowed by their lists of foolish government interventions. That
the individual, alone and in groups, best knew his own interest was a nearly
universal assumption. Neither Bentham, the economists, nor the landlords
doubted it. It was a dominant theme of John Stuart Mill's *Political Economy*.
"The great majority of things are worse done by the intervention of the government," he told his many readers, "than by the individual." Mill also told
Auguste Comte that "what is done for people benefits them only when it assists them in doing what they can do for themselves," a rather severe test
when the needed benefits might include elaborate waterworks or expensive
asylums, whose beneficiaries might include the utterly destitute or mentally
ill. Mill always had difficulty overcoming his belief that government was inept
and unwise.[62] For the Radical Thomas Hodgskin, that difficulty was insuperable, and it suffuses his *Popular Political Economy,* as indeed it did the popu-
larization of political economy by Jane Marcet and Harriet Martineau and in
journals like *Chambers' Edinburgh Journal*—even by the paternalist Southey
when he insisted that "more may be done by . . . active individuals than could
be effected by legislative interference," a sentiment Coleridge echoed in ex-
alting "free agency" and condemning "Act of Parliament Reform."[63] Disraeli
and Peel had no higher estimate of government. Twice Disraeli told the
Commons that government had never built a single road, bridge, or canal,
adding the second time that neither had government established a university
or an empire. Such failures would not have surprised Peel, who decried the
"torpid hand of government."[64] The Peelite William MacKinnon saw no reason to contest Peel's opinion, since he believed that "except for teaching the
poor that they are responsible for distress the government is without
power."[65] Distress, for some, was providential and so beyond government, so
at least declared the Tory evangelical Henry Drummond. "No House," he
said, "will have the power to relieve distress," adding that "misery is the lot of
man."[66] Many Whigs and Radicals knew that economic crises, not God, created economic distress, but they too doubted government's ability to end it.
No M.P. had a more compassionate interest in helping the working classes
than the Whig Robert Slaney, chair of various select committees and the

author of five works investigating social conditions. Yet he wrote of the "impossibility of increasing employment by legislation," that the only answer for jobless handloom weavers lay in their own conduct, and that the government should not adopt "a uniform and complete plan of education."[67]

From 1843 to 1845, five select committees and five royal commissions, along with special reports of the Poor Law Commission, investigated the plight of handloom weavers, lack of schooling among the poor, the distress of textile towns, the exploitation of women and children in workshops and fields, the need for allotments, and an improvement in the conditions of Irish peasantry. These were thorough investigations that revealed pervasive and acute social evils, yet not one committee or commission dared recommend that government act to remove them. For the weavers, the answer was only free trade and education, an education that was unlikely, since the 1838 Committee on Education had said it that it was "not prepared to propose any means for meeting the deficiency"; nor did any of the voluminous reports on distress in textile towns and the exploitation of women and children in workshops dare to propose a government remedy; and neither did the Devon Commission on Ireland, which announced, "we can not recommend any direct legislation," nor the allotment committee, which rejected the idea of a compulsory act of Parliament.[68]

Fear of offending vested interests certainly lay behind much of their timidity, but so did the belief of the M.P.'s that government was inept and unwise, a sentiment just as widespread in the journals that the M.P.'s read. The liberal *Athenaeum* argued strenuously that the belief that the legislature could greatly help the working class was "a fatal delusion" and called government interference "the monstrous fallacy of the age." Also a delusion, said the Radical *Sun*, was the belief that acts of Parliament were "remedies for great ills."[69] For the Unitarian *Christian Teacher,* the remedy for the evil of women working in factories lay in educating them and not legislation, since "laws have proved but sorry preventives."[70]

Paternalist journals had no higher an estimate of government. "Government can neither wholly prevent nor effectively cure," insisted the *Quarterly Review*, "the evils arising from economic distress," and neither was "any set of laws adequate to the permanent cure . . . of the evils of Ireland." The *Christian Remembrancer* also found "many ills of our social system . . . beyond the power of legislation." It later insisted that "all legislative enactments must be powerless," since "Christianity is the only cure." Finally, the *Morning Post*, in opposing the Public Health Act, claimed that "there can be no remedy of social evils but by the rich."[71] Paternalism and laissez-faire had little trouble coexisting.

Many others considered the problem of Ireland to lie beyond legislation. It was a bog of hopeless ills, ills so deeply rooted and perplexing that only knowledgeable landlords, not inept government, could solve them, and then only partly. The *Edinburgh Review's* Nassau Senior looked to the rich in Ireland, free of any compulsion, to aid the poor. In 1846, he denied that poor law relief was "a right" and, despite a serious shortage of workhouses, opposed any outdoor relief for the destitute. In 1848, he criticized John Stuart Mill's proposed public works, allotments, and allowances. "Government," wrote Senior in 1841, "has laboured to fetter and direct the people." Thomas Spring Rice and Charles Trevelyan, Senior's colleagues on the *Edinburgh Review*, were no keener about government. When confronted with manufacturing distress, Rice concluded that "it is on moral remedies we must rely" while Trevelyan denounced the use of public works during the Irish famine, preferring instead the voluntary work of the Society of Friends.[72]

There was little that government was wise enough to remedy: not the evils of exploitative company stores and not costly burials in overcrowded church graveyards, according to Peel's home secretary, Sir James Graham; not London's water supply, said the Whig Lord Seymour; certainly not prices, said the Board of Trade's Henry Labouchere; not diseased towns, said the *Economist* and the *Morning Post*; and not the distress of the poor, said a nearly unanimous Commons to Ferrand's motion of 1842 to spend a million pounds for poor relief.[73] Even Edwin Chadwick and Lord Ashley, those stalwart advocates of sanitary reform, opposed public housing because of skepticism of government.[74] It was folly too, declared G. Calvert Holland, Sheffield's leading paternalist, "to look to government to remedy ignorance and misery." "To call upon government for their redress," he wrote, "would be about as effective as a prayer offered up to Jupiter." Even Ireland's famine lay beyond government. "It is only by the power of God himself," declared Liverpool's leading evangelical, the Reverend Dean M'Neil, "that the calamity can be removed."[75] Loud and widespread was the opinion that a government too often inept and unwise should have but limited ends.

THE LIMITED ENDS OF GOVERNMENT

As unwise and inept as the Victorians thought government, and as oppressive, unjust, and costly, it was a necessity. There were things government should do as well as not do. A rule was needed, a clear definition of the duties of the state was needed. Many thought they had found one in Adam Smith's neat and succinct definition of them as threefold: protection from "violence and invasion," "the exact administration of justice," and the establishment of "public works and public institutions which it can never be for the interest of the individual . . . to erect."[76] This attractive definition, happily in consonance with John Locke's view of government as little more than the protection of life and property, became the basis, along with Locke's dictum, of the pithy and popular phrase "the protection of person and property." For countless early Victorians, government was ideally to consist of little more than the law courts, the military, and the police. The "protection of person and property" defined the ends of government along the entire spectrum of opinion that ranged from the *English Chartist Circular* to the Tory *Fraser's* and included the *Leeds Mercury, British Quarterly, Congregational Magazine,* and *Edinburgh Review.* It was also held by such disparate thinkers as Burke, Coleridge, Nassau Senior, Frederick Maurice, Dr. Channing, and the utilitarian John Arthur Roebuck.[77] The language could vary. *Fraser's* spoke of "life and property" and Maurice of "individual rights and possession." It could also be amended. The *Westminster's* caveat was "until the government grew wiser"; Burke added "to protect and encourage industry"; and the *Leeds Mercury* included foreign affairs and revenue, although these could be subsumed under a wider interpretation of "protection."[78] Coleridge added four vague positive ends, but concluded that since they had been already largely achieved, "nothing was asked of the state than to withhold or retract all extrinsic and artificial aids to an injurious system." The *Economist* was even more negative, saying: "Unless it be for the punishment of crime we know not for what purpose governments subsist."[79]

Neither Adam Smith's threefold duties nor "protection of person and property" logically precluded an expanded role for the state. Could not protection of persons mean the protection of labor from endless hours in a factory, or of the poor from squalid, diseased slums? And could not Adam Smith's "institutions which it can never be to the interest of the individual to erect" include old age pensions and a national health service? Did not the economists add on function upon function? All true! Yet the definition of the state as no more than a protector of persons and property, as constantly used in the press, invariably carried negative implications. Burke followed its use with the injunction that "in all other respects the less they do the better." *Fraser's* used the definition in an article denouncing the income tax as inquisitional. Roebuck assumed it when he declared that "to do more . . . would bring immediate mischief."[80] The Nonconformist *British Quarterly, Congregational Magazine,* and *Leeds Mercury* used it to attack government education, and Nassau Senior, J. R. McCulloch, Jane Marcet, and the *Morning Chronicle* as an expression embodying the wisdom of laissez-faire.[81] For Marcet, it meant that government should "annul every law that interferes with property," a thoroughly negative view of government that was shared by Lord Brougham and the Liberal M.P. Thomas Wyse. Brougham asserted that "the only duty of government was to remove obstacles." Wyse declared that "all the state can do [for education] . . . is to shovel away the obstacles [and] let society work of itself."[82] It was advice that Wyse himself, who introduced a progressive education bill, never followed.

The widespread belief that the state was evil, or at least inept, faced little competition. There was no positive theory of government intervention, no modern collectivism. There was, to be sure, collectivism—Owenite, Fourier-ist, and Christian Socialist—but it was unmistakably local and communal, with scarcely any room for an active central government.

It is also true that the economists wrestled with the problem. John Stuart Mill, Nassau Senior, and J. R. McCulloch each devoted a chapter to the scope of government, chapters that, although they showed that the three were not blind apostles of laissez-faire, also made it clear that they thought laissez-faire was the best rule. Their lists of justifiable interferences were ample. They included education, public health, roads, canals, harbors, and all those public works blessed by Adam Smith. Then there were laws defining commerce and property and finance, to which they would add laws controlling corporation property and laws protecting factory children, lunatics, and animals. But ample as were the lists of these three economists, they do not add up to a theory of collectivist government. The interventions were random, disconnected exceptions, reflecting no compelling logic. Most of the exceptions listed also were already part of the law of the land. Neither Mill, Senior, nor McCulloch outlined or campaigned for new schemes of intervention, and all three opposed the ten-hour day—even for women. They wanted government limited. "Untenable," declared McCulloch "is the doctrine that government can interfere advantageously with its subjects"; it was "a most fatal error," argued Senior, "to interfere other than for protection," and Mill echoed these sentiments in his section "The Inferiority of Government Agency," with its celebration of "spontaneous action."[83] Although the economists silently accepted government intervention when it came to a matter of economic advantage (like banking acts), their real trust was in the invisible hand of the market and the self-reliance of an educated people.

The paternalists also looked to what Coleridge called "free agency." Although collectivist in rhetoric, full of the organic unity of all classes, they reserved their collectivism for the smaller spheres defined by property, parish church, and locality. The utilitarians, even though the greatest happiness principle would prove to be the preeminent rationale for government interference, looked askance at a government seen as repressive, corrupt, arbitrary, and Tory, all hateful features that led the working class to an even greater hostility to government.

There was, in fact, no ideology or theory in early Victorian England urging a larger, more active state. Government in itself continued to be perceived as a vast evil. It was unjust, costly, corrupting, inept, and unwise. Furthermore, it was "unnecessary," because the early Victorians had such an overflowing confidence in the invisible hand of the economists, the paternal rule of property, the mission of the Church, the self-help of a better-educated people, and the beneficial work of philanthropy and voluntarism. More widespread even than this confidence was a belief in Coleridge's exhortation to be "better people" and Carlyle's command "reform yourself." Similar pleas were heard in all the pulpits, High Church, evangelical, Nonconformist, and Catholic. The call to be better Christians expressed a Christian laissez-faire more pervasive than that preached by the economists.

That in the very period when these laissez-faire attitudes were dominant, hundreds of laws and scores of agencies expanded the role of government as never before poses a paradox, one whose resolution is necessary before one can understand the social conscience of the early Victorians.

CHAPTER 14

The Inexorable Growth of Government

However evil the Victorians considered government, it never ceased to grow. In twenty-three years, from 1833 to 1855, Parliament passed 6,898 acts (2,522 public, 735 private, and 3,031 local). It also created more than twenty central departments, although the exact number is hard to state, since there can be differences on what to include. Should one, for example, include the inspector of Welsh highways, the commissioner of saving banks, the inspector of quarantine, and the inspector of salmon fisheries? The larger departments employed hundred of commissioners, assistant commissioners, agents, inspectors, and surveyors, who investigated and reported on every conceivable problem and every possible institution, ranging from the meanest dame school to the most sacred cathedral close, from the smallest workshop to the most imposing mill, and from the filthiest slums to the wealthiest Oxford college. Neither the most remote lighthouse nor nearest London theater escaped the tentacles of government.

More than one-third of Parliament's acts strengthened local government, enlarging the functions of the J.P.'s, already at the height of their power, and of England's over 15,000 parish vestries, 587 poor law unions, 178 municipal corporations, 708 statutory authorities, and 182 new local boards of health, all of whom regulated Her Majesty's subjects in an unprecedented ways, forbidding, for example, women from cleaning windows six feet above the ground. The same government that many called evil proved repeatedly useful, as did that accursed continental device "centralization." By 1851, the 22,000 civil servants of 1815 had become 39,000. They and some 25,000 local officials governed England.

A powerful central government, however, had not been unknown in earlier times. In George III's reign, 8,000 officials worked to raise and manage the finances for what John Brewer, in *Sinews of Power*, calls Britain's "fiscal-military juggernaut." To defeat Napoleon, the central government spent a larger share of the nation's income than it did in the 1840s, but hardly any of it went to new departments performing new functions.[1]

England's central government, after 1832, grew in three areas, the regulation of the economy, the supervision of local authorities, and the continuance of a firm, law-and-order, moral governance. The first of these areas, the economic, proved one of the most contentious and ambivalent. Political economists determined on achieving a laissez-faire society demanded the end of the Corn Law, the Navigation Act, and every vestige of an anachronistic mercantilism; at the same time, humanitarians and workers clamored for factory and mining acts and a growing middle class called for a more rational and safer system of railways and steamships. The result was factory, mining, merchant marine, and railway acts. Parliament passed factory acts in 1833, 1844, 1847, and 1853. The Factory Act of 1833 excluded children below nine years of age, limited those aged from nine to thirteen to eight hours of work, which the 1844 act cut to six and a half. The 1844 act also required that no child could work half-time without receiving half a day of schooling, and that machinery be fenced, and contained a host of strict regulations to prevent evasions. The 1847 act gave the young and women a ten-and-a-half-hour day, which effectively included men, and the 1853 Act declared illegal the use of children in relays to work men more than ten and a half hours. The mining acts of 1842, 1849, and 1854 excluded women and children and required stricter measures to reduce accidents. The merchant marine acts of 1849 and 1854 took the first faltering steps toward improving the dismal conditions of the seamen, toward enforcing stricter qualifications for its previously untested and often incompetent officers, and toward the establishment of better and safer standards of navigation. Passenger acts added to the regulation of ships, ending the fatal overcrowding of emigrants on filthy, ill-provided, disease-ridden, and disastrously unsafe vessels. And finally the Railway Act of 1844 gave the humbler classes cheaper, faster, covered trains.[2] Beyond these acts, there were few that substantially improved the fate of the jobless and destitute or relieved the underpaid, overworked, and exploited. Britain's 100,000 factory operatives constituted only a small fraction of the workforce. Millions of workers had no protection whatever: workshop workers in the fifty trades investigated by the Children's Employment Commission; weavers, whose plight the Handloom Commissioners described; railway navvies, whose squalid dormitories and harsh and dangerous work a select committee exposed; and the one and a half million agricultural laborers, the worst paid, worst housed, and most neglected, although no more neglected than the costermongers, scavengers, and street people of Henry Mayhew's London.[3]

That Parliament fell short of protecting the lower orders did not mean it was unalterably opposed to government interference in the economy. On the contrary, intervention grew and grew. It did so because the middle and upper classes (including the economists) found government useful. They repealed a Combination Act outlawing trade unions in 1825 only to pass an act severely restricting them in 1826, just as the repeal of the Corn Law in 1846—a triumph of laissez-faire—was followed by a Drainage Act offering low interest loans to landowners—a clear case of government intervention. The 1849 repeal of the Navigation Act, a triumph of laissez-faire, was followed by an 1854 Merchant Marine Act with 548 clauses, a triumph of interventionism.[4]

Property far more than humanitarianism demanded act upon act of Parliament. Property, sacred and inviolate when legislation threatened to harm it, was less sensitive if the legislation helped it—and much of it did help. Just as landowners welcomed drainage acts, so in 1836, 1841, and 1843, they welcomed the tithe, copyhold, and enclosure commissioners whose intervention commuted tithes in kind to cash (and lessened them), turned copyholds into freeholds, with ampler rents, and made enclosures cheaper and landed estates more profitable. By 1860, over half a million acres had been enclosed, to the gain of landowners and the loss of holders of small plots and of rights to the commons.[5] For centuries, Parliament had legislated on how land was held, how it could be entailed and how bought and sold. Legislation also defined its rights over game and determined that the eldest son should inherit the estate intact. Railway acts even required landowners to sell rights-of-way to railway companies. A pure laissez-faire never existed. Two thousand laws, wrote Ramsay McCulloch in 1843, regulated commerce.[6] Parliamentary acts granted railway companies the right to buy land, regulated the companies in order to lessen accidents, and determined what they could charge other companies. They also appointed inspectors to see that the lines were safe.[7] Devastating shipwrecks, over 500 a year, led to the 548-clause Merchant Marine Act of 1854, an act that also increased government power over lighthouses, the examination of pilots and masters, the construction of the ships, the working conditions of the seamen, and much more, an act that insurers, shipowners, and the middle and upper classes, who desired safety, felt it was to their interest to support, just as it was to their interest to support the Bank Act and the Joint Stock Company Act of 1844. The Bank of England and no other bank could issue paper money, and then only in a fixed ratio to its gold reserves; and the law now excused owners of stock in joint stock companies from liability for their losses.[8] The extent of government interference was great. Parliament not only passed laws against the adulteration of food, it established weights and measures, regulated the fares of hackney coaches, established the competency of physicians, and prevented the sale of poison. Parliament also promoted public utilities, docks, harbors, and the Thames embankment, and created a Department of Art and Science that would establish schools for the training of industrial designers. The government also supported a Museum of Practical Geology to help mine owners. Government legislation to encourage and organize capitalism and to ensure that railways and ships were safe and hackney coaches inexpensive far outweighed legislation to protect adult workers.[9]

Extensive too, although usually blunted, was government interference to supervise local authorities and to improve society, a second area of government's inexorable expansion, the area of the hated centralization. From the New Poor Law of 1834 to the Police Act of 1856, the failure of local government to cope with the acute problems of the growth of populations, towns, and industries led to greater central supervision. In 1835, came the prison inspectors; in 1842, the commissioners of lunacy; in 1848, the General Board of Health. Like the Poor Law Commission, they all had inspectors or assistant commissioners and powers to inspect, report, and advise, but to do little more. The Poor Law Commission could issue regulations, confirm local appointments, settle local disputes, and give grants to and require the appointment of good medical officers, auditors and schools. Yet imposing as these powers seemed, local guardians persisted in assisting 85 percent of the paupers out of doors, refused to establish district schools, and tolerated not a little abuse. The other commissioners and inspectors had even less power and therefore had to depend on persuasion and publicity to make a partnership effective in which the lion's share of power remained with local authorities who enjoyed sovereign control over rates.[10]

For all the outcry against centralization, in day-to-day governing power, the local authorities gained more power than the central government. The inexorable growth of government was as much local as central. The 587 poor law unions and 182 boards of health expanded the role of local government, as did the county justices and parish and borough officials, all given greater powers by lunacy, prison, police, and highway acts. Centralization did not mean less government, as the Benthamite jurist John Austin argued, but more.[11] The 1834 Highway Act left power to parish vestries and turnpike trusts, while the Police Act of 1839 allowed the counties to establish, only if they wished, a more effective police, which, by 1841, half the counties did. Some 15,000 parishes continued to manage, and often with scandalous negligence, four-fifths of England's roads.[12] And although seventeen out of twenty-six counties did establish county police, their performance was a mixed one, some excellent, many more so ineffectual that Parliament in 1856 placed them

under tighter Home Office supervision. Local boards of health, largely independent after the 1854 abolition of the General Board of Health, also had
mixed results; again, some were excellent, but most, even in great towns, fell
prey to small-minded, factious officials, to powerful vested interests, and to
an overwhelming resistance to higher rates.

But not all was resistance to rates. When civic pride was involved and
when amenities were desired, towns were quick to use Parliament's many acts
of permissive legislation to create a vigorous and expanding local government. From 1808 to 1851, Parliament passed acts that permitted towns to establish, regulate, and fund common lodging houses, libraries, markets and
fairs, museums, baths and washhouses, and schools of design, the fruits, not
of an evil government, but of a government that formed a new and growing
dimension of the social conscience of the early Victorians. As many a magnificent town hall reveals, civic pride had no hesitation about expressing itself
in local government.[13]

Local government, although imposing in its town halls and increased
powers, was not without its weaknesses and failings. More acts and departments did not always mean a kinder, more generous government. Poor law
unions not only had many new powers, but also the harsh workhouse test, the
bastardy clauses that forbade the unwedded mother from gaining help from
the father, and the separation in workhouses of man and wife. And for the
many destitute able-bodied males who were denied any relief but that in a
workhouse, the local administration of the New Poor Law meant either a
negligent or a harsh government. From 1835 to 1850, despite a 50 percent increase in population, a huge increase in wealth, and severe economic depressions, 20 percent less was spent on poor relief by local unions in control of
rates than in the previous fifteen years.[14] The expanded local government was
no less harsh or negligent as regards the imprisoned and mentally ill, imposing treadmills, solitary confinement, and leg irons in some prisons, and per-
mitting wretched, dirty, overcrowded common rooms in others. Asylums
varied from enlightened Lincoln to miserable Bedlam, the embodiment of all
that was wrong with local government.

Local government could also be both extravagant and neglectful. Proud
towns like Sheffield and Leeds disdained to establish a local board of health
by means of an order in council through the General Board of Health, which
cost £88, preferring to create a board through a local act, whose passage cost
£1,600 or more. Their boards then failed to make many needed improvements because their elected members opposed higher rates. Fifteen years after
Parliament abolished the General Board of Health in 1854, the Sanitary
Commission of 1869 reported that all but a few exemplary towns, such as Liv-

erpool, had failed to provide an adequate sanitary system.[15] But all was not failure and neglect. It is quite undeniable that local government, prompted and supervised by the central government, as well as prodded by its own vigorous critics, grew and improved inexorably. In twenty years, by working through Parliament, it added 3,631 local and personal acts to the statute book, the vast majority being local. And undeniable, too, is the fact that these acts, like the central government's mining and prison acts, often suffered from lack of funding and from powers too meager for the challenges faced. They nevertheless did much good. Many of the 587 poor law unions, despite some Scroogelike niggardliness and continued abuses, did vaccinate children, set up dispensaries, give 85 percent of relief outside the workhouse, improve the care of the elderly sick and orphaned in more commodious workhouses, send the insane to asylums, and teach children to read. In 1847, local schools taught 40,000 pupils to read and write. And most improved of all was medical service, on which they spent 64 percent more in 1852 than in 1838. Some even gained and used the power to indict those who failed to remove nuisances.[16]

Prisons and asylums, despite the excesses of the treadmill and solitary confinement and barracklike housing of the mentally ill, were also substantially more comfortable, clean, and orderly. The asylums were freer of chains and of cold, unheated, and overcrowded wards. Despite the sanitary failings revealed by the 1869 commissioners, England was laying sewers, building waterworks, employing health officers, and laying the basis for healthy towns. That sanitary improvements lagged behind growing squalor is unhappily true; but though they produced no Valhalla they did avoid Stygian depths. The growth of local government for all its tentativeness and its surrenders to selfish ratepayers and vested interests forms a positive and salutary aspect of the growth of the early Victorian social conscience.[17]

For many, quite as salutary as these improvements in local government was the government's role in guaranteeing law and order and in providing a moral governance. That government should guarantee law and order was beyond dispute. From time immemorial, it had been the government's unquestioned obligation to protect persons and property. Nothing was more necessary than that government jail thieves, put down riots, and hang murderers. Only radicals protested against the imprisoning of Chartists who conspired to riot, and even fewer protested the coercion bills that denied the Irish their constitutional freedoms or objected to the militia suppressing riots. Nor did many protest when Lord Palmerston refused to grant, because it would create a "public nuisance," the right of the Total Abstainers Society to march in Birmingham.[18] Most early Victorians who boasted of English liberties much preferred law and order and thus did not consider as evil those old, entrenched institutions that preserved order. Vagrants, poachers, drunkards, blasphemers, and all manner of criminals quailed in terror before the more than 3,000 county justices in their petty and quarter sessions and assizes. Nor did early Victorians object to the lord lieutenants whose militias suppressed riots, and the sheriffs, bailiffs, coroners, and constables who apprehended wrongdoers. These officials, along with governors of prisons, workhouses, and asylums, made up the elaborate, much-disciplining, and greatly esteemed local governments of England, whose activities and powers, along with those of the central courts, never abated. From 1805 to 1842, the prosecution of crime increased sevenfold. Legislation also greatly increased the J.P.'s power to dispense with juries and to whip or send miscreants to prison by summary powers.[19]

Two events convinced early Victorians of the need of a greater moral governance: a constantly increasing crime rate and the constant growth of the cities, where Mayhew found "criminal tribes," Dickens "a menacing savagery," and *Blackwood's* the breakdown of "restraints of character, relationships and vicinity."[20] The early Victorians' fear of sinful man and of unchecked appetites and impulses led to a threefold demand for a greater moral governance: (1) a demand for legislation to prohibit immorality, (2) a demand that law itself inculcate morality, and (3) a demand that government help schools educate children in righteousness. Although prohibition of immorality had a long history, much remained to be done. From 1835 to 1845, the early Victorians thus passed laws outlawing bearbaiting, cockfighting, bare-knuckled prize fighting, gaming houses, and obscene publications, as well as laws for censoring the theater. Blasphemy and homosexuality still earned one a prison term, and profanity and nonattendance at church a fine. Both in the press and in Parliament, some Nonconformists and Scottish and Anglican evangelicals demanded sabbatarian laws forbidding trading or railway travel on Sundays, but an increasingly secular and capitalist England said no.[21]

There was, however, no opposition to the use of law as an instructor of morality. Secular as well as ecclesiastical courts enforced new divorce laws, new county courts using new laws continued putting debtors in prison, and charity commissioners demanded that endowments be honest. Laws multiplied and deviance was increasingly made criminal, in keeping with the 1840 Bankruptcy Commission's report that "the law is the most powerful of teachers."[22] Laws could also be more positive in their moral governance. Law created post office savings accounts to promote thrift, and law, by regulating friendly societies, promoted self-reliance. That cleanliness and enlightenment might prosper, law insisted on sanitary regulations and allowed towns, if they wished, to apply rates to baths and washhouses, libraries, parks, and art galleries.[23]

The promotion of libraries and galleries was, of course, more than mere law, an inculcator of morality. It involved the use of knowledge and beauty to further morality itself, part of the third form of moral governance. An expanding government spent millions on the British Museum, the National Gallery, schools of design, art unions, the Great Exhibition, and geological and natural science museums.[24] It also decided to help Church schools educate England's children.

In 1839, Parliament created the Committee on Education with two inspectors of schools and £30,000 in grants that went to some 400 schools of the Church of England and the nondenominational but largely Nonconformist British and Foreign School Society. Twenty years later, in 1859, there were thirty-four inspectors and grants worth £723,115. Grants, which had begun as aids to building, now covered payment of teachers and pupil teachers, retirement benefits, and school supplies.[25] No other department of government experienced so rapid and substantial a growth. That growth in 1839 did not at all seem inexorable. The Church of England proclaimed loudly and clearly that it and not the government was the educator of the people, and Nonconformists, ever jealous of the state, were loud and clear in their voluntarism. Yet despite intentions, two underlying forces were at work, a growing awareness that England, the world's preeminent industrial and capitalist society, had the most inadequate system of public education in western Europe, and a recognition that England was preaching self-help to the poor without providing them with the instrument for its attainment. Desire as they did, and passionately, that Church schools teach everyone, they could not fund them.

There was nothing too venerable or sacred to escape the government's insinuating and proliferating touch—neither Oxford University (in 1854 thoroughly investigated by a commission) nor the Church of England itself. In 1836, the Whigs established a permanent Ecclesiastical Commission, and in 1836, 1838, and 1840, they passed acts equalizing (somewhat) the very unequal incomes of the bishops and clergy. They sought to prohibit a clergyman from holding more than two benefices and to suppress nonresident livings so as to terminate the more useless prebends and canonries and redistribute their funds to the poorer clergy. The bishops soon gained control of the commission and reforms lessened, but the precedent was clear, Parliament and its commissions could regulate the Church. In 1850, through the Privy Council, the government even forced the bishop of Exeter to give a living to a Reverend G. C. Gorham, whose doubts about baptismal regeneration the bishop and other High Churchmen considered rank heresy. The bishops found themselves part of government, and a government that by an act of Parliament in 1846 created the two new bishoprics of Manchester and Ripon.[26]

The pervasive and constant growth of government bettered, if falteringly, the people's lot. Although often imperfect, even woefully so, it represented the more generous aspect of the early Victorian social conscience. Government did considerably more good than harm. Its 6,300 statutes passed between 1832 to 1855 and scores of commissions and departments did not diminish English liberties, bring unbearable taxes, or check an expanding economy. Its main weakness was that it did not do enough. Viewed collectively, to be sure, these thousands of acts did seem to sound the death knell of a pure laissez-faire (if it ever existed), but viewed individually, and particularly in each act's pronounced weaknesses, they reveal the great impact that laissez-faire thinking had on the growth of government. The early Victorians were impelled to make many tentative and exploratory first steps, and they left huge areas of wretchedness and misery untouched, a part of the large domain of a laissez-faire society. Still, the inexorable growth of government made of England a more civilized and humane society. It was a profoundly significant event. But why did it occur from 1833 to 1858, in a country where so many people believed government to be evil?

THE FORCES BEHIND THE GROWTH
OF GOVERNMENT

Three powerful and three supplementary forces led to the expansion of the state. The three dominant ones were those old, familiar, and reliable friends of historians of Victorian England, the classic triad of population growth, industrial revolution, and urbanization; the three supplementary ones were emerging classes, advancing knowledge, and the dynamics of government itself.

From 1801 to 1851, the number of people in England and Wales doubled, from 8.9 to 17.9 million, a not entirely disagreeable fact for economic expansion, except that so many were destitute paupers, declining handloom weavers, homeless vagrants, and the underclass of London. They just kept multiplying, from 1810 to 1820 by 18 percent, an explosion that aggravated the vast destitution caused by the acute economic depressions of 1816–17 and 1825. It alarmed a generation raised on Malthus's *Essay on Population* and led them to look to government for remedies. One of them, Sir Robert Wilmot Horton, under-secretary of state for the colonies, had, in 1823 and 1824, persuaded the prime minister, Lord Liverpool, to set aside £56,000 for the emigration of distressed paupers to Canada. Horton's Select Committee on Emigration heard many a landlord urge state-assisted emigration, as did Malthus himself, who wanted the government to pay for the emigration of 500,000 Irish, although only if their cottages were destroyed to prevent repopulation. The

Tory government dismissed the idea as too expensive. Too expensive was the view also of later Whig governments, which in 1831 gave only a token grant to assist female emigration.[27]

A great many of overpopulation's flood of poor were crammed into unsafe, overcrowded, and filthy ships, were given meager rations and foul water, and died of disease or shipwrecks. So grievous were these evils that from 1823 to 1852, Parliament passed eleven acts, put numerous agents-general in English ports, and established a Land and Emigration Commission to regulate the passenger trade. Overpopulation had again helped cause an expansion of government.[28]

Emigration, great as it was, did not stem a population explosion rooted in falling death rates and rising birthrates, an explosion that flooded rural England with vast numbers of unemployed and underemployed paupers and seemingly caused an unending, unnecessary rise in the poor rate. It was this specter, the fruit of overpopulation, that haunted the outlook of both the landed classes and the writings of the economists and that helped lead to the age's most revolutionary act of centralization, the New Poor Law.

The sheer numbers of a multiplying population not only overwhelmed bloated towns and drove up crime but helped drive down the meager wages of weavers to a barely subsistence level and filled to overflowing poor houses, prisons, and asylums. "Understaffed and overcrowded," is the historian Kathleen Jones's judgment of the country lunatic asylum at York in 1816—103 patients in quarters designed for 55.[29] Prisons, too, were overcrowded as crime rose and people multiplied. Select committees and the press demanded more and better prisons and a reformed and efficient police, demands that led to the growth of government, both local and central.[30]

Population growth alone did not, of course, lead to that expansion. Industrialization and urbanization played a role, although not always an indispensable one. In largely rural Ireland, an exploding population helped foster the expansion of government; by 1830, it had no fewer than nineteen public departments, including prison and education inspectors.[31] England and Scotland, however, experienced, despite the arguments of revisionist historians to the contrary, an industrial revolution. The revisionists deny both that economic growth was revolutionary and that vast numbers poured into strictly industrial firms. But though growth was not as explosive as the more zealous historians claim nor steam-driven factories so universal, by 1850, Britain's per capita income was twelve times what it had been in 1750. And quite as revolutionary as steam-driven factories was the division of labor and rationalization of production that characterized the cutlery trades of Sheffield, the potteries of Staffordshire, and the hardware manufacturers of the Black Country.[32]

There were also railways and steamships, and soon thereafter, railway and merchant marine departments and inspectors. And although factories were not ubiquitous, they were both numerous enough and scandalous enough in their exploitation of children to lead to factory acts and factory inspectors and the growth of government. No abuse equaled the exploitation of factory children in arousing the social conscience of the early Victorians. It led many to a new awareness of society. "A new social state," declared Charles Buller, M.P., in the 1844 factory debate, and "masses of labour place them [factories] more completely under the control of the government." For the *Westminster Review,* in the same year, England was experiencing "a new era in the social life because of machinery . . . and the factory system."[33]

But not all areas won the dramatic attention that the satanic mills did; those on the periphery often went unnoticed. Iron making and iron fashioning, a great industrial triumph, brought no government intervention; neither did the navvies building the railways nor the overworked and underpaid women and children in England's dismal workshops. These women and children outnumbered those in textile mills.[34] In widely dispersed preindustrial workshops, they went unnoticed until the Commission on Women and Children in Manufactures of 1843—and then were only passingly noticed and soon forgotten. Meanwhile, images of monstrous factories whose relentless machines enslaved and deformed six-year-olds who worked fourteen and sixteen hours a day filled the debates in Parliament, speeches at great gatherings, and pamphlets and the press. Featured prominently by Michael Sadler's Select Committee of 1832, these images forced the Whig-Utilitarian dominated Royal Commission of 1833 to admit that cruel abuse of children did occur. These same abuses inspired Blake's phrase "satanic mills," Southey's "moral excrescences," Coleridge's indignation, and Lord Ashley's tireless campaign to prevent them. They persuaded Parliament to vote for a larger central government and for the first significant regulation of capital and labor.

The industrial revolution also led to an expanded state in less dramatic ways. By the late 1850s, there were inspectors of railways, steamships, mines, and smokestacks. There were some protests by doctrinaire economists, mine-owning lords, and railway stockholders, but no clash of ideas. In 1849, Disraeli, with a bow to his Lord Londonderry, opposed a bill empowering inspectors to see that mines were safe, but he invoked no great principles. It was a bill that Joseph Hume, so often and belligerently laissez-faire, supported.[35] Rare was the M.P. who took a consistent position on government intervention. Few also wanted railways more dangerous, steamships more likely to sink, towns smokier and more disease-ridden. Acts to make things safer and cleaner were a part of the technological imperatives of the industrial revolution. And just as technologically imperative as safe railways and steamships were the engineering advances that made mines safer, advances demanding enforcement by government inspectors.

Industrial advances also joined other economic developments and population growth to promote urbanization, the third leg of the classical triad of forces leading to government growth. In 1851, 54 percent of the people, not the 20 percent of 1801, lived in large towns. In the thirty years after 1801, the population of the towns in Lancashire and the West Riding of Yorkshire increased fourfold, with Leeds increasing fivefold. Londoners, 864,000 in 1801, numbered 2,367,000 in 1851.[36] Urbanization had exploded with a suddenness unparalleled in world history. It evoked an energetic voluntarism and a dedicated philanthropy, only to see both fall short of removing the more persistent and deeply rooted abuses. It also revealed the shortcomings of self-reliance and paternalism. Manchester cotton lords knew no more how "property's duties" could remove Manchester's slums and destitution than philanthropists knew how to lessen London's massive poverty. It forced the early Victorians to build a more active central government.

Two facts defined the impact of urbanization, the concentration of abuses, and the rise of urban social reformers. Rural England, of course, also knew crime and ignorance, and, although less in extent, disease. But urban crime, ignorance, and disease were so visible! so immediate! so dramatically concentrated! They haunted the minds of the early Victorians as dispersed rural evils did not, filling the pages of journals, government reports, pamphlets, and novels with stories of dreadful murders, raging cholera, and a drunkenness and profligacy unchecked by education. Those "moral maladies," said the *Sun* in 1847, are "consequent upon the congregation of men."[37] Good as well as evil was also consequent on the congregation of men. It was largely urban, not rural, England that produced the reformers who grappled with these issues. London, above all, with its great societies and dominant press, was the most demanding of social reforms. It was the Prison Discipline Society, established by William Wilberforce in 1816, that demanded improved prisons. He was aided by pamphlets from London's Law Amendment Society and the Philanthropic Institute, which pioneered in the establishment of reformatories.[38] It was the Central Society of Education, aided by the statistical societies of Liverpool, Manchester, Birmingham, and Sheffield that championed public education, aided by the Church of England's National Society and the Nonconformists' British and Foreign Society, both centered in London. It was also, in the 1850s, Manchester, allied with other towns, that formed the Lancashire Public Schools Association, soon to become the National Public Schools Association. And strengthening sanitary reform was the

Health of Towns Association, whose very title reflected those urban problems and urban forces behind the creation of the General Board of Health.[39]

London was, of course, the home of Parliament, Whitehall, the law courts, and, in season, many of the country's wealthy landowners. It might thus seem a national as well as an urban center. It was both. A city of two million, dwarfing all others in wealth and importance, it was a huge demographic fact, from which the early Victorians' social conscience could never escape.

Provincial towns, however, also produced, as rural England seldom did, social reformers. It was Birmingham and Bristol, not Norfolk and Suffolk, that produced M.D. Hill and Mary Carpenter, the two most important crusaders for the Reformatory Act of 1854. Aiding that crusade were also Manchester's Thomas Beggs, Liverpool's Edward Rushton, and "those benevolent persons in every large town" that Mary Carpenter found "willing to rescue their fellow creatures."[40]

The benevolent of large towns also demanded better education of the poor to reduce the moral corruption spawned by towns. In 1833, fearful of "the vast mass of manufacturing population," the *Edinburgh Review* announced that "we can no longer defer the great education question." From cities came those most zealous for education; their statistical societies made the most reliable investigations and their members the most eloquent pleas before the 1835 and 1838 select committees on education, pleas backed by resolutions from the northern manufacturing towns.[41]

Even more purely urban was the sanitary movement that responded to the fact that not only was the death rate in towns twice that in the countryside, but their stench and filth were far more vivid and disagreeable. Edwin Chadwick's 1842 Sanitary Report and the 1844 Report of the Royal Commissions on the Health of Towns were powerful and entirely urban, as were the many Health of Towns associations that demanded government action. It was an urban evil and an urban movement that quite overwhelmed the staunchest laissez-faire principles of the *Globe*, the *Examiner*, the *Daily News*, and, in the provinces, the *Manchester Guardian*, *Carlisle Journal*, and the *Scotsman*.[42]

Less formidable than the triad of population, industrial and urban growth was the first of the three supplementary forces, the emergence of more powerful middle and working classes. A great increase of people, industry, and towns characterized the first thirty years of the century as much as the next thirty years, although it was the latter thirty, the years after the Reform Act of 1832, that saw the revolutionary growth of government. Before 1832, French wars, postwar dislocations, Tory repression, the struggle for Catholic emancipation, and the concentration of the rising middle classes on the political reform of Parliament limited social reform to some weak and nearly unenforceable truck, factory, prison, and lunacy acts. After 1833, came acts enforced by central inspectors and commissioners, acts as unwelcome to the unreformed Tory as welcome to the reformed Whig Parliament. Although land still dominated the reformed Parliament, the middle classes had a much larger voice, a voice that from 1833 to 1856, allied to Whig and liberal gentry, created some twenty central departments. Only two of the departments, the single 1842 mining commissioner and the 1845 Lunacy Commission came into being during the rule of the Tories, but both were private, not government, bills.[43] That more voters from the varied middle classes returned more M.P.'s, that Nonconformists now accounted for 15 percent of the electorate, and that workers became a more organized force, with their press, unions, friendly societies, and petitions must not be omitted from the forces leading to a larger government. Kay-Shuttleworth, who as an assistant poor law commissioner and secretary to the Education Committee, was at the center of social reform, observed, in 1866, in his *Law of Social Progress*, that the Reform Act brought in the middle classes and that they brought in thirty years of social reform.[44] He could also have added the Municipal Reform Act of 1835, which brought elected mayors and town councils and a broader franchise to local government. Whether government was a vast evil or not, emerging forces wished it larger, more representative, and more active.

That they did so was in part due to the second supplementary force, the revolutionary advances in knowledge, advances both in the discovery of new knowledge and the greater dissemination of existing knowledge. From 1832 to 1844, claimed Toulmin Smith, Parliament created 166 commissions to investigate everything from the navigation of the Shannon to the Thames embankment. From 1833 to 1852, more than 200 select committees also probed into every aspect of British life.[45] Their many large folio volumes joined the even more numerous folio volumes of the reports of scores of permanent commissioners, assistant commissioners, and inspectors and the reports of hundreds of private and voluntary authorities, the most important of which were multiplied many times over by countless newspapers, journals, pamphlets, and books. That the rich did not know how the poor lived, a claim Disraeli made in *Sybil*, is a dubious claim.[46] Victorians were flooded with scientific knowledge and social facts. That it furthered their humanitarianism is quite probable, that it led to a larger government a near certainty. Engineers, physicians, chemists, geologists, and inventors filled their reports with findings that demanded a directive government. Disastrous mining accidents led the government in 1844 to appoint England's leading geologist, Sir Charles Lyell, and its leading physicist, Michael Faraday, to a government commission on mining accidents, and in 1845, it added the geologist Henry de la

Beche and the chemist Dr. Lyon Playfair to the commission, and all four recommended state action. That better ventilation, firmer buttressing, and the wider use of Davy lamps would reduce accidents persuaded that most devoted votary of laissez-faire, Thomas Chalmers's *North British Review*, that government must intervene.[47]

Science also made it difficult for the government not to intervene in the nation's public health. The discovery by medical men that where there were foul cesspools, filthy courtyards, no sewers, pollution, acute overcrowding, and contaminated water, there were disease and death called for action; and particularly so given the engineers' development of a system that used the continuous flow of water to flush refuse through improved glazed tubular drains, which made continued lethargy intolerable and government action inevitable. Moreover, since local government often lacked the needed scientific knowledge, some central supervision became necessary.[48] Railway accidents, like mining explosions and polluted towns, brought in the engineers. "If the government needs an officer of a high capacity," declared Henry Labouchere, president of the Board of Trade, "we choose a royal engineer." All eight of the railway inspectors came from the Royal Engineers. Education and scientific knowledge was also esteemed by county asylums, who welcomed the lunacy commissioners for their knowledge of mental illness.[49]

Science and technology insinuated themselves everywhere. There were soon smokestack inspectors and inspectors of salmon fisheries, Welsh roads inspectors, inspectors of Thames steamers, examiners of physicians, pilots, and engineers, and commissioners to inspect lighthouses—all bringing to bear advances in science.[50] These advances joined an equally impressive advance in society's knowledge of itself, of its failings and possibilities, as developed in investigation upon investigation, and made known to the public by the press, by learned journals, by books and pamphlets, and by endless government reports. The proliferating government reports point to the third supplementary force, government itself.

In 1832, there already was much government, both local and central, in England. The country was perhaps more misgoverned than undergoverned. The statute books bulged with powers that Parliament had given to local J.P.'s, to parishes, and to statutory authorities that they might firmly rule England, powers that came from a central government that was free of large, continental bureaucracies. But although free of large bureaucracies, Parliament and the courts were clearly and incontestably centralized and sovereign. It was a government that had defeated the armies of Louis XIV and Napoleon, built an empire, passed more than 2,000 laws regulating commerce, and presided over the birth of industrial capitalism. Its magistrates, many of whom were M.P.'s and active in supervising highways, police, prisons, bridges, asylums, and law and order, were experienced governors, governors who saw their cherished eighteenth-century model of government—a Parliament legislating, local officials administering, and law courts enforcing—fail to meet the problems of an industrial and urban society, problems ranging from child labor and a growing pauperism to cruelties in prisons and asylums and accidents to railways and steamships. These M.P.'s and J.P.'s had not been shy of passing poor laws and factory, prison, lunatic, railway and merchant marine acts to meet these challenges. Furthermore, neither they nor Whitehall officials began with a tabula rasa. The officials at the Board of Trade who fashioned the Merchant Marine Board, for example, began with forty statutes passed by their predecessors.[51]

They expanded the functions of government by strengthening their own departments, encouraging local government, and calling for new departments to enter new areas. The factory, mining, railway, and emigration inspectors were particularly anxious to strengthen their modest powers and staff. The Factory Act of 1844 gave the government far stricter powers to regulate working and meal times, to fence machinery, to grant certificates of age, and to be more strict in requiring the schooling of children; and the Mining Act of 1854 greatly increased the power of inspectors to enforce the law. Both acts not only reflected the constant recommendations of the inspectors but were largely drawn up by them.[52] No fewer than six general acts and hundreds of private acts increased the powers of the Railway Department from 1840 to 1846, and from 1828 to 1849, five acts added to the powers of the emigration commissioners.[53] The inspectors not only helped draft the acts but, by means of their reports, read by M.P.'s and summarized by the press, and by appearances before select committees, argued for an expanded role. They also, by persuasion, increased that role in their visits to mines, factories, railways, and ships.

Poor law assistant commissioners and lunacy commissioners, and health, prison, and education inspectors not only expanded the powers of their departments but those of local authorities. The engineering inspectors of the General Board of Health played a crucial role in the creation of 182 local boards of health, as did many education inspectors in multiplying the number of schools and lunacy commissioners in promoting county asylums.[54] Prison inspectors were also active. Frederick Hill drafted the Scottish Prison Act that established a General Board, and Whitworth Russell and William Crawford campaigned for the adoption of cellular prisons suitable for separate confinement. They promoted such changes both throughout their districts and for the Home Office's Pentonville and Parkhust prisons.[55]

Frederick Hill teamed up with Joseph Fletcher, an education inspector, to help establish juvenile reformatories, and both had an influence on Mary Carpenter. Inspectors and commissioners did not reserve their wish for a more active government to their own departments. Edwin Chadwick, who wrote the 1833 Factory Act and wrote half of the famous report that led to the New Poor Law of 1834, also became the secretary of the new commission. From that position, he wrote the Constabulary Report of 1839 and the famous Sanitary Report of 1842 that led to the 1839 Constabulary Act and 1848 Public Health Act. The movement that culminated in the Public Health Act had its beginnings in the 1838 Report on Fever in London by three poor law assistant commissioners, Neil Arnott, Southwood Smith, and James Kay-Shuttleworth.[56] Kay-Shuttleworth joined another assistant commissioner, E. C. Tufnell, in a powerful report on England's scandalous lack of schooling. Kay-Shuttleworth also testified to that failing and to the need for a better system before the 1838 Select Committee on Education.[57] Frederick Hill and Leonard Horner, both in their reports and separate publications, repeatedly called for better education not only in prison and factory but throughout England, pleas that helped in the establishment of the Committee on Education. Since Parliament refused to support a normal school, Tufnell and Kay-Shuttleworth did so from their own incomes. Tufnell as a member of the 1833 Factory Commission was one of the first to inform the nation of the cruel treatment of children in mines. The ceaseless probings of inspectors stung the early Victorian social conscience.[58]

They were, however, more than gadflies. Their experiences and remedies informed many a statute. Seymour Tremenheere, whose many voluminous reports as a mining commissioner and education inspector probed society's every failing, was also instrumental in drawing up nineteen acts of Parliament. William Blamire, a tithe commissioner and expert on rural property, gave invaluable testimony to the Select Committee on Enclosures and became first an enclosure commissioner and then a copyhold commissioner. He was, said his biographer, "at the heart of the great rural reforms."[59] The growth of government was in part self-generating. It had a dynamism of its own, and at the heart of that dynamism were the commissioners and inspectors.

So inexorable were these forces, so pervasive the view that government was evil, and so weak the ideas favoring a larger government, that many historians see the growth of government as reflective of economic, social, and institutional, not ideological, forces. An "intolerable state of things," argues W. L. Burn, along with "prejudices and habits and interests" was far more important than "pseudo-philosophical theories." Burn was praising Oliver MacDonagh's *Patterns of Government Growth*, a pioneering study of the passenger acts as a model of government growth. According to this model, a historical process begins when "a blaze of ascertainable abuse" that is able to "melt economic doctrine" interacts with "the rub and wear of experience" and "the most ordinary of everyday reactions." The result is a "self- generating" process, largely independent of "human purpose"[60] Harold Perkin also praises MacDonagh, especially his emphasis on industrialization, urbanization, and "ordinary, uninstructed humanitarianism," as the "prime movers" of government growth. Derek Fraser underscores this view in his *Evolution of the Welfare State*, calling government growth "practical, unplanned, and ad hoc." It was a process, Karl Polanyi observes, that took place in all Western countries "irrespective of national mentalities" and that was implemented by "peoples who were mere puppets."[61]

They were not mere puppets! It was not merely a blaze of grievances and ordinary humanitarianism, exclaims Jennifer Hart in her 1965 article in *Past and Present*, but principles and standards. "Ideas," she writes, after attacking MacDonagh, Burn, Kitson Clark, Roylston Lambert, and myself, "can influence people." The "general climate of opinion" does count. Abuses, she argues, do not become problems without principles and standards, and certainly do not provide solutions.[62]

MacDonagh and Perkin do not, in fact, omit ideas from their account of historic processes. MacDonagh admits that ideas influence that process, just as that process molds ideas, while Perkin sees at work an ideology that is the "crystallization of the accepted wisdom as hitherto unvoiced assumptions."[63] Viewed largely, over a half century, from Berlin to New York, and in terms of the growth of many different agencies, particular ideas often do not seem crucial. Factory acts, boards of health, and education committees were bound to come, even if a decade earlier or later. But viewed closely, in terms of Peel or Disraeli and their followers, or Russell and Palmerston and their supporters, or in terms of a particular journal or party, ideas were at work, were influential. Two ideas that were at work were the idea of a paternal government and the idea of a utilitarian state.

CHAPTER 15

The Idea of a Paternal Government

Large and inexorable forces, when viewed one issue at a time, and one M.P., editor, or clergyman at a time, seem less divorced from ideas than if viewed from a distance. No debate over a factory act or poor law ever occurred without a clash of opposing ideas, clashes whose outcome was not inevitable, but closely fought and revolving around differing intellectual outlooks.

Among the ideas forming these outlooks, two above all, although in differing degrees, promoted the growth of government: the idea of a paternal government and the idea of a utilitarian state. Many other ideas, of course, also played a role and helped form the early Victorian social conscience. The concepts of a paternal government and a utilitarian state must be seen in the context of the larger, more complex intellectual development that included the romantic movement, religious revivals, the rationalism of the Enlightenment, and the overall advance of knowledge. But most of these, certainly those that helped define the vision of a laissez-faire society, did little directly to create a more active state. Neither political economy nor a belief in the inviolability of property, society's providential harmony, nor the importance of self-reliance and voluntary societies led to greater government. Even natural law ideology, whose roots ran back both to medieval thought and to the triumph of Newtonian science, and whose masterful exposition by John Locke had an unrivaled influence on the English, checked more than it favored a powerful state. A belief in natural law and natural rights, so powerfully stated by Thomas Paine and William Godwin, led not to radicals who demanded a more active government but to men such as William Cobbett, who opposed state education, denounced centralization, and told workers to win the ten-hour day on their own. The natural rights philosophy also underpinned Owenites, who looked to rural communities, O'Connorite Chartists, who espoused private land schemes, and humanitarians like Dickens, Jerrold, and Mayhew, for whom government was mostly a vast evil. Nor would the outlook of Nonconformists—ruggedly individualistic, jealously independent, and dedicated to the ways of God, not the ways of Caesar—ever encourage the growth of government.

The first of these two key ideas, belief in a paternal government, had roots that ran back to Tudor England and was woven not only into the laws of the land but into the inherited attitudes of the wealthy and powerful.

THE MEANING OF A PATERNAL GOVERNMENT

Four features in particular define the early Victorians' idea of a paternal government: (1) it protected the weak, helpless, and poor; (2) it promoted industry; (3) it guided and instructed faith and morals; and (4) it protected life, property, and the social order. "Protection" was a key word—protection of industry, morality, order, and most particularly, the weak and helpless. As Edward Cayley, Tory M.P., pamphlet writer, and outspoken paternalist, said in praise of the "Patriarchal System," all law was to "protect the weak against the strong, who care for themselves."

It was not an uncommon sentiment among paternalists of both parties. For the Tory Montague Gore, "the object of all society is to protect the weak . . . [and] for that government is instituted"; and for the Whig and evangelical William Cowper, the Ten Hour Bill was justified by "the old principle of protection of the weak." "What is needed," proclaimed Carlyle, "is the parental care of the poor."[1]

It was a principle that lay at the heart of the factory debate. In 1844, the Tory Thomas Acland pled for the "principle of the protection of labour," which the Whig-Utilitarian Charles Buller called protection of "the helpless" and the Radical John Fielden protection of "the weak." The Tory Henry Liddell agreed, insisting that the state should put itself "*in loco parentis.*" From 1832 to 1847, the factory debate absorbed the early Victorians and forced them to consider the role of government in an industrial economy.[2] The exploitation of children in Britain's textile mills evoked Wordsworth's compassion, Coleridge's indignation, Oastler's vehement *Slavery in Yorkshire,* and the harrowing revelations of cruelties by Sadler's Select Committee of 1832, revelations that aroused a nation. Wordsworth demanded that "the state" should stand "*in loco parentis* to its subjects," Coleridge that government should regulate factories, and Oastler and Sadler that there be a Ten Hour Act.[3]

No one was more compassionate of children than Lord Ashley. "The State," he told the Commons, "should show herself a faithful parent." But the state was not to be a faithful parent to factory children alone, but to chimney sweeps, blind children, the thousands in mines and workshops, and those juvenile offenders and London's outcasts for whom he established ragged schools and reformatories. The plight of lunatics, too, many as helpless as children, led him to plead for a more paternal, a more protecting government.[4]

The plea to protect the weak involved no radical ideas but an old and honored principle of English law. The sovereign, the keeper of the King's Peace, was bound to protect, announced the *Law Magazine*, "incapable persons . . . since the state is *parens patriae* and stands *in loco parentis* to orphans and bastard children as it does to lunatics." It was a law that ran back to feudal times, one that determined that "the duty of the sovereign to protect his liege subjects" was "of the most extensive character."

The extensive character of the sovereign's duty to protect had long included a mercantilist encouragement of industry—the second feature of a paternal government. Even Burke, a disciple of Adam Smith, added "the promotion and encouragement of industry" to his short list of government functions. It also appears in Robert Southey's list of functions as tariffs for the protection and promotion of handicraft guilds, and the Tory M.P. Charles Newdegate announced that "Protection" considered "the regulation of trade . . . as much a part of the duty of Government as protection of the person."[5] At the center of that protectionism, which lay at the heart of Toryism, were the corn laws, flanked by the long cherished navigation acts and by recent public works in Ireland. In the never-ending corn law debates of the 1840s, in the many speeches of the members of the Protection Society, and in the writings of Edward Cayley, Michael Sadler, and David Urquhart, the protection of agriculture, trade, and manufacturing formed the most popular feature of a paternal government, the one most reflective of vested interests.[6]

For the seriously religious, the most popular feature was the third characteristic of a paternal government, its spiritual and moral guidance for the improvement of the people. For Southey, that meant a national education run by the Church of England and funded in part by the state. "They must be fed," he insisted, "sound doctrine." If such a "foundation" were to be laid, he added, there would be "a superstructure of prosperity and happiness." Coleridge agreed, and the fourth and final function of his "God-like State" was "the development of faculties, moral and rational," a function given over to a "nationality" headed by the king, which would be the people's "guide, guardian and instructor."[7]

The state would also guide and instruct through its powerful magistracy, backed by the majesty of its vast and formidable laws and an active clergy. Very little errant behavior fell outside their jurisdiction, neither drunkenness, absence from Church, poaching, nor vagrancy. "Men are made happy," said the paternalist *Blackwood's*, "only by rendering them orderly, moral, and religious," a view, Carlyle argued, that the populace themselves held when they cried, "Govern me, guide me."[8]

R. B. Seeley, in his classic work on paternalism, *Perils of the Nation*, would establish in every parish, as governors and guides, "guardians of the poor and courts of morals, and stricter surveillance over their houses." A devout evangelical, he joined his fellow believers in demanding that Parliament pass stricter laws on drink, gambling, the theater, the press, and the observance of the Sabbath.[9]

Strict laws were needed to guarantee peace and order, the fourth characteristic of a paternal government. The protection of property and life was the summum bonum. For early nineteenth-century Tories, this meant acts muzzling the radical press, outlawing seditious meetings, and denying Catholics, Nonconformists, and workers any role in government. "Curb the seditious press," cried Southey, "and keep it curbed." "To learn obeying," Carlyle wrote in 1843, "is the fundamental art of governing." In 1850, he praised the rule of the hero-king, the drill sergeant and "wise command and wise obedience." Tory paternalists from Benjamin Disraeli to Henry Drummond looked to a revived monarchy, Drummond because "the duty of kings and fathers is still the same . . . the duty of supervision."[10] A revived Crown was a favorite with advocates of a paternal government, not only with the giants, Burke, Coleridge, Southey, and Carlyle, but with many a High Churchman and Young Englander and with the Christian Socialists like Charles Kingsley. It reflected an authoritarian outlook, but a fanciful one, since their vision of a strong monarchy was more rhetorical than actual. Less fanciful was their strong fear of crime and disorder and their belief in the suppression and punishment of blasphemy and sedition by imprisonment.

Obedience was the refrain of countless sermons reminding all that the laws of man are ordained by God. "Submit yourself," said the High Church Reverend Charles Hewitley, since the laws of "those lawfully appointed over us [are] God's laws." Even the Nonconformists, who denounced all government interference in religion and education, preached obedience to God's ordained laws. The state, said the Methodists' *Watchman* is "the great conservator of public morals."[11] Most Nonconformists and many Anglicans were evangelicals and as such likely to be authoritarian. Many, like the much-read Reverend Edward Bickersteth, looked to the "Righteous Kings of Israel" as the model for "Civil Government," while others, like R. B. Seeley, the publicist for the "Patriarchal System," demanded that "the State be a terror to evil doers."[12] Prisons, transportation, the whipping of erring juveniles, the treadmill, and solitary confinement all became part of a paternal government that led the radical George Jacob Holyoake to declare "paternal government is the government of the Tories, of tyranny, and of retrogression."[13] But it was not only the government of the Tories and of tyranny, but of many who were less repressive and less reactionary but of great influence.

INFLUENCE IN HIGH PLACES

A majority of the 1841 House of Commons had attended either Oxford or Cambridge, and their graduates constituted an even higher proportion of the front bench, the House of Lords, and, perhaps, the magistracy. Almost all the clergy of the Church of England (who also made up nearly one-third of the county J.P.'s) had attended those two august seats of learning, and in the 1820s and 1830s, paternalist ideas of an earnest religious tone were gaining the ascendancy. Their sermons, published and spoken, had an influence second only to the press, and the press, long deemed a vulgar profession, witnessed an invasion of Oxford and Cambridge men, some as owners, some leader writers, and a few as editors. Unreformed and narrow in curriculum, leisurely and sybaritic in lifestyle, Oxford and Cambridge were nevertheless influential in forming the social conscience of the early Victorians. And in the 1820s and 1830s, paternalist ideas of an earnest religious tone were gaining the ascendancy.

The news from Cambridge was that Paley's utilitarianism was in retreat. Not only were William Whewell, Thomas Peacock, and Adam Sedgwick, the great luminaries of the university, attacking Paley's dominance (along with the errors of Bentham), but at Trinity College the scholarly Julius Hare and his pupil the philosophical Frederick Maurice, the founder of Christian Socialism, were proclaiming Coleridge and Wordsworth the reigning monarchs. Their votaries, to cement their rule and win disciples, refashioned the Cambridge Apostles club. The Apostles, twelve in number and all serious, intellectual, and religious, formed a select and powerful group. They included the poet Tennyson, the historian Connop Thirlwall, future bishop of St. David's, and four future M.P.'s, Edward Horsman, Sir Spencer Walpole, Charles Buller, and Richard Monckton Milnes. It was Monckton Milnes who told the Commons that England needed a paternal government. Also calling for such a government was the Apostle Arthur Helps, whose *The Claims of Labour* and *Friends in Council* popularized paternalist ideals, and John Sterling, whose writings, nobility, and early death won him biographies by Julius Hare and Carlyle. John Sterling, in his essay "State of Society," denounced utilitarianism and the worship of mammon and looked to an "alteration of mind" inspired by Wordsworth and Coleridge.[14]

Two Apostles became editors, John Kemp of the *British and Foreign Review* and Frederick Maurice of the *Athenaeum* and the *Education Magazine*, and two others, George Venables and James Spedding, wrote leaders for the *Times*. Some became clergymen; Julius Hare and Charles Merivale became archdeacon of Lewes and dean of Westminster respectively. Small in number but powerful, they considered, said Charles Merivale, that "Coleridge and Wordsworth are our principal divinities and Hare and Thirlwall . . . their prophets."[15]

Cambridge undergraduates like George Smythe, Lord John Manners, and Alexander Baillie Cochrane, the core of Disraeli's Young England, also adored Coleridge and Wordsworth. Smythe was tutored by Hare and Maurice, and Cochrane attended Trinity College, as did Manners's friends Lord Littleton, Beresford-Hope, and Stafford O'Brien. Manners and his friends, along with Peter Borthwick (of Jesus College, Cambridge) became Tory M.P.'s and friends of Young England, Borthwick also becoming editor of the Tory *Morning Post*. Beresford Hope, a poet, was like Stafford O'Brien, outspoken in praise of Coleridge and Wordsworth. Seven Tory M.P.'s from Cambridge, all prominent in debates, thus brought the ideas of Coleridge and Wordsworth to Parliament. There was, indeed, as Thomas Arnold had said much earlier, a Cambridge movement stemming from Coleridge.[16]

But what of Oxford? Was it still mired in Aristotle and Locke? Not at all. Coleridge and Wordsworth also entered its sacred halls, although not without the help of missionaries from Cambridge. In 1827, Frederick Maurice arrived at Oxford, where he joined William Gladstone's Essay Club, founded on the model of the Apostles. Most of its leading members became Peelites, many of whom rose high in government: Lord Lincoln became Peel's man at Woods and Forests, Edward Cardwell Gladstone's successor at Trade, Sydney Herbert, secretary to the Admiralty and Lord Francis Egerton, secretary of war. Other members of the Essay Club were Thomas Acland Jr., a leading advocate in Parliament of Church education and ten-hour bills, and Roundell Palmer, M.P., leader writer for the *Times* and at Oxford a "reveller in the poetry of Wordsworth and Coleridge." They all welcomed Gladstone's *The State and Its Relation to the Church* with its praise of Coleridge as "masterly . . . [and] full of substantial truth" and its call for a government that stands "in a paternal relation to the people."[17]

The Essay Club was by no means the only place nourishing the idea of a paternal government. There was also Oriel College, which the Broad Churchmen Edmund Copleston, Richard Whatley, and Thomas Arnold had made the intellectual center of Oxford, and which continued so under the High Churchmen John Keble, William Pusey, and John Henry Newman. Arnold, whom his editors thought "the true disciple of Coleridge," shared Coleridge's vision of a state and Church united for the paternal care of the people, a vision Copleston and Whately only shared in part, being, as followers of Burke, much more persuaded of the truths of political economy, and as bishops, more jealous of the Church's prerogatives. Their successors at Oriel, Keble, Pusey, and Newman, although no lovers of political economy and fearful of Arnold's comprehensive paternal government, were nonetheless lovers of Wordsworth and Coleridge and keen for a Church-dominated paternal government.

At Oriel, the reign of Aristotle and Locke was yielding to Burke, Wordsworth, and Coleridge. John Campbell Colquhoun, an Oriel graduate who was tireless in Parliament for Church causes, wrote a biography of Coleridge, who, he said, had "influenced many lives," including those of other Oriel men such as Sir George Grey, Sir John Yarde-Buller, John Pakington, Edmund Denison, and Sir William Heathcote, all of whom became M.P.'s and all but Grey, Tories. Oriel also produced Dean Church, High Church editor of the *Guardian*.[18] Oriel was not alone; at Exeter College, William Sewell, in 1836 Oxford's professor of moral philosophy, was denouncing utilitarianism and celebrating paternalism.[19] The graduates of Oxford and Cambridge not only brought their ideal of a more paternal government to a Parliament and a Church in which they were dominant, but to the press and the world of publishing, in which they were not. But although not dominant, neither were they weak, especially when allied to Burkians and Coleridgeans from beyond Oxford and Cambridge. John Delane, an Oxford man, who become editor of the *Times* in 1841, hired as leader writers the Oxford High Churchmen Thomas Moseley and Roundell Palmer, the Cambridge Apostles' Archdeacon George Venables and James Spedding, and, from a Trinity College steeped in Coleridge, Henry A. Woodham, who wrote more of the *Times*'s leaders of the 1840s than anyone else.

The *Times*'s rival, the utilitarian *Morning Chronicle*, ceased to be utilitarian in 1847 when William Gladstone, Sydney Herbert, and Lord Lincoln, all once members of Oxford's Essay Club, joined with the Cambridge Young Englander Beresford Hope to purchase it. They immediately hired the Apostle George Venables and Young England's George Smythe to rescue it from utilitarianism.[20]

The *Standard*'s editor and the director of a chain of provincial papers was Wordsworth's and Coleridge's friend and fervent admirer Alaric Watts; the editor of *John Bull* was William Mudford, unstinting in his admiration of Burke and Coleridge; the Apostles' John Kemble edited the *British Foreign Review*; and Oxford's Thomas Moseley, Dean Church, and Richard Jelf edited, respectively, the *British Critic*, the *Guardian*, and the *English Review*. From Edinburgh came John Gibson Lockhart, a Coleridgean and son-in-law to Sir Walter Scott, to edit the *Quarterly Review*.[21] Tory paternalists controlled *Blackwood's*, and Thomas Chalmers dominated the *North British Review*. Many books also promoted paternalism. The writings of Coleridge, Arnold, and Gladstone ran to many editions. And, from 1828 to 1835, according to Gladstone "a furor for Church establishment came down upon the Conservatives." The paternal government was to be an ecclesiastical paternal government, whose bold outlines also appeared in 1839 in Frederick Maurice's *The Kingdom of Christ* and in 1838 in Oxford's W. G. Ward's *The Ideal of a Christian Church*. The works of Sewell and Helps and of Seeley and Sadler spelled out the details of a paternal government, whose necessity no one presented more powerfully than Carlyle. "Coleridge and Carlyle," argued the Reverend R. W. Dale, were for the young "masters of thought." Little wonder that Maurice concluded that Coleridge's *On the Constitution of Church and State* (1829) had "influenced [the] men who ultimately rule the masses."[22]

Powerful among England's rulers and powerful in its plea for a more paternal, protective, and guiding government, it nevertheless had only a mixed impact on the growth of government.

A MIXED IMPACT

The idea of a paternal government had only a mixed impact on the growth of government, because it was only one strand in a larger paternalism. Michael Sadler urged a "Patriarchal System," not a paternal government, just as the *Quarterly Review* spoke of "paternal relations" and Arthur Helps insisted that the analogy of the father should be the basis "of all social government," that is, government by masters, landlords, clergymen, and schoolmasters. "What we need," said Frederick Lucas, editor of the Catholic *Tablet*, "is the parental, sovereign care exercised by the rich."[23] Those who were all-powerful in society, not just government, were to be paternal. Government indeed would be but one of four elements defining paternalism, one joined by property, Church, and locality—locality being a fusion of local property, voluntary institutions, and local government. For most paternalists, the term "paternal government" usually meant Parliament, the law courts, and Whitehall, which limits the idea of a paternal government and makes it ambivalent. In the regulation of the economy, it confronted a jealous property, in the moral guidance of the people, a proud Church, and in solving society's many problems, an entrenched locality.

In the first area, the economy, paternal government's proclaimed mission was to protect the weak and helpless, particularly by those factory acts that won such enthusiastic support. The Factory Act of 1833, with its central inspectors enforcing the exclusion of those under nine years of age and limiting the labor of those aged nine to thirteen to eight hours a day, and the 1847 Ten Hour Act radically enlarged the scope of government. The passage of those two acts owed much to the idea of a paternal government, an idea held by the leaders of the factory movement, Richard Oastler, Michael Sadler, the Reverend G. S. Bull, the Reverend John Raynor Stephens, and Lord Ashley, as well as by a large array of M.P.'s and editors ranging from Disraeli to Alaric Watts and including Tory backbenchers, the Tory press, and some Anglican clergy from the north of England. Whig governments may have proposed, Benthamites drawn up, and Liberals supplied votes for these two acts, but the beginnings of the factory movement, its early agitations, and the sustained pressure it kept up for seventeen years came from strong supporters of a paternal government. It was the out-and-out paternalist Richard Oastler whose revelations of the cruel exploitation of children first aroused public opinion; it was Michael Sadler, proponent of the "Patriarchal System," whose Select Committee persuaded a nation of the truth of Oastler's revelations; it was Lord Ashley who said "let the state show herself a faithful parent" and aroused the conscience of Parliament to these evils; and it was the M.P. John Fielden, who argued that government should "protect the weak from the strong," whose Ten Hour Bill won the day in 1847.[24] Three Apostles, Monckton Milnes, Charles Buller, and Connop Thirlwall, two from Oxford's Essay Club, Lord Francis Egerton and Thomas Acland Jr., and three from Oriel, John Colquhoun, Sir George Grey, and Sir John Pakington, joined the Cambridge Young Englanders Lord John Manners and Baillie Cochran in support of the Ten Hour Bill. Even the bishop of London spoke for it in terms of a "parental function of the state."[25]

The bill also won the support of the Tory *Standard, Morning Post, John Bull, Blackwood's,* and *Fraser's,* and the *Times,* which invoked "the whole paternal character of government."[26] In 1847, 78 percent of the Conservatives allied with 58 percent of the Liberals to pass the Ten Hour Act, which, along with the 1848 Public Health Act, led John Stuart Mill to conclude that England was "to be governed paternally."[27]

The idea of a paternal government also played a role in the passage of the Mines Act of 1842, which excluded children and women from the mines, and Gladstone's 1843 and 1844 acts protecting coal whippers from wage frauds and giving third class passengers covered coaches and faster and less expensive trains. But the idea of a paternal government fared less well on other issues, bowing over and over again to sovereign property, which had its own paternal duties and rights. Where were the 78 percent of Conservatives who voted for the Ten Hour Bill when Henry Halford proposed the protection of frame-work knitters, Lord Grosvenor relief for overworked London bakers, and Thomas Duncombe some justice for the lace workers? All lost. Halford picked up only 58 votes, and Grosvenor and Duncombe only nineteen and six, with most of those votes coming from Whigs and Radicals.[28] An absence of Tory votes was no less marked on bills for the protection of agricultural tenants and laborers, especially if Irish. Burke, Coleridge, and Southey had said government was never to interfere in agriculture, and it did not—except, of course, for drainage, tithe, enclosure, and copyhold bills that benefited the landlords. No bill compensating the tenant for the improvements he made had a chance in a landlord Parliament and neither did many Tory paternalists support a reform in the game laws, an end to the Act of Settlement that bound laborers to their parish, or the establishment of an effective poor law for the Irish. When in 1847 and 1849, efforts were made to strengthen the Irish poor law, the Young Englander Lord John Manners and the Apostle Edward Horsman denounced it as "socialism" and "crushing" to property.[29] The agricultural tenant and laborer lay beyond the pale of a paternal government.

So did child labor, if it was not in textile mills. Lord Ashley's Children's Employment Commission's four-volume compendium of abuse that told of five-, six-, and seven-year-old girls making buttons, lace, and gloves, and plaiting straw for twelve hours a day for four or five shillings a week, and of boys from six up in the metal trades making pins, nails, screws, and chains for twelve hours on end for five or six shillings, some of which went for petty fines or overpriced goods at company stores. Most exploited of all were milliners and needlewomen who for the scantiest of wages worked in the months of the London season from eighteen to twenty hours a day.[30] There was no paternal government for these suffering children, whose numbers far exceeded those in regulated textile mills.

The idea of paternal government had its limits. It was indeed not decisive in defining the enforcement powers of the 1833 Factory Act. Sadler, Ashley, Oastler, and Fielden, along with the *Times* and *Leeds Intelligencer,* had never wanted the inspectors who in fact kept the 1833 act from becoming a dead letter like earlier factory, truck, and chimney sweep acts.[31] Most Tories, furthermore, were not natural supporters of a Ten Hour Act. In 1844, only 46 percent of them supported Lord Ashley's ten-hour amendment. Their devotion to sacred property had long engendered hostility to all government meddling. Why then, in 1847, did 78 percent support the Ten Hour Act? According to seven newspapers (the Tory *Standard* included) and two M.P.'s (Ashley and Milner Gibson), many did so in retaliation for the repeal of the

Corn Law. From 1844 on, many Tories, brimming with hostility toward anti–Corn Law manufacturers, economists, and Whigs and Liberals saw in the passage of a Ten Hour Act, so anathema to the enemies of land, sweet revenge. But though it pleased many a Tory to support on this occasion a paternal government's intervention in the economy in order to protect the weak and helpless in this, it was more of an exception than a rule. The Tories' new leader in the House, Disraeli, said in opposing the Mines Act of 1849, that the rule should be "no interposition between capital and labor."[32] Perhaps the idea of a paternal government would have a fuller expression in its second function, the moral and religious guidance of the people.

A PATERNAL CHURCH

It was not more laws, commissioners, and inspectors regulating the economy that inspired the young paternalists of Oxford and Cambridge but more bishops, vicars, and deacons guiding the people in the ways of the kingdom of God, ways outlined in the much-acclaimed works of Coleridge, Arnold, Gladstone, and Maurice. The ways of the kingdom of God were also outlined in the many charges to the clergy by bishops and archdeacons, the editorials of the burgeoning religious press, and the seemingly infinite outpouring of sermons. Although they differed on many issues, almost all called for a more active, more paternal Church, led by a national clerisy, that would strengthen and be strengthened by a paternal government and foster a juster and more caring society. It would, said Thomas Arnold, create a "Kingdom of God for the most effective removal of all evil and the promotion of all good." It was a sentiment, wrote the *Quarterly Review*, with which Arnold and Coleridge agreed, since both believed that "the Christian Church . . . alone is able to put down the evil which [is] . . . daily growing."[33]

It was the vision of the more reforming bishops, a vision of newly built churches rising in urban wastelands, of parishes divided and subdivided and endowed with vicars and curates who visited the sick, and deacons and sisters caring for the poor, all part of one, great, unified national Church. It was a noble and inspiring vision and had an impact, although a mixed one, on the growth of government.

Among the many social problems that the Church was to address, none was more important than the ignorance of the lower orders, itself the greatest source of so many other evils. The Church of England, said the archbishop of Canterbury in 1839, was to be the teacher of the people. And by 1859, with thirty-four inspectors and more than 80 percent of government grants, it was, if not the only, certainly the greatest teacher of the people. What better example of the impact of the idea of a paternal government on the expansion of the state! What an admirable example of the impact of Coleridge's idea of a clerisy on the young Tory paternalists from Oxford and Cambridge! Yet the story was not that simple. Forces far more complex were at work, forces reflecting and defining the outlook of both the Tory and Whig-Liberal parties.

Three facts in succession defined the educational outlook of the Tory paternalists: they were, at first, for a paternal government educating the people, but only if it was exclusively Anglican; then, second, they saw in the Whig scheme of government aid and inspection to essentially voluntary church schools a form of a paternal government promoting a clerisy; and, finally, their own dominance in that scheme and the narrowness of their goals greatly limited the effectiveness of the idea of a paternal government providing education for all.

That the Tory paternalists wanted a paternal government to provide education only if exclusively Anglican became clear in 1839, when the Whigs proposed the granting of £30,000 to both the schools of the Church's National Society and those of the nondenominational British and Foreign School Society. The Whig proposal also called for the appointment of government inspectors and the establishment of a normal school to train desperately needed teachers. The proposal evoked a storm of protest from Churchmen and Tories of every hue. "Insidious," "unconstitutional," "perfectly despotic," "socinian," and "poisonous" shouted Ashley, Gladstone, Graham, Plumptre, and the bishop of London. A "monstrosity," "state control," "a tyranny," and "your children are to be taken from you," wrote the Tory *Standard*, *Morning Herald*, the evangelical *Record*, and the *Times*. After the idea of a normal school was dropped, the measure was passed by the Commons by only two votes, and hardly one of the votes for it was Tory; not even a Cambridge Apostle or an Oxford Essayist, except the Whig Charles Buller. Even the liberal Maurice, although not in the Commons, opposed it.[34]

Despite talk of the Whig proposal being "perfectly despotic" and "state control" the Tory paternalists were not voluntarists. They had no objection at all to government grants for education if it were exclusively Anglican. In 1843, a Tory government proposed a bill that would establish rate-financed factory schools to be run by trustees, a majority of whom would be Anglicans. All of the teachers in these schools must also be Anglican and be approved by a local bishop, and all would teach the Anglican catechism and liturgy and a smattering of knowledge taken from the Bible. That Catholic and Nonconformist pupils would be excused from Anglican religious instruction (but only if they requested it) in no way allayed the outrage felt by thousands of Nonconformists and Catholics. It was their children's meager earnings and the parents' modest incomes that would support these Anglican schools. Tory hopes that the Church of England would be the exclusive educator of the people collapsed after 2.6 million people signed petitions of protest and thousands attacked the proposal in angry meetings and told their M.P.'s how utterly intolerable it was to have their money support teachings they considered heretical.[35]

The Tory Factory-Education Bill also had a more lasting effect; its threat of a Church-dominated education made Dissent ever more hostile to any government aid to education and thus far more voluntarist, as well as far less trusting of Tory paternalists, who almost to the man supported the Factory-Education Bill. Publicly financed education didn't bother Tory consciences if it financed their schools alone.

Finance Church schools, however, is just what the 1839 Committee on Education did—along with Nonconformist ones, a fact that evoked Tory denunciations. By 1847, nearly nine out of ten grants went to Anglican schools. The Church itself, of course, contributed much. It had by 1839 established twenty-four diocesan boards of education and schools in hundreds of parishes, schools greatly expanded by the help of increased grants and inspection.[36] By 1859, there were thirty-four inspectors and £723,000 in grants, the nearest thing to a clerisy the Victorians would ever achieve. It was the government's largest department dealing with social issues, testifying to the impact that—with Whig help, and despite the Tories' initial opposition—the idea of a paternal government had on the growth of the state.

The idea of a paternal government bringing together Church and state was not the sole monopoly of the Tories. Some important Whigs also held these ideas, as Richard Brent makes clear in his study of *Liberal Anglican Politics*. Whigs like Lords John Russell, Morpeth, and Howick, along with Thomas Spring Rice, were far more religious than their latitudinarian and Foxite predecessors, and in their own way, they were as paternalist as the Tories, only in the liberal manner of Thomas Arnold, not in the conservative way of Coleridge; their Arnoldian clerisy included Catholics and Dissenters. It was Spring Rice, writing in the *Edinburgh Review* in 1839, whose educational plans most approximated the proposals of the Whigs' 1839 Committee on Education, with its decision to work through the schools of the various churches rather than through rate-supported schools. This was a departure from the efforts of the utilitarians and the Central Society for Education to create a national system of local schools supported by the ratepayers that would offer nondenominational religious instruction.[37] Although the growing power of Enlightenment ideas, whether among Owenites, utilitarians, or Whigs, along with the growing demand of the middle and working classes for good schools, put great pressure on the Whigs to act, it was, nevertheless liberal Anglican Whigs of paternalist beliefs who decided on an essentially voluntary system involving all churches and modestly aided and supervised by a paternal government. It was a merger of the idea of the paternalism of the leading churches with the idea of a paternal government, a partnership between the churches and the state. But it was a partnership, unfortunately, in which the Church of England blunted as well as promoted an effective system of education, the third fact about the effort of Tory paternalists to achieve Coleridge's idea of a clerisy.

It was, for example, churchmen who made the Peel government play such a reluctant role in 1839 and afterward. In 1844, after three years in office, Peel's government asked for only £40,000 for the Committee on Education, a mere £10,000 more than in 1839. When the Congregational Board of Education asked for more, Lord Wharncliffe, the Tory head of the Committee on Education retorted, "Who and what are these Congregationalists?" Peel made it clear that he believed that education should depend largely on the voluntary exertions of the local clergy and gentry.[38]

Two underlying fears still blunted Tory efforts at education reform, the fear of churchmen that education would become too secular or heretical and the fear of many rural Tories that education would encourage the lower orders to rise above their station. The result was that from 1841 to 1846, Peel's government did little in the field of education to advance a paternal government. It was again the Whigs who acted. It was Lord John Russell's government that in 1847 voted £100,000 in education grants, appointed more inspectors (four for poor law schools), gave stipends for pupil teachers, provided additional income and retirement benefits to long-serving teachers, and provided grants for school books and apparatus. It also established a normal school.[39] Larger grants and more inspectors followed in the 1850s, as well as greater voluntary efforts by the churches to make the partnership work. But the system was imperfect.

The very reports of the Church-approved inspectors reveal its imperfections: abysmal state of schools, "crowded, ill ventilated, poorly taught . . . teachers ill educated," "only 1 in 9 teachers adequately trained," "only 1 in 7 [pupils] can read with ease," instruction "monotonous and mechanical," "children's minds left utterly uncultivated," education "dry, meager and inaccurate," "great deficiency of education," and "religious knowledge about a nullity."[40] The reasons for these failures were the scanty years of actual schooling, a want of funds and a want of support. "Nearly ¾ leave before 10," "National Society funds in a depressed state," "2/3 of local funds come from the local school fees," and over and over again, "inadequacy of funds" and "want of funds," a result of the "apathy of the gentry," the "indifference of the wealthy" and the fact that "landlords and manufactures give so little."[41] That grants were given only if there was a matching grant left the poorer areas without support. In one area of 30,000 people, there was only one Church of England school. Schools expanded, but less than the population. That voluntarism had failed, said an inspector, was admitted by "all not blinded by bigotry."[42] In 1850, the *Education Times* reported that "the inefficiency of religious education is a fact as notorious as the inefficiency of secular education and is more scandalous." Church education was, concluded the Reverend Richard Dawes, "in some measure a national deception retarding the cause of education." In 1848, Connop Thirlwall, bishop of St. David's, lamented the hopelessness "of [poor children] acquiring the first element of instruction."[43]

A better system would be one that was locally managed, rate-supported, and under a Board of Education, and with either nondenominational religious instruction or excused time for instruction in one's own faith. But Tory paternalists (the Reverend W. F. Hook and a rare few excepted) would have none of it; from 1818 to 1849, Tories helped defeat eight bills presenting some variation of a rate-financed public education. Even in the mid 1850s, with Dissenters moving away from voluntarism toward a rate-supported system, Parliament rejected four bills for locally financed schools—an effective solution that had to wait until 1870, an enlarged electorate, and a generation less stubbornly attached to the Church of England and Coleridge's idea of a clerisy.[44]

That a revitalized, paternalist Church and a renewed Christian morality—the doing of good—could end the ignorance of the lower orders and solve England's pressing social evils was a powerful belief among early Victorians—a belief eloquently expressed by Burke, Coleridge, Southey, and Wordsworth. It was an admirable but illusory vision. Reality was quite otherwise. Half of England's churchgoers were not Anglican. And of the half that were Anglican, many were indifferent. Even good Anglicans and some clergymen were not very generous to their own schools. That the Church of England, or even Arnold's improbable clerisy of all faiths, could end ignorance, feed the poor, cleanse towns, and relieve widespread destitution was a pipe dream; one that was nevertheless held by very profound and earnest minds. Why they did is complicated, although it is clear that at least two reasons played a role, their emotional attachment to the Church of England and their sanguine hope that its Christian faith would make men good. Their allegiance was to a paternal Church more than to a paternal government, just as the gentry's allegiance was to a paternalism of property and locality more than to a paternal government. The paternalism of Church and property often weakened the allegiance to a paternal government, as did the paternalism of locality.

LOCALITY

Sir Henry Halford, M.P. for South Leicestershire and author of bills in defense of hosiery workers and framework knitters, was the purist of paternalists. In an 1840 pamphlet entitled *Some Remarks on the Constabulary Force Report*, he distinguishes between an arbitrary and encroaching central government of odious, despotic, and officious functionaries who endanger liberty and a "paternal power," a local one, of unpaid magistrates and unpaid constables representing "a subordination of rank each doing its duties." The central government, unlike the "paternal power" does not "prepare mankind for manhood" but "enervates, blunts and reduces all to a flock of industrious animals."[45] Halford was not alone. His fellow Tory M.P. Sir Arthur Brooke identified "paternal government" with "landlords doing their duty," as did even the Liberal M.P. Samuel Peto, who, upon hearing of landlords destroying cottages, asked "Where is the local government, the paternal care of which we hear so much." For the Tory Richard Vyvyan, the answer was clear: local authority resided in "the people of varying grades . . . entrusted by the constitution with the administration of internal affairs."[46] It was a view widely held. The *Oxford and Cambridge Review* defined patriarchal government as the "supervision, care, and kindness carried out in all relations of society," while *Fraser's* argued that the "Constitution confers on the English gentry and English clergy a sort of paternal guardianship." The *Quarterly Review* put the matter more bluntly, paternal government would be a mockery unless landlords were monarchs and the clergy did their duty.[47] Few believed more fully in that view than Disraeli in his praise of that "territorial constitution" that gave landowners responsibility for governing. Paternalism in *Coningsby* and *Sybil* is always clerical, landed, and local, never central. And for Coleridge, true democracy lay in the corporations, vestries, and joint stock companies, while Southey saw in every parish a "little commonwealth."[48] There were, of course, many for whom paternal government meant both local and central government. For a few, it meant mostly central. For R. B. Seeley, government made up what Sadler called a "Patriarchal System." Even the very unpaternal *NonConformist* spoke of "paternal relationships."[49] The term "paternal government" was, in fact, used in various ways and often vaguely. How, then, could it have had much of an impact on the growth of government? H. T. Liddell, a Tory and County member, knew how it could—so did Halford, Pakington, the duke of Richmond, and many others for whom the eighteenth century provided the model. "The country," said Liddell, "should be governed by statute and not by the unconstitutional authority of expensive boards." Unsaid, since universally assumed by the House, was the fact that the J.P.'s would administer the statutes. The J.P., in 1830 at the apex of power, was an indispensable part of the idea of a paternal government, although not without rivalry—or rather help—from the clergy, 1,322 of whom were also among the some 3,000 county J.P.'s.[50] But most landlords and clergy were not J.P.'s, and those that were, were often much more majestic as great landlords. A tenant or laborer bowed just as deferentially to his landlord on his estate or the clergyman in his church as he did when he stood before a J.P. in petty session. There was in locality no firm line between a legal and an informal government. Many were the gradations of authority defining both formal local government and the world of property and of voluntary institutions. The world of voluntarism included dispensaries, clothing clubs, benefit societies, and hospitals, the governors of which might also be landlords, the wealthy, and the clergy. Among these might also occasionally be found a J.P. who was at the heart of a locality, busy paternally enforcing the law. And to the extent that multiplying statutes gave them greater and greater powers, the idea of a paternal government added to the growth of government.

Sir John Pakington, M.P. for Warwickshire, chairman of its quarter session, and an Oriel man, believed that government should expand through the magistracy. He saw Parliament pass three of his bills, in 1840 a bill to regulate beer houses more strictly, in 1844, one to expand the coroner's power, and in 1847, one to give J.P.'s the summary power to have juvenile offenders whipped. Magistrates would supervise beer houses and punish juvenile offenders, just as they would have protected, if Halford's bills had passed, the hosiery workers and framework knitters. Sir John Pakington, one of the Tories' most effective paternalists, supported, as his centralization-hating squires did not, the Police Act of 1839.[51] He saw, as the duke of Richmond realized of the Prison Act of 1835, that the local J.P.'s gained the greatest share of power. In his 1845 lunacy bills, Lord Ashley followed the pattern accepting central inspection while adding to the J.P.'s dominant, rate-raising power. In such measures, the J.P.'s powers were enhanced, and government grew and grew. It was a growth not always to their liking, but if local power was enhanced, they supported it.[52]

The idea of a paternal government as largely local had its negative as well as its positive impact. It often led Tory squires to a consuming hatred of centralization. "Centralization" said Lincolnshire's R. A. Christopher, was one of the "greatest evils," because it endangered the government in which "everyone however humble bore his part . . . [under] those that it pleased Providence to place in a better situation."[53] There were 129 county members in the House of Commons, 24 of whom spoke often, whether to denounce the centralizing Police Act of 1839 (against which three wrote hostile pamphlets) or the despotic Public Health Act of 1848. None of the 24 voted for the Health

Act. Although they divided on the New Poor Law, it was country squires such as Banks, Sibthorp, Liddell, Halford, Henley, and Floyer who joined urban Radicals to form the hard core of opposition to that centralizing law.[54] But it was a quite small hard core. In 1842, even though they had vociferously condemned it in the 1841 election, most Tories—83.2 percent of them—voted to renew the Poor Law, which left local power in charge and saved ratepayers £2 million a year.[55] But the squires' hatred of centralization did lead to a steady opposition to the growth of the central government, and it was a hostility rooted in their sovereign place in local government. John Floyer, M.P. for Dorset, was, for example, a J.P., deputy lieutenant, sheriff, and chairman of the quarter sessions; Joseph Henley, the squire of the House, was also chairman of the quarter sessions and a deputy lieutenant; and Sir John Walsh was lord lieutenant and justice rotulorum of Radnorshire and J.P. deputy lieutenant and high sheriff for Berkshire.[56] A great number of the county M.P.'s were magistrates, not a few were colonels of the militia or captains of the yeomanry, and many enjoyed honorific offices in voluntary institutions. For these men of large estates and high local office, a profound love of locality joined with their unquestioned belief in property to form a conception of paternal government quite inimical to centralization.

But was this true of Peelites like Gladstone and Milnes, Lord Lincoln and Lord Francis Egerton, men inspired at Oxford and Cambridge by Coleridgean ideals? The answer is yes if one examines two of London's most powerful dailies, the *Morning Chronicle* and the *Times*.[57] In 1847, Gladstone, Lord Lincoln, Sydney Herbert, and Beresford Hope, all High Church, paternalist university men, bought the *Morning Chronicle* and had Young England's George Smythe write some of its editorials. Ireland, public health, and the Ten Hour Bill were the great issues. On public health, the paper endorsed a resounding No! It employed Toulmin Smith to fill its columns with his vehement anti-centralizing polemics. On Ireland, noes again resounded, no to the 1849 Irish Poor Law, no to bills helping tenants, no to funds for promoting emigration, no to wastelands for the landless, and no to a labor-rate to help the destitute. The *Morning Chronicle* declared the Ten Hour Bill, "pernicious" and followed with praise of Malthus.[58] It also supported the use of relays of children to evade the ten-hour day. An income tax or an audit of railways was no part of government, and the *Morning Chronicle* praised Carlyle's attack on "clever red tapists." Negative also was its response to Lord Ashely's ragged schools and emigration schemes. The *Chronicle* declared Ashley's ideas "false." The evils besetting these unfortunates, it added, were only "heightened by government interference."[59]

The Oxford and Cambridge men at the *Times* could also be negative, and also obsessive in their hatred of centralization. The New Poor Law—dictatorial, despotic and unconstitutional—was still in 1848 the *Times*'s bête noire.[60] Also instruments of a wicked centralization were the Committee on Education and the new police. It condemned the sanitary reports of the Poor Law Commission as "expensive and inquisitorial." It opposed both the Metropolitan Building Act with its "host of surveyors" and the "inquisitorial" Charities bill.[61] It did see in 1848 the need for a General Board of Health and, after five years of opposition, the need for a Committee on Education—although in 1852 it condemned the idea of rate-supported schools and in 1854 rejoiced at the fall of "the autocratic General Board of Health." In 1853, it condemned Fielden's factory bill that outlawed relays and thereby guaranteed a ten-hour day, pronouncing it "socialist."[62] The *Times* did, to be sure, support some measures of government interference—Ashley's ten-hour amendment in 1844, the 1849 Mines Act, and the 1850 Merchant Marine Acts—but the list was short, since, as it announced in 1843, "That legislation will cure all the social evils, we dare not venture to hope."[63]

Neither the *Morning Chronicle* nor the *Times* championed, in a sustained way, any great expansion of the state. Tenacious attachments to a paternalism that rested on property doing its duties, the Church guiding and instructing, and locality administering to social needs discouraged a belief in a larger, more active central government. For such a belief one must look to the idea of a utilitarian state.

CHAPTER 16

The Idea of a Utilitarian State

The story of the impact of the idea of an utilitarian state on the growth of government has been often told in terms of Jeremy Bentham and his disciples. It is a story of Benthamite collectivist ideas and their implementation by Benthamite bureaucrats, Benthamite M.P.'s, and Benthamite editors. It is a story with both a core of truth and considerable exaggeration.

BENTHAMITE COLLECTIVISM

That Bentham's ideas were collectivist is perhaps the most solid part, but only if taken as a latent collectivism. The young Bentham's beliefs and sentiments were anything but collectivist: he believed in the laissez-faire principles of political economy and felt a radical's deep anger at the aristocracy's corrupt, oppressive, and mischievous government. In his *Defense of Usury*, published in 1787, he denounced not only all regulation of the rate of interest but much of the mercantilists' meddling in the economy. In both that book and his 1811 *Manual of Political Economy*, he insisted that the government play only the most modest of roles in the economy. The individual, not the government, knew best his own interests, his own happiness. Adam Smith's *Wealth of Nations* became Bentham's Bible.[1]

But as his ever-curious, ever-assiduous mind probed deeper into political economy, he saw that government intervention could both help the economy and help repair society's deeper flaws. He filled his manuscripts with endless government schemes, schemes for social insurance to cover illness, old age, and unemployment, and schemes to regulate poisons, impure foods, noxious trades, unhealthy towns, roads. and canals. The government was even to provide post houses on Britain's highways. Government was also to enforce savings in order to increase capital, to help the poor with subsidies, and, in times of crisis, to set a maximum price on bread and to store food.

Government would also foster science and provide hospitals.[2] Although

Bentham would be known after his death as a political economist of the lais-sez-faire school, his own economic thought had become more collectivist.

Far deeper was Bentham's radical anger at a corrupt and sinister aristo-cratic government. He was the author of the phrase "government itself a vast evil." It was a government of Tory repression, blunders, and misrule, of the Six Acts against sedition and the Peterloo Massacre; of sinecures and pensions and bribery at the hustings—in short, a government of sinister influences, corrupting the whole. Yet these beliefs did not—as they did with Priestley, Godwin, and Cobbett—discourage a readiness to use government to remove greater evils. True, government could be evil, but there were, Bentham added, even greater evils, which government could lessen. And there was a great utilitarian yardstick to decide when government should intervene. It should do so when that intervention was a lesser evil than that which it would re-move, namely, when intervention would lead to the greatest happiness of the greatest number. It was a yardstick that increasingly pointed toward collec-tivism.[3]

In 1789, Bentham announced and amply defended the greatest happiness principle in his *Introduction to the Principles of Morals and Legislation*. In 1830, according to his *Constitutional Code*, a dedication to the greatest happiness principle should be the oath taken by all legislators. That *Code* was a blue-print for a more collectivist state. First of all, it would be a democracy, since who but the many know what brings happiness to the many? The government would also have fourteen ministries, ranging from finance and trade to inter-communications and domain, which would include ministries of education, health, indigent relief, and a preventive ministry.[4] It would be a centralized government, with many inspectors superintending scores of local headmen, who would do much of the governing. Bentham was certainly right in con-fessing, "I never had any horror, sentimental or anarchic, of the hands of gov-ernment." Bentham described in detail the health minister's *aqua procurante* and malaria-obviating functions, replete with sewers, drains, and healthy dwellings. He also described an education ministry with a central authority, inspectors, and locally financed schools. But, perhaps still being hesitant to interfere in the economy, Bentham is very sketchy on the finance, trade, and indigent ministries. And he still believed that a deterrent severity, copious in-struction, and positive conditioning would further a world of free, independ-ent individuals.[5] The *Constitutional Code* is a positive document, its ministries energetic in their "inspective, statistic and ameliorative functions." The "Posi-tive Ends of Government" were the "maximization of subsistence, abun-dance, security against all evil in every shape, against evil from every source."[6] To insist that government constantly investigate "every" social evil and provide security against evil from "every source" and in "every shape" was a powerful formula for collectivism.

But did many read the *Constitutional Code*? It does not make lively reading. Bentham was not, John Stuart Mill confessed, read by the general public. Edward Bulwer-Lytton concurred, noting that "none [of his works] have been read by large numbers," and the *Athenaeum* observed "the little progress which the doctrines of Bentham have made on the public."[7]

If Bentham's ideas were to further the growth of a utilitarian state, it would have to be through disciples. But again, according to John Stuart Mill in 1843, the remaining disciples of Bentham numbered only one or two, and the historian Élie Halévy has Romilly, Bowring, and James Mill the "only" visitors to "the hermit of Queens Square." Yet his ideas, Mill insisted, had a powerful influence. They did so, argues Samuel Finer (1972), through the writings and actions of an elite—some two or three dozen—who read or heard about Bentham.[8]

A BENTHAMITE ELITE

There is a core of truth to this picture of active, dedicated, politicking, and propagandizing Benthamites, but also a problem: how does one know who among the M.P.'s, bureaucrats and journalists whom Finer cites were actually inspired by Bentham? and by how much? The term "Benthamite" in the following discussion does not mean that they necessarily were, or were not, influenced by Bentham, but only that they shared with him a common set of ideas. Such was certainly true of James Kay-Shuttleworth and Matthew and Frederick Hill, three of the many powerful Benthamite bureaucrats whose views were well formed by the time they had arrived in London and met Bentham and his friends. Kay-Shuttleworth's views were shaped by a Nonconformist Sunday school, a cotton-manufacturing father, medical studies at Edinburgh University, and social investigations in industrial Manchester. The Hills were influenced by a schoolmaster father who raised them on Priestley, Unitarianism, Pestalozzi, and English radicalism, ideas well formed before they met Bentham.[9]

Neither did Bentham play a crucial role in the development of Benthamite editors, John Black of the *Morning Chronicle* (before 1847), Robert Rintoul of the *Spectator*, Albany Fonblanque of the *Examiner* and John Wilson of the *Globe*. Black and Rintoul left Scotland at twenty-six and twenty-eight, with their outlooks firmly in place; Fonblanque was distinguished above all as a man utterly independent in opinion, and Wilson for an anonymity and mystery he still enjoys.

The *Westminster Review* of the 1840s was owned and run by W. E. Hickson, with many contributions by William Ellis, Alexander Bain, and W. R. Greg. All but Greg, a Unitarian, a failed Cheshire cotton manufacturer, and a prolific writer on social issues, were from the London circle around John Stuart Mill and clearly were utilitarians. So were such occasional reviewers as John Bowring, William Molesworth, John Roebuck, and Edwin Chadwick. Ellis believed both that pleasure and pain should underline morality and that happiness is the end of education, while Hickson, who wrote many of the *Westminster*'s articles of the 1840s, insisted that amelioration of labor was "the most important problem of the day." They were not, however, disciples of Bentham, a name absent from Hickson's *Dutch and German Schools* of 1840 and his *Malthus* of 1849 as it is absent from Ellis's *Social Economy* of 1846. But the editor and contributors of the *Westminster* were clearly utilitarians. They shared Bentham's zeal for education, for social investigation, and for the amelioration of all evil and the maximization of happiness, but they gained that zeal from a wider basis than a reading of Bentham. Hickson inherited his zeal for "the thoroughgoing reform of society" and the money to run the *Westminster* from a Baptist father keen on education and cooperative farms.[10]

Also varied and elusive are the rich intellectual sources of the ideas of the twelve Philosophical Radicals who in the 1830s and 1840s brought utilitarianism to Parliament. What led twenty-two-year-old Charles Buller to write to his former tutor, "I have adopted utilitarianism" when that tutor was Thomas Carlyle, who was hostile to that ethic? Buller attended Cambridge, as did five other Philosophical Radicals, William Molesworth, Perronet Thompson, Henry Warburton, Charles Villiers, and Edward Strutt. Even at the Cambridge of the Apostles and Coleridgean ideas, William Paley's *The Principles of Moral and Political Philosophy* was still the required text, a text whose lucid, sensible, God-centered utilitarianism had long filtered into the minds of many an undergraduate. Only one of Parliament's twelve Philosophical Radicals, John Leader, attended Oxford. John Arthur Roebuck read Locke in Quebec City's library and learned democracy from the American experience across the border. The Scotsman Joseph Hume, the oldest of the twelve, like the editors Black and Rintoul, came south with a radicalism rooted in a natural rights philosophy that Bentham pronounced a fiction. That same natural rights philosophy ran deep in that Priestleyan Unitarianism that defined John Bowring's opinions long before he became Bentham's friend.[11]

Many and diverse as were the sources of the utilitarianism of the Benthamite bureaucrats, journalists, and M.P.'s, their commitment to refashioning society according to the greatest happiness principle was firm enough to serve as a sample of those Benthamite-like ideas that might have had an impact on the growth of government. The growth of government itself being a force for its further growth, the role of the bureaucrat becomes of paramount importance.

From 1832 to 1856, Benthamites occupied key bureaucratic posts in four areas that saw the largest growth of government: factories, poor law, education, and health. That Benthamites were influential in these areas owes much to the astonishing career of Edwin Chadwick. He was the secretary of the Factory Commission of 1832, secretary to the Poor Law Commission from 1834 to 1846, and, with Senior, co-author of the groundbreaking 1834 Poor Law Report. He was also a member and wrote the report of the Constabulary Commission of 1839 and authored the famous 1842 Sanitary Report. From 1848 to 1854, he was one of three commissioners of the General Board of Health. The area of education alone escaped him, but not really, for as secretary of the Poor Law Commission, he encouraged his friends and assistant commissioners E. C. Tufnell and James Kay-Shuttleworth to expand poor law education, just as he encouraged Kay-Shuttleworth, Southwood Smith, and Neil Arnott (all friends of Bentham) to investigate fever in the East End and to write England's first significant sanitary report.[12]

Kay-Shuttleworth became, in 1839, the powerful secretary to the Committee in Council on Education, and Southwood Smith a commissioner on the General Board of Health. Meanwhile, Frederick Hill, the longest-serving prison inspector—1835 to 1851—and his brother Matthew, recorder of Birmingham, became leading champions of reformatories. These leading bureaucrats, whose investigations revealed so much misery and suffering, shared Bentham's belief that the object of government was to lessen such misery and suffering wherever it existed, to fight "evil in every shape . . . from every source," and to maximize human happiness.

Their outlook was also Benthamite in a second way: a passion for practical reforms. No one was more fertile in such reforms than Bentham. Scheme upon scheme, device upon device, some eccentric and some eminently useful, flowed endlessly from one of the boldest and most inventive minds in all England. Also bold and inventive were the practical schemes of Benthamite bureaucrats, far bolder and more inventive that the Apostles' schemes for a paternal government. One of the most efficient of these schemes was that of government inspectors overseeing local and private authorities. It was not a new idea: the judiciary, the military, the revenue departments, and the government of Ireland had long employed inspectors. But to impose inspectors on sacred local authorities and sacrosanct property was to commit the cardinal sin of centralization. Yet just such a recommendation emerged in Chadwick's factory, poor law, constabulary, and health reports and in the acts that followed them. Bureaucratic input also emerged in the orders in council on education issued by the Whig Lords Russell and Lansdowne (but fashioned by Kay-Shuttleworth), in Frederick Hill's Scottish Prison Act of 1838, and in the Reformatory Act of 1854, which owed so much to Bentham's dinner guest Matthew Hill. The use of inspectors, a leitmotiv of Bentham's *Constitutional Code*, was a shrewd move. It not only tactfully allowed a supervision (at first modest) of prickly and jealously independent local authorities but initiated those constant investigations and reviews that increased the role of government. It increased, in Bentham's words, "the inspective, statistic, recordative and amelioration-suggestive functions."[13]

It was the nature of the utilitarian state to abound in inspections, statistics, reports, and ameliorative ideas. It led not a few—like the county and Tory M.P.'s Colonel Sibthorp, Joseph Henley, and Robert Christopher—to complain of statistics as they did of centralization.[14]

Matching Bentham's theoretical inventions were Edwin Chadwick's practical ones. Little did Lord Melbourne, the home secretary, realize in 1832 and 1833, when Edwin Chadwick became an assistant factory commissioner and a member of the Royal Commission on the Poor Law, what a flood of "amelioration-suggestive" ideas would flow from this former secretary to Bentham and most assiduous of all bureaucrats. In an early draft of the Factory Bill of 1832, he proposed inspectors and subinspectors, proposals that were adopted, and clauses providing for locally financed schools, medical certificates of age, fenced machinery, employer liability for accidents, and half pay for the sick, which were not.[15] Then in 1834, as the co-author of the Poor Law Report of 1834, Chadwick recommended the system of commissioners, assistant commissioners, and the workhouse test, all proposals that were adopted, and separate asylums for orphans, the aged, lunatics, and the ill, as well as good schools and excellent medical care, which were rejected.[16] At the General Board of Health, Chadwick developed yet more schemes, schemes for inspectors and local boards, for the provision of pure, constantly flowing water, and for glazed drainage pipes six inches in diameter to flush sewerage. There were also schemes for the cleansing of filthy courts, streets, and dwellings, schemes for smoke abatement, and schemes for the use of sewerage on farms and for the municipal management of gas and water. These proposals all reflected some underlying doubts about laissez-faire and voluntarism. Chadwick believed it was the government's mission to care for the welfare of the people. Almost alone among early Victorians, he urged that inspectors be appointed to end the exploitation of the thousands of unprotected children in England's workshops.[17]

Kay-Shuttleworth served his apprenticeship as bureaucrat as an assistant poor law commissioner under Chadwick, with whom he shared a stern belief in the corrupting effect of outdoor relief and the healthy deterrent influence of the workhouse test. But, convinced that education and good health prevented pauperism, he also championed district poor law schools and effective medical relief and was co-author of the 1838 Report on Fever. His vigorous work to improve poor law schools won him appointment as secretary of the Committee on Education, where in 1839, he suggested rate-supported schools and a teacher training college (proposals that were not adopted) and inspectors and grants to church schools (which were). It was a weak compromise that, seven years later, in 1847, Kay-Shuttleworth and the returning Lord John Russell and Lord Landsdowne tried to strengthen with larger grants, particularly for higher teacher salaries, for the development of pupil teachers, and for an expanded training college. In 1849, frustrated and ill, Kay-Shuttleworth retired, and two years later, though retired, he urged Russell to adopt a national system of rate-supported schools, an amelioration-suggestive idea again not adopted.[18] In 1840, frustrated by the Church of England's veto of a government teacher training college, Kay-Shuttleworth and Tufnell, with their own money, initiated just such a college at Battersea. By 1846, and with the Whigs again in power, a government training college was established. And although the college was thoroughly Anglican, it was still too liberal for the High Churchmen.

The ameliorative schemes of the Hills suffered the same mixed fate. Matthew Hill, the Birmingham judge, saw his reformatory ideas partially realized in the 1854 Act. Frederick Hill, the prison inspector, consoled himself that although still deficient, England's prisons had improved. Matthew Hill's many charges as Recorder and his books *Public Education* (1822) and *Repression of Crime* (1857) were, like Frederick Hill's prison reports and his books *National Education* (1837) and *Crime: Its Amount, Causes and Remedies* (1852), chock-full of schemes for improved schools, reformed prisons, workers recreations, hospitals, asylums, and improved police. Matthew visited France's Mettray reformatory and brought back to the visiting magistrates of Stretton-on-Dunsmore school a belief in the reformative power of placing the errant young in family-sized groups run by skilled teachers, inspired by Christian kindness and an unbound faith in industrial training. Industrial training, not the treadmill and the solitary hours of separate confinement, lay at the heart of Frederick Hill's schemes of prison reform, schemes that drew on Captain Maconochie's mark system and, like those of other Benthamite bureaucrats, were sometimes adopted and sometimes not.[19]

Those that were adopted furthered the growth of government far more than the far fewer schemes—allotments that were voluntarily given, schools that were exclusively Anglican, the whipping of juveniles—inspired by the idea of a paternal government. In 1848, eight of the education inspectors came from Oxford and Cambridge and were ordained in the Church of England. None of their reports urged a substantially larger government role in education, even though their reports revealed the inadequacies of the system. The reports of the Congregationalist Reverend J. D. Morell did urge a larger role for government, as did those of Jelinger Symons and E. C. Tufnell, inspectors of poor law schools who believed in a utilitarian state.[20]

BENTHAMITE M.P.'S AND JOURNALISTS

Bureaucrats are hired and fired by ministers dependent on the support of a majority of M.P.'s, who depend in turn on an electorate informed by the press. Benthamite bureaucrats needed the help from Benthamite M.P.'s and editors, help they received from the twelve Philosophical Radicals in Parliament and some five journals favoring a utilitarian state. A dozen would seem to count for little in a Commons of 658, and five periodicals for little more in the giant world of journalism, but garrulous and prolific in ideas as they all were, they threw down the gauntlet for others to take up. They challenged all to show that their respective measures brought the greatest happiness. "The business of government," John Arthur Roebuck told them, "was to increase by all means . . . the happiness and wellbeing of its subjects," a sentiment shared by his fellow Philosophical Radicals, Grote, Molesworth, and Bowring, who invoked "the happiness of the people," "the happiness of each individual," and "the greatest sum of enjoyment," and echoed by Warburton's "the public good is the only test."[21]

The *Westminster Review*, a Benthamite journal, joined in the chorus, demanding that all legislation bring the greatest happiness to the greatest number, while at the *Globe* the Benthamite editor John Wilson told his readers that "the great object of government was to promote the interests of the many."[22] John Black, an intimate of Bentham and the Mills, constantly applied the criterion "did the good out-weigh the evil" at the *Morning Chronicle*, and the Mills' friends Albany Fonblanque ("an early disciple" of John Stuart Mill) and Robert Rintoul applied the utilitarian yardstick at the *Examiner* and *Spectator*, which also published many articles by the younger Mill (who thought Rintoul's *Spectator* "one of our best journals").[23]

The utilitarian yardstick challenged long-accepted criteria of religious truth, ancient tradition, and natural law. An expanded electorate and a wider reading public found in utilitarianism a more practical yardstick than the evangelicals' moral pronouncements, Burke's historical prescriptions, and the Radicals' natural rights. But did that yardstick always demand a larger government? Did a larger government always increase happiness? Not always. That yardstick often called for a smaller, cheaper government with no corn laws, no income taxes, no ten-hour days, no grants to the Church of England, no stamp taxes on newspapers, and no capital punishment. The utilitarians believed in political economy and had no love of high taxes or oppressive laws and expensive bureaucracies. They were also intensely individualistic, exceedingly sanguine about education, and unbounded in their hopes of a free society of the self-reliant. They opposed the ten-hour day, which the workers wanted, and supported the New Poor Law, which the poor hated. In Parliament, they denounced any regulation of labor, rents, or prices as "unnecessary and mischievous" and "delusory." The regulation of London's coal whippers was objectionable, an unwise departure, said Bowring, from the principles of political economy. No one invoked political economy more than Joseph Hume and John Arthur Roebuck.[24] The truths of political economy were also sacred to the utilitarian press. An "uncontrolled and free industry," declared the *Morning Chronicle* in 1841, "best promoted progress," while the *Westminster Review* pronounced laissez-faire "the fundamental axiom of commercial policy."[25] Few newspapers could rival the *Examiner* and *Globe* in denouncing corn laws, income taxes, and ten-hour and railway acts. Only Rintoul's *Spectator* had doubts about political economy, a fact that led John Wilson of the *Globe* to denounce it "for departing from the laws of political economy."

The utilitarians' faith in political economy often lessened when confronted with practical problems. In 1844, as M.P. for industrial Bolton, whose workers wanted the ten-hour day, Bowring chose not to oppose it, just as earlier he joined the workers' attack on the New Poor Law.[26] Joseph Hume, an inveterate foe of the ten-hour day, nevertheless supported government regulation of mines, railways, emigration, charities, passenger vessels, tenant rights, enclosures, tithes, public health, and Church property. He also joined Bowring in urging a kinder poor law and Roebuck in demanding the regulation of railways, since, as Roebuck said, it was "for the benefit of the public."[27]

Just as strong as political economy in furthering the utilitarians' laissez-faire outlook was their intense belief in an independent, self-reliant working class. That belief even defined Hume and Roebuck's opposition to the ten-hour day. No wage fund or supply and demand theory informed their arguments against it, but old radicalism's hatred of laws that denied workers their liberty. An educated, free, and self-reliant working class could determine its own destiny. To ensure that such self-reliance be not corrupted by easy relief, the utilitarians in the 1830s supported the New Poor Law, which they saw as one of the bases of a laissez-faire society. Its stern refusal of a corrupting relief would help create, in the self-reliant individual, the needed building block of a new society. Easy relief, declared Hume, "would destroy that self-reliance upon which alone they could depend for the well being of the people."[28] Utilitarians, like puritans, wished to make men free by making them virtuous. "The object of government," proclaimed Molesworth, "was to make good men, good citizens, industrious members of society," an objective, added Roebuck, that demanded schools that will make "the individual a good child, a good parent, a good citizen, in short, a good man." The New Poor Law would make men good, added Charles Villiers, "by making them independent."[29]

The dream of a well-educated, industrious, healthy, independent citizenry forming a society so free and self-reliant that government would grow smaller was an illusion. To educate them required public schools and education boards and inspectors; and to make them industrious, poor law guardians, commissioners, and workhouses that disciplined and trained the errant, cared for the orphans; and for those falling ill, an expanded medical care, since disease was a principal cause of pauperism. Nor could disease be reduced when the poor lived in unsanitary slums. Utilitarians thus demanded a national system of schools, a larger, more active poor law, and central and local boards of health. In order to reform juvenile offenders and criminals, England needed reformatories and reforming prisons. And to ensure that charities, universities, and medical colleges contributed to a freer and happier society, England needed a more active, reforming government. It was a tendency made even greater by the principle that government should intervene wherever such interference would do more good than evil, as would happen if there was close regulation of passenger ships, railways, merchant seamen, and matters such as protecting the well-off from exorbitant fares on London's hackney coaches.[30] For Charles Buller and for Rintoul's *Spectator,* the greater happiness included the ten-hour day; and for all twelve utilitarian M.P.'s, the greater happiness certainly demanded the exclusion of women and children from mines.

All five utilitarian journals supported an increased role for government, but it was the pre-1847 *Morning Chronicle* and the *Westminster Review* that best revealed the Benthamite propensity to collectivism. Backed by its owner, John Easthope—"a thorough utilitarian" said a fellow journalist—the *Chronicle*'s editor and Bentham's friend John Black displayed a utilitarian zeal for reforms. The *Morning Chronicle* supported the exclusion of women and children from mines and of young children from factories and urged the usual reforms in the fields of education, health, and the poor laws. It also championed bills to regulate smoke pollution, enclosures, banking, print works, lunacy, the medical profession, and charities.[31] Free enterprise was not an inviolate principle. "Free enterprise in railways," the *Chronicle* declared, must be checked, and to do so, "legislation was indispensable." The *Chronicle* also chastised Roebuck for being so vehement against the Ten Hour Bill, raised doubts as to the use of "non-interference" as an argument, and defended the principle of centralization.[32] It found the efforts of the Education Committee inadequate and thought that a national system of education was a necessity. If "noes" to government intervention distinguished the Peelite *Morning Chronicle* after 1847, before 1847 it was the "yeses."

The *Westminster Review*, long the home of Benthamites, was no less latently collectivist. Its schemes ranged from penny postage, government-run lighthouses, and public cemeteries to government colonization and municipal-run gas and water works, warehouses, and hospitals. Government would also promote science and reclaim Irish wastelands for the poor.[33] In arguing for greater control of railways, it announced that "the laissez faire system should be abandoned." It did see government as evil, although, as the years passed, less and less. It soon realized that "legislation to control industry expressly on behalf of humanity and public morals marks a new era of social life."[34] Humanity and public morals also required that the government protect the thousands of children in the some fifty trades investigated by the Children's Employment Commission. Powerful and distressing as were the commission's revelations, no journal and no M.P. called for government intervention except the *Westminster*. In 1842 and 1846, it called for legislation to protect overworked and miserably treated children.[35] Other journals, but not many, wrote of the plight of the mentally ill, but none more fully and compassionately than the *Westminster*, and neither did many journals rival it in demanding a truly public education—in 1840, on the model of the Dutch, and in 1851, according to the scheme of the National Public Schools Association.[36] "Certain things," it wrote, "require to be done by the State"; and not only, it said earlier, "in redress of abuse" but for "the reconstruction of the edifice of society."[37]

In the reconstruction of that edifice, few played a more important role than the political economists, who were not untouched by utilitarianism.

THE "UTILITY" OF THE POLITICAL ECONOMISTS

Nassau Senior, J. R. McCulloch, and John Stuart Mill were the most renowned economists of the 1840s, and all held utilitarian assumptions. "The only rational foundation of government," wrote Senior in 1847, "is expedi-

ency—the general benefit of the community . . . the welfare of the governed."
McCulloch was no less explicit. "The only general rule," for government interference, he wrote, was when "expediency was strong," a rule J. S. Mill used
in his very popular *Political Economy* (1848).[38] And as early as 1833, Poulett
Scrope, a political economist and the M.P. from Stroud from 1833 to 1867, declared that "the welfare of the people is now universally acknowledged as the
only legitimate end of state policy," which made political economy a "branch
of the science of happiness." Herman Merivale, professor of political economy at Oxford, told students in 1837 that not just economists but all political
philosophers had "the happiness of man . . . for the ultimate object."[39] Backed
by such claims, it is little wonder that both Peel and his home secretary, Sir
James Graham, told their fellow M.P.'s that the aim of political economy was
"the greatest happiness to the greatest number." Both were urging the repeal
of the Corn Law. But protectionists like Philip Bennett replied that because
"happiness was certainly the duty of government," there was all the more reason for the Corn Law.[40] Many M.P.'s did not equate the economists' rigid
dogma with the greatest happiness. Above all they disliked the dogma of laissez-faire, which even its supporters espoused in general but violated in practice. William Gladstone, Peel's president of the Board of Trade, urged, in
1844, that the government regulate the hiring and payment of the coal whippers who unloaded coal at the port of London. Gladstone announced that
although "the legislature should not interfere with labor," the "evils from interference were as nothing to the vices of this system," a utilitarian yardstick
that he used again when, in introducing his huge 1844 Railway Bill, he confessed that, although "adverse in general to interference . . . the need is so
great." It was a frequent refrain. Lord Francis Egerton, after praising "the
truths . . . of the science of political economy" and expressing his "dislike of
meddling," supported the Ten Hour Bill as an "exception."[41] John Easthope,
although he believed that "the railway companies and public interests were
identical," found government regulation necessary for the "public conven-
ience." William Clay, a doctrinaire political economist, nonetheless found
the Joint Stock Company Act "expedient."[42] Increasingly, doctrinaire economists bowed to the practical and useful, to "utility" and to a concern for the
public good. "Look at the statute book," exclaimed William Wynn, and "the
spirit of meddling with every detail."[43]

So abundant was the meddling, so abundant were the exceptions, that another rule of thumb, another theory, however rough-hewn, was needed, a
criterion like Senior's, McCulloch's, and Mill's "the expedient." Political
economy and utilitarianism had more similarities between them than just the

expedient; both dealt in the quantitative, both sought maximization, both weighed supply and demand and pain and pleasure, and both worried about distribution. The magnitude of an evil was Bentham's criterion, and the magnitude of capital was Ricardo's, as well as the exact amount of rent, wages, and profits. Both wealth and happiness were to be maximized, and both were to be distributed fairly. The empirical, the quantitative, and the expedient in political economy undermined its earlier abstract deductions. Both Ricardo's theory of wages, rents, and profits and Malthus's law of population suffered from empiricism's dissolving powers. Both political economy and utilitarianism were embedded in the British empiricism of Bacon, Hobbes, Locke, Hume, and, most particularly, Adam Smith and Jeremy Bentham.

British empiricism was also a pragmatic tradition eminently suitable for the construction of the legislative framework needed for a laissez-faire economy and society. "Utility" means useful and expedient, and extraordinarily useful and expedient were laws that not only made property a reality but laid down the rules, often highly detailed, for property's use, sale, and inheritance. Peel and his lieutenants, learned in political economy, thus added to the more than 2,000 existing laws governing commerce, which regulated pilots, lighthouses, enclosures, and tithes, among other things. They gave loans for agricultural drainage and, in Ireland, for railway operations, the construction of harbors, and the erection of buildings. They passed laws regulating banks and joint stock companies. Useful and expedient, too, was a social framework defined by law. There was, said political economists from Smith to Mill, great utility to public education, health measures, prisons, hospitals, reformatories, poor laws, police, lunatic asylums, and all those things—and they were many—that were indispensable for the greater happiness, but that it was not to the interest of the individual to perform. "The real business of the political economist," said George Pryme, professor of political economy at Cambridge, "is to ascertain . . . what laws and lawgivers can do to promote it [property]," since "in so doing they will promote happiness."[44] In ascertaining those laws, the lawgivers, every year better educated in economics and more concerned about the public good, added to the size of government. And among such lawgivers, few were more active in enlarging government than the Whigs.

UTILITARIANISM AND THE WHIGS

The social conscience of all early Victorians was a fusion of different attitudes. There was no pure utilitarian and no pure paternalist, but rather utilitarians who were somewhat paternalist and paternalists who were a bit utili tarian; and both wove into their outlook other strands—political economy, self-reliance, voluntarism, the worship of property, a belief in a providential order—a compound made more complex by the conflicting strands of philanthropy and humanitarianism, mixing with self-, vested, and class interests. This fusion and convergence was particularly true of those Whigs who governed from 1830 to 1841 and from 1847 to 1857 (1852 excluded). They governed because the Whig-Liberal Party of the 1830s and the Whig-Liberal-Peelite Party of the 1850s were the largest; and they were the largest because they were the nearest to the political middle, as well as the most welcoming to different groups. They ranged from great Whig landlords, who differed little from Tory ones, to Radicals sympathetic to Chartists; from Nonconformists hostile to the Church and state to Anglicans wedded to Church and state; and from political economists wedded to laissez-faire to Benthamites ready to expand the government.

Just how the idea of a utilitarian state fitted in with the final convergence of these strands is not easy to determine, especially when it comes to a utilitarianism that rested not merely on the greatest happiness principle but on an insistence upon the investigation of every problem, on a love of facts of every kind, on a zeal for inventive schemes, and a liking for bureaucracy, even if centralized. It was the outlook of the Chadwicks, Kay-Shuttleworths, and the Hills, but how deep did it run in the Whig leaders who hired them? No one ever called Lord John Russell and Lord Palmerston, two of the most powerful of such Whigs, utilitarians. They were, if anything, paternalists, inheriting that natural outlook of all great landed families. Palmerston, an eldest son who inherited huge estates in England and Ireland, was a model paternalist, most especially on his Irish estates, where he built schools and roads, banished exploiting middlemen, and imported Scottish farmers to improve agriculture. No less generous in England, he gave to charity "a quarter of his salary."[45] Lord John, although as a younger son he did not inherit the huge Bedford estate, was nonetheless imbued, as were most great peers, with the traditional sense of property and privilege—a paternalist tradition strengthened in Palmerston and Russell, and other sons of peers, by high government office. As colonial secretary and as the man who introduced the Reform Bill, Lord John knew the duties of government. And he showed himself to be very much the paternalist when he urged landlords to relieve the poor and to perform other duties that went with wealth. Lord Palmerston also praised the gentry for using the militia "to cement a bond of union" with the lower classes.[46]

But their inherited Whig paternalism precluded neither a belief in political economy, the necessity of self-help, and the value of voluntary benevolence nor a utilitarian belief in government. Palmerston in 1847 told his electors that "the science of government demanded investigation to some practical result," which would lead to "practical utility" and "the general interest of the whole," a sentiment Lord John echoed in telling the Commons that "the government should interfere wherever beneficial and wherever calculated to do good."[47] Both Palmerston and Russell attended the lectures of Dugald Stewart, and although Stewart condemned the utilitarianism of Paley and was rivaled by few in his laissez-faire economics, he did insist that progress needed "the superintending care of government," and that happiness was "the only object of legislation." It was a view Lord Palmerston met again at the Cambridge of Paley, and a sentiment that must have remained embedded in the young Russell, who was "full of Dugald Stewart" and who praised, as "one of the best letters" his father ever wrote, a letter that told his son that "governments are made for the happiness of the many."[48] Although they were no Philosophical Radicals, no intimates of Bentham, the utilitarian strand in Palmerston's and Russell's social conscience does help explain their consistent support for education and public health measures and for the Ten Hour Bill and an adequate Irish poor law. It also explains why Palmerston's record at the Home Office was one of ceaseless activity. He ordered that reeking cemeteries be closed, that London improve its sewers, and that mill owners fence dangerous machinery. He also demanded that belching chimneys be controlled, that prisons be improved (with useful labor replacing the treadmills), that reformatories be established, and that a definitive Ten Hour Act for factory operatives be passed. He ended his stay at that office with a failing effort, eloquently made, to preserve the General Board of Health. These accomplishments, said Lord Ashley, added up to more than those of his ten predecessors.

Utilitarianism also played a role in Lord John Russell's career. From 1830 to 1841 and 1847 to 1857 (1852 excepted), as home, colonial, and foreign secretary, and as prime minister and president of the Council, he played a leading role in the seven Whig-Liberal ministries that created almost all of the new central departments that constituted the early Victorians' administrative revolution. As prime minister, his greatest personal contribution was his strong backing of Kay-Shuttleworth's 1847 expansion of education, the establishment of the General Board of Health, with Chadwick in command, his successful fight for improved Irish poor laws and the passage of acts to lessen, by the use of inspectors, mining accidents and abuses in the merchant marine. As home secretary, he effected dramatic humanitarian reforms in criminal law and worked with inspectors to reform prisons, and as colonial secretary, he worked to further emigration.[49]

The idea of a utilitarian state was also alive among other ministers, M.P.'s, and journalists who belonged to the large and diffuse Whig-Liberal party, a party that was, after all, also the home of Benthamite M.P.'s, bureaucrats, and journalists. The convergence of the many elements that formed the early Victorian social conscience was not always as harmonious as the blending of paternalist caring and utilitarian benevolence. Rather, it was often a battle of conflicting ideas both within and between the various groups and interests constituting the Tory and Whig-Liberal parties. A tension between outlooks often occurred in the same person. Such was certainly true of those who wrote for the Whig *Edinburgh Review*.

Macvey Napier, editor of the *Edinburgh Review*, welcomed utilitarian reviewers such as John Austin, M. D. Hill, John Hill Burton, and John Stuart Mill and such utilitarian ideas as found expression in other reviewers. No red pencil obliterated Nassau Senior's boast, in his 1848 review of Mill's *Political Economy*, that on the question of government interference, "there is no limit, no exception, to the rule of expediency," and neither did anyone cross out William Empson's declaration that "nothing would be more conducive at present to public welfare than . . . legislation . . . forged anew out of recent facts and the exigencies of our modern societies."[50] Proudly did the *Edinburgh Review* champion the factory, poor law, education, and sanitary measures of the 1830s and 1840s. With great emphasis, it devoted six articles to that great panacea, education. The first article appeared in 1833 and urged the creation of a ministry of public instruction and the provision of nondenominational religious instruction. An article in 1850 urged the establishment of ratepayer-supported schools. The four articles in between urged with great vigor an expanded educational system.[51] The *Edinburgh Review* favored factory legislation, but only for children, which was in keeping with the opinion of many utilitarians, John Stuart Mill included. It also joined Mill in support of the New Poor Law, which, however severe, even cruel, greatly expanded government and did considerable good in schooling the poor, caring for their illnesses, and making relief uniform, certain, and free of undue cruelties and abuse. The General Board of Health also did much good and won the support of the *Edinburgh Review,* despite loud cries elsewhere protesting its centralization.[52] In January 1847, the *Edinburgh Review* answered the outcry against centralization by publishing John Austin's article "Centralization," which judged it "beneficial." George Cornewall Lewis concurred, in an 1846 article, saying that centralization "enormously increased the practical efficiency and responsibility of the local authorities."[53] The *Edinburgh Review* had much less fear of an expanding state than did the *Quarterly Review* or *Blackwood's*, a fact that owed much to its welcoming of the idea of a utilitarian state.

But that welcome was not always warm. The columns of the *Edinburgh Re-*

view, like sprawling Whig country houses, had other guests: political economy, the sacredness of property, the doctrine of self-reliance, voluntarism,
and even the paternalism of property. Since it had long been a friend of political economy, it is not surprising that it published articles by Nassau Senior,
John Stuart Mill, and Herman Merivale, or that it employed W. R. Greg,
Thomas Spring Rice (chancellor of the Exchequer from 1835 to 1839), Charles
Trevelyan (secretary to the Treasury), and G. C. Lewis (a poor law commissioner), to spell out, in a most orthodox manner, the principles of a laissez-
faire economy. In its columns, Malthusianism, dying elsewhere, was kept
moderately alive by Mill and Greg, while G. C. Lewis insisted that a
"systematic relief of the poor is an interference with a natural order . . . resting on property." Senior also believed in a natural order resting on property.
Nature had provided, he insisted, that the interests of the public coincide with
"the wise laws of nature." G. C. Lewis condemned the ten-hour day and truck
acts as a form of slavery and insisted that legislation would provide the workers with no panacea.[54] Senior also chided Mill for the "wild theories" that led
him to support government measures for employing Irish wastelands, developing free emigration, and guaranteeing fixity of tenure, but praised him for
his condemnation of public works, outdoor allowances, and allotments for
the poor. He also praised Mill for his claim that the aim of government
should be to make men safe, not happy, a sentiment that would have pained
Bentham.[55] Mill's articles on de Tocqueville's *Democracy in America* and Arthur Help's *Claims of Labour* listed more toward laissez-faire than toward
government intervention, as did, even more strongly, Charles Trevelyan's articles which insisted that government should never shield the workers from
economic vicissitudes, most of which were of their own making.[56]

That laissez-faire did not always work for Ireland's destitute, those good
Whigs Senior, Trevelyan, and Lewis realized. Yet disliking big government
and great expenditures, they turned to the paternalism of property. Both
Senior and Trevelyan, citing Henry Drummond's "property has its duties,"
looked to landlords more than to government to care for the starving, landlords whom Lewis saw as a part of "a natural order resting on property," an
order that for Spring Rice included "model manufacturers."[57]

Paternalism was, however, far from being a major theme of the *Edinburgh*'s outlook, and it never rivaled the use of political economy. It also had
a strong belief in the "moral remedy," based both on the self-reliance of the
lower orders and the benevolence of the upper. There were "no remedies for
insufficient wages" wrote Senior, citing J. S. Mill, that did not operate
"through the minds and habits of the people." It was on "moral remedies,"
said Spring Rice, "that we must depend," remedies, he added, that Thomas

Chalmers expressed as a "Christian benevolence . . . beautifully blended with true philosophy."[58]

Self-reliance was crucial. They preached it constantly: fewer children, urged Greg, Mill, and Senior; less corrupting relief, demanded Senior, Lewis, and Trevelyan; more intelligence and education, insisted Rogers, Greg, Mill, and Empson, and from Merivale, "the labourers are themselves responsible . . . for most of the evil that besets their condition."[59] "Education," Mill told *Edinburgh Review*'s readers, was "not the principal, but the sole remedy."[60]

Mill and other reviewers also favored voluntary efforts from above, from organizations like the Labourer's Friend Society, the Society for the Diffusion of Useful Knowledge, and the Society for Distressed Needlewomen. They also looked to the better association of workers and employers, whether by means of a caring paternalism or profit sharing. The "higher classes," complained Mill, had not "done their duties."[61]

But although Mill was never as keen for a utilitarian state as was Bentham, nor the utilitarians of the *Edinburgh Review* as keen for it as the purer Benthamites of the *Westminster*, the *Edinburgh* reviewers nevertheless desired to educate the workers, to reform them by a disciplining poor law, to save juveniles from crime by reformatories, and to guarantee healthy towns, desires that led them to urge an expanded and utilitarian state.

But not without compromises. The eclectic Whigs, as rulers of a large and motley party and a large and diverse nation, had long shown themselves masters at compromise. The Whig party had in its own ranks M.P.'s hardly friendly to a utilitarian state, ardent localists like Sir Benjamin Hall, M.P. for Marylebone, who persistently expressed that London borough's hatred of centralization, and Lord Seymour, soon to be duke of Somerset, who with equal persistence expressed the rural localism of his Totnes constituents. To this lordly duke, Bentham was "a destructive fanatic" and Chadwick "loathsome."[62] There were also Whig churchmen who, in the 1850s, in combination with the Peelites, determinedly prevented the achievement of the viable system of public education so dear to utilitarians.

Yet utilitarianism in its various forms and degrees was alive in Whigs like Viscount Howick, Robert Slaney, Poulett Scrope, even in Thomas Macaulay, who in 1828 was so scathing about Benthamites. Howick, in 1844 urged a ten-hour bill, since the "concern of government" should be the "moral and physical welfare of the great body of people," and most especially "the happiness . . . of labour."[63] Even more energetic than Howick was Shrewsbury's M.P., Robert Slaney, who was not only the author of five pamphlets on the condition of the working classes but the mover and chairman of many select committees for their improvement. Slaney announced in his first pamphlet, in 1819, that he sought "the happiness of the poor," and in 1842, in his fourth, that the first principle of government should be "the protection of the weak" (the view of the complete paternalist) and "the welfare of the many" (the core of utilitarianism). In Slaney, a model landlord, paternalism and utilitarianism converged, and did so while blending in political economy and the morality of self-reliance, culminating in education as the grand panacea.[64]

Poulett Scrope also fused together these attitudes, a fusion, however, whose emphasis lay in a utilitarian political economy. Few M.P.'s could rival Scrope in urging a greater role for government. In 1833, in his *Political Economy*, he declared the aims of state policy to be "the greatest happiness to the greatest number." To achieve this, he not only advocated the usual Whig measures to protect children and improve education and health, but also a ten-hour day, government reclamation of Irish wastelands for the poor's use, and a government guarantee that tenants be compensated for their improvements.[65]

In 1846, Macaulay, the Whigs' philosopher, declared for the ten-hour day. He also urged a much greater role for government in education and health. Long a critic of the utilitarians for their lack of imagination, their indifference to the aesthetic, their mechanical view of human nature, and their cold rationalism, he prided himself on being a practical man of the middle way, one sophisticated enough to observe that there was no general rule for government intervention. But since arguments are stronger when based on general truths, he succumbed and declared that government should intervene whenever it was "for the public interest." Drawing up law codes in India, he leaned heavily on Bentham.[66] He had attended Cambridge, as had Viscount Howick, Slaney, and Scrope, and many other M.P.'s. Cambridge was Whig, Oxford Tory, and it was at Cambridge that all were required to read Paley, a Whig who combined paternalism and utilitarianism and one in whom, Scrope confessed, he firmly believed. Macaulay, however, thought more highly of the Scottish philosopher, and great favorite of Whigs, Sir James Mackintosh. Although Mackintosh believed, as utilitarians did not, in an innate moral conscience, he did admit that "in the largest sense there was a universal coincidence of virtue and utility."[67] The idea of "utility" insinuated itself in many ways into the Whig social conscience. It even did so, although not nearly so strongly, with Tories.

UTILITARIANISM AMONG THE TORIES

To Viscount Howick's claim that the object of government is "the welfare . . . of the people," Peel answered that Howick was right, and that government should attend "to the social happiness . . . of the people."[68] The Tories were not about to give the Whigs and Radicals a monopoly on one of the nation's most appealing arguments. In the Corn Law debate, Philip Bennet, M.P. for Suffolk, announced that for five years he had "advocated the happiness of the people" and had always consulted the welfare of the greatest number, a refrain picked up by fellow Tories, Plumptre, Newdigate, Borthwick, and the earl of Winchelsea, who variously expressed the principle of the "happiness of the largest extent of the people," "happiness and welfare of the people," "the most good to the greatest number," "happiness of the people" and simply "felicity."[69]

These utilitarian phrases also found themselves expressed in the Tory press, as they did at the hustings in 1841 and 1847. In 1847, at York the Tory George Hudson, the railway king, appealed to "the welfare and happiness of the working classes," while Mr. Neeld in Wiltshire appealed to "the great benefit of the whole community" and "of all classes." For Lord Farnham, the Church itself was "the mainspring of temporal happiness," and Lord Courtenay's aim was "the general welfare of the country."[70] Such expressions, although clichés, were not as common among Tories as cheers for Church and queen and praise of local government and talk of the duties of property—all of which, of course, promoted the well-being of the people. Two facts led to a broader appeal: a larger electorate and an intellectual tradition not inimical to utilitarianism. Paternal solicitude might work in pocket boroughs, but not in the larger boroughs and in counties with expanded electorates, where many, many new voters wanted greater happiness for a greater number. Such appeals were also not entirely alien to British empiricism and pragmatism, a tradition that led the middle aged Coleridge to insist that "the happiness of mankind is the end of virtue." And he did not mean this loosely, adding that "reason and conscience can have but one moral guide, utility."[71] It was a rule expounded by the evangelical paternalist R. B. Seely in his *Life of Michael Sadler* in which he announced, in capital letters, that Sadler's great aim was "TO EXTEND THE UTMOST POSSIBLE DEGREE OF HUMAN HAPPINESS TO THE GREATEST POSSIBLE NUMBER." Evangelicals need not fear appealing to the greatest happiness, since one of the greatest of them, William Wilberforce, had declared happiness to be "the end for which men unite in civil society."[72]

Utilitarianism, dominant through Paley at Cambridge, also had a foothold in an Oxford steeped in Aristotle and Locke. Although some philosophers would insist that neither Aristotle nor Locke was formally a utilitarian, their writings were not without utilitarian ideas. Not only did Aristotle insist that "ethical virtue and ethical vice [were] connected with pleasure and pain" and that we should "guide the education of the young by means of pleasure and pain," but that people agreed that "happiness [was] the highest of all goods" and "virtue"—all reflections that would have delighted John Locke, who argued that "things are good or evil only as they refer to pleasure and pain," since "God has joined virtue and public happiness together." Richard Whatley who taught Aristotle to many an undergraduate at Oriel College had no trouble in also recommending Paley's *Moral and Political Philosophy* as a great book. Oriel's Thomas Arnold also had no trouble teaching its students that "the supreme problem of politics was the science of human happiness."[73] Utilitarianism was everywhere, not only in Paley, Aristotle, and Locke but Hobbes, Hume, Priestley, Tucker, Brown, and, as "prudence" and "utility" (borrowed from Cicero) in Burke.[74]

But its very universality makes it suspect. It was so commonplace, so platitudinous and obvious, that it was nearly a tautology, merely another form of humanitarianism. How could it be a decisive force in the growth of government? How could it be distinguished from paternalism if Coleridge, Seely, and Wilberforce embraced it and if Paley could so successfully fuse paternalism and utilitarianism?

The idea of a paternal government and a utilitarian state did converge, often in one person and often in partnerships. From 1848 to 1854, at the General Board of Health, England's most active Benthamite and her most active evangelical, the rationalist Chadwick and the pious Lord Ashley, worked amiably and diligently to improve the public's health. The pious rationalist Sir Samuel Romilly and the rational evangelical Thomas Fowell Buxton likewise worked together to civilize a barbaric criminal code. To establish reformatories in England, the Benthamite M. D. Hill worked with the evangelical Reverend Sydney Turner, both aided by Mary Carpenter, who was inspired by Unitarian piety and utilitarian rationalism. In the prison inspectorate, the Benthamite Frederick Hill worked with the evangelical Whitworth Russell; in Parliament many evangelical paternalists like Grosvenor and Buxton joined utilitarians like Buller and Scrope and Whigs like Howick and Russell to urge the Ten Hour Bill, while angry Radicals and backbench Tories denounced the cruelties of the New Poor Law and both paternalists and utilitarians urged a General Board of Health. One of them was Monckton Milnes, whose early Young England paternalist sentiments merged gradually with a later utilitarian liberalism to make him one of Parliament's most consistent humanitarians.

Although the Tories talked of the welfare and happiness of the people and were not untouched by a general utilitarianism, it neither ran very deep nor made their idea of a paternal government effective. They never, for example, vigorously pursued the happiness of the greatest number. Although they employed the rhetoric of the well-being of the people and their greatest happiness, their positions on most issues resisted the use of statistics and calculations of aggregate welfare. Tory paternalists focused on the concrete, on the parish, the town, and the county, the individual neighbor, on paupers with names, always expressions of Coleridge's "home born feelings." Carlyle and Sibthorp scoffed at statistics, while Dickens, no Tory, but also no utilitarian, ridiculed the utilitarian obsession of Gradgrind and Bounderby with "facts, facts, facts." But it was just such a passion for statistics and aggregates, of thinking of the larger public good, and of all kinds of investigation to further it, that made the idea of a utilitarian state a more productive idea than paternalism in an age of growing populations, towns, and industry. Admirable and helpful as were Tory paternalists in furthering factory, mine, juvenile, lunacy, and many other reforms, it was seldom Tory bureaucrats and ministers who made the investigations and invented the schemes that made reform possible. It was Chadwick, not Ashley, at the Board of Health, and Kay-Shuttleworth, not the Anglicans, at the Committee on Education, who drew up the efficient measures. Not only did Tory aversion to aggregates and statistics hamper the impact of the idea of a paternal government, but so, too, did their aversion to centralization.

A second trait that made the idea of a utilitarian state so forceful was the quiet, ad hoc, and constant addition of scores of inspectors and commissioners to the central government. Centralization, so strong in Bentham's *Code*, so deep in the minds of Benthamite bureaucrats and M.P.'s, and so eminently practical and useful, played a crucial role in the growth of government. That growth came nowhere near the establishment of an adequate and comprehensive welfare state or a planned economy. The essence of the administrative revolution that occurred from 1833 to 1856 was, first of all, the laying down of a foundation for the central government's supervision of local authorities—poor law guardians, health boards, county magistrates, town councils, and a vast array of statutory authorities—as well as inspectors and commissioners to check the worst abuse of capitalism and the worst failings of voluntary institutions. That supervision and those checks were, to be sure, jealously limited and narrow, and they fell far short of the socialism that their grandchildren brought to the Labour Party and England, but utilitarians did bring to bear a passion for investigating social evils and a passion for schemes to bring happiness to the greatest number, a passion that, positioned within the framework of a growing centralized bureaucracy, would convert an administrative revolution into a continual administrative evolution.

There was a third crucial characteristic informing the idea of a utilitarian state: the resolve to end all evil, "evil in every shape, in every place." It was a resolve that was far weaker among paternalists who were not only convinced of man's sinfulness and the inevitability of evil but closely tied to institutions that were involved in the continuance of social evils. That evil in every shape could be ended, should be ended, and must be ended inspired believers in a utilitarian state, as it did not believers in a paternal government. A vigorous optimism informed utilitarians, the optimism of the Enlightenment that all things can be done, that tubular glazed drains and the banishing of effluvia could free towns of disease, that emigration, wastelands for the poor, and fixed tenure could solve Irish ills, that an education not mired in Scripture and the catechism could create the sober, industrious, and provident working class and the rational and benevolent governing class that would bring about a brave new world. There would be no evangelical sermons on "Famine, the Rod of God" or "Cholera, a Divine Warning," no fasts, no day of prayer, no fear of educating a person beyond his or her station, and no Sabbatarian and paternal control of the morals of sinners.

Two great intellectual events helped define England's response to the inexorable forces demanding change: a religious revival in all its forms and the advance of knowledge and rationalism that came from the Enlightenment. Although the religious revival (along with romanticism and new historical learning) did promote the idea of a more active paternal government, it was the Enlightenment's legacy of increasing knowledge, vigorous reason, and mounting optimism that rational man could end evil that most decisively promoted in the early Victorians' social conscience a resolve to create a larger and more caring government.

Conclusion

The early Victorians bequeathed to their successors a powerful vision of a laissez-faire society. It was an amalgam of the old—a paternalism based on the sacredness of property and the rightness of the providential order—and the new—the truths of political economy and, in terms of a greater emphasis, the virtues of self-reliance and the philanthropic benevolence of voluntary societies. It was an outlook that lay at the center of their social conscience, one with great strengths and weaknesses. A Britain guided by that outlook created the world's largest empire, wealthiest economy, and most prosperous of peoples. Little wonder that the early Victorians had such an unbounded faith in this vision of a laissez-faire society, a faith undiminished even though they had at every turn employed an expanding government whose interference they denounced, and even though their society was still plagued by grievous social evils and injustices.

For many, the most important part of that vision was political economy, with its certainties that nothing benefited society more than freeing the economy from the dead hand of government. Works of the greatest learning and acuteness had revealed self-regulating laws that would lessen poverty and increase prosperity. It was a science that made the term "laissez-faire" a commonplace and supplied the emerging outlook with a coherent theory. It is not surprising that many saw political economy as the core of a vision of a laissez-faire society.

But most early Victorians did not. Only a few understood its axioms, and many hated them. Tories were furious at political economy's attacks on protectionism, Christians were alarmed at its praise of selfishness, workers saw themselves as exploited by it, and humanitarians were saddened by its severities. The vision of a laissez-faire society needed a more popular base, and it found it in the age's exceptionally moral and individualistic cast of mind. Increasingly, the early Victorians looked to a revived and strengthened morality emphasizing the duties of the individual. Improved men and women, not government, would provide the sovereign remedies, which would be the work of the reformed men and women of a free society. For most early Victorians, moral truths were far more real and important than those of political economy.

A belief in solving social problems through individual moral improvement took two fundamental forms, more self-reliance among workers and greater benevolence on the part of the propertied. These both found eloquent expression in two of the age's most popular forms of literature, novels and sermons, which were read by far more people than ever read works on political economy. Far more, certainly, read Charles Dickens. Thousands followed the exciting adventures of Oliver Twist, Nicholas Nickleby, David Copperfield, Martin Chuzzlewit, and Pip. The readers of these adventures neither sought nor found a well-rounded social philosophy, and it was never Dickens's intention to impart such. But in the dogged endurance of his heroes as they were buffeted by misfortune, there was powerfully evident a persevering self-reliance and moral strength that proved the single best way to overcome social evil, a far more useful lesson than any wage fund theory and far more basic to a laissez-faire society.

But admirable as was their self-reliance, Oliver, Nickleby, Copperfield, and Pip needed the benevolence of a Mr. Brownlow, the Cheerybles, Miss Trotwood, and Magwich to triumph over the cruel and hardhearted. That society needs the powerful and rich to be kindhearted and benevolent was Dickens's second moral lesson. Dickens looks to self-reliance and benevolence and never to government.

It was also an outlook found in most other widely read novelists, in Bulwer-Lytton, Douglas Jerrold, William Thackeray, and Mrs. Gaskell. Even silver fork novels of the Newgate schools saw the resolving of society's conflicts in the moral virtues of individual heroes and benefactors.

That self-reliance and benevolence offered two of the best answers to social evils was not argued only by novelists. It also informed countless sermons—and most educated Victorians attended church. "Charity," announced J. B. Sumner shortly before becoming, in 1848, archbishop of Canterbury, "is the appointed preventive of the evils of a highly civilized country."[1] "The root of all these [social] evils," declared the Reverend Edward Bickersteth, one of the most widely read evangelicals, was "the love of money," "the selfishness of men of wealth," and "WANT OF PITY IN THE HEART." And the remedy was plain: "Let Christian love be paramount," "love thy neighbor as thyself," and have "mercy on the poor."[2] Throughout the country, from pulpits of every faith, came pleas to love thy neighbor and be merciful to the poor, moral commands unrivaled in frequency by any axiom of political economy. For the vast majority of Christians, such commands lay at the core of their social conscience. There were also commands calling on the poor to be self-reliant. "Charity," said Richard Whatley, archbishop of Dublin in 1830, is "a *reward* not on those in mere want, but on those of *extraordinary* sobriety, industry, and general good conduct."[3] Calls for moral improvement were particularly strong from Nonconformists. Their ministers fused their calls to the rich to be kind and to the poor to be self-reliant into a call to all Christians to be righteous. For Thomas Binney, London's most popular Congregationalist, "Righteousness takes in all personal values . . . rectitude, purity, kindness, benefice, sobriety, industry . . . [and] brotherly sympathy with all mankind." These Christian virtues would "cure all the disorders of the world." George Dawson, Birmingham's most famous Baptist, called for taking such righteousness—manly, earnest, humane—"into the polling booth, newspapers, in literature, everywhere," including on weekly visits to the sick and needy. He found these virtues best expressed in Thomas Carlyle, who demanded that people be "righteous and noble," and that "man must reform from within," since "the final reform [is] the making the people righteous."[4] Binney and Dawson raised the intense morality of the puritan tradition, with its ingrained individualism, to a broader, more secular level. Nonconformists, Broad Church Anglicans, and liberal evangelicals all increasingly placed the morality of the Sermon on the Mount at the center of a Christianity that would produce the many righteous, benevolent, and self-reliant Christians needed to create a society free of social evils.

It is difficult to overestimate the early Victorians' faith in man's capacity to improve. It was a faith fundamental to their vision of a laissez-faire society. Two intellectual movements, the Enlightenment and evangelicalism, along with an unprecedented upward social mobility, underpinned this pervasive and limitless faith. Only education would produce self-reliant workers and benevolent rulers. "Knowledge is power," Francis Bacon had said, and John Locke had explained that knowledge came through the sensations and expanded by associations. Moral, far more than economic, beliefs thus inspired the early Victorians' vision of a laissez-faire society. John Stuart Mill called for no great changes in the economic and political structure of England. Instead, he found the two "great desiderata" to be "the regeneration of the individual character among the lettered and opulent . . . and . . . our educational institutions." And "since the primary causes of social evil are ignorance and want of culture," he argued, "the future of the labouring class [is] principally dependent on their own mental cultivation." "The refined classes must end their moral effeminacy," and laborers had to substitute "self dependence" for "dependence and protection."[5] The answer lay in education. Only education would produce self-reliant workers and benevolent rulers. Only an educated, self-reliant, and generous people could build a just society.

Such people would not only be better educated but purer Christians. Most educated Victorians attended church. If asked how best to fashion a better society, far fewer would recommend economic reforms than would urge that there be more and better Christians doing their social duties. The evangelicals among them, nearly a third of the Anglicans, and most of the Nonconformists, would agree with one of their great preachers, Thomas Chalmers, who said he looked to "no great change in the external aspect of society . . . [but] a moral and spiritual change," a time when "Christianity becomes universal . . . and the rule of real Christians . . . binds all . . . into one consenting brotherhood." The evangelical *Christian Observer* and *Record* shared Chalmers's optimism about the rule of virtuous Christians. The *Observer* argued that "our welfare cannot be much affected by . . . merely worldly politics but by the vigorous maintenance of public and private virtue." The *Record* found the answer to the "misery" of distressed cotton towns like Paisley in "private benevolence." It said nothing of the need of a good poor law in a town that faced massive unemployment and had no good poor law. Personal benevolence was also the remedy for famine in Ireland, since "as Christianity shines more brightly and warmly on any land, this benevolence largely increases."[6]

Boundless were the expectations of those inspired by the Enlightenment of an educated and self-reliant populace, and great if not boundless were the expectations of the evangelicals of the triumph of the Gospel and Christian virtues. And even more powerful were the promises of those who combined the two.

Few combined the two more successfully than Broad Church Anglicans and Liberal Nonconformists. What great vistas lay ahead for a nation both rationally educated and deeply Christian! Such certainly was the bright hope of Thomas Arnold when he became headmaster of Rugby. No longer would fagging, pranks, and chapels full of dreary catechisms be the rule, but solid learning, earnest religion, and sermons resounding with an enlightened and manly Christianity. The remedy for the evils besetting the land, Arnold said, was "a general and earnest application of the principles of the Gospel to our dealing with each other."[7] It was a message also delivered by many others, from Oxford University to the workhouse schools that promised to transform young paupers into sober, industrious, Christian adults. It greatly influenced the Anglican and Nonconformist schools that received government grants. The reports and visits of the education inspectors brought enlightened ideas to Church schools that were already deeply Christian. Throughout Britain, the confident promises of rationalism fused with the moral seriousness of Christianity to hold out a nearly limitless prospect of a free society.

Great were the promises and optimistic the expectations in the working of a laissez-faire society. Political economists promised that a free economy would benefit all; enlightened liberal reformists that a universal education, a disciplining, educating poor law, reformed prisons and reformatories, would produce a self-reliant working class; and Christianity awakened to a new benevolence would alleviate the misery and suffering that a free economy and self-reliance had not ended. Christian benevolence would join a larger voluntarism that was far more extensive.

Voluntarism's promises were legion: for Joseph Hume, it promised a ten-hour day "voluntarily" agreed to; for Owenites, the right to build utopian communities; for civic reformers, free baths and washhouses; for landlords, the right to give or not give allotments; and for philanthropists, the opportunity to form societies for every conceivable purpose. While voluntarism for most meant, above all, freedom from government interference, for some it also meant the formation of societies upon the principles of association, societies that would substitute cooperation and mutual aid for capitalism's ruthless competitive spirit. It formed the basis of Owenite communities, Christian Socialist workers' workshops, John Minton Morgan's Christian commonwealth, and countless other schemes that also proved impractical. But societies based on the principle of association could also be practical. Association not only formed the basis of the friendly and benefit societies that assured their members decent burials, aid if sick, convivial monthly meetings, and, sometimes, aid if jobless, but allowed workers to establish savings banks, building societies, and consumer cooperatives. For John Stuart Mill, partnerships of employers and employees and joint stock companies where employees participated were among the most desirable forms of association. Mill seldom, in his *Political Economy* of 1848, urged the government to expand its role any further. His socialism, like that of many others, looked primarily to the voluntary expansion of the principle of association.

Based on a long-standing, deeply rooted belief in the sacredness of property and the rightness of Providence, powerfully supported by a political economy that revealed the wondrous working of capitalism, and by an unlimited faith in the growth of a self-reliant working class, Christian virtue, and voluntary philanthropy, the vision of a laissez-faire society become the dominant theme of the early Victorian social conscience.

Dominant, yes, but how successful? Did it answer the demanding problems of an industrial and urban Britain? Were its weaknesses greater than its strengths? Not at all—the weaknesses were far fewer, would have been the response of the Victorians of 1860, who could point to triumphant capitalism, a self-reliant people, and far-reaching philanthropy. By 1850, Britain produced 40 percent of the world's hardware and 50 percent of its cotton and iron, and by 1860, one-third of the world's steel. In 1850, Britain's gross national product was £523 million; by 1870, it was £916 million. Its per capita income was £32 6s. a year, compared to France's £21 1s. and Germany's £13 3s. Such an economy put no strain on a belief in the advantages of laissez-faire.

Neither did the improved condition of a more self-reliant working class. Their life after 1860 to a considerable extent no longer resembled Friedrich Engels's dark picture of 1844, with its unrelieved slums, destitution, ignorance, child labor, and long hours of work. British workers were more and more the educated, provident, law-abiding, and prosperous class that F. M. L. Thompson describes so well in his *The Rise of Respectable Society* (1988). Increasingly, says Thompson, workers lived in neat row houses, two rooms up and two down, which spread throughout England. The front room was a parlor for a family life as respectable as that of the middle class. Workers were also better educated, because of both a bewildering variety of Church, voluntary, and private schools and their astonishing success at self-education.[8]

Not everyone, of course, was educated or prosperous, and misery, suffering, and ignorance persisted. But also persisting was the belief that they could be lessened by the voluntary outpouring of benevolence, both by individuals and by philanthropic societies. The early Victorians had infinite pride and confidence in these societies. There was no nook or cranny that they did not reach. Thirsty? Turn to the town's drinking fountain, a gift from voluntarism. Drowning at sea? Expect rescue by the Royal Life-Boat Institute, a philanthropic society. Down and out in London? Join the some 1,200 who nightly received a bed from the Houseless Poor Association. Filthy? Visit the nearest public baths or washhouse. Hungry and destitute? Go to the nearest soup kitchen or await a visit from a district visiting society.

Voluntarism also did far more than relieve distress. It left no area uncovered. Few were those it did not attempt to educate or reform, since hardly an educational institution, from the universities to the meanest ragged school, was not run by voluntarists. Most sickness was also alleviated by voluntary hospitals or dispensaries. Voluntarists reformed juvenile offenders and cared for discharged prisoners. They also built and supported half of British churches and founded the colony of Sierra Leone for freed slaves. Voluntarists built model houses for workers, established clothing clubs and penny banks, and cared for orphans and the deaf and blind. Scores of societies, like the Prison Discipline Society and the Health of Towns Association, campaigned for social reform. Nearly everyone participated, if only by attending a charity ball or dropping pennies in the offertory. And beyond formal philanthropies, there was the individual benevolence of millions, including landlords, lady bountifuls, and captains of industry acting within a still lively paternalist tradition. Voluntary benevolence in all its forms helped millions of early Victorians and formed one the great strengths of a laissez-faire society.

There was a fourth strength, one so accepted as to often go unnoticed, namely, the "English Liberties" that distinguished constitutional England from Continental monarchies. They, too, were an essential part of Britain's laissez-faire society, and they, too, had grown larger and more secure by 1860, making Victorians prouder of the rightness of the social outlook that they left the next generation.

But should they have been so proud? For all its impressive strengths, the laissez-faire society had glaring weaknesses. Triumphant capitalism, for example, could not rid itself of periodic breakdowns or continuing injustices. The breakdowns were painful and frequent. They occurred in 1811, 1816, 1819, 1825–26, 1839–42, and 1847. Manufacturing towns suffered from overproduction, gluts, closed mills, and joblessness. In 1826, in the manufacturing towns of Lancashire and Yorkshire, between 30 percent and 75 percent were unemployed, and in 1842 in Bolton nearly 60 percent. Agriculture had its winter layoffs, caused by rain and snow, and even worse were the severe crises resulting from bad harvests.

There were also continuing injustices. Underemployment never ceased as a population explosion flooded agriculture and spilled over into the towns. Rural pauperism seldom fell below 10 percent, and in manufacturing Oldham from 1800 to 1850, 40 percent or more lived in poverty. Massive London knew massive underemployment. Henry Mayhew estimated that one-third of the workers worked only half time and another third only occasionally, only day by day. With such underemployment and with trade unions harassed and kept weak, there was little that workers could do about pitiful wages, long hours and wretched conditions. Nor was anything done about the children who worked long hours in every workshop and factory in the land except textile mills and mines. That factory and mining inspectors prevented such exploitation in textiles and mines only made more shameful the fact that an even wider extent of exploitation went unchecked. Capitalism could still be cruel.

How then could early Victorians believe in the invisible hand that benefited all? Did not the economists suffer some profound illusions? They did, and not just about the invisible hand; they also believed that there was a fixed wage fund, that wages fell to subsistence, that the cost of labor determined a good's value, that population increased faster than food, and that gluts and

depression could never occur in a genuine laissez-faire society—all propositions posterity has judged false.

Economists were not alone in holding illusions. The moralists of self-
reliance held such when many of them argued that the poor's laziness and
improvidence were the main cause of their poverty. The moralists underestimated both the industry and toughness of the workers and the enormous barriers that depressions and underemployment placed before even the most
self-reliant. They never fully admitted that pauperism and poverty rose and
fell with the fluctuations of the economy. Did the moralists really believe that
economic depressions and mass unemployment came because of a sudden
increases in laziness and improvidence? Did they really think that a modest
outdoor relief to the jobless would dissuade them from returning to work
when jobs reappeared? Had they read Henry Mayhew on the industry, re-
sourcefulness, and resolve to never go on parish relief of hawkers, street per-
formers, coal heavers, porters, carmen, and crossing sweepers, they might
have freed themselves of their illusions. Or they could have read the Sanitary
Report of 1842, which revealed that sickness was the greatest cause of pauperism, or the 1842 inquiries of the Leeds Society for the Suppression of Mendicity, which showed that unemployment and sickness, not idleness and improvidence, caused 85 percent of poverty.

The voluntarists and the philanthropists also had their illusions. That they
did much good was not illusory, but quite illusory was the amount of good
they promised. Church of England schools did teach many children, but that
the Church could be the teacher of the whole nation was a will-o'-the-wisp.
Voluntary industrial schools, such as those of William Allen and Lady Byron,
did reform delinquent youth, but they only reformed the tiniest fraction of
the juveniles needing reform. Some hospitals and dispensaries did come close
to covering the needs of the ill, yet most fell far short. Soup kitchens were invaluable to the hungry of depression-ridden mill towns and famine-stricken
Ireland, but only until they were closed from want of funds. Lord Ashley's
model housing was noble but helped far less than 1 percent of London's
homeless. Throughout England, the zeal for voluntarism not only fell short
but often inspired opposition to government reforms.

One of the most pervasive illusions was the promise made by the religious
that a true Christianity would spread, and with it such doing of good that
there would be a fair and just society. That Christians had for centuries made
similar promises and all had fallen far short meant little to those men of the
cloth who assured their congregations of the Christian rule of the virtuous.

Rationalists also had their illusions. If all received the vote, a sound education, and freedom from bad laws and superstition, then crime, destitution, injustice, and misery in every form would vanish. And though rationalists had not seen their promises fail for as many centuries as the religious had, their sanguine expectations were just as unattainable. Many and great, then, were the illusions underlying the early Victorians' vision of a laissez-faire society.

It is perplexing. How could a social outlook based on so many illusions prove so powerful? Why did that outlook dominate the Victorians' social conscience for a century, keep itself alive in the collectivist twentieth century, and be revived by Margaret Thatcher? There are two possible answers: either that its strengths and successes were far greater than its illusions and weaknesses, or that it relied, without acknowledging it, on government action. Its strengths certainly exceeded its weaknesses. The proverbial glass was considerably more than half full. Lord Ashley's model housing did fall short, but by 1900, thanks to capitalism, only about one-tenth of the working class endured slum conditions. Fewer lived in poverty thanks to a 50 percent rise in real wages from 1875 to 1900, the product of both capitalism and the fact that the workers were "fiercely self-reliant."[9] They were also better educated. For all the failings of the educational system, there were in 1870 some 14,000 schools, only a third or fewer of which were state-aided, and then only partially.

But, of course, it was not all a matter of capitalism, self-reliance, and voluntarism, but of more and more government. Yet though the Victorians used government to meet its deficiencies, they did not let the fact diminish their vision of the ideal laissez-faire society. Although they seldom mentioned government's invaluable role, they were nonetheless pleased to see it lessen society's grievous evils. It was a position full of contradictions, which raise a perplexing question: how could the early Victorians have developed both a powerful vision of a laissez-faire society and a greatly expanded government?

They did so, in part, because they acted in separate channels, channels that met different needs. The vision of a laissez-faire society met intellectual and psychological needs, the growth of government the need to solve social and economic problems. In sermons, lectures, books, periodicals, and pamphlets, Victorians developed a satisfying intellectual picture. Even though the promises of an invisible hand that benefited all and of an expanding Christianity bringing a just and fair society fell short of fulfillment, they still offered a way of using distant promises to explain away the reality of destitution, cruelty, and injustice. People were psychologically relieved to believe in great solutions, in grand, optimistic schemes. Members of the anti-Corn Law League found it highly satisfying to believe that repealing that law would raise wages, end unemployment, banish poverty, and bring world peace. Self-made men reassured themselves that destitution would disappear if all were as self-reliant as they. And blaming the poor for their own poverty gave satisfaction to many, since it was an easy way to avoid responsibility.

There was also an intellectual satisfaction in a coherent system, one that appeared as logical and coherent as political economy or as tightly connected as the theology and morality of evangelicalism. And best of all were outlooks that were not only intellectually coherent but supportive of one's favorite institution, whether it was a Methodist chapel or a cathedral chapter, a town council or a county session, a chamber of commerce or an agricultural association. Few things exceeded the institutional and local loyalties of the English. They were loyalties that when joined with omnipresent self-interest and the satisfactions of a coherent system could explain away the worst realities of poverty and injustice. They formed a social outlook that, although it left so many social problems unremedied, was nonetheless passed on from generation to generation.

But there were still pressing social problems, problems that had to be answered by Parliament, town councils, county quarter sessions, and myriad boards and agencies. This channel also had its own history, one often separate from the history of those ideas that gave intellectual and psychological satisfaction. There was in these local and national bodies much talk of practical problems and little of economic theories, educational panaceas, or a purer Christianity. In their debates and votes, two powerful forces, neither very intellectual, contended, vested economic, political, and social interests, on the one hand, and a humanitarian feeling that certain abuses could no longer be tolerated, on the other. Such was the case with children in mines and mills, the mentally ill in barbarous asylums, and the disease, crime, destitution, and widespread lack of education in mushrooming towns. The feeling that glaring abuses were intolerable constantly battled the power of vested interests and increasingly gained hard-fought reforms by struggles that seemed quite separate from the world of social theories.

But these channels also were not so separate if humanitarian feelings are considered as ideas. Humanitarianism was one of the most powerful forces defining the early Victorian social conscience. It was in everyone's breast to be aroused by vivid accounts of cruelty and suffering. It rightly made Dickens one of the age's greatest moralists, however confused his ideas on social reform. If humanitarianism was not a distinct idea or theory, it was nonetheless a feeling that infused other ideas and theories with a greater humanity. These ideas and theories in turn often promoted humane feelings. In the great evangelicals Wilberforce and Ashley, an evangelical Christianity inspired a humanity that freed slaves and rescued factory children, just as an existing pervasive humanitarianism also softened the outlook of many a hard, sin-obsessed evangelical. And certainly Enlightenment ideas made a widespread humanitarianism even more widespread. It was Fenelon and other Enlightenment philosophers who inspired the young Bentham to dream of altruistic schemes for saving mankind, just as Bentham's utilitarian arguments in turn strengthened a widespread humanitarianism. Humanitarianism also infused a narrow paternalism with a greater benevolence to dependents, while paternalist writers—from Coleridge to Carlyle—used paternalist theories to expand humanitarian feelings. Nor did humanitarianism leave Nonconformist apostles of individualism and self-reliance untouched. Humanitarian feelings led Bible-oriented Dissenters to invoke the Sermon on the Mount, and those who did, like Thomas Binney and George Dawson, responded by preaching a far more humanitarian gospel than did their predecessors.

Although humanitarianism was everywhere, it was not everywhere powerful. Diffuse and undefined, it could not overcome universal selfishness and widespread institutional and local loyalties. To better effect reform, humanitarians needed a clear-cut ideology. Two outlooks offered themselves as humanitarianism's vehicle, the idea of a paternal government and the idea of a utilitarian state. The idea of a paternal government proved only moderately successful. It did much good, as Lord Ashley's career shows. But it fell short, because its deepest roots were in a land, Church, and local government that could not abide a strong, active, central government. It thus fell to the idea of a utilitarian state to give an effective form to humanitarianism. Since utilitarians did not fear a stronger central government, they were more successful in helping humanitarianism overcome vested interests and institutional and local loyalties. Not only were Benthamite M.P.'s and bureaucrats full of zeal for social facts and practical schemes, but the utilitarians' great yardstick—the greatest happiness of the greatest number—was the most popular and widely used moral rule, and so an excellent way for humanitarianism to express itself. A widespread utilitarian ethic (one not always admitted) reached far beyond the Benthamites to give expression to a powerful humanitarianism, thus laying the foundations of a caring government and greatly expanding the dimensions of the early Victorian social conscience.

M.P.'s of Religious and Rationalist Outlook

RELIGIOUS	RATIONALIST
Thomas D. Acland	John Bowring
Charles Adderley	Charles Buller
Lord Ashley	William D. Christie
Frederick Thornhill Baring	Richard Cobden
William Colquhoun	Thomas Duncombe
William Cowper	John Easthope
Henry Drummond	William Ewart
Viscount Ebrington	George Grenville, Lord Nugent
Thomas Estcourt	Charles Grey, Lord Howick
Henry Goulburn	Sir John Hobhouse
William Gladstone	Joseph Hume
Sir George Grey	John Leader
Robert Grosvenor	Charles Lushington
John Hardy	Thomas B. Macaulay
Henry Halford	William MacKinnon
Sydney Herbert	William Molesworth
Charles Talbot, Viscount Ingestre	Lord Nugent
Sir Robert Inglis	Lord Palmerston
Forster McGeachy	John Roebuck
Lord John Manners	Lord John Russell
Sir John Pakington	George Poulett Scrope
Robert Palmer	Edward Strutt
Henry Pelham, Lord Lincoln	Thomas N. Talford
John Plumtre	Henry Temple, Lord Palmerston
Richard Spooner	Charles Villiers
	Thomas Wakley
	William Williams
	Thomas Wyse

Notes

CHAPTER 1

1. Thomas Starkey, *England in the Reign of King Henry the Eighth . . . A Dialogue Between Cardinal Pole and Thomas Lupset*, ed. J. M. Cowper (London, 1878), pt. 2, cxxix.

2. William Dunham and Stanley Pargellis, *Complaint and Reform in England, 1436–1714* (New York, 1938), pp. 196–198; Thomas Elyot, *The Book Named The Governor* (1531), ed. S. E. Lehmberg (London, 1962), pp. 1–2.

3. Robert Benton Seeley, *Memoirs of the Life and Writings of Michael Thomas Sadler, Esq.* (London, 1842), p. 32; Cecil Driver, *Tory Radical: The Life of Richard Oastler* (New York, 1946).

4. Edmund Burke, *The Works of Edmund Burke* (9 vols.; Boston, 1839), 4: 252; Charles Parkin, *The Moral Basis of Burke's Political Thought* (Cambridge, 1956), pp. 31, 36, 61.

5. Samuel Taylor Coleridge, *Letters, Conversations and Recollections* (London, 1836), p. 172; id., *On the Constitution of Church and State* (London, 1829), p. 119; Robert Southey, *Sir Thomas More, or, Colloquies on the Progress and Prospect of Society* (2 vols.; London, 1829–31), 1: 299.

6. Burke, *Works*, 1: 213; 4: 245, 232; Parkin, *Moral Basis of Burke's Political Thought*, p. 36; Coleridge, *Church and State*, p. 55; id., *Two Lay Sermons: Statesman's Manual* (London, 1839), p. 416; id., *Table Talk* (London, 1835), 2: 135.

7. Coleridge, *Statesman's Manual*, pp. 224–225, 416, 430; id., *Letters, Conversations and Recollections*, p. 62; Parkin, *Moral Basis of Burke's Political Thought*, p. 30; Southey, *Sir Thomas More*, 1: 165.

8. *The Life and Correspondence of Robert Southey*, ed. Rev. Charles Cuthbert Southey (6 vols.; London, 1849), 6: 87; Coleridge, *Statesman's Manual*, pp. 359, 593, 416, 419.

9. Robert Benton Seeley, *The Perils of the Nation: An Appeal to the Legislature, the Clergy, and High and Middle Classes* (London, 1843), p. 28; William Sewell, *Christian Politics* (London, 1844), pp. 278–279.

10. Thomas Carlyle, *Chartism* (London, 1839), pp. 34, 36; Thomas Arnold, *Miscellaneous Works* (New York, 1845), pp. 432–433.

11. Arthur Helps, *Claims of Labour* (London, 1844), pp. 9, 34, 35, 48, 58, 63, 64, 75, 92, 94, 97, 118, 129, 131, 140.

12. Coleridge, *Table Talk*, 2: 227; Thomas Chalmers, *The Christian and Civic Economy of Large Towns* (3 vols.; Glasgow, 1821–26), 1: 132, 139, 296; Thomas Carlyle, *Latter Day Pamphlets* (1850; London, 1872), p. 56; William Sewell, *Christian Communism* (Oxford, 1848), p. 19.

13. Augustus Welby Northmore Pugin, *Contrasts, or, A Parallel Between the Noble Edifices of the Fourteenth and Fifteenth Centuries and Similar Buildings of the Present Day* (London, 1836).

14. Southey, *Sir Thomas More*, vol. 2; Kenelm Digby, *The Broad Stone of Honour, or, Rules for the Gentlemen of England* (London, 1823; new ed., 1845), bk. 4, *Orlandus*, pp. 82, 90, 94 (quotation); bk. 1, *Godefridus*, pp. 86ff.

15. William Cobbett, *A History of the Protestant Reformation* (London, 1829), 1: 142–157, 183–186.

16. John Wade, *The Extraordinary Black Book: An Exposition of Abuses in Church and State, Courts of Law, Representation, Municipal and Corporate Bodies, with a Précis of the House of Commons, Past, Present, and to Come* (1831; new ed., London, 1832), pp. 20, 57; W. Wordsworth, *The Poetical Works* (London, 1940), 2: 455.

17. Coleridge, *Church and State*, pp. 43–64; id., *Table Talk*, 1: 199.

18. Chalmers, *Christian and Civic Economy*, 1: 8, 29, 169–358.

19. Arnold, *Miscellaneous Works*, pp. 263, 514–516.

20. Sewell, *Christian Politics*, pp. 78, 266–67, 314–318, 363–366, 393; *Christian Communism*, p. 20; Seeley, *Perils of a Nation*, pp. 217, 224, 307; *Remedies*, p. 130.

21. Frederick Denison Maurice, *The Kingdom of Christ* (London, 1843); C. K. Gloyn, *The Church and the Social Order* (Forest Grove, Ore., 1942), pp. 118–142; N. C. Masterman, *John Malcolm Ludlow: The Builder of Christian Socialism* (Cambridge, 1963), pp. 62–63, 71, 85, 98–99; *Politics for the People*, July 15, 1848; John Minter Morgan, *Religion and Crime* (London, 1840), pp. 29–30.

22. Sewell, *Christian Politics*, pp. 308, 313; Seeley, *Remedies Suggested for Some of the Evils Which Constitute "The Perils of the Nation,"* 2d ed. (London, 1844), p. 165.

23. Coleridge, *Church and State*, pp. 83–86; id., *Table Talk*, 2: 311, 324, 283; Arnold, *Miscellaneous Works*, pp. 88–94, 263–449, 500–502; A. P. Stanley, *Life of Thomas Arnold* (London, 1901), pp. 343, 386.

24. Maurice, *Kingdom of Christ*, pp. 240, 278, 557–569; id., *The Life of Frederick Denison Maurice, Chiefly Told in His Own Letters*, 4th ed. (2 vols.; London, 1885), pp. 32–33.

25. Chalmers, *Christian and Civic Economy*, 1: 109–358; Carlyle, *Latter Day Pamphlets*, pp. 79, 125, 135, 141–143.

26. Carlyle, *Latter Day Pamphlets*, pp. 79, 125, 135, 141–143; id., *Past and Present* (London, 1897), pp. 88–140.

27. Coleridge, *Church and State*, pp. 43–64; id., *Table Talk*, 1: 200–201.

28. Sewell, *Christian Politics*, pp. 313, 368.

29. Arnold, *Miscellaneous Works*, pp. 266–310, 414, 446–449.

30. Masterman, *John Malcolm Ludlow*, pp. 1–73, 85; *Politics of the People*, July 1848, pp. 205–210.

31. Terence Kenny, *The Political Thought of John Henry Newman* (London, 1957), p. 172.

32. Sewell, *Christian Politics*, pp. 222–223, 330.

33. Seeley, *Sadler*, p. 448.

34. Driver, *Tory Radical . . . Oastler*, pp. 296–297.

35. Sir Arthur Helps, *Friends in Council: A Series of Readings and Discourse Thereon*, 2 vols. (London, 1847–1849), 1: 142; id., *Claims of Labour*, pp. 20, 78, 111, 115, 116; *Quarterly Review*, Mar. 1828, p. 565; July 1828, pp. 60, 62, 64, 77; May 1830, pp. 252–253; Southey, *Sir Thomas More*, 2: 221; Driver, *Tory Radical . . . Oastler*, pp. 296–297, 435.

36. Burke, *Works*, 1: 251, 254, 257, 265, 270, 278.

37. Coleridge, *Statesman's Manual*, pp. 418, 430; John Colmer, *Coleridge, Critic of Society* (Oxford, 1959), p. 148.

38. Southey, *Sir Thomas More*, 1: 165; id., *Essays, Moral and Political* (2 vols.; London, 1832), 1: 192, 195; 2: 26, 29, 116, 158; Sewell, *Christian Politics*, pp. 133, 142, 209.

39. Chalmers, *Christian and Civic Economy*, 1: 6–8, 13, 29, 248, 283–284, 295–297; 2: 44, 132, 201.

40. Coleridge, *Statesman's Manual*, p. 421; id., *Letters*, 1: 27; *Life and Correspondence of Robert Southey*, ed. C. C. Southey, 6: 231; Southey, *Essays*, 1: 149. On Southey and the Poor Law, see also Donald Winch, *Riches and Poverty: An Intellectual History of Political Economy in Britain, 1750–1834* (New York, 1996), pp. 309–315.

41. Burke, *Works*, 4: 261.

42. Colmer, *Coleridge*, pp. 44–45; F. M. Todd, *Politics of the Poet: A Study of Wordsworth* (London, 1957), p. 215; Coleridge, *Table Talk*, 2: 74.

43. Driver, *Tory Radical . . . Oastler*, p. 507; Seeley, *Sadler*, pp. 80, 135, 417; Southey, *Sir Thomas More*, 1: 134; Sewell, *Christian Politics*, pp. 165–167, 209; Helps, *Claims of Labour*, pp. 6, 40–45, 58; Burke, *Works*, 4: 243.

44. Coleridge, *Statesman's Manual*, pp. 415, 417; Colmer, *Coleridge*, pp. 109–110.

45. Seeley, *Sadler*, pp. 45, 339, 604.

46. Burke, *Works*, 7: 44; Coleridge, *Table Talk*, 1: 202; 2: 148, 281–290, 311, 347, 324.

47. Geoffrey Carnall, *Robert Southey and His World* (Oxford, 1960), p. 149; Southey, *Essays*, 1: 219; 2122, 125; id., *Sir Thomas More* 1: 93; Sewell, *Christian Politics*, p. 330.

48. Coleridge, *Table Talk*, 2: 148; Carlyle, *Latter Day Pamphlets*, p. 135; id., *Past and Present*, p. 146.

49. Seeley, *Sadler*, p. 33; Sadler, *Ireland*, pp. 187, 193; Southey, *Sir Thomas More*, 1: 105; 2: 221; id., *Essays*, 1: 109; 2: 23–25; *Quarterly Review*, Mar. 1828, p. 565; July 1828, pp. 60–62, 64, 77; May 1830, pp. 252–253, 255, 260, 276–277; Wordsworth, *Poetical Works*, 2: 416.

50. Carlyle, *Latter Day Pamphlets*, pp. 79, 125, 135, 140–143.

CHAPTER 2

1. George Croly, *A Memoir of the Political Life of the Right Honourable Edmund Burke* (Edinburgh, 1840); *Blackwood's Magazine*, Aug. 1842, p. 220; Oct. 1842, p. 542; Jan. 1843, p. 9; July 1843, p. 66; *Quarterly Review*, Sept. 1846, p. 565; Dec. 1849, pp. 183–184; Dec. 1847, p. 177.

2. Theodore Martin, *Memoir of William Edmonstoune Aytoun* (London, 1867), p. 11; Ann M. Stoddart, *John Stuart Blackie* (London, 1895), p. 18; Samuel Warren, *The Intellectual and Moral Development of the Present Age* (London, 1853), p. 32.

3. H. A. Kennedy, *Professor Blackie* (London, 1895), pp. 129, 158; G. S. Merriam, *The Story of William and Lucy Smith* (London, 1889), p. 17; Thomas De Quincey, *Reminiscences of the English Lake Poets* (London, n.d.), p. 1.

4. John F. Murray, *The World of London* (London, 1845), 1: 131; J. Campbell Smith, *Writings by the Way* (London, 1885), p. 471.

5. Sir Archibald Alison, *Some Account of My Writings: An Autobiography* (2 vols.; Edinburgh, 1883), 1: 187; Margaret Oliphant, *William Blackwood and His Sons* (London, 1897), 1: 420.

6. Andrew Lang, *The Life and Letters of John Gibson Lockhart* (London, 1897), 2: 285; 1: 136;

Critic, July 7, 1860, p. 41; John Croker, *Correspondence and Diaries* (London, 1884), 2: 412; *Quarterly Review,* Dec. 1841, pp. 10–11, 79, 387.

7. Katherine Lake, *Memorials of William Charles Lake* (London, 1901), p. 23; Thomas Mozley, *Reminiscences Chiefly of Oriel College and the Oxford Movement* (Boston, 1882), p. 150; R. C. Church, *Essays and Reviews* (London 1854), p. 343; *Christian Remembrancer,* July 1849, p. 67; Thomas Vargish, *Newman: The Contemplation of Mind* (Oxford, 1970), p. 59.

8. *Fraser's Magazine,* May 1857, p. 613; *Memoirs of the Life and Correspondence of Henry Reeve,* ed. J. K. Laughton (London, 1898), 1: 36, 44.

9. Charles Whibley, *Lord John Manners and His Friends* (London, 1925), pp. 133, 260; M. M. H. Thrall, *Rebellious Fraser's* (New York, 1934), pp. 11, 26, 30–33, 89, 95–96; *Fraser's Magazine,* Feb. 1840, p. 160; *The Wellesley Index to Victorian Periodicals,* ed. Walter E. Houghton, vol. 2 (Toronto, 1979), 309–310.

10. Stoddart, *Blackie,* p. 154.

11. Merriam, *Story of William and Lucy Smith,* p. 154.

12. *Quarterly Review,* Mar. 1842, pp. 10–46; Sept. 1840, p. 447.

13. *Blackwood's Magazine,* Apr. 1830, p. 680.

14. *Blackwood's Magazine,* Nov. 1841, p. 673; Mar. 1849, p. 313; *Quarterly Review,* Dec. 1841, pp. 26–27.

15. *Blackwood's Magazine,* Dec. 1841, pp. 26–27.

16. *Oxford and Cambridge Review,* Aug. 1845, p. 153; *Fraser's Magazine,* July 1846, p. 93; *Blackwood's Magazine,* May 1845, p. 543; June 1849, p. 715.

17. *Quarterly Review,* Sept. 1841, pp. 341–342; *Fraser's Magazine,* Feb. 1841, pp. 129–130, 133.

18. *Quarterly Review,* Sept. 1840, 469, 447–502.

19. *Quarterly Review,* Sept. 1840, p. 569; 1842, 70: 491; Sept. 1846, p. 569; *Blackwood's Magazine,* Mar. 1849, p. 312; July 1843, pp. 65–66.

20. *British Critic* 29 (1840): 334, 357–358; *Quarterly Review,* Sept. 1840, p. 501.

21. *English Review,* Jan. 1844, pp. 48–104; Dec. 1844, pp. 126–151; May 1845, pp. 179–180; Dec. 1846, pp. 418–431; *British Critic* 23 (1838): 174–179, 164–186; 26 (1839): 359–371; *Christian Remembrancer* 47 (1845): 1–28, 453–471; 51 (1847): 276–291; 53 (1849): 1–16.

22. *Blackwood's Magazine,* May 1848, p. 561; *English Review,* Jan. 1844, pp. 71, 86; Dec. 1844, p. 427; *Oxford and Cambridge Review,* July 1845, p. 7; June 1846, p. 458; Oct. 1846, p. 343; Nov. 1846, pp. 492ff; *Quarterly Review,* Sept. 1848, p. 359.

23. *Oxford and Cambridge Review,* Sept. 1845, p. 313, Aug. 1845, p. 178.

24. *Fraser's Magazine,* June 1843, pp. 748–749.

25. *Oxford and Cambridge Review,* July 1846, p. 82; *English Review,* Dec. 1844, p. 261; *Quarterly Review,* Sept. 1840, pp. 501–502; 1841, 68: 343; *Blackwood's Magazine,* June 1849, p. 714.

26. *Blackwood's Magazine,* June 1846, pp. 733–734.

27. *English Review,* Dec. 1848, p. 267; *Oxford and Cambridge Review,* Jan. 1846, p. 47; *British and Foreign Review,* Jan. 1840, p. 231; J. C. Smith, *Writings by the Way,* pp. 471–472.

28. Alison, *Autobiography,* 1: 24, 35; *Blackwood's Magazine,* Nov. 1841, pp. 659, 672; Oct. 1842, pp. 459–466.

29. *Quarterly Review,* Dec. 1843, pp. 554–555; Dec. 1849, p. 150; *Christian Remembrancer,* Oct. 1846, p. 315.

30. *Blackwood's Magazine,* Sept. 1840, p. 311; *Fraser's Magazine,* May 1843, p. 511.

31. *British Critic* 33 (1843): 249–250, 252, 271.

32. *Fraser's Magazine*, Aug. 1844, p. 251; *Blackwood's Magazine*, Apr. 1842, p. 520.

33. *Quarterly Review*, Apr. 1835, pp. 485–536; *Blackwood's Magazine*, Nov. 1846, pp. 555–570.

34. *Parliamentary Papers* [hereafter cited as *P.P.*], 1835, 28: 50; *Fraser's Magazine*, Apr. 1841, pp. 377–389; *Blackwood's Magazine*, June 1841, p. 706; Nov. 1846, pp. 555–570; Nov. 1857, p. 642.

35. *British Critic* 33 (1843): 254; *Fraser's Magazine*, May 1844, p. 623; *English Review*, Dec. 1844, p. 261; *Quarterly Review*, June 1845, pp. 15–16.

36. *Quarterly Review*, Dec. 1841, pp. 181, 173–182.

37. W. F. Hook, *Letter to the Bishop of St. David's on. . . the Education of the People* (London, 1846); *Quarterly Review*, Sept. 1846, pp. 377–424; *Fraser's Magazine*, Sept. 1846, pp. 371–372; *Oxford and Cambridge Review*, Oct. 1846, p. 330; *English Review*, Sept. 1840, p. 136.

38. *Blackwood's Magazine*, Mar. 1840, p. 428; May 1848, pp. 540–562; May 1849, pp. 568ff; *Quarterly Review*, Dec. 1848, pp. 238, 238, 243.

39. *Blackwood's Magazine*, May 1844, p. 649; *Quarterly Review*, Dec. 1846, pp. 245, 252–253, 262; Mar. 1847, pp. 466, 470, 471, 478.

40. *Fraser's Magazine*, Feb. 1843, p. 239; Dec. 1843, pp. 732–739; *Oxford and Cambridge Review*, Nov. 1846, p. 361.

41. *Quarterly Review*, Dec. 1846, pp. 245, 248; Sept. 1849, p. 530.

42. *Fraser's Magazine*, May 1844, pp. 506, 507–515; *Quarterly Review*, June 1844, pp. 234, 257, 224–280; *Blackwood's Magazine*, Aug. 1845, pp. 173–176; Nov. 1845, pp. 637–638, 644.

43. *Blackwood's Magazine*, Dec. 1846, pp. 722, 727; Aug. 1845, pp. 139–140; Nov. 1849, p. 519; *Quarterly Review*, Dec. 1847, pp. 177, 175–203; Dec. 1841, pp. 43–48; June 1841, pp. 92–94; *Oxford and Cambridge Review*, July 1846, pp. 87–89; July 1846, p. 93; *Blackwood's Magazine*, Aug. 1845, pp. 139, 129–140; *Fraser's Magazine*, Jan. 1846, p. 8; Apr. 1848, p. 402; Nov. 1848, p. 557; Sept. 1848, pp. 294–299.

44. *Quarterly Review*, June 1840, pp. 116, 123.

45. *Quarterly Review*, Mar. 1843, pp. 436, 449; *Blackwood's Magazine*, Oct. 1842, pp. 646, 652.

46. *Fraser's Magazine*, Sept. 1847, pp. 371, 366–377; Nov. 1847, pp. 505–515.

47. Alison, *Autobiography*, 1: 13.

48. T. T. Carter, *A Memoir of John Armstrong, D.D., Late Lord Bishop of Grahamstown* (Oxford, 1857), pp. 6–7, 67.

49. Martin, *Aytoun*, p. 106; *Athenaeum*, May 12, 1883, p. 604; *Blackwood's Magazine*, Aug. 1845, p. 173.

50. *Quarterly Review*, June 1841, p. 255; Croker, *Correspondence and Diaries*, 2: 222, 250.

51. Marion Lochhead, *John Gibson Lockhart* (London, 1954), p. 245; Lang, *Lockhart*, 2: 195; Rosaline Masson, *Pollok and Aytoun* (London, 1898), p. 97; Alison, *Autobiography*, 1: 131, 559, 602.

52. Lang, *Lockhart*, 2: 191, 195; Lochhead, *Lockhart*, pp. 173, 243, 245.

53. Oliphant, *Blackwood's Magazine*, 2: 263, 268, 346, 355, 367, 369, 381.

54. "Stanley Lees Giffard, the Complete Independent" (MS), in the Halsbury Papers (listed at the National Registry of Archives); *Standard*, Nov. 9, 1858, Sir Robert Peel Papers, Add. MSS 40, 563, British Library, S. L. Giffard to Sir Robert Peel, Mar. 21, 1845; Arthur Aspinall, *Politics and the Press* (London, 1949), pp. 335–337; 440; Alice Fox, *The Earl of Halsbury, Lord High Chancellor* (London, 1929), pp. 11–15, 30, 32, 38; Alaric Alfred Watts, *A Narrative of My Life* (London, 1884), 1: 152, 229–237, 240.

55. The Times, *The History of The Times* (London, 1935–), 2: 7, 46, 47, 119–133; Arthur I. Dasent, *John Thaddeus Delane, Editor of The Times* (London, 1908), 1: 20, 13–55; H. R. Fox Bourne, *English Newspapers: Chapters in the History of Journalism* (London, 1887), 2: 70–72.

56. *Dictionary of National Biography* (London, 1894) [hereafter cited as *DNB*], 39: 915; *Canterbury Magazine*, Sept. 1834, pp. 121–123.

57. G. P. R. James, *Charles Tyrrel* (New York, 1839), 2: 39.

58. Catherine Gore, *Peers and Parvenues* (London, 1846), 1: 168.

59. G. P. R. James, *The Gentleman of the Old School* (New York, 1893), 1: 113, 115.

60. Catherine Gore, *Men of Capital* (London, 1846), 2: 56–67.

61. J. F. Murray, *Viceroy* (London, 1841), 1: 69, 93–97, 196.

62. William Sewell, *Hawkstone* (London, 1845), 1: 79, 90, 94–95, 124, 133; 2: 22, 239, 286.

63. Francis Trollope, *Jesse Phillips* (London, 1844), p. 40; id., *Michael Armstrong, Factory Boy* (London, 1840), 2: 164, 214, 215, 227.

64. Elizabeth Gaskell, *Mary Barton* (London, 1848), pp. 482–483; id., *North and South* (London, 1855), pp. 164–165.

65. Charles Kingsley, *Alton Locke* (London, 1848), pp. 228–229, 286, 345, 360–361; id., *Yeast* (London, 1858), pp. 88–89, 182, 183, 185; Benjamin Disraeli, *Coningsby* (London, 1844), p. 251; Sewell, *Hawkstone*, 2: 284.

66. Elizabeth Sewell, *Amy Herbert* (London, 1846), 1: 23, 25, 242; 2: 54; Charlotte Elizabeth [Tonna], *Helen Fleetwood* (1844; reprint, London, 1858), pp. 17, 94, 133, 303.

67. Francis Paget, *The Pageant; or, Pleasure and Its Price* (London, 1843), pp. xvi, 7, 8, 39, 61, 78, 190; id., *The Warden of Berkingholt* (London, 1843); William Gresley, *Clement Walton* (London, 1848), pp. 39, 124, 132, 145, 146, 152, 169, 174; id., *Church Clavering* (London, 1845); id., *Charles Lever* (London, 1845); id., *Frank's First Trip to the Continent* (London, 1845); Robert Armitage, *Ernest Singleton* (London, 1848), 1: 88, 90, 105, 108, 133, 229; 2: 57, 110, 131, 296; 3: 35; id., *The Penscellwood Papers* (London, 1846), 2: 14; id., *Doctor Hackwell* (London, 1842), 2: 21, 85, 90, 273; 3: 107.

68. Charles Dickens, *Nicholas Nickleby* (London, n.d.), p. 424; id., *Hard Times* (London, 1858).

69. Dickens, *Nicholas Nickleby*, pp. 341, 354, 359; id., *A Christmas Carol* (London, 1843), p. 31; id., *Pickwick Papers* (Boston, n.d.), p. 224.

70. Dickens, *Nicholas Nickleby*, pp. 76, 257–275, 312–314, 359, 444–447; *The Chimes*, in *Christmas Books* (New York, 1868), pp. 153–154.

71. Douglas Jerrold, *The History of St. Giles and St. James* (London, 1851), pp. 127, 152–153, 211.

72. Charlotte Brontë, *Shirley* (London, 1898), pp. 118, 218, 221, 248, 253, 437; Harriet Martineau, *Deerbrook* (London, 1878), pp. 263, 344, 360–361, 419, 472, 479.

73. Theodore Hook, *Peregrine Bunce* (London, 1873), pp. 12, 26, 29.

74. Charles Dickens, *Dombey and Son* (New York, 1912), 558.

CHAPTER 3

1. *Northampton Mercury*, Oct. 26, 1844; *Leeds Intelligencer*, Mar. 30, 1844; *Western Luminary*, Jan. 19, 1844; *Shrewsbury Chronicle*, Nov. 5, 1841; *Western Times*, Jan. 19, 1841; *Farmer's Magazine*, Sept. 1844, pp. 259–263; Dec. 1844, pp. 529–550.

2. *Sussex Agricultural Express*, June 15, 1844; Dec. 14, 1844; June 18, 1844, Oct. 28, 1843; Dec. 7, 1844; Jan. 25, 1845; June 13, 1846.

3. *Sussex Agricultural Express*, Feb. 8, 1840; Jan. 1, Dec. 30, 1842; July 19, 1845; Jan. 7, 1843; Nov. 1, 1845; Feb. 8, Dec. 5, 1840; Jan. 13, 1841.

4. John Mordant, *The Complete Steward* (London, 1761), pp. 377–401; Thomas Gisborne, *An Enquiry into the Duties of Men of the Higher and Middle Classes* (London, 1794), pp. 416–424.

5. Lord Sydney Godolphin Osborne, *The Savings Bank* (London, 1835); id., *Hints to the Charitable* (London, 1838); id., *A View of the Low Moral and Physical Condition of the Agricultural Labourers* (London, 1844); John Sandford, *Parochialia; or, Church, School, and Parish: The Church System and Services, Practically Considered* (London, 1845). See also G. W. Perry, *The Peasantry of England* (London, 1846), and *Meliora, or, Better Times to Come*, ed. Charles Talbot, Viscount Ingestre (London, 1852).

6. *Northampton Mercury*, Aug. 24, 1844; *P.P.*, 1843, 7: 203.

7. F. M. L. Thompson, *English Landed Society in the Nineteenth Century* (London, 1963), pp. 209–210.

8. David Spring, *The English Landed Estate in the Nineteenth Century* (Baltimore, 1963), p. 52; *Journal of the Statistical Society of London* 1 (1839): 407; *P.P.*, 1852, 40: 445; *Salisbury Journal*, Aug. 3, 1844; *Hansard*, 1847, 91: 167.

9. John Glyde, *The Moral, Social, and Religious Condition of Ipswich* (London, 1850), p. 357; Great Britain, Public Record Office [henceforth cited as P.R.O.], *Poor Law Papers*, Ministry of Health [henceforth cited as M.H.] 32/21, Earle to LeFevre, Mar. 31, 1835; H. T. Ryall, *Portraits of Conservatives* (London, 1836); George Douglas Campbell, 8th duke of Argyll, *Autobiography and Memoirs* (London, 1906), pp. 129–135, 228, 291–294.

10. P.R.O., *Poor Law Papers*, M.H. 32/21, Earle to LeFevre, May 31, 1837; *Chambers' Edinburgh Journal*, Sept. 24, 1842, p. 286; *Leeds Intelligencer*, Nov. 30, 1844; G. W. F. H. Carlisle, *The Viceregal Speeches and Addresses, Lectures and Poems, of the Late Earl of Carlisle, K. G.*, ed. J. J. Gaskin (Dublin, 1866), pp. xvi, lxxxii; P.R.O., *Poor Law Papers*, M.H. 32/27, Gilbert's diary, Jan 5, 1839; *Witness*, Jan. 22, 1842.

11. Edwin Hodder, *The Life and Work of the Seventh Earl of Shaftesbury* (London, 1886), 2: 367; Sir Arthur Gordon, *The Earl of Aberdeen* (London, 1893), pp. 11–12.

12. John Prebble, *The Highland Clearances* (London, 1963), pp. 291, 295, 301.

13. *Hansard*, 1845, 78: 317; *P.P.*, 1846, 24: 396–397; James Grant, *Memoirs of Sir George Sinclair* (London, 1870), p. 313; David Spring, "Agents of the Earl of Durham," *Durham University Journal*, June 1962, pp. 104–112; id., *English Landed Estate*, p. 52.

14. Owen Chadwick, *Victorian Miniatures* (London, 1960), pp. 61, 65; *Memoirs and Literary Remains of Lieutenant-General Sir Henry Bunbury*, ed. Charles Bunbury (London, 1868), p. 84; Charles R. Strutt, *The Strutt Family of Terling* (London, 1939), pp. 77–78.

15. Chadwick, *Victorian Miniatures*, pp. 63, 72–74; Bunbury, *Memoirs*, pp. 85, 114, 196–202; Strutt, *Strutt Family*, pp. 77–78.

16. Chadwick, *Victorian Miniatures*, p. 71; Strutt, *Strutt Family*, pp. 78–79; Bunbury, *Memoirs*, pp. 203–205.

17. John Glyde, *Suffolk in the Nineteenth Century* (London, 1852), pp. 354, 325–355.

18. Hodder, *Life and Work of the Seventh Earl of Shaftesbury*, 2: 367; *P.P.*, 1843, 12: 35–40, 73, 88, 92–93, 153, 165, 214–215, 216, 226, 236.

19. *P.P.*, 1847, 11: 13–14, 37, 40, 48, 49, 134, 210, 224, 354, 375, 406, 484, 509, 552; *Oxford and Cambridge Review*, July 1845, p. 87; for *Times* citations, see *A Century of Municipal Progress, 1835–1935*, ed. H. J. Laski, I. Jennings, and W. A. Robson (London, 1935), p. 43.

20. *P.P.*, 1837, 17: 18–20; 1843, 12: 21, 29, 44–47, 58, 73, 75, 80, 311.

21. *P.P.*, 1846, 9: 28, 52, 197; 1848, 7: 21–33.

22. *P.P.*, 1843, 7: 255; 1848, 7: 31–33, 64, 67–70; *Farmer's Magazine*, Jan. 1845, p. 61.

23. *P.P.*, 1842, 33: 207–208; 1845, 35: 4, 101, 102, 147; 1847, 45: 211–212; 1852, 40: 208.

24. *P.P.*, 1846, 9: 21, 33, 52, 54, 131–148, 179, 258–267.

25. *P.P.*, 1843, 12: 19–39, 65.

26. *P.P.*, 1850, 28–80; 1839, 38: 647; 1843, 25: 121; 1855, 26: 7, 24, 31, 34, 37, 57–60, 77, 85; *Stamford Mercury*, Aug. 22, 1851.

27. *P.P.*, 1843, 12: 19–39, 65.

28. P.R.O., *Poor Law Papers*, M.H. 32/21, Earle to LeFevre, July 11, July 22, 1835; May 31, 1837; M.H. 32/39, Hawley to Nicholls, July 9, 1837; *P.P.*, 1837, 17: 10–11; 1838, 38: 189–194.

29. P.R.O., *Poor Law Papers*, M.H. 32/34, Hall to Nicholls, Feb. 18, 1836; M.H. 32/44, Head to commissioners, June 1, 1836; M.H. 32/26, Gilbert to commissioners, Jan. 21, 1836.

30. Anthony Brundage, "The Landed Interests and the New Poor Law," *English Historical Review* 87, no. 342 (1972): 27–48; for an opposing view, see Peter Dunkley, "The Landed Interest and the New Poor Law: A Critical Note," *English Historical Review* (Oct. 1973): 1836–1841.

31. *P.P.*, 1843, 7: 204–206, 208, 217, 229, 247, 288, 294, 305–306, 352.

32. William Hawley, archbishop of Canterbury, *A Charge Delivered at His Visitation* (London, 1844), p. 27; Leonard Prestige, *Pusey* (London, 1953), p. 168; Charles James Blomfield, bishop of London, *A Pastoral Letter to the Clergy of the Diocese of London* (London, 1847), p. 7; John Bird Sumner, *A Charge to the Clergy* (London, 1844), p. 11; George Kitson Clark, *Churchmen and the Condition of England* (London, 1973), p. 145.

33. Hugh M'Neil, *The Famine: A Rod of God* (Liverpool, 1847), p. 30; John Bird Sumner, *Christian Charity* (London, 1841), p. 22; A. R. Ashwell, *Life of the Right Reverend Samuel Wilberforce* (London, 1880), 1: 227–228.

34. William Gresley, *Practical Sermons* (London, 1848), p. 363; Christian Instruction Society, *A Course of Thirteen Lectures to Socialists and Others* (London, 1840), p. 130; Rev. Arthur Martineau, *What Is My Duty?* (London, 1847), pp. vii, 28, 36.

35. Edward Denison, bishop of Salisbury, *A Charge to the Clergy* (London, 1843), p. 43; William J. Copleston, *Memoir of Edward Copleston, D.D., Bishop of Llandaff* (London, 1851), p. 246; Rev. Thomas Dale, "The Principle of Christian Stewardship," in id. et al., *Hints on the Culture of Character* (London, 1855), p. 72.

36. *Sermons for Sundays, Festivals and Fasts*, ed. Rev. Alexander Watson (London, 1846), p. 356; Sumner, *Charge*, p. 22; Rev. Francis Close, *Occasional Sermons*, pp. 338–340; Rev. William Gresley, *Parochial Sermons* (London, 1842), p. 366; Rev. Henry Melvill, *Sermons on Public Occasions* (London, 1846), pp. 47–48; Paget, *Warden of Berkingholt*, p. 64.

37. Rev. T. R. Bentley, "The Christian Law of Forgiveness," in *Sermons for Sundays, Festivals and Fasts* (London, 1846), ed. Watson, p. 325; Francis Close, *Eighty Sketches of Sermons* (London, 1861), p. 142.

38. Ian Anstruther, *The Scandal of the Andover Workhouse* (London, 1973), p. 16; Diana McClatchey, *Oxfordshire Clergy, 1777–1869: A Study of the Established Church and of the Role of Its Clergy in Local Society* (Oxford, 1960), pp. 98–101; Rev. W. J. Conybeare, *Sermons; Preached in the Chapel Royal* (London, 1844), p. 181; id., *Essays Ecclesiastical and Social* (London, 1855), p. v.

39. Anstruther, *Andover*, pp. 81–84, 11, 16, 116–117, 123–133; *P.P.*, 1837, 17: 1ff; *Times*, Aug. 11, 25, 1840; Oct. 23, 1843; G. R. W. Baxter, *The Book of the Bastilles* (London, 1841), pp. 116–117, 118, 140, 464. Reports on the workhouses in Baxter are not dependable.

40. J. C. Gill, *Parson Bull of Byerley* (London, 1963), pp. 49–72, 106–117; Baxter, *Book of Bastilles*, p. 276.

41. Georgina Battiscombe, *John Keble* (New York, 1964), p. 176; Armitage, *Penscellwood Papers*, 2: 294; Charles James Blomfield, *1842 Charge* (London, 1842), pp. 63–64; *1846 Charge* (London, 1847), p. 37; Thomas Hussey, *The Christian Obligation to the Poor* (London, 1844), pp. 5–6; Edward Denison, *1845 Charge* (London, 1845), pp. 33–34.

42. W. R. W. Stephens, *A Memoir of Richard Durnford* (London, 1899), pp. 5–7; *The Memoirs and a Selection from the Letters of the Late Rev. Charles Jerram*, ed. James Jerram (London, 1855), pp. 326–327; Osborne, *Hints to the Charitable*, pp. 7–63.

43. Edward Denison, *1842 Charge* (London, 1842), pp. 30–32; id., *1845 Charge*, pp. 26, 44; H. P. Liddon, *Walter Kerr Hamilton, Bishop of Salisbury* (London, 1890), pp. 32–33, 43, 67, 72; R. Arnold, *Our Bishops* (London, 1875), p. 214; Sydney Herbert, *Proposals for the Better Application of Cathedral Institutions* (London, 1849), pp. 22–38.

44. G. F. A. Best, *Temporal Pillars: Queen Anne's Bounty, the Ecclesiastical Commissioners, and the Church of England* (London, 1964), p. 360; "National Education in England, 1800–1870," *Cambridge Historical Journal* 12 (1956): 163–164; Denison, *1845 Charge*, p. 26; Frank Smith, *The Life and Work of Sir James Kay-Shuttleworth* (London, 1923), pp. 147–148.

45. W. R. Stephens, *The Life and Letters of Walter Farquhar Hook* (London, 1879), 2: 160, 164, 306; Walter F. Hook, *The Duty of English Churches* (London, 1851), p. 201; Blomfield, *Charge*, p. 42.

46. Alfred Blomfield, *A Memoir of Charles James Blomfield* (London, 1864), p. 181; P. J. Welch, "Bishop Blomfield" (Ph.D. diss., London University, 1952), p. 159.

47. Close, *Occasional Sermons*, p. 336; *Cheltenham Examiner*, Feb. 3, 1841; Jan. 31, 1844; *Cheltenham Journal*, June 27, 1842; *Cheltenham Chronicle*, Aug. 14, 18, 1847; Kitson Clark, *Churchmen and the Condition of England*, p. 72.

48. Walter F. Hook, *An Inaugural Discourse Preached in the Parish Church at Leeds* (London, 1837), pp. 5–10; id., *The Duty of English Churchmen* (London, 1851), pp. 7–26; Stephens, *Hook*, 2: 159, 163, 319; C. J. Stranks, *Dean Hook* (London, 1954), pp. 58–59.

49. *Cheltenham Examiner*, Jan. 27, Feb. 10, Apr. 14, Oct. 6, 1841; Jan. 31, Feb. 2, 1844; *Cheltenham Chronicle*, Feb. 9, 16, 23, June 22, Aug. 17, Dec. 21, 1843; Apr. 14, May 19, 26, June 16, 23, Sept. 15, Oct. 6, 20, Nov. 3, 17, 1847; *Cheltenham Journal*, June 27, 1842; Close, *Occasional Sermons*, pp. 220–226; W. E. Adams, *Memoirs of a Social Atom* (London, 1903), 1: 11–17, 83–84.

50. Gresley, *Parochial Sermons*, p. 171; Sandford, *Parochialia*, p. 323; Hussey, *Christian Obligation to the Poor*; Francis Paget, *Sermons on Duties of Daily Life* (London, 1844), p. 265.

51. F. Bennett, *The Story of W. J. E. Bennett: Founder of S. Barnabas', Pimlico, and Vicar of Froome-Selwood: And of His Part in the Oxford Church Movement of the Nineteenth Century* (London, 1909), pp. 35–67.

52. Wade, *Extraordinary Black Book*, p. 48; Élie Halévy, *History of the English People* (London, 1961), 1: 396ff; Best, *Temporal Pillars*, pp. 198, 362–367; M. H. Port, *Six Hundred New Churches* (London, 1961), pp. 125–126; K. S. Inglis, *Churches and the Working Classes in Victorian England* (London, 1963), pp. 2, 7, 18 (the churches in London were half empty); C. H. Bromley, *The Church, the Privy Council, and the Working Classes* (London, 1850), pp. 22–23; *P.P.*, 1851, 42: 525–526.

53. *P.P.*, 1846, 32: 565; 1847, 45: 103, 323; 1848, 50: 60, 390–391; 1851, 42: 432–434; 1852, 40: 84, 344, 346; 1853, 80: 456.

54. George Eliot, *Scenes of Clerical Life* (London, 1858), 1: 7, 36, 39; 2: 14, 21, 22; Anthony Trollope, *The Warden* (London, 1855), pp. 1–25.

55. Smith, *Life and Work of Sir James Kay-Shuttleworth*, p. 102; Thomas Birks, *Memoir of the Rev. Edward Bickersteth* (London, 1851), 2: 9, 133, 164–169; Rev. Isaac Wilberforce, *A Charge* (London, 1843), pp. 8–11.

56. *Cheltenham Chronicle*, Jan. 5, June 22, 1842; *Cheltenham Examiner*, Jan. 10, 1844.

57. William Charles Henry, "A Biographical Notice of the Late Rev. Richard Dawes," *Hereford Times*, Mar. 16, 1847, pp. 10–14; Richard Dawes, *Remarks Occasioned by the Present Crusade against the Educational Plans of the Committee of Council on Education* (London, 1850), p. 8.

58. J. T. Ward, *The Factory Movement, 1830–1855* (London, 1962), pp. 87, 178, 423, 425; *Leeds Mercury*, Apr. 13, 1844; *Leeds Times*, Mar. 16, 1844; C. F. G. Masterman, *The Life of Frederick Denison Maurice* (London, 1907), p. 69.

59. Walter F. Hook, *On the Means of Rendering More Efficient the Education of the People* (London, 1846); Stephens, *Hook*, 1: 206–212; Rev. Francis Close, *National Education* (London, 1852); Blomfield, *1846 Charge*, pp. 44–47.

60. Bromley, *The Church, the Privy Council, and the Working Classes*, p. 23; G. A. Denison, *Notes of My Life, 1805–1878* (London, 1878), pp. iii, 147–158; id., *Church Education: The Present State of the Management Question* (London, 1849); P.R.O., Home Office [henceforth cited as H.O.], 65/5569, registrar general to Lord Palmerston, Apr. 27, 1856.

61. W. C. Taylor, *Notes of a Tour in the Manufacturing Districts of Lancashire* (London, 1842), pp. 21–28, 61–66; *Journal of the Statistical Society of London* (1839): 418–419; Andrew Ure, *The Philosophy of Manufactures, or, An Exposition of the Scientific, Moral, and Commercial Economy of the Factory System of Great Britain* (London, 1835), pp. 349–352; William R. Greg, *Enigmas of Life* (London, 1891), pp. x–xiii; *Westminster Review*, Sept. 1840, pp. 390–404, fully describes the Greg mills without naming them; *DNB*, 8: 530.

62. Rhodes Boysen, *The Ashworth Cotton Enterprise: The Rise and Fall of a Family Firm, 1818–1880* (Oxford, 1970), pp. 127–132.

63. Ibid., pp. 95–96, 112, 123, 126, 128.

64. George Unwin, *Samuel Oldknow and the Arkwrights* (London, 1924), pp. 135, 175; Sidney Pollard, "The Factory Village," *English Historical Review* 79 (July 1964): 513–531; Ure, *Philosophy of Manufactures*, p. 16; Neil Smelser, *Social Change in the Industrial Revolution* (Chicago, 1959). See also Richard Bendix, *Work and Authority in Industry* (New York, 1963).

65. Boysen, *Ashworth Cotton Enterprise*, pp. 120, 205; *Westminster Review* Sept. 1840, pp. 392–398.

66. *P.P.*, 1839, 19: 506, 528–531, 533–536; Report of Prison Inspectors, 1846, 20: 574–575; Thomas Beggs, *An Inquiry into the Extent and Causes of Juvenile Depravity* (London, 1849), p. 139.

67. William R. Greg, *Essays on Political and Social Science* (London, 1853), 1: 210–213, 354–355, 367–368; Boysen, *Ashworth Cotton Enterprise*, pp. 91, 99, 108, 121.

68. Ure, *Manufactures*, pp. 329, 352, 353, 415, 417; Taylor, *Notes*, pp. 68, 81, 113, 118–121; E. S. Cayley, *Reasons for the Formation of the Agricultural Protection Society* (York, 1836), p. 5.

69. *Fraser's Magazine*, Nov. 1844, pp. 627–628; *Eclectic Review*, Sept. 1843, p. 333.

70. Charles Dickens, *Notes on America* (Boston, n.d.), pp. 92–100; James Silk Buckingham, *The Eastern and Western States of America* (London, 1842), pp. 292–309; William Scoresby, *American Factories* (London, 1845); *Christian Teacher* (1842): 2; *Westminster Review*. Feb. 1843, p. 154; *Eclectic Review*, Apr. 1843, p. 384; *Leeds Mercury*, June 21, 1845; Oct. 10, 1846; *Athenaeum*, Feb. 19, 1842, p. 159; *Mirror*, Mar. 19, 1842; *Hansard*, 1846, 83: 389–390.

71. Papers praising Ashworth, Greg, or Ashton are: *Athenaeum*, July 14, 1840, p. 528;

Morning Chronicle, Mar. 18, 1843; *British Quarterly* 1 (1845): 144; *Christian Observer* 42 (1842): 699; *Eclectic Review*, Sept. 1842, p. 458; *Journal of the Statistical Society of London* 1 (1839): 416; *People's Journal*, Mar. 13, 1847; *Westminster Review*, Sept. 1840, pp. 390–398; *Weekly Chronicle*, Sept. 13, 1840.

72. *Leeds Mercury*, Oct. 23, 1841; Mar. 11, 1843; Jan. 17, 1846; *Leeds Intelligencer*, July 31, 1847; W. G. Rimmer, *Marshall of Leeds, Flax Spinner* (Cambridge, 1960), pp. 108, 120–121, 149, 203–218, 222–223, 261.

73. *Journal of the Statistical Society* 1 (1838): 418; W. H. Elliot, *The Story of the "Cheeryble" Grants* (London, 1906), pp. 123, 125, 175, 184, 200; Charles Whibley, *Lord John Manners and His Friends* (2 vols.; Edinburgh, 1925), 2: 102–103; Boysen, *Ashworth Cotton Enterprise*, p. 126; *P.P.*, 1842, 22: 465; Ivan Melada, *The Captain of Industry in English Fiction* (Albuquerque, N.M., 1970), pp. 115–116.

74. Taylor, *Notes*, p. 117; Rev. Robert Balgarnie, *Sir Titus Salt* (London, 1878), pp. 113–147, 160–163.

75. Nassau Senior, *Letters on the Factory Act* (London, 1837), p. 33; *P.P.*, 1843, 27: 309, 346–348; 1844, 28: 535, 540; 1848, 26: 159; Ward, *Factory Movement*, pp. 161, 211.

76. *Fraser's Magazine*, Nov. 1844, p. 625; *Examiner*, May 18, 25, 1844; *Westminster Review*, Aug. 1843, p. 102; *P.P.*, 1848, 26: 159.

77. *P.P.*, 1842, 90: 23, 33, 41–45, 46, 87, 127, 132, 138, 144–145, 161, 178, 267–270; 16: 21, 37, 177, 189, 204, 206, 209, 308, 310.

78. Ibid., 1843, 14: Report A, p. 11; Report B, pp. 14, 26; Report D, p. 2; vol. 15, Report L, p. 3.

CHAPTER 4

1. *Oxford University and City and County Herald*, July 10, 1847.

2. *Economist*, Feb. 20, 1847, p. 197; *Oxford and Cambridge Review*, July 1846, pp. 81–82; *Edinburgh Review*, Apr. 1845, p. 507; *Hansard*, 1846, 86: 1029.

3. Thomas Mun, *England's Treasure by Foreign Trade* (London, 1664); Sir William Petty, *Treatise of Taxation* (London, 1662); John Locke, *Consequences of Lowering the Interest and Raising of the Value of Money* (London, 1691); David Hume, *Essays and Treatises on Several Subjects* (London, 1752) and *Political Discourses* (London, 1753). See also Mark Blaug, *Economic Theory in Retrospect* (Homewood, Ill., 1962; reprint, London, 1968), pp. 12–30.

4. Élie Halévy, *The Growth of Philosophical Radicalism* (Boston, 1955), p. 269.

5. Mrs. Marcet, *Conversations on Political Economy* (London, 1824); Harriet Martineau, *Illustrations of Political Economy* (London, 1832); Mark Blaug, *Ricardian Economics: A Historical Study* (New Haven, Conn., 1958), pp. 37–38.

6. D. P. O'Brien, *John Ramsay McCulloch: A Study in Classical Economics* (London, 1970), p. 61; Rev. Richard Jones, *Literary Remains, Consisting of Lectures and Tracts on Political Economy*, ed. Rev. William Whewell (London, 1859), p. xix; *The Economic Writings of Mountifort Longfield*, ed. R. D. Collison Black (London, 1971), pp. 6–7; William Shee, *Papers, Letters, and Speeches in the House of Commons on the Irish Land Question* (London, 1863), p. 21; *DNB*, 51: 245.

7. *Wellesley Index to Victorian Periodicals*, ed. Houghton, vol. 1 (Toronto, 1966), 872, 990, 1011, 1078, 1080; vol. 3 (1979): 843–885; John M. Robson, "The Rhetoric of J. S. Mill's Periodical Articles," *Victorian Periodicals Review*, Sept. 1977, p. 125.

8. Blaug, *Ricardian Economics*, pp. 37–40, 44; Barry Gordon, *Economic Doctrine and Tory*

Liberalism (London, 1979), pp. 11, 13; Robson, "The Rhetoric of J. S. Mill's Periodical Articles," *Victorian Periodicals Review*, Sept. 1977, p. 125.

9. Frank Fetter, *The Economists in Parliament, 1780–1868* (Chapel Hill, N.C., 1980), pp. 3–33, 231, 227–242.

10. Seeley, *Sadler;* Michael Sadler, *Law of Population* (London, 1830); E. S. Cayley, *On Commercial Economy* (London, 1830); *Reasons for the Formation of the Agrarian Protection Society* (London, 1844); *Selected Economic Writings of Thomas Attwood,* ed. Frank Fetter (London, 1964); Frederick Muntz, *The True Cause of the Late Sudden Change in the Affairs of the Country* (London, 1837); C. M. Wakefield, *Life of Thomas Attwood* (London, 1885), pp. 359–397; Anna Gambles, *Protection and Politics: Conservative Economic Discourse, 1815–1852,* Royal Historical Society Studies in History, n.s., 0269–2244 (Suffolk, Eng.; Rochester, N.Y., 1999).

11. Élie Halévy, *Thomas Hodgskin* (London, 1956); Thomas Hodgskin, *Labour Defended Against the Claims of Capital; or, The Unproductiveness of Capital Proved with Reference to the Present Combinations Amongst Journeymen* (London, 1825); Noel W. Thompson, *The People's Science: The Popular Political Economy of Exploitation and Crisis, 1816–34* (London, 1989); William Thompson, *Labour Rewarded. The Claims of Labour and Capital Conciliated; or, How to Secure to Labour the Whole Product of Its Exertion* (London, 1827).

12. David Ricardo, *On the Principles of Political Economy* (London, 1819), pp. 109–134, esp. 132–133; O'Brien, *J. R. McCulloch,* pp. 23, 291; Jones, *Literary Remains,* ed. Whewell, pp. 79–82; 115–116, 144–149; p. 228; *Economic Writings of Mountifort Longfield,* ed. Black, pp. 172–176, 200–215; 234–236; James Mill, *Elements of Political Economy* (London, 1824), pp. 40–67; John Stuart Mill, *Principles of Political Economy* (London, 1848), 1: 406–497; J. R. McCulloch, *A Discourse on the Rise, Progress, Peculiar Objects, and Importance of Political Economy* (Edinburgh, 1824), pp. 328–331; Blaug, *Ricardian Economics,* pp. 125–126; E. West, *Price of Corn and Wages of Labour* (London, 1815), pp. 80–86; Perronet Thompson, *The True Theory of Rent* (London, 1827), p. 16.

13. Adam Smith, *The Wealth of Nations* (1776; London, 1846), suppl. n. 2, pp. 437–444; Ricardo, *Principles,* pp. 1–46; James Mill, *Elements of Political Economy,* pp. 41–46, 73–84; J. S. Mill, *Principles of Political Economy,* 1: 546–561; Blaug, *Ricardian Economics,* pp. 48, 52–53; George Poulett Scrope, *Principles of Political Economy Deduced from the Natural Laws of Social Welfare, and Applied to the Present State of Britain* (London, 1833), 168–175; *Economic Writings of Mountifort Longfield,* ed. Black, pp. 11–12, 29–43.

14. Blaug, *Ricardian Economics,* pp. 62, 80–96, 154, 208; *Economic Writings of Mountifort Longfield,* ed. Black, pp. 133, 154, 181–187; Jones, *Literary Remains,* ed. Whewell, pp. x–xiii, 41, 228, 595; Scrope, *Principles of Political Economy,* pp. 168–170; 265–268; Thomas Malthus, *Principles of Population* (London, 1836), pp. 319–20; William D. Grampp, *The Manchester School of Economics* (Stanford, Calif., 1960), p. 33.

15. Political Economy Club of London, *Minutes of Proceedings, 1899–1920* (London, 1921), Mallet's diary, pp. 223, 265; Frank Fetter, *Development of British Monetary Orthodoxy* (Cambridge, Mass., 1965), p. 285; *Blackwood's,* Sept. 1842, p. 340; *Journal of the Statistical Society* 1 (1839): 317; *Standard,* Mar. 2, 1842, which also refers in May 27, 1841, to "cant of political economy"; Blaug, *Ricardian Economics,* p. 187; *Daily News,* Feb. 7, 1845.

16. *Hansard,* 1847, 89: 494.

17. Grampp, *Manchester School of Economics,* p. 22.

18. Blaug, *Ricardian Economics,* pp. 165–171, 182, 186; J. S. Mill, *Principles of Political Economy,* 1: 189–195, 406–429.

19. *Leeds Intelligencer*, Mar. 5, 1842.

20. Halévy, *Growth of Philosophical Radicalism*, p. 266.

21. David Roberts, "The Utilitarian Conscience," in *The Conscience of the Victorian State*, ed. Peter Marsh (Syracuse, N.Y., 1979), pp. 39–71; Joseph Hamburger, *Intellectuals in Politics: John Stuart Mill and the Philosophical Radicals* (London, 1965), pp. 11–15, 118, 141–142, 166–168, 201–204, 220, 271.

22. Fetter, *Economists in Parliament*, p. 80; *Hansard*, 1947, 89: 1070, 1127; 1844, 71: 87.

23. *Hansard*, 1834, 24: 1061, 25: 1096; 1838, 40: 436; 1839, 45: 76; 1842, 64: 159–160, 168–170, 554; 1844, 73: 1263, 1460; 1847, 92: 312; 1846, 85: 268.

24. *Hansard*, 1843, 71: 231; 1846, 86: 950; 1847, 93: 270; 1848, 97: 1113.

25. Roberts, "Utilitarian Conscience," in *Conscience of the Victorian State*, ed, Marsh, pp. 41–57; "Who Ran the Globe?" *Victorian Periodicals Review*, June 1971, pp. 6–11; *DNB*, 5: 107; 26: 362; John Stuart Mill, *Autobiography* (New York, 1964), pp. 79, 84, 130–131; *The Earlier Letters of John Stuart Mill, 1812–1848*, ed. Francis E. Mineka (London, 1963), vol. 13 of *The Collected Works of John Stuart Mill*, pp. 254, 365, 391; William Beach Thomas, *The Story of the Spectator* (London, 1928); Thomas Escott, *Masters of English Journalism* (London, 1911), p. 238; *London Journal*, Aug. 30, 1845, p. 431; Sept. 6, 1845, p. 438.

26. *DNB*, 59: 316; 33: 164; H. G. Ward, *Chapters in the Political History of Sheffield* (Sheffield, 1884), pp. 1–48; *London Journal*, 1845, 1: 6, 397; 1846, 2: 133; Emilie I. Barrington, *The Servant of All* (London, 1927); Escott, *Masters of English Journalism*, p. 236; Charles W. Dilke, *Papers of a Critic* (London, 1875), p. 66.

27. David Roberts, "Charles Dickens and the *Daily News*," *Victorian Periodicals Review*, Summer 1989, pp. 51–63; Justin McCarthy and John Robinson, *Daily News: A Jubilee* (London, 1896), p. 53; Charles Mackay, *Forty Years' Recollections of Life, Literature, and Public Affairs, from 1830 to 1870* (London, 1877), pp. 71–75, 105, 123; James Hedderick, *Backward Glances* (London, 1891), p. 287; James Grant, *Portraits* (London, 1841), 1: 265.

28. Mackay, *Forty Years' Recollections*, pp. 73–76; Barrington, *Servant of All*, p. 58; Walter Bagehot, *Literary Studies* (London, 1879), 1: 84; Robson, "J. S. Mill's Periodical Articles," p. 125.

29. *The Collected Works of Dugald Stewart*, ed. Sir William Hamilton (11 vols.; Edinburgh, 1854–60), 10: liii–lviii; O'Brien, *J. R. McCulloch*, pp. 48–54; *Worthies of Cumberland* (London, 1867), 3: 133; Lord Northbrook, *Journals and Correspondence, 1808–1852* (London, 1867), pp. 120–125; Martha McMackin Garland, *Cambridge before Darwin: The Ideal of a Liberal Education* (New York, 1980), p. 57; George Pryme, *Autobiographical Recollections* (London, 1870), pp. 92, 119; Political Economy Club of London, *Minutes of Proceedings*, pp. 360–361.

30. Roylance Kent, *The English Radicals: A Historical Sketch* (London, 1899), p. 374; *Hansard*, 1838, 32: 1042.

31. S. Leon Levy, *Nassau Senior* (Boston, 1943), pp. 148, 221, 223, 230–233.

32. Barrington, *Servant of All*, pp. 20–21, 58, 66–69, 93, 146–147; Harriet Martineau, *Autobiography*, ed. Maria Weston Chapman (2 vols.; Boston, 1877), 1: 70; *Daily News*, Mar. 2, 1847; J. B. Atlay, *The Globe and Traveller Centenary* (London, 1903), p. 17.

33. *Hansard*, 1846, 83: 1295–1296; 86: 506, 1303, 1319.

34. *Hansard*, 1847, 89: 1275, 1371; Fetter, *Economists in Parliament*, p. 43.

35. John Prest, *Lord John Russell* (Columbia, S.C., 1972).

36. John Bird Sumner, *A Treatise on the Records of the Creation: And on the Moral Attributes of the Creator* (2 vols.; London, 1816); Levy, *Nassau Senior*, p. 174; Donald H. Akenson, *A Protestant in Purgatory: Richard Whatley, Archbishop of Dublin* (Hamden, Conn.,

1981); E. J. Whatley, *Life and Correspondence of Richard Whatley* (London, 1866), pp. 53, 111; Samuel Finer, *The Life and Times of Edwin Chadwick* (London, 1952), pp. 39–49.

37. Marion Bowley, *Nassau Senior* (London, 1937), pp. 258–261; Finer, *Edwin Chadwick*, pp. 28–29, 52–53.

38. Jones, *Literary Remains*, ed. Whewell, pp. xxix–xxx; Henry Lonsdale, M.D., *A Biographical Sketch of the Late William Blamire* (London, 1861), pp. 30–35; Oliver McDonagh, *A Pattern of Government Growth, 1800–60: The Passenger Acts and Their Enforcement* (London, 1961), pp. 56, 59, 66–67, 71, 85–86, 131–132, 136, 143, 290, 326–327; Fetter, *Economists in Parliament*, pp. 268–273, 276–277; P.P., *General Index to the Reports of Select Committees, Printed by Order of the House of Commons, 1801–1852* (London, 1853).

39. Lucy Brown, *The Board of Trade and the Free Trade Movement* (Oxford, 1958), pp. 29–31, 140–158, 213.

40. Grampp, *Manchester School of Economics*, pp. 3, 16, 20, 107–108.

41. On the Ten Hour Bill, see *Hansard*, 1844, 73: 1263, 1460; 74: 330–333, 1108; on the Corn Law, 1846, 86: 721; on the Poor Law, 1841, 69: 1086; 1842, 65: 511; 1847, 92: 998, 1112, 1154; Wendy Hinde, *Richard Cobden* (London, 1987), pp. 39–40; *Manchester Guardian*, Mar. 13, 20, 27, 1844; Jan. 18, 1845; *Leeds Mercury*, May 12, 1837; Feb. 17, 1838; Feb. 10, 1844; Feb. 7, 1846.

42. *Hansard*, 1819, 41: 935; 1824, 10: 740; 1839, 46: 777; 1842, 63: 662; 1846, 83: 72; 1847, 95: 660; 1849, 106: 1449–1461.

43. Arvel Erickson, *The Public Career of Sir James Graham* (London, 1952), pp. 50–56; id., *Edward Cardwell: Peelite* (Philadelphia, 1959), pp. 6–10; John Morley, *The Life of William Ewart Gladstone* (London, 1903), 1: 240–245, 250, 255–57, 262–268, 279–280; Norman Gash, *Sir Robert Peel* (London, 1972), pp. 92, 123, 427, 459, 470–471; F. Darrell Munsell, *The Unfortunate Duke: Henry Pelham, Fifth Duke of Newcastle, 1811–1864* (Columbia, Miss., 1985), pp. 21–57; *Times*, Apr. 4, 1844.

44. Edward Copleston, *A Reply to the Calumnies of the Edinburgh Review* (London, 1810), pp. 107, 154; Pryme, *Autobiography*, p. 166; E. J. Whatley, *Life and Correspondence of Richard Whatley*, pp. 10, 16, 53.

45. E. J. Whatley, *Life and Correspondence of Richard Whatley*, p. 53; Richard Whatley, *Introductory Lectures on Political Economy* (London, 1831–1832); Charles Merivale, *Herman Merivale* (London, 1884), p. 2.

46. Bourne, *English Newspapers*, p. 153; Escott, *Masters of English Journalism*, pp. 230–231.

47. *Morning Chronicle*, Feb. 24, Apr. 3, 15, June 19, July 12, 1848; Jan. 31, Feb. 23, Mar. 27, May 2, June 27, 1849.

48. David Roberts, "Early Victorian Newspaper Editors," *Victorian Periodicals Review*, Dec. 1971, pp. 7–10.

49. Henry Cockburn, *Memorials of His Time* (New York, 1861), pp. 32, 50, 177; *Memoirs of Sir Thomas Dyke Acland* (London, 1902), pp. 9–11; *Works of Dugald Stewart*, ed. Hamilton, 10: xxxiii, xlviii–lxxii.

50. Boyd Hilton, *The Age of Atonement* (Oxford, 1988), pp. 55–70, 87–89, 108–10, 116–222; O'Brien, *J. R. McCulloch*, pp. 45–68; Henry Cockburn, *Journals of Henry Cockburn* (Edinburgh, 1874), 1: 177–78.

51. Blaug, *Ricardian Economics*, pp. 37–39, 130–138; Robert K. Webb, *Harriet Martineau* (London, 1960), pp. 97–127, 148–150; William Chambers, *Memoir of Robert Chambers* (London, 1872), p. 237; R. H. Horne, *A New Spirit of the Age* (2 vols.; London, 1844), 2: 71; Charles Knight, *Capital and Labour* (London, 1845); *DNB*, 21: 246; G. J. Holyoake, *Sixty Years of an Agitator's Life* (London, 1906), p. 77.

52. Strutt, *Strutt Family of Terling*, p. 80; *North of England Magazine*, Jan. 1843, p. 136; *The Norwich Post: Its Contemporaries and Successors* (Norwich, 1951), p. 5; *Sussex Advertiser*, Mar. 26, Apr. 2, 23, May 21, 1844, Mar. 19, 1878; H. Wharlow, *The Provincial Newspaper* (London, 1886), p. 89; Frederic Boase, *Modern English Biography, Containing Many Thousand Concise Memoirs of Persons Who Have Died since the Year 1850* (6 vols.: Truro, 1892–1921), 1: 120; *Worthies of Buckinghamshire* (Aylesbury, 1888), p. 167; Richard S. Lambert, *The Cobbett of the West: A Sketch of Thomas Latimer* (London, 1939), pp. 61–63; *Western Times*, Apr. 10, 1847.

53. *Punch*, 4: 42–44; 12: 91.

54. *Douglas Jerrold's Magazine*, 1845, 1: 27; 2: 86–88; Richard Garnett, *The Life of W. J. Fox* (London, 1910), p. 283; Roberts, "Charles Dickens and the *Daily News*," *Victorian Periodicals Review*, Summer 1989, pp. 51–63.

55. Halévy, *Thomas Hodgskin*, pp. 19–23, 43–44; Garnett, *W. J. Fox*, pp. 264–266; W. J. Fox, *Reports of Lectures delivered at the Chapel in South Place, Finsbury* (London, 1838), 5: 2; *Daily News*, Feb. 9, 1845; Roberts, "Charles Dickens and the *Daily News*," *Victorian Periodicals Review*, Summer 1989, pp. 51–63.

56. *Christian Remembrancer* 16 (1848): 316; *Christian Observer* 18 (1848): 336; *Manchester Guardian*, May 10, 1848.

57. *British Quarterly* 1 (1845): 599; *Eclectic Review*, Mar. 1846, p. 257, Sept. 1848, p. 365; *Prospective Review* 3 (1847): 18–19; Arthur Miall, *Life of Edward Miall* (London, 1884), p. 10.

58. *Christian Socialist*, Nov. 2, 1850, p. 3.

59. *Quarterly Review*, Dec. 1846, pp. 136–137.

60. David Roberts, "Early Victorian Newspaper Editors" and "More Early Victorian Editors," *Victorian Periodicals Review*, Jan. 1972, pp. 1–13, and June 1972, pp. 15–28; *Times*, July 7, 1853.

61. *Economic Writings of Mountifort Longfield*, ed. Black, pp. 1–2; George Pryme, *A Syllabus of a Course of Lectures on the Principles of Political Economy* (London, 1852), p. xi.

62. *Hansard*, 1846, 83: 650; 1849, 103: 622–623.

CHAPTER 5

1. *Hansard*, 1837, 37: 596–601; 1838, 41: 909–931; Lucy Brown, *The Board of Trade and the Free Trade Movement* (London, 1958), pp. 54, 79–80; Millicent Garrett Fawcett, *Life of the Right Hon. Sir William Molesworth, Bart.* (London, 1901), p. 243.

2. Harriet Grote, *The Philosophical Radicals of 1832* (London, 1883); Roberts, "Utilitarian Conscience," in *Conscience of the Victorian State*, ed. Marsh, pp. 41–43, 51–52, 60–61; Joseph Hamburger, *Intellectuals in Politics* (New Haven, Conn., 1965), pp. 11–29; Fawcett, *Life of the Right Hon. Sir William Molesworth*; *Free Trade Speeches of the Right Hon. Charles Pelham Villiers* (London, 1957), pp. 129–134; 141–142.

3. Grampp, *Manchester School of Economics*, pp. 47–48, 107; *Hansard*, 1842, 61: 1043–1045; 62: 24–25; 1846, 83: 1124.

4. *Hansard*, 1838, 41: 917; Susan Fairlie, "The Corn Laws and British Wheat Production, 1829–76," *Economic History Review*, Apr. 1969, pp. 88–113; Thomas Tooke, *History of Prices* (London, 1838–1857), 5: 56–58.

5. O'Brien, *J. R. McCulloch*, pp. 96–97. Blaug, *Economic Theory in Retrospect*, pp. 192, 215.

6. D. C. Moore, "The Corn Laws and High Farming," *Economic History Review* 18 (1965): 545; Susan Fairlie, "The Nineteenth-Century Corn Law Reconsidered," *Economic History Re-*

view 18 (1965): 562; 22 (1969): 88–113; Grampp, *Manchester School of Economics*, p. 41; *P.P.*, 1841, 10: 64.

7. *Hansard*, 1846, 83: 81.

8. *NonConformist*, Aug. 18, 1841, p. 328; Nicholas Edsall, *Richard Cobden, Independent Radical* (London, 1986), p. 93; *Hansard*, 1842, 62: 58; 1846, 87: 323.

9. *Hansard*, 1842, 64: 1036; 1845, 81: 342, 349.

10. R. C. O. Matthews, *A Study in Trade Cycle History: Economic Fluctuations in Great Britain, 1833–1842* (Cambridge, 1954), pp. 214–217.

11. *Standard*, Jan. 29, Apr. 20, 1841; Feb. 5, Mar. 7, 1842; Mar. 18, 1843; Mar. 28, 1844; May 10, June 10, 1847.

12. *John Bull*, Nov. 6, 1841; Jan. 1, 1842; *Morning Post*, Apr. 15, 1840; July 16, 1842; Feb. 24, July 27, 1843; May 25, 1844.

13. *Morning Herald*, Apr. 22, 1844; and for the *Standard*, see *Manchester Guardian*, Feb. 8, 1842.

14. *Daily News*, Jan 22, 29, Feb. 5, 1846; *Weekly Chronicle*, Jan. 7, 1844; *Morning Advertiser*, Mar. 18, 29, 1844; *Globe*, June 3, 1842; *Sheffield Independent*, Jan. 29, 1842.

15. *Hansard*, 1842, 60: 422–433; 62: 820; Edsall, *Richard Cobden*, pp. 109, 129, 163; Hinde, *Richard Cobden*, pp. 103–104, 160.

16. *Hansard*, 1845, 78: 786–808; Gash, *Sir Robert Peel*, pp. 470–471; Edsall, *Richard Cobden*, p. 149; Hinde, *Richard Cobden*, p. 147.

17. *P.P.*, 1842, 35: 69–98, 171–179, 213, 227; *P.P.*, 1843, 7: 3–5; E. J. Hobsbawm, *Labouring Men: Studies in the History of Labour* (New York, 1964).

18. *Weekly Chronicle*, Sept. 6, 1840; June 23, 1842; Mar. 31, May 4, Oct. 20, 1844; *Weekly Dispatch*, July 3, 1842; Jan. 7, 1844.

19. *Globe*, July 4, 1842; May 18, 1843; *Morning Chronicle*, Jan. 21, 1841.

20. *Leeds Mercury*, Mar. 22, 1845.

21. *The Croker Papers: The Correspondence and Diaries of the Late Right Honourable John Wilson Croker . . . Secretary to the Admiralty from 1809 to 1830*, ed. L. J. Jennings (2 vols.; New York, 1884), 2: 248, 252, 271–272; (3 vols.; London, 1884), 3: 40, 43–44; *Hansard*, 1846, 83: 118.

22. Boyd Hilton, "Peel: A Reappraisal," *Historical Journal* 22 (1979): 585–614; British Museum, *Peel Papers*, Add. MS 40342, Peel to C. Lloyd, 1819; *Hansard*, 1824, 10: 740; 1834, 22: 445; 1846, 83: 68–69; 1849, 106, 1450.

23. William Aydelotte, "The Country Gentlemen and the Repeal of the Corn Laws," *English Historical Review*, Jan. 1967, p. 57.

24. *Hansard*, 1846, 84: 155; 1845, 81: 333; 1845, 80: 1410; 1846, 83: 1296.

25. *Memoirs of Sir Thomas Dyke Acland*, pp. 8–9, 23; Erickson, *Edward Cardwell*, pp. 6–7; Munsell, *Unfortunate Duke*, pp. 10–16, 38–57; Bernard Falk, *The Bridgewater Millions* (New York, 1942), pp. 165–166; F. C. Mather, *After the Canal Duke* (Oxford, 1970), pp. 40, 345; Francis, 1st earl of Ellesmere, *Personal Reminiscences of the Duke of Wellington* (London, 1903), pp. 38–42; David Roberts, *Paternalism in Early Victorian England* (New Brunswick, N.J.), pp. 253–255, 280.

26. Sir James Graham, *Corn and Currency* (London, 1826); J. T. Ward, *Sir James Graham* (London, 1967), p. 67; *Hansard*, 1845, 81: 333; 1846, 83: 55–61; 86: 640, 1374–1398; Edmund Burke, *Thoughts and Details on Scarcity* (London, 1800).

27. Grampp, *Manchester School of Economics*, p. 18; O'Brien, *J. R. McCulloch*, p. 391; J. R. McCulloch, *Statements on the Proposed Repeal of the Corn Laws* (London, 1841), p. 25; Adam

Smith, *An Inquiry into the Nature and Causes of the Wealth of Nations* (1776), ed. Edwin Cannan, 6th ed.(2 vols.; London, 1950), 1: 427.

28. *Hansard*, 1846, 83: 652, 763–768; 86: 319, 657.

29. Lionel Robbins, *The Theory of Economic Policy in English Classical Political Economy* (London, 1952); Warren J. Samuels, *The Classical Theory of Economic Policy* (New York, 1952); P. S. Atiyah, *The Rise and Fall of Freedom of Contract* (Oxford, 1979); and also see Gunnar Myrdal, *The Political Element in the Development of Economic Theory* (London, 1953).

30. Robbins, *Theory of Economic Policy*, pp. 43, 45.

31. Adam Smith, *Wealth of Nations*, ed. Cannan, 1: 429; 2: 214, 269–273; J. S. Mill, *Principles of Political Economy*, 2, bk. 5, pp. 337ff.

32. J. R. McCulloch, *Principles of Political Economy* (1825; new ed., London, 1843), pp. 268–269.

33. J. Grunswick, *Labour and the Poor in England and Wales, 1849–1851: Letters to the Morning Chronicle* (London, 1983); *Journal of the Statistical Society*, 1: 22, 65, 124, 416; 2: 19, 173, 299, 303; 3: 14, 25, 146, 195, 257; 4: 156, 294; 5: 222, 226, 268, 274; 6: 17, 25, 28, 44, 133, 300; 9: 204, 339; 10: 259; 11: 21, 101, 193, 344.

34. *P.P.*, 1843, 14: A 10–11; 15: I 41–44; Q 1–11; F 29–31.

35. *P.P.*, 1843, 14: C 3–6; E 1–15.

36. *P.P.*, 1843, 14: A 7–9.

37. *P.P.*, 1843, 12: 17–93, 143–236.

38. David Roberts, *Victorian Origins of the British Welfare State* (New Haven, Conn., 1960); pp. 106–118, 272–292; P. W. J. Bartrip and S. B. Burnham, *The Wounded Soldiers of Industry: Industrial Compensation Policy, 1833–1897* (Oxford, 1983).

39. *Hansard*, 1848, 97: 1104, 1113; 1846, 86: 914–950; 1845, 82: 1452, 1517; 1847, 90: 1103; 92: 406, 418–419; 93: 262; 1848, 99: 86–100; 1845, 86: 1419–1427; 1848, 97: 856–890.

40. *Hansard*, 1846, 83: 190–191; 1843, 71: 78; 1846, 86: 407, 1031; 1847, 89: 1136.

41. *Hansard*, 1844, 74: 665, 681–682.

42. *Hansard*, 1847, 89: 1136; 1844, 73: 1245; 1846, 86: 1078; 1844, 73: 1388; 1847, 90: 175–177; 91: 146–147; 92: 312–313.

43. *Hansard*, 1847, 87: 1080.

44. Adam Smith, *Wealth of Nations*, ed. Cannan, 2: 184; *Morning Herald*, Mar. 31, May 5, 1843.

45. McCulloch, *Discourse on . . . Political Economy*, p. xxii and table of contents; Bowley, *Nassau Senior*, pp. 168, 176, 186–187; Nassau Senior, *An Outline of Political Economy* (London, 1838), pp. 128–141; F. L. van Holthoon, *The Road to Utopia: A Study of John Stuart Mill's Social Thought* (Assen, Netherlands, 1971), p. 139; J. S. Mill, *Principles of Political Economy*, vol. 1, bk. 1, ch. 6; Robert Torrens, *Letter to the Right Hon. Lord Stanley on Colonization* (London, 1849), p. 89.

46. Senior, *Letters on the Factory Act*, pp. 4; Bowley, *Nassau Senior*, pp. 255–258.

47. *Hansard*, 1844, 73: 1108, 1112; 1844, 74: 308; 1846, 86: 473, 1055; 85: 1237–1238; 1842, 61: 395; 1843, 68: 967, 1844, 73: 1108–1112, 1243–1244, 75: 1080–1081; 1844, 74: 308; 1846, 85: 1237–1238; 86: 473, 1055.

48. Political Economy Club of London, *Minutes of Proceedings*, pp. 273–275.

49. *P.P.*, 1845, 25: 20; *Hansard*, 1847, 89: 1109.

50. *P.P.*, 1841, 10: 49.

51. Adam Smith, *Wealth of Nations*, ed. Cannan, 2: 184–85.

52. *Hansard*, 1847, 89: 649, 1329; 1848, 95: 1173.

53. *Hansard*, 1844, 73: 1122; 72: 250; 1845, 77: 174.

54. *Hansard*, 1848, 98: 1173; 1847, 89: 649, 1141–1142.

55. *Hansard*, 1847, 92: 420; 1844, 74: 656.

56. *Hansard*, 1844, 73: 1263; 74: 1106–1110; 1847, 92, 312–313.

57. *Weekly Chronicle*, May 18, 1844.

58. *Hansard*, 1842, 60: 420–431; 1847, 90: 141–153.

59. *Manchester Times*, Mar. 29, 1844; *Morning Chronicle*, Mar. 21, 1844; *Economist*, May 18, 1844, p. 808; *Sun*, Mar. 18, 1844, *Morning Advertiser*, Mar. 29, 1844 (agricultural gentlemen voted for Ashley "from feelings of vindictiveness"); *Hansard*, 1846, 85: 1219–1220; 1847, 90: 792; *Standard*, Apr. 22, 1847 (quotes Roebuck), and Mar. 30, 1844. The best combination of anger at manufacturers and support of Ten Hour Bill, *Hansard*, 1847, 90: 141–153.

60. *Hansard*, 1847, 92: 312–313.

61. For the views of the economists on the poor laws, see J. R. Poynter, *Society and Pauperism* (London, 1969); Gertrude Himmelfarb, *The Idea of Poverty* (London, 1984); Raymond Cowherd, *Political Economists and the English Poor Laws* (Athens, Ohio, 1977); Kenneth Smith, *The Malthusian Controversy* (London, 1951), and Harold A. Boner, *Hungry Generations: The Nineteenth-Century Case Against Malthusianism* (New York, 1955).

62. *Hansard*, 1834, 22: 874–892.

63. Great Britain, Poor Law Commissioners, *The Poor Law Report of 1834*, ed. S. G. Checkland and E. O. A. Checkland (Baltimore, 1974), pp. 82–242, esp. pp. 140–149; *P.P.*, 1834, 27: 1–180.

64. *Poor Law Report*, ed. Checkland and Checkland, pp. 88, 104–105, 114–124; 129–135; 145–150, 156–181, 219–242; *P.P.*, 1834, 22: 25–26; 36–37, 44–53, 123–127.

65. *Poor Law Report*, ed. Checkland and Checkland, pp. 31–82; Mark Blaug, "The Myth of the Poor Law," *Journal of Economic History* 1 (June 1963): 151–178; id., "The Poor Law Report, Re-examined," ibid, 1964, pp. 229–245; James Taylor, "The Mythology of the Old Poor Law," ibid., 1969, 293–297 (critical of Blaug).

66. *Hansard*, 1834, 24: 477–478; *Poor Law Report*, ed. Checkland and Checkland, pp. 242–261; *P.P.*, 1847, 11: 1–556.

67. *Hansard*, 1834, 22: 874–897, 23: 314–330, 805–838, 954–1001, 1281–1348; 1836, 31: 1137–1138; 35: 590–596, 708–730; 1837, 36: 989–1089; 39: 321–338; 1838, 41: 747–756; 42: 725–746, 1003–1080; 1841, 56: 375–445; 67: 400–503; 1842, 63: 192–197, 427–453.

68. *Hansard*, 1836, 35: 717. Poor rates fell from £6,377,000 in 1834 to £4,711,000 in 1836.

69. John Austin, "Centralization," *Edinburgh Review*, Jan. 1847, pp. 221–258.

70. *P.P.*, 1836, 29: 145–168, 189–206; 1838, 28: 279–284; 1842, 19: 154–155; *P.R.O.*, M.H. 32/48, June 30, 1836, Kay-Shuttleworth's 70-page report.

CHAPTER 6

1. *Hansard*, 1842, 63: 46; 1846, 83: 938; 84: 1395; 1847, 95: 37.

2. *Hansard*, 1847, 42, 89; 1842, 65: 103–104, 106; 1840, 55: 436–437.

3. *Hansard*, 1844, 92: 1194.

4. *Hansard*, 1844, 74: 641; 1844, 73: 1108, 1111–1112; 1846, 83: 399–400; *Examiner*, Mar. 6, 1847.

5. *Hansard*, 1844, 73: 255; 1844, 73: 428; 1844, 75: 295–6; 1844, 76: 1417; 1845, 82: 619; 1845, 79: 1068; 1841, 56: 316; 1844, 76: 1416; 1845, 79: 369; 1845, 82: 18; 1847, 92: 387; 1849, 102: 621; 1849, 103: 688–689; 1846, 83: 199; 1846, 88: 198–199; 1847, 91: 1221–2; 1847, 93: 727, 1093–1094.

6. *Hansard*, 1846, 84: 1203; 1847, 90: 1296; 1847, 91: 359, 871–878.

7. *Hansard*, 1848, 97: 1313; 1849, 103: 1329–1331.

8. *Hansard*, 1849, 102: 811; 1849, 104: 126; 1849, 103: 174–175, 177–178, 1330.

9. *Hansard*, 1849, 103: 177–178; 1849, 102: 174–175.

10. John Locke, *Two Treatises of Government* (Cambridge, 1960), Second Treatise, §§ 25–51, 124; Alexander Welsh, *The Hero of the Waverley Novels* (New Haven, Conn., 1963), ch. 4 and pp. 911f; C. B. Macpherson, *The Political Theory of Possessive Individualism: Hobbes to Locke* (Oxford, 1964), pp. 194–214.

11. Locke, *Two Treatises*, Second Treatise, §§ 25–51, 124. By the 1840s, there were twelve editions of the *Two Treatises*, twelve editions of Locke's *Works*, and six of smaller collections.

12. William Blackstone, *Commentaries on the Laws of England* (1765–1769; Philadelphia, 1860), bk. 2, ch. 1, and pp. 393–399.

13. Richard Schlatter, *Private Property* (London, 1951), pp. 161, 178–181; *The Writings and Speeches of Edmund Burke*, ed. Paul Langford and William B. Todd (Oxford, 1981–), vol. 3, *Reflections on the French Revolution*, pp. 202–205, 224, 270–272.

14. William Paley, *The Principles of Moral and Political Philosophy* (1785), 13th ed. (London, 1801), pp. 110–121.

15. H. L. Hart, *Essays on Bentham* (Oxford, 1982), pp. 57–58.

16. McCulloch, *Discourse on . . . Political Economy*, pp. 61ff; J. S. Mill, *Principles of Political Economy*, 1: 244.

17. John Hartley, "Literary Aspects of Christian Socialism in the Works of Frederick Maurice and Charles Kingsley" (Ph.D. diss., London University, 1962), p. 82; Thomas Hodgskin, *Labour Defended* (London, 1825), p. 237; Halévy, *Thomas Hodgskin*, pp. 108, 115.

18. J. S. Mill, *Principles of Political Economy*, 1: 248–251.

19. *Chartist Circular*, 1: 68.

20. *Blackwood's* July 1841, p. 4; Feb. 1842, p. 263; Dec. 1846, p. 756; Dec. 1840, p. 81; Aug. 1842, p. 272; Sept. 1842, p. 411; Mar. 1843, p. 397; May 1845, 539; *Quarterly Review*, June 1844, pp. 260, 273; Dec. 1847, pp. 267–306, esp. 283 and 299; Jan. 1830, p. 105; Sept. 1841, p. 341; Mar. 1844, p. 452; Sept. 1846, p. 572; Dec. 1846, pp. 237–239, 465; Mar. 1847, p. 476; June 1849, p. 271, 296; Croly, *Memoir of . . . Edmund Burke*; id., *Sermons* (London, 1848), pp. 4–5; *Croker Papers*, ed. Jennings, p. 84.

21. *Fraser's*, Sept. 1844, p. 374; Michael Sadler, *Speech . . . to the Merchants and Ship-Owners of Whitby* (Warrington, 1829), p. 8; *Sussex Agricultural Express*, Oct. 23, 1841 and Aug. 23, 1845; *Standard*, Apr. 23, 1844.

22. *Blackwood's*, June 1841, p. 715; Nov. 1841, p. 659; *Fraser's*, Feb. 1840, p. 160; Feb. 1841, 135; Apr. 1841, p. 386; Sept. 1844, p. 374.

23. *Standard*, July 5, 1847; Apr. 22, 1845.

24. *Railway Times*, Feb. 1, 1840; Sept. 21, 1844, p. 1079; June 29, 1844; July 6, 1850, pp. 660–662; *Farmer's Magazine*, Dec. 1844, pp. 484–485; Feb. 1845, pp. 146–147; Apr. 1844, p. 307.

25. *Mirror*, July 4, 1840.

26. *Witness*, May 7, 1842.

27. *Eclectic Review*, Oct. 1840, p. 411; *North British Review*, Aug. 1849, p. 407, 416; *Non-Conformist*, Sept. 15, 1847, p. 673; June 26, p. 469.

28. *Westminster Review*, Sept. 1840, pp. 384–385; *Prospective Review*, 1847, 3: 351.

29. *Hansard*, 1833, 15: 350; 1849, 104: 286.

30. *Hansard*, 1844, 76: 1507; 1847, 90: 668; 1848, 98: 1154, 1161; 1845, 79: 369; 1849, 103: 1040;

1841, 66: 164; 1844, 73: 1111; 1846, 83: 398; 1842, 65: 103; 1842, 69: 429–466; 1846, 83: 615; 1844, 76: 473; 1848, 98: 1107; 1848, 99: 912.

31.   *Hansard*, 1836, 35: 346, 346–347; 1840, 65: 1012; 1846, 85: 150–153, 156–157; 1844, 75: 295; 1845, 82: 25–26, 33; 1834, 21: 1053; 1835, 27: 645; 1836, 33: 510; John Hill Burton, *Political and Social Economy* (London, 1844), p. 62.

32.   *Hansard*, 1834, 22: 877; 23: 821; 25: 259.

33.   *Worcester Chronicle*, July 3, 1841; *Dorset Chronicle*, June 3, 1841; *Leeds Mercury*, June 26, July 3, July 10, 1841; *Nottingham Journal*, June 25, 1841; *York Herald*, July 3, 1841; *Oxford Journal*, July 3, 1841; *Shrewsbury Chronicle*, June 24, 1841; and the *Durham Chronicle*, July 2, 1841, which said Tory attacks on the New Poor Law had become "the common claptrap subject of the present election."

34.   *Hansard*, 1846, 87: 1045.

35.   *P.P.*, 1843, 12: 17–398; 1847, 11: 38–554; 1848, 7: 3–70; 1846, 9: 1–311.

36.   Cecil Woodham Smith, *The Great Hunger, Ireland 1845–1849* (London, 1962), pp. 314–17; 374–376, 408–410.

37.   *Hansard*, 1847, 92: 89–90; 1849, 102: 279, 290, 356; 103: 1330.

38.   Abraham Tucker, *The Light of Nature* (Cambridge, 1831), 2: 247.

39.   M. L. Clarke, *Paley: Evidences for the Man* (Toronto, 1974), pp. 94–95.

40.   William Wilberforce, *A Practical View of the Prevailing Religious System* (Boston, 1829), pp. 96–97.

41.   Edward Bickersteth, *The Works of Edward Bickersteth* (16 vols.; London, 1853); id., *The Signs of the Times in the East: A Warning to the West* (London, 1845); Birks, *Memoir of . . . Bickersteth*, p. 18.

42.   Ashhurst Turner Gilbert, *God's Blessing the Only Security Against National Want* (Chichester, 1847), pp. 6, 23; id., *A Sermon . . . in Obedience to Her Majesty's Letter for the Relief of the Irish and Scotch* (London, 1847), pp. 8, 19.

43.   M'Neil, *Famine*, pp. 8, 31.

44.   Paley, *Moral and Political Philosophy*, 1: 65.

45.   Tucker, *Light of Nature*, 2: 241, 258.

46.   Sumner, *Treatise on . . . Creation*, 2: 160.

47.   Burke, *Thoughts and Details on Scarcity*, p. 270.

48.   Charles Neave, *A Lecture on the Character and Writings of William Paley* (London, 1873), p. 7; William Smith, *A Discourse on the Ethics of the School of Paley* (London, 1837), p. 7; Warren, *Intellectual and Moral Development*, p. 56.

49.   George Combe, *Lectures on Moral Philosophy* (Boston, 1840), pp. 42, 52.

50.   *The Works of Thomas Chalmers* (25 vols.; New York, 1842), 6: 366–367.

51.   Jonathan Dymond, *Essays on the Principle of Morality* (London, 1842), p. 1; Adam Sedgwick, *Discourse on the Studies of the University of Cambridge* (London, 1833), pp. 12–19; Thomas Southwood Smith, *The Divine Government* (London, 1826), pp. vi, 19, 24; George Ramsay, *An Enquiry into the Principles of Human Happiness and Human Duty* (London, 1843), pp. 37, 183–188; Samuel Spalding, *Philosophy of Christian Morals* (London, 1843), pp. 3–5; 45–47, 184.

52.   *Hansard*, 1847, 92: 64.

53.   Mrs. Marcet, *Rich and Poor* (London, 1851), p. 21; Paley, *Natural Theology* (London, 1836), ch. 26, "Of the Goodness of the Deity."

54.   *Christian Teacher*, 1843, 5: 259; Andrew and Charles Reed, *Memoirs of the Life and*

Philanthropic Labours of Andrew Reed (London, 1863), p. 242; Edward Lucas, *Life of Frederick Lucas* (London, 1886), p. 17; Sandford, *Parochialia*, pp. 331–332; Sewell, *Christian Politics*, p. 34.

55. *Westminster Review*, Oct. 1842, 38: 398; *Athenaeum*, Apr. 11, 1840, p. 288; Sept. 11, 1847, p. 1244; Dec. 4, 1847, Sanitary Reform; June 16, 1849, p. 613.

56. Sumner, *Treatise on . . . Creation*, 2: 43, 51, 68–69, 92–93, 180–181; Chalmers, *Works*, 6: 128.

57. J. H. S. Kent, "The Clash Between Radicalism and Liberalism in Methodism" (Ph.D. diss., London University), p. 274; *Christian Penny Magazine* 3 (1848): 57.

58. W. F. Hook, *Sermons* (London, 1841), p. 61; John Medway, *Memoirs of the Life and Writings of John Pye Smith* (London, 1853), pp. 385–386.

59. Paley, *Moral and Political Philosophy*, 2: 152–153.

60. Wilberforce, *Practical View of the Prevailing Religious System*, pp. 169, 182, 270, 274–275.

61. *Quarterly Review*, Dec. 1840, pp. 501–502; *Devises and Wiltshire Gazette*, Apr. 18, 1844; *Hansard*, 1844, 73: 1465–1466.

62. Wilberforce, *Practical View of the Prevailing Religious System*, p. 96; Tucker, *Light of Nature*, 2: 383, 404; Sumner, *Treatise on . . . Creation*, 2: 211; Chalmers, *Works*, 4: 63; Paley, *Moral and Political Philosophy*, 2: 383.

63. Wilberforce, *Practical View of the Prevailing Religious System*, p. 96; Tucker, *Light of Nature*, 2: 383, 404; Sumner, *Treatise on . . . Creation*, 2: 211; Chalmers, *Works*, 4: 63; Paley, *Moral and Political Philosophy*, 2: 142; Clarke, *Paley*, pp. 295, 298, 344.

64. *Economist*, Feb. 13, 1847, pp. 169–170; Jan. 20, 1848, p. 127.

65. Sir James Mackintosh, *Ethics* (Edinburgh, 1836), ed. William Whewell, preface, pp. 13, 16; Thomas Brown, *Lectures on Ethics* (Edinburgh, 1846), xvi; Combe, *Lectures on Moral Philosophy*, p. 11; Spalding, *Christian Morals*, p. 128; *Works of Dugald Stewart*, ed. Hamilton, 6: 13, 20; Sedgwick, *Discourse*, pp. 39–50.

66. Spalding, *Christian Morals*, p. 184; Ramsay, *Enquiry into the Principles of Human Happiness and Human Duty*, pp. 34, 183; Brown, *Ethics*, pp. 217, 251, 255.

67. Bernard Mandeville, *Fable of the Bees* (6th ed., 1729), ed. Phillip Harth (Harmondsworth, Eng., 1970); Adam Smith, *Theory of Moral Sentiments* (1759; Boston, 1817), 2: 164; id., *Wealth of Nations*, ed. Cannan, 1: 16.

68. George Combe, *Constitution of Man* (Boston, 1829), p. 211; Chalmers, *Works*, 6: 63, 82; Wilberforce, *Practical View of the Prevailing Religious System*, pp. 180, 270; *NonConformist*, June 22, 1842, p. 450; See also Richard W. Hamilton, *Nugae Literariae: Prose and Verse* (London, 1851), p. 421; Clarke, *Paley*, p. 335; Paley, *Moral and Political Philosophy*, 1: 108–109.

69. Marcet, *Rich and Poor*, p. 21; H. Martineau, *Autobiography*, ed. Chapman, 2: 245.

70. Halévy, *Thomas Hodgskin*, p. 51; Burton, *Political and Social Economy*, p. 29; Scrope, *Principles of Political Economy*, p. 11.

71. Samuel Hollander, *The Economics of Adam Smith* (Toronto, 1973), p. 248; Hamilton, *Nugae Literariae*, p. 421.

72. Wilberforce, *Practical View of the Prevailing Religious System*, p. 199; Tucker, *Light of Nature*, 2: 253.

73. *John Bull*, May 13, 1848; *Christian Remembrancer* 12 (1846): 376; Gresley, *Parochial Sermons*, p. 361; A. Martineau, *What Is My Duty?* p. 46; Henry Melville, *Sermons Preached on Public Occasions* (London, 1846), p. 47; George Croly, *The Closing of the Exhibition* (London,

1851), p. 9; Rev. Thomas Stevens, *Poor Law Relief No Charity* [sermon on John 15:17] (London, 1845), p. 18; Rev. Samuel Warren, *Sermons on Practical Subjects* (London, 1845), pp. 15, 177; *Sermons for Sundays, Festivals and Fasts*, ed. Watson, p. 345.

74. *Blackwood's*, Apr. 1848, p. 518; Rev. Legh Richmond, *Annals of the Poor* (1815; London, 1851), pp. 65, 231; Wilberforce, *Practical View of the Prevailing Religious System*, pp. 275, 277; Chalmers, *Works*, 6:107.

75. Clarke, *Paley*, p. 38; Paley, *Natural Theology*, 300, 301; id., *Moral and Political Philosophy*, 1: 21–42.

76. Sumner, *Treatise on . . . Creation*, 2: 286–297, 300–302.

77. Tucker, *Light of Nature*, 2: 258; Paley, *Moral and Political Philosophy*, 1: 100–113.

78. Sumner, *Treatise on . . . Creation*, 2: 58.

79. Smith, *Divine Government*, pp. 240, 293–295; Spalding, *Christian Morals*, pp. vi, 51, 366.

80. Burke, *Works*, 9: 249–281, 366, esp. 253, 265, 270; Paley, *Natural Theology*, p. 330.

81. Sumner, *Treatise on . . . Creation*, 2: 203, 315–318.

82. Wilberforce, *Practical View of the Prevailing Religious System*, p. 273; Chalmers, *Christian and Civic Economy*, pp. 8–9.

83. M'Neil, *Famine*, p. 8.

84. Paget, *Warden of Berkingholt*, p. xi; A. Martineau, *What Is My Duty?* p. iii.

85. *Fraser's*, Aug. 1844, pp. 249, 251; *Leeds Intelligencer*, July 16, 1842; *Leeds Conservative*, Sept. 3, 10, 1842.

86. *Hansard*, 1849, 107: 870; 104: 76–78; 1842, 61: 546; 1845, 80: 928.

87. *Hansard*, 1840, 54: 1005; 1844, 73: 1434; 1839, 48: 579.

88. Tucker, *Light of Nature*, 2: 343; Burke, *Works*, 4: 279.

89. *Hansard*, 1842, 61: 315–317; 1846, 84: 291; 1846, 85: 178.

90. Mountifort Longfield, *Four Lectures on the Poor Law* (Dublin, 1834), p. 57; Jones, *Literary Remains*, ed. Whewell, p. 71; Scrope, *Principles of Political Economy*, p. 1.

CHAPTER 7

1. W. Sewell, *Christian Communism* (Oxford, 1848), pp. 15–16, 19.

2. *Blackwood's Magazine*, Apr.–May 1842, pp. 518–520; July 1843, p. 122.

3. *Fraser's Magazine*, May 1843, p. 511; Oct. 1849, p. 439; Nov. 1849, p. 526; Apr. 1841, p. 385; *Morning Post*, May 19, 20, 1848; *Morning Herald*, June 28, 1842.

4. *Morning Chronicle*, June 23, 1849; Apr. 22, 1848.

5. Rev. Charles Girdelstone, *The Causes and Cure of Abject Poverty* (London, 1847), p. 8.

6. Gresley, *Clement Walton*, p. 161; Osborne, *Hints to the Charitable*, p. 8; Melville, *Sermons on . . . Public Occasions*, p. 66; Sandford, *Parochialia*, p. 339.

7. Sumner, *Treatise on . . . Creation*, 2: 1–2, 136, 162–163; Stanley, *Addresses and Charges of Edward Stanley*, p. 62; Whately, *Political Economy*, p. 194; Welch, *Bishop Blomfield*, p. 216; John Allen, bishop of Ely, *Charge to the Clergy* (London, 1841), p. 15; Charles, Thomas Langley, bishop of Ripon, *Charge to the Clergy* (London, 1841), pp. 9–10; George Murray, bishop of Rochester, *Charge to the Clergy* (London, 1843), p. 34; Ashley Turner Gilbert, *A Pastoral Letter* (Chichester, 1843), p. 16.

8. Burke, *Works*, 9: 253; Blaug, *Economic Theory in Retrospect*, pp. 68–77.

9. *British Critic* 33 (1843): 250.

10. Southey, *Essays*, 1: 149, 217, 2: 25–26.

11. Chalmers, *Works,* 6: 120, 255, 289; id., *Christian and Civic Economy,* p. 9; *North British Review,* Nov. 1844, pp. 8, 27; J. B. Sumner, *Evidences of Christianity* (London, 1824), p. 404; id., *Treatise on . . . Creation,* 2: 95, 220, 285–6, 328.

12. *North British Review,* Nov. 1846, p. 113; Aug. 1848, p. 350; Thomas Chalmers, *Institutes of Theology* (New York, 1849), 2: 406; id., *Works,* 6: 129; Sumner, *Treatise on . . . Creation,* 2: 69, 88, 162–163.

13. *Hansard,* 1845, 78: 806; *Devises and Wiltshire Gazette,* Dec. 26, 1844; *Sussex Agricultural Express,* Sept. 11 and Oct. 9, 1841.

14. *Fraser's,* Nov. 1844, p. 626; *Quarterly Review,* Mar. 1844, p. 507.

15. Sophy Hall, *Dr. Duncan of Ruthwell, Founder of Savings Banks* (London, 1910), p. 60; Southey, *Essays,* 1: 217; Rev. T. S. Grimshawe, *A Memoir of the Rev. Legh Richmond* (London, 1840); Richmond, *Annals of the Poor.*

16. Osborne, *Hints to the Charitable,* pp. 11, 16–18, 26, 34, 49, 59.

17. *Hansard,* 1845, 78: 309–310; *Sussex Agricultural Express,* Jan. 6, 1844, Dec. 12, 1840; *Salisbury Journal,* Aug. 3, 1844.

18. *Poor Law Report,* ed. Checkland and Checkland, pp. 82–277; *P.P.,* 1834, 39: 127–207; *Manchester Guardian,* May 17, 1834; *Hansard,* 1834, 24: 1061, 25: 1096; 1841, 56: 451; 1842, 64: 168–170.

19. *Spectator,* Sept. 18, 1841.

20. Blaug, *Ricardian Economics,* pp. 106–107, 111–121; Poynter, *Society and Pauperism,* pp. 144–185.

21. Peter Dunkley, *Crisis of the Old Poor Law and England* (New York, 1982), pp. 101–102, 106, 118, 122–123, 127.

22. Poynter, *Society and Pauperism,* pp. 190–222, 249–271, esp. 310–316; William Blamire, *Remarks on the Poor Law* (London, 1800); J. Willis, *On the Poor Laws of England* (London, 1800); Sir George Nicholl, *A History of the English Poor Law* (London, 1898), 2: 191–226, 3: 52–116; Sydney and Beatrice Webb, *English Poor Law History* (London, 1927), pt. 1: 396–428, pt. 2: 82–103.

23. *Manchester Guardian,* Aug. 3, 1842.

24. *Hansard,* 1838, 28: 50; 1834, 25: 211ff, 222–224.

25. *Poor Law Report,* ed. Checkland and Checkland, pp. 115–135, 145–149; *P.P.,* 1836, 29: 510–14; 1837, 17: pt. 1, 80–90, 481–493; 1838, 18: pt. 1, 73–101, pt. 2, 67–68; 1838, 28: 289–294; 1840, 17: 212–216.

26. *Hansard,* 1834, 25: 211–251.

27. *P.P.,* 1838, 28: 279–283.

28. Bowley, *Nassau Senior,* p. 254; David Philips and Richard Storch, *Policing Provincial England, 1829–1856* (Leicester, 1999), pp. 111–135.

29. Anthony Brundage, *The Making of the New Poor Law* (New Brunswick, N.J., 1978), p. 67; *Hansard,* 1842, 64: 170–171.

30. *Hansard,* 1849, 103: 189; 1847, 92: 1224.

31. *Hansard,* 1842, 64: 116; 1841, 61: 399–400; 1847, 93: 668, 887, 898–899.

32. Seeley, *Remedies,* pp. 284, 309.

33. *Fraser's,* Apr. 1841, 380; *John Bull,* Oct. 30, 1841.

34. *Quarterly Review,* Apr. 1835, pp. 476–539; 1841, 68: 530–531; *Blackwood's,* Apr. 1842, p. 520; Mar. 1847, p. 272.

35. *Hansard,* 1849, 102: 618, 811, 829; 103: 178; 107: 846, 853; *Quarterly Review,* Mar. 1843, p. 438.

36. *Hansard*, 1847, 92: 562.

37. *Hansard*, 1846, 85: 735; 1847, 91: 877.

38. *Hansard*, 1847, 91: 877; 1849, 102: 392–391; 104: 565, 585; 1847, 90: 1274, 1277.

39. *Edinburgh Review,* July 1843, p. 2; *Poor Law Report,* ed. Checkland and Checkland, p. 156.

40. A. Blomfield, *Memoir of Charles James Blomfield*, p. 134; Sumner, *Treatise on . . . Creation*, 2: 107, 113, 114, 116, 128–130, 133–134, 153–154, 161, 164, 271, 184–188, 412; id., *Christian Charity* (London, 1841), pp. 2, 132; R. A. Soloway, *Prelates and People* (London, 1969), pp. 118, 129, 185.

41. Political Economy Club of London, *Minutes of Proceedings,* pp. 252, 265, 404–412; O'Brien, *J. R. McCulloch*, pp. 330–331; *Hansard*, 1834, 28: 972, 1321–1332.

42. Thomas Spencer, *Objections to the New Poor Law Answered* (London, 1841), pp. 1–11; *The New Poor Law, Its Evils and Their Remedies* (London, 1841), pp. 4–6; id., *The Outcry Against the New Poor Law* (London, 1841), pp. 1–7.

43. Stevens, *Poor Law Relief No Charity*, p. 18; Rev. Charles Kingsley, *Politics for the People* (London, 1848), 1: 34.

44. *P.P.*, 1836, 29: 211–221.

45. *P.P.*, 1852–53, 89; *Journal of the Royal Statistical Society* 18 (1855): 146.

46. Clyde Binfield, *So Down to Prayers: Studies in English Nonconformity, 1780–1920* (London, 1977), pp. 115–116.

47. G. I. T. Machin, *Politics and the Churches in Great Britain, 1832–1868* (Oxford, 1977), pp. 54–60.

48. Edward Baines Jr., *Life of Edward Baines* (London, 1851); Charles Mitchell, *The Newspaper Press Directory* (London, 1854), pp. 1–4; *P.P.*, 1842, 26: 562–567.

49. Thomas W. Laqueur, *Religion and Respectability: Sunday Schools and Working Class Culture, 1780–1850* (New Haven, Conn., 1967), p. 42; *Baptist Guardian,* Oct. 3, 1845.

50. Horton Davies, *Worship and Theology in England: From Watts and Wesley to Maurice* (Princeton, N.J., 1961), p. 154; A. J. Calman, *A Biography of John Ashworth* (Manchester, 1875), pp. 30–33.

51. *Baptist Magazine*, Apr. 1842, p. 177; Sept. 1847, pp. 552–554; July 1846, p. 343.

52. Rev. James Evans, *Sermons* (London, 1858), p. 163; Arthur Miall, *Life of Edward Miall,* pp. 2, 6–8, 28, 39–40; *NonConformist,* Sept. 11, 1844, p. 637; Mar. 10, 1847, p. 141; *Patriot,* Apr. 29, 1845.

53. *Christian Penny Magazine*, 1849, 4: 281; *Congregational Magazine,* Jan. 1845, p. 131.

54. A. C. Underwood, *A History of the English Baptists* (London, 1947), pp. 161–194; Albert Peel, *One Thousand Years of Congregationalism* (London, 1931), p. 128; R. W. Dale, *History of English Congregationalism* (London, 1931), pp. 636, 701–704.

55. *Watchman,* Mar. 17, 1847; *Baptist Examiner,* Jan. 1844, p. 6; William Benson, *Life and Letters of James Bourne* (London, 1875), p. 358.

56. *Congregational Magazine,* Feb. 1845, pp. 130–131; July 1845, p. 498; Thomas Binney, *Sermons Preached in the King's Weigh-House Chapel, London, 1829–1869* (London, 1875), p. 322; Rev. R. W. Hamilton, *Posthumous Works of the Rev. John Ely* (London, 1848); *Baptist Examiner,* June 1841, pp. 161–163.

57. *Congregational Magazine* 8 (1844): 42–43; Wright Wilson, *The Life of George Dawson* (Birmingham, 1905), pp. 38–39, 41, 44, 48, 52, 85; George Dawson, *Biographical Lectures* (London, 1886), pp. 358–389.

58. E. J. Hobsbawm, *Industry and Empire: An Economic History of Britain since 1750*

(London, 1972), diagrams 10 and 22; E. L. Woodward, *The Age of Reform* (Oxford, 1958), p. 1; Binfield, *So Down to Prayers*, pp. 56–57.

59. Binfield, *So Down to Prayers*, pp. 7–9; David Thompson, *Nonconformity in the Nineteenth Century* (London, 1972), p. 13.

60. *Congregational Yearbook*, 1848, pp. 101–102; 1846, pp. 177–178; *Congregational Magazine*, Feb. 1847, pp. 68–73.

61. *Congregational Yearbook*, 1846, pp. 130–140; Kenneth Brown, *A Social History of the Nonconformist Ministry* (Oxford, 1980), pp. 20–24, 44–50; p. 21, tables 1.1, 1.5, 1.6, and 1.7.

62. Raymond Holt, *The Unitarian Contribution to Social Progress in England* (London, 1952), pp. 24–25, 43–44, 49, 58–59, 187, 198; R. G. Wilson, *Gentlemen Merchants: The Merchant Community in Leeds* (Manchester, 1971), pp. 161, 172, 177–180, 187; *Leeds Mercury*, Sept. 18, 1841; A. Temple Patterson, *Radical Leicester* (Leicester, 1954), chs. 3 and 4; Asa Briggs, *Victorian Cities* (New York, 1963), pp. 68–69, 84, 123–125, 195–204.

63. Binfield, *So Down to Prayers*, pp. 30–34, 65, 73–74; Alan D. Gilbert, *Religion and Society in Industrial England* (London, 1976), pp. 83–85, 90, 96–97, 104, 111–112, 115–116, 145–147; Thompson, *Nonconformity in the Nineteenth Century*, pp. 13, 20, 22, 39–43.

64. Binfield, *So Down to Prayers*, pp. 72–74, 115, 266; *Leeds Times*, Jan. 9, 16, 1841; *Leeds Mercury*, Sept. 18, 1841; Apr. 1, May 20, 1843; June 7, 1845.

65. E. Paxton Hood, *Thomas Binney* (London, 1874), p. 144; *Christian Pioneer*, Dec. 1846, p. 69; *Baptist Pioneer*, Aug. 1846, pp. 21–22; *Christian Penny Magazine*, 1849, 4: 244; *Christian Teacher*, 1841, 3: 38–39.

66. *Congregational Magazine*, Dec. 1845, p. 905; *Prospective Review*, 1845, 1: 107; *NonConformist*, Apr. 17, 1844, p. 244; *Baptist Pioneer*, Aug. 1846, p. 23; Sept. 1846, pp. 25–26, 28.

67. Binney, *Sermons . . . in the King's Weigh-House Chapel*, p. 361; John Ely, *Posthumous Works of Rev. John Ely* (London, 1848), pp. 74–75, 423; *Eclectic Review*, Dec. 1848, p. 714; Thomas Jackson, *The Life of the Rev. Robert Newton* (London, 1855), p. 95.

68. *Sussex Agricultural Express*, Apr. 10, 1841; Roberts, *Paternalism*, p. 181; *P.P.*, 1843, 27: 309, 346–348.

69. Gresley, *Frank's First Trip to the Continent*, p. 161; id., *Church Clavering*, p. 254; id., *Practical Sermons*, p. 363; Sandford, *Parochialia*, pp. 111–112; Mrs. Hippesley Tuckfield, *Education for the People* (London, 1839), pp. 6, 50, 115; G. P. G. Cosserat, *How Is the Character of the Church to Be Maintained* (Exeter, 1849), p. 17.

70. Adam Rushton, *Life of Adam Rushton* (London, 1909), ch. 15; J. Evans, *Sermons*, pp. 65, 105, 121, 127, 163; James Griffin, *Memories of the Past* (London, 1858), p. 155; G. J. Holyoake, *Life of Joseph Raynor Stephens* (London, 1882), p. 63.

71. *Leeds Mercury*, Dec. 5, 1840; June 6, 1846; John Daniel Morell, *On the Progress of Society in England as Affected by the Advancement of National Education* (London, 1859), pp. 17–18.

72. *Athenaeum*, Oct. 14, 1843, pp. 921–922; Mar. 18, 1847, p. 258; *Westminster Review*, June 1840, pp. 114–115; June 1845, p. 459; Oct. 1846, pp. 189–216; *Edinburgh Review*, Oct. 1848, p. 399; *Morning Chronicle*, Mar. 4, 1843.

73. *The Autobiography of Samuel Smiles, LL.D.*, ed. Thomas Mackay (New York, 1905), pp. 132–133; *Westminster Review*, Apr. 1834, p. 300; Lady Noël Byron, *What De Fellenberg Has Done for Education* (London, 1839), p. 37.

74. *Edinburgh Review*, Apr. 1847, p. 527; *P.P.*, 1842, 35: 144–145; Southey, *Essays*, 1: 149; *Quarterly Review*, June 1845, p. 26; Jelinger Symons, *Popular Economy* (London, 1840), p. 41–44; *Chambers' Edinburgh Journal*, Mar. 13, 1847; Thomas Bailey, *A Discourse on the Causes of*

Political Revolution (London, 1831), pp. 4–5; *Records of Longevity* (London, 1857), p. 4; Brian Simon, *Studies in the History of Education, 1780–1870* (London, 1960), p. 44; John Gray, *The Social System* (London, 1831), p. 96.

75. Mackintosh, *Ethics*, ed. Whewell, p. 34.

76. Simon, *Studies in the History of Education*, p. 146; J. S. Mill, *Dissertations and Discussions, Political, Philosophical and Historical* (New York, 1873), 1: 54; *James and John Stuart Mill on Education*, ed. F. A. Cavenagh (Cambridge, 1931), p. ix.

77. *Morning Chronicle*, Jan. 9, Apr. 22, 1840; Jan. 7, Mar. 4, 1843 Apr. 30, 1845; May 6, 1846; Apr. 12, June 19, 1847; Ethel Ellis, *Remains of William Ellis* (London, 1873), p. 43; Dilke, *Papers of a Critic*, 1: 66; Leslie A. Marchand, *The Athenaeum: A Mirror of Victorian Culture* (Chapel Hill, N.C., 1941), pp. 31–32, 69; *Athenaeum*, July 9, 1836, pp. 481–482; Apr. 4, 1840, p. 267, June 20, 1840, p. 491; Dec. 31, 1842, pp. 1124–1125, 1137.

78. *Westminster Review*, June 1840, pp. 111–115; Apr. 1834, pp. 302–307; July 1842, p. 220; Joseph Payne, *Pestalozzi: The Influence of His Principles and Practices on Elementary Education* (London, 1875); Henry Holman, *Pestalozzi: An Account of His Life and Work* (London, 1908); Byron, *What De Fellenberg Has Done for Education*.

79. J. H. Thom, *Preventive Justice and Palliative Charity* (London, 1845), pp. 9–11; id., *A Spiritual Faith* (London, 1895), pp. ix–xi; *Christian Teacher*, 1841, 3: 221, 421; 1842, 4: 106–108; 1843, 5: 268; *Prospective Review*, 1845, 1: 105.

80. Graham Wallace, *William J. Fox, 1786–1854* (London, 1924), p. 16; Garnett, *The Life of W. J. Fox*, pp. 214, 225, 253, 261; Smith, *Divine Government*, pp. 31, 155, 173, 202, 206, 215–216, 218; id., *The Probable Influence of the Development of the Principles of the Human Mind on Its Future Progress in Knowledge and Goodness: A Discourse* (London, 1818), pp. 7, 9, 17; id., *The Philosophy of Health*, 1: 85–87; 98; William E. Channing, *Works* (Boston, 1845), 3: 359.

81. Smith, *Divine Government*, pp. 173, 218; id., *Discourse*, pp. 7, 9; id., *Philosophy of Health*, 1: 94, 98; Garnett, *Fox*, pp. 208, 214, 225–226, 252; *People's Journal*, Jan 17, 1846, pp. 30–31; Mar. 14, 1846, p. 147; Channing, *Works*, 1: 377–378, 2: 356.

82. Garnett, *Fox*, pp. 51, 55, 63, 183–4, 198, 247, 252, 253; Holt, *The Unitarian Contribution to Social Progress* (London, 1952), pp. 22, 60, 134, 173–178, 187, 198, 204, 262–72, 335.

83. Robert Theobald, *Memorials of John Daniel Morell* (London, 1891), pp. 12, 14–17, 21, 23–24, 26; Boase, *Modern English Biography*, 2: 962; Morell, *On the Progress of Society in England*, pp. 10–11, 17, 18, 20; *P.P.*, 1850, 44: 468, 496, 507; 1853, 80: 628.

84. *P.P.*, 1845, 35: 102–103, 120; 1848, 50: 180–181; John P. Norris, *Easy Lessons on Confirmation* (London, 1877), p. 32; id., *The Education of the People* (London, 1869), pp. 1–2; id., *Ten School Room Addresses* (London, 1849), pp. 6, 16–17, 23; id., *The Catechism and Prayer Book* (London, 1872), p. 401.

85. Symons, *Popular Economy*, pp. 38–41; *P.P.*, 1841, 20: 195; *P.P.*, 1852, 39: 57; 1846, 32: 266, 277; 1838, 28: 288; M.H. 32/48, Kay-Shuttleworth to Lewis, Oct. 27, 1835.

86. *P.P.*, 1838, 28: 274–284, 298–308; M.H. 32/48, June 30, 1836; *P.P.*, 1839, 20: 103–112; 1840, 17: 247–262; Boase, *Modern English Biography*, 6: 714; *Journal of the Society of Arts*, July 16, 1886, p. 898; *Times*, July 12, 1886.

87. *P.P.*, 1839, 20: 107–109; 1840, 17: 247–262; 1860, 54: xxix, 1–20.

88. *P.P.*, 1843, 25 and 26: 453–454; 1846, 37: v–xiv; 1838, 11: 9.

89. *P.P.*, 1839, 42: 357–382, 417–426; 1842, 22: 445; 1843, 27: 309, 321–322, 335–356; 1847, 15: 467; 1848, 26: 109, 121.

90. Welsh, *Bishop Blomfield*, pp. 47–50; John Kaye, *A Charge to the Clergy* (London, 1840), p. 32.

91. *Spectator,* Sept. 3, 1842, p. 853.

92. Mary Alden Hopkins, *Hannah More* (New York, 1947), pp. 211–220; G. H. Spinney, *Cheap Repository Tracts* (London, 1940); Marcet, *Rich and Poor,* pp. 117–118; id., *Conversations on Political Economy* (London, 1824), pp. 25, 41, 98, 132, 155, 158, 168; H. Martineau, *Autobiography,* ed. Chapman, 1: 399–400.

93. R. K. Webb, *The British Working Class Reader* (London, 1955), pp. 66–74; Chester W. New, *The Life of Henry Brougham* (Oxford, 1961), pp. 332–351; Charles Knight, *The Rights of Industry Addressed to the Working-Men of the United Kingdom* (London, 1831), p. 170.

94. *DNB,* 31: 245–248; Knight, *Rights of Industry,* p. 170; Mabel Tylecote, *The Mechanics' Institutes of Lancashire and Yorkshire* (Manchester, 1957), pp. 28, 34, 44, 57, 66, 124; New, *Brougham,* p. 346; Society for the Diffusion of Useful Knowledge [henceforth cited as SDUK], *Report on the State of Literary, Scientific, and Mechanics' Institutes in England* (London, 1841), pp. 13, 23.

95. *Leeds Mercury,* Oct. 16, 1841; June 25, Sept. 10, 1842; Nov. 1, 1845; Feb. 18, 1843; Feb. 22, 1845; Dec. 4, 1847.

96. SDUK, *Report on. . . Mechanics' Institutes,* p. 23; *A Manual for Mechanics' Institutions* (London, 1839), pp. 23, 38; *Leeds Mercury,* Mar. 19, 1842; June 17, 1848; Simon, *Studies in the History of Education,* p. 254.

97. *Scotsman,* Mar. 20, 1847; *Westminster Review,* Aug. 1843, p. 110; William Chambers, *Memoirs of Robert Chambers* (London, 1872), p. 237; Smiles, *Autobiography,* pp. 87–131; *Leeds Mercury,* Feb. 18, 1843; Mar. 1, 1845; and, for the *Penny Magazine,* see Patricia Anderson, *The Printed Image and the Transformation of Popular Culture* (London, 1991), pp. 3, 49, 50–83 passim.

98. *Chambers' Edinburgh Journal,* Apr. 2, 1842, p. 81.

99. *Leeds Mercury,* June 25, Sept. 10, 1842; Feb. 18, 1843; May 4, 1844; Feb. 15, 22, 1845; Jan. 24, Mar. 27, June 6, 1846; Oct. 30, 1847.

100. Knight, *Rights of Industry,* p. 101; id., *Capital and Labour,* p. 207.

101. Smiles, *Autobiography,* pp. 132–133; id., *Education of the Working Classes* (London, 1842); *Leeds Times,* May 14, Sept. 17, and Oct. 1, 1842.

102. David Roberts, "Early Victorian Newspaper Editors," *Victorian Periodicals Review,* Dec. 1971, pp. 1–2.

103. Chambers, *Memoirs of Robert Chambers,* 119–120.

104. *English Chartist Circular,* 1842, 1: 10, 17, 163, 460; 2: 3, 110, 169; Holyoake, *Sixty Years of an Agitator's Life,* pp. 150–188; *The Movement* 1, no. 2: 14; no. 1: 3; 2, no. 67: 103; *The Union,* 1842, Apr. 1, p. 32, Oct. 1, p. 256, and Nov. 1, p. 330.

105. David Roberts, "Early Victorian Newspaper Editors," *Victorian Periodicals Review,* Dec. 1971, pp. 1–12, June, 1972, pp. 15–28, Dec. 1972, pp. 12–26, June 1973, pp. 33–41; Lambert, *Cobbett of the West,* p. 61; Simon, *Studies in the History of Education,* pp. 211–273, 259.

106. William Lovett, *The Life and Struggles of William Lovett: An Autobiography* (London, 1967), pp. 9, 18–19, 21, 25–29, 31–33, 44–45, 50–51, 53–55; Thomas Cooper, *Eight Letters to the Young Men in the Working Class* (London, 1851), pp. 5–8, 11, 17; id., *The Life of Thomas Cooper* (London, 1872), pp. 163–165; Robert J. Conklin, *Thomas Cooper, the Chartist* (Manila, 1935), p. 321.

107. Laqueur, *Religion and Respectability,* pp. 42–43; 91–92, 101–102, 106, 192–193, 241.

108. Brian Harrison, *Drink and the Victorians: The Temperance Question in England, 1815–1872* (Pittsburgh, 1971), pp. 107–119, 150.

109. Henry Carter, *The English Temperance Movement* (London, 1933), pp. 2–24; E. C.

Irwin, *A Weaver at the Loom of Time: A Sketch of the Life of Joseph Livesey* (London, 1923), pp. 1–24; Lilian Lewis Shiman, *Crusade Against Drink in Victorian England* (London, 1988), pp. 30–34, 43–73.

110. Philip Gardner, *The Lost Elementary Schools of Victorian England* (London, 1984), pp. 5–6, 29, 32, 48, 83, 90–91, 94–101, 173.

111. Henry Mayhew, *London Labour and the London Poor: A Cyclopædia of the Condition and Earnings of Those That Will Work, Those That Cannot Work, and Those That Will Not Work,* 4 vols. (London, 1861–62; reprint, London, 1968), 1: 35, 57, 95, 110, 114, 132, 149, 289, 321–322, 329.

112. Samuel Smiles, *Self-Help* (Boston, 1869), p. 76; id., *Autobiography*, pp. 114–115.

113. Hobsbawm, *Labouring Men*, pp. 74–76; J. G. Kohl, *England and Wales* (1844; reprint, London, 1968), p. 106; Leeds Society for the Suppression of Mendicity, *Twenty-Fifth Report* (Leeds, 1843), p. 14.

114. *Hansard*, 1837, 36: 1088; 1842, 60: 188.

115. Osborne, *Hints to the Charitable*, pp. 5, 7, 8–63; id., *A View of the Low Moral and Physical Condition of the Agricultural Labourer* (London, 1844), pp. 17, 1–30.

116. *P.P.*, 1838, 18: 46–50, 185–191; *Hansard*, 1846, 84: 1191.

117. W. P. Alison, *On the Management of the Poor* (London, 1840), pp. 42, 92; id., *Observations on the Famine of 1846–1847* (London, 1847), pp. 32–33; id., *Observation on the Epidemic Fever of 1843 in Scotland* (Edinburgh, 1844).

118. R. D. Collison Black, *Economic Thought and the Irish Question, 1817–1870* (Cambridge, 1960), pp. 94–95.

119. Hugo Reid, *What Should Be Done for the People* (London, 1848), p. 14.

CHAPTER 8

1. *Leeds Intelligencer*, Apr. 10, 1847; Arthur Miall, *Life of Edward Miall*, p. 112; *Patriot*, Feb. 27, 1847.

2. *Baptist Magazine,* Feb. 1847, p. 98; Rev. J. E. Giles, *Two Lectures in Explanation of the Objects of the Proposed Anti–State Church Association Conference* (Leeds, 1844), p. 3; Denison, *Notes of My Life*, p. iii.

3. Gash, *Reaction and Reconstruction in English Politics*, pp. 11–12, 70–72, 83–91; Owen Chadwick, *The Victorian Church* (London, 1966), 1: 54–60, 70, 101–157.

4. Chadwick, *Victorian Church*, 1: 60–79, 197–198, 493–494; *Remains of the Late Reverend Richard Hurrell Froude*, ed. J. H. Newman and J. Keble (4 vols.; London, 1838–39), 1: 396; *Christian Remembrancer* 12 (1846): 45.

5. *Oxford and Cambridge Review*, Oct. 1846, pp. 330–331; *Spectator*, June 7, 1845, p. 540.

6. R. W. Hamilton, *Sermons* (Leeds, 1846), pp. 203, 207.

7. *NonConformist*, May 6, 1844, pp. 303–304.

8. Rev. J. E. Giles, *Anti–State Church*, p. 3; *Eclectic Review,* Mar. 1844, p. 353; Jan. 1844, p. 19.

9. Gilbert, *Religion and Society in Industrial England*, pp. 78–79, 80, 84; Machin, *Politics and the Churches in Great Britain*, pp. 16, 45–46, 103–107, 160–162; D. Thompson, *Nonconformity in the Nineteenth Century*, pp. 64–65; William G. Addison, *Religious Equality in Modern England* (London, 1944), pp. 60–68; *Patriot*, Feb. 1842, a weekly column on Church rates persecutions; *Congregational Yearbook*, 1846, p. 51; *NonConformist*, May 6, 1844, p. 305; R. W. Dale, *History of Congregationalism* (London, 1907), pp. 619–630.

10. *Leeds Mercury*, Apr. 1, 1843, and Oct. 30, 1847; *Patriot*, Apr. 29, 1845, Feb. 11, and Apr. 5, 1847.

11. Chalmers, *Christian and Civic Economy*, 1: 27–28, 91, 267–268, 2: 90–94; *Record*, Mar. 26, 1840; Donald Lewis, *Lighten Their Darkness: The Evangelical Mission to the Working Class* (New York, 1986), pp. 17–20.

12. *Hansard*, 1842, 60: 186–188; 1844, 75: 877; 76: 1480; 1845, 79: 358, 380–381; 81: 1426–1428; 1846, 85: 1128; 86: 1059; 87: 284; 1847, 92: 79; 1848, 96: 1304; 97: 881, 1331; 98: 527; 99: 95, 1069–1071; 101: 2–11; 1849, 103: 688–689; 104: 102–104.

13. *John Bull*, 1841: Feb. 6, p. 69; 1847: Jan. 4, p. 9, Feb. 15, p. 100; Mar. 6, p. 149; *Economist*, 1843: Sept. 23, p. 51; July 6, 1844, p. 974; 1845: May 10, p. 431, May 24, p. 480; 1847: Apr. 10, 441, May 1, p. 493; *Christian Teacher*, 1843, 5: 265.

14. *Patriot*, June 5, 1848; *North British Review*, Feb. 1845, p. 437.

15. *Sussex Agricultural Express*, Apr. 11, 1840; *New Moral World*, July 18, 1840, pp. 33–34.

16. *British Critic*, Oct. 1837, pp. 461, 466–467; Apr. 1838, pp. 350–351; Oct. 1839, pp. 344–345; *Christian Remembrancer* 12 (1846): 45; Sewell, *Christian Politics*, p. 368.

17. *Hansard*, 1839, 48: 579; 1847, 87: 1255.

18. Sewell, *Christian Politics*, p. 368.

19. *Record*, June 8, 1840.

20. D. G. Paz, *The Politics of Working-Class Education in Britain* (Manchester, 1980), pp. 62–63; Gash, *Reaction and Reconstruction*, pp. 78–79; *Christian Observer*, July 1843, p. 510.

21. A. Blomfield, *A Memoir of Charles James Blomfield*, pp. 174–178, 191–208; Welch, *Bishop Blomfield*, pp. xiii–xviii, 50–58; C. J. Blomfield, *National Education* (London, 1838); id., *A Charge, 1840* (London, 1840), pp. 1–8; William Howley, *A Charge to the Clergy, 1844* (London, 1844), pp. 20–21, 36–40; id., *Charge to the Clergy, 1840* (London, 1840), p. 16; Desmond Bowen, *The Idea of the Victorian Church* (Montreal, 1968), pp. 39, 70–72, 76, 78, 199.

22. John Hurt, *Education in Evolution* (London, 1971), pp. 32–36; G. F. A. Best, "National Education in England," *Cambridge Historical Journal* 12 (1956): 163–167; Paz, *Working Class Education*, p. 82; Machin, *Politics and the Churches in Great Britain*, p. 151; Richard Brent, *Liberal Anglican Politics* (Oxford, 1987), p. 249; N. Gash, *Reaction and Reconstruction*, pp. 78–79; *P.P.*, 1840, 40: 389–406; James Kay-Shuttleworth, *Four Periods of Education* (London, 1862), pp. 179–281.

23. *Hansard*, 1819, 41: 933; 1841, 56: Feb. 15; 57: 127; 1842, 60: 186, 64: 179; 1843, 67: 107–111; 71: 419; 1847, 89: 763; 1849, 104: 102–103.

24. Paz, *Working Class Education*, p. 117; Machin, *Politics and the Churches in Great Britain*, pp. 153–155; Kay-Shuttleworth, *Four Periods*, pp. 187–196.

25. Thompson, *Nonconformity*, p. 67; Machin, *Politics and the Churches in Great Britain*, pp. 155–160; David Hempton, *Methodism and Politics in British Society* (London, 1984), pp. 164–171; *Leeds Mercury*, Apr. 15, 1843; *Watchman*, Apr. 12 and 19, May 17, and June 28, 1843; Elizabeth Isichei, *Victorian Quakers* (Oxford, 1970), pp. 191, 198; Langley, *Charge to the Clergy, 1844*, p. 13; *Hansard*, 1843, 67: 1412–1469; 69: 1567–1570; 70: 1331–1341.

26. Smith, *Life and Work of Sir James Kay-Shuttleworth*, pp. 72–93; Kay-Shuttleworth, *Four Periods*, pp. 179–281.

27. *P.P.*, 1847, 45: 1–40; Kay-Shuttleworth, *Four Periods*, pp. 437–522; Smith, *Life and Work of Sir James Kay-Shuttleworth*, pp. 162–174, 184–185; Paz, *Working Class Education*, pp. 130–136; Hurt, *Education in Evolution*, pp. 93–95.

28. *Eclectic Review*, Nov. 1847, pp. 589–591, 608–616; Nov. 1848, pp. 597–598; *NonConformist*, Apr. 1847, pp. 207–210; *Baptist Magazine*, Aug. 1846, pp. 494–497; Feb. 1847, pp. 98–

99, Apr. 1847, pp. 265–270; *Patriot,* Feb. 15, 18, 25, Apr. 8, 1847; *Cheltenham Free Press,* Oct. 1847, 30; *Leeds Mercury,* Feb. 13, 20, and 27, and Mar. 6 and 20, 1847. The *Mercury* also lists the *Evangelical Magazine* and *Christian Witness* as opposed to government education.

29. *Watchman,* Apr. 14, 21, and 28, and June 23, 1847; *Wesleyan,* Apr. 28, 1847; *Leeds Times,* Apr. 24, 1847; David Hempton, *Methodism,* pp. 172–174; N. Gash, *Reaction and Reconstruction,* pp. 101–103; Machin, *Politics and the Churches in Great Britain,* pp. 163–165, 184–190; *Scotsman,* May 15, 1847.

30. Gash, *Reaction and Reconstruction,* 107; Machin, *Politics and the Churches in Great Britain,* pp. 184, 197; *Watchman,* Feb. 10, 1847 (eight out of nine of the grants to the Church of England); *Athenaeum,* May 29, 1847, pp. 565–566; *Leeds Intelligencer,* June 15, 1847; *Hansard,* 1852, 119: 379–395, 1195–1198.

31. *Baptist Examiner,* 1844: Jan., p. 25, Mar., p. 85; *Baptist Pioneer,* 1846: July, p. 3, Aug., p. 23, Sept., pp. 25–26, Dec. p. 67, 1 (after 1846, *Christian Pioneer; Congregational Magazine,* Feb. 1845, pp. 141, 145; *Baptist Guardian,* Nov. 21, Dec. 19, 1845; *Baptist Magazine,* 1847: Apr., p. 268, June, p. 410.

32. *Leeds Mercury,* May 21, 1842; *Congregational Magazine,* Jan. 1842, p. 34; Addison, *Religious Equality in Modern England,* p. 83; Ely, *Posthumous Works,* p. 70.

33. A. and C. Reed, *Memoirs of Andrew Reed,* p. 205.

34. *Manchester Guardian,* Apr. 24, 1847; J. Hurt, *Education in Evolution,* pp. 12, 42; *P.P.,* 1849, 42: 245ff, reports of four inspectors of poor law schools; 1850, 43: reports of fourteen inspectors of voluntary schools.

35. *Congregational Yearbook,* 1846, pp. 46–47, 1848, p. 27; Albert Peel, *These Hundred Years: A History of Congregational Union in England and Wales* (London, 1931), p. 178; *Leeds Mercury,* Apr. 3, 1847; W. T. Whitley, *A History of the British Baptist* (London, 1923), p. 289; D. Hempton, *Methodism,* pp. 171, 156–174.

36. *Westminster Review,* Jan. 1848, p. 432; *Leeds Intelligencer,* June 19, 1847; *Athenaeum,* May 29, 1847, p. 566.

37. *P.P.,* 1845, 35: 484; 1847, 45: 101, 221–223; Henry Moseley, *Faith in the Work of Teachers* (London, 1854), p. 16.

38. Henry Moseley, *A Sermon Preached on the Seventeenth Anniversary of the Bath and Wells Diocesan Society* (London, 1856), pp. 13–16; *Hansard,* 1850, 109: 45.

39. Simon, *Studies in the History of Education,* pp. 34, 211–253, 266–269.

40. *Howitt's Journal,* Jan. 9, Apr. 3, 10, May 29, 1847; *People's Journal,* Apr. 16, 25, 1846; Dawson, *Biographical Lectures,* p. 396; Wilson, *Life of George Dawson,* pp. 27, 37.

41. *Edinburgh Review,* 1844: Jan., pp. 155–156; 1847: Apr., pp. 527–528; 1848, Jan., p. 166, Oct., p. 399; *Westminster Review,* 1840: Sept., pp. 386–387, 400–403; 1842: Oct., pp. 399, 407–408; 1844: June, pp. 418–431; 1846: Oct., pp. 207–211; 1847: Apr., p. 272; 1848: Jan., pp. 427–447; 1848, Oct., pp. 65–67, 76; *Athenaeum,* 1840: June 20, pp. 491–492; 1843: Mar. 18, p. 258; 1844, June 8, pp. 517, 574–577; 1846: July 18, pp. 729–730; 1847: May 29, pp. 565–566; *Morning Chronicle,* July 13, 1840; Mar. 4, 25, 1843; June 19, 1847; *Daily News,* Feb. 4, 1846; Feb. 6, 17, Mar. 15, Apr. 12, 1847; *Weekly Chronicle,* Aug. 9, 1840; May 4, 1844; Apr. 18, 1847; *The Spectator,* 1843: Apr. 15, pp. 346–347, Apr. 29, p. 396; 1844: Apr. 13, p. 347; Sept. 7, p. 853, Oct. 5, p. 947; 1846: Sept. 5, p. 853; Oct. 24, p. 1021; 1847: Apr. 17, p. 373, Apr. 24, p. 398; McCulloch, *Discourse on . . . Political Economy,* p. 432.

42. Denison, *Present State of the Management Question,* p. 25; Dawes, *Remarks Occasioned by the Present Crusade,* pp. 11, 19–22; *Hansard,* 1853, 128: 29; S. E. Maltby, *Manchester and the Movement for National Elementary Education* (Manchester, 1902), pp. 84–88; Na-

tional Public Schools Association, *Explanations of the Objects of Education Proposed by the Public Schools Association* (London, 1851).

43. *Hansard*, 1838, 43: 727; 1841, 57: 127; 1845, 81: 1422; 82: 132; 1848, 96: 1304. "The inefficiency of religious education is in fact as notorious as the inefficiency of secular education," said the *Education Times*, Apr. 1850, p. 147. Education grants were only 2 percent of government expenditures, noted the *Times*, Feb. 27, 1850.

44. Lewis, *Lighten Their Darkness*, pp. 36–39, 117; *Record*, May 21, 1840; *Cheltenham Chronicle*, Dec. 21, 1842; *Leeds Mercury*, Dec. 19, 1840; Jan. 2 and Dec. 18, 1841.

45. *Baptist Magazine*, Sept. 1846, p. 544; *Congregational Magazine*, Nov. 1843, p. 777; *Wesleyan Times*, Jan. 8, 1849; *Watchman*, May 17, 1848.

46. *Leeds Mercury*, Feb. 6, 1841; Apr. 3, 1841; Jan. 27, 1844; Lewis, *Lighten Their Darkness*, p. 55.

47. Lewis, *Lighten Their Darkness*, pp. 120–121, 129; *Leeds Mercury*, Jan. 8, 1842; Jan. 6, 1844; Dec. 12, 1846; Dec. 23, 1848; *Baptist Magazine* June 1847, p. 407; *Congregational Yearbook*, 1846, p. 70; *Mirror*, July 3, 1841.

48. Prestige, *Pusey*, pp. 113–118; Harry Parry Liddon, *Life of Edward Bouverie Pusey* (4 vols.; London, 1893–97), 3: 1–19, 22; Southey, *Colloquies*, 2: 330; Chadwick, *Victorian Church*, 1: 506–507; *Christian Remembrancer*, Jan. 1849, pp. 6–15; *Hansard*, 1840, 55: 296, 273–326.

49. *Oxford and Cambridge Review*, 1846: July, pp. 44–53, Oct., pp. 330–343, 346; *Eclectic Review*, July 1841, p. 3.

50. *Watchman*, Mar. 17, 1847; *Baptist Examiner*, Jan. 1844, p. 6.

51. *Baptist Examiner*, Jan. 1844, p. 6; *Christian Remembrancer*, 1846, 12: 375–376.

52. Chalmers, *Civic and Christian Economy*, 1: 26–27, 67–70, 91, 268–269, 273, 291, 295–304.

53. *North British Review*, 1844: Feb., pp. 426–437; Nov., p. 38; 1846, p. 261.

54. J. H. Thom, *Spiritual Blindness and Social Disruption: A Sermon* (London, 1849), p. 23; id., *Preventive Justice and Palliative Charity*, pp. 7–9.

55. Chadwick, *Victorian Church*, 1: 505–511; Prestige, *Pusey*, pp. C 113–120; Liddon, *Pusey*, 11–14.

56. Dr. Campbell, *Jethro: A System of Lay Agency* (London, 1839), pp. 7–33, 54; *Congregational Yearbook*, 1848, 102.

57. *Select Writings of the Rev. James Dixon*, ed. Rev. Edward Lightwood (London, 1890), p. 74; Sumner, *Christian Charity*, p. iii, lx.

58. E. J. Whatley, *Life and Correspondence of Richard Whatley*, pp. 246–247; *Christian Teacher*, 1843, 4: 109; *Eclectic Review*, Nov. 1848, p. 618.

59. Sewell, *Christian Communism*, pp. 15, 19, 41–42, 111, 131–146, 169.

60. Lewis, *Lighten Their Darkness*, p. 174; *Baptist Magazine*, June 1847, p. 407; *North British Review*, Nov. 1846, p. 261; *Congregational Magazine*, 1840, 4: 44.

61. *Congregational Magazine*, Dec. 1843, pp. 903–913; July 1845, pp. 537–538.

62. *Christian Teacher*, 1840, 2: 110–114; *Prospective Review*, 1845, 6: 114; Rev. Charles Wickstead, *The Commonweal* (London, 1848), p. 11.

63. *Congregational Magazine*, Dec. 1845, pp. 905–907; *Baptist Examiner*, June 1844, p. 164; *Wesleyan*, June 16, 1847.

64. Mayhew, *London Labour and the London Poor*, 1: 6.

65. *Baptist Magazine*, June 1847, p. 407; *Congregational Yearbook*, 1846, p. 70; *Leeds Mercury*, Mar. 13, 1841; Bickersteth, *Works*, 8: 310.

66. *Leeds Mercury*, Dec. 26, 1840; Jan. 6, 1844.

67. *Westminster Review,* May 1843, pp. 408–409.

68. Sampson Low, *The Charities of London* (London, 1851).

69. *Bentley's Miscellany* 1840, 7: 601; *Athenaeum,* Jan. 30, 1847, p. 117.

70. *British Critic* 26 (July 1839): 196–197, 223; *Christian Remembrancer,* 1849, 16: 342.

71. *Englishman's Magazine,* Oct. 1842, p. 234; Rev. John Armstrong, *Church Endowments* (London, 1839), p. 18; *Western Times,* Jan. 20, 1844.

72. Gresley, *Practical Sermons,* p. 171; Prestige, *Pusey,* p. 113; *Christian Remembrancer,* Jan. 1849, pp. 1–9; *Quarterly Review,* Dec. 1846, pp. 127–141; Dec. 1847, 142ff.

73. F. K. Prochaska, *The Voluntary Impulse: Philanthropy in Modern Britain* (London, 1988), p. 59; Ian Bradley, *The Call to Seriousness* (New York, 1978), p. 136; Low, *Charities,* pp. vii–xi.

74. David Owen, *English Philanthropy, 1660–1960* (Cambridge, Mass., 1964), p. 163; Ralph Wardlaw, *Lectures on Female Prostitution* (Glasgow, 1842), pp. 136–139; Mary Carpenter, *Reformatory Schools* (London, 1850), pp. 38–39, 53–55, 210–260, 324–345; Ford K. Brown, *Fathers of the Victorians: The Age of Wilberforce* (Cambridge, 1961), pp. 329–340.

75. R. Wardlaw, *Female Prostitution,* pp. 9–160; *Quarterly Review,* Dec. 1846, pp. 127–141.

76. Rosamond and Florence Davenport-Hill, *The Recorder of Birmingham: A Memoir of Matthew Davenport Hill* (London, 1878); Owen, *English Philanthropy,* pp. 102, 103, 111, 117, 152; Harriet Martineau, *Biographical Sketches* (London, 1876), pp. 319ff; William Allen, *The Life of William Allen* (London, 1846), 1: 72, 117, 252–253, 269, 344, 349; 2: 205–206, 355, 392; 3: 19, 22, 29, 141, 188, 292–294.

77. John Woodward, *To Do the Sick No Harm* (London, 1974), p. 144; Brian Abel-Smith, *The Hospitals, 1800–1898* (London, 1964), p. 40; Ruth G. Hodgkinson, *The Origins of the National Health Service: The Medical Services of the New Poor Law, 1834–1871* (Berkeley and Los Angeles, 1967), p. 199.

78. Woodward, *To Do The Sick No Harm,* pp. 38–43, 46, 48–50, 64, 128; Abel-Smith, *Hospitals,* pp. 24–27; Hodgkinson, *Origins of the National Health Service,* pp. 198–200.

79. *Metropolitan Magazine,* 1834, 10: 331; 11: 1; Thom, *Preventive Justice and Palliative Charity,* p. 17; Melville, *Sermons . . . on Public Occasions,* p. 200.

80. Wardlaw, *Female Prostitution,* pp. 157–158; Benjamin Love, *Chapters on Working People* (London, 1843), p. 19; Burton, *Political and Social Economy,* p. 159; W. L. Burn, *Age of Equipoise* (New York, 1964), p. 125; *Westminster Review,* June 1845, pp. 451, 459.

81. *Watchman,* Jan. 19, 1842.

82. *Manchester Guardian,* Dec. 21, 1842; *Leeds Mercury,* Mar. 12, 1842; Jan. 7, May 13, 1843; Feb. 5, 1848.

83. *Scotsman,* Mar. 17, 1847; Mary Daly, *The Famine in Ireland* (Dublin, 1986), pp. 68, 79, 87–93.

84. Addison, *Distress in Manchester,* p. 41; Benjamin Love, *The Handbook of Manchester* (Manchester, 1842), pp. 96, 128–137.

85. *Leeds Mercury,* June 7, Nov. 1, 1845; Jan. 1, Mar. 21, Apr. 11, June 13, Oct. 10, 1846; *North of England Magazine,* 1842: Apr., pp. 164–166, Nov., p. 45; Briggs, *Victorian Cities,* pp. 25, 47–48, 135–139, 153, 157, 160–162, 170–172, 246, 255, 274; A. Temple Patterson, *Radical Leicester,* pp. 369, 379; Peter Bailey, *Leisure and Class in Victorian England* (London, 1978), pp. 36–38, 50–53.

86. *Spectator,* Nov. 25, 1843, p. 1117.

87. Hodgkinson, *National Health Service,* pp. 254–257.

88. *Sussex Agricultural Express,* Jan. 25, 1845; *Manchester Times,* Jan. 2, 1841; *Spectator,* Nov. 25, 1843, p. 1117.

89. *Spectator*, Nov. 9, 1844, p. 1067; *Scotsman*, Sept. 1, 1847.

90. Owen, *English Philanthropy*, pp. 182–198; 247–275, 277.

91. Carpenter, *Reformatory Schools*, pp. 38, 120–132, 148–149, 154–155, 211, 258; *Quarterly Review*, Dec. 1846, pp. 127–141; Owen, *English Philanthropy*, pp. 120–132.

92. *Quarterly Review*, Dec. 1847, pp. 142–152; Owen, *English Philanthropy*, pp. 376–378.

93. *Manchester Guardian*, Dec. 21, 1842; *Woolmer's Exeter and Plymouth Gazette*, Feb. 20, 1847; *Leeds Mercury*, Dec. 19, 1840, May 28, 1842, May 13, 1843; Mary Daly, Kevin Nowland, "The Political Background," and Thomas P. O'Neil, "The Organization and Administration of Relief" in *The Great Famine*, ed. R. Dudley Edwards and T. Desmond Williams (Dublin, 1956), pp. 174–175, 227–228, 235–237, 241, 255, 258; Woodham Smith, *Great Hunger*, pp. 296, 411.

94. Love, *Handbook of Manchester*, p. 106; *Journal of the Statistical Society*, Oct. 1842, 289–290; William C. Henry, *A Biographical Notice of the Late Very Reverend Richard Dawes* (London, 1867), pp. 11–13; R. Dawes, *Hints of an Improved and a Self-Paying System of National Education* (London, 1847).

95. *P.P.*, 1849, 14: 79; *Westminster Review*, Apr. 1828, p. 387; J. M. Baernrether, *English Associations of Workingmen* (London, 1889), p. 162; P. H. J. H. Gosden, *Self-Help: Voluntary Associations in Nineteenth-Century Britain* (New York, 1974), pp. 12, 227; *Spectator*, Feb. 14, 1846, p. 990.

96. Sydney and Beatrice Webb, *The History of Trade Unionism* (London, 1902), p. 18; J. H. Clapham, *An Economic History of Modern Britain* (3 vols.; Cambridge, 1926–38), vol. 1, *The Early Railway Age, 1820–1850*, p. 296.

97. Grimshawe, *Memoir of … Legh Richmond*, pp. 82–86; Osborne, *Hints to the Charitable*, pp. 36–44; Sandford, *Parochialia*, pp. 348–351; Girdlestone, *The Cause and Cure of Abject Poverty*, pp. 10–11; Rev. Thomas Dale, *Address to the Parishioners of St. Pancras* (London, 1847), p. 13.

98. *P.P.*, 1848, 26: 44, 60; Gosden, *Self-Help*, pp. 33–34.

99. *Morning Post*, June 5, 1848.

100. Gosden, *Self-Help*, pp. 22–24, 29–30, 42–47; *P.P.*, 1848, 26: 4, 14, 24–30; 1849, 14: 5, 74–75.

101. *Leeds Mercury*, May 21, 1842.

102. *P.P.*, 1848, 26: 3–4, 24–25, 40–48, 57–59; 1849, 14: 21–22, 66, 78.

103. Gosden, *Self-Help*, pp. 22–24; *P.P.*, 1848, 26: 11–12, 20, 40–42; 46–48, 58, 72; 1849, 14: 21–22, 34, 78, 85–86; G. Calvert Holland, *The Vital Statistics of Sheffield* (London, 1843), pp. 206–207.

104. *Eclectic Review*, Apr. 1848, pp. 457–458; *Christian Teacher*, 1840, 2: 111; *Leeds Mercury*, Dec. 21, 1844; *Witness*, Oct. 5, 1844; *North British Review*, Nov. 1847, pp. 68–69; *Spectator*, Feb. 14, 1846, p. 132.

105. Hall, *Dr. Duncan*, pp. 29–49; Gosden, *Self-Help*, pp. 208–214; Southey, *Essays*, 1: 217; Oliver Horne, *A History of Savings Banks* (London, 1947), pp. 28–30, 43–44, 93–101, 141; *The Works of Jeremy Bentham*, ed. J. Bowring (London, 1838–43), 8: 409–411; Poynter, *Society and Pauperism*, pp. 289–291; *Journal of the Statistical Society*, Mar. 1846, pp. 1–4; SDUK, "Cottage Evenings," *Working Man's Companion*, 1831, pp. 20–26.

106. Hall, *Dr. Duncan*, pp. 1–86; Rev. Henry Duncan, *An Essay on the Nature and Advantages of Savings Banks* (Edinburgh, 1815), p. 13; Gosden, *Self-Help*, pp. 207, 211, 213–221; G. Calvert Holland, *An Inquiry Into the Moral, Social and Intellectual Condition of Sheffield* (London, 1839), p. 131; Love, *Handbook of Manchester*, p. 110.

107. Gosden, *Self-Help*, pp. 144–157.

108. *Manchester Times*, Feb. 27, 1841; *Howitt's Journal*, Mar. 13, 1847, pp. 144–146; *People's Journal*, Aug. 14, 1847, pp. 270–273; *Union*, Oct. 1, 1842, p. 288; *Mirror*, 1841, Feb. 13, p. 101; Feb. 20, p. 114; Mar. 13, p. 165.

109. *People's Journal*, Nov. 14, 1846, pp. 270–273; Mar. 27, 1846, pp. 136–137; Smiles, *Autobiography*, p. 104; *P.P.*, 1848, 26: 30–31; Gosden, *Self-Help*, pp. 1–2.

110. Harold Perkin, *The Origins of Modern English Society* (London, 1969), p. 383; *P.P.*, 1848, 26: 25, 44–45; 1849, 14: 25, 47, 74, 77.

111. W. H. G. Armytage, *Heavens Below: Utopian Experiments in England, 1560–1960* (London, 1961), pp. 216–217; *Times*, May 27, 1846.

112. G. J. Holyoake, *A History of Co-operation in England: Its Literature and Its Advocates* (2 vols.; London, 1875–79), 1: 193.

113. Torben Christensen, *Origin and History of Christian Socialism, 1848–54* (Arhus, Denmark, 1962), p. 227; *Democratic Review*, 1849: Aug., p. 132; Sept., p. 135; Nov., p. 206; Dec., p. 248; *Red Republican*, 1850, Sept. 14, p. 101; *People's Journal*, Mar. 20, 1847, pp. 157–159.

114. Armytage, *Heavens Below*, pp. 134–137, 185–191; G. D. H. Cole, *The History of Socialist Thought: The Forerunners* (Manchester, 1945), 1: 3–6, 38–72; Richard Pankhurst, *The St. Simonians, Mill and Carlyle* (London, 1957), pp. 1–5; Holyoake, *History of Co-operation in England*, 1: 229.

115. Thompson, *Labour Rewarded*, pp. v, 90–91; Holyoake, *History of Co-operation in England*, 1: 229; Pankhurst, *St. Simonians*, pp. 31–35, 147–148; *Christian Socialist*, Mar. 22, 1851, p. 164; Packe, *Life of John Stuart Mill*, pp. 308–314; J. S. Mill, *Autobiography*, pp. 125–126; *Edinburgh Review*, Apr. 1845, p. 516.

116. Cole, *History of Socialist Thought*, 1: 71–73; Boase, *Modern English Biography*, 6: 33; *DNB*, 3: 234; 28: 122–125.

117. J. F. C. Harrison, *Quest for the New Moral World: Robert Owen and the Owenites in Britain and America* (New York, 1969), pp. 45–91, 151–197; Robert Owen, *A New View of Society* [1813–14]; *and, Report to the County of Lanark* [1821], ed. V. A. C. Gatrell (Harmondsworth, Eng., 1970), pp. 43, 7–83; Cole, *Century of Co-operation*, pp. 23–25.

118. Christensen, *Christian Socialism*, pp. 59–160; *Christian Socialist*, Nov. 2, 1850, pp. 1–5.

119. J. S. Mill, *Dissertations and Discussions*, 1: 196; id., *Principles of Political Economy*, 2: 324–325; *Westminster Review*, July 1848, pp. 298–299, Jan. 1849, p. 523; *Howitt's Journal*, 1847: Mar. 6, p. 141, Mar. 20, p. 171; *People's Journal*, 1846: June 20, pp. 346–348, Nov. 14, pp. 270–273; *Edinburgh Review*, Apr. 1848, p. 446; J. F. C. Harrison, *Social Reform in Victorian Leeds: The Work of James Hole, 1820–1895* (Leeds, 1954), p. 42.

120. Harrison, *Quest for a New Moral World*, p. 49; John Minter Morgan, *Colloquies on Religion and Religious Education* (1837; reprint, London, 1850), pp. 122–135, 185–187.

121. *Christian Socialist*, Feb. 22, 1851, p. 135; Christensen, *Christian Socialism*, p. 128; *New Moral World*, July 18, 1840, p. 35.

122. Holyoake, *History of Co-operation in England*, 2: 351; *Howitt's Journal*, 1847: Feb. 6, p. 77, Feb. 20, p. 15; J. S. Mill, *Dissertations*, 1: 196–197, 214.

123. Maurice, *Life of F. D. Maurice*, 1: 277; Holyoake, *History of Co-operation in England*, 2: 363; *The Movement*, 2: 103.

124. Armytage, *Heavens Below*, pp. 86–90; *People's Journal*, Sept. 19, 1846, p. 161.

125. Armytage, *Heavens Below*, pp. 213–214; *The Land For the Labourers and the Fraternity of Nations*, ed. Thomas Cooper (London, 1848), pp. 8–9; Harrison, *Social Reform in Leeds*, p. 2.

126. Harrison, *Quest for the New Moral World*, pp. 173, 163–194; Holyoake, *History of Co-operation in England*, 1: 271–277, 282–290; Cole, *Century of Cooperatives*, pp. 21, 32, 34, 35.

127. John Minter Morgan, *The Christian Commonwealth* (London, 1845), pp. 35–54; Harrison, *Quest for the New Moral World*, pp. 76, 172–173, 180–190.

128. Christensen, *Christian Socialism*, pp. 142–148, 162; Masterman, *John Malcolm Ludlow*, p. 95; Cole, *Century of Cooperatives*, pp. 24–25.

129. *Edinburgh Review*, Apr. 1845, pp. 516, 519; J. S. Mill, *Principles of Political Economy*, 2: 324–328; *P.P.*, 1850, 19: 253–255, 257, 258.

130. Christensen, *Christian Socialism*, pp. 162–165, 227, 287–290, 319–320, 358–361.

131. *P.P.*, 1850, 19: 255–256; Holyoake, *History of Co-operation in England*, 2: 35–52; Cole, *Century of Cooperatives*, pp. 57–73; Gosden, *Self-Help*, pp. 182–186.

132. Cole, *Century of Cooperatives*, pp. 38–66; Holyoake, *History of Co-operation in England*, 2: 39, 51.

CHAPTER 9

1. Brown, *Fathers of the Victorians*, p. 317; *Edinburgh Review*, July 1844, p. 306.

2. *Watchman*, May 19, 1847; *Economist*, July 17, 1847, p. 809.

3. Melville, *Sermons . . . on Public Occasions*, p. 46; R. W. Hamilton, *Sermons, Second Series* (Leeds, 1846), pp. 608–609; Rev. William Stowell, *Twelve Sermons* (London, 1850), p. cxxxiii.

4. Charles Dickens, *Illustrated Cabinet Edition* (Boston, n.d.), *Sketches by Boz*, 1: ch. 6, pp. 49–56, ch. 19, pp. 233–240; *Bleak House*, 1: ch. 4, pp. 94–95, ch. 8, pp. 149, 152, ch. 7, p. 158, ch. 14, pp. 272, 276, ch. 15, p. 302, ch. 16, p. 329; 2: ch. 3, p. 68; *Our Mutual Friend*, bk. 2, ch. 1, pp. 322–327. Norris Pope, *Dickens and Charity* (New York, 1978).

5. *The Philanthropist*, July 1, 1843, p. 13; Thomas Carlyle, *Critical and Miscellaneous Essays* (London, 1899), 4: 162, 170, 172; id., *Latter Day Pamphlets*, pp. 43, 58.

6. *The Oxford English Dictionary*, 2d ed., s.v. "philanthropist."

7. *The Works of Percy Bysshe Shelley*, ed. Harry Buxton Forman (London, 1880), 5: 385–386; William Godwin, *Enquiry Concerning Political Justice* (London, 1776), p. 388.

8. Godwin, *Enquiry Concerning Political Justice*, p. 379; Jeremy Bentham, *Deontology* (London, 1834), 1: 299, 2: 36, ch. 3, "Extra-regarding Prudence," pp. 133, 259–260.

9. Dugald Stewart, *The Philosophy of the Active and Moral Powers of Man*, vol. 7 of *Works of Dugald Stewart*, ed. Hamilton, pp. iii–v, xi, 18–19, 23, 35, 39, 45, 183–184; Thomas Brown, *Lecture on Ethics* (Edinburgh, 1846), p. 254; *The Second Report and Address of the Philanthropic Society* (London, 1788).

10. *The English Chartist Circular*, 1842, 2: 205; *New Moral World*, July 18, 1840, p. 35; Thomas Cooper, *The Triumph of Perseverance and Enterprise* (London, 1854), pp. 166–167.

11. Horne, *New Spirit of the Age*, introduction and table of contents.

12. *Plymouth Times*, Jan. 27, 1844; Celina Fox, "The Development of Social Reportage in England," *Past and Present*, Feb. 1977, pp. 107–108.

13. *People's Journal*, June 6, 1846, pp. 312–313; *Howitt's Journal*, Aug. 21, 1847, pp. 123–125.

14. Holyoake, *History of Co-operation*, 1: 120.

15. James Mill, *Essays on I. Government and Education* (London, n.d. [1828]; reprinted from supplement to the *Encyclopaedia Britannica*); Byron, *What De Fellenberg Has Done for Education*; Thomas Hodgskin, *Popular Political Economy* (London, 1827).

16. William Allen, *The Life of William Allen* (Philadelphia, 1847), 1: 91–92; Alexander Bain, *Life of James Mill* (London, 1882), 1: 81ff.

17. Jo Manton, *Mary Carpenter and the Children of the Streets* (London, 1976), pp. 83–84, 112–113; R. and F. Davenport-Hill, *Recorder of Birmingham*, pp. 156, 160–166, 171–175.

18. *Christian Teacher*, 1841, 3: 439.

19. *Eclectic Review*, Apr. 1841, p. 421; *Blackwood's*, Dec. 1840, p. 814; Mar. 1841, p. 370; Mar. 1849, p. 312; Sept. 1844, p. 274; *Quarterly Review*, Jan. 1831, p. 277.

20. James Grant, *Memoirs of Sir George Sinclair* (London, 1870), p. 225; *Mirror*, Aug. 2, 1845, p. 88; *Leeds Intelligencer*, Aug. 15, 1840.

21. Carter, *Memoir of John Armstrong*, p. 169 (Armstrong writing in the *Christian Remembrancer*).

22. J. Giles, *Socialism* (Leeds, 1839), p. 72.

23. Wilberforce, *Practical View of the Prevailing Religious System*, p. 271; Chalmers, *Christian and Civic Economy*, pp. 71–73.

24. Owen, *English Philanthropy*, p. 93; R. W. Church, *The Oxford Movement, Twelve Years, 1833–1845* (London, 1891), pp. 12–13; Gisborne, *Enquiry into the Duties of Men*, pp. 114–115.

25. *Christian Observer*, Nov. 1845, p. 692; *Congregational Magazine*, Oct. 1842, p. 705.

26. Francis Close, *Occasional Sermons*, pp. 220–226, 336, 340–346, 385–386, 397–398; id., *The Sin and Danger of Rebellion* (London, 1848); W. E. Adam, *Memoirs of a Social Atom* (London, 1903) 1: 11–18; Simona Pakenham, *Cheltenham: A Biography* (London, 1971), pp. 105–115; *Cheltenham Examiner*, Jan. 27, Feb. 10, 24, Mar. 10, 24, Apr. 11, Oct. 6, 1841; Jan. 24, 31, Feb. 14, 21, Apr. 10, 1844; *Cheltenham Chronicle*, Feb. 2, 9, 16, June 22, Sept. 28, Nov. 9, Dec. 21, 1842; Jan. 6, 20, Apr. 7, 14, May 19, 26, July 16, Oct. 6, 1847.

27. Brown, *Fathers of the Victorians*, pp. 329–340; 353–360.

28. William Allen, *Life of William Allen*, 1: 55, 75, 68, 91, 131; Alexander Bain, *James Mill: A Biography* (London, 1882), 81, 160.

29. *Christian Observer*, Apr. 1848, p. 262; Elizabeth Fry, *Memoir of the Life of Elizabeth Fry, with Extracts from Her Journal and Letters*, ed. by two of her daughters (2 vols.; 1847; 2d rev. ed., London, 1848), 1: 18, 36, 41, 47.

30. *Memoirs of Sir Thomas Fowell Buxton*, ed. Charles Buxton (London, 1866), pp. 34, 42, 44; Elizabeth Isichei, *Victorian Quakers* (Oxford, 1970), pp. 6–7.

31. Ellen Gibson Wilson, *Thomas Clarkson: A Biography* (London, 1989), pp. 55, 93, 102, 134; Thomas Clarkson, *Essay on the Slavery and Commerce of the Human Species* (London, 1786), pp. 13–14.

32. *Edinburgh Review*, July 1844, pp. 259–260; Wilberforce, *Practical View of the Prevailing Religious System*, p. 147.

33. Wilson, *Life of George Dawson*, pp. 14–17, 20–34; Thomas Binney, *Righteousness Exalteth a Nation* (London, 1840), pp. 3–33; Arthur Miall, *Life of Edward Miall*, pp. 23, 107–113; Thomas Bunting, *The Life of Jabez Bunting* (London, 1859); Rev. Samuel Coley, *The Life of the Rev. Thomas Collins* (London, 1869); Gordon Rupp, *Thomas Jackson, Methodist Patriarch* (London, 1954); Thomas Jackson, *The Life of the Rev. Robert Newton* (London, 1855); Geoffrey Finlayson, *The Seventh Earl of Shaftesbury, 1801–1885* (London, 1981), p. 196.

34. Brown, *Fathers of the Victorians*, p. 123.

35. Kitson Clark, *Churchmen and the Condition of England*, pp. 71, 71–75, 106, 178, 186, 199, 211, 276, 328, 332; McClatchey, *Oxfordshire Clergy*, pp. 70–74, 92, 132–134.

36. *Athenaeum*, Jan. 30, 1847, p. 117; *British Studies*, Autumn 1983, p. 87.

37. *Fraser's*, Sept. 1848, p. 444.

38. *People's Journal*, Mar. 7, 1846; *Decorator's Assistant*, Oct. 1848, p. 232; *Athenaeum*, June 27, 1846, p. 655.

39. George Boole, *The Right Use of Leisure* (London, 1847), p. 25; Owen, *English Philanthropy*, p. 175.

40. Richard Whately, *Remains of the Late Edward Copleston* (London, 1854), p. 97.

41. *Blackwood's* June 1846, pp. 733–734; *Westminster Review*, Feb. 1843, p. 149; Sept. 1844, p. 384; June 1845, pp. 461, 463. And see Caroline Sheridan Norton, *The Child of the Islands: A Poem* (London, 1845).

42. *John Bull*, Dec. 26, 1840, p. 619; *Devizes and Wiltshire Gazette*, Apr. 18, 1844.

43. *Edinburgh Review*, Apr. 1845, p. 499–506; Ure, *Philosophy of Manufactures*, p. 8.

44. *Blackwood's*, June 1846, p. 733; Feb. 1841, p. 198; *John Bull*, Apr. 10, 1841, p. 176; Jan. 4, 1847, p. 39; Feb. 15, 1847, p. 100.

45. Sewell, *Christian Politics*, p. 30; *Quarterly Review*, 1842, 70: 338–339; 71: 312–313; June 1848, p. 139; Carter, *Memoir of John Armstrong*, p. 169; John Armstrong, *A Further Appeal For the Formation of Church Penitentiaries* (London, 1851), p. 10.

46. *British Critic*, 1838, 23: 186–187; *Englishman's Magazine*, Oct. 1842, p. 234; *English Review*, Jan. 1844, pp. 85–87.

47. William Parry-Jones, *The Trade in Lunacy* (London, 1972), p. 16.

48. Sandford, *Parochialia*, p. 314; F. G. Hopgood, *An Address on the Principles and Practices of Christian Almsgiving* (London, 1839), pp. 2–5; Hussey, *Christian's Obligation to the Poor*, p. 16.

49. H. P. Liddon, *Walter K. Hamilton, Bishop of Salisbury* (London, 1890), p. 15; Paget, *Warden of Berkingholt*, p. 133; Rev. J. E. N. Molesworth, *Common Sense, or, Everybody's Magazine* 1: 167; *Western Times*, Apr. 3, 1847.

50. Gresley, *Parochial Sermons*, p. 181; Sandford, *Parochialia*, p. 314; Rev. F. Paget, *Sermons* (London, 1844), p. 265.

51. *English Review*, Jan. 1844, pp. 48–104; Herbert, *Proposals for the Better Application of Cathedral Institutions*, pp. 11–27.

52. Thomas Dale, *Address to the Parishioners of St. Pancras, Middlesex* (London, 1847), p. 17; Rev. Francis Close, *An Apology for the Evangelical Party, Being a Reply to the Pamphlet of the Rev. W. Gresley* (London, 1846), p. 14.

53. *British Critic*, July 1839, p. 196.

54. Brian Harrison, "Philanthropy and the Victorians," *Victorian Studies*, June 1966, p. 372; William Thom, *Rhymes and Recollections of a Hand-Loom Weaver* (London, 1845), p. 136; Walter Jerrold, *Douglas Jerrold and Punch* (London, 1910), p. 83; *Times*, Dec. 5, 1850.

55. *Weekly Chronicle*, Mar. 23, 1844; *Daily News*, Mar. 12, 1846; *Westminster Review*, June 1840, p. 149; *Bentley's Magazine* 7 (1840): 134.

56. Brian Harrison, "Two Roads to Social Reform: Francis Place and the Drunken Committee," *Historical Journal* 11 (1968): 293; *Monthly Repository*, n.s., 8 (1834): 628; *British Quarterly* 1 (1845): 558–559.

57. Harriet Martineau, *Poor Law and Paupers* (London, 1833), pp. 64, 137, 196–202; Scrope, *Principles of Political Economy*, p. 329; Marcet, *Rich and Poor*, pp. 1–2; Burton, *Political and Social Economy*, p. 159.

58. Thom, *Preventive Justice and Palliative Charity*, pp. 1–5, 14–16; *Christian Teacher*, 1842,

4: 106, 109–110; Holland, *Vital Statistics of Sheffield*, pp. 29, 41, 137–138; id., *An Inquiry into the Moral, Social and Intellectual Condition of the Industrious Classes of Sheffield* (London, 1839), pt. 1, pp. 17, 29, 30.

59. *Weekly Dispatch*, July 3, 1842; *Daily News*, May 20, 1846; *Spectator*, Jan. 20, 1844, p. 60; Edward Edwards, *A Letter on the Present Position of the Education Question* (London, 1847), p. 24.

60. *Bentley's Miscellany*, 1839, 6: 575; *Spectator*, May 1, 1841, p. 421; *Sunday Times*, May 9, 1847; Joshua Toulmin Smith, *Local Self-Government Un-Mystified: A Vindication of Common Sense, Human Nature, and Practical Improvement, against the Manifesto of Centralism Put Forth at the Social Science Association* (London, 1857), p. 28; *Athenaeum*, Nov. 2, 1844, p. 992; *Westminster Review*, Feb. 1843, p. 149.

61. *Economist*, Aug. 5, 1854, p. 837; Nov. 29, 1845, p. 1192.

62. *Durham Chronicle*, July 16, 1847.

63. Harrison, "Philanthropy and the Victorians," p. 364; E. P. Thompson, "Political Education of Henry Mayhew," *Victorian Studies*, Sept. 1967, pp. 52–53.

64. *Athenaeum*, Aug. 19, 1848, p. 828; *Eclectic Review*, Nov. 1849, p. 548; Cyrus Redding, *Fifty Years' Recollections, Literary and Personal, with Observations on Men and Things* (3 vols.; London, 1858), 3: 319.

65. *Punch*, 4: 53; *Fraser's*, June 1846, p. 669.

66. *Sun*, Mar. 18, 1844; Beggs, *Inquiry into the Extent and Causes of Juvenile Depravity*, p. 135; Mayhew, *London Labour and London Poor*, p. 317.

67. Owen, *English Philanthropy*; F. K. Prochaska, *Women and Philanthropy in Nineteenth-Century England* (New York, 1980) and *Voluntary Impulse*.

68. Woodward, *To Do The Sick No Harm*, pp. 25–27, 36, 48, 53, 57–59, 60, 64–66, 70, 128, 130–131, 142; Melville, *Sermons . . . on Public Occasions*, p. 201.

69. Kohl, *England and Wales*, pp. 107, 113–115, 120–121; Love, *Handbook of Manchester*, pp. 87–88, 96, 101, 106, 119–145, 170–184; *Manchester Times*, Feb. 20, 27, Apr. 17, 24, 1841.

70. *P.P.*, 1843, 40: 351–361; Carpenter, *Reformatory Schools*, pp. 5off, 242–243; 263, 338–343, 400; Manton, *Mary Carpenter*, pp. 9, 83–84, 112–116.

71. James Hammerton, *Emigrant Gentlewomen, Genteel Poverty and Female Emigration* (London, 1979), pp. 53–65; *Hull Advertiser*, Apr. 16, 1847.

72. Birks, *Memoir of . . . Bickersteth*, 2: 366–367.

73. Brown, *Fathers of the Victorians*, pp. 70, 261, 249, 250, 273, 336; Low, *Charities of London*, pp. vii–xi; Prochaska, *Voluntary Impulse*, p. 59; Owen, *English Philanthropy*, p. 128; Bradley, *Call to Seriousness*.

74. Prochaska, *Women and Philanthropy*, pp. 30, 37, 42–43, 49, 163–170, 176; Fry, *Memoir of the Life of Elizabeth Fry*, 1: 201–202, 252–254, 265–274, 289–295, 367; *Congregational Magazine*, 1840, 4: 34.

75. Rev. Hugh M'Neil, *Anti-Slavery and Anti-Popery: A Letter Addressed to E. Cropper, Esquire, and T. B. Horsfall, Esquire* (London, 1838), p. 3; Owen, *English Philanthropy*, pp. 165–167.

76. Lewis, *Lighten Their Darkness*, pp. 113, 116; Bickersteth, *Works*, 8: 302; Peel, *These Hundred Years*, p. 151; Owen, *English Philanthropy*, p. 140; Kohl, *England and Wales*, p. 114; *Leeds Mercury*, Dec. 26, 1840; Dec. 14, 1844; Dec. 12, 1846.

77. *Sun*, June 2, 1847; *Sunday Times*, May 9, 1847.

78. *John Bull*, May 13, 1848, p. 458; *Hull Advertiser*, May 17, 1847; *Westminster Review*, Sept.

1840, p. 386; *Christian Teacher*, 1841, 3: 439; Harriet Ritvo, *The Animal Estate: The English and Other Creatures in the Victorian Age* (Cambridge, Mass., 1987), pp. 125–160.

79. *Hansard*, 1846, 84: 17; *Sussex Agricultural Express*, June 26, 1841; *Edinburgh Review*, Jan. 1844, pp. 129–131.

80. *Quarterly Review*, June 1848, p. 141.

81. Owen, *English Philanthropy*, pp. 142–143; Prochaska, *Voluntary Impulse*, pp. 68–69.

82. Norris Pope, review of *George Williams and the Y.M.C.A.: A Study in Victorian Social Attitudes*, by Clyde Binfield (London, 1973), *Victorian Studies*, June 1974, p. 440; Owen, *English Philanthropy*, p. 164.

83. Anon., *Destitution, Prostitution and Crime in Edinburgh* (Edinburgh, 1850), pp. 6–7; *Punch*, 2: 26; W. P. Alison, *Observations on the Epidemic Fever of 1843* (Edinburgh, 1844), p. 23.

84. Lewis, *Lighten Their Darkness*, p. 116.

85. Rev. Henry Worsley, *Juvenile Depravity* (London, 1849), pp. 192–193.

86. *Times*, Jan. 23, 1854.

87. Carpenter, *Reformatory Schools*, pp. 50, 245, 339; *P.P.*, 1852, 7: 30–39; Allen, *Life of William Allen*, 2: 323; *Journal of the Statistical Society*, 1842, 5: 282; *North British Review*, May 1849, pp. 78–84, 90.

88. Lucas, *Life of Frederick Lucas*, p. 24; Standish Meachem, *Lord Bishop: The Life of Samuel Wilberforce* (Cambridge, Mass., 1970), p. 104; *Christian Observer*, June 1845, p. 692.

89. Sandford, *Parochialia*, p. 334; Rev. John Ely, *Works*, pp. lxxvi, 18–19.

90. Chalmers, *Works*, 4: 54; Campbell, *Jethro*, pp. 54, 65; Lewis, *Lighten Their Darkness*, pp. 168, 174.

91. Lewis, *Lighten Their Darkness*, pp. 39, 54, 60–61, 107, 111.

92. Hilton, *Age of Atonement*, pp. 10, 96–97; 131–132; 107, 211–215; Lewis, *Lighten Their Darkness*, pp. 100–102; Edward Paxton Hood, *The Age and Its Architects* (London, 1952), p. 163.

93. Bickersteth, *Works*; Rev. T. R. Birks, *The Sin of England* (London, 1845); *Protestant Truth, the Basis of National Prosperity* (London, 1848), p. 28; Rev. Hugh M'Neil, *England's Caesar* (London, 1844); id., *The State in Danger* (London, 1847); id., *Collected Works of the Rev. Hugh M'Neil* (London, 1877); id., *Anti-Slavery and Anti-Popery*; id., *Famine*, p. 27.

94. David Mole, "The Church of England and Society in Birmingham" (Ph.D. diss., Cambridge University), pp. 76–79.

95. Fry, *Memoir of the Life of Elizabeth Fry*, 1: 252–268, 304; Martin Wiener, *Reconstructing the Criminal: Culture, Law, and Policy in England, 1830–1914* (Cambridge, 1990), pp. 133–134; Caroline Fox, *Memoirs of Old Friends* (London, 1882), 1: 313–314.

96. Rev. J. Field, *Prison Discipline: The Advantage of the Separate System* (London, 1846), pp. 88–89; 186; G. L. Chesterton, *Revelations of Prison Life* (London, 1856), pp. 171, 183–188; Ursula Henriques, "The Rise and Decline of the Separate System," *Past and Present*, Feb. 1972, p. 72; J. Gurney, *Thoughts on Habits and Discipline* (London, 1844); Rev. George Heaton, *The Clergyman in the Gaol* (London, 1847), pp. 18, 48, 56; *Record*, Apr. 14, 1842; Mar. 1, 1847; Joseph Adshead, *Our Present Gaol System* (London, 1849), p. 72; id., *Prisons and Prisoners* (London, 1845), p. 86.

97. Elaine Hadley, "Natives in a Strange Land," *Victorian Studies*, Spring 1990, pp. 411–430; *Times*, May 5, 1839; Brian Harrison, "Philanthropy," *Victorian Studies*, June 1966, p. 369; Bradley, *Call to Seriousness*, pp. 99, 101, 104, 109.

98. *Hansard*, 1841, 57: 749; 1842, 65: 74–75, 511–513; Hilton, *Age of Atonement*, pp. 104, 108;

Chalmers, *Works*, 6: 121–124; *North British Review*, 1844, 2: 40–41; Chalmers, *Christian and Civic Economy*, 1: 8; Melville, *Sermon ... on Public Occasions*, p. 200; J. E. N. Molesworth, *Sermons for Sunday, Festival and Fasts* (London, 1855), p. 167.

99. *Christian Observer*, 1841, 41: 465–466; 1842, 42: 181–188; 1845, 45: 629; 1847, 47: 127; 1847, 47: 244–245; 1849, 49: 82–88; *Record*, Apr. 2, 6, 1840; Jan. 9, 1840, June 30, 1842; Feb. 18, 1847; Daly, *Famine in Ireland*, pp. 83, 89.

100. Sumner, *Christian Charity*, p. 100; Melville, *Sermons ... in Public Occasions*, p. 200; Christian Instruction Society, *Thirteen Lectures to Socialists*, p. 136.

101. *Blackwood's*, July 1844, p. 8.

CHAPTER 10

1. J. S. Mill, *Dissertation and Discussions*, 1: 197; *Journal of the Leeds Polytechnic Exhibition*, 1845, p. 42; Randall McGowen, "A Powerful Sympathy," *Journal of British Studies*, July 1986, p. 333.

2. *Athenaeum*, Mar. 23, 1844, pp. 263–264; *People's Journal*, Jan. 31, 1846, p. 68.

3. *Sunday Times*, Jan. 14, 1844; *Morning Herald*, July 25, 1844; *Standard*, June 9, 1842; *Morning Chronicle*, Sept. 21, 1848.

4. *Westminster Review*, Oct. 1842, p. 390; *Christian Teacher* 4 (1842): 30, 34.

5. *Spectator*, Apr. 13, 1844, p. 346; *Punch*, 2: 19.

6. *Hansard*, 1842, 65: 104, 573.

7. *Hansard*, 1849, 102: 621; 1848, 97: 359; 1844, 74: 134–135; 1843, 71: 90–91.

8. *Leicestershire Mercury*, July 31, 1847; *Edinburgh Review*, Apr. 1846, pp. 375, 377; *Mirror*, Jan. 18, 1845.

9. Driver, *Tory Radical ... Oastler*, p. 473.

10. *Punch* 4: 129; see also 1: 118; 2: 26, 118; 3: 19, 160; 4: 53; 10: 25; 11: 132; Anne Humphrey, *Henry Mayhew* (London, 1984), p. 99; *Weekly Chronicle*, Oct. 20, 1844, and Oct. 9, 1847.

11. *Edinburgh Review*, July 1844, 259.

12. *Blackwood's*, Nov. 1845, p. 644; *North British Review*, May 1845, pp. 83–84; Aug. 1847, p. 572.

13. *Christian Remembrancer* 9 (1845): 301; Helps, *Claims of Labour*, p. 73.

14. *Punch*, 12: 56; *North British Review*, Nov. 1846, pp. 116, 259.

15. Holyoake, *Life of Joseph Raynor Stephen*, pp. 59–60; Robert Vaughan, *Religious Parties in England* (London, 1839), pp. 109–113; *North British Review*, Nov. 1846, p. 116.

16. *Westminster Review*, June 1844, pp. 373–374; *Jerrold's Shilling Magazine*, 1845, 1: preface; *Mirror*, Sept. 14, 1844.

17. H. Carter, *Temperance Movement* (London, 1933), p. 22.

18. Christine Walkley, *The Ghost in the Looking Glass: The Victorian Seamstress* (London, 1985), pp. 18–25; *P.P.*, 1843, 14: F30; T. J. Edelstein, "Iconography of the Seamstress," *Victorian Studies*, Winter 1980, p. 186; Lindsay Errington, *Social and Religious Themes in English Art* (London, 1984), p. 113.

19. John Clubb, *Selected Poems of Thomas Hood* (Cambridge, Mass., 1970), p. 305.

20. Susan P. Casteras and Ronald Parkinson, *Richard Redgrave, 1804–1888* (New Haven, Conn., 1988), pp. 118–119.

21. *Mirror*, May 24, 1845; *Edinburgh Review*, Apr. 1846, p. 376; *Morning Chronicle*, Sept. 21, 1848; *People's Journal*, Jan. 10, 1846, p. 21.

22. Charles Dickens, *The Chimes*, ch. 3 of quarter 3, p. 185.

23. Mrs. Elizabeth Gaskell, *Ruth* (London, 1967); G. W. M. Reynolds, *The Seamstress* (London, 1853); Camilla Toulmin's painting *The Orphan Milliner*; Mark Lemon, *The Semptress* (London, 1886).

24. Douglas Jerrold, "The Story of a Feather," in *Works*, 2: ch. 2: 20, 32, ch. 4: 37.

25. Errington, *Themes in English Art*, figs. 47 and 50 and p. 131; Blanche Jerrold, *The Life of George Cruickshank* (London, 1882).

26. Errington, *Themes of English Art*, p. 120; Casteras and Parkinson, *Redgrave*, p. 20.

27. Clubb, *Thomas Hood*, p. 317; Errington, *Themes of English Art*, fig. 55 and pp. 55, 180; B. Jerrold, *Cruickshank*, pp. 90–91.

28. *Licensed Victuallers Almanack*, 1862, p. 99; Boase, *Modern English Biography*, 1: 1201; David Roberts, "Who Ran the Globe?" and "Early Victorian Newspaper Editors," *Victorian Periodicals Review*, June 1971, p. 6, and Dec. 1971, pp. 1–12; Halévy, *Growth of Philosophical Radicalism*, p. 309.

29. Charles Pebody, *English Journalism* (London, 1882), p. 138; *DNB*, 59: 4, 13: 237; 29: 336, 35: 120; William Jerdan, *Autobiography* (London, 1852), p. 27, Arthur A. Adrian, *Mark Lemon* (London, 1966), pp. 5–16.

30. *DNB*, 56: 88–106.

31. *DNB*, 47: 379; 49: 284; 13: 252; 32: 388; 35: 120; *DNB* 2d supp., 3: 610; S. Squire Sprigge, *The Life and Times of Thomas Wakley* (London, 1897), pp. 6–30.

32. Humphrey, *Henry Mayhew*, pp. 1–7; *DNB*, 1: 30; 37: 153; 48: 43, 1–9; *The Life and Labours of Albany Fonblanque*, ed. E. B. de Fonblanque (London, 1874), pp. 1–9; Escott, *Masters of English Journalism*, p. 237; Clubb, *Poems of Thomas Hood*, pp. 1–6; *DNB*, 48: 43 (1896).

33. Mackay, *Forty Years' Recollections*, pp. 16–20; Richard Kelly, *Douglas Jerrold* (New York, 1912), pp. 16–17; Blanche Jerrold, *The Life of Douglas Jerrold* (London, n.d.), p. 32.

34. W. Jerrold, *Douglas Jerrold of Punch* (London, 1910); *DNB*, 1: 31; *DNB*, 35: 120; Pebody, *English Journalism*, p. 130; Alexander Andrews, *A History of British Journalism* (London, 1859), 2: 273–275.

35. B. Jerrold, *Jerrold*, pp. 123, 126–127, 132, 147, 172, 187, 215–217, 221–223, 226; R. Kelly, *Douglas Jerrold*, pp. 18, 20, 24; Earl Lytton, *The Life of Edward Bulwer, First Lord Lytton* (London, 1913), 2: 135; B. Jerrold, *The Life of George Cruickshank*, p. 250; Robert L. Patten, *George Cruickshank's Life and Times and Art* (New Brunswick, N.J., 1992), 1: 391; Clubb, *Thomas Hood*, pp. 22, 24; Charles Mackay, *Thoughts Through the Long Day* (London, 1887), p. 181; *DNB*, 35: 120.

36. G. Robert Stange, "The Victorian City and the Frightened Poets," *Victorian Studies*, Summer 1968, p. 629.

37. W. Jerrold, *Douglas Jerrold and Punch*, p. 50; Alexander Welsh, "Satire and History: The City in Dickens," *Victorian Studies*, Mar. 1968, p. 395; Anne Humphrey, *Travels into the Poor Man's Country* (Athens, Ga., 1978), pp. 38–39; *Edinburgh Review*, Apr. 1847, pp. 553–554.

38. *Fraser's*, Jan. 1844, p. 211; W. Jerrold, *Douglas Jerrold and Punch*, p. 6; Patten, *Cruickshank*, p. 36; B. Jerrold, *Cruickshank*, p. 58.

39. *Illustrated London News*, June 18, 1842, p. 81; *Douglas Jerrold's Shilling Magazine*, 1845, 1: preface.

40. Kelly, *Douglas Jerrold*, ch. 3; B. Jerrold, *Jerrold*, pp. 184–215; W. Jerrold, *Jerrold and Punch*.

41. Mackay, *Thoughts Through the Long Day*, pp. 354–355; id., *Voices in the Crowd* (London, 1846), p. 40.

42. *Illustrated London News*, Aug. 6, 1842, p. 193.

43. *Hood's Journal,* Jan. 6, June 5, 1847; *Howitt's Journal,* Jan. 16, Nov. 6, 1847; *Punch,* 1843, 1: 107; 2: 240; 4: 44–46; 11: 43; *Lancet,* June 5, 1841, p. 371; June 6, 1844, p. 313–315; *Morning Advertiser,* Mar. 6, 1840, Mar. 5, June 18, 1847; *Medical Times,* Mar. 12, 1842, May 4, 1844; *Spectator,* May 1, 1841, Apr. 13, 1844; *Sun,* Feb. 24, 1843, Mar. 23, 1844, Mar. 10, 1847; *Sunday Times,* Feb. 4, 1844; *Times,* Oct. 18, 1842; Jan. 5, Mar. 13, 1844; *Weekly Dispatch,* Oct. 25, 1840; May 23, 1847; *Illustrated London News,* May 28, p. 38, June 25, p. 97, 1842, Jan. 30, 1847 p. 101; *Pictorial Times,* Sept. 30, 1843.

44. Thomas, *Story of the Spectator;* William Norrie, *Dundee Celebrities of the Nineteenth Century* (Dundee, 1873), pp. 175–178; British Museum, Peel MS, Add. MS 40,579, Oct. 30, 1845; *DNB,* 48: 311; 28: 280; 28: 297; *Licensed Victuallers Almanac,* 1862, p. 99; Joseph Hatton, *Journalistic London* (London, 1882), p. 156.

45. Times, *History of the Times,* 1: 179, 187–201, 210–211; 2: 5–6; Arthur Dasent, *John Thaddeus Delane* (London, 1908), 1: 15–22, 42–49; *Times,* May 19, 1835; May 18, 1838; Feb. 16, Sept. 17, 23, Oct. 2, 4, 12, 1841; Jan. 28, 29, 1842; July 9, 1849; July 7, Oct. 13, 1853.

46. Dickens, *Oliver Twist,* ch. 2; Edward Bulwer-Lytton, *Paul Clifford* (London, 1840), pp. 13–15; William Ainsworth, *Jack Sheppard* (London, n.d.), pp. 2, 10–11; D. Jerrold, "The Story of a Feather," in *Works,* 2: 20, 36.

47. *DNB,* 21: 56; 50: 325; G. A. Sala, *The Life of George Sala* (London, 1895), p. 218.

48. *Lloyd's Weekly,* Feb. 11, 1844, Feb. 21, 1847; *Howitt's Journal,* Feb. 6, 1847.

49. David Roberts, "How Cruel Was the New Poor Law?" *Historical Journal* 6, no. 1 (1963): 97–107; *Punch,* 1849, 17: 49; 1850, 18: 15; 1844, 7: 243; 1846, 10: 170; 1843, 4: 47; 1845, 8: 92; 1858, 35: 15; Simon Houfe, *John Leech and the Victorian Scene* (Suffolk, Eng., 1984), p. 89.

50. Casteras and Parkinson, *Redgrave,* pp. 62, 118–119; Errington, *Themes in English Art,* pp. 57, 91, 97, 180, figs. 55, 56.

51. Philip Collins, *Dickens: The Critical Heritage* (New York, 1971), pp. 54, 198; *Westminster Review,* June 1844, p. 374; *Edinburgh Review,* Oct. 1838, p. 73.

52. *Oxford and Cambridge Review,* Jan. 1846, p. 47.

53. Clubb, *Thomas Hood,* pp. 305, 317; Albert Wertheim, "Childhood in John Leech's Pictures of Life and Character," *Victorian Studies,* Sept. 1973, pp. 60–87; Errington, *Themes in English Art,* pp. 57–68, 89–99, 115–120, 132, 180–190, 202–204, 208–209, and figs. 4, 17, 18, 19, 50, 55, 56.

54. Bulwer-Lytton, *Paul Clifford,* pp. x, 200, 263; Ainsworth, *Jack Sheppard,* p. 10; Jerrold, "St. Giles and St. James," in *Works,* 1: 3, 8, 12, 20.

55. Dickens, *The Chimes,* ch. 3 of quarter 3, pp. 192–194.

56. Clubb, *Thomas Hood,* p. 321.

57. Patten, *Cruickshank,* pp. 309, 367; Charles Dickens, *Pickwick Papers* (Boston, n.d.), ch. 4, p. 482; id., *Barnaby Rudge* (London, 1953), ch. 70, p. 487; id., *David Copperfield* (Boston, n.d.), ch. 23; *Bleak House* (Boston, n.d.), ch. 1.

58. John Leech, *Early Pencillings in Punch* (London, n.d.), p. 21; Jerrold, "St. James and St. Giles," in *Works,* 1: 155–160; 392–394.

59. *Punch,* 5: 37; 10: 9, 49; 11: 158.

60. *Punch,* 4: 44, 134; 5: 55; 10: 9, 25, 197; 11: 437; 12: 56, 78; B. Jerrold, *Douglas Jerrold,* p. 190.

61. Dickens, *The Chimes,* first quarter, pp. 139–141; Clubb, *Thomas Hood,* pp. 274–278.

62. *Educational Times,* Aug. 1849, 243ff.

63. Walkley, *Ghost in the Looking Glass,* pp. 9, 23, 28, 44; William S. Holdsworth, *A History of English Law* (London, 1956), pp. 187–193, 633–639.

64. T. J. Edelstein, "Iconology of Seamstresses," *Victorian Studies*, Winter 1980, pp. 196–205.

65. *Punch* 1: 118, 131; A. Humphreys, *Henry Mayhew*, pp. 121, 140–141, 143.

66. Dickens, *The Chimes*, ch. 3, p. 194; Kelly, *Jerrold*, p. 78.

67. *Westminster Review*, July 1847, pp. 120–121; *Watchman*, June 15, 1842; *Leeds Mercury*, June 11, 1842; *Hansard*, 1842, 63: 1357.

68. *Eclectic Review*, Aug. 1842, p. 202; *P.P.*, 1842, 15: 32–40, 44–46, 53–54, 87, 138–142, 145–146, 187–198.

69. *Hansard*, 1833, 17: 99; 19: 227, 230.

70. *Spectator*, July 4, 1844, pp. 636–637; *Sheffield Mercury*, Feb. 13, 1847.

71. *Hansard*, 1833, 19: 246.

72. *Hansard*, 1844, 73: 1263, 1410; 74: 1106.

73. *Sussex Agricultural Express*, Aug. 14, 1847; *Hansard*, 1847, 90: 768.

74. Peter Mandler, "Cain and Abel: Two Aristocrats and the Early Victorian Factory Acts," *Historical Journal* 27, no. 1 (1984): 102–107.

75. *Sun*, Mar. 23, 1844.

76. Political Economy Club of London, *Minutes of Proceedings*, J. L. Prevost, p. 286; Patrick Joyce, *The Historical Meaning of Work* (Cambridge, 1987), pp. 156–164, 171–174; Ward, *Factory Movement*, pp. 20, 53, 91, 414; *P.P.*, 1844, 28: 535–537; 1845, 25: 20–21.

77. Ward, *Factory Movement*, pp. 414–416; *Standard*, Apr. 22, 1847; *Lloyd's Weekly*, May 5, 1844; *Morning Chronicle*, Mar. 21, 1844; *Sun*, Mar. 18, 1844; *Manchester Times*, Mar. 29, 1844; *Economist*, May 18, 1844.

78. Ward, *Factory Movement*, p. 414; Joyce, *Work*, pp. 171–174; Robert Gray, *The Factory Question and Industrial England* (London, 1996), pp. 189–191.

79. *P.P.*, 1816, 6: 40–42; 1827, 6: 75ff; Kathleen Jones, *Lunacy, Law and Conscience* (London, 1955), pp. 133–139.

80. Jones, *Lunacy, Law and Conscience*, pp. 93–98.

81. Robert Gardiner Hill, *Total Abolition of Personal Restraint in the Treatment of the Insane* (London, 1839), pp. 10–13, 20, 24–25; Daniel H. Tuke, *Chapters in the History of the Insane in the British Isles* (London, 1882), pp. 79–83, 90–91, 99–100, 127–128, 154–157, 167–169; Vida Skultans, *English Madness: Ideas on Insanity, 1580–1890* (London, 1979), pp. 57–80, 60–61, 99–100, 111–112.

82. *P.P.*, 1854, 29: 42; Sir James Clark, *A Memoir of John Conolly, M.D., D.C.L., Comprising a Sketch of the Treatment of the Insane in Europe and America* (London, 1869), pp. 30–42, 57, 73–83; Hill, *Total Abolition of Restraint*, pp. v–iv, 6–12, 37–46; John Conolly, *The Construction and Government of Lunatic Asylums and Hospitals for the Insane* (London, 1848; reprint, 1968), pp. 1–45; id., *An Inquiry Concerning the Indications of Insanity with Suggestions for the Better Protection and Care of the Insane* (London, 1830; reprint, 1964), pp. 1–34; *DNB*, 10: 114–115; Jones, *Lunacy, Law and Conscience*, pp. 140, 150–153; Anne Digby, *Madness, Morality, and Medicine: A Study of the York Retreat, 1796–1914* (New York, 1985), pp. 13–15.

83. *Quarterly Review*, Oct. 1844, pp. 416–417; *Hansard*, 1845, 81: 199–200.

84. See Michel Foucault, *Madness and Civilization: A History of Insanity in the Age of Reason*, trans. Richard Howard (New York, 1965, 1973); *Madhouses, Mad Doctors, and Madness*, ed. Andrew Scull (Philadelphia, 1981), pp. 105–166; Digby, *Madness, Morality, and Medicine*, mild but telling criticism of Foucault and Scull, pp. 64–66; Skultans, *English Madness*, not so mild on Foucault and Scull, pp. 11–14, 55–56, 104–105.

85. Jones, *Lunacy, Law and Conscience*, p. 116; *DNB*, 57: 301; Clark, *Conolly*, pp. 16–40; Tuke, *Chapters in the History of the Insane*, pp. 108–137, 179–213.

86. *P.P.*, 1847, 33: 53–54.

87. Digby, *Madness, Morality, and Medicine*, pp. 24–29, 34–36, 62–65, 88–102; Tuke, *Chapters in the History of the Insane*, pp. 131–135; Clark, *Memoir of John Conolly*, p. 3; Conolly, *Inquiry Concerning the Indications of Insanity*, pp. 5–91; *DNB*, 46: 344–346; Skultans, *English Madness*, pp. 13–14, 23–41, 66; Henry Munro, *Remarks on Insanity, Its Nature and Treatment* (London, 1951), pp. ii–vii; James Cowles Prichard, *The Different Forms of Insanity in Relation to Jurisprudence* (London, 1842), pp. 146, 163–164; Gardner, *Total Abolition of Restraint*, pp. 9–19; *P.P.*, 1848, 32: 496, 636, 778, 882; 1854, 23: 5–6; Jones, *Lunacy, Law and Conscience*, pp. 33–60.

88. *Blackwood's*, July 1840, p. 69.

89. W. A. Mumford, *William Ewart, M.P. 1798–1869* (London, 1960), p. 59; Lord Nugent, *On the Punishment of Death* (London, 1840), pp. ii–iv.

90. Leon Radzinowicz, *A History of English Criminal Law and Its Administration from 1750* (London, 1948), 1: 574–583, 598; *Hansard*, 1848, 97: 557–558; Mumford, *Ewart*, p. 60; V. A. C. Gatrell, *The Hanging Tree* (Oxford, 1994), p. 581.

91. Radzinowicz, *History of English Criminal Law*, 1: 601–605; 4: 304, 317–324; *Hansard*, 1837, 37: 709–731; 1840, 55: 1081.

92. Radzinowicz, *Criminal Law*, 1: 326–327.

93. *Hansard*, 1849, 104: 1084; 1841, 58: 1410; *Edinburgh Review*, 1831, 54: 238.

94. *Hansard*, 1840, 55: 1101; 1847, 90: 1098; *Northampton Mercury*, June 2, 1847.

95. *Hansard*, 1832, Mar. 27, 947; 1834, 25: 1023; 1837, 37: 709–716, 38: 908–918; *P.P.*, 1836, 36: 187, 206–210; Mumford, *Ewart*, pp. 59–62, 74–76.

96. George Rude, "Protest and Punishment in Nineteenth-Century Britain," *Albion*, Spring 1973, p. 21.

97. Radzinowicz, *History of English Criminal Law*, 1: 574–606; 4: 303–330, 344; *Hansard*, 1840, 50: 742; *Hansard*, 1840, 50: 1084; *P.P.*, 36: 187–209.

98. Gatrell, *Hanging Tree*, pp. 10–21; *Hansard*, 1847, 90: 1095–1096; 1840, 52: 940; 1848, 97: 566–569, 586–588.

99. Margaret May, "Innocence and Experience: The Evolution of the Concept of Juvenile Delinquency," *Victorian Studies*, Sept. 1973, p. 10.

100. *Times*, Aug. 2, 1853; Leon Radzinowicz and Roger Hood, *The Emergence of Penal Policy*, vol. 5 of *History of English Criminal Law*, pp. 142–147.

101. *P.P.*, 1837, 19: 44.

102. *Daily News*, Jan. 11, 1847.

103. R. and F. Davenport-Hill, *Recorder of Birmingham*, pp. 152–153, 156, 160; W. S. Childe Pemberton, *Life of Lord Norton* (London, 1909), p. 128; Carpenter, *Reformatory Schools*, pp. 229–232; *P.P.*, 1852, 7: 30.

104. Carpenter, *Reformatory Schools*, pp. 50, 230–232, 245, 341, 339; *Journal of the Statistical Society*, 1842, 5: 282; Radzinowicz and Hood, *Emergence of Penal Policy*, p. 161.

105. *P.P.*, 1847, 7: 382; 1850, 17: vi, 29.

106. *Eclectic Review*, Dec. 1848, pp. 646–648; M. May, "Juvenile Delinquency," *Victorian Studies*, Sept. 1973, pp. 15–16; Wiener, *Reconstructing the Criminal*, pp. 14–15.

107. Carpenter, *Reformatory Schools*, pp. 343–344; Wiener, *Reconstructing the Criminal*, pp. 132–135; Radzinowicz and Hood, *Emergence of Penal Policy*, pp. 147–154; *Spectator*, Jan. 10, 1846, p. 36.

108. *P.P.*, 1847, 7: 382; 1850, 17: 29; 1852, 7: 45, 93, 102, 198; *Hansard*, 1847, 90: 430–439; 99:

430–469; 1853, 129: 1099–1101, 1103; *Edinburgh Review,* Apr. 1847, p. 528; *Eclectic Review,* Dec. 1848, pp. 646–648; *Times,* Aug. 2, 1853; *Daily News,* Jan. 11, 1847; *Athenaeum,* Feb. 21, 1846, p. 181; William B. Neale, *Juvenile Delinquency in Manchester* (London, 1840); W. C. Osborne, *Lectures on the Prevention of Crime* (London, n.d.); Joseph Adshead, *Our Present Gaol System* (London, 1849).

109. *P.P.,* 1852, 7: 10, 52–57; *Douglas Jerrold's Magazine,* 1845, 2: 228.

110. *Hansard,* 1848, 100: 81–84; Manton, *Mary Carpenter and the Children of the Streets,* pp. 105–110; *P.P.,* 1852, 7: 16, 42–44, 105; R. and F. Davenport-Hill, *Recorder of Birmingham,* p. 182.

111. Childe-Pemberton, *Lord Norton,* p. 136; Beggs, *Inquiry into the Extent and Causes of Juvenile Depravity,* pp. 14–27; Worsley, *Juvenile Depravity,* Symons, *On the Reformation of Young Offenders,* pp. 82–118; T. Beames, *The Rookeries of London* (London, 1850); Neale, *Juvenile Delinquency in Manchester,* pp. 11–23, 40–53; John Mirehouse, *Crime and Its Causes* (London, 1840), pp. 11–20; *Edinburgh Review,* Oct. 1847, pp. 520–522, 528–535; *Spectator,* Nov. 26, 1842, pp. 1140–1141; *Journal of the Statistical Society,* 1847, 10: 38.

112. *Hansard,* 1846, 87: 1336–1346; 88: 691; 89: 594; 91: 197, 1142; 1849, 104: 927–930; Ritvo, *Animal Estate,* pp. 126–130, 144; *Chambers' Edinburgh Journal,* Mar. 6, 1847, p. 153; G. R. Scott, *The History of Corporal Punishment* (London, 1938), pp. 71–85, 98–104; *Spectator,* Aug. 21, 1847, p. 805; *Examiner,* Mar. 25, 1848; *Edinburgh Review,* July 1842, p. 422.

113. McDonagh, *Pattern of Governmental Growth,* pp. 17–19; *Spectator,* July 22, 1843, p. 683; May 7, 1842, p. 443; July 24, 1847, p. 710; *Examiner,* Apr. 1, 1843; Mar. 4, 1848; *Athenaeum,* July 26, 1844, p. 741.

114. *Hansard,* 1848, 99: 86–89; E. P. Thompson, *The Unknown Mayhew* (London, 1972), p. 161, 137–216; Love, *Handbook of Manchester,* p. 109.

115. *P.P.,* 1836, 22: 39–45, 56–64; Major General Charles Napier, *Remarks on Military Law and the Punishment of Flogging* (London, 1837), pp. 1–202; John Gardner, *On the Inhuman and Disgraceful Punishment of Flogging in the Army and Navy* (London, 1832), pp. 5–12.

116. *Hansard,* 1834, 22: 253; 25, 283–284, 1102; 1846, 87: 381–460, 1344; Edward M. Spears, *Radical General: Sir George de Lacy Evans* (Manchester, 1983), p. 59.

117. Eugene Razor, *Reform in the Royal Navy* (Hamden, Conn., 1976), p. 45; Jonathan Gathorne-Hardy, *The Old School Tie* (New York, 1977), pp. 8–10.

118. Harry Hopkins, *The Long Affair: Poaching Wars in Britain* (London, 1985); D. V. Jones, "The Poacher: A Study in Victorian Crime and Protest," *Historical Journal* 22, no. 4 (Dec. 1979): 825–895; *Hansard,* 1845, 78: 70; *P.P.,* 1846, 9: 433–434.

119. MacDonagh, *Pattern of Government Growth,* pp. 189–190, 218; P. W. I. Bartrip, "State Intervention in Mid-Nineteenth Century," *British Studies,* Fall 1983, pp. 66–67; *Law, Economy and Society, 1750–1914,* ed. G. R. Rubin and David Sugarman (Worcester, Eng., 1984), pp. 241–245.

120. *Times,* Feb. 16, 1841; *Athenaeum,* July 26, 1844.

121. Keith Thomas, *Man and the Natural World* (London, 1983), pp. 149, 154, 173, 186–189; Ritvo, *Animal Estate,* pp. 133, 137, 155; Antony Brown, *Who Cares for Animals; 150 Years of the R S.C.P.A.* (London, 1974), pp. 12–27; Bailey, *Leisure and Class in Victorian England,* p. 18; Great Britain, Parliament, *The Statutes of the Realm,* 2d rev. ed. (1849), 8: 581.

122. *Hansard,* 1840, 53: 342–350, 422–434; 1842, 60: 247; 61: 1042–1047; *Nottingham Journal,* July 2, 9, 1841; *Leeds Intelligencer,* Jan. 4, 1840.

123. *Hansard,* 1847, 91: 617–636; 1848, 96: 387–402; Lewis, *Edwin Chadwick,* pp. 41–56, 114–131; Edwin Chadwick, *The Sanitary Condition of the Labouring Population of Great Britain,* ed. Michael Flinn (1842; Edinburgh, 1965), pp. 254–276.

124. *Hansard*, 1837, 36: 1085; 1841, 57: 646, 59: 881; 1844, 76: 341.

125. *Hansard*, 1844, 76: 321.

126. *Standard*, Mar. 20, 1841; *Morning Herald*, June 29, 1842; *Morning Post*, Mar. 10, 1840; *Times*, Apr. 30, 1834, May 14, 1838, Feb. 22, 1841; *Weekly Dispatch*, Oct. 25, 1840; *Sun*, Mar. 24, 1841; *Lancet*, Feb. 22, 1840, p. 812; *Howitt's Journal*, Jan. 16, 1847, pp. 33–38.

127. *Hansard*, 1834, 22: 876–882; 23: 812, 986–987, 993, 999.

128. *Spectator*, May 1, 1844, p. 421; *Economist*, June 5, 1847, p. 640; *Westminster Review*, Apr. 1847, p. 255.

129. *Hansard*, 1841, 57: 646, 660–666; 1843, 66: 1188–1189; 1844, 76: 341; *Illustrated London News*, June 25, 1842, p. 97; *Weekly Dispatch*, Oct. 25, 1840; *Lancet*, Feb. 22, Apr. 6, 1841; *Times*, Jan 4, 8, 1841; *Fraser's*, Apr. 14, 1841, pp. 379–388.

130. David Ashworth, "The Urban Poor," in *The New Poor Law*, ed. Derek Fraser (London, 1976), pp. 135–139; Michael Rose, "The Allowance System under the New Poor Law," *Economic History Review* 19 (1966): 612–615; Anne Digby, *Pauper Palaces* (Boston, 1978), pp. 11, 13, 71–72, 166, 183; Lynn Lees, *The Solidarities of Strangers* (Cambridge, 1998), p. 187.

131. Digby, *Pauper Palaces*, pp. 4–6, 12, 22, 80; Rose, "Allowance System," p. 613; M. A. Crowther, *The Workhouse System* (London, 1984), p. 35.

132. Ashworth, "Urban Poor Law," p. 139; P.R.O., M.H. 12/15066, Jan. 1843; Crowther, *Workhouse System*, pp. 49; Hodgkinson, *National Health Service*, pp. 149, 187–194; *P.P.*, 1843, 45: 67–70, 86–90, 204–215; Roberts, "How Cruel Was the New Poor Law?" *Historical Journal* 6 (1963): 104.

133. Ursula Henriques, "How Cruel Was the New Poor Law?" *Historical Journal* 11 (1968): 365–370; Digby, *Pauper Palaces*, pp. 77, 166–167, 180–182; Hodgkinson, *National Health Service*, pp. 111, 149, 157; *P.P.*, 1838, 28: 145–162, 201, 279–280; 1839, 17: 92–99.

134. University College, London, Bentham MSS, 154b, 607 T, Tufnell to Bentham, 1845.

135. Smith, *Life and Work of Sir James Kay-Shuttleworth*, pp. 46–54, 62–74, 80; *Journal of the Arts*, May 21, 1875, pp. 607–608; Finer, *Edwin Chadwick*, pp. 147–164, 209–230, 297–311; C. L. Lewis, *Dr. Southwood Smith* (London, 1898), ch. 4; *P.P.*, 1839, 20: 104–110.

136. Hodgkinson, *National Health Service*, pp. 187–194; Crowther, *Workhouse System*, p. 49; P.R.O., M.H. 12/12457, Apr. 28, 1838; M.H. 12/15225, Jan. 20, 1842; M.H. 12/968, Feb. 27, 1836; M.H. 12/968 (a), Nov. 1836, Neave to commissioners; M.H. 12/5593, Mar. 30, 1841, 12 Mar. 1843; M.H. 12/12460, Apr. 27, 1842; M.H. 12/12855.

137. Peter Dunkley, "The Hungry Forties and the New Poor Law," *Historical Journal* 17, no. 2 (1974): 329–345.

138. Roy Porter, *English Society in the Eighteenth Century* (London, 1990), pp. 154–155, 306–307; Sydney and Beatrice Webb, *English Prisons under Local Government* (London, 1902), pp. 107–110.

139. Sean McConville, *A History of English Prisons* (London, 1981), 1: 86–104, 136–163; Margaret Delacy, *Prison Reform in Lancashire, 1700–1850* (London, 1987), p. 114; Rev. Sydney Smith, *Sermons Preached at St. Paul's Cathedral* (London, 1846), p. 375.

140. *P.P.*, 1835, 11: 20, 16–46, 67–71, 118–119, 123, 129, 177, 290, 469–78.

141. *P.P.*, 1850, 17: 113–115; 1848, 36: iii–v; 1849, 36: v–xi; 1841, 5: iv–v; Williams's reports: 1842, 21: iii–iv, 4–7, 185–188; 1836, 35: 4–25, 69–80; 1838, 31: 1–120; reports of Russell and Crawford: 1846, 20: 308–310, 359–366; 1843, 25 and 26: 1–30; 1838, 31: 112–113; Hill's reports: 1836, 35: 357–372; 1838, 31: 307–308; 1843, 25 and 26: 6–15; 1844, 29: 593–597; 1845, 24: 99–136; 1846, 20: 463–483.

142. *P.P.*, 1843, 25 and 26: 7; Dickens, *American Notes*, pp. 140–161; Henriques, "Separate System," *Past and Present*, Feb. 1972, pp. 16–93.

143. Frederick Hill, *Autobiography* (London, 1892), pp. 259–260; *P.P.*, 1843, 25 and 26: 7.

144. *Gloucester Journal*, Jan. 9, 1847; *Eclectic Review*, Oct. 1847, pp. 455–460.

145. Radzinowicz and Hood, *Emergence of Penal Policy*, p. 147; Henriques, "Separate System," *Past and Present*, Feb. 1972, pp. 64–66, 68, 72, 75, 80–81, 84–85; *Hansard*, 1849, 103: 404–406, 418; 105: 553–557; 106: 1006–1007, 1012, 1015–1018; 109; *Times*, Oct. 13, 1853; *Christian Observer*, Apr. 1847, p. 244; Feb. 1849, p. 136; *North British Review*, Nov. 1848, p. 28.

146. *Works of Jeremy Bentham*, ed. J. Bowring, 4: 71; R. and F. Davenport-Hill, *Recorder of Birmingham*, pp. 154–156, 160–164, 182–190, 272, 322–324, 337–338; Frederick Hill, *Autobiography*, pp. 182–184, 287; id., *Crime, Its Causes and Remedies* (London, 1853), p. 274; *P.P.*, 1842, 21: 7; 1845, 37: xv–xvi; 1849, 26: xiv.

147. Radzinowicz and Hood, *Emergence of Penal Policy*, pp. 156, 233 (index); *Law Magazine*, 1845, 34: 38–48; S. and B. Webb, *English Prisons*, pp. 150, 164–170.

148. *P.P.*, 1848, 36: 363–84; Henriques, "Separate System," *Past and Present*, Feb. 1972, pp. 62–92; *Times*, July 29, 1854, p. 8; *P.P.*, 34: 199–211.

CHAPTER 11

1. *Edinburgh Review*, Apr. 1847, p. 523.

2. *Times*, July 15, 1853; Thomas Cooper, *The Purgatory of Suicides* (London, 1845), p. 32.

3. *Eclectic Review*, Sept. 1843, pp. 331–338; *Edinburgh Review*, Oct. 1840, p. 44; Feb. 1843, pp. 194–197; Sept. 1843, p. 338; Robert Vaughan, *The Age of the Great Cities* (London, 1843), pp. 196–197; Mayhew, *London Labour and the London Poor*, 1: 35, 233; 2: 54; 3: 328, 349, 369.

4. *Blackwood's*, J. F. Murray's "World of London" series, Apr., May, June, Aug., Sept. 1841 and Jan. and Feb. 1842; *Quarterly Review*, 1841, 67: 173–180; Dec. 1846, pp. 127–141; Dec. 1847, pp. 142–152; *Fraser's*, Feb. 1849, pp. 127–128.

5. R. and F. Davenport-Hill, *Recorder of Birmingham*, pp. 164–166; Childe-Pemberton, *Life of Lord Norton*, pp. 126, 136; Nugent, *On the Punishment of Death*; *Hansard*, 1840, 55: 1082; 1841, 56: 462.

6. Nugent, *On the Punishment of Death*; *Hansard*, 1834, 25: 91; 1840, 55: 1082; 1841, 56: 462.

7. Thomas, *Man and the Natural World*, pp. 181, 186, 297; Ritvo, *Animal Estate*, p. 129; James Turner, *Reckoning with the Beast* (Baltimore, 1980), pp. 40–45; Edward Fairholme and Wellesley Pain, *A Century of Work for Animals* (New York, 1924), pp. 60–73.

8. Napier, *Military Law and the Punishment of Flogging*; *P.P.*, 1836, 22: 43–49, 81–88; S. and B. Webb, *English Prisons*, pp. 128, 150, 164–170, 173, 182, 188, 213.

9. R. K. Webb, *The British Working Class Reader*, p. 22; P. Gardner, *The Lost Elementary Schools of Victorian England*; Laqueur, *Religion and Respectability*.

10. Peter Jupp, "The Landed Elite and Political Authority," *British Studies*, Jan. 1990, pp. 68–71.

11. Asa Briggs, *Victorian Cities* (arts), pp. 137–138, 152, 164, 166, 183; (learned societies), pp. 20, 47, 109, 160–164, 166, 255; (hospitals) 25, 199, 272; (parks) 135, 201, 273, 301, 323; (libraries) 136, 196–197, 201.

12. Derek Fraser, *Power and Authority in the Victorian City* (New York, 1980), pp. 11, 19–20, 27–48, 58–61, 63–69, 111, 115, 119, 140, 160.

13. Michael Cullen, *The Statistical Movement* (New York, 1975), pp. 77–104.

14. P. Jubb, "Landed Elite," *British Studies*, Jan. 1990, pp. 69–70.

15. C. R. Sanders, *Coleridge and the Broad Church Movement* (Durham, N.C., 1962), pp. 14–16, 91–93, 122–128, 193–195; Colmer, *Coleridge*, p. 165; Peter Allen, *The Cambridge Apostles* (Cambridge, 1978), pp. 36, 47, 68, 78–81, 89, 90, 132–133, 139, 142, 206.

16. Alan John Hartley, "Literary Aspects of Christian Socialism" (Ph.D. diss., London University, 1963), pp. 141–142; Coleridge, *Table Talk*, 2: 74, 281, 317; *Church and State*, pp. 71, 417; John Colmer, *Coleridge, Critic of Society* (Oxford, 1959), p. 173.

17. Gertrude Himmelfarb, *Victorian Minds* (New York, 1968), pp. 35, 37, 39, 40, 45, 46; "Bentham's Utopia: The National Charity Company," *British Studies*, Nov. 1970, p. 100; Michael Ignatieff, *A Just Measure of Pain: The Penitentiary in the Industrial Revolution, 1750–1850* (New York, 1978), pp. 75, 77, 110; Michel Foucault, *Discipline and Punish: The Birth of the Prison*, trans. Alan Sheridan (New York, 1977), pp. 205, 208–209.

18. *Works of Jeremy Bentham*, ed. J. Bowring, 8: 361–457, esp. 385, 387, 390, 396–397, 402, 412–413, 420, 424–425, 430, 433, 437; *Times Literary Supplement*, Oct. 29, 1993; Himmelfarb, *Victorian Minds*, pp. 45–51; Ignatieff, *Just Measure of Pain*, p. 75; Radzinowicz, *History of English Criminal Law*, 1: 390; Sean McConville, *English Prison Administration* (London, 1981), 1: 121; Jeremy Bentham, *Principles of Morals and Legislation* (Oxford, 1879), pp. 311, 268; id., *Deontology* (London, 1834), 1: 229.

19. "Utilitarian Moral Philosophy," *British Critic* 28 (July 1840): 93–125, p. 125; Henry Carlisle, *Correspondence of Abraham Hayward* (London, 1886), p. 9; *Athenaeum*, May 28, 1843, p. 473; George B. Hill, *The Life of Sir Rowland Hill* (London, 1880), 1: 170–171.

20. Alexander Bain, *James Mill*, p. 71; J. S. Mill, *Autobiography*, p. 86.

21. *Eclectic Review*, Apr. 1845, pp. 382–383; *Manchester Guardian*, Oct. 3, 1840; *North British Review*, Nov. 1850, pp. 4–7; *Spectator*, Jan. 4, 1840, p. 36, Apr. 29, 1843, pp. 396–398.

22. *Edinburgh Review*, Oct. 1854, p. 570–571, 601; *Christian Teacher*, 1843, 5: 312; *Athenaeum*, Apr. 5, 1845, pp. 327–328; James Grant, *Portrait of Public Characters* (London, 1841) 2: 143.

23. William Wordsworth, *Poetical Works*, ed. William Knight (London, 1884), 3: *The Excursion*, bks. 6, 7, and 8; F. M. Todd, *Politics of the Poet, A Study of Wordsworth* (London, 1957), pp. 97–98; Horne, *New Spirit of the Age*, 1: 329; *Quarterly Review*, 1842, 69: 27–45.

24. H. Cockburn, *Memorials of His Time*, p. 32.

25. Jasper Ridley, *Lord Palmerston* (New York, 1971), pp. 14–18; John Prest, *Lord John Russell*, pp. 12, 399; *Works of Dugald Stewart*, ed. Hamilton, 10: xlv–lv; *Memoirs of Sir Thomas Dyke Acland*, p. 8.

26. Hilton, *Age of Atonement*, pp. 56–57; Keith Leask, *Hugh Miller* (New York, 1896), p. 50.

27. *Works of Dugald Stewart*, ed. Hamilton, 2: 77; 8: 49, 202; 9: 277.

28. Ibid., 6: 226–230, 301; 7: 239; Paley, *Moral and Political Philosophy*, 1: 168, 220, 236–238, 270; 2: 279–298, 300–301.

29. Kitson Clark, *Churchmen and the Condition of England*, p. 72; McClatchey, *Oxfordshire Clergy*, p. 91; Mole, "Church of England and Society in Birmingham," p. 84; Kathleen Heasman, *Evangelicals in Action: An Appraisal of Their Social Work in the Victorian Era* (London, 1962), p. 211; Lewis, *Lighten Their Darkness*, pp. 50–52.

30. Kitson Clark, *Churchmen*, p. 143.

31. *Hansard*, 1845, 78: 1383.

32. Kitson Clark, *Churchmen*, p. 73; E. R. Norman, *Church and Society in England* (Oxford, 1976), pp. 127–128.

33. J. B. Summer, bishop of Chester, *Charge to the Clergy* (London, 1835, 1841); William

Bloomfield, bishop of London, *Charge to the Clergy* (London, 1842, 1846); William Howley, archbishop of Canterbury, *Charge to the Clergy* (London, 1844); Henry Phillpotts, bishop of Exeter, *Charge to the Clergy* (London, 1842, 1845, 1848).

34. Gill, *Parson Bull*, pp. 114, 117, 124, 127, 131; Finlayson, *Seventh Earl of Shaftesbury*, p. 196.

35. M'Neil, *Famine*, pp. 8–9; F. Bennett, *Story of W. J. E. Bennett*, pp. 13–14.

36. Lewis, *Edwin Chadwick*, pp. 210–211.

37. Christian Instruction Society, *Lectures to Socialists* (London, 1840), p. 180; Donald Lewis, *Lighten Their Darkness*, p. 100.

38. *Christian Teacher*, 1841, 41: 638; Gresley, *Clement Walton*, p. 161; *Sermons at St. Mary's Church, Warwick* (London, 1843), p. 4; Mole, "Church of England and Society in Birmingham," p. 285.

39. Sumner, *Christian Charity*, p. ix.

40. Gresley, *Frank's First Trip to the Continent*, p. 161; Kitson Clark, *Churchmen and the Condition of England*, p. 215; Stevens, *Poor Law Relief No Charity* (London, 1845), p. 12.

41. Melville, *Sermons . . . on Public Occasions*, p. 46.

42. Rev. James Davies, *The Filling Up of the Christian Ministry* (London, 1848), pp. 8–9; Rev. James Joyce Evans, *Memoirs and Remains of the Rev. James Harington Evans* (London, 1852), p. 25; Rev. William Stowell, *Twelve Sermons by the late Rev. William Hendy Stowell* (London, 1850), pp. cxxxvi–cxxxvii; William Stowell, *William Stowell* (London, 1859), pp. 29–30, 99.

43. John Kent, "The Clash Between Radicalism and Conservatism in Methodism" (Ph.D. diss., Cambridge University, 1950), pp. 4–5, 37–39, 89–91; 214–249, 256, 258–259; Thomas Jackson, *Recollections of My Own Life and Times* (London, 1878) (524 pages and not one word on a social question); Holyoake, *Life of Joseph Raynor Stephens*, pp. 47–60.

44. Binney, *Sermons . . . in the King's Weigh-House Chapel*, pp. 45–47, 73, 322, 361 (religion, true or false, if carried out would cure all the disorders and make society virtuous); Paxton Hood, *Thomas Binney*, pp. 5–6, 33–35, 41, 197, 222; Binney, *Righteousness Exalteth a Nation*, pp. 5–10; Arthur Mursell, *James Philip Mursell, His Life and Work* (London, 1886), pp. 13–14; W. F. Conybeare, *A Sermon Preached in the Chapel Royal Whitehall*, p. 64; Wilson, *Life of George Dawson*, pp. 5, 14, 19, 25, 67, 76–77, 95; Dawson, *Biographical Lectures*, p. 400.

45. *Hansard*, 1844, 73: 1263, 1460; 1846, 86: 1080; 1847, 90: 820–821; the votes for and against a corn law or a ten-hour bill come from various divisions on the issue, not just one; Coleridge, *Church and State*, p. 430.

46. *Hansard*, 1847, 93: 645; 1848, 1342.

47. *Hansard*, 1842, 64: 1365; 1843, 69: 407; 1844, 75: 1547; 1846, 85: 265; 1841, 57: 749; 1842, 64: 168.

48. *Hansard*, 1840, 52: 946; 55: 1101; 1841, 57: 1418; 1948, 97: 591; 1849, 104: 1090; 1840, 53: 1136; 1847, 92: 5.

49. *Hansard*, 1842, 62: 537; 1846, 88: 462; 1849, 103: 404; 105: 552; 106: 1012–1016.

50. *Hansard*, 1849, 103: 314; 104: 279; 1848, 97: 362.

51. *Hansard*, 1842, 63: 1321–1352; 1844, 73: 1073–1101, 1122–1123; 1845, 77: 638–666; 81: 181–198; 1848, 99: 430–455; 1849, 107: 897–914.

52. *Hansard*, 1843, 71: 78–82; 1845, 78: 311–315; 1848, 99: 86–89; 1849, 107: 481–485; 1847, 92: 406–418.

53. *Hansard*, 1843, 71: 90.

54. Gill, *Parson Bull*, p. 69; Hilton, *Age of Atonement*, pp. 213–214.

55. Hilton, *Age of Atonement*, pp. 213–214.

56. *Chambers' Edinburgh Journal,* May 1, 1847, p. 2; *Decorator's Assistant,* Aug. 26, 1848; *English Chartist,* 2: 205.

57. *Magistrate,* Dec. 1, 1848, p. 50; *P.P.,* 1846, 20: 309–310; *Eclectic Review,* Sept. 1842, p. 433.

58. Napier, *Remarks on. . . the Punishment of Flogging,* pp. 146–147; *City of London Magazine,* 1: 78.

59. *Hansard,* 1840, 52: 946; 55: 1101; 1848, 97: 591; 1849, 104: 1090.

60. *Hansard,* 1849, 103: 314; 104: 279; 1847, 93: 645; 1848, 97: 362.

61. *Hansard,* 1842, 62: 537; 1846, 88: 462.

62. Sprigge, *Thomas Wakley,* pp. 11–36; W. A. Munford, *William Ewart, M.P., 1798–1869* (London, 1960), pp. 19–42.

63. *Hansard,* 1841, 57: 749; 1842, 64: 168; 1844, 73: 1263, 1460; 1846, 86: 1080; 1847, 90: 820; 93: 280; 1848, 97: 1113; 1846, 86: 950; 1847, 93: 645; 1848, 97: 1342.

64. F. R. and Q. D. Leavis, *Dickens: The Novelist* (New Brunswick, N.J., 1979), p. 188.

65. *Social Control in Nineteenth-Century Britain,* ed. A. P. Donajgrodzki (Totowa, N.J., 1977), pp. 63–73.

66. Ruth Richardson, *Death, Dissection and the Destitute* (London, 1987), pp. 101–102, 113, 151, 153 (citing Roger Cooter), 191, 203.

67. *Madhouses, Mad-Doctors, and Madmen: The Social History of Psychiatry in the Victorian Era,* ed. Andrew Scull (Philadelphia, 1981), pp. 105–116.

68. Foucault, *Madness and Civilization,* pp. 75, 77–78, 176, 182, 186, 207, 227, 252, 267.

69. Ignatieff, *Just Measure of Pain,* pp. 193, 218; Foucault, *Discipline and Punish.*

70. Wiener, *Reconstructing the Criminal,* pp. 115–116.

71. Richard Johnson, "Educating the Educators: Experts and the State," in *Social Control in Nineteenth-Century Britain,* ed. A. P. Donajgrodzki, pp. 100–102; Ritvo, *Animal Estate,* p. 131.

72. *Edinburgh Review,* Oct. 1841, pp. 14–15; July 1842, p. 491; Oct. 1842, p. 206; July 1847, p. 217; Oct. 1854, p. 601; Apr. 1845, pp. 523–524; Jan. 1837, pp. 319–320; Jan. 1848, pp. 231–319.

73. *Edinburgh Review,* Apr. 1843, pp. 391–407; Jan. 1844, pp. 131–2, 131–154; Oct. 1846, pp. 268–313; Jan. 1848, pp. 232–319; Jan. 1849, pp. 223–267; Apr. 1849, pp. 403–434; Oct. 1849, pp. 261–274.

74. *P.P.,* 1844, 26: 535; P.R.O., M.H. 32/49, Kay-Shuttleworth to Poor Law Commission, July 11, 1837; M.H. 32/70, E. C. Tufnell to John LeFevre, Jan. 12, 1838; E. J. Whatley, *Life and Correspondence of Richard Whatley,* pp. 230, 248, 250.

75. *P.P.,* 1846, 32: 571; 1846, 24: 394–395.

76. *P.P.,* 1849, 46: 383–385; 1850, 223: 372.

77. *Journal of the Society of Arts,* July 16, 1886, pp. 608–609; Smith, *Life and Work of Sir James Kay-Shuttleworth,* pp. 86–194; *P.P.,* 1842, 22: 445–446; 1847–1848, 26: 152; 1855, 15: 3–9; E. J. Whatley, *Life and Correspondence of Richard Whatley,* p. 248.

78. British Museum Catalogue; Brent, *Liberal Anglican Politics,* p. 150.

79. David Hartley, *Observations On Man* (London, 1749).

80. Simon, *Studies in the History of Education,* pp. 146, 194; Frederick Hill, *Autobiography,* p. 182.

81. Conolly, *Inquiry Concerning the Indication of Insanity,* p. 8.

82. Thomas, *Man and the Natural World,* pp. 175–176.

83. *Edinburgh Review,* Apr. 1845, p. 502.

84. *Eclectic Review,* July 1849, p. 112; *Hansard,* 1841, 58: 1413; 1847, 90: 1079–1080; Armitage, *Penscellwood Papers,* 2: 279.

85. Sheldon Rothblatt, *The Revolution of the Dons: Cambridge and Society in Early Victorian England* (London, 1981), pp. 101–106; J. S. Mill, *Autobiography*, p. 164.

86. Morell, *On the Progress of Society in England*, p. 4; G. Combe, *The Constitution of Man*, pp. 160–161, 224; Smith, *Divine Government*, pp. 157, 171.

87. Henry Moseley, *Faith in the Works of a Teacher* (London, 1854), p. 8.

88. Conolly, *Construction . . . of Lunatic Asylums*, p. 1; Alexander Maconochie, *On Reformatory Discipline in County and Borough Prisons* (Birmingham, 1851), pp. 11–12, 16, 18; id., *Crime and Punishment: The Mark System, Framed to Mix Persuasion with Punishment, and Make Their Effect Improving, yet Their Operation Severe* (London, 1846); *Blackwood's*, Aug. 1845, p. 136; W. Slaney, *A Plea to Power and Parliament for the Working Classes* (London, 1847), pp. 141–142.

89. John Stuart Mill, *System of Logic* (1843), in id., *The Logic of the Moral Sciences*, ed. A. J. Ayer (La Salle, Ill., 1988), pp. 26, 50.

90. *Westminster Review*, Feb. 1842, p. 18.

91. *Hansard*, 1844, 73: 1434–1435.

92. *Blackwood's*, May 1844, p. 542; *John Bull*, Feb. 13, 1844, p. 79.

93. Manton, *Mary Carpenter*, p. 108.

94. *Journal of the Statistical Society*, 1846, 9: 177; 1847, 10: 38; Humphrey Woolrych, *The History and Results of the Present Capital Punishments in England* (London, 1832), p. 181.

95. *P.R.O.*, M.H. 32/72, Twisleton to commissioners on Paisley; *P.P.*, 1838, 18: pt. I, pp. 11–40 (Nottingham); 1842, 19: 10–11; 35: 69–98 (Bolton), 195–335 (Stockport); 1843, 7: 3–5, 1–139 (Paisley).

96. Lewis, *Edwin Chadwick*, pp. 45–46; Chadwick, *Sanitary Report of 1842*, pp. 254–298.

97. W. A. F. Browne, *What Asylums Were, Are, and Ought to Be* (London, 1837), pp. 4–5, 69; Munro, *Remarks on Insanity*.

98. Roger Cooter, *The Cultural Meaning of Popular Science* (London, 1984), pp. 32, 120, 124; Conolly, *Inquiry Concerning the Indications of Insanity*, p. 7; Browne, *Asylums*, p. viii.

99. Combe, *Constitution of Man*, p. 30.

100. Gerald McNeice, *Shelley and the Revolutionary Ideal* (Cambridge, Mass., 1969), p. 10.

101. Marchand, *Athenaeum*, pp. 30–31; Henry Crabb Robinson, *Diary, Reminiscences and Correspondences* (London, 1869).

102. *Howitt's Journal*, Nov. 27, 1847, p. 348; Henry Cole, *Fifty Years of Public Work* (London, 1884), pp. 16–18.

103. *Westminster Review*, Jan. 1849, p. 371; Oct. 1842, p. 315.

104. *Westminster Review*, June 1846, p. 405; Apr. 1842, pp. 305–319; Mar. 1845, pp. 163–185; Oct. 1847, pp. 119–130; Apr. 1848, pp. 70–83.

105. *Westminster Review*, Oct. 1842, p. 390; June 1844, pp. 310, 374; Dec. 1843, pp. 327–330, 465–466.

106. *Westminster Review*, July 1832, pp. 52–62; Jan. 1842, pp. 202–216; June 1845, p. 469.

107. Bain, *Autobiography*, p. 64.

108. Bentham, *Deontology*, p. 229.

109. *Hansard*, 1845, 78: 1394; 80: 1094; 1847, 89: 594; 1846, 88: 395, 456.

110. Manton, *Mary Carpenter*, p. 27; Raymond Holt, *The Unitarian Contribution to Social Progress in England* (London, 1952), pp. 157–271; Isichei, *Victorian Quakers*, p. xix and passim.

111. Manton, *Mary Carpenter*, pp. 10–35; *DNB*, 9: 157; Hill, *Life of Sir Rowland Hill*, 1: 1–67; R. and F. Davenport-Hill, *Recorder of Birmingham*, pp. 2–8; *DNB*, 6: 76; Weaver, *John*

Fielden, pp. 31–37, 50, 291; Conolly, *Inquiry Concerning the Indications of Insanity,* p. 11; Frederick Hill, *Autobiography;* Lewes, *Southwood Smith.*

112. Wilson, *Thomas Clarkson,* p. 14; Thomas Clarkson, *The Grievances of Our Mercantile Seamen, a National and Crying Evil* (London, 1845), pp. 4–27; Earl Leslie Griggs, *Thomas Clarkson* (London, 1836).

113. Isichei, *Victorian Quakers,* pp. 247–250; Rufus Jones, *The Later Periods of Quakerism* (London, 1921), pp. 335–348.

114. Digby, *Madness, Morality, and Medicine,* pp. 15–33; Tuke, *Chapters in the History of the Insane,* pp. 92–160; Isichei, *Victorian Quakers,* p. 244; Thomas, *Man and the Natural World,* pp. 159, 162, 180, 297.

115. Jones, *Later Periods of Quakerism,* pp. 335–347.

116. Wilson, *Thomas Clarkson,* p. 15; *The Memoirs of Sir Thomas Fowell Buxton,* ed. Charles Buxton, p. 122; E. Fry, *Memoirs,* 1: 17.

117. Southwood Smith, *Divine Government,* pp. 1–52, 154, 168, and 202, and pt. 4 on Scripture; id., *Probable Influence of the Development of the Principles of the Human Mind,* p. 39; Mary Carpenter, *Morning and Evening Meditations* (London, 1845); Weaver, *John Fielden,* pp. 30–35.

118. Simon Maccoby, *English Radicalism, 1832–1852* (London, 1935), p. 76; Weaver, *John Fielden,* pp. 54, 220–221.

119. Brent, *Liberal Anglican Politics,* pp. 134, 136; Peter Mandler, "Cain and Abel," *Historical Journal* 27 (1984): 86; Carlisle, *Viceregal Speeches and Addresses,* ed. Gaskin, pp. xix–xxii, lxxix, 46; *Leeds Mercury,* July 10, 1841; Lord Morpeth, *The Last of the Greeks* (London, 1828).

120. R. A. Slaney, *On Sources of Happiness* (London, 1857), p. 31; *Reports of the House of Commons on Education and on Health* (London, 1841), p. 12; Hilton, *Age of Atonement,* 241; *DNB,* 52: 367.

121. Philanthropic Society, *Second Report,* p. iii.

122. *Chambers' Edinburgh Journal,* May 1, 1847, p. 2; North Waterloo Academic Press brochure announcing a planned ten-volume *Waterloo Directory of English Newspapers and Periodicals, 1800–1900* (Waterloo, Ontario, 2000), p. 2; Richard Altick, *The English Common Reader* (Chicago, 1957), p. 286.

123. R. W. Hamilton, *Nugae Literariae,* p. 146.

124. Michael J. Cullen, *The Statistical Movement in Early Victorian Britain* (New York, 1975), pp. 15, 19, 29, 35, 77, 105, 119–132; M. W. Flinn, *Sanitary Report of 1842,* p. 21.

125. *Hansard,* 1837, 37: 715; 1840, 55: 914, 1081; 1847, 90: 1079–1090; 1848, 97: 543, 551, 559, 571; 1849, 104: 1061, 1073.

126. *Hansard,* 1847, 90: 1082–1083; 1848, 97: 543; 1849, 104: 1066–1068; *Journal of the Statistical Society,* June 1845, pp. 177–178.

127. T. Wrightson, *On the Punishment of Death* (London, 1837), pp. 53–54. *Hansard,* 1849, 104: 1061–1062.

128. *Journal of the Statistical Society,* 1838, 1: 242.

129. *Hansard,* 1847, 90: 1091–1093; 1849, 104: 1067–1070.

130. *Blackwood's,* Nov. 1841, pp. 666–668; *Oxford and Cambridge Review,* Nov. 1846, p. 595.

131. *Journal of the Statistical Society,* 1841, 4: 331; 1843, 6: 233–236; 1846, 9: 29–30; 1849, 11: 204.

132. R. D. Grainger, *Unhealthiness of Towns* (London, 1845), p. 47; Browne, *Asylums,* p. 50.

133. General Board of Health, *Report on Cholera* (London, 1850), app. A, p. 3; Flinn, *Sanitary Report of 1842,* p. 44, 64; *P.P.,* 1839, 20: 100–106; Munro, *Remarks on Insanity,* pp. i–ii.

134. Digby, *Madness, Morality, and Medicine*, pp. 14–48.

135. Skultans, *English Madness*, pp. 58–61; Jones, *Lunacy, Law and Conscience*, pp. 57–65, 149–156; Browne, *Asylums*, p. 185; Conolly, *Construction . . . of Lunatic Asylums*, p. 48; Prichard, *Forms of Insanity*, pp. 19, 31.

136. Flinn, *Sanitary Report of 1842*, pp. 9, 23, 32.

137. Chadwick, *Sanitary Report of 1842*, pp. 13, 15, 21–22; *P.P.*, 1839, 17: Fever, app. C.

138. James Smith, *Report on Lancaster* (London, 1849), p. 5; Edward Crecy, *Report on Derby* (London, 1849), pp. 9–10; William Ranger, *Report on Edmonton* (London, 1850), p. 9; Sir Robert Rawlinson, *Report on Birmingham* (London, 1849), pp. 2–4.

139. Sir Robert Rawlinson, *Report on Whitehaven* (London, 1849), pp. 4–5; William Lee, *Report on Over Darien* (London, 1851), pp. 19–20.

140. *Hansard*, 1854, 135: 984; *P.P.*, 1855, 2: 151.

141. *P.P.*, 1837–1838, 21: 1–2, 68; 1840, 25: 1; 1836, 35: 68, 72; *Times*, Dec. 1894, obituaries; Boase, *Modern English Biography*, 5: 608; *Lancet*, Dec. 15, 1894, pp. 1454–1455; for Hawkins: *P.P.*, 1836, 35: 6, 29, 62; 1838, 31: 1–5; 1839, 27: 44; 1840, 25: i; 1855, 26: 17, 24, 38–40, 86–87; P.R.O., H.O. 12/4591, report on Northampton Gaol; for John Perry: *P.P.*, 1845, 24: 36; *P.P.*, 1850, 17: 103, 113–114; 1854, 26, p. 7; 1855, 26: 57; H.O. 12/4591; *Monthly Notices of the Astronomical Society*, Feb. 10, 1871, p. 102; *Medical Times*, Jan. 22, 1870; for Donatus O'Brien: *P.P.*, 1848, 36: 127–129; 1849, 26: 8; 1850, 103: 113–114; Boase, *Modern English Biography*, 6: 314; for John Williams: *P.P.*, 1838, 31: 7; 1839, 22 i–iii, xi; 1842, 21: 7; 1850, 28: 58, 36.

142. Hodgkinson, *National Health Service*, pp. 47, 61, 132, 135, 143, 148.

143. *Hansard*, 1842, 62: 521–523.

144. *Hansard*, 1849, 107: 103–104.

145. *P.P.*, 1855, 15: 583, 597, 651–664, 691; MacDonagh, "Coal Mines Regulations," in *Ideas and Institutions in Victorian Britain*, ed. Robert Robson (New York, 1967), pp. 84, 58–84.

CHAPTER 12

1. *Examiner*, Oct. 15, 1842.

2. *Lloyd's Weekly*, Mar. 3, 1844, Feb. 21, 1847; *Leeds Times*, Sept. 17, 1842; *Educational Times*, Nov. 1, 1847; *Northern Star*, May 28, 1842.

3. *Fraser's*, Mar. 1847, p. 325; *Morning Post*, Mar. 24, 1847.

4. *Blackwood's*, May 1845, pp. 537, 530–537; *Quarterly Review*, Dec. 1849, 178.

5. John Murray, *The World of London* (London, 1845), 1: 65; *Oxford and Cambridge Review*, Aug. 1845, p. 154.

6. *Edinburgh Review*, Jan. 1845, p. 208; *Sussex Advertiser*, May 28, 1844; *Educational Times*, Nov. 1, 1847.

7. *Hansard*, 1845, 78: 581; 1842, 62: 500, 870; 1844, 73: 1437; 1848, 99: 87–88; Chalmers, *Works*, 4: 59.

8. Brown, *Fathers of the Victorians*, p. 75; Bickersteth, *Works*, 7: 299–302, 14: 126–127, 130; Hilton, *Age of Atonement*, p. 96.

9. M'Neil, *Famine*, p. 27.

10. *Western Times*, Apr. 3, 1847; Paget, *The Pageant*, pp. 27, 33–34, 68, 146.

11. Binney, *Sermons . . . in the King's Weigh-House Chapel*, pp. 46–48; Hamilton, *Nugae Literariae*, pp. 421–422.

12. *Eclectic Review*, July 1844, p. 110; *NonConformist*, Apr. 17, 1844, p. 344, and May 18, 1842, p. 335, May 25, 1842, p. 361.

13. Charles Dickens, *Nicholas Nickleby* (1838–39; London, 1957), pp. 619 and 6–17, 117–123, 177, 223–246, 405–406, 432–448, 619–635, 745, 758; id., *Martin Chuzzlewit* (1844; Boston, n.d.), 1: ch. 8: 183, 2: ch. 11, 229–254; id., *Little Dorrit* (1855–57; London, n.d.), ch. 13, pp. 541–542. William Thackeray, *Vanity Fair* (1848; London, 1968), pp. 13, 109, 128, 157; Bulwer-Lytton, *Paul Clifford*, pp. 127, 168, 199–200.

14. Thackeray, *Vanity Fair*, pp. 13, 109, 128, 157; Bulwer-Lytton, *Paul Clifford*, pp. 127, 168, 199–200.

15. Bulwer-Lytton, *Paul Clifford*, pp. 127, 199; Disraeli, *Sybil*, pp. 54, 118, 142, 144, 154, 162–163, 167, 202; C. Gore, *The Cabinet Minister* (London, 1839), 1: 185; id., *Mammon* (New York, 1859); id., *Peers and Parvenu* (London, 1846), 1: 94.

16. Coleridge, *Church and State*, p. 67; Carlyle, *Chartism*, pp. 162–163; Southey, *Essays*, 1: 178, 195, 223; *Life and Correspondence of Robert Southey*, ed. C. C. Southey, 6: 87; *P.P.*, 1850, 19: 55–56; *Quarterly Review* 74 (Oct. 1844): 483; Arnold, *Miscellaneous Works*, p. 175.

17. Phyllis Deane and W. A. Cole, *British Economic Growth* (London, 1962), p. 282; Jeffrey Williamson, *Did British Capitalism Breed Inequality?* (Boston, 1985), p. 40; W. D. Rubinstein, *Elites, and the Wealthy in Modern British History* (New York, 1987), pp. 28, 50, 114; Perkin, *Origins of Modern English Society*, pp. 21, 138–140; Phyllis Deane, *The First Industrial Revolution* (Cambridge, 1965), pp. 241–253; Eric Hobsbawm, "The British Standard of Living," *Economic History Review*, Aug. 1957, pp. 51–61; Simon Kuznets, "Economic Growth and Income Inequality," *American Economic Review*, Mar. 1955, pp. 17–19.

18. James Caird, *English Agriculture in 1850–1851* (London, 1852), pp. 510–511; Williamson, *Did British Capitalism Breed Inequality?* pp. 8–9; K. D. M. Snell, *Annals of the Labouring Poor* (London, 1985), pp. 60, 101, 121, 123, 126, 128–131, 172–179, 190–195.

19. Osborne, *View of the … Condition of the Agricultural Labourer*, pp. 10–16; *P.P.*, 1843, 12: 80–81, 14: A–10–12, D–6, 15: I–41–43, 49; Pamela Horn, *The Rise and Fall of the Victorian Servant* (New York, 1975), pp. 184–185.

20. Clapham, *Early Railway Age*, p. 559; *P.P.*, 1846, 13: 427–436, 450–451, 464, 477, 485, 512; Bartrip and Burman, *Wounded Soldiers of Industry*, p. 69.

21. *P.P.*, 1843, 14: E, 1–6.

22. MacDonagh, "Coal Mines Regulation," in *Ideas and Institutions*, ed. Robson, pp. 83–85; *P.P.*, 1843, 14: C, 3–5.

23. Bartrip, "State Intervention," pp. 69, 74; *Mining Journal*, Jan. 27, 1855.

24. F. L. M. Thompson, *English Landed Estate in the Nineteenth Century*, pp. 218–220, 231, 241, 253; Caird, *English Agriculture in 1850–1851*, pp. 447, 475–477, 510–511, 513; Digby, *Pauper Palaces*, p. 199.

25. Chadwick, *Sanitary Report of 1842*, p. 7; *P.P.*, 1848, 6: 23, 33, 35.

26. *P.P.*, 1846, 9: 28, 51, 79, 81, 128–130, 170–179, 196–197, 258, 267; 1844, 5: 14, 22, 33, 44, 61–62, 79–80, 85, 118, 157.

27. *P.P.*, 1843, 12: 40, 43, 78, 80–81, 87–93, 153, 157, 161, 164–165, 216, 226–227; Chadwick, *Sanitary Report*, pp. 6, 80–99, 114, 117–120, 221, 136, 189–204, 299–300, 326–327, 336–337; Enid Gauldie, *Cruel Habitations: A History of Working-Class Housing, 1780–1918* (London, 1974), pp. 73–169.

28. Chadwick, *Sanitary Report of 1842*, pp. 6–7, 9, 114, 136, 221; *Journal of the Statistical Society*, 3: 18, 11: 20, 6: 17, 11: 1–19 and 193–216; Gauldie, *Cruel Habitations*, pp. 74–76, 81–84, 157, 159, 189.

29. Chadwick, *Sanitary Report of 1842*, pp. 136, 221; Gauldie, *Cruel Habitations*, pp. 157–158.

30. *P.P.*, 1843, 12: 78; Chadwick, *Sanitary Report of 1842*, p. 327.

31. Gauldie, *Cruel Habitations*, p. 189; Donald Olsen, *Town Planning in London* (New Haven, Conn., 1964), pp. 169–170; Chadwick, *Sanitary Report of 1842*, p. 334.

32. *P.P.*, 1845, 40: 7; E. J. Hobsbawm and George Rude, *Captain Swing* (New York, 1968), p. 51.

33. *P.P.*, 1848, 53: 15; Edwin Chadwick Papers, History Library, University College, London University, memo "On the inadequate payment to High Service" (Nov. 1849); *Standard*, Mar. 15, 1842.

34. Glyde, *Suffolk in the Nineteenth Century*, pp. 183–184.

35. Rhodes Boysen, "The New Poor Law in Northeast Lancashire," *Transactions of the Lancashire and Cheshire Antiquarian Society*, 1960, 60: 450–455; Ashworth, "Urban Poor," in *New Poor Law*, ed. Fraser; Digby, *Pauper Palaces*, pp. 12–13, 109, 143–144, 166; *The Poor and the City: The English Poor Law in Its Urban Context, 1834–1914*, ed. Michael E. Rose (New York, 1985), pp. 7–8; id., *The Relief of Poverty* (London, 1986), pp. 12ff; id., "Allowance System," *Economic History Review* 19 (1963): 607–620.

36. Anstruther, *Scandal of the Andover Workhouse*, pp. 111–152; Roberts, "How Cruel Was the New Poor Law?" *Historical Journal* 6 (1963): 97–107.

37. P. Dunkley, "The Hungry Forties and the New Poor Law," *Historical Journal* 17, no. 2 (1974): 335, 338; Snell, *Annals of the Labouring Poor*, pp. 123, 131; *New Poor Law*, ed. Fraser, pp. 38, 41, 68–69, 140; Hodgkinson, *National Health Service*, pp. 35, 37, 81–87, 107, 132.

38. Digby, *Pauper Palaces*, p. 166.

39. Karel Williams, *From Pauperism to Poverty* (London, 1981), pp. 71 (in 1858, 12 percent of trade unionists were jobless and only 12,000 able-bodied men received outdoor relief), 75, 86–87; Digby, *Pauper Palaces*, pp. 56–57.

40. *P.P.*, 1837, 17: pt. 2, 3d report, p. 76; Mayhew, *London Labour and the London Poor*, 2: 68; Digby, *Pauper Palaces*, p. 143; Baxter, *Book of the Bastilles*, pp. 116, 118, 119, 125–126; Karel Williams, *From Pauperism to Poverty*, pp. 71–72, 74–75.

41. K. Williams, *From Pauperism to Poverty*, pp. 64, 76–77.

42. Ashworth, "Urban Poor," in *New Poor Law*, ed. Fraser, p. 140; Digby, *Pauper Palaces*, pp. 5–6, 22.

43. *P.P.*, 1847, 2: 13–14, 37, 40, 48–49, 134, 210, 224, 354, 375, 406, 484, 509, 552; *Oxford and Cambridge Review*, July 1845, p. 87.

44. *P.P.*, 1842, 35: 69–98, 171–179, 193–199, 203, 260; 1843, 7: 80–82, 94–95, 120–121; *Poor and the City*, ed. Rose, p. 8; Ashworth, "Urban Poor," in *New Poor Law*, ed. Fraser, p. 142; Digby, *Pauper Palaces*, p. 87.

45. *P.P.*, 1837, 17: pt. 1, 1st report, pp. 19–21, 38, 42, 133–134, 141–143, 146, 148; 2d report, p. 48; 3d report, pp. 25–35, 37–59; pt. 2, 10th report, pp. 5–6, 10–11, 20–27. For general moralizing claims, see pt. 1, general report, pp. 7–11; 1st report, 62–63, 69–74, 89; 6th report, pp. 33–34; 7th report, 2–15, 33–34; pt. 2, 20th report, pp. 1–2; 1838, 18: pt. 1, general report, pp. 11–12, 16–18, 20–29, 33; pt. 2, pp. 185–194.

46. W. P. Alison, *On the Management of the Poor*, pp. 7, 33, 36–37, 42, 55–57, 63–72, 101; Perry, *Peasantry of England*, p. 38.

47. Woodham Smith, *The Great Hunger*, pp. 60, 82, 106–107, 111, 164, 172, 185, 198, 285, 296–297, 302, 307–308, 314, 318, 375, 379, 408; Edwards and Williams, *Great Famine*, pp. xi, 141–142, 149–150, 154, 158, 163, 218–220, 223, 232, 235, 244–246; Daly, *Famine in Ireland*, pp. 60, 67, 71, 75, 78, 81, 88, 94, 96, 113–114.

48. *Hansard*, 1847, 89: 725; 90: 1311; 1849, 102: 279, 393–394, 598; 103: 63, 210, 1312, 1329; 104: 74, 77.

49. *Hansard*, 1847, 89: 666–667; 90: 294ff; 1848, 97: 362; 1849, 104: 279.

50. *Hansard*, 1847, 90: 1310–1312; 92: 89–90; 1849, 105: 1286.

51. Robert Rawlinson, *Further Inquiries . . . of Macclesfield* (London, 1851), pp. 13–14; Joseph Adshead, *State of Education in the Borough of Manchester* (London, 1852).

52. *Leeds Mercury*, June 26, 1841; *Nottingham Journal* July 9, 1841.

53. *Hansard*, 1849, 109: 876–877; R. J. White, *The Political Thought of Samuel Taylor Coleridge* (London, 1938), p. 42.

54. *Leeds Mercury*, July 10, 1841; *Staffordshire Mercury*, July 17, 1847.

55. *Times*, May 9, 1848, Jan. 2, 1855.

56. *Liverpool Chronicle*, May 6, Aug. 5, 1856.

57. *Leeds Mercury*, Jan. 21, 1841.

58. *Guardian*, Jan. 21, 1886, p. 8; *Blackwood's*, Feb. 1847, p. 244; *Morning Post*, Feb. 6, 1843, May 25, 1844; William Aydelotte, "The House of Commons in the 1840s," *History*, 1954, pp. 248–262.

59. *Westminster Review*, 1837, 26: 208–209; MacDonagh, *Government Growth* (London, 1977), pp. 61, 65, 68, 152, 204, 213; id., "Coal Mines," in *Ideas and Institutions of Victorian Britain*, ed. Robson, pp. 58–84.

60. P. R. O., H.O. 45/1851, Aug. 8, 1851, L. Horner to Sir George Grey; *Mining Journal*, Aug. 17, 1850; Oliver MacDonagh, *Early Victorian Government, 1830–1870* (New York, 1977), pp. 189–190, 204, 213, 219–220.

61. R. W. Kostal, *Law and the English Railways* (Oxford, 1994), p. 29; Henry Parris, *Government and the Railways* (London, 1965), pp. 83–86.

62. Kostal, *Law and the English Railways*, pp. 4, 11, 31, 41.

63. Clapham, *Early Railway Age*, p. 392; Kostal, *Law and the English Railways*, pp. 327–328.

64. *Railway Times*, Mar. 8, 1845; John Francis, *A History of the British Railways* (London, 1851) 2: 95–219; W. T. Jackman, *The Development of Transportation in Modern England* (Cambridge, 1916), p. 489.

65. Francis, *British Railways*, 2: 111, 218–219.

66. Henry G. Lewin, *The Railway Mania and Its Aftermath* (New York, 1968), pp. 107–108; Kostal, *Law and the English Railways*, p. 126.

67. Richard S. Lambert, *The Railway King, 1800–1871* (London, 1934), pp. 234–236, 248–255, 273–274, 299.

68. Finer, *Edwin Chadwick*, p. 440; *Fraser's*, Aug. 1847, 214; *Times*, Oct. 4, 1852, and Mar. 25, 1853.

69. *Liverpool Chronicle*, Feb. 16, Mar. 9, Apr. 20, 1850.

70. Roberts, *Welfare State*, p. 8; Robert Rawlinson, *Preliminary Inquiry into Dover* (London, 1849), pp. 1–3; Lewis, *Edwin Chadwick*, pp. 288–289; R. H. Mottram, "Town Life," in *Victorian England*, ed. G. M. Young (London, 1934), 1: 204, 153–224; Chadwick, *Sanitary Report 1842*, p. 381.

71. Roberts, *Welfare State*, pp. 272–287; *P.P.*, 1850, 17: 65–66.

72. Finer, *Edwin Chadwick*, p. 307; Lewis, *Edwin Chadwick*, pp. 94–95, 271, 330.

73. Royston Lambert, *Sir John Simon* (London, 1963), p. 59.

74. Lewis, *Edwin Chadwick*, pp. 94–95, 271, 330, 340–341; Finer, *Edwin Chadwick*, pp. 403–405, 409–502, 471–472.

75. Finer, *Edwin Chadwick*, 327–328, 374, 390–393, 412–422, 403–429;. Lewis, *Edwin Chadwick*, pp. 358–375; R. Lambert, *Sir John Simon*, pp. 66, 68, 86, 122–123, 126–127, 147, 178, 221; *Hansard*, 1852, 102: 1305, 1311.

76. R. A. Lewis, *Edwin Chadwick*, p. 136; *P.P.*, 1849, 24: 61; Henry Austin, *Report on Taunton* (London, 1850); Edward Crecy, *Report on Eton* (London, 1850), pp. 7–11.

77. *Westminister Review*, July 1848, pp. 422–439; Royston Lambert, *Sir John Simon*, pp. 66–87, 122–161.

78. Roberts, *Paternalism*, pp. 198, 200, 251–252, 258; id., *Welfare State*, pp. 77, 82, 97–98; *Hansard*, 1848, 98: 72, 711, 738–739.

79. Roberts, *Paternalism*, pp. 225–226, 256, 258; *Hansard*, 1847, 92: 1005; 93: 667, 714, 716, 727, 729–301, 885; 1848, 98: 712, 717, 719, 723–724, 728–729, 740, 753, 764–765, 771, 789, 792, 794, 798–799.

80. Finer, *Edwin Chadwick*, p. 98; *Standard*, May 5, 1834, May 9, 1848; *Morning Herald*, May 28, 1834; *John Bull*, May 13, 1848.

81. Owen, *English Philanthropy*, pp. 191, 182–203.

82. Smith, *Life and Work of Sir James Kay-Shuttleworth*, pp. 148–149, 157–159; *Eclectic Review*, Nov. 1847, 608; Jan. 1848, pp. 96–119; Dec. 1848, 707–714; *NonConformist*, 1847: Apr. 7, pp. 206, 213, 230–231, June 9, 428–430; *Westminister Review*, July 1842, pp. 219–220; Edwin Chadwick Papers, Rough Notes on Central Administration (n.d.); *Times*, Sept. 26, 1842; *Hansard*, 1850, 110: 438.

83. David Roberts, "Lord Palmerston at the Home Office," *The Historian*, Nov. 1958, pp. 63–81; P.R.O., H.O. 45/5276; *Hansard*, 1854, 133: 1267; 134: 750; *Manchester Guardian*, June 24, 1854; Radzinowicz, *Criminal Law*, 4: 243–302; *Hansard*, 1845, 77: 719.

84. *Edinburgh Review*, Jan. 1847, pp. 221–258; *Hansard*, 1854, 135.

85. *Hansard*, 1854, 135: 990; J. Toulmin Smith, *Government by Commissions Illegal and Pernicious: The Nature and Effects of All Commissions of Inquiry and Other Crown-Appointed Commissions* (London, 1849), pp. 39–45, 67, 76–95, 121, 151, 165–303; id., *Local Self-Government Un-mystified* (London, 1857), p. 29.

86. J. S. Mill, *Autobiography*, p. 144; Lambert, *Sir John Simon*, p. 237; Edwin Chadwick Papers, undated letter of 1847 on the *Morning Chronicle*.

87. J. S. Mill, *Autobiography*, pp. 134–136; Packe, *John Stuart Mill*, p. 203; *Edinburgh Review*, Oct. 1840, p. 15; J. S. Mill, *Principles of Political Economy*, 2: 178, 507, 515, 558–603; Toulmin Smith, *Government by Commissions*, pp. 165, 176.

88. *John Bull*, May 13, 1848; Coleridge, *Table Talk*, 2: 53.

89. Ross Harrison, *Bentham* (London, 1983), p. 200; Jeremy Bentham, *Church-of-Englandism and Its Catechism Examined . . .* (London, 1817); *Punch*, 3: 152; *Manchester Guardian*, Sept. 29, 1841.

90. *Westminster Review*, Sept. 1844, pp. 166–167; Sumner, *Charge*; C. Woodham-Smith, *The Reason Why* (London, 1953), p. 31.

91. *Hansard*, 1850, 108: 374; *Westminister Review*, Sept. 1844, pp. 136–137; *Lancet*, Oct. 10, 1842, p. 101; May 13, 1843, pp. 234–235; Jeanne Peterson, *The Medical Profession in Mid-Victorian London* (Berkeley and Los Angeles, 1978), pp. 8–11, 168, 172; Ivan Waddington, "General Practitioners," *Health Care and Medicine in Nineteenth Century England* (New York, 1977), p. 172; W. J. Reader, *Professional Men: The Rise of the Professional Classes in Nineteenth-Century England* (New York, 1966), pp. 191–192.

92. *Douglas Jerrold's Shilling Magazine* 2 (1845): 507.

93. Reader, *Professional Men*, pp. 14–25, 47, 75–76, 128; Woodham-Smith, *Reason Why*, pp. 21–23; Gwyn Jenkins, *The Army in Victorian Society* (London, 1973), p. 9.

94. William Holdsworth, *A History of English Law* (London, 1965), 10: 234–235; *P.P.*, 1846, 10: 509–531.

95. *P.P.*, 1846, 10: pp. 498–509; Woodham-Smith, *Reason Why*, p. 140; *Punch*, 10: 170–171.

96. *Lancet*, 1840: Jan. 4, p. 538; Sept. 26, pp. 1–2; 1841, Feb. 6, pp. 698, 732; May 22, pp. 331–333; 1842: Oct. 15, pp. 101–103; 1847: Nov. 20, p. 555; Ivan Waddington, "General Practitioners," in *Health Care and Popular Medicine*, ed. John Woodward and David Richards (New York, 1977), pp. 168–178; Peterson, *Medical Profession*, pp. 7, 9, 30; Edward O'Brien, *The Lawyer, His Character and His Rule of Holiness* (London, 1842), pp. 13–21, 55.

97. *Law Magazine*, 1844, 31: 15, 24; 32: 174–175; *Punch*, 2: 108.

98. Harrison, *Bentham*, p. 202; Dickens, *Pickwick Papers*, ch. 43; *Punch*, 2: 108.

99. British Museum, Peel Papers, Add. MSS 40448, Peel to Graham, Dec. 28, 1842; Best, *Temporal Pillars*, pp. 362–368; *Western Times*, Jan. 20, 1844; *Hansard*, 1850, 108: 324; 111: 170.

100. *Hansard*, 1842, 42: 521–539; 1846, 87: 1337–1342; 88: 377–466, 685–694; 1847, 89: 594–595; 91: 1142; Woodham-Smith, *Reason Why*, pp. 43, 49–52, 140–141.

101. Peterson, *Medical Profession*, p. 30.

102. Reader, *Professional Men*, pp. 25–31, 54–58; Holdsworth, *History of English Law*, 15: 128.

103. *Law Magazine*, May 1840, p. 359; Feb. 1841, pp. 98, 131–141, May 1841, pp. 311–324; Nov. 1841, pp. 243–245; May 1842, pp. 270–275; Aug. 1842, pp. 1–34; May 1844, p. 311; 1845, 33: 58, 269–271; and 1849, 41: 14.

104. *Hansard*, 1845, 80 or 81: 497; *Law Magazine*, 1844, 31: 253; 1847, 38: 36.

105. Henry Phillpotts, bishop of Exeter, *A Charge to the Clergy* (London, 1840), p. 60; Ian D. C. Newbould, "The Whigs, the Church and Education," *British Studies*, June 1987, pp. 334, 342; Geoffrey Best, "National Education in England, 1800–1870," *Cambridge Historical Journal* 12 (1956): 163–164; Paz, *Working Class Education in Britain*, pp. 82, 85, 100–102, 109; Denison, *Church Education*, pp. 4–25; id., *Notes of My Life*, pp. 99, 149, 155, 168.

106. Dawes, *Remarks Occasioned by the Present Crusade*, pp. 11, 31; Hook, *Means of Rendering More Efficient the Education of the People*, pp. 7, 33; Smith, *Life and Work of Sir James Kay-Shuttleworth*, pp. 170, 174–175.

107. *P.P.*, 1845, 35: 343, 466; 1846, 32: 543; 1847, 45: 104; 1852, 40: 346.

108. Hook, *Means of Rendering More Efficient the Education of the People*, pp. 2–71; *Hansard*, 1850, 111: 792–795.

109. *Leeds Times*, Aug. 14, 1847; *Hansard*, 1853, 124: 38.

110. George Trevelyan, *The Life of John Bright* (Boston, 1913), p. 394; *Hansard*, 1847, 91: 1008.

111. E. P. Thompson, *The Making of the English Working Class* (London, 1966), pp. 711–832; Asa Briggs, *Chartist Studies* (London, 1967), p. 297; id., "The Language of 'Class,'" in *Essays in Labour History* (London, 1960); Perkin, *Origins of English Modern Society*, pp. 176–217. For further discussion of "class," see Gareth Stedman Jones, *The Language of Class* (London, 1983), Dror Wahrman, *Imagining the Middle Class* (London, 1995), David Cannadine, *The Rise and Fall of Class* (New York, 1999), and Patrick Joyce, *Visions of the People* (London, 1991).

112. Francis E. Mineka, *The Dissidence of Dissent: The Monthly Repository, 1806–1838* (Chapel Hill, N.C., 1944), p. 199; *Hansard*, 1846, 83: 134, 758; *Economist*, Sept. 16, 1843, p. 33; George Porter, *Progress of a Nation* (London, 1847), p. 658.

113. Anon., *Young England: Addresses Delivered by Lord John Manners* (London, 1844), p. 6.

114. *Hansard*, 1846, 84: 1361; *York Herald*, Aug. 24, 1844; A. P. Stanley, *Memoirs of Edward and Catherine Stanley* (London, 1879), p. 278.

115. *Spectator*, Aug. 20, 1842, p. 833; *Hansard*, 1843, 71: 88; 1846, 83: 1311.

116. Nassau Senior, *Outline of Political Economy*, p. 89.

117. Arnold, *Miscellaneous Works*, p. 226; *Congregational Yearbook*, 1848, pp. 101–102; *Edinburgh Review*, Jan. 1846, pp. 68–69.

118. Robert Vaughan, *The Modern Pulpit* (London, 1842), pp. 35–36; *Patriot*, June 22, 1848; *Leeds Mercury*, May 16, 1835.

119. *Hansard*, 1840, 51: 1222; 1846, 86: 406; 1845, 81: 287; 1842, 61: 327, 64: 568.

120. *Leeds Mercury*, Mar. 16, 1844; J. S. Mill, *Dissertations and Discussions*, 1: 195.

121. Robert Shoyen, *The Chartist Challenge* (London, 1958), pp. 96, 102, 183–184, 198, 204, 218, 225, 231; Patricia Hollis, *Class and Class Conflict in Nineteenth-Century England* (London, 1973), pp. 82–84; Briggs, *Chartist Studies*, pp. 13, 38, 77–78, 269, 296; *London Democrat*, 1839, p. 12; *Northern Star*, Apr. 13, 1844.

122. Briggs, *Essays in Labour History*, p. 59; J. S. Mill, *Dissertations and Discussions*, 2: 190, 195; William MacKinnon, *History of Civilization* (London, 1846), 1: 3–4, 10, 15; William L. Alexander, *Memoirs of the Life and Writings of Ralph Wardlaw* (Edinburgh, 1866), p. 380.

123. Driver, *Tory Radical . . . Oastler*, pp. 42–44, 282–302; Oastler, *Slavery in Yorkshire; Fleet Papers*, Jan. 2, June 26, July 3, 17, 1841; May 1, 1842; *Hansard*, 1842, 63: 1321, 1657; 64: 582; 65: 500; 1844, 73: 1075, 1231, 1413, 1449, 1620, 1667; 1845, 77: 638, 664; 1846, 83: 379, 411; 86: 938; 1847, 93: 843; John Fielden, *The Curse of the Factory System* (London, 1838), pp. 1–74.

124. *Chartist Circular* 1: 9 (refers to two classes, slave and master), 7, 29, 91; 2: 3, 41, 169; Hollis, *Class and Class Conflict*, pp. 72–73, 81–82, 138–139, 140–142, 261–270; *Political Register*, Nov. 2, 1816, Nov. 27, 1830.

125. *Northern Star*, Jan. 18, July 30, 1842.

126. *Chartist Circular*, 1: 21; 2: 341; *Northern Star*, Jan. 13, 1844; *Morning Chronicle*, Apr. 21, 1842; *Hansard*, 1846, 83: 1347; *New Monthly Magazine*, May 1842, pp. 463–464.

127. *Northern Star*, Mar. 28, 1840; *Fraser's*, Apr. 1848, p. 586; *Standard*, Dec. 9, 1845; *Leeds Times*, Dec. 17, 1842.

128. *Westminster Review*, June 1846, p. 405; *Hansard*, 1846, 87: 1205–1206; *Morning Advertiser*, Mar. 6, 1844; *NonConformist*, Jan. 12, 1842, p. 25.

129. *Northampton Mercury*, July 24, 1847; *Times*, Jan. 23, 1854.

130. *Standard*, June 10, 1847; *Spectator*, Apr. 27, 1844, p. 396; *Chambers' Edinburgh Journal*, Apr. 9, 1842, p. 92; Mayhew, *London Labour and the London Poor*, table of contents of vols. 1, 2, and 3.

131. *Christian Teacher*, 1842, 4: 210; *Hansard*, 1845, 82: 408; *Patriot*, Feb. 21, 1842; *Hansard*, 1849, 103: 450.

132. *North British Review*, May 1845, pp. 212–213.

133. James Grant, *Newspaper Press* (London, 1872), 3: 116–117; *Oxford and Cambridge Review*, Sept. 1845, pp. 324–325.

134. William Pitt Lennox, *Memoir of Charles Gordon Lennox, Fifth Duke of Richmond* (London, 1862), pp. 249, 259; *Sussex Agricultural Express*, June 13, 1846; Woodham-Smith, *Reason Why*, pp. 36–44, 59–63; 66, 68, 86; *Hansard*, 1847, 90: 4–9; Prebble, *Highland Clearances*.

135. Gathorne Hardy, *Old School Tie*, pp. 60–66, 71–72, 109–113; *Hansard*, 1849, 106: 1378–1379, 1364–1388.

136. *Hansard*, 1844, 72: 225; 75: 877; David Cecil, *Lord Melbourne* (London, 1954), p. 247.

137. *Hansard*, 1842, 64: 540.

138. *Hansard*, 1842, 63: 10–11; 65: 1054; 1840, 55: 433–438; 1843, 68: 319–320; 1845, 81: 1205–1207; 1847, 92: 552; 1847, 95: 929; *Hull Advertiser*, May 14, 1847; *Scotsman*, May 12, 1847; Ed-

wards and Williams, *Great Famine,* p. 163; *Times,* May 28, 1839; *Westminster Review,* July 1842, pp. 219–220; Edwin Chadwick Papers, Rough Notes on Central Administration; *P.P.,* 1841, 10: 400.

139. Constantine Henry Phipps, marquis of Normanby, *The English in Italy* (3 vols.; London, 1825), 1: 225–227; 2: 18, 105, 263; 3: 274.

140. Richard Deacon, *The Cambridge Apostles* (London, 1985); Church, *Oxford Movement*; Lord Ashburton, *The Commercial Crisis* (London, 1847), p. 27.

141. F. M. L. Thompson, "The Landed Elite," in *European Landed Elites,* ed. David Spring (Baltimore, 1977), p. 37; Phipps, *English in Italy,* 2: 294–296.

142. Mrs. Hardcastle, *Life of John Lord Campbell* (London, 1881), pp. 161–162.

143. Patrick Joyce, *Work, Society, and Politics: The Culture of the Factory in Later Victorian England* (New Brunswick, N.J., 1980), pp. 1–41; John Garrard, *Leadership and Power in Victorian Industrial Towns* (Manchester, 1983); G. R. Serle, *Entrepreneurial Politics in Mid-Victorian Britain* (Oxford, 1993); Richard H. Trainor, *Black Country Elites: The Exercise of Authority in an Industrialized Area, 1830–1900* (Oxford, 1993).

144. Joyce, *Work, Society, and Politics,* pp. 50–82; Anthony Howe, *The Cotton Masters, 1830–1860* (New York, 1984).

145. *Leeds Mercury,* Feb. 20, Oct. 23, 1841; Apr. 15, 1843; Jan. 25, 1845; July 18, Aug. 8, 1846; July 17, 1847; *Punch,* 2: 102; a 4: 216–219; 5: 37; 10: 9, 21, 25, 49, 52, 83, 88, 125, 197, 217; 11: 173; 12: 152, 185, 195; *Leeds Times,* Feb. 13, May 1, 1841; Jan. 22, Feb. 26, 1842; Mar. 2, 16, 1844.

CHAPTER 13

1. *English Chartist Circular,* 1: 10, 17; *Leeds Mercury,* June 26, 1841; *London Democrat,* Apr. 20, 1839, pp. 13–14; May 4, 1839, p. 25; *Red Republican,* July 13, 1850; *Democratic Review,* Sept. 1847, p. 156; Cooper, *Purgatory of Suicides,* pp. 2–4, 11, 19, 85, 115, 131, 152–153, 161, 202.

2. *Northern Star,* Apr. 25, Mar. 26, June 25, 1840; Feb. 13, 1847; Halévy, *Growth of Philosophical Radicalism,* p. 191.

3. Owen, *New View of Society,* pp. 36, 45, 54, 235, 255, 261.

4. *The Movement,* 1849, no. 18: 139; no. 54: 460; *Prometheus,* Jan. 1842, pp. 1, 12.

5. Halévy, *Thomas Hodgskin,* pp. 48–49, 86–87, 109, 115; Hodgskin, *Popular Political Economy,* pp. 24, 109, 120, 125–126; 253; id., *Travels in North Germany* (Edinburgh, 1820), 1: 179–180.

6. Thompson, *Making of the English Working Class,* pp. 746–749; Holyoake, *History of Cooperation,* 1: 146–147, 203, 237, 247–248; Robert Collis, *Pitman of the Northern Coal Fields* (Manchester, 1987), pp. 37, 70; *Spectator,* Aug. 19, 1844, p. 781; *Pictorial Times,* Sept. 30, 1843; *Hansard,* 1841, 59: 816.

7. *Eclectic Review,* Jan. 1841, p. 101; *NonConformist,* Apr. 28, 1841, p. 60; Jan. 12, 1842, p. 17; *Patriot,* Feb. 21, 1842, Feb. 11, 1847; Machin, *Politics and the Churches in Great Britain,* pp. 104–107; *Leeds Mercury,* May 2, 1840.

8. Halévy, *Thomas Hodgskin,* pp. 21–23; 30; Hodgskin, *An Essay on Naval Discipline* (London, 1813).

9. Joel H. Wiener, *The War of the Unstamped: The Movement to Repeal the British Newspaper Tax, 1830–1836* (Ithaca, N.Y., 1969), p. 125.

10. Ibid., pp. 1–20, 125, 237–303.

11. Ibid., p. 125; *Weekly Dispatch,* Mar. 15, 1840; *Morning Post,* July 17, 1844.

12. Armytage, *Heavens Below,* pp. 130–132; *Weekly Dispatch,* Nov. 1, 1840; Thompson, *Labour Rewarded,* pp. 90–91; *The Promethean,* Jan. 1842, p. 12; Feb. 1842, pp. 25–26, 34–35; *The*

Union, Aug. 1, 1842, pp. 129–135; *Northern Star*, Jan. 25, 1840; *Chartist Studies*, ed. Briggs, pp. 304–342.

13. *Red Republican*, July 13, 1850, p. 27; Sept. 14, 1850, p. 101; *Democratic Review*, July 1849, p. 50; *London Democrat*, Apr. 20, 1839, pp. 13–14, Apr. 27, 1839, pp. 23–24 (quotation); May 4, 1839, p. 25; May 18, 1839, p. 47.

14. *Hansard*, 1841, 56: 451; 57: 449, 749; 1842, 63: 258; 64: 168–169, 259; 65: 79, 512.

15. *Hansard*, 1841, 57: 449, 748–749; 1842, 63: 259; 64: 168–169, 258–259, 653, 684.

16. *Hansard*, 1844, 74: 518.

17. *Leeds Mercury*, Aug. 7, 1847; *Somerset County Gazette*, July 3, 1841; J. A. Roebuck, *Pamphlets for the People* (London, 1835) 3: 7–8; Weaver, "The Political Ideology of Short Time," in *Worktime and Industrialization: An International History*, ed. Gary Cross (Philadelphia, 1988), p. 93.

18. *Howitt's Journal*, Jan. 16, p. 38; *Pictorial Times*, Aug. 26, Sept. 30, 1843; *Illustrated London News*, May 28, June 25, July 23, Oct. 22, Nov. 12, 1842; *Weekly Dispatch*, Oct. 25, 1840; *Sunday Times*, Feb. 4, 1844.

19. *Daily News*, Feb. 7, 1846; *Douglas Jerrold's Shilling Magazine* 1 (1845): 509.

20. *Economist*, May 18, 1844, p. 811; *Leeds Mercury*, Dec. 5, 1840; Apr. 2, 1842; *Leeds Times*, July 27, 1842.

21. *Western Times*, Mar. 16, 1844; *Punch* 10: 25; *Weekly Chronicle*, Mar. 28, 1844; *Spectator*, Sept. 27, 1845, p. 927.

22. *Economist*, Mar. 22, 1845, p. 262; *Punch*, 1: 50; 5: 165; *Spectator*, Sept. 27, 1845, p. 927; *Examiner*, Sept. 20, 1840; Feb. 26, 1842; Apr. 27, 1844; Jan. 9, 1847; *NonConformist*, July 14, 1847, p. 506.

23. *Lloyd's Weekly*, May 12, 1844; May 23, 1847; *The Sun*, May 3, June 11, 1842; Mar. 18, 1844; Feb. 12, 1847; *Weekly Dispatch*, Mar. 24, 1844; May 23, 1847; *Weekly Chronicle*, Apr. 21, 1844.

24. *Howitt's Journal*, Apr. 3, 10, 1847; *People's Journal*, Apr. 18, 1846.

25. *Westminster Review*, Sept. 1840, pp. 384–5.

26. *Douglas Jerrold's Shilling Magazine* 2 (1845): 88; Hodgskin, *Labour Defended*, pp. 30–31; Halévy, *Thomas Hodgskin*, pp. 120, 130; Fox, *Reports of Lectures Delivered at the Chapel in South Place*, 6: 16; B. Jerrold, *Life of Douglas Jerrold*, pp. 39, 110; Godwin, *Enquiry Concerning Political Justice* (swayed the minds of the poets); Sumner, *Treatise on … Creation*, p. 304 (quotes Godwin); Paul Bloomfield, *Edward Gibbon Wakefield* (London, 1961), pp. 17–18; Holyoake, *Sixty Years of an Agitator's Life*, p. 216; Marchand, *Athenaeum*, p. 31.

27. David Roberts, "Charles Dickens and the *Daily News*," *Victorian Periodicals Review*, Summer 1989, pp. 51–62; Halévy, *Thomas Hodgskin*, pp. 120, 130; Godwin, *Enquiry Concerning Political Justice*, p. 76; Desmond King-Hele, *Shelley, His Thought and Work* (London, 1960), pp. 18, 28; Percy Bysshe Shelley, *The Mask of Anarchy* (London, 1832), cantos 3–7; Muhammad Siddiq Kalim, "The Use of Shelley in the Writings of the Owenites" (M.A. thesis, London University, 1960), pp. 66, 90–99.

28. *Baptist Magazine*, Apr. 1847, p. 268; *Eclectic Review*, May 1843, pp. 580–581, Nov. 2, 1847, pp. 491–492; *Leeds Mercury*, Feb. 27, 1847; *NonConformist*, June 1847, p. 428; Mar. 10, 1847, p. 141; *Patriot*, Feb. 25, Apr. 8, 12, 16, 1847; Paxton Hood, *Thomas Binney*, pp. 19–20; Stowell, *Memoir of R. W. Hamilton*, pp. 404–406; Baptist Noel, *Union of Church and State* (London, 1848), pp. 11–12; Rev. Benjamin Parson, *Education, the Want and Birthright of Every Human Being, or, Education as It Is, and as It Ought to Be* (London, 1850), pp. 64–65; id., *The Unconstitutional Character of the Government Plan for Education* (London, 1851), pp. 6–8; Thomas Binney, *The Doctrine of the Bible in Reference to Religious Education* (London, 1843),

p. 100; Dale, *History of Congregationalism*, p. 9; Rev. Andrew Reed, *The Inspectors Inspected* (London, 1852), pp. 4, 13, 16–18.

29. *NonConformist*, June 22, 1842, p. 450; Mar. 27, 1842, p. 197; May 6, 1844, p. 301; Aug. 28, 1844, p. 612; June 9, 1847, p. 428; *Baptist Guardian*, Oct. 3, 10, 1845; Arthur Miall, *Life of Edward Miall*, pp. 25–26; *Patriot*, June 9, 1842; Apr. 21, 29, July 3, 1845; June 24, 28, 1847; Mar. 13, 1848.

30. *Hansard*, 1848, 98: 738–739, 1172.

31. *Hansard*, 1840, 54: 1271–1275; 55: 21, 29, 38, 47–48; Henry Halford, *Remarks on the Report of the Constabulary Force Commissioners* (London, 1840), pp. 21, 29, 53, 59.

32. *Hansard*, 1839, 50: 357; 1848, 98: 711.

33. *Hansard*, 1839, 48: 269, 626, 652.

34. *Times*, Oct. 10, 1833; Apr. 20, 30, May 8, 1834; Feb 5, Mar. 20, May 14, 1838; Feb. 1, Mar. 21, 1839; July 15, Sept. 26, Dec. 15, 1842; Oct. 24, 1843; Feb. 29, June 29, July 10, 11, 1844; Dec. 26, 1845.

35. *Standard*, May 12, 1834; May 21, 1839; May 9, 1848; *John Bull*, Mar. 20, 1841; May 13, 1848.

36. MacDonagh, *Early Victorian Government*, pp. 12–15.

37. Wade, *Extraordinary Black Book*, pp. 85, 113, 132, 162, 164–165, 169–170, 207, 255, 262–263, 275, 284, 350–351, 377–379, 381, 392–393.

38. L. T. Hume, *Bentham and Bureaucracy* (London, 1961), pp. 177–178, 194, 201; *Works of Jeremy Bentham*, ed. Bowring, 9: 27, 67, 89.

39. J. F. Rees, *A Short Fiscal and Economic History of England* (London, 1921).

40. *Hansard*, 1833, 20: 134.

41. *Hansard*, 1840, 51: 1240–1244; 1841, 57: 646–664; 1847, 91: 979–995.

42. *Hansard*, 1833, 18: 292–297; 1849, 102: 1219–1220; 107: 571–572; 578, 590; 1842, 61: 993, 999–1000.

43. *Punch*, 10: 25; 13: 143; *Westminster Review*, June 1844, p. 561.

44. *Eclectic Review*, Aug. 1842, 224; *NonConformist*, Mar. 13, 1842, p. 201; *Patriot*, June 27, 28, 1847; *Baptist Examiner*, Jan. 1844, p. 8.

45. *Hansard*, 1849, 107: 408–412, 430, 478, 571, 599.

46. British Library, Peel Papers, Add. MSS, 40,560, W. Miles to Peel, Feb. 22, 1845; *Western Times*, Aug. 7, 1847; John Packington, *A Charge on the Subject of the County Expenditure* (Worcester, 1853), pp. 7–8; *Nottingham Journal*, Aug. 6, 1847; Henry Willougby, *Apology of an English Landlord* (London, 1827), p. 7.

47. *Northern Star*, Mar. 26, 1842; *Weekly Dispatch*, Mar. 13, May 8, 1842; *Examiner*, Mar. 19, 26, Apr. 9, 16, 23, 1842; *Leeds Times*, Mar. 19, 1842; *Morning Chronicle*, Mar. 16, 1848; *Morning Post*, May 4, 1842.

48. *Eclectic Review*, Aug. 1842, p. 224; Jan. 1848, p. 104; *Hansard*, 1847, 92: 1178–1179; 93: 1104–1105; 1848, 97: 1010–1011; 98: 711–712.

49. Toulmin Smith, *Government by Commissions*, p. 298.

50. *Hansard*, 1835, 25: 437; 1849, 102: 618.

51. *Hansard*, 1848, 102: 413–414; 1849, 104: 167; 106: 848; 107: 838.

52. *Hansard*, 1849, 103: 57–58, 63, 74, 189, 212, 268; *Fraser's*, Dec. 1843, p. 739; Dec. 1849, p. 709.

53. *Hansard*, 1842, 60: 186–188; 1848, 102: 421.

54. *North British Review*, May 1847, p. 139; *Hansard*, 1848, 100: 910–911.

55. Edward Denison, bishop of Salisbury, *A Sermon Preached at St. Margaret's* (London, 1839), pp. 21–22; Wilson, *Life of George Dawson*, pp. 95–96.

56. Binney, *The Bible and Education*, pp. 100–101; Medway, *Memoirs of John Pye Smith*, p. 511; *English Review*, July 1844, p. 392; Sept. 1846, p. 136.

57. *Leeds Mercury*, Feb. 7, 1846; *Leeds Times*, July 27, 1844.

58. *Hansard*, 1848, 97: 1322; *North British Review*, Nov. 1849, p. 39.

59. *Edinburgh Review*, Oct. 1841, pp. 15, 33; Jan. 1846, pp. 83–84; Oct. 1848, p. 334.

60. J. S. Mill, *Principles of Political Economy*, II: 19–20, 375, 511–514, 560–562, 589; *Autobiography*, p. 135; *Earlier Letters of John Stuart Mill*, ed. F. E. Mineka, vol. 13 of *The Collected Works of J. S. Mill*, pp. 716–717; Packe, *The Life of J. S. Mill*, p. 306; MacDonagh, *Early Victorian Government*, p. 69.

61. *Blackwood's*, Oct. 1848, pp. 410, 427; *Christian Remembrancer*, Oct. 1848, pp. 315, 332, 336, 342–43; Toulmin Smith, *Government by Commissions*, pp. 165–166; *Spectator*, May 13, 1848, pp. 467–469.

62. J. S. Mill, *Principles of Political Economy*, 2: 511–512; MacDonagh, *Early Victorian Government*, pp. 68–69.

63. Hodgskin, *Labour Defended*, p. 93; Marcet, *Rich and Poor*, pp. 47–48; Coleridge, *A Lay Sermon*, p. 416; Southey, *Essays*, 5: 192–193.

64. Edwin Chadwick Papers, "Memo on administrative payments for hands of government" (n.d.); *Hansard*, 1839, 48: 579; 1841, 56: 375–376; 1844, 72: 250.

65. *Hansard*, 1842, 60: 186; MacKinnon, *History of Civilization*, 1: 366.

66. *Hansard*, 1848, 99: 913–914.

67. Robert Slaney, *Essay on the Employment of the Poor* (London, 1819), § 2: 17, 45–46; id., *A Plea to Power and Parliament for the Working Classes*, pp. 50–51, 97, 112–113, 138. id., *State of the Poor in Great Towns* (London, 1841); id., *Reports of the House of Commons on Education and Health*; Osborne, *View of the . . . Condition of the Agricultural Labourer*, p. 17; see also Paul Richards, "Robert Slaney," *Social History*, Jan. 1979.

68. *P.P.*, 1835, 13: iii–xx, and 1841, 10: 398–402 (handloom weavers); 1835, 13: 3–19, and 1838, 7: 159–167 (education); 1841, 7: 3–271 (distress in Scotland); 1842, 35: 69 (Bolton), and 195–335 (Stockport); 1843, 7: 3–5 (Paisley); 1843, 7: 202–206 (allotments); 1843, 12: 17–398 (children in agriculture); 1843, 15: §§ A to Q (children in manufactures); 1845, 19: 6–15 (Ireland).

69. *Athenaeum*, Dec. 23, 1848, p. 1290; July 7, 1849, p. 692; *Sun*, June 13, 1842.

70. *Christian Teacher*, 1841, 3: 37; *Daily News*, Mar. 17, Apr. 14, May 12, 21, 1846, Jan 4, 1847; *Edinburgh Review*, Oct. 1848, 326.

71. *Quarterly Review*, 1842, 70: 491; Mar. 1847, p. 470; *Christian Remembrancer*, 1846, 12: 375–376; 1848, 16: 343; *Morning Post*, June 14, 1842.

72. *Edinburgh Review*, July 1841, p. 507; Feb. 1843, pp. 205, 226; Apr. 1846, pp. 377, 480–481; Oct. 1846, pp. 273–274, 279, 286, 299–300, 308–309; Jan. 1848, 253–255, 271–272; Oct. 1848, pp. 325–327.

73. *Hansard*, 1842, 63: 1640–1657; 1843, 67: 76; 1845, 79: 339; 1847, 90: 260; Lewis, *Edwin Chadwick*, pp. 244, 367; Chadwick Papers, "1854 memo on Lord Seymour."

74. *Quarterly Review*, Dec. 1847, pp. 142–151; Ursula R. Q. Henriques, *Before the Welfare State: Social Administration in Early Industrial Britain* (London, 1979), p. 117.

75. *Hansard*, 1849, 106: 848; M'Neil, *Famine*, p. 8; G. Holland, *Moral, Social, and Intellectual Condition of the Industrious Classes of Sheffield*, p. 11.

76. Smith, *Wealth of Nations*, ed. Cannan, 2: 184.

77. *British Quarterly*, 1845, 1: 149; *Congregational Magazine* 1843, 7: 835; *English Chartist Circular*, 2: 169; *Fraser's*, Mar. 1845, p. 376; *Edinburgh Review*, Oct. 1848, p. 331; *Leeds Mercury*,

Dec. 12, 1840; Marcet, *Rich and Poor*, p. 48; E. Baines Jr., *Life of Edward Baines*, p. 333; id., *Letter to the Right Hon. Lord John Russell on State Education* (London, 1847), p. 11; *Morning Chronicle*, Apr. 1, 1843; *Westminster Review*, Oct. 1846, p. 6; Robert Montgomery, *Edmund Burke: A Selection* (London, 1853), p. 198; Bowley, *Nassau Senior*, pp. 242–243; Sanders, *The Broad Church Movement*, pp. 259–260; Coleridge, *Church and State*, p. 86; McCulloch, *Discourse on . . . Political Economy*, pp. 257–258; *Hansard*, 1847, 89: 648–649.

78. *Fraser's*, Mar. 1845, p. 376; *Westminster Review*, Oct. 1846, p. 6; Sanders, *Broad Church Movement*, pp. 259–260.

79. Coleridge, *Lay Sermon*, p. 417; Colmer, *Coleridge*, pp. 109–110; *Economist*, May 31, 1845, p. 503.

80. Montgomery, *Burke*, p. 198; *Fraser's*, Mar. 1845, pp. 374–375; *Hansard*, 1847, 89: 648–649.

81. *British Quarterly*, 1845, 1: 149; *Congregational Magazine*, 1843, 7: 835; Baines, *Letter to Lord John Russell*, p. 11; J. R. McCulloch, *A Statistical Account of the British Empire, Examining Its Extent, Physical Capacities, Population, Industry, and Civil and Religious Institutions* (2 vols.; London, 1837), 1: 644; Marcet, *Rich and Poor*, pp. 1–65.

82. Marcet, *Rich and Poor*, p. 48; *Hansard*, 1847, 89: 612; Thomas Wyse, *Education Reform* (London, 1836), p. 447.

83. J. S. Mill, *Principles of Political Economy*, 2: 339–343; 511–512, 515–516, 523, 526, 519–542; McCulloch, *Discourse on . . . Political Economy*, pp. 255–294, esp. 294; id., *The Literature of Political Economy: A Classified Catalogue of Select Publications in the Different Departments of That Science, with Historical, Critical and Biographical Notices* (London, 1845), pp. 37, 293; id., *Statistical Account of the British Empire*, 1: 644; Bowley, *Nassau Senior*, pp. 242, 243–249, 264–267, 277.

CHAPTER 14

1. Sydney Checkland, *British Public Policy, 1776–1839* (London, 1983), p. 11; Fraser, *Power and Authority in the Victorian City*, pp. 134, 150, 152, 203; Joseph Redlich and Francis Hurst, *Local Government in England* (London, 1903), p. 131; John Brewer, *The Sinews of Power: War, Money, and the English State, 1688–1783* (New York, 1989), pp. 127, 251.

2. Henriques, *Before the Welfare State*, pp. 70–112; MacDonagh, *Early Victorian Government*, pp. 22–95; M. H. Thomas, *The Early Factory Legislation* (London, 1948), pp. 209–222, 235, 285; Atiyah, *Rise and Fall of Freedom of Contract*, pp. 238–253.

3. Checkland, *British Public Policy*, pp. 70, 82–83; *P.P.*, 1841, 10: 302–400; 1842, 12: 17–398; 1843, 14: A,1 to B,22; 1846, 13: 427–437; Mayhew, *London Labour and London Poor*.

4. Lonsdale, *Biographical Sketch of the Late William Blamire*, pp. 44, 46–48; Roger Prouty, *The Transformation of the Board of Trade* (London, 1957), pp. 95–97.

5. Roberts, *Welfare State*, pp. 51, 56, 130, 134; *P.P.*, 1848, 26: 97; 1852, 18: 393, 517, 597; Lonsdale, *Biographical Sketch of the Late William Blamire*.

6. J. R. McCulloch, *The Principles of Political Economy with a Sketch of the Rise and Progress of the Science*, 2d rev. ed. (London, 1830), p. 263.

7. Parris, *Government and Railways*, pp. 28–102; Frank Fetter, *The Development of British Monetary Orthodoxy* (Cambridge, Mass., 1965), pp. 185–194, 198.

8. Prouty, *Transformation of the Board of Trade*, pp. 30, 41, 50, 65–66, 87–88, 90, 93, 95; Checkland, *British Public Policy*, p. 70; Fetter, *Monetary Orthodoxy*, pp. 165–197; Roberts, *Welfare State*, p. 92; Black, *Economic Thought on the Irish Question*, 38–40, 117.

9. Atiyah, *Rise and Fall of Freedom of Contract*, pp. 252, 336, 370, 521, 543–547, 548, 552–558, 566; Daly, *Famine*, pp. 24, 41.

10. Roberts, *Welfare State*, pp. 105–117; Henriques, *Before the Welfare State*, pp. 26–64, 128–148; Finer, *Edwin Chadwick*, pp. 69–192, 338–353.

11. Charles Reith, *British Police and the Democratic Ideal* (Oxford, 1943), pp. 26, 29–30; J. M. Hart, *The British Police* (London, 1951), pp. 27–33; Jones, *Lunacy, Law and Conscience*, pp. 74–78, 141–142, 171–172, 191–193; Roberts, *Welfare State*, pp. 47, 113, 115, 117, 283; *Edinburgh Review*, Jan. 1847, pp. 221–258.

12. B. and S. Webb, *English Local Government: The Story of the King's Highways* (London, 1913), pp. 166–167, 176, 201–209; Derek Fraser, *Power and Authority* (New York, 1980), pp. 62–69, 94–99, 115–118, 125–128, 134–136, 141–142; David Philips and Robert D. Storch, *Policing Provincial England* (Leicester, 1999), p. 231.

13. T. S. Ashton, *Economic and Social Investigations in Manchester* (London, 1934), pp. 45–50; Briggs, *Victorian Cities*, pp. 45, 52, 135, 158–160, 20, 206–207, 273, 301, 323, 352; S. Checkland, *British Public Policy*, pp. 156–157; Kohl, *England and Wales*, pp. 107–108; 111–114, 117–120, 122, 130, 138–139; John Prest, *Liberty and Locality* (Oxford, 1990), pp. 6–47.

14. Hodgkinson, *National Health Service*, pp. 28, 30, 39, 195, 205–213, 219, 335–575; Henriques, *Before the Welfare State*, pp. 26–59, 140, 213–214; Fraser, *New Poor Law*, pp. 67–86, 128–170; *Poor Law Report*, ed. Checkland and Checkland, pp. 256–273; S. and B. Webb, *English Poor Law History*, pt. 2: 134–135.

15. Lewis, *Edwin Chadwick*, pp. 292, 301–318; Briggs, *Victorian Cities*, p. 20.

16. Hodgkinson, *National Health Service*, pp. 28, 30, 195, 205–213, 219, 335, 575; Henriques, *Before the Welfare State*, pp. 26–59, 213–214; Lionel Rose, *Rogues and Vagabonds* (London, 1988), pp. 17–22; Prest, *Liberty and Locality*, pp. 14, 178; *Hansard*, 1844, 76: 348; *P.P.*, 1855, 46: 2–3.

17. Jones, *Lunacy, Law and Conscience*, 145–201; *P.P.*, 1850, 28: 795; Briggs, *Victorian Cities*, pp. 111, 145–146, 211, 225; Lambert, *Sir John Simon*, pp. 122–127, 159–169, 191–199, 222–230.

18. P. R.O., H.O., 45/5128.

19. Wiener, *Reconstructing the Criminal*, pp. 15, 50.

20. Ibid., pp. 19, 24; *Blackwood's*, July 1844, pp. 7–8.

21. Checkland, *British Public Policy*, pp. 104–106, 149; *North British Review*, May 1848, pp. 123–140; *Record*, Sept. 17, 1840; Apr. 14, 21, 1842; *Hansard*, 1848, 100: 450–462.

22. Checkland, *British Public Policy*, pp. 152–153; Rubin and Sugarman, *Law, Economy and Society*, pp. 241–242; Owen, *English Philanthropy*, pp. 66–68; Wiener, *Reconstructing the Criminal*, p. 46.

23. Gosden, *Self-Help*, pp. 66–68, 72, 100, 191, 220; Lewis, *Edwin Chadwick*, pp. 127, 343; Thomas Greenwood, *Edward Edwards* (London, 1902), p. 20; Janet Minihan, *Nationalization of Culture* (New York, 1977), pp. 92–93.

24. Minihan, *Nationalization of Culture*, pp. 14–16, 18–19, 35, 41, 50–52, 54, 57, 74, 77, 83, 101.

25. *P.P.*, 1840, 40: 388–404; 1860, 54: 1–30; Kay-Shuttleworth, *Four Periods*, pp. 179–183.

26. Chadwick, *Victorian Church*, 1: 103–106, 126–142, 169, 235–236, 336–346.

27. Raymond Coward, *Political Economists and the English Poor Laws* (Athens, Ohio, 1977), pp. 158–164; H. J. M. Johnston, *British Emigration Policy, 1815–1830* (London, 1972); James Hamerton, *Emigrant Gentlewomen, Genteel Poverty and Female Emigration* (London, 1979), pp. 55–65.

28. MacDonagh, *Pattern of Government Growth*, pp. 55, 59, 65–66, 69, 73, 77–78, 85, 117–118, 124–126, 143–147, 163, 166, 171–174, 189–190, 194, 198, 213, 244–245.

29. Jones, *Lunacy, Law and Conscience*, pp. 84, 97–98, 112, 126, 149.

30. Wiener, *Reconstructing the Criminal*, p. 14; *P.P.*, 1835, 11: 20, 68, 123, 177, 373, 463–466, 517–519; 1836, 35: 1–48, 69; Prison Discipline Society, *Report on the Select Committee on Secondary Punishments* (London, 1835); *Morning Chronicle*, Aug. 17, 1835.

31. R. H. Gretton, *The King's Government* (London, 1913), p. 114.

32. David Landes, "The Fable of the Dead Horse," in *The British Industrial Revolution*, ed. Joel Mokyr (Oxford, 1992), pp. 151, 135–167.

33. Thomas, *Early Factory Legislation*, pp. 9–33, 66–70, 209–222, 295–296, 326–327; *Westminster Review*, July 1842, pp. 86–87.

34. Checkland, *British Public Policy*, pp. 82–83; *P.P.*, 1843, 12: 17–398; 14: A–11–15, B–14–26, D–2–8; 15: S–4–7, Q–1–16; 1846, 13: 426–503.

35. *Hansard*, 1849, 106: 1336; 1850, 112: 114–115; 113: 759.

36. Burnett, *Social History of Housing*, pp. 6–7; MacDonagh, *Early Victorian Government*, pp. 1–2; Olsen, *Town Planning in London*, p. 14; F. M. L. Thompson, "Town and City," in *Cambridge Social History of Britain, 1750–1950* (Cambridge, 1990), 1: 5–6.

37. *Sun*, Mar. 6, 1847.

38. Thomas Fowell Buxton, *Memoirs* (London, 1848), p. 64; Owen, *English Philanthropy*, pp. 120–121.

39. Central Society of Education, *First Reports* (London, 1837); B. Binns, *A Century of Education* (London, 1908), pp. 32–33, 49–58, 263, 298; Cullen, *Statistical Movement*, pp. 14, 23, 65–69, 121–125, 131, 139–145; Maltby, *Manchester and the Movement for National Elementary Education*, pp. 67–92; Paz, *Politics of Working Class Education*, pp. 63–90; Finer, *Edwin Chadwick*, pp. 236–240, 293–294, 311, 357, 422.

40. R. and F. Davenport-Hill, *Recorder of Birmingham*, pp. 150–170; Manton, *Mary Carpenter*, pp. 112–124; W. L. Rushton, *Letters of a Templar* (London, 1903).

41. *Edinburgh Review*, Oct. 1833, p. 350; Manchester Statistical Society, *The State of Education in the Borough of Bury* (London, 1835), *The State of Education in the City of York* (London, 1836–1837), *The State of Education in the Borough of Salford* (London, 1835); *Journal of the Statistical Society*, Apr. 1840, p. 25; *P.P.*, 1838, 7: 62–66; *Manchester Guardian*, June 5, 1839; *Hansard*, 1838, 43: 710–38.

42. Chadwick, *Sanitary Report of 1842*, pp. 77, 223; P. P., 1844, 17: 12–153; *Globe*, Mar. 15, Apr. 10, 1848; *Daily News*, Apr. 6, 1847, Mar. 24, 1848; *Examiner*, Apr. 8, May 13, June 24, Aug. 5, Sept. 2, 1848; *Scotsman*, May 29, 1847; *Manchester Guardian*, Mar. 4, Apr. 28, 1848; *Carlisle Journal*, Apr. 2, 1847; *Times*, June 15, 1847.

43. Finlayson, *Seventh Earl of Shaftesbury*, pp. 183–187, 224–226, 229–231.

44. Brent, *Liberal Anglican Politics*, pp. 252–253; Sir James Kay-Shuttleworth, *The Laws of Social Progress* (London, 1866), p. 43.

45. Smith, *Government by Commission*, pp. 20–27; *P.P.*, General Index to the Reports of Select Committees, 1801–1852 (London, 1853).

46. Disraeli, *Sybil*, p. 67.

47. R. Nelson Boyd, *Coal Mines Inspection: Its History and Results* (London, 1879), pp. 68–78; MacDonagh, "Coal Mines Regulation," in *Ideas and Institutions*, ed. Robson, pp. 69–70; *North British Review*, Nov. 1847, pp. 80–81.

48. Lewis, *Edwin Chadwick*, pp. 181–238; 279–301; Finer, *Edwin Chadwick*, pp. 154–164, 209–243, 333–379, 439–453.

49. Whitworth Porter, *History of the Corps of Royal Engineers* (3 vols.: London, 1889–1915), 1: 1, 326; 2: 324–327, 433, 486–487; 3: 233–259; Parris, *Government and the Railways*, pp. 232–235, see also 33–35, 110–112, 176–181.

50. P.R.O., H.O., 45/5677; *Times,* Dec. 27, 1854; *P.P.,* 18: xxxiii, 348; Daly, *Famine,* p. 44; Porter, *Royal Engineers,* 3: 466–487; Prouty, *Transformation of the Board of Trade,* pp. 4, 48–51, 89, 93, 95; Peterson, *Medical Profession,* pp. 35–38.

51. Prouty, *Transformation of the Board of Trade,* p. 85.

52. Thomas, *Early Factory Legislation,* pp. 117, 209–221; MacDonagh, "Coal Mines," in *Ideas and Institutions,* ed. Robson, pp. 79–84; Roberts, *Welfare State,* pp. 83, 92, 107–109, 113, 116–117, 144, 319; Parris, *Government and Railways,* pp. 33, 109–111.

53. MacDonagh, *Pattern of Government Growth,* pp. 65–66, 146–147, 151, 202, 212; Cleveland Stevens, *English Railways and Their Development,* pp. 62–64, 134, 147; *Statutes at Large,* 3 & 4 Vict. c. 97; 5 and 6 Vict. c. 55; 7 & 8 Vict. c. 18, 35; 9 & 10 Vict. c. 105; Prouty, *Transformation of the Board of Trade,* pp. 10–12.

54. Roberts, *Welfare State,* pp. 205–208, 213–217, 226, 228, 235–236; 263–271, 287, 289, 301; Lewis, *Edwin Chadwick,* pp. 279–319; Jones, *Lunacy, Law and Conscience,* pp. 133–213.

55. Hill, *Autobiography,* pp. 130–132, 180–182, 195–196, 296–305; Henriques, "Separate System," *Past and Present,* Feb. 1972, pp. 77–79, 89; Walter Clay, *Memoir of Rev. John Clay* (London, 1861), pp. 178, 185; Carpenter, *Reformatory Schools,* pp. 7–8, 27, 45; *P.P.,* 1845, 37: ii–vi, 129–130; F. Hill, *National Education* (London, 1853), pp. 22–52; id., *Crime, Its Amount, Causes and Remedies,* p. 61 (cites Jelinger Symons, *School Economy,* on the reformatory school at Quatt); *P.P.,* 1843, 21: 135–150; 1846, 32: 596–609; 1838, 31: 1.

56. Carpenter, *Reformatory Schools,* p. 45; Finer, *Edwin Chadwick,* pp. 39–96, 156–157, 164–180, 209–230, 297–311; Lewis, *Edwin Chadwick,* pp. 3–83, 158–181.

57. Smith, *Life and Work of Sir James Kay-Shuttleworth,* pp. 45–68; B. C. Blomfield, *The Autobiography of Sir James Kay-Shuttleworth* (London, 1964), pp. 39–69; Sir James Kay-Shuttleworth, *Recent Measures for the Promotion of Education in England* (London, 1839); *P.P.,* 1838, 7: 173–198, 203–214; 1835, 11: 1–26, 31–43, 115; Manchester Statistical Society reports on the state of education in Bury, York, and Salford cited in n. 41 above; Thomas Adkins, *The History of St. John's College, Battersea* (London, 1906), pp. 17–18.

58. *Journal of the Society of Arts,* July 16, 1886 (obituary of C. Tufnell); *P.P.,* 1848, 26: 254–262; for poor law assistant commissioners: *P.P.,* 1838, 28: 156ff; 1839, 20: 104–111, 119–122; 1840, 17: 247–262; James Kay-Shuttleworth and E. C. Tufnell, *On the Training of Pauper Children* (London, 1839); for prison inspectors: *P.P.,* 1836, 35: 360–372; 1838, 31: 308; 1843, 25 and 26: 453–454; 1845, 24: 401; 1846, 20: 308–310; for factory inspectors: *P.P.,* 1837, 31: 62; 1838, 28: 95–96, 123; 1839, 19: 357–382, 417–426; 1842, 22: 368–426; 1843, 27: 292–293; Boyd, *Coal Mines Inspection,* pp. 32–33; for education inspectors: *P.P.,* 1841, 20: 195–198; 1843, 40: 351–361; 1847, 45: 567–570; 1852, 40: 343–344.

59. *Times,* Sept. 1893 (obituary of Seymour Tremenheere); Roberts, *Victorian Origins,* p. 60 (citing *P.P.,* 1842, 12: 255–257); Lonsdale, *William Blamire,* pp. 4, 31–44.

60. W. L. Burn, review of Oliver MacDonagh, *A Pattern of Government Growth, 1800–60: The Passenger Acts and Their Enforcement* (London, 1961), *Historical Journal* 6 (1963): 140; MacDonagh, *Pattern of Government Growth,* pp. 9, 15–16, 143, 117–118.

61. Harold Perkin, "Individualism versus Collectivism," *British Studies,* Fall, 1977, pp. 106–108; Derek Fraser, *The Evolution of the British Welfare State: A History of Social Policy since the Industrial Revolution* (London, 1973), p. 128; Karl Polanyi, *The Great Transformation* (1944; New York, 1957), p. 217.

62. Jennifer Hart, "Nineteenth-Century Social Reform: A Tory Interpretation," *Past and Present,* July 1965, pp. 39–46.

63. MacDonagh, *Pattern of Government Growth*, p. 16; H. Perkin, "Individualism versus Collectivism," *British Studies*, Fall 1977, p. 108.

1. Montague Gore, *Letter to the Middle Classes* (London, 1939), p. 9; *Hansard*, 1846, 83: 1283–1295; 85: 1228; 86: 400–401, 490.

2. *Hansard*, 1844, 73: 1434, 1633; 74: 686, 944; Richard Oastler, *Slavery in Yorkshire* (York, 1835).

3. Wordsworth, *Poetical Works*, 5: *Excursion*, bk. 8, pp. 335–349; Alfred Cobban, *Edmund Burke and the Revolt Against the Eighteenth Century* (New York, 1929), p. 209; Coleridge, *Lay Sermon*, p. 430; Seeley, *Sadler*, pp. 338–339, 592–595.

4. *Hansard*, 1845, 77: 655–666; Finlayson, *Seventh Earl of Shaftesbury*, pp. 36–37, 74, 124, 129, 183–186, 189–190, 223, 228–232, 273–276, 346–347, 351–352, 410–417.

5. *Law Magazine*, Aug. 1849, pp. 89–93, 101; Robert Montgomery, *Edmund Burke* (London, 1853), p. 198; Southey, *Essays*, 2: 24, 155–56; id., *Correspondence*, 6: 87; id., *Colloquies*, 2: 420–425.

6. Robert Walker Smith, *The Protectionist Case in the 1840s* (London, 1933), pp. 1–81; Gambles, *Protection and Politics*, p. 76.

7. Southey, *Essays*, 1: 231; 2: 25, 125, 132, 149, 162; Coleridge, *Church and State*, pp. 43–44, 88; Ben Knights, *The Idea of the Clerisy in the Nineteenth Century* (London, 1978), p. 42; Colmer, *Coleridge*, p. 165.

8. *Blackwood's*, Jan. 1844, p. 536; Carlyle, *Chartism*, pp. 147, 157.

9. Seeley, *Perils of a Nation*, pp. 218, 234, 317, 319, 326.

10. Southey, *Essays*, 2: 23–24; Carlyle, *Past and Present*, p. 88; id., *Latter Day Pamphlets*, pp. 91, 103, 125–126, 142; Henry Drummond, *Speeches in Parliament* (London, 1860), pp. 319 and 124, 131, 143, 257–258, 313.

11. Rev. Charles Hewitley, *Parochial Sermons* (London, 1849), p. 190; *Watchman*, June 23, 1847.

12. Bickersteth, *The Sign of the Times in the East*, pp. 317, 334, 343; id., *Divine Warnings*, p. 122 (vol. 14 of *Works*).

13. G. J. Holyoake, "The Paternal Form of Government," *The Movement*, no. 18: 139.

14. John Sterling, "State of Society," in *Essays and Tales*, ed. Julius Hare (London, 1848), 2: 30–31.

15. Deacon, *Cambridge Apostles*, pp. 2, 7, 8–9, 11, 14–15, 26; Dasent, *John Thadeus Delane*, pp. 40–44, 48; *Men of the Times* (London, 1872), p. 700; Laughton, *Memoirs of the Life and Correspondence of Henry Reeve*, ed. Laughton, 1: 12, 36, 44; Garland, *Cambridge Before Darwin*, pp. 17, 58, 68, 86–87; *DNB*, 37: 97–105; N. Merrill Distad, *Guessing at Truth: The Life of Julius Charles Hare (1795–1855)* (Shepherdstown, W. Va., 1979), pp. 25–26; *Victorian Studies*, Winter 1980, pp. 278–279; J. A. Merivale, *Autobiography of Dean Merivale* (London, 1899), p. 80.

16. Susan Faye Cannon, *Science and Culture: The Early Victorian Period* (New York, 1978), pp. 29–59; *Men of the Times*, 1872, p. 504; *DNB*, 27: 309; Alexander James Beresford Hope, *Poems* (London, 1841), p. 21; Richard Faber, *Young England* (London, 1987), pp. 13–16, 41, 96, 117–119, 156, 176; *DNB*, 12: 374.

17. *DNB*, 37: 97; 26: 212; supp. 3: 94; 17: 153; Munsell, *Unfortunate Duke*, p. 13; Morley,

Gladstone, 1: 54, 59–60; *Memoirs of Sir Thomas Dyke Acland*, pp. 9, 23, 29, 48, 50; Faber, *Young England*, p. 176; St. Vincent Beechy, *Two Sermons on the Occasion of the Funeral of Francis Egerton, Earl of Ellesmere* (London, 1857); Francis Egerton, *Personal Reminiscences of the Duke of Wellington*, ed. Lady Ellesmere (London, 1903), pp. 38, 59–60; Erickson, *Edward Cardwell*, p. 6; Gladstone, *The State in Its Relation with the Church*, pp. 6, 17–18, 83.

18. Mandell Creighton, *Sir George Grey* (London, 1901), pp. 14–16; Munsell, *Unfortunate Duke*, pp. 14–15; J. C. Colquhoun, *Scattered Leaves of Biography* (London, 1864), pp. 225, 142; Thomas Arnold, *Principles of Church Reform* (London, 1962), pp. 30, 56.

19. *DNB*, 51: 290.

20. Dasent, *John Thadeus Delane*, 1: 44–48; *Men of the Times*, 1872, p. 700; Times, *History of the Times*, 2: 125, 127; Pebody, *English Journalism*, p. 117.

21. Watts, *Alaric Watts*, 1: 99–101, 152, 229–230, 240; 2: 175–180; *DNB*, 39: 253, 29: 290; *Canterbury Magazine*, Sept. 1834, p. 121; Deacon, *Cambridge Apostles*, p. 24; Times, *History of the Times*, 2: 125; Lochhead, *John Gibson Lockhart*, p. 148; Andrew Lang, *The Life and Letters of John Gibson Lockhart* (London, 1898), 1: 207–236; 371; 2: 4, 87, 222–226, 240, 277, 284.

22. Henry Rogers, *The Superhuman Origins of the Bible* (London, 1893), p. xxi; Coleridge, *Church and State*, "Memoir" by R. W. Dale, pp. x–xi.

23. Seeley, *Sadler*, p. 32; Helps, *Claims of Labour*, pp. 153–154; *Quarterly Review*, 1840, 66: 501–502.

24. Seeley, *Sadler*, pp. 33, 168; Driver, *Tory Radical . . . Oastler*, on Ashley, pp. 212–218, 249, 450–451, 454, 464, 470, 483; on Fielden, pp. 149, 261–263, 311, 323, 456, 464, 470, 483; on Sadler, pp. 93, 116–117, 124, 125, 139, 153, 164, 170–176; *Hansard*, 1844, 74: 683–684; Finlayson, *Seventh Earl of Shaftesbury*, pp. 79–85, 124–127, 192–194, 219–229; Ward, *Factory Movement*, pp. 44–155 (Sadler), 139–159, 321–392 (Oastler), 166–390 (Shaftesbury), 333–392 (Fielden).

25. *Hansard*, 1844, 73: 1195–1197, 1263 (division list), 1511–1514, 1632; 74: 688, 1022, 1106; 1846, 86: 407, 467, 496–497, 950 (only Lord John Manners of Young England votes yes on lace bill), 1080 (only Disraeli and Manners); 1847, 89: 1107–1125, 91: 1130–1131 (on the ten-hour day the only yes votes were by Disraeli and Manners), 92: 311, 893–895, 926, 945–946.

26. *Standard*, Jan. 10, 1842; *Morning Post*, Mar. 20, 1844; *Morning Herald*, Apr. 1, 1844; *John Bull*, Jan. 15, 1842; *Fraser's*, May 1844, pp. 619–626; *Times*, Feb. 29, Mar. 11, 1844.

27. Lubenow, *Politics of Government Growth*, p. 147; MacDonagh, *Early Victorian Government*, p. 69.

28. *Hansard*, 1846, 86: 950; 1847, 93: 278–279; 1849, 107: 493.

29. *Hansard*, 1847, 90: 1385; 91: 253–254; 1848, 98: 62–63; 99: 805ff, 913–914, 975, 1057; 100: 907, 932; 106: 851–852.

30. *P.P.*, 1843, 11: 295, 352; 12: 10; 14: A, 52, F, 39, 55, 58; Ivy Pinchbeck, *Women Workers in the Industrial Revolution* (London, 1930), pp. 49–311; Friedrich Engels, *The Condition of the Working Class in England* (1845), trans. and ed. W. O. Henderson and W. H. Chaloner (Oxford, 1958), pp. 218–240, 296–300.

31. *Leeds Intelligencer*, as quoted in Ann Hobson, *On Higher Than Commercial Grounds* (London, 1985), p. 75; *Times*, Feb. 29, 1844.

32. *Morning Advertiser*, Mar. 29, 1844; *Economist*, May 18, 1844; *Scotsman*, May 8, 1847; *Morning Chronicle*, Mar. 21, 1844; *Standard*, Mar. 20, 1844, Apr. 22, 1847; *Sun*, Mar. 18, 1844; *Manchester Guardian*, Mar. 27, 1844; *Hansard*, 1846, 85: 1218–1219; Ward, *Factory Movement*, p. 415.

33. Arnold, *Principles of Church Reform*, pp. 20, 29; *Quarterly Review*, Oct. 1844, p. 597.

34. *Hansard*, 1839, 48: 269–279, 626, 652, 1257–1259; *Standard*, May 27, June 5, 1839; *Morning Herald*, July 4, 9, 20, 1840; *Times*, Feb. 1, 21, 1839; *Record*, Mar. 2, 1840; F. Maurice, *The Life of Frederick Denison Maurice* (London, 1885), 1: 277.

35. Paz, *Working Class Education*, pp. 115–126; Chadwick, *Victorian Church*, 1: 340–341; Smith, *Life and Work of Sir James Kay-Shuttleworth*, pp. 185–189, 215–229.

36. G. F. A. Best, "National Education," *Cambridge Historical Journal* 12 (1956): 163–164; Smith, *Life and Work of Sir James Kay-Shuttleworth*, pp. 149–150.

37. Brent, *Liberal Anglican Politics*, pp. 218–251; *Edinburgh Review*, Oct. 1839, pp. 149–169.

38. Smith, *Life and Work of Sir James Kay-Shuttleworth*, pp. 154–156, 172–182; *P.P.*, 1847, 45: 1–28.

39. *P.P.*, 1847, 45: 1–18; Smith, *Life and Work of Sir James Kay-Shuttleworth*, pp. 172–182; Kay-Shuttleworth, *Four Periods*, p. 495.

40. *P.P.*, 1845, 35: 342–344, 406, 409, 463–465, 578; 1846, 32: 361–362, 506–508, 532–533; 1847, 45: 84–87, 105–106, 136–88, 156; 1848, 50: 391, 482–483; 1852, 40: 208; 1855, 42: 503, 601.

41. *P.P.*, 1845, 35: 211–212, 549–550, 579; 1846, 32: 366–367, 373–374–378–380; 1847, 45: 94, 97, 104; 1848, 50: 394–396; 1852, 40: 346.

42. *P.P.*, 1847, 45: 104; 1853, 80: 625.

43. *Education Times*, Apr. 1, 1850, p. 147; Dawes, *Present Crusade Against the Education Plan of the Committee in Council*, p. 147; Connop Thirlwall, *Remains Literary and Theological of Connop Thirlwall*, ed. J. J. Stewart Perowne (3 vols.; London, 1877–80), 1: 117.

44. Maltby, *Manchester and the Movement for National Education*, pp. 60–98.

45. H. Halford, *Some Remarks or the Constabulary Force Report* (London, 1840), pp. 1–65, esp. 21, 29, 53, and 60–61.

46. *Hansard*, 1849, 103: 216–217; 106: 662–663; Brian T. Bradfield, "Sir Richard Vyvyan and Tory Politics" (Ph.D. diss., London University), p. 335.

47. *Oxford and Cambridge Review*, July 1846, p. 82; *Fraser's*, Dec. 1843, p. 730.

48. *Hansard*, 1846, 83: 1340–1346; 86: 83–86; Coleridge, *Table Talk*, 2: 53; Best, *Templar Pillars*, p. 165; *Quarterly Review*, 1820, 23: 564.

49. Seely, *Sadler*, p. 33; *NonConformist*, Apr. 3, 1844, p. 213.

50. *Durham Chronicle*, July 9, 1841 ("I see the county governed, as it ought to be, by statute not by the unconstitutional authority of expensive boards"); H. E. Zangert, "The Social Composition of the County," *British Studies*, Nov. 1971.

51. *DNB*, 43: 94–95; *Men of the Time*, 1872; *Dod's Parliamentary Companion*, 1849, p. 223; T. C. Tuberville, *Worcestershire in the Nineteenth Century* (London, 1952), pp. 294–295, 300, 303, 315–316; Packington, *Charge on the Subject of the County Expenditure*, pp. 7, 13; *Hansard*, 1840, 54: 1413; 1846, 86: 950.

52. Finlayson, *Seventh Earl of Shaftesbury*, pp. 230–231; *Statutes at Large*, 8 & 9 Vict. c. 100 and c. 101; Jones, *Lunacy, Law and Conscience*, pp. 191–195. For an excellent discussion of the growth of local government, see Prest, *Liberty and Locality*.

53. *Stamford Mercury*, Aug. 13, 1847.

54. Roberts, *Welfare State*, pp. 224, 257, 281; *Hansard*, 1842, 64: 683; 65: 340–341; 1847, 93: 887, 898–899.

55. W. C. Lubenow, *Politics of Government Growth* (London, 1971), pp. 40, 49; *Manchester Guardian*, Aug. 3, 1842.

56. Joseph Foster, *Alumni Oxonienses: The Members of the University of Oxford, 1715–1886*, 1 & 2: 472; Boase, *Modern English Biography*, 1: 1072; *Men of the Time*, 1872, Joseph Henley; *St. James Magazine*, 1870, 4: 771–772; *DNB*, 25: 416–417; 59: 216.

57. Munsell, *Unfortunate Duke*, p. 99; Pebody, *English Journalism*, p. 117, and on the staff, Archdeacon Venables, Abraham Hayward, Lord Strangford.

58. Pebody, *English Journalism*, pp. 117–120; Escott, *Masters of English Journalism*, pp. 230–231; Bourne, *English Newspapers*, 2: 151–153; J. Grant, *Saturday Review*, p. 8; *Morning Chronicle*, Feb. 26, Apr. 4, 8, June 21, July 12 (decries breakdown of *in loco parentis* in Europe), 1848; Jan. 17, 31, July 27, 1849.

59. *Morning Chronicle*, Mar. 16, May 20, 1848; Jan. 31, Apr. 14, June 27, July 13, 26, 1849; July 8, 15, Aug. 1, 1854.

60. *Times*, Apr. 30, May 26, June 30, July 5, 1834; May 18, 1848.

61. *Times*, Apr. 11, May 21, 25, July 8, 1839; July 15, Sept. 26, Dec. 15, 1842; Oct. 24, Dec. 15, 1843; July 10, 11, 19, 1844; Apr. 9, 1846.

62. *Times*, Apr. 23, 1847; May 9, 18, 1848; Feb. 27, 1850; Jan. 8, 1852; July 7, 1853; May 7, July, 7, 8, 11, 1854.

63. *Times*, July 5, 1842; Feb. 29, Mar. 11, 1844; Feb. 12, 1850; *Morning Post*, Feb. 1, 1843 (cites the *Times*, "that legislation can cure social evils we dare not hope").

CHAPTER 16

1. Jeremy Bentham, *In Defense of Usury* (London, 1787); id., *Manual of Political Economy* (London, 1811); Werner Stark, *Jeremy Bentham's Economic Writings* (London, 1952), 1: 14, 26–27, 34, 49–53; 3: 26, 32, 41, 52, 58–59; *Works of Jeremy Bentham*, ed. Bowring, 3: 31–85; Halévy, *Growth of Philosophical Radicalism*, p. 265.

2. Werner Stark, *Bentham's Economic Writings*, 1: 52; 2: 12–14, 47–51; 3: 32; T. W. Hutchinson, "Bentham as an Economist," *Economic Journal*, June 1956, pp. 302–304; *Works of Jeremy Bentham*, ed. Bowring, 9: 24 (government in itself is one vast evil), 273–275, 441, 431, 439, 443–445, 577, 612–637; Polanyi, *Transformation*, pp. 139ff.

3. *Works of Jeremy Bentham*, ed. Bowring, 9: 24.

4. Jeremy Bentham, *Leading Principles of a Constitutional Code, for Any State* (London, 1825); id., *Constitutional Code*, ed. F. Rosen and J. H. Burns (3 vols.; New York, 1983); id., *An Introduction to the Principles of Morals and Legislation* (1789; reprint, London, 1879), pp. 2–4; *Works of Jeremy Bentham*, ed. Bowring, 9: 199–200.

5. *Works of Jeremy Bentham*, ed. Bowring, 9: 431–439, 441–445, 612–637.

6. Ibid., 9: 199.

7. F. R. Leavis, *J. S. Mill on Bentham and Coleridge* (London, 1950), p. 42; Edward Lytton Bulwer [Bulwer-Lytton], *England and the English* (1833; Chicago, 1970), p. 318; *Athenaeum*, May 28, 1842.

8. Hamburger, *Intellectuals in Politics*, pp. 14, 272; Leavis, *Mill on Bentham and Coleridge*, p. 142; Halévy, *Growth of Philosophical Radicalism*, pp. 304, 480; Samuel Finer, "The Transmission of Benthamite Ideas," in *Studies in the Growth of Nineteenth Century Government*, ed. Gillian Sutherland (London, 1972), pp. 11–32.

9. Smith, *Life and Work of Sir James Kay-Shuttleworth*, pp. x, 1–35; Frederick Hill, *Autobiography*, pp. 7–64; R. and F. Davenport-Hill, *Recorder of Birmingham*, pp. 2–44.

10. *DNB*, 5: 106–107; 48: 311–312; David Roberts, "Early Victorian Newspaper Editors," *Victorian Periodicals Review*, Dec. 1971, pp. 7–8; and id., "Who Ran the *Globe*?" ibid., June 1971, pp. 6–11; W. E. Hickson, *Malthus* (London, 1853), pp. 1–2; Edmund Kell Blythe, *The Life of William Ellis* (London, 1889), p. 8; *Wellesley Index to Victorian Periodicals*, ed. Houghton (Toronto, 1979), 3: 536–554.

11. For a fuller discussion of Benthamite M.P.'s and editors, see David Roberts, "The Utilitarian Conscience," in *The Conscience of the Victorian State,* ed. Peter Marsh (Syracuse, N.Y., 1971).

12. Finer, *Edwin Chadwick,* pp. 147–163, 149–254, 281.

13. *Works of Jeremy Bentham,* ed. Bowring, pp. 441, 443.

14. *Hansard,* 1845, 79: 363, 366, 370.

15. Finer, *Edwin Chadwick,* pp. 50–68; MacDonagh, *Early Victorian Government,* pp. 42–48.

16. Finer, *Edwin Chadwick,* pp. 69–96; MacDonagh, *Early Victorian Government,* pp. 101–114.

17. Lewis, *Edwin Chadwick,* pp. 181–357; Finer, *Edwin Chadwick,* p. 475; Edwin Chadwick Papers, "Rough Draft of a Central Administration" (n.d.).

18. Smith, *Life and Work of Sir James Kay-Shuttleworth,* pp. 50–51, 62, 72, 84–85, 104, 137, 152–154, 170, 278–279; *P.P.,* 1846, 32: 11, 209; 1847, 45: 1–18; Kay-Shuttleworth, *Four Periods,* pp. 182–183.

19. R. and F. Davenport-Hill, *Recorder of Birmingham,* pp. 8, 61–63, 96, 123, 153–154, 160, 167, 191, 322–324, 378–380, 383; Frederick Hill, *Crime: Its Amount, Causes and Remedies* (London, 1853), pp. 83, 103, 135, 195–196; id., *Autobiography,* pp. 71, 76, 94, 109, 121–123, 180, 183, 196, 213, 219, 256, 279.

20. Joseph Fletcher, *Education, National, Voluntary and Free* (London, 1851), pp. 25, 40; Morell, *On the Progress of Society in England,* p. 12; Jelinger Symons, *A Plea for Schools* (London, 1847); *P.P.,* 1843, 40: 351; 1852, 39: 57; 1852, 40: 83, 345–360, 373; 1853, 80: 625.

21. *Hansard,* 1843, 69: 530–531; 1836, 34: 827; 1835, 29: 290; 1838, 41: 927; 1842, 60: 409; 1835, 30: 954.

22. *Westminster Review,* Sept. 1844, p. 34; *Globe,* June 10, 1840: Atlay, *Globe and Traveller Centenary,* pp. 10, 11; Roberts, "Who Ran the *Globe*?" pp. 6–10.

23. *DNB,* 5: 107–108; *Morning Chronicle,* May 6, 1846; *Albany Fonblanque,* ed. E. B. de Fonblanque, pp. 20, 31–33, 35; *Earlier Letters of John Stuart Mill,* ed. Mineka, pp. 254, 367, 391, 699.

24. Roberts, "Utilitarian Conscience," in *Conscience of the Victorian State,* ed. Marsh, pp. 57–61; *Hansard,* 1845, 77: 660; 1846, 86: 928–929; 1847, 93: 275–276; 1834, 23: 1096–1097; 1843, 71: 86–87.

25. *Morning Chronicle,* June 9, 1841; Anon., *Hints to Employers: The Elevation of the Working Class* (reprint from *Westminster Review,* no. 67), pp. 5–6.

26. G. F. Bartles, "The Political Career of Sir John Bowring" (M.A. thesis, London University), pp. 186, 327, 332–333, 394; *Blackburn Gazette,* June 6, 1832.

27. Roberts, "Utilitarian Conscience," in *Conscience of the Victorian State,* ed. Marsh, pp. 62–69.

28. *Hansard,* 1848, 97: 658; 1836, 35: 730.

29. *Hansard,* 1847, 91: 1183; 1833, 20: 142; 1836, 35: 730.

30. *Hansard,* 1834, 73: 1434–1436; *Spectator,* Apr. 3, 1844, p. 347; Apr. 20, 1844, p. 370.

31. Grant, *Portraits of Public Characters,* 1: 46, 82; *Morning Chronicle,* 1834, May 12; 1839, June 4, 22; 1840, Jan. 17, 22, Feb. 24, Mar. 12, July 13; 1841, Jan. 1, Feb. 3, 11, Mar. 10, 17; 1842, Apr. 13, May 7, 24, June 9, 15; 1843, Jan. 18, June 21; 1844, May 6, 9; 1845, Apr. 30, June 7, July 7; 1845, Apr. 4; 1846, May 6; 1847, Feb. 4, 6, Mar. 23, 26, 31, Apr. 29, May 3, June 11, 19.

32. *Morning Chronicle,* 1845, Mar. 22; 1846, May 6; 1847, Feb. 6, 8, 11, May 3.

33. *Westminster Review,* Apr. 1838, pp. 225–253; Apr. 1842, p. 422; June 1844, pp. 446–459; Jan. 1842, pp. 202–213; Mar. 1846, pp. 133–145; July 1848, p. 533; Oct. 1847, pp. 83–84; July 1848, pp. 447–448, Oct. 1848, pp. 179–187.

34. *Westminster Review,* July 1842, pp. 6–7; June 1846, p. 476; Oct. 1847, pp. 383–84; July 1848, p. 447.

35. *Westminster Review,* July 1842, p. 138; Oct. 1846, p. 205; Apr. 1842, pp. 305–317; June 1840, pp. 61–83.

36. *Westminster Review,* Mar. 1845, 168–191; Jan. 1851, pp. 403–411.

37. *Westminster Review,* May 1843, p. 499; Oct. 1846, p. 202.

38. Bowley, *Nassau Senior;* Blaug, *Ricardian Economics,* p. 194; J. S. Mill, *Principles of Political Economy,* vol. 2, bk. 4.

39. Scrope, *Principles of Political Economy,* pp. xi–xii; C. Merivale, *Herman Merivale,* p. 29; H. Merivale, *Introductory Lectures on the Study of Political Economy* (Oxford, 1837), pp. 7, 29.

40. *Hansard,* 1844, 73: 1213.

41. *Hansard,* 1843, 71: 78, 81; 1844, 76: 484.

42. *Hansard,* 1844, 76: 1178; 1847, 92: 893; 1840, 55: 1183.

43. *Hansard,* 1846, 63: 774.

44. George Prynne, *The Autobiographical Recollection of George Prynne* (London, 1870), p. 124.

45. E. Ashley, *The Life and Correspondence of Henry John Temple Viscount Palmerston* (London, 1879), 2: 7; Mabell Ogilvy, countess of Airlie, *Lady Palmerston and Her Times* (London, 1922), pp. 35–36; *Western Times,* Aug. 7, 1847.

46. Brent, *Liberal Anglican Politics,* p. 54; *Hansard,* 1854, 136: 468.

47. *Western Times,* Aug. 7, 1847; *Hansard,* 1844, 74: 658.

48. *Works of Dugald Stewart,* ed. Hamilton, 8: 23, 181; Jasper Ridley, *Lord Palmerston* (New York, 1971), pp. 14–15; John Prest, *Lord John Russell* (Columbia, S.C., 1972), pp. 9, 12.

49. Ridley, *Palmerston,* pp. 293, 409–410; David Roberts, "Lord Palmerston at the Home Office," *Historian,* Nov. 1958, pp. 63–81; Prest, *Lord John Russell,* pp. 54, 85–91, 101–102, 105, 127, 129, 136–138, 148, 150, 197–198, 243–244, 264–265, 267, 296–298, 307, 311.

50. *Edinburgh Review,* Oct. 1848, p. 331; Jan. 1848, p. 169.

51. *Edinburgh Review,* Oct. 1833, pp. 1–30; 1850, pp. 94–124; Jan. 1838, pp. 439–450; Apr. 1842, pp. 116–138; Oct. 1847, p. 512; Oct. 1849, pp. 149–161.

52. *Edinburgh Review,* Oct. 1841, pp. 14–41; Apr. 1843, p. 391; Jan. 1844, pp. 131–156; Jan. 1850, pp. 210–222; Apr. 1850, p. 377; Oct. 1852, pp. p. 403.

53. *Edinburgh Review,* Jan. 1846, p. 66; Jan. 1847, pp. 221–258.

54. *Wellesley Index to Victorian Periodicals,* ed. Houghton, 1: 416–429; *Edinburgh Review,* Jan. 1840, p. 240; Feb. 1843, pp. 205–226, esp. 205–206; Apr. 1845, pp. 499–500; Jan. 1846, pp. 66–96, esp. 89–91; Oct. 1846, pp. 273–274; Jan. 1848, pp. 297, 231–319; Oct. 1848, p. 325; Oct. 1849, pp. 265–272.

55. *Edinburgh Review,* Oct. 1848, pp. 325–328.

56. *Edinburgh Review,* Oct. 1840, pp. 2–47; Apr. 1845, pp. 498–525; Jan. 1848, pp. 231–319; Oct. 1849, pp. 261–274.

57. *Edinburgh Review,* Jan. 1843, pp. 216, 226–227; Oct. 1846, p. 274; Jan. 1848, p. 298.

58. *Edinburgh Review,* Feb. 1843, pp. 205–206; Oct. 1848, pp. 325–326.

59. *Edinburgh Review,* Oct. 1841, pp. 15–24; Jan. 1844, p. 15, 1–154; Apr. 1845, pp. 499–500;

Oct. 1845, pp. 509–512; Jan. 1846, pp. 83–84; Oct. 1846, pp. 308–331; Apr. 1847, pp. 527–528; Jan. 1848, pp. 288, 297–298, 314–315; Oct. 1848, p. 325; Oct. 1849, pp. 267–268.

60. *Edinburgh Review*, Apr. 1845, p. 509.

61. *Edinburgh Review*, Apr. 1845, pp. 512–513.

62. Chadwick Papers, July 1854, Memo on Lord Seymour; Lewis, *Edwin Chadwick*, pp. 234–235, 249–250, 266, 268, 273, 325–326, 334–335, 360–361, 367–368, 395; Finer, *Edwin Chadwick*, pp. 387–388, 397–404, 409, 414–417, 424–426, 463–473; Gwendolen Ramsden, *Letters, Remains, and Memoirs of Edward Adolphus Seymour* (London, 1893), p. 451; *Hansard*, 1853, 126: 551; 129: 1497, 1573–1577, 1580–1587.

63. *Hansard*, 1844, 74: 636, 642; 1845, 80: 971.

64. Slaney, *Essay on the Employment of the Poor*; id., *State of the Poorer Classes in Great Towns*, p. 13; id., *Essay on the Beneficial Directions of Rural Expenditure* (London, 1824), p. 18; id., *Reports of the House of Commons on Education and Health*; id., *A Plea to Power and Parliament on the Working Classes*, pp. 93, 98; id., *On The Sciences of Happiness*; *Hansard*, 1834, 23: 816; 1839, 48: 296–298; 1840, 51: 1222–1232; 53: 2981; 1846, 83: 319; 1848, 99: 462.

65. Scrope, *Principles of Political Economy*, pp. xi–xv, 2, 4, 10, 17, 26, 33–35, 51, 127, 259, 293–294, 300–307, 315, 322, 333, 337–338, 427, 429, 448–450; id., *Suggested Legislation of the Dwellings of the Poor* (London, 1849); *Hansard*, 1834, 23: 317; 1846, 83: 215; 84: 1002; 85: 585, 630–642; 1847, 92: 1124; 1848, 97: 1006, 1363–1367; 99: 982–983.

66. *Hansard*, 1846, 86: 1029–1041; 1847, 91: 1006–1021; John Clive, *Macaulay: The Shaping of an Historian* (New York, 1973), pp. 64–65, 126–127, 129–130, 134–135, 227, 334, 347, 352–353, 384, 435, 452–453, 497.

67. Scrope, *Principles of Political Economy*, p. 2; Mackintosh, *Ethics*, ed. Whewell, p. 355.

68. *Hansard*, 1844, 74: 642–643, 652.

69. *Hansard*, 1846, 83: 1283; 86: 436–437, 437–439, 1224.

70. *Durham Chronicle*, Aug. 6, 1847; *Sussex Agricultural Express*, Aug. 7, 1847; *Devise and Wiltshire Gazette*, July 29, 1847.

71. Coleridge, *The Friend*, 2: 200; id., *Marginalia* in Thomas Malthus, *Essay on the Principles of Population* (London, 1803), pp. vii, 11, copy in British Library under S. T. Coleridge.

72. Seeley, *Perils of a Nation*, p. xv; *Sadler*, pp. 42, 145; Wilberforce, *Practical View of the Prevailing Religious System*, p. 273.

73. Aristotle, *Nicomachean Ethics*, ed. and trans. Hippocrates G. Apostle (Boston, 1975), pp. 3, 9, 11, 133, 181, 214; John Locke, *Essay Concerning Human Understanding* (London, 1965), pp. 29, 189; W. Tuckwell, *Tractarian Oxford* (London, 1905), pp. 90–91, 111–112.

74. *Edmund Burke: Select Writings*, ed. Peter J. Stanlis (New York, 1963), p. 30.

CONCLUSION

1. Sumner, *Christian Charity*, p. iii.

2. Bickersteth, *Works*, 14: 131–132; id., *Signs of the Times*, pt. 2, 211, 323.

3. E. J. Whatley, *Life and Correspondence of Richard Whatley*, p. 56.

4. T. Binney, *Righteousness Exalteth a Nation* (London, 1840), p. 4; id., *Sermons Preached at the King's Weigh-House Chapel*, p. 361; Wilson, *Life of George Dawson*, pp. 16, 30; Dawson, *Biographical Lectures*, pp. 400–401.

5. J. S. Mill, *Dissertations*, 1: 54, 206, 218; id., *Political Economy*, 2: 318–324, 584–585.

6. Chalmers, *Works*, 6: 127, 129; *Christian Observer*, Feb. 1844, p. 127; *Record*, Feb. 4, 1842, Jan. 25, 1847.

7. *North British Review*, Feb. 1845, p. 437.

8. Engels, *Condition of the Working Class in England*, pp. 31–73, 124–129, 165–170, 218–237, 296–310; F. M. L. Thompson, *The Rise of Respectable Society: A Social History of Victorian Britain, 1830–1900* (Cambridge, Mass., 1988), pp. 143–149, 151–197, esp. 183–188.

9. Thompson, *Rise of Respectable Society*, p. 199.

Index

In this index an "f" after a number indicates a separate reference on the next page, and an "ff" indicates separate references on the next two pages. A continuous discussion over two or more pages is indicated by a span of page numbers, e.g., "57–59." "Passim" is used for a cluster of references in close but not consecutive sequence.

A Beckett, Gilbert, 264f
Aberdeen, earl of, 47
Aberdeen school of industry, 331
Acland, Thomas, Jr., 99, 415, 419, 422
Acland, Thomas, Sr., 314
Adderly, Charles, 187, 213, 283, 285, 309f
Adey, D. G., 47
Age of Great Cities (Vaughan), 297
agricultural associations, 44f, 143
agricultural labor, 11, 38, 48–53, 103, 121f, 143, 173, 337ff, 366, 397, 463
Ainsworth, William, 264, 268f, 270
Albert, Prince, 210
Albion, 353
Alison, Archibald, 29f, 36, 118, 126
Alison, W. P., 181, 211, 252, 256, 344
Allen, William, 206, 222, 233f, 236f, 248, 250ff, 322f, 464
allotments, 46, 48f, 51, 54, 68, 103, 144, 187, 260, 310, 367, 383, 392
Almanac (Cruickshank), 265
Althorp, Lord, 109, 120, 146, 290
Alton Locke (Kingsley), 39ff
American Notes (Dickens), 294
Amy Herbert (E. Sewell), 41
Analogy of Religion (Butler), 127
Anglicans, 34, 123, 128, 140, 360f, 367f, 371, 417. *See also* Church of England
Animal Estate (Ritvo), 287
animals, treatment of, 265, 287, 295, 314, 316, 323, 394, 402
Anster, John, 260

Anti–Corn Law Association, 82, 465
Anti–Corn Law League, 82, 85, 92ff, 96, 100, 108
Apostles Club, Cambridge, 300, 418f, 422
apothecaries, 356
arboretum (Derby), 208
Argyl, duke of, 46
aristocracy, 2, 17, 22, 38, 40, 96ff, 99, 367, 370f, 414–434 passim, 453, 460
Aristotle, 12, 87, 419, 452
Armitage, Robert, 41, 57
Armstrong, John, 36, 241
army, 311, 356ff, 367, 376f
Army and Victorian Society (Jenkins), 356
Arnold, Thomas, 14, 17, 22f, 26, 164, 308, 336, 363, 367; and aristocracy, 419, 421, 424, 426, 453, 460; and clerisy, 19f, 22, 426, 428
Arnott, Neill, 299, 329, 412
art galleries, 240, 402
Ashley, Lord (later Seventh Earl of Shaftesbury), 4, 297, 392; legislative reforms, 34, 107, 250f, 274f; as paternalist, 29, 47, 49, 63, 90; as philanthropist, 205f, 210, 229, 244, 252, 255, 431, 464
Ashton, Thomas, 65
Ashworth, Edmund, 65
Ashworth, Henry, 65ff
Association of Philanthropists (Shelley), 232
associationism: (philosophical idea), 164f; (social ideal), 188, 217–225, 450, 461
associationists, 218–225f